A legacy of Swedish tycoon Alfred Nobel, the Nobel Peace Prize has been hailed as "the greatest honor a man can receive in this world." Since the first Peace Prize was handed out in 1901, recipients have included Theodore Roosevelt, General George Marshall, Bertha von Suttner, Dag Hammarskjöld, Lech Walesa, Bishop Desmond Tutu, Albert Schweitzer, Martin Luther King, Jr., Mother Teresa, and dozens of others whose struggles for a better world have earned them the distinction of Nobel Peace Prize winners.

In 1987, the laureate and award of $350,000 were conferred upon Oscar Arias, president of Costa Rica. On what grounds did he win? Who else was nominated? What other figures throughout history have won the Nobel Peace Prize and with it the title of "Hero of Humanity"? Irwin Abrams's *The Nobel Peace Prize and the Laureates* holds the answers to those and countless other questions about the prize, the selection process, and the men and women it has gone to through the years.

This immense body of chronologically arranged work details the evolution of the Nobel Peace Prize, delves into the role and mechanics of the Norwegian Nobel Committee, and profiles each of the eighty-seven laureates. The author also provides an insightful evaluation of the Nobel Committee's decisions over time. Infinitely useful as a reference tool, the book includes surveys, tables, and both general and specific bibliographies.

The Nobel Peace Prize and the Laureates

An Illustrated Biographical History, 1901–1987

Alfred Nobel

The Nobel Peace Prize and the Laureates

An Illustrated Biographical History, 1901–1987

IRWIN ABRAMS

G.K. Hall & Co.
Boston

Manufactured in the United States of America.

Designed and produced by John Amburg.
Copyediting supervised by Michael Sims.
Set in 11/12 Garamond No.3 by Huron Valley Graphics, Inc.

All photographs courtesy of The Nobel Foundation.

Library of Congress Cataloging-in-Publication Data

Abrams, Irwin.
The Nobel Peace Prize and the laureates: An Illustrated Biographical History, 1901–1987 / Irwin Abrams.
p. cm.
Bibliography: p.
Includes index.
ISBN 0-8161-8609-X
1. Pacifists—Biography. 2. Nobel prizes—History. 3. Peace—Awards—History. I. Title.
JX1962.A2A25 1988
327.1'72'0922—dc19
[B] 88-16313
CIP

To Freda
and to
David and Carole
and in memory of James

Contents

Foreword

I was in Norway in September 1981 at a symposium on Population Growth and World Economic Development, sponsored by the Norwegian Nobel Institute, and visited the offices of the Norwegian Nobel Committee that awards the Peace Prize. Photographs of the laureates are very naturally displayed around the walls, from the beginning of the prize awards in 1901. I was shocked to find how few I could identify, especially in the earlier years. Having been a member of the peace movement for more than fifty years and one of the very early members of the peace research movement (and one of the founders of the *Journal of Conflict Resolution* in 1956), I was a little shocked to find how ignorant I was of the history of one of the major concerns of my life. Reading Irwin Abrams's history of the Nobel Peace Prize and the laureates, covering the last eighty-seven years, has therefore been a most salutary experience, filling in many gaps of my knowledge of the past, all of which is relevant to the present, and giving me a much clearer picture than I had before of the uphill, Sisyphus-like, but nevertheless persistent, movement of the human race towards the abolition of war and the establishment of stable peace.

What I confess surprised me a little was that this experience of learning turned out to be such a delight. Irwin Abrams writes with a succinct charm and brings every one of the eighty-seven Nobel award recipients to life. It is something of an accident, incidentally, that the number of awards just equals the number of years that the Peace Prize has been in existence. The number of double awards exactly counterbalances the nineteen years in which no awards were given. Of the awards, some fifteen were given to institutions and associations; the rest were to individuals. Altogether the list constitutes a not-quite-random sample of the upper and more visible end of something profound that has been happening to the human race in these eighty-seven years. These years have seen a major change in the nature of war, thanks largely to the airplane, the missile, and the nuclear weapon, which have transformed large-scale war into genocide rather than fighting. This change is reflected also in what might almost be called "surrogate wars" in the Third World, especially since 1945, using more conventional weapons. It is particularly appropriate that Alfred Nobel created the Peace Prize, because the enormous change in the nature of war and peace can well be dated from his discovery of nitroglycerin, which started off an extraordinary increase in the human capacities for destruction.

The Peace Prize is one out of five prizes established by Alfred Nobel. The other four are administered in Sweden and the Peace Prize, in Norway. This itself perhaps has a significance more than Nobel could have recognized at the time. It was the peaceful separation of Norway from Sweden in 1905 which set the pattern for the enormous dismembership of European empires, largely peaceful, with a few exceptions, that followed the Second World War. It is indeed particularly appropriate that the Peace Prize should have originated in Scandinavia, which is where stable peace between independent countries originated in the nineteenth century, at that time between Sweden and Denmark. Stable peace can be defined as a situation where two independent countries have no plans whatever to go to war with each other. I have argued in my little book *Stable Peace* (Austin: University of Texas Press, 1978) that stable peace spread to North America after about 1871 and to Western Europe after the Second World War. It now extends across the Pacific to Australia, New Zealand, and Japan. In the nuclear age this is really the only form of national security that is genuinely secure. National defense can no longer give security. Deterrence cannot be stable in the long run. The great problem of the human race now is how to expand the area of stable peace from the "great triangle" (from Australia, to Japan, across North America, to Western Europe) which it now occupies, first to include the Soviet Union and its allies, and then to spread to the Third World, where it still has a long way to go. The Nobel Peace Prize is a symbol of this radical and irreversible movement in human history, imperfect, no doubt, like all symbols, but nevertheless of great importance.

The Peace Prize is awarded by an independent committee whose task is not to be envied. Their choices have sometimes been subject to severe criticism, but mostly with approval ranging from mild to enthusiastic. There is no doubt, however, that the committee has operated over the years, with changing membership, with honesty and dignity. There has been a movement over the years away from awards to representatives of the organized peace movement, though not entirely, towards representatives of humanitarian and human rights organizations and to organizations as well as individuals. Awards to statesmen peaked somewhat in the 1919–39 period, but have risen somewhat in recent years. In the earliest period, international law and jurists were recognized, but none since 1919, which perhaps reflects a certain decline in the effectiveness of international law.

What is striking is the complete absence of any recognition of the international peace research movement, which begins in the 1950s and is represented by such organizations as the International Peace Research Association and a good many research institutes and programs around the world (one of the earliest, incidentally, in Oslo itself, the International Peace Research Institute). This is now a very noticeable movement not only in research but in education. I have argued indeed that a new discipline both in research and in education has developed in the last thirty years, what the French call *polemologie,* in English usually called by the name of peace and conflict studies. This has gone completely unrecognized by the Nobel Peace Prize, but perhaps that will come.

The Peace Prize is a very good example of the slow, but very significant, development of what might be called "integrative power." On a world scale, the economic power of the Nobel Committee is not very large, but for some reason the prestige of the prize and its publicity value seem to have grown steadily over the years. All the threat power of Hitler could not prevent the prize being of some impact on the treatment of Ossietzky in the Nazi period. The prize has certainly helped to legitimate some of its recipients who have been in dangerous political situations.

Irwin Abrams has brought to life a remarkable episode in the history of the human race, which is still continuing. This book is a work of literature as well as of careful research. The vignettes of the prize winners, both the people and the organizations, make them all come alive in the minds of the reader. It is like looking through a number of fascinating keyholes at some significant episodes in the history of the human race, which can then be much more widely appreciated and understood. Whoever reads this book will experience both insight and pleasure.

Kenneth E. Boulding
Institute of Behavioral Science
University of Colorado-Boulder

Preface

When Alfred Nobel was planning the establishing of his Peace Prize, he wrote his friend Baroness Bertha von Suttner in 1893 that he expected it to be awarded for no longer than thirty years. If the world had not become peaceful by then, he said, it would go directly back to barbarism. Thirty years after Nobel wrote these words, the so-called civilized nations were locked in a world war unprecedented in its deadliness, and after a short truce they were plunged into a second world war that produced unheard-of weapons of destruction and untold human suffering. Since then, violent conflicts have proliferated all over the world, and an uneasy peace prevails between the two rival power blocs, both of which are aware that the use of their nuclear weapons could result in the extermination of life on our planet.

In the century since Nobel made his dire prediction, the world has indeed gone far toward barbarism. Should the Norwegian Nobel Committee, then, have closed up shop and returned their funds to the Nobel Foundation, as a leading critic urged during the Second World War? Nineteen times the committee has in fact decided to give no prize, and the prospect of an end to war often seems as frail as the pitiful figure of peace cynical cartoonists delight to confront in their drawings with a gigantic war god or a tower of guns.

Certainly Nobel's Peace Prizes have not brought peace on earth. But the Norwegian Nobel Committees have acted from a different conception. In his will Nobel directed them to give the prize to champions of peace who organize peace congresses, promote disarmament, or work for "fraternity between nations," and in their awards the committees have acknowledged efforts of all sorts to tighten human bonds, recognizing that this must be the basis for any enduring political organization of peace.

The Peace Prize has been given not only to peace activists but to international lawyers, humanitarians, religious figures, labor leaders, international civil servants, and recently to champions of human rights. Although statesmen have won prizes for their efforts to end particular wars and international conflicts, these have been among the most criticized awards. The most respected of these awards have been those given to political leaders who have demonstrated a lasting dedication to peace.

The Norwegian Nobel Committees have become used to criticism for their decisions. Unlike the other Nobel Prizes, there are no "authorities" in the field of peacemaking, and everyone feels confident in expressing an opinion. There is general agreement, however, that the Nobel Peace Prize has come to represent the most prestigious world prize for service to humanity. In the midst of stories about violence, terrorism, and conflict, twice a year peace makes news—in October, when the Nobel Prize is announced, and in December, when it is awarded.

Although the Nobel pantheon of peace includes some lesser figures, nevertheless it is filled with distinguished personalities who have dedicated themselves to improving the human lot, some on the world scene, at the League of Nations or the United Nations, some in tiny places such as a hospital in the African jungle or a house of charity in the slums of Calcutta. Others whose names are not so well remembered worked with the same dedication in organizations that have been awarded the prize. What so many of the peace laureates have had in common was what Martin Luther King, Jr., phrased so well—the determination "to leave a committed life behind." And among their contributions to humanity, perhaps their greatest legacy is their demonstration that even in a barbaric world an individual committed to service to humanity and peace can make a difference.

It was the late Jacob Oser, emeritus professor of economics at Syracuse University, who, out of his own commitment to peace, drew the attention of G. K. Hall and Company to the need for a biographical reference book on Nobel Peace Prize winners. When the publishers asked me to undertake the project, I was much attracted to it. Years ago I had published the first critical analysis of the correspondence between Alfred Nobel and Bertha von Suttner, and in an article in 1962 I had sought to draw the balance of the prize up to that time. Over the years I had met a number of the laureates, beginning before the Second World War when I was working on my doctoral dissertation on European peace societies, and during the war when I served with the American Friends Service Committee in its relief work, for which it, along with the British Quakers, received the 1947 Peace Prize.

As I was considering G. K. Hall's invitation, I happened to be attending a conference where a report was presented on the results of a public opinion poll on the heroes of American teenagers. I was appalled by the list of film and television stars and rock and roll performers whom they seemed to want to emulate. Another report had it that American youth have no heroes at all! I could see that a book presenting Nobel heroes of humanity could make an important contribution.

I also realized that there was a need for a book that would give full and accurate information on the prize itself. I had come across so many examples of ignorance and misconceptions about it. Nominations have often been sent to Stockholm, not Oslo, for example, and editorial writers have exhibited much confusion about who hands out the tokens of the prize and where. The relationship of the Norwegian Nobel Committee to the Norwegian government and parliament is not well understood, nor do many would-be nominators know who is eligible to submit proposals and how and when they are to be submitted.

So I accepted the assignment, with the intention of producing a book that would not only try to make the mechanics of the prize clear but also provide an account of its origins and development and an evaluation of the work of the committee in its first eighty-seven years. This is Part One of the present work. Part Two deals with the laureates, grouped in four periods, with a brief historical introduction to each period and an essay and bibliography for each recipient.

It is my hope that this book can be the first port of call for those looking for basic facts and an interpretation of the Nobel Peace Prize and its winners and for recommendations as to where to look for further information.

While much of Part One and a number of the biographical essays have been based upon original research, I preferred that the text not be studded with monographic footnotes to facilitate ease of use, and I trust that the comments below and the bibliographical listings will give sufficient indications of the materials I have used.

A good part of the research for the book was conducted at the Norwegian Nobel Institute in Oslo. I am much in debt to Dr. Jakob Sverdrup, institute director and secretary of the Norwegian Nobel Committee, who has helped this project along in innumerable ways. I was able to use selected documents from the committee archives, which are open up to the 1930s, and Dr. Sverdrup arranged interviews for me with past and present members of the committee, with his two predecessors as institute director and committee secretary, and with committee advisers. Dr. Sverdrup also kindly arranged for my attendance on three occasions at the award ceremonies and festivities. I extend thanks as well to his staff, who assisted me in using the institute's invaluable book collection on the prize and in the inevitable photocopying.

In this country I worked primarily at the Swarthmore College Peace Collection, whose holdings on the organized peace movement are unique. I want to thank Dr. Jean Soderlund, the former curator, and her staff for their help. In Philadelphia, Jack Sutter, archivist of the American Friends Service Committee, made available to me documents relating to the prizes for the Quakers and Carl von Ossietzky. For preparation of a preliminary bibliography, I am grateful to Mrs. Patricia Dugan, formerly librarian at Utica College.

Several of the laureates kindly accorded me interviews: Linus Pauling, Willy Brandt, Alva Myrdal, García Robles, and Dr. Bernard Lown, one of the two co-presidents who represented International Physicians for the Prevention of Nuclear War at the presentation ceremony. I also talked with Pérez Esquivel, Elie Wiesel, and Oscar Arias. Of the earlier recipients I met Henri La Fontaine, Ludwig Quidde, Christian Lange, Ralph Bunche, and Martin Luther King, Jr.

For most of the biographical essays I depended upon secondary sources, finding particular assistance from the scholarly entries in the *Biographical Dictionary of Internationalists* and the *Biographical Dictionary of Modern Peace Leaders,* and for more recent figures, *Current Biography.* I also had access to documentary collections on certain of the laureates: the papers of Jane

Addams and Emily Greene Balch at Swarthmore; those of Norman Angell at Ball State University; the Carl von Ossietzky materials at the University of Oldenburg in West Germany and at the International Institute of Social History at Amsterdam; and the papers of Christian Lange in the Library of the University of Oslo. For earlier peace leaders I have seen the records of the International Peace Bureau and the papers of Bertha von Suttner and Alfred Hermann Fried in the Library of the United Nations in Geneva. Documents of Frédéric Passy, once made available to me by his son, Paul Passy, are now in the Library of the Peace Palace at The Hague. At the National Archives in Washington, D.C., I had opportunity to use the diplomatic correspondence of the Department of State with Oslo only for 1936.

I am grateful to Joe Cali, librarian of the Olive Kettering Library at Antioch College, and his staff, who know how to make the resources of a small college library go a long way. I wish to thank Werner Simon, archivist at the Library of the United Nations in Geneva, for so helpfully reviewing the entire manuscript, and also Professor Sandi Cooper for her carefully considered comments, although any errors that may still linger are mine. Meghan Robinson Wander, executive editor at G. K. Hall, has wielded the editorial pen with discrimination and judiciousness, and she has been supportive and patient. She, Cecile Watters, the skilled copy editor, and her other associates ably helped turn my pages into the present book.

Finally, I want to thank my daughter, Carole Abrams-Reis, for her invaluable help, not only as general assistant in the early going, but for critical comments and important translations from Norwegian and Swedish materials throughout.

My wife, Freda Morrill Abrams, served as in-house editor and in a variety of other ways, sometimes as director of logistics, sometimes as work foreman, always as purveyor of good sense and wisdom. Without her help this book would have been a poorer thing.

Irwin Abrams

Acknowledgment

I owe a special debt of gratitude to the Nobel Foundation of Stockholm, especially to Baron Stig Ramel, the Executive Director, and to Margaretha Ehrén and Birgitta Lemmel, Information Officers, who provided me with most helpful advice and materials.

The foundation kindly made available the illustrations, which are printed with its permission, and also granted permission to quote from the Nobel lectures and other speeches presented at the award ceremonies in Oslo, which have been published by the foundation annually in *Les Prix Nobel.* Quotations from these addresses have also been drawn from *The Nobel Lectures: Peace, 1901–1970,* 3 vols., edited by Frederick W. Haberman (Amsterdam, London, and New York: Elsevier, 1972) and used with the permission of the Elsevier Publishing Company and the Nobel Foundation.

Abbreviations

The following abbreviations are used in the bio-bibliographies.

BDI: *Biographical Dictionary of Internationalists.* Edited by Warren Kuehl. Westport, Conn.: Greenwood, 1983.

CB: *Current Biography Yearbook,* New York: H.W. Wilson, 1940–.

FNP: *Der Friedens-Nobelpreis von 1901 bis heute,* 12 vols. (in process). Vol. 1. *Der Friedens-Nobelpreis von 1901 bis 1904,* edited by Michael Neumann. Zug, Switzerland, and Munich, West Germany: Edition Pacis, 1987.

DAB: *Dictionary of American Biography.* New York: Scribners, 1928–.

DNB: *Dictionary of National Biography.* Oxford: Oxford University Press, 1921–22–.

MPL: *Biographical Dictionary of Modern Peace Leaders.* Edited by Harold Josephson. Westport, Conn.: Greenwood, 1985.

WEP: *World Encyclopedia of Peace.* 4 vols. Oxford: Pergamon, 1986.

Part One

The Nobel Peace Prize

1

Alfred Nobel and the Establishment of the Peace Prize

In January 1897, Stockholm newspapers reported that Alfred Nobel, the wealthy Swedish inventor of dynamite who had died the month before, had left the greater part of his large fortune for the establishment of a fund, "the interest on which shall be annually distributed in the form of prizes to those who, during the preceding year, shall have conferred the greatest benefit on mankind."

There were to be five prizes: three in science, for persons who had made the most important discoveries in physics, chemistry, and physiology or medicine; one for the person "who shall have produced in the field of literature the most outstanding work of an idealistic tendency"; and one for the person "who shall have done the most or the best work for fraternity between nations, for the abolition or reduction of standing armies and for the holding and promotion of peace congresses."

The prizes for physics and chemistry were to be awarded by the Swedish Academy of Sciences; that for medicine by the Karolinska Institute in Stockholm; that for literature by the Swedish Academy; and "that for champions of peace by a committee of five persons to be elected by the Norwegian Storting" (parliament). Nobel's directives concluded with these words: "It is my express wish that in awarding the prizes no consideration whatever shall be given to the nationality of the candidates, but that the most worthy shall receive the prize, whether he be Scandinavian or not."

The century about to close had seen monumental progress in science, and it was not surprising, except for the magnitude of the award, that a scientist and inventor like Nobel might want to establish prizes for achievements in these fields. Royal academies had recognized distinguished work of scientists as well as that of writers. But a prize for peace? Had not Europe been at peace for a generation, ever since the Franco-Prussian War of 1870–71? To be sure, it was an armed peace, and the costs of maintaining armies and armaments were becoming more and more burdensome. But what were these peace congresses whose organizers were to be rewarded, and what was an inventor of high explosives doing endowing a prize for peace?

Such might have been the thoughts of a European reading the report about Nobel's peace prize in the newspapers. As we look back upon it from the vantage point of the late twentieth century, however, Nobel's action does not seem so strange. He drew up his will in 1895. In less than twenty years the European armed peace was to dissolve in the first of two terrible wars that would engulf the whole world in violent bloodbaths, engaging not just armies but entire societies in a new kind of total warfare made more lethal by the very technological progress that the nineteenth century had celebrated. Civilization would somehow survive these tragic episodes of destruction only to face the prospect of thermonuclear annihilation. As Dr. Tore Browaldh, deputy chairman of the Nobel Foundation, declared at the Stockholm award ceremonies in 1982, in the Atomic Age "the unthinkable has been made possible: to transform Spaceship Earth into a nova, an exploding star, by means of new world war. Today the Nobel Peace Prize stands as the symbol of the struggle to prevent the extinction of man as a species."

Of course, Nobel could not have foreseen this turn of events. But as a scientist who knew at first hand the awful force of his new explosives, he recognized that the science and technology of his day were changing the shape of warfare, and he even had some conception of how a state of "mutual terror" might keep the peace. He once remarked to a peace activist, his friend Baroness von Suttner: "My factories will perhaps make an end to war sooner than your congresses. The day that two army corps can annihilate one another in one second, the civilized nations will shrink from war and discharge their troops."

As a rationalist and humanitarian thinker, Nobel had long been interested in the cause of peace, but it was through Baroness Bertha von Suttner, a longtime friend and peace activist, that he learned that an international movement to prevent war was emerging in the 1890s. Since 1889 two types of international peace meetings had been taking place almost every year: the Universal Peace Congresses of representatives from European and American peace societies, and the conferences of peace-minded deputies from some fifteen national legislatures, which evolved into the Interparliamentary Union. By the early 1890s each had established a coordinating bureau at Bern in Switzerland. These two branches of the peace movement overlapped in membership to some extent and in general did not differ in their approach to the problems of peace. The strongest support for both came from England and the United States, where religious groups had founded peace societies early in the nineteenth century and were later joined in mid-century by free-traders in international congresses that were largely Anglo-American in composition.

Now at the end of the century other elements were participating in the movement: liberal nationalists who drew inspiration from the conception of a federation of republics, jurists working to develop international law, utilitarians who saw war as irrational and wasteful, and humanitarians appalled by the suffering it caused. There were important differences among the various groups. The religious pacifists opposed all war as evil, whereas most of the others approved of "just" wars. Moreover, some of the politicians, uneasy at the prospect of being compromised in the company of "impractical idealists," insisted that their interparliamentary conferences keep a separate identity from the more popular congresses organized by the Peace Bureau.

All agreed, however, on the necessity of some kind of tribunal of arbitration where international disputes could be settled, which most peace leaders of the time thought of as a great panacea. They also agreed that the building of larger military establishments was more likely to lead to war than to the maintenance of peace. Some saw the reduction of armaments as a first step to be taken to reduce international tension; others pointed out that arms reduction could come only as a consequence of international organization. All warned that a new war would surely break out if the rule of force in relations between states were to continue unchecked. Parliamentarians and citizen activists alike saw the dangers of the international anarchy of their day much more clearly than did most of their contemporaries.

These were the developments that the baroness reported to Alfred Nobel, seeking to win his support for the cause. He responded with generous contributions, and in 1892 at her urging he came to Bern where the fourth Universal Peace Congress was meeting, not to take any part in it, but to learn from her how the young peace movement was doing. He was impressed with the quality of most of the peace leaders, but he expressed some doubts about the practicality of their proposals. All the same, he declared himself willing to be convinced that the peace movement could become effective. "Inform me, convince me," the baroness recalled his words, "and then I will do something great for the movement." She understood that he meant to endow with a small fortune persons who were able to make an important contribution to peace so that they could give themselves entirely to the work.

A few months later, in January 1893, Nobel wrote Baroness von Suttner that he planned to dispose of a part of his fortune by founding a prize to be "awarded to him or her who had caused Europe to make the longest strides toward ideas of general pacification." He spoke of the award being given every five years, six times in all: if Europe had not reformed the present system in thirty years, it was headed straight back to barbarism. In her reply the baroness raised an objection to the idea of a prize, arguing that the cause of peace was so compelling no such incentive was necessary. All that committed workers for peace needed was support for their efforts. If the queen of England convoked a peace conference, would *she* get the prize? Or if some philanthropist gave great sums for peace, would he?

Nobel took some account of these comments in the will he drafted and signed in March 1893, which included a bequest for Bertha von Suttner's Austrian Peace Society along with provision for prizes to be awarded every three years for scientific and intellectual achievements "in the wide field of knowledge and progress." These were to include prizes for persons who "are successful in word and deed in combating the peculiar prejudices still cherished by peoples and governments against the inauguration of a European peace tribunal." Nobel was explicit that the prizes were to go "to the most deserving without any regard to the question whether he be a Swede or a foreigner, a man or a woman."

In November 1895, Nobel drew up and signed the final version of his testament, which omitted the bequest to the Austrian Peace Society, but established the Peace Prize. There was no mention of a peace tribunal, but reference was made to the organization of peace congresses and efforts for disarmament, activities in which Bertha von Suttner and her fellow activists were engaged. Nobel's nephew Emanuel, the relative who knew him best, later told a member of the Storting prize committee that it was the baroness who was responsible for the peace clause in the will. His uncle had told him once in Paris, "I want to do something for Bertha von Suttner and the cause of peace."

Alfred Nobel: Man of Contradictions

The world loves a paradox, and whenever the Nobel award is discussed in the public prints, the irony of an inventor of powerful explosives leaving a legacy for peace is frequently pointed out. This is not the contradiction that it may seem to be, however, although it is true that Nobel's personality was complex. Baroness von Suttner drew the best pen-portrait in a letter she wrote him on the twentieth anniversary of their first meeting:

> A thinker, a poet, a man bitter and good, unhappy and gay—given to superb flights of mind and to malicious suspicions, passionately in love with the far horizons of human thought and profoundly distrustful of the pettiness of human folly, understanding everything and hoping for nothing; so you seemed to me. And twenty years have done nothing to efface this image.

This was indeed Alfred Nobel—cynic and idealist, pessimist and optimist, a melancholy and lonely man, yet witty and charming on such occasions as he chose to take part in social occasions. Always feeling himself to be Swedish, he was nonetheless a true man of the world, living most of his life outside Sweden and speaking fluently English, French, German, and Russian. It was consistent with his cosmopolitanism that his prizes, as we have seen, were to be awarded without any consideration of nationality.

Alfred Nobel's longest sojourn in Sweden was the first years of his life. At the age of nine he traveled with his mother and brothers to St. Petersburg to join the father, who was rebuilding his finances after an earlier bankruptcy in Sweden. Immanuel Nobel was a talented architect, engineer, inventor, and entrepreneur. His children followed in his footsteps. Alfred's brothers developed the oil industry in the empire of the tsars. Alfred himself not only invented dynamite but, more important, the process to set off the blast, and these became the basis for a worldwide industry, with Nobel factories and companies located throughout Europe and the United States. Alfred Nobel was a brilliant organizer and businessman, but his greatest joy came from his scientific research. He much preferred to work on experiments in his laboratory than travel about the world on business affairs, especially in his later years when the ill health that had always plagued him became more serious. It is an indication of the extent of his scientific work that at the time of his death he held at least 355 patents in many countries.

Busy as he was, Nobel managed to find the time for wide reading. The prize for literature was no mere afterthought. He loved literature and had even tried his hand at creative writing himself. As a youth of eighteen he composed an autobiographical poem in English, and later he wrote a play that was privately printed. His prolific output of letters display a mordant wit and a playful use of language. He intended to do some serious writing in Swedish when he could find the leisure.

This, however, was one luxury he never felt he could afford. He was too often on the move, monitoring the progress of his far-flung network of companies. For a long time his base was his well-appointed apartment on the Avenue Malakoff in Paris. Then he bought a villa in San Remo on the Italian Riviera and later a home in Sweden, where he intended to spend his summers. But his death in San Remo at the age of sixty-three put an end to his plans.

He died virtually alone, as he had lived so much of his life. Attending him were only a valet and his Italian doctor, who could not understand the Swedish words that were all Nobel could manage after suffering a stroke. His two nephews and Ragnar Sohlman, his young assistant, were summoned by telegraph, but they arrived only after his death.

Alfred Nobel had not known much true happiness in his life. He once wrote to his sister-in-law in St. Petersburg:

> What a contrast between us! You live a warm and glowing life, surrounded by loved ones whom you care for and who care for you; you are anchored in contentment. I drift about without rudder or compass, a wreck on the sea of life; I have no memories to cheer me, no pleasant illusions of the future to comfort me, or about myself to satisfy my vanity. I have no family to furnish the only kind of survival that concerns us, no friends for the wholesome development of my affections, or enemies for my malice.

Although there is exaggeration here and a self-deprecation that we often find in his letters, these lines poignantly convey his sense of loneliness, his regret at having no family of his own and few close friends. He was no recluse, but he gave his first loyalty to his work and limited his social life. Indeed, many of the personal relationships he did have failed to nourish in him a faith in humankind. Like other wealthy men, he was a constant target for begging letters, all of which he took pains to answer personally. In his business affairs he frequently found himself dealing with rascals and sharpsters, and often he had to go to law to protect his patents from unethical associates.

Nor did Nobel find happiness in relationships with women, except for his mother, whom he adored. We know of his first romantic love only through a tender passage in his autobiographical poem, which tells of her early death. When he was in his forties, he advertised for a lady to serve as secretary and manager of his Paris household. The beautiful Countess Kinsky, who came from Vienna to apply for the job, charmed him but left after a week to elope with an Austrian nobleman whom she loved. The next time Nobel saw her was some years later, when the lady, now Baroness von Suttner, visited him in Paris with her husband. She was to remain Nobel's good friend until his death, with the fateful consequences for the peace prize that we have seen.

Nobel next became interested in an Austrian shop girl, installed her in an apartment in Paris, tried in vain to make her into a cultured lady who would be a suitable companion, and ended up supporting her at a distance for the rest of his life. After his death, she sold his letters to the executors of his will. For many years thereafter these letters remained confidential, and it is only the more recent biographies of Nobel that tell of this unfortunate liaison.

Nobel's distrust of his fellow human beings, although seemingly well founded, contended with an even more deeply rooted idealism about humanity in general. In the phrases of Baroness von Suttner, the "malicious suspicions" were interred with his bones; the good that he did lived after him in the "superb flight of mind" that gave us the Nobel prizes.

What, then, of explosives and peace? This apparent contradiction has generated a serious misconception that persists today in certain quarters that the munitions maker left his "tainted money" to peace in order to salve his conscience. But actually, Nobel's dynamite was primarily used for nonmilitary purposes, for building roads, tunnels, railroads, and canals, and for mining. It is true that among his experiments were some that involved the improvement of military weapons, but this was a consequence of his relentless scientific curiosity. The greater part of his fortune resulted from the sale of explosives manufactured for civilian use.

It was toward the end of his life, in the late 1880s, that he devised his one important purely military invention, that of smokeless powder, which would have a significant influence on military tactics: it gave the defense an advantage over the offense by reducing the visibility of the defense's guns. It has been estimated, however, that his income from this source represented no more than one-tenth of his estate. Also in his last years he purchased the Bofors factory in Sweden, which produced war materials, but on this investment he actually lost money.

In Nobel's mind there was no contradiction between his military inventions and peacemaking. As he told Baroness von Suttner, his factories might bring an end to war sooner than her peace congresses, as war became more terrible. When the baroness first wrote him about her antiwar novel, *Die Waffen Nieder* (*Lay Down Your Arms*), and her commitment to the cause of peace, he jokingly asked her where, in case of universal peace, he could place his new smokeless powder. But when he read the book, he was so impressed that he thought it should be translated into all languages. Referring to the literary weapons she had wielded so skillfully and should *not* lay down, he spoke of the weapons of war as "instruments of hell." Elsewhere he called war "the horror of horrors and the greatest of all crimes."

The Will

Alfred Nobel's will, surely one of the most consequential ever written, was actually a defective legal instrument. Because of his long troublesome experiences with lawsuits, Nobel had come to distrust lawyers and to regard them as "niggling parasites." Thus when at age fifty-five he decided to make his will, he simply had a friend in Stockholm send him a specimen form, and he drew it up himself. No record of this first effort exists, only the revision of 1893 and the final will of 1895.

In the final version Nobel stated his general intentions clearly enough, but some basic elements were lacking. What Nobel, otherwise such an experienced businessmen, failed to do in the document was to provide for a legatee to carry out his high purposes. He directed that a fund be established from the bulk of his estate and specified how the income was to be used, but included not a word about who was to manage the money. Moreover, although Nobel was specific about the five prizes and the institutions that were to award them, he had not bothered to let these groups know what he was planning and to secure in advance their acceptance of the assignment. If any one of the five had refused, the whole will might have been thrown out.

Nobel did name the executors in the will—Ragnar Sohlman, his trusted assistant, and Rudolf Lilljequist, a Swedish industrialist. Their first move was to engage a lawyer, and the choice was a happy one: Carl Lindhagen, then a young jurist who was to become a prominent politician, the well-respected lord mayor of Stockholm from 1903 to 1930, and a leading worker for world peace whose own candidacy for the peace prize made the Norwegian committee's short list on four occasions. With Lindhagen as his legal adviser and close associate, Sohlman, who was only twenty-seven in 1897, took the major responsibility in the long struggle to see the will through the courts, negotiating with the Nobel relatives and other concerned parties.

The first legal question was that of jurisdiction. Which had been the actual domicile of this vagabond millionaire: Paris, where he had lived the longest; San Remo, where he had moved in 1891 and where he died; or the home near the Bofors factory in Sweden, where he had begun to spend the summer and autumn months in his last years? Many advantages would accrue if the will could be probated in Sweden; such a loosely drawn document was certain to be treated less rigorously there than in a French court and the taxes would be far less. Lindhagen could argue that Nobel was, after all, a Swedish subject, that he had had Swedish witnesses sign the will in the Swedish Club of Paris, that he had chosen Swedish executors, and that four of the five prizes were to be awarded by Swedish bodies.

Unfortunately, however, most of Nobel's funds and securities were in Paris banks. So before the French authorities or Nobel's relatives could realize what was happening, Sohlman secretly removed these holdings from France, escorting the boxes of documents to the railroad station post office in Paris with a loaded gun in his hand to protect them from any mishap. Some of the securities were sold in London; the rest went to Stockholm. The total net worth of Nobel's estate was more than 31 million Swedish crowns, almost $9 million, an immense fortune at the time. When it was safely in Sweden, the executors managed to have jurisdiction established in the Bofors district court.

The problems were just beginning, however. First, there were the interests of the relatives, for whom the will provided only minor bequests. Then there were the bodies named in the will who were to make the awards. Although the Norwegian Storting accepted its role with alacrity, some members of the Swedish institutions had grave reservations about taking on the formidable responsibilities envisaged, and some of the scientists would have preferred to use the funds to support their own research. Since these were all public bodies, the will became a matter of state, and its disposition ultimately required agreement by the Nobel family and the award-making bodies and finally approval by the king of Sweden.

In the beginning King Oscar II opposed the will and thought that Nobel's whole estate should go to the family. He told Emanuel Nobel, who headed the Russian branch, not to neglect the interest of his relatives "in favor of some fantastic ideas of your uncle," who had been influenced by "peace fanatics and particularly by women." But Emanuel was not swayed and remained faithful to his uncle's wishes. Telling Sohlman to remember the Russian concept of the executor as the "spokesman of the soul," Emanuel gave full support to the executors when the Swedish branch of the family started an action to contest the will. But in time, a settlement was finally reached with the family.

Sohlman and Lindhagen also had to contend with the opposition of Swedish conservatives, who claimed that Nobel had been "unpatriotic" in providing for international awards instead of designating his funds for Swedish use. They were particularly critical that the Norwegian Storting was to select the committee to make the peace award. It was a time when Norwegians were growing restive with their union with Sweden under a common monarch, and the conservatives claimed the peace prize would be used to win friends for the Norwegian cause.

Opponents of the will maintained, too, that the money that would come to each laureate would be excessive. Sohlman wrote confidentially to Baroness von Suttner that the peace leaders could undercut much of the opposition if they would agree in advance to keep only one-third of a prize for themselves and to contribute the rest to their peace societies. The baroness rejected this suggestion as contrary to Nobel's intentions to endow a prizewinner with major resources. Such a provision was not adopted, but as it turned out, the peace laureates have in fact given most of their money to their organizations or have used it for similar purposes.

To establish the validity of the will, Lindhagen made effective use of the sworn testimony of the witnesses who had signed it. He showed that Nobel firmly believed that large inheritances disadvantage heirs, who thereby lose their desire to work. In this regard he spoke of himself as something of a socialist. Moreover, in the final will of 1895 Nobel reduced the bequests for his relatives because he knew they had prospered since the first will was drawn. As for the lack of specifications for implementing the will, Lindhagen produced testimony that this had always been Nobel's way: he would engage someone in whom he had confidence, tell him what he wanted done, and then leave it to that person to accomplish the task.

The two young Swedish engineers who had

witnessed the will, R. W. Strehlenert and Leonard Hwass, testified that Nobel had told them his prizes were intended to give promising persons "such *complete independence* that they would in the future be able to devote whole energies to their work. His wish was not to reward work that had been done, or talents that showed promise, but to give an opportunity for fruitful development." A few months before his death Nobel had declared, "I would not leave anything to a man of action, as he would be tempted to give up work. On the other hand I would like to help dreamers, as they find it difficult to get on in life." Had Nobel written this condition into the will, it is possible that the Swedish bodies designated to make awards might have rejected the assignment altogether. It was going to be difficult enough to agree on distinguished achievement that should be rewarded. As it was, the juries were free to work out their own policies and methods of selection and to make changes in the future if needed.

Paradoxically, the fact that the testament was loosely drawn made possible a number of compromises in the final settlement, which satisfied the various parties. And on 29 June 1900, King Oscar II approved the statutes of the Nobel Foundation, which was created to supply the missing legatee and to receive the designated assets from the executors. Three and a half years had elapsed since Nobel's death, hardly a long time considering the many difficulties the executors had had to overcome.

The Nobel Foundation

With the machinery in place, the first prize awards were made in 1901 on 10 December, the anniversary of Nobel's death, which was selected as the foundation's Festival Day when all awards would be made. The statutes governing the administration of the Nobel Foundation also laid down the principles and procedures for the award-making bodies to follow, and although some amendments have been adopted, the most recent edition of the statutes, approved by the Swedish government in 1982, shows little fundamental change.

The statutes provide that each prize is to be awarded at least once in every five-year period, beginning with the first award. After 10 percent of the annual income has been added to the capital, the remainder is to be divided into five parts, corresponding to the five prizes. Each prize-awarding body retains one-fourth of its share for its own expenses; three-fourths represent the prize funds for that year. Under no circumstances can the money awarded be less than 60 percent of this portion, nor may it be shared by more than three prizewinners. Thus while the amount of money for any one prize is always equal to each of the other four, a laureate may have to share it with others.

The statutes provide not only that a given prize can be divided into as many as three parts but also that it can be awarded to an institution or an association. Bertha von Suttner opposed both provisions. She was against any division of the prize because of Nobel's expressed desire that the sum be large enough to be effective: "The inventor of dynamite knew better than anyone the effectiveness of accumulated forces." As to endowing institutions, the baroness declared that they were only "a form, a body—but the soul of a society always resides in an individual. It is the energy, the dedication, the sacred fire which fills a heart and a spirit, that is what propels a movement." Lindhagen agreed that her evidence that Nobel had wanted to endow only individuals was entirely convincing, but said that in view of the opposition it had been impossible to arrange matters in any other way. He asked her to recognize that Nobel had "only stated an idea, without indicating the practical execution, which he left, with confidence, in other hands." This was the argument that Lindhagen had used to get the will accepted by the probate court.

The Norwegian Nobel Committee was the only one of the award-making bodies to make explicit provision for granting prizes to institutions and associations in its Special Regulations, and fifteen such awards have been made since 1901 (see appendix A, table 5). All five bodies have made divided awards, most frequently in the scientific fields, where the prize money has sometimes been divided into three parts. The Peace Prize has often been shared by two laureates but never by three (see appendix A, table 3). The literature prize has rarely been divided.

The statutes also modify specific directives that Nobel did write into the will. His intention to award achievements of "the preceding year" was interpreted to permit prizes for earlier achievements whose significance had only recently become apparent. This was a reasonable modification, especially in the sciences, where theories and discoveries need time to be accepted. But in practice it has enabled the committees to reward graybeards whose most creative work is long past, obscuring Nobel's original idea of facilitating rather than rewarding achievement. George Bernard Shaw is said to have likened the awarding of Nobel Prizes to throwing a life preserver to a man who has already reached the shore.

Although Nobel specified that the prizes were to be granted annually, the statutes permit postponing the decision to the following year. If no nominee is deemed worthy by one of the juries and if upon reconsideration the decision is still not to grant a prize, then its amount reverts to the main fund. Before an amendment was adopted in 1974, only half of such unused monies would go to the main fund and the rest would be allocated to that prize section for its own purposes.

The statutes direct each awarding body to establish its own criteria of competence for nominators, who must submit their proposals to the appropriate body by 1 February for the prize of that year. Personal applications for an award are not acceptable. Each Swedish awarding body is to appoint a Nobel Committee of three to five persons to give their opinion on the candidates, but for the Peace Prize the will stipulated that the Storting is to elect the committee that itself decides the award. The Swedish Nobel Committees may include non-Swedes and the Norwegian Committee persons who are not Norwegians. The prize-awarding bodies are authorized to set up scholarly institutes to assist them; called Nobel Institutes, they belong to the foundation.

Amendments in 1974 made two noteworthy changes in the statutes. Originally a person who died after having been nominated could be given the award posthumously and the heirs could collect the prize money. There have been only two such awards—in literature for the Swedish poet Erik Karlfeldt in 1931 and the Peace Prize in 1961 for Dag Hammarskjöld, late secretary-general of the United Nations. Questions were raised about the propriety of posthumous awards, however, since Nobel had envisioned that the laureates would *use* the money. The 1974 amendment finally limited such awards to persons living when the announcement is made that they have won the prize (usually in October) but who die before the presentation ceremony on 10 December. The very presence of a posthumous-award provision in the statutes, however, is an indication of the disposition to treat the Nobel Prize as an honor rather than a financial boon for the laureate.

The second change of 1974 tightened up the confidentiality of the selection process. The formulators of the statutes had anticipated the controversies ahead over the naming of laureates and inserted a clause declaring, "No appeal may be made against the decision of a prize-awarding body with regard to the award of a prize." It also stipulates that no record is to be made of any differences of opinion in the deliberations, nor are any to be revealed. By the amendment of 1974 even the nominations and any investigations or opinions concerning the nominees are not to be divulged; only after fifty years may documents relating to a particular award be examined by a researcher. The Norwegian Nobel Committee has had a remarkable record over the years of observing these obligations of confidentiality, although it must be noted that in comparison with the larger Swedish award-making bodies, the deliberations in Oslo involve only five committee members and the committee secretary.

The statutes provide for a board and trustees of the Nobel Foundation. The board is composed of six members, who are Swedish or Norwegian citizens; one, the chairman, is appointed by the government, and the others are elected by the trustees, who represent the five award-making institutions. The board elects one of its members to serve as executive director of the foundation. There have been six executive directors since 1901, all prominent in Swedish public life. Most notable was Ragnar Sohlman, Nobel's assistant and executor of his will, who served the foundation in a number of capacities until his death in 1948. The present executive director is Baron Stig Ramel, who has served since 1972.

The major purpose of the foundation is to administer the funds. The total assets turned over to the foundation by the executors of Nobel's will, after taxes and expenses had been paid and various settlements made, amounted to well over 31 million crowns or about $8,610,000 at the rate of exchange of the time, an unprecedented philanthropic endowment. A certain proportion of the money was used for a building fund and for the establishment of the Nobel Institutes. This left something over 27 million crowns in the main fund in 1901; the amount available for each of the five prizes was the equivalent of about $41,800 (twenty-five times the annual income of a Swedish university professor of the period).

Nobel had directed in his will that the capital be invested in "safe securities." This meant that a conservative policy had to be pursued, and most of the money was invested in Swedish and Norwegian gilt-edged bonds and mortgages on real estate. The foundation gradually broadened this policy, with the approval of the government, but after fifty years a Nobel Prize was worth less than $32,000, and by 1953 the assets of the foundation had declined two-thirds in real value.

In 1946 the Swedish parliament exempted the foundation from payment of most taxes, and in 1953 the foundation received approval from the government to invest more freely and to put a large percentage of the funds in common stocks. Later the proportion of permitted overseas investments was raised. This has meant that the amount of the prize money has continued to rise since 1953. Whereas in 1950 the amount was only 13,500 Swedish crowns more than in 1901, by 1960 it had risen by 61,700 crowns over the 1950 level. In 1970 the amount had increased 174,000 crowns over 1960, and in 1980 it was more than double the 1970 amount.

Baron Ramel has been particularly successful in

his investment policies. Since he took office in 1972, the amount of the prize money has soared. In 1983, on the 150th anniversary of Nobel's birth, the prize, appropriately, was worth 1.5 million crowns (the equivalent of about $230,000). This was an increase of 30.4 percent over 1982, compensating both for inflation and Sweden's devaluation of the crown. In 1986 the prize was worth 2 million crowns (about $270,000). The value of the 1988 prize increased by 15 percent to 2,500,000 crowns.

Since being liberated from the limitations of conservative investments in 1953, the foundation's finances have made a remarkable upswing. By the end of 1987 its assets amounted to 1.3 billion Swedish crowns, and it calculated that the real value of its holdings considerably surpassed that of the original Nobel estate of some 32 million 1900 crowns.

A Sixth Prize

In 1968 the Bank of Sweden established the Bank of Sweden Prize in Economic Sciences in Memory of Alfred Nobel, pledging an annual amount to the Nobel Foundation equal to that of each of the other prizes. The laureate is chosen by the Swedish Royal Academy of Sciences in accordance with the Nobel Foundation statutes governing nomination of candidates, adjudication of the prize, and its presentation.

The Nobel Foundation agreed to the institution of this award in economics, since this was a field in which Nobel was deeply interested, like the five fields he had stipulated. It is not anticipated that other such prizes will be established, although a number have been proposed.

$337,500

2

The Norwegian Nobel Committee

In the complicated process of settling the will, the Peace Prize presented special difficulties. First of all, there was the matter of the award being made in Norway. By the terms of Nobel's earlier will of 1893, all the prizes were to be awarded by Swedish bodies, but in the final will of 1895 Nobel specified that the Peace Prize was to be given by a committee of five to be appointed by Norway's parliament.

Nobel never told anyone why he made this change. Since Norway was then associated with Sweden under a common monarch, he may simply have wanted to distribute responsibilities within the union. The Norwegians preferred to think that Nobel wanted to give recognition to the Storting because it had been the first national legislature in the world to vote support for the newly organizing peace movement. Nobel may also have been influenced by his admiration for the leading Norwegian writer, Bjørnstjerne Bjørnson, who was a strong peace advocate.

Whatever the reason for Nobel's designation of a Norwegian committee, this choice could only heighten the opposition to the will in Sweden. In the 1890s many Norwegians were becoming restive with the union, and a movement was developing that was to bring full independence to Norway in 1905. There was apprehension in Sweden that the Storting might use the Peace Prize as a political instrument to win foreign support for Norwegian independence. Critics in Sweden also pointed out that a committee selected by a political body was not likely to be free of political partisanship, in contrast to the scholarly and scientific bodies in Sweden that were to award the other prizes. But the Storting, unmoved by political considerations, readily accepted Nobel's mandate; the group looked upon it as a high honor, considering it to be the consequence of its support for the peace movement. After receiving formal notification from the executors on 24 March 1897, the Storting voted to accept the responsibility on 26 April, over a year before the designated Swedish bodies took such action. In August the Storting adopted a resolution on the selection and tenure of the committee and proceeded to elect the five members.

According to the resolution, every three years the Storting was to elect members and alternates of the Nobel Committee for six-year terms, acting on the report of its Committee on Elections at the last session of each Storting term. Two members were to be replaced at the end of three years, three at the next election, and so on, alternately, every three years. Those whose terms came to an end were eligible for reelection. In 1984, for example, the terms of three members expired; two retired and one was reelected.

The Independence of the Norwegian Nobel Committee

It is not always understood that the Peace Prize is awarded by an independent committee. Although the members are selected by the Norwegian parliament, the committee is in no way responsible to the Storting or to the Norwegian government for its decisions.

Over the years, in fact, it has become increasingly distanced from the Storting.

In its early history the committee did indeed have governmental connections, although not constitutionally; the Storting felt it was important to have the country's political leaders among its members. In 1937, however, the Storting decided that cabinet ministers in office should not serve. This decision was a result of the prize's being awarded in 1936 to Carl von Ossietzky, who had been imprisoned in a Nazi concentration camp. In anticipation of the committee's choice and the reaction to be expected from Hitler, Foreign Minister Halvdan Koht and a former premier both withdrew from the committee's discussions. The Third Reich actually warned Norway that such a peace award would be considered an unfriendly act. The Norwegian government answered that the committee was quite separate, but to avoid any such situation in the future, the Storting in the following year moved to ban members of the government from the committee.

Members of the Storting who were not cabinet ministers continued to play an important part in the committee until 1977, when, for reasons unrelated to the Nobel Committee, the Storting decided its members should not participate in any nonparliamentary committees it might appoint. The Nobel Committee fell in this category. As a consequence, its base is broader than before, with those politicians who are members likely to have already completed their active political careers.

Coincidentally, in the same year, 1977, the committee resumed its original name of the Norwegian Nobel Committee, after having been known since the earliest years as the Nobel Committee of the Storting. It remains a committee of the Storting, of course, but its only formal obligation to the legislature is an annual report, which has become more and more of a routine summary over the years.

The independence of the committee is symbolized in the award ceremony itself. In Sweden the king has always presented the other four prizes to the laureates, whereas in Norway the committee plays the principal role. In the first years the committee's chairman made the announcement at a session of the Storting. Since Norway became independent with its own monarch, the prize has been awarded in the royal presence, but the presentation of the diploma, the medal, and the check for the amount of the prize is made by the chairman or a representative of the committee.

Despite all these efforts to dissociate the Nobel Committee from the Norwegian government, there are still occasions when the Norwegian Foreign Office is officially asked by foreign diplomats to assist with nominations of the head of state or foreign minister of their countries. Moreover, when an award is viewed with disfavor by other governments, such as the prize for Menachem Begin in 1978, Norwegian diplomats at their posts abroad find themselves again and again having to explain that the Nobel Committee is not an agency of their government. The only formal governmental protest, however, was the remonstrance of the Third Reich over the Ossietzky award. After the Lech Wałesa prize was announced in 1983, the Polish government made a formal protest, not because of the award, but because the Norwegian premier publicly congratulated Wałesa.

The Personnel of the Norwegian Nobel Committee

When the Storting established the committee in 1897, there was some discussion as to whether non-Norwegians should be included in the membership. The deputies who were to make the nominations decided that "this time" they would recommend "Norwegians exclusively," and the Storting approved their list. In 1900, following the regulations, another election was held to replace the two members who were chosen by lot to retire in order to start the two-three alternation. But by that time, the statutes of the Nobel Foundation had been adopted and included a clause that stated, "Persons other than Norwegians may be members of the Norwegian Committee." The question consequently was debated in the Storting and in the press.

A minority argued for the inclusion of one or two distinguished foreigners, pointing out that Nobel himself had transcended national and Scandinavian considerations in setting up prizes for laureates from all countries. This would give the committee the benefit of expert knowledge and answer any criticism that the committee was influenced by narrow political considerations. The foreign members would be chosen not by nationality, with all the problems this could cause, but by office—for example, the presiding officers of the Institute of International Law or the Interparliamentary Union.

Critics of this proposal pointed out the advantages for "little Norway" in having the exclusive honor of administering the Peace Prize and called the idea a vote of no confidence in Norwegian competence. There was little objection in the country when the Storting reelected the two retiring members and the committee remained all-Norwegian.

The question arose only once more, many years later. In 1973, during the controversy in Norway over the much-criticized award to Henry Kissinger, the suggestion was put forward that the committee should be internationalized. It received serious attention among a few Storting deputies, and there was an effort to schedule debate about the committee in the parliament. The matter was eventually dropped. Even for those who agreed with the principle, the difficulties in the way of fashioning an international committee that would be free from national and political loyalties seemed insurmountable.

The composition of the committee since World War II has reflected the strength of the political parties in the parliament. The slate is prepared by the Committee on Elections of the Storting with that aim in mind, and it is always approved by that body without debate. In recent years the Labor party has been the largest in the Storting, and two members of that party have held seats on the committee. Despite this arrangement, however, committee members are not expected to represent a political party or persuasion.

In 1987 the members of the committee included two former politicians, Egil Aarvik, long prominent in the Christian People's party and at one time a cabinet minister, and Odvar Nordli, who had been prime minister from the Labor party; Gidske Anderson, a well-known author-journalist and the only woman member; Francis Sejersted, professor of history at the University of Oslo; and Gunnar Stålsett, secretary general of the Lutheran World Council in Geneva. Aarvik chaired the committee and Anderson was his deputy.

Once elected to the committee, it has been the custom for members to be reelected until they decide to step down. This has made for an extraordinary continuity until very recently, as can be seen from the following list of chairpersons. Jorgen Løvland, who chaired from 1901 to 1922, was Norway's first foreign minister after the separation from Sweden. His successor, Frederik Stang, jurist and rector of the University of Oslo, was chairman until 1941. He was followed by Gunnar Jahn, who headed Norway's Statistical Bureau and was later director of the National Bank. Jahn joined the committee in 1937 and chaired it from 1942 until 1966. After the two-year term of Nils Langhelle, Aase Lionaes, who came to the committee in 1949 as a Labor deputy and the first woman member, chaired from 1969 to 1978. Dr. John Sanness, director of the Norwegian Institute of Foreign Policy, was chairman from 1979 to 1981.

The member who served the longest was Hans Jakob Horst, who took his seat in 1901 and remained on the committee until his death in 1931. He was a prominent deputy of the Left and one of the international leaders of the Interparliamentary Union. Another longtime member was Bernhard Hannsen, shipping magnate, member of parliament, and a leader of the Norwegian peace societies, who served from 1913 until 1938. Horst and Hannsen represented the two branches of the organized peace movement, the parliamentarians and the peace activists. Since the Second World War, the peace movement as such has not had direct representation on the committee.

Continuity has also been provided in the persons of Christian Lange and Halvdan Koht. Lange was the first secretary of the committee (1901–09), then honorary adviser in the history of internationalism, and finally a member of the committee (1934–38). Professor Halvdan Koht was one of the earliest advisers (1904–13) and served as a member from 1919 to 1937. A further contribution to continuity has been the succession of long-term secretaries of the committee. When Lange left this position in 1909 after organizing the basic procedures of the committee, he was followed by Ragnald Moe, who remained in that post until 1947. Moe's successor was August Schou, who retired as secretary in 1973 but stayed on as adviser for several years. Moe and Schou made their careers serving in the double capacity as secretary of the committee and director of the Nobel Institute. Thereafter, Tim Greve, diplomat, historian, and journalist, remained for only four years in this position, and he was succeeded in 1978 by Dr. Jakob Sverdrup, who already had had a prominent career as journalist and university teacher of history and held a professorship at the University of Oslo along with his Nobel responsibilities.

The committee has been led by some of the most prominent figures in Norwegian public life, who have sought to carry out their mandate conscientiously over many years of their lives, most of them serving until their death. In the past decade the tenure of both chairpersons and staff has become shorter, and there are those who have lamented the passing of the strong leaders of earlier years, like Løvland, Stang, and Jahn. It remains to be seen whether this change will affect the work of the committee.

The Norwegian Nobel Institute

According to the statutes of the Nobel Foundation, each of the prize-awarding bodies was to establish a scholarly institute to aid it in its work. Thus, in 1904 the Norwegian committee established the Norwegian Nobel Institute "to follow the development of international relations, especially the work for their peaceful adjustment, and thereby to guide the Committee in the matter of the award of the prize." In addition, "it shall also work for mutual knowledge and respect, for peaceful intercourse, justice and fellowship between nations." The institute was to have a library with a selection of periodicals and a reading room. With these were to be associated "scholarly activities and popular educational work." Other such activities at home and abroad could be supported by the institute from its revenues.

Some international jurists at the time urged the committee to go further and make the institute international in membership, give it a key role in the award selections, and even have it play a part in the reconciliation of international conflicts. Although the Norwegian Nobel Committee cherished no such ambitions for the institute, its first director, Christian Lange, who remained secretary of the committee, did have high hopes of making it a world center for the scholarly study of peace and internationalism: "the best place for the study of international problems."

Unfortunately, such hopes were never realized. Lange did succeed in putting together a collection of periodicals and books on peace that was unique for its time, and the institute later published an excellent series of monographs on internationalism. But these publications have not been continued, and the available resources have never made it possible to establish the research center of which Lange and others dreamed. Nor has the institute ever carried on or supported in any significant way "popular educational work" for peace. For a time the committee made grants to peace societies and peace journals, as well as to individual peace activists and scholars, and once the institute planned programs of lecturers and even appointed lecturers on its staff, but no longer. Recently there has been a program of seminars for Norwegian teachers of international relations, but it is supported by a special fund.

In general the institute has worked mainly on its first objective, to serve as a support staff for the committee in the selection of laureates. In the first years Lange as secretary had written all the reports on nominees chosen by the committee for special consideration. After the institute was established, he shared this work with three part-time advisers representing international law, history, and political economy. Today the advisers, all at the University of Oslo, are professors of economics, of history, and of conflict and peace research.

The institute is still housed in the old classic mansion that was renovated with funds from the Nobel Foundation. It opened in 1905 on the occasion of an award ceremony highlighted by the presence of newly independent Norway's first monarch. There were the usual critics who declared that the money should have been spent not on an impressive building but on peace activities. Actually, the building at 19 Drammensveien near the gardens of the royal palace is a dignified structure, but modest indeed compared to the grandiose Palace of Peace that Andrew Carnegie built a few years later in The Hague for the Permanent Court of Arbitration. Nor have the Nobel Committees since then used very much money to keep up appearances; on visits in the early 1980s I found very little changed since my first visit before World War II. In 1985, however, the committee finally arranged to spruce up its headquarters and, for the first time, to install an elevator.

Today the Nobel Institute stands in stark contrast to the sparkling American embassy farther down the street, which can boast of an architectural award. Outside the institute a bust of Alfred Nobel faces the street. One proceeds through the brighter but still unpretentious entry hall and takes the elevator or the great stairway to the more welcoming library on the second floor. On the third floor is the committee's conference room, where the great decisions are made, and the small auditorium, once the scene of the award ceremony and the lectures of the laureates, both of which now take place in the more spacious great auditorium of the university (the Aula).

The library holds a modest collection of over 100,000 books, including government and United Nations publications, with a small assortment of general periodicals and journals of peace and international affairs. The library subscribes to a limited number of daily newspapers from various countries, fewer proportionately than before 1914. Publications by and about the laureates, in part sent along to support nominations, are very complete until the year of the award and thereafter rather spotty. Invaluable for the researcher are the scrapbooks of news clippings on the prize from 1901 until recently. In its early years few other libraries in the world made any attempt to keep up with the publications of the organized peace movement or to follow carefully the developments in international law and arbitration. For the committee's advisers to prepare solid reports, then, the institute library was indispensable. But today these experts are more likely to do their research in the libraries of the University of Oslo. The institute library has always been open to the general public, however, and it is especially used these days by students. In recognition of this service, the Storting makes a regular contribution to the library budget.

Thus the Norwegian Nobel Institute never realized the fond hopes of its founders that it might become a center for the study of international affairs, and its pursuit of its second stated objective, education for peace, has steadily diminished. Today great centers have been established in other parts of the world for international studies and for peace education and research, with public and private support. In light of these developments, the committee and its institute cannot be faulted for concentrating all their energies and resources on their primary task, the selection of the peace laureates.

The Selection Procedure

The process of selecting the laureates begins each autumn when the secretary of the committee sends out some five thousand circulars inviting nominations for the following year's award to be submitted by 1 February of that year. The right to make a nomination is restricted to the following people:

1. Past and present members of the committee and its advisers
2. Members of national assemblies and governments and members of the Interparliamentary Union
3. Judges of the International Arbitration Court and the International Court of Justice at The Hague
4. Members of the Commission of the Permanent International Peace Bureau (now in Geneva)
5. Members of the Institute of International Law
6. University professors of political science and jurisprudence, history, and philosophy
7. Former winners of the Peace Prize

By the deadline several hundred communications will have been received, submitted in many forms. The committee files contain nominations casually scribbled on a visiting card, sent in telegrams of one line, and presented in handsomely printed booklets. The most acceptable form of nomination is a well-considered letter accompanied by substantial documentation.

Along with the bona fide nominations, the committee often receives a host of proposals from ineligible persons, sometimes from individuals nominating themselves, which is not permitted. There may be supporting letters and petitions as the result of an organized campaign for a nominee. The committee once received a letter from members of a religious group, saying that they were writing as they had been instructed to by their superiors. Then there are the nominations sent in by members of parliaments who are merely doing a favor for someone in their constituency. There have been persons who secured nominations in this way and then went about advertising themselves as "nominated for the Nobel Peace Prize." It is the secretary's job to sort out all this material and to screen it for the committee. He discards all the ineligible proposals and prepares an annotated list of the nominees for the first meeting of the committee after 1 February.

The members assemble in the simply appointed room at the institute that is used only for their meetings. They sit at an oval table beneath a candelabrum, surrounded by pictures on the walls of Alfred Nobel and all the laureates. To the right of the chairperson is the deputy chairperson, and to the left, the secretary, who is the only nonmember admitted. The secretary prepares the materials for each meeting and answers questions, but takes no part in the decision-making deliberations.

During the first meeting the committee members exercise their own right of nomination. Often their purpose is to tidy up the list by formally proposing a nominee of the previous year, who must be renominated to be given consideration since no names are carried over from year to year, or by proposing separately a name that has been submitted in a joint nomination.

The number of nominations considered in recent years has risen to over eighty. Once the whole list was released to the press, but the amended statutes of 1974 barred this practice, since it seemed unfair to those not chosen. The press, lacking official information, has relied upon speculation and news releases supplied by some nominators, despite the committee's discouragement of this practice.

From the secretary's annotated list of all the nominees, the committee at its first meeting selects about twelve to be reported on for further consideration. The secretary distributes these assignments among the three advisers and himself. By the next meeting in the late summer, the reports are available in printed form for the eyes of the committee alone. These are the reports that are open for inspection by scholars only after fifty years have elapsed. Those now available from the first three decades of this century are most impressive documents—thorough, conscientious, and authoritative, a tradition that has been maintained to the present. One adviser told me he was permitted by the committee to submit samples of his reports along with other evidence of his professional scholarship to buttress his case for advancement in his university.

The advisers strive for objectivity in their reports, citing both pros and cons. It is only natural, however, that on occasion an adviser may become attached to the subject of his report and feel a sense of accomplishment if the committee selects that nominee. On the other hand, in one case the adviser was so convinced that a candidate's claims were specious that the committee found his highly negative report inappropriate and refused to keep it in the printed records.

It is in the advisers' reports that a particularly substantive initial nomination may have its influence. On at least one occasion the adviser's report seems to have been almost entirely based upon a well-documented proposal. It is in these reports also that a communication from a person ineligible to nominate but deemed worthy of a hearing, such as a laureate in one of the other four fields, may be brought to the attention of the committee. It is here that the results of a campaign may weigh in the balance.

Committee members maintain that they are unimpressed by campaigns and that they consider each nomination on its merits, quite apart from the identity of the nominator or the supporters. Indeed, one campaign seems to have been counterproductive: an organized effort in the Storting in behalf of Alva Myrdal may only have stirred up the committee's desire to show its independence of that body and delayed her award. Yet there have been successful campaigns, beginning with the very first prize, that for Henry Dunant. Other noteworthy organized efforts that succeeded were those in behalf of Norman Angell, Carl von Ossietzky, Emily Greene Balch, and Eisaku Sato. Despite their disclaimers, committee members can hardly remain impervious to compelling manifestations of public opinion. Judging from the earlier reports of advisers now accessible, the committee must still see evidence as to how a candidacy is judged by worthy and creditable persons who have gone to the trouble of sending well-documented letters of nomination or have otherwise written in support of a candidate. On the other hand, committee members may not give so much weight to someone who merely signs a group nomination. Committee members are not naive, and it is unlikely that they were much impressed, for example, by the number of American congressmen who were annually mobilized by their constituents to lend their names in support of Elie Wiesel, whose major credentials for the prize lay elsewhere.

After the committee members have studied the advisers' reports, the substantial discussions begin on the selection of the laureate. According to the statutes, if the prize for the preceding year has been reserved, the committee must first reach its decision about the current year before addressing the question of the previous year's prize. The deliberations may continue in more than one meeting, but when the chair feels that the discussion has gone on long enough, each member is asked to declare his or her choice and to give the reasons. After they have gone around the table a second time, the chair attempts to express the consensus.

Much depends upon the chair's skill in understanding each member's feelings and moving toward agreement. The committee strives for unanimity, but in case opinions are divided, the majority decides. We know of two occasions when the selection was made by a vote of three to two: the prize for Woodrow Wilson in 1920 and that for Henry Kissinger and Le Duc Tho in 1973. The latter instance led to the unprecedented resignation of two members of the committee.

In the earliest years of the prize, the announcement of the winner was made on 10 December, when the chair reported to the Storting in a session that lasted no more than thirty minutes. Until that moment the identity of the laureate was known only to the committee, the prizewinner, and a few others. Until 1906 the announcement of the prize to the Storting was regularly made in the hall of the parliament. Thereafter, the scene shifted to the new building of the institute, where in 1907 the laureate was present to receive the award on 10 December for the first time. The ceremony returned to the Storting only once, in 1920, when the parliament wanted to present the award for President Wilson to his representative. In 1910, by an amendment to the statutes of the Nobel Foundation, the prize-awarding bodies were permitted to announce the award before 10 December. Today each of these bodies releases the news to the press in October, but at different times to ensure greater publicity. The Peace Prize is usually announced before the middle of the month.

In contrast to the others, the Norwegian committee for many years announced its prize without citing the reasons for it, although these were usually referred to in the presentation speech given by a committee member. This practice was changed in 1975, at the instance of the committee secretary, Tim Greve, who from his journalistic experience was well aware of the needs and uses of the media. He pointed out that the moment when the world is listening most attentively is when the name of the winner is revealed, not when the award ceremony takes place in December. The most effective time to make public the message the committee wants to convey with its prize is when the chairperson is standing outside the door of the committee room in front of television cameras and microphones. Consequently, since 1975 the chairperson has read a press communiqué with the reasons for the award detailed, and the media coverage has substantially improved.

The Ceremony of Award

The statutes of the Nobel Foundation call for all the prizes to be presented on 10 December, the anniversary of Nobel's death. But that month in Oslo is often bitterly cold, and visitors who come for the ceremonies may reflect, as they trudge through the snow in the icy air, that it would have been better to have selected the anniversary of his birth in October.

In early December, however, the Christmas holidays are approaching, Yuletide decorations are beginning to appear in the streets, and despite the weather, the mood in Oslo is bright and festive. The award and its attendant festivities represent a high point in the winter season, for the presentation of the Peace Prize is a great event in the life of this small country. Norwegians are proud to be, even briefly, the center of world attention, as they watch the great numbers of foreign media representatives descend upon their capital to report the affair. The Wałesa award of 1983, for example, brought a record number of several hundred.

The official ceremonies include the presentation of the prize at one o'clock in the afternoon of 10 December, the banquet for the laureate that evening, and the laureate's Nobel lecture, usually delivered on the following day. When appropriate, there may also be an ecumenical church ceremony in the cathedral. An unofficial event that takes place only for prizewinners especially favored by the populace is the torchlight parade in their honor on one of the evenings of their sojourn. It may be organized by the university students, by peace activists, or by other groups. In 1983 it was the trade unionists who organized the procession for Wałesa, but the hundreds of people who moved past the balcony of the Grand Hotel where Danuta Wałesa and her son Bogdan stood, carrying burning torches and chanting slogans of support, included all sections of the populace. Pérez Esquivel insisted on joining the parade instead of reviewing it, which disrupted the schedule for the evening banquet.

The scene of the formal presentation of the award, once the small lecture hall of the institute, for the past four decades has been the large auditorium of the university, the Aula. There a crowd of 650 can find seats, whereas the institute could seat only 150. In the exceptional circumstances of 1978, when Premier Begin of Israel came to receive his award, the event was moved to the Aarhus fortress for security reasons (occasioning comment more ironic than irenic).

The Aula provides an appropriate setting for the ceremony. On its walls are the murals of the great national painter Edvard Munch, which seem to evoke the spirit of Norway and the characteristic Norwegian love of nature. The hall is large enough to seat all the leading personages of the political and cultural life of the country and the diplomatic corps, who have all received special invitations, as well as others who have managed to get tickets, yet it is not too large for a certain sense of intimacy as the laureate receives the tokens of the award and speaks directly to an audience that is neither huge nor remote. It is a friendly hall and a warm and responsive audience, many of whom know one another.

The ceremony has its traditions and is carefully planned. After everyone is seated, the laureate is escorted to a place in the front row. Then, on the stroke of one o'clock, the king of Norway appears at the rear of the hall, and while he and his party are escorted to special seats set up in mid-aisle, all rise solemnly and silently. When the audience is once again seated, the program begins with selections from the orchestra. For Martin Luther King, Jr., they played selections from *Porgy and Bess,* for Danuta Wałesa, a polonaise.

Now it is the turn for the chairperson of the committee and the laureate to walk up the steps to the flower-decked stage. The chairperson makes a speech setting forth the reasons for the award and then presents the laureate with a diploma and medal. The laureate gives a speech of acceptance, which is translated into Norwegian, if necessary. Both return to their seats, and the orchestra plays once more. The king comes forward to congratulate the new laureate. Then all stand while the royal party leaves the hall, and the ceremony is over. It usually takes about an hour. The presentations in Stockholm later the same day are not so simple. There the attenders are in formal attire, and it is the king of Sweden who hands out the tokens of the five awards amid fanfares and bows.

The diploma and the medal were both designed by Norwegian artists. Gerhard Munthe designed the diploma, which is presented to the laureate in an artistically carved wooden box. The gold medal of the Peace Prize was executed on the model created by Gustav Vigeland, whose famous sculpture park is a leading cultural attraction of Oslo. On one side of the medal is pictured the head of Alfred Nobel, on the other, three figures join arms within the inscription "For peace and fraternity of peoples."

In the evening the committee gives a gala dinner at the Grand Hotel for the laureate and his or her party, with a select guest list. This is the occasion when the laureate can meet the committee members and other Norwegian leaders. It is also an eagerly anticipated social event. The story goes that when Mother Teresa learned that so much money was to be spent upon a feast in her honor, she insisted that instead the money should be given to her to feed the starving in Calcutta. There is no provision, however, for the laureate to receive more money than the amount of the prize, except for travel expenses to and from Oslo. So it was arranged that the item for food in Mother Teresa's travel account was greatly increased, and the hungry in Calcutta were fed. But to relieve the disappointment in Oslo, the committee found other funds so that the banquet could be replaced by a reception for Mother Teresa.

If the laureate is unable to attend the ceremony, a representative may be designated. In Oslo the diplomatic representative of the laureate's country has often served in that capacity. Andrei Sakharov and Lech Wałesa naturally preferred to be represented by their wives. If for some reason the laureate is not represented at the ceremony, he or she has until 1 October of the following year to collect the prize money.

The Nobel Lecture

The only obligation that comes with any Nobel Prize is the requirement that, whenever possible, the prizewinner deliver a public lecture in the city of the award within six months of receiving it. Permission to do this later is easily secured. The record postponement was that of Theodore Roosevelt, who received the award for 1906 and gave his lecture in 1910, when he had finished his presidency and was on his travels. Roosevelt delivered his lecture in the National Theater to an audience of over two thousand. Most of the Nobel lectures have been presented in the institute auditorium, since interest in the lecture is rarely as keen as that in the award ceremony itself. In more recent years the event has been shifted to the Aula, but it rarely draws a packed house.

Of the eighty-six prizewinners since 1901, fifty-one individual laureates have presented their lectures in person or had representatives read it for them, as have fifteen representatives of award-winning institutions. Of those who missed the assignment, most won their prize before the Second World War. Between 1901 and the First World War, of the seventeen individual laureates, a number of them old or ill, seven did not come to the Norwegian capital to present a lecture. In the years between the two world wars, nine of the twenty individual prizewinners gave no lectures (one came for the award but did not lecture).

Since 1945, however, only five have failed to appear: Cordell Hull (1945) was unwell; Henry Kissinger (1973) and Anwar Sadat (1978) pleaded the pressure of affairs of state, although Sadat sent a short text that was read by a representative; Sakharov (1975) was not allowed by his government to come but sent a carefully prepared address that was read by his wife; and Wałesa (1983) feared that if he left Poland, the government would not let him return. He sent his wife to accept the award, and his lecture was read by a Solidarity comrade and the translation by a popular Norwegian actor.

These lectures, which have all been published together with the Stockholm prize lectures by the Nobel Foundation in the series *Les Prix Nobel,* reflect not only a variety of approaches to peace but differences in form and style, and they are of uneven quality. They are the products, of course, of lives of activism rather than of scholarship. Some of the laureates were clearly too busy to do more than contribute reflections on current problems of peace. Others went to considerable effort to present thoughtful accounts of their own peace efforts or the particular approach to peace they advocated. Some laureates were obviously speaking to an unseen audience that extended far beyond Oslo; others spoke directly to their immediate auditors. There is high inspiration here and moving eloquence. Altogether the lectures represent an important documentation of the rich diversity of peacemaking and the high caliber of some of the best of the peacemakers.

3

The Transformation of the Prize: Nobel's Wishes and the Record of the Norwegian Nobel Committee

Has the committee in its decisions been faithful to the intentions of Alfred Nobel? To answer this question we will examine a number of Nobel's expectations:

1. Nobel expected the Peace Prize to support the organized peace movement. How have the peace leaders fared in comparison to other categories of laureates?
2. Nobel wanted the prizes to be awarded annually. How often has the prize been withheld? How often divided?
3. According to the will, "no consideration whatever shall be given to the nationality of the candidates." How international is the list of laureates?
4. Nobel wanted his prize to go to individuals, but the statutes permit institutional laureates. What has the committee done in this regard?
5. Nobel wrote Bertha von Suttner of awards "to him or her." What does the record show for women laureates?
6. Nobel wanted the prize to be awarded for an achievement of "the preceding year." To what extent have the peace awards been given for recent achievements?
7. Nobel wanted to foster rather than to honor achievement. Which has meant more to the laureates, the diploma and the medal or the check?

How Has the Organized Peace Movement Fared?

As soon as Nobel's will was made public, Bertha von Suttner and the other peace leaders began to congratulate one another. This was what Nobel had led her to expect when he said he would do something important for the peace movement, and his will even specified efforts for the reduction of armaments and the promotion of peace congresses, activities about which he had expressed some criticisms.

Great was the disappointment of the peace workers, however, when the first prize was announced in 1901: Frédéric Passy, the acknowledged doyen of the organized peace movement, was to share it with Henry Dunant, founder of the Red Cross. To Baroness von Suttner and her colleagues the Red Cross was not working for peace at all. However admirable its efforts to alleviate the human suffering that war caused, the true objective should be to reduce the incidence of war so that such suffering would be prevented in the first place. But the Nobel Committee took a different view. Nobel had also specified awarding work for "fraternity between nations," and what greater demonstration could there be of such fraternity than the works of mercy of the Red Cross in the midst of hostilities?

In Nobel's original Swedish, *folkens förbrödande* conveys a stronger sense of forging the bonds of brotherhood between peoples than does the official English translation, "fraternity between nations," and successive Nobel Committees have used this phrase to give an ever broader interpretation to peacemaking. On the one hand, they have honored statesmen for their efforts to bring individual wars to an end, to resolve international conflicts, and to organize and nurture the structures of international organization. On the other, they have acknowledged efforts to relieve human suffering, to bring about social justice and right human relationships, recognizing the spiritual and material foundations on which any enduring peace must rest. Some of the most acclaimed awards have gone to works inspired by a faith in human brotherhood.

The independence the committee has shown from the first in its interpretation of Nobel's testament was illustrated in the words of the present chairman, Egil Aarvik, in an interview with me in 1983. Referring to the new emphasis on human rights, he said, "The will does not state this, but the will was made in another time. Today we realize that peace cannot be established without a full respect for freedom."

To show the proportion of awards that have been given to representatives of the organized peace movement, table 1 in appendix A is organized by categories in which all the laureates can be classified. In the peace movement category are listed those laureates whose primary efforts, when they were given the award, were directed to influencing public opinion in favor of peace through their societies and their own writings and propaganda and to pressuring governments to follow peaceful policies.

The laureates in this category are easiest to classify in the period 1901–18. The committee was giving recognition to leaders of the two wings of the movement of Nobel's own time, the politicians of the Interparliamentary Union and the heads of the peace societies who met in the international congresses, a number of whom were also parliamentary deputies. In this period twelve of the twenty awards went to these leaders and their international bureau.

In subsequent periods it is harder to make a firm classification for this group. Some laureates, like Cecil (1937), Noel-Baker (1959), and Myrdal (1982), had made important peace contributions when they were holding government positions, but were recognized for subsequent activities after they had left office. Pérez Esquivel (1980) headed an important international peace society but seems more properly classified in the human rights category.

Carl von Ossietzky (1935) is a special case. In making this award to an inmate of a Nazi concentration camp, the committee, mindful of Norway's relations with the Third Reich, emphasized his work for peace as an opponent of militarism and German rearmament in the Weimar Republic. But it was really responding to the pressure of a world campaign, which, as one of the organizers, Willy Brandt, then a young emigré in Oslo, remembers was "to save a victim of the Brown Terror, condemn Nazism, and honor the other Germany."

Of the total of eighty-seven selections, then, at most twenty-seven fall in the category of the organized peace movement, twenty in the first thirty-seven years. Twenty-five statesmen have been named, if we include in that category all those who by dint of their office have been involved with top policy in relations between states: heads of state, foreign ministers, ambassadors, and United Nations statesmen.

The humanitarian category is based on the committee's own broad interpretation of its mandate to recognize works that demonstrate brotherhood among peoples. I include here Léon Jouhaux (1951), the French labor leader who, in the words of the committee representative, "devoted his life to the work of promoting brotherhood among men and nations," and the International Labor Organization (1969), which was also cited for its work for social justice. Included also is the American agricultural scientist Norman Borlaug (1970), whose Green Revolution has provided more food for a hungry world. Boyd Orr (1949) has worked for peace with the same objective.

Bertha von Suttner and her colleagues were right to view the first humanitarian award in 1901 with alarm. Although the peace leaders garnered a good share of the prizes in the early years, their successors have received far fewer awards. Not since the first two periods has the organized peace movement in Norway had a member on the committee, and peace activists have often been critical of the awards.

When the Committee Disagrees

In the eighty-seven years of the prize there have been nineteen years in which no award was given, the highest number for all the Nobel prizes. Nine of these were years of world war, which brought disruption to all the prizes, but to the Peace Prize most of all. In 1940 Norway was occupied by Germany and two committee members went into exile; only the legal connection with neutral Sweden kept the Quisling government from laying hands on the Norwegian Nobel Institute and provided a basis for the committee's continuance.

In years of peace the committee has postponed the award twenty times, on ten of these occasions finally deciding to withhold the prize for the previous year altogether. Table 2 in appendix A indicates the distribution of these negative decisions in the four periods. Given Nobel's desire for an award every year, there seem to be a fairly large number of omissions, although the recent record indicates a more hopeful trend, with prizes regularly awarded since 1972 and only one year when the prize was reserved for the next decision time.

We can only speculate about the reasons for postponing or completely withholding a prize. Reserving the award in 1925, for example, made it possible the next year to give awards to four statesmen at the same time who were all responsible for the easing of international tensions. The decisions to make no award for 1932 and to postpone the award for 1933, on the other hand, seem to have been a result of the worsening international situation. The prize for 1976, which in the following year was given to Mairead Corrigan and Betty Williams for their reconciliation work in Northern Ireland, may have been postponed to allow for more time to observe how their peace movement, which had started so dramatically, would develop.

The withholding of the prize for 1948 had to do with considerations about posthumous awards. Word leaked out that the committee was considering two such awards—to Gandhi, assassinated in that year by a Hindu opposed to Gandhi's policy of reconciliation with Pakistan, and to Prince Bernadotte of Sweden, assassinated a few months later by Israeli terrorists opposed to his United Nations mediation mission. The committee's inquiries in Stockholm about the appropriateness of posthumous awards were not conclusive, and the decision was made to reserve the prize rather than go ahead. In 1949 the committee decided to make no award for 1948. Presumably no living candidate seemed as worthy as the two who had died as martyrs to peace.

There is evidence in the archives of the committee that on at least two occasions a prize was reserved because of strong disagreement among committee members. In 1919 the candidacy of Woodrow Wilson met with resistance in the committee because of his war policies and the punitive aspects of the Versailles Treaty. The committee could agree on no other candidate, and the decision was left for the next year. In 1920 the opposition was overcome and Wilson was given the prize for his part in establishing the League of Nations.

In 1935 the leading candidate was Carl von Ossietzky, with a growing movement of public opinion in his behalf. The committee was clearly divided, however, and the prize was reserved for 1936. By that time the movement of opinion was even stronger and the composition of the committee had changed. Two members with governmental connections withdrew from the committee so that the government would be dissociated from such a decision, which was sure to infuriate Hitler. The committee then made the courageous decision to give the 1935 award to Ossietzky, and Hitler, true to form, decreed that henceforth no citizen of the Third Reich would be allowed to accept any of the Nobel prizes.

Such disagreements may have been the major reason for decisions to give no prize. Certainly it has not always been the lack of worthy candidates. The very first peacetime year for which no prize was awarded was 1923. In that year, two candidates who were considered by the committee but passed over, Jane Addams and Lord Cecil, were given the prize later, and there were other strong candidates, such as President Masaryk of Czechoslovakia, Charles Evans Hughes, and the Interparliamentary Union. Again in the following year, when no prize was given, Addams and Cecil were considered, and there were two other nominees who were to be found qualified for the award later, Ludwig Quidde (1927) and the Quakers (1947).

Nobel's directive for annual awards seems more to the point today than ever, insofar as the Peace Prize is concerned. Now that it has become so prestigious and newsworthy, every award means a rare opportunity to turn the attention of a violent world to the ways of peace. The making of the award has become in itself a form of peacemaking. And a decision to make no award sends to the world a message of discouragement that can delight only war makers and political cartoonists.

The practice of dividing a prize, unanticipated by Nobel but permitted by the foundation statutes, has probably been used by the Oslo committee to reconcile differences of opinion, judging from such odd couplings as Addams/Butler (1931), and MacBride/Sato (1974). Although the awards often proved controversial, more appropriate divisions were joint awards to statesmen for bilateral agreements, such as Briand/Stresemann (1926), Kissinger/Le Duc Tho (1973), and Begin/Sadat (1978). There have also been joint awards for shared achievement: English/American Quakers (1947), and Corrigan/Williams (1976). In the earliest period divided prizes were used to reward a number of the aging peace veterans before it was too late. Here, too, there were a few surprising pairings, which may well have represented compromises. Table 3 in appendix A shows the distribution.

"Whether Scandinavian or Not"

Nobel's admonition that his prizes should be awarded internationally, not just to Scandinavians, has been well heeded by the Norwegian Nobel Committee.

Only two fellow countrymen have been named, and only five from Sweden and one from Denmark. Twenty-four countries are represented in the roster of laureates (twenty-five, if the declined award to Le Duc Tho of the Democratic Republic of Vietnam is included). Heading the list is the United States with eighteen, followed by Great Britain with ten and France with nine.

Western Europe and the United States remained the main source of laureates through the Second World War. It was only with the award for 1960 to Albert Lutuli, the Zulu chieftain from South Africa, that the committee began to think more globally. The narrow Western orientation continued, however, and voices were raised in protest, proposing that the committee itself be reorganized to include international personalities from outside Norway, who would provide some balance in the selections. With the naming of the first representative from Asia in 1974, former prime minister Sato of Japan, and the broader based choices of the years since then, this criticism has been stilled. Committee members have individually expressed to me their genuine concern to distribute the awards among the different regions of the world. Table 4 in appendix A, which gives the figures on the awards by country, shows a strong trend toward this objective. In the awards of the last ten years, Israel, Egypt, India, and South Africa have been represented, and there have been three Latin American laureates.

"To the Person"

Nothing was further from Nobel's mind than to set up awards for institutions. The whole point of his prizes was what they would do for individuals. In the compromises of the settlement of the will, however, the statutes of the Nobel Foundation were written to permit each of the prize-awarding bodies to decide whether "institutions and associations" would also be eligible for its award, and the regulations of the Norwegian Nobel Committee made explicit provision for this.

The committee has given fifteen such awards, 17 percent of the total, but only four before World War II. Most favored have been the Red Cross, with four prizes, and international refugee agencies of the League of Nations and the UN, with three. Table 5 in appendix A gives the distribution. The decision to permit these impersonal awards was criticized at the time, especially by the peace activists. Bertha von Suttner, who knew Nobel's intentions, had protested, as we have seen, declaring that "the soul of a society always resides in an individual." Engaged in the best of good works as these bodies have been, both the international recognition and the money have usually meant far less to them than to an individual laureate.

Moreover, in the broadest context—the meaning of a prize for the world—the best of the individual awards have represented the greatest glory of the Peace Prize, the celebration of the service for humanity of great human beings, whose lives are an inspiration for us all. Three times the committee has directed the world's attention to the desperate plight of refugees and the fine work that international agencies have done in trying to meet this crying human need. But it may not be unfair to compare the impact of these awards with what it means for the world to have its attention called to the great qualities of mind and spirit of Fridtjof Nansen and the epic story of his herculean labors in behalf of the homeless and the stateless. An award to an institution may mean more than inconsistency with Nobel's original intentions; it may mean an opportunity missed to put the Peace Prize to its highest use.

"To Him or Her"

There are few women laureates in all five prize lists. If peace has the most, seven, with six in literature and fewer in the other fields, it is because the Oslo committee has named four in the last seven years (see table 6, appendix A). This augurs well for the future in the peace awards, but the past record is dismal. It is more of a reflection upon our civilization in general, of course, than upon the Norwegian Nobel Committee in particular, but since it was a woman who had so much to do with Nobel's setting up the award in the first place, one might somehow have expected better of the committee.

Bertha von Suttner had to wait for her award until 1905, when she received the seventh prize (in 1901 and 1902 the prizes were divided). The committee did not give her special consideration until 1903, when she was passed over in favor of the English politician William Randal Cremer, cofounder of the Interparliamentary Union, although Baron Pirquet, the Austrian parliamentarian, sent along with his nomination copies of her correspondence with Nobel. In 1904, nominated by most of the peace leaders, she made the short list again, but the committee decided to honor an institution, the Institute of International Law.

In 1905 the baroness had the largest number of nominations of all the twenty-four nominees. Her nominators included not only her coworkers, who called her their "commander in chief," but the Swedish Interparliamentary group and fourteen deputies from Hungary. Even so, to get a decision in her favor required a letter from Bjørnstjerne Bjørnson to his fellow members of the committee, reporting what he had learned from Emanuel Nobel about his uncle's wishes. Bjørnson insisted that this was an order from Nobel himself to give Bertha von Suttner the prize. The committee thereupon gave her not only the prize for 1905 but an undivided prize, the second to be granted. This was two years after Marie Curie had become the first woman Nobel laureate, in physics.

It was twenty-six years before the next peace award went to a woman, although in 1911 Marie Curie picked up her second prize, in chemistry, and there had been three women laureates in literature by 1928. In 1931 the Oslo committee divided the prize between Jane Addams and Nicholas Murray Butler. She had first been considered by the committee in 1916 for her mediation efforts during the war, but no prize was given for that year or for 1923, when she was considered but passed over again. In that year among her thirty nominators were eminent personalities like Woodrow Wilson, John Dewey, Senator Robert La Follette, Sidney Webb, Graham Wallas, George Lansbury, and Clement Attlee. The report of the committee's adviser was highly positive, characterizing the candidate as "the most outstanding representative of practical American idealism." Jane Addams was on the committee's short list again in 1924 and 1928, both years for which no prize was awarded, as well as 1929 and 1930, when it was awarded to others. Finally the committee gave her the prize in 1931, four years before her death. Another fifteen years went by before another woman, Emily Greene Balch, colleague of Jane Addams in the work of the Women's International League for Peace and Freedom, and a renowned scholar in international affairs, was corecipient in 1946 with John Mott.

On the eve of the Second World War, in response to pressure from the women's movement in Norway, the Storting elected women alternate members to the committee, but it was only in 1947 that Aase Lionaes, a Labor deputy, became the first woman to hold a regular seat. There has been a woman member ever since, and beginning in 1969 Mrs. Lionaes chaired the committee until 1979. Still, after 1946 it was another thirty years before Corrigan and Williams shared the prize for 1976; then Mother Teresa received it in 1979 and Alva Myrdal (divided) in 1982.

It is true that very few women were nominated in the period up to 1939; in that time the committee gave special consideration only to ten.[1] This has not been the case in the last forty years, however. A particularly strong candidate would have been Eleanor Roosevelt, who chaired the United Nations Commission on Human Rights from its creation in 1946 until 1953. In 1947 she was nominated to share the prize with Alexandra Kollontai, who was well known in Scandinavia as Soviet envoy to Sweden and who had played an important role in the peace negotiations between the Soviet Union and Finland. Such a joint peace award in those early days of the cold war could have been a significant demonstration of the possibilities of the superpowers reaching an understanding. The 1947 prize, however, went to the Quakers (in whose behalf Eleanor Roosevelt herself had written to Oslo), and the prize for 1948 was withheld.

"During the Preceding Year"

Nobel's will called for prizes for those who "during the preceding year shall have conferred the greatest benefit on mankind." The foundation statutes state that this is to be interpreted as meaning "most recent" achievements and "older works only if their significance has not become apparent until recently." This procedure is particularly advisable in the science fields, where time is needed to assess the true significance of discoveries. In the field of peace, however, the Norwegian committee's heeding of the injunction for timeliness has resulted in several awards that have failed to stand the test of time. Awards for recent actions have mainly gone to statesmen, many of whom, it seems, the committee should have left to history to judge.

The first award for an achievement in "the preceding year," for example, was given to U.S. president Theodore Roosevelt in 1906 for his mediation efforts to end the Russo-Japanese War, which was concluded by the Treaty of Portsmouth in 1905. In time Roosevelt himself would declare that his greatest service to peace was his sending the American battle fleet around the world. And historians, basing their judgment on relevant documents, would one day point out that the war had been about to end anyway and that Roosevelt had, after all, been primarily motivated by considerations of power politics in the Orient.

The next four statesman awards stand up better. In 1913 Elihu Root was given the 1912 award, not for any immediate achievement, however, but for his conciliatory policies toward Latin America when he was secretary of state in 1904–9, for his subsequent peaceful contributions as a United States senator, and for his work through the Carnegie Endowment for International Peace. In this case, the committee could take a long look at the candidate, and his later career seems to have confirmed their choice.

In 1920 the committee gave Woodrow Wilson the 1919 prize for his role in the establishment of the League of Nations through the Treaty of Versailles, signed in 1919. This was debated in the committee, as we have seen, but the prize has worn well. In the same year the committee gave the 1920 award to Léon Bourgeois, then president of the French Senate and of the Council of the League of Nations, for his part in the establishment of that institution, acknowledging at the same time his sustained service for peace; he had represented his country at the First Hague Conference of 1899. In 1921 the committee honored Prime Minister Hjalmar Branting of Sweden for his recent contribution in connection with the League of Nations, but again the committee was also recognizing his work of many years in behalf of peace and internationalism.

The next awards to statesmen of the Great Powers may have been timely but are now dubious: Austen Chamberlain, General Dawes, Briand, Stresemann, and Kellogg were honored for recent treaties, but had demonstrated no long commitment to peace. The diplomatic world they constructed collapsed soon afterward. More important, under the scrutiny of historians the high motives they professed have been called into question. It was no doubt these awards that evoked the private comment from Albert Einstein in 1935 at the time of the Ossietzky campaign that the list of Peace Prizes would make "good old Nobel . . . turn in his grave."

This was not the case with the award to Arthur Henderson in 1934 for his work with the League of Nations Disarmament Conference, even though it was about to end in failure. This prize was timely, and Henderson's accomplishments for peace as British foreign secretary in 1920–31 were also fresh in mind. Moreover, disarmament had been specified by Nobel in the will. Above all, however, Henderson was not just the very soul of the League's disarmament effort, but a thoroughly committed man who had long worked for peace and who literally wore himself out for the cause of disarmament, dying within a year of receiving the prize.

The statesman awards after the Second World War were well timed: Cordell Hull for the United Nations, George C. Marshall for the Marshall Plan, Lester Pearson of Canada for his United Nations policies, Willy Brandt for his *Ostpolitik,* the policy of reconciliation with states of Eastern Europe. All these awards were made soon after the actions they honored had been taken, and a case can be made for each. Not so the later awards to Kissinger and Le Duc Tho (1973) and to Begin and Sadat (1978), which were timely but much criticized. The former duo were honored for negotiations so fragile that Le Duc Tho declined to accept the prize, and Kissinger tried to return it later. Begin's is the only prize that gave rise to a widespread movement to have it withdrawn and voices of protest were raised even in the Storting. The prize for Sadat has not been so criticized—his trip to Jerusalem was courageous and his stand for peace, after all, led to his assassination—but the jury is still out, as it is with former premier Sato of Japan (1974), in whose behalf a costly campaign was waged that drew much notice in the press. The most recent statesman award, to President Arias of Costa Rica in 1987, was so much of the moment that critics called it premature. He was named for his achievement made only shortly before the committee's decision, the Central American peace accord, which the committee wanted to support with its prize. For such a purpose the committee recognized that it was making a gamble. Only time will tell whether it will pay off in the long run.

This review of the timely awards to statesmen suggests that this may be the category for which the committee most needs the yardstick of time. Statesmen are able to make a contribution to peace because of their office, not necessarily because of personal qualities or any long-term commitment to the cause. In those awards that seem to stand up best in the light of history, the committee considered the person as well as the policy.

In fields other than international diplomacy, there have been some notable timely awards: to Nansen (1922) for his postwar work for prisoners of war and refugees; to Linus Pauling (1962) for organizing world opinion in behalf of the nuclear test ban; to Williams and Corrigan in Northern Ireland (1976); and to Lech Wałesa (1983) for his struggle for human rights in Poland. A different kind of timely prize is the award to a person associated with a certain cause, given in a year when that cause is receiving special recognition, such as that to Cassin in Human Rights Year (1968), to Amnesty International in the Year of Prisoners of Conscience (1977), and to Myrdal and Robles in the year of the special United Nations session on disarmament (1982).

Great moments in the history of peace do not come so often. A champion of peace is more likely to "confer the greatest benefit on mankind" through years of dedicated effort, like Schweitzer in the African jungle, Mother Teresa in the slums of Calcutta, and Noel-Baker in a lifetime of work for disarmament. Nobel's directive about the "preceding year" is the one the committee is most justified in interpreting very liberally.

Decorations or Development Grants?

I have spoken of the young Swedish engineers Hwass and Strehlenert, who witnessed Nobel's will and later gave testimony about his intentions. In 1914, after having observed the first fourteen years of the awards in Stockholm and Oslo, these two felt compelled in all conscience to speak out in protest against the direction they saw the awards taking, which they believed was contrary to what Nobel had told them he wanted. They wondered what had become of Nobel's hopes, as they had heard it from his own lips, of making life easier for "dreamers," those noble and idealistic poets and inventors whose high promise is so often lost because they are impractical and without means. Nobel had spoken of lightening the everyday burdens of these creative souls so they could make the contributions they were capable of. He had spoken of his prizewinners as his "spiritual heirs." But where were the dreamers on the list of laureates? The awards had been given to those already famous, to laureates as rich as the poet of India, Rabindranath Tagore, who had received the most recent literature prize in 1913, and as old as the German historian Theodor Mommsen, who was eighty-five when he received the literature prize in 1902.

Even older was peace laureate Ferdinand Buisson, who at eighty-six was the oldest of any Nobel Prize winner. The average age of the peace laureates, sixty-four, is the highest for all the five prizes established in 1901, and the average time they had left to live after receiving the prize was eleven years. As table 7 in appendix A shows, two-thirds of the recipients were over sixty when given the award, one-third were over seventy, and five were octogenarians. Moreover, one award was given posthumously. In recent years, the oldest laureate has been Alva Myrdal, who died a little more than three years later. The trend recently, however, has favored younger laureates. The last twenty-five years have seen awards given to Wałesa (forty), Tutu (fifty-three), Wiesel (fifty-seven), and Arias (forty-six), and to the three youngest laureates of all, Corrigan (thirty-three), Williams (thirty-four), and Martin Luther King, Jr. (thirty-five).

How Laureates Have Used the Prize Money

Although Nobel's money could not be used by older beneficiaries quite as he intended, some peace laureates have used the funds to support themselves so they could work more effectively for peace. Bertha von Suttner was one, although she had less than nine years to enjoy her prize and she was so generous in response to the pressing needs of relatives and friends and good causes that she was not entirely relieved of financial cares until in her last years she received a pension from Andrew Carnegie. In the case of Linus Pauling, Nobel's objective came closest to being realized. Pauling had already won a Nobel Prize in chemistry and was sixty-two when he was awarded the Peace Prize. But the prize money made it possible for him to resign from the California Institute of Technology, where his peace activities had alienated the Board of Trustees. Twenty-five years after receiving the Peace Prize, Pauling was still working for the cause.

Some laureates have kept the money, others have given it to their own organization or others in the field, and still others have used it for new projects that would not otherwise have been possible. A good proportion of the laureates, especially in the earlier years, made no mention of how they spent the money, and it can be assumed that they used it for private purposes. Not all were so frank as Aristide Briand, the French statesman, who said he would use the prize money for his farm, or García Robles, the Mexican statesman, who declared that he would devote his half of the prize to his family.

When the laureate is closely identified with a movement, coworkers seem to expect that that is where the money will go. When Betty Williams and Mairead Corrigan kept their prize funds, making it possible to take themselves off the payroll of the Peace People, they were severely criticized. The controversy weakened the movement and helped shatter the relationship between the two women.

In some instances the prize money has helped relieve economic problems. Ludwig Quidde, the German peace leader, was a man of means until the inflation of the 1920s. His share of the 1927 prize enabled him to continue his work for peace in Germany until Hitler came to power. After he had fled to Switzerland, grants from the Oslo committee for a book he was writing on the peace movement helped him keep body and soul together. It was Norman Angell's financial problems that led him actively to seek the prize. His successful campaign led to his receiving the award in 1934. After paying his debts and arranging for an annuity, he used what money he could spare to establish a fund to help other peace workers. Angell remained active in the peace movement until after World War II. Alva Myrdal made grants to peace causes but kept enough to hire the secretary she had needed for so long. She continued to work for peace even when she was confined to a hospital bed in the two years before her death.

Henry Dunant, the founder of the Red Cross who shared the first prize of 1901, might well have used the money for himself. A few years earlier he had been discovered living on a meager allowance in a hospital room in a small Swiss town, where he had retired in obscurity after financial reverses had made him something of an outcast in his native Geneva. A campaign waged in his behalf won the prize for him and rehabilitated his reputation, but he remained in his retreat, saved most of the money, and at his death left it to peace and charitable associations.

Many laureates gave away all the money to their organizations. William Randal Cremer, the veteran English labor leader who won the third prize in 1903, gave it to his International Arbitration League. Cremer was anything but selfless in maintaining his claim as initiator of the Interparliamentary Union. Nevertheless he unselfishly passed along the funds to the league and continued to live as modestly as before. Jane Addams gave the prize money to her Women's International League for Peace and Freedom, as did her colleague and successor as honorary president, Emily Greene Balch, whose prize was the result of a campaign undertaken by the organization. Albert Schweitzer was able to expand his hospital complex at Lambaréné, adding a house for lepers. Lord Boyd-Orr gave his money for a building to house peace organizations in London. His friends, however, thought that he should have kept enough to hire a secretary so that his wife would not have to type all his letters with her two fingers. Martin Luther King, Jr., worked out a formula to divide the prize money among civil rights associations, and Pérez Esquivel turned it over to his Service for Peace and Justice.

In a spirit similar to that of the laureates who endowed the work in which they were engaged, President Anwar el-Sadat of Egypt gave his prize money to his childhood village in the Nile Delta, to which he also contributed the royalties from his autobiography. And President Arias of Costa Rica told reporters he would use the money to form "a foundation for Costa Rica's neediest citizens."

The only case we know of where a laureate sought the prize because he wanted the money for his organization was that of Father Pire of Belgium. When looking for a rich foundation to which he could apply for a grant to support refugee work, he wrote to the Nobel Foundation in Stockholm. Informed that the Norwegian Nobel Committee had given prizes for such endeavors, he naively sent an account of his work to Oslo. The Nobel Foundation statutes forbid a candidate from nominating himself, but more sophisticated supporters, including the Norwegian ambassador to Belgium, took Father Pire's case in hand, and he was awarded the prize in 1958. He used the money in the construction of two of the villages he was building so that refugees could leave displaced persons' camps.

Some laureates contributed the prize money to other good causes. Charles G. Dawes, for example, gave his to the Walter Hines Page School of International Relations at Johns Hopkins University, and Lech Wałesa contributed much needed medical supplies to Polish hospitals. Theodore Roosevelt allocated his funds to establish arbitration for industrial conflicts, but this project never materialized. René Cassin, the co-author of the UN Declaration of Human Rights, established an Institute for Human Rights in Strasbourg. Henry Kissinger set up a scholarship fund for children of GIs who died in Vietnam, and Bishop Tutu founded such a fund to help South African blacks study in the United States. Elie Wiesel announced he would establish a Foundation for Human Rights, the first project of which would be a conference on hate and the second a conference to consider the implications for humanity of the Hiroshima bomb.

A New Visibility

Also helpful to laureates is the distinction the prize bestows upon them. As the Nobel Committee has made the prize more prestigious by expanding the field of candidacy, those crowned with its laurels achieve a new visibility and find the world more attentive to their words. Mairead Corrigan pointed out that "it gives you an audience wherever you go," and Marion Wiesel said in Oslo in 1986 that her husband now had "a big microphone." A laureate, automatically identified as a Nobel Peace Prize winner, is suddenly more newsworthy and receives more space whatever he or she does.

The Nobel Peace Prize has been particularly important for dissidents at odds with their own governments. Linus Pauling, who had been refused a passport by the State Department because of his peace activities, said to me that winning the Nobel Prize made working for peace respectable: "Its effect was not so much on me and my actions, but on my reputation with the American people, who realized that what I said was in the interests of the United States and not just the Soviet Union."

The first such dissident to receive the prize, antimilitarist publicist Carl von Ossietzky, was transferred from a Nazi concentration camp to a police hospital in Berlin when the international campaign for his prize gained momentum. When the prize was announced, Hermann Goering tried to persuade him to reject it, fearing the unfavorable publicity for the Reich if he accepted. Ossietzky was not permitted to go to Oslo to receive his prize, but he was allowed to enter a private sanatorium, where he lived out what was left of his life under police surveillance.

Albert Lutuli, the Zulu leader of the African National Congress, became a world figure when the Nobel Committee awarded him the prize in 1960. He got to use the "big microphone" only briefly, however. The South African government, under international pressure, gave him and his wife an eight-day passport to travel directly to Oslo and back, with no side trips. And after his return, he was again restricted in his movements and his voice was stifled by the government. Bishop Tutu was already well known before receiving his prize, but the award immensely increased his stature in the eyes of the world and certainly gave him the "big microphone," which, unlike Lutuli, he has been able to use with significant effect.

Although Andrei Sakharov was not permitted to leave the Soviet Union to receive the prize in 1975, he cherished it nevertheless, and many of his appeals and statements, typed single-spaced on onionskin paper and smuggled out to the West, were signed "A. Sakharov, Nobel Prize laureate." The prize helped keep Sakharov in the public eye and was one more element in the international pressure that eventually secured his return to Moscow from his Gorki exile.

Lech Wałesa hoped to win the prize because he felt it would give him bargaining power with the Polish government. A few days before he heard the good news from Oslo in 1983, he told a visiting journalist that he thought the Nobel Committee would not give him the prize, since it would have really helped him the year before, "when the situation was still fluid." This was, however, a misconception about the motives of the committee that awarded Wałesa the prize. Its chairman told me that although every award may have political implications, his committee had acted to honor a deserving human rights candidate, not to intervene in Poland's internal affairs.

For Pérez Esquivel, the Argentinian leader of the nonviolent human rights movement in Latin America, the prize made all the difference. As in the case of Ossietzky, he was nominated when, with no charge brought against him, he was incarcerated by the military government; the purpose of his nomination was to bring international attention to his situation. Betty Williams and Mairead Corrigan, after gaining the right to make nominations, proposed him for the 1978 prize while he was still in prison, and in the next two years as well. Amnesty International adopted him as a prisoner of conscience, and religious leaders protested his imprisonment. He was released finally after thirteen months of confinement and torture. In 1980, when his prize was announced, Pérez Esquivel was still virtually unknown in the world. The Norwegian News Agency even identified him as a Brazilian. Argentina's controlled press declared that the award maligned the country, and when he returned from Oslo, Pérez Esquivel and his family lived for months under constant threats of violence. But he kept up his work with the Service for Peace and Justice and continued his protests against human rights violations. In the face of his Christian witness, the military government found it harder to maintain that by its repressive acts it was defending Western civilization.

Pérez Esquivel believes that his Nobel Prize marked the beginning of the decline of the military government and helped strengthen the democratic forces that were ready to take over the country after the defeat in the Falkland/Malvinas War. Ironically, because of an earlier law, the repressive government was obliged to pay Pérez Esquivel an annual pension in recognition of his winning the award. The Nobel Prize also made Pérez Esquivel a familiar figure on the university lecture circuit in the United States, where for a generous fee he has spoken out on the Latin American struggle for peace and justice, not sparing his criticism of the policies of the Reagan administration in Central America.

A New Sense of Responsibility

The winning of such a high honor as the Nobel Peace Prize can heighten a laureate's sense of commitment. A few months after Martin Luther King, Jr., was awarded the prize, Coretta Scott King told me that until they had gone to Oslo, they "had not realized what the world expected of Martin." In his excellent biography of King, David Garrow says that the Nobel Prize increased the burden of responsibility that King felt he had to carry, and that this was a factor in his decision, contrary to the advice of some of his colleagues, to come out publicly in opposition to the Vietnam War.

Often in the acceptance speech at Oslo the laureate affirms a renewed determination to work for peace. Father Pire declared, "I am no old admiral who receives the last and finest decoration of his life. . . . The Nobel Peace Prize is not the end of a career but a beginning, a fresh start, the continuation with renewed zeal. . . . It puts immense responsibility upon me." He said that he wanted to leave the prize greater by his service as a laureate, and he presented the committee with "the rest of my life." Unfortunately, he died eleven years later at the age of fifty-nine.

Willy Brandt declared when accepting the prize in 1971, "The Nobel Peace Prize is the highest honor, but also the most demanding, which can be granted to a man with political responsibility. I thank you sincerely and will everything I can in my future work to bring nearer to realization what many expect of me." Even after leaving the office of chancellor of West Germany, Brandt has continued to work for peace on the world stage through the international socialist movement and in other ways.

Albert Schweitzer had always avoided making

political statements, but after being given the Peace Prize, he said, "I should do something to earn it," and he was open to the persuasive arguments of Norman Cousins that he should make a public statement against nuclear testing. Schweitzer's Declaration of Conscience was consequently read over the Oslo radio in April 1957, and he used the same station a year later to appeal for the renunciation of nuclear weapons. Throughout his last years Schweitzer remained active in his peace efforts.

Recognizing and Endowing Potential

To what extent is it possible to recognize the potential for distinguished peacemaking? An association of American Nobel laureates recently announced the establishment of Nobel Laureate Fellowships, awards of fifty thousand dollars to be given to outstanding researchers at the graduate level in the three scientific fields of the Nobel prizes and in economics. Literature and peace were not included. "Peace is an uncertain area," the spokesman of the group explained. "It's a lot harder to identify." He went on to say that fellowships for peace would be considered if a donor were found who would "help set the criterion."

To recognize a potential for peacemaking of the highest order at an early age is surely more difficult than to spot great scientific promise. What is distinctive about the finest peace laureates is not their intellectual talents but their spiritual gifts, and these are not so likely to be apparent in the very young. As we have seen, the youngest peace laureates were in their early thirties: Martin Luther King, Jr., Betty Williams, and Mairead Corrigan. Albert Schweitzer was only twenty-one when he made his great decision to serve humanity, but he was almost thirty before he realized how he would go about it and thirty-eight when he set out for Africa. Mother Teresa became a religious early in her life, but she was thirty-six when she heard the call to work in the slums of Calcutta. Linus Pauling first became concerned about peace after Hiroshima, when he was forty-four. Alva Myrdal turned her attention to disarmament only when she was fifty-nine.

Distinguished peacemaking demands a deep commitment that can inspire persistent effort over a long period despite disappointment and frustration. One peacemaking act of state or one peace campaign is not enough; the track record should be substantial. This is perhaps why the award to Betty Williams and Mairead Corrigan, based on a single peace campaign, spectacular as it was, did not lead to more significant achievement. On the other hand, the prize for King is a prime example of an award that spurred a dedicated laureate to still higher accomplishment. His early death prevented even greater achievement.

The Oslo committees, however, need not have waited so long to honor Jane Addams at seventy-one, Lord Cecil at seventy-three, Albert Schweitzer at seventy-eight, Philip Noel-Baker at seventy, and Alva Myrdal at eighty. They were all likely candidates in years when the prize was withheld. The recent human rights awards represent a new trend in the right direction: Sakharov, fifty-four; Pérez Esquivel, forty-nine; Wałesa, forty; Tutu, fifty-three; and Wiesel, fifty-seven. In all these cases the committees were acknowledging superior achievement but at the same time equipping the recipients with the means to accomplish even more at a stage in their lives when there was still time to do so.

Although over the years the committees have compiled a very good record in their difficult task, these recent awards may indicate that they are considering more carefully the possibility of choosing laureates who have the energy, the resolve, and the time to accomplish something greater than that for which they won the prize. Such awards could realize Alfred Nobel's fondest hopes.

Statesmen and the Prize

The largest number of prizes since World War I has gone to statesmen, a category Bertha von Suttner was certain Nobel did not have in mind. As we have seen, such prizes have been among the most controversial of all the awards and have been most vulnerable to the researches of historians. Most statesmen laureates who were adjudged to have made an outstanding contribution to peace were enabled to do so by dint of the office they held; at best they may have recognized that the national interest coincided with the end of a war or a policy of détente. Such laureates are hardly to be compared with champions of peace whose dedication to the highest ideals of humanity has inspired long years of service.

Leaving aside the messages of gratitude statesmen have always sent to Oslo, an interesting question concerns their real thoughts about the prize—how important was it to them? Although a proper answer would require a great deal of research among their papers, it is clear, that overall, statesmen have regarded the prize as an asset to their reputation. There are indications, in fact, that many of them made or encouraged efforts to receive it. The Foreign Office of Norway and its diplomats have had to explain repeatedly that they and their government have nothing to do with the award decisions and that they are not in a position to aid the candidacy of one or another head of state.

In a few cases we have documentation of statesmen's efforts to win the prize. We know, for example, that Saavedra Lamas, the Argentinian foreign minister, asked Cordell Hull, the American secretary of state, to support his candidacy, which Hull did in the interest of the Good Neighbor policy. Few statesmen have shared the humility of Hull, who tells in his memoirs how he asked that his own name be withdrawn in favor of President Franklin Roosevelt, whom he felt better qualified. It seems clear that former premier Sato of Japan aided the campaign that was successfully waged to bring him the prize. Henry Kissinger has said that President Richard Nixon, who hoped to go down in history as a distinguished peacemaker, was much disappointed that he did not win the prize that went to his secretary of state.

We can gain some indication of how a statesman laureate regards the prize by his willingness to come to Oslo to receive it and to give the expected Nobel lecture. The Norwegian committee has always been willing to waive the six-month provision and schedule the lecture at the laureate's convenience. The first statesman laureate was President Theodore Roosevelt, who won the prize in 1906. He delivered his lecture in 1910 only after Andrew Carnegie had persuaded him that if he did not accept the committee's invitation, there might be prejudice against future American candidates. Elihu Root, the second American prizewinner, was more willing. Awarded the prize in 1913, he prepared a lecture to be delivered in September 1914, but when war broke out in August, it was called off.

In the period between the wars, 1919–39, ten statesmen received the award, of whom only four came to Oslo: Hjalmar Branting from nearby Sweden, Foreign Minister Gustav Stresemann of Germany, former secretary of state Frank Kellogg (who did not, however, give a formal Nobel lecture), and Arthur Henderson of Britain, who was at the time the president of the fading Disarmament Conference in Geneva. Since World War II, of the ten statesmen or diplomat laureates, six delivered lectures in Oslo, including Brandt, Begin, and Arias, who were still in office at the time. General Marshall was in poor health but made the effort to travel to Europe on rough December seas.

Kissinger asked to be excused ostensibly because of the pressure of state business; he has admitted, however, that it was because he wished to avoid a likely demonstration against his Vietnam policy. There has been a feeling at the Norwegian Nobel Institute that Kissinger distanced himself from the prize. He never gave a Nobel lecture, although he has been to Oslo since the award, and he is the only laureate unrepresented in a volume of essays by living prizewinners which was edited by the secretary of the institute.

For Arias the prize has meant increased support for his peace plan for Central America and has provided what the *New York Times* called a "splendid pulpit" in Oslo. The prize has helped Arias not only abroad but also at home, where he has been criticized for paying too much attention to foreign affairs.

Conclusion: "Who Shall Have Conferred the Greatest Benefit on Mankind"

Clearly, the Peace Prize has become something very different from what Nobel originally intended: most of the prizes have been used to reward rather than to facilitate individual achievement; the prize money has frequently been given away, making philanthropists of the laureates; more than a few awards have gone to impersonal institutions; the organized peace movement has received little assistance after the first years; the prizes have often been reserved and in a number of years have not been awarded at all; the grants have not often been given for recent activities; and there have been few women laureates. Nobel's desire that the awards should span all countries has, however, been honored from the beginning, and in recent years the prize has become even more global.

In rendering this account, we must not forget that Carl Lindhagen reminded Bertha von Suttner that Nobel had only "stated an idea," leaving it to others in whom he had confidence to execute it, as was his custom. In discharging its mandate, Chairman Stang said as long ago as 1930, the Norwegian Nobel Committee has considered it its duty to be on the watch for *all* developments that may have a potential for bringing peace. This has produced a pantheon in which an agricultural scientist like Norman Borlaug can take his place with Mother Teresa, a workers' leader like Lech Wałesa can stand with President Wilson, and Archbishop Söderblom can join Andrei Sakharov.

Scholars engaged in the new study of peace research have faulted the committee for its lack of "a clear peace theory," but in the long run, it is all to the good that the committee has held no one theory of peace and has been free to use its own discretion. Consider only the recent move to human rights awards, which, as Chairman Aarvik pointed out, Nobel's will said nothing about.

The committee is accustomed to the brickbats that seem to follow each year's decision. Few nonscientists are competent to challenge the science prizes, and it is mostly the literati who are prepared to pass judgment on the literature award. But there are no "authorities" on peacemaking, and everybody can have an opinion on the merits of the Norwegian committee's verdicts. The most persistent criticism in recent years has been that the committee is pro-Western in the East-West conflict. There have been a few indications that this might change. In 1973 the committee named a Communist leader for the first time in pairing Le Duc Tho with Henry Kissinger, although the North Vietnamese diplomat chose to decline the prize. The prizes for Sakharov and Wałesa were condemned in the East, but in 1985 the award to the International Physicians for the Prevention of Nuclear War (IPPNW), which was presented to the copresidents, Dr. Chazov of the Soviet Union and Dr. Lown of the United States, was applauded in Moscow and denounced by Western conservatives. In making the IPPNW award, Chairman Aarvik acknowledged that the committee was sending a message to the two superpowers to work for arms control at the coming summit.

Almost any prize can have political implications, but in recent years the committee has seemed to move more purposefully in using the prize to influence governmental actions. As we have seen, the human rights prizes for dissidents aided their efforts by endowing them with a new status. The committee's deputy chair, Gidske Anderson, said in a recent interview that the prize can be used to encourage a political process: "When we gave it to Bishop Tutu, we were supporting a process, or when we gave it to Sakharov."

Certain prizes to statesmen have been intended not only to reward them for a peacemaking achievement but to encourage them to make further efforts. Kissinger and Le Duc Tho were honored for negotiating the January 1973 armistice in Vietnam, but the committee's statement urged them to work toward a peace settlement. In 1978 Begin and Sadat were both recognized for the Camp David agreements and bidden to proceed with treaty negotiations for the implementation.

The 1987 award for President Arias was perhaps the most explicitly political of all the Peace Prizes. Chairman Aarvik told the press:

> If the Peace Prize has any meaning, it must support a process that is going on. The prize has two aspects: the one to honor what has been achieved—the peace plan signed in Guatemala in August—and the other aspect is the support from the prize for the process which we think should go on.
>
> We think the direction taken by President Arias is the right one, and therefore we want to throw the prestige of the Nobel Peace Prize to support a plan working in the right direction.

This policy may mark a new departure in the committee's decision making. It has its risks, as Aarvik acknowledged in the same interview, and critics have claimed that in intervening in a continuing political process, the committee is exceeding its mandate. Defenders of the committee, on the other hand, maintain that Nobel's basic purpose in establishing the Peace Prize was, after all, to promote peace and that it is consistent with this purpose for the committee on occasion to try some peacemaking itself.

What Nobel's will said explicitly was that the Peace Prize, like the others, was to be given to persons who "shall have conferred the greatest benefit on mankind." To this highest aim of Alfred Nobel, the Norwegian committee has tried to remain faithful throughout its long history, however the circumstances and the thinking of the time may have influenced a particular award and whatever the criticisms from advocates of different conceptions of peace.

That the committee has largely succeeded in this effort is attested to by the high prestige the Peace Prize enjoys in the world—no other award for service to peace and human brotherhood is ever mentioned in the same breath. Today in the nuclear age, peace has a most urgent meaning. But survival is not the only goal. Again and again in its selections, the Norwegian committee has emphasized the *positive* meaning of peace, pointing to the foundation on which a true peace must rest. And through its happiest choices, the committee has set before us an array of inspiring human beings, who sustain in the rest of us what they themselves had in such abundance, what Martin Luther King, Jr., called "an audacious faith" in humankind.

Note

1. Bertha von Suttner (1903, 1904, 1905), Priscilla Peckover (1905), Lucia Ames Mead (1913), Belva A. Lockwood (1914), Jane Addams (1916, 1923, 1924, 1928, 1930, 1931), Elsa Brandström (1928), Annie Besant (1931), Lady Aberdeen (1931), Etienne Clémentel (1933), and Carrie Chapman Catt (1939).

Bibliographical Notes

The Nobel Peace Prize

There have been few scholarly studies of the Peace Prize beyond the accounts by the directors of the Norwegian Nobel Institute: Ragnald Moe, *Le Prix Nobel de la Paix et l'Institut Nobel Norvégien* (Oslo: Aschehoug, 1932), and August Schou, "The Peace Prize," in Nobel Foundation, *Nobel: The Man and His Prizes,* 3d ed. (New York: Elsevier, 1972), pp. 485–607.

I first examined the history of the prize in "Nobel Peace Prize: A Balance Sheet," *American Journal of Economics and Sociology* 21 (July 1962): 225–43. The first fruits of research for this book appeared in "The Transformation of the Nobel Peace Prize," *Peace and Change: A Journal of Peace Research* 10 (Fall–Winter 1984): 1–25, much of which has been used here. The first study in a journal of peace research was the highly critical article by Solveig Häll, irreverently entitled "Who is the Establishment Peacenik? A Study of Nobel Peace Prize Recipients," *Instant Research on Peace and Violence* (Tampere, Finland) 3, no. 2 (1973): 84–94.

The World Encyclopedia of Peace, edited by Ervin Laszlo and Jong Youl Yoo, 4 vols. (London: Pergamon, 1986), has an article on "The Nobel Peace Prizes" by me, as well as biographies of all the laureates through 1985 and useful bibliographies on the peace movement.

A new German-Swiss series, Der Friedens-Nobelpreis von 1901 bis heute, is planned to cover all the laureates in twelve volumes. Articles are written by scholars and are intended for the general reader. Special care has been taken with the illustrations, many of which are in color. The first volume, *Der Friedens-Nobelpreis von 1901 bis 1904,* edited by Michael Neumann, was published in 1987 (Zug, Switzerland and Munich, West Germany: Edition Pacis).

Popular accounts of the prize are by Mortimer Lipsky, *Quest for Peace: The Story of the Nobel Award* (South Brunswick, N.J.: A. S. Barnes, 1966), and Tony Gray, *Champions of Peace* (London: Paddington, 1976). A sprightly survey by John Bovey, who had served in the U.S. embassy in Oslo, is "Peace and Its Prizes," *Studia Diplomatica* (Brussels) 28 (1975):75–88, condensed as "Nobel's Legacy," *Christian Science Monitor,* 8 December 1983, pp. 35–36.

Alfred Nobel and the Nobel Foundation

Two biographies of Nobel have been authorized by the Nobel Foundation: Ragnar Sohlman and Henrik Schück, *Nobel: Dynamite and Peace,* translated by Brian and Beatrix Lunn from the Swedish edition of 1926 (New York: Cosmopolitan, 1929), and Erik Bergengren, *Alfred Nobel: The Man and His Work,* translated by Alan Blair from the Swedish edition of 1960 (London: Thomas Nelson & Sons, 1962). Sohlman was Nobel's assistant and later executor and executive director of the Nobel Foundation. Both contributed chapters on Nobel to *Nobel: The Man and His Prizes.*

The Sohlman-Schück biography was the first

about Nobel and the standard work until the Nobel Foundation commissioned Bergengren, a former Swedish Red Cross official, to write a more definitive account based on a thorough examination of Nobel's extensive correspondence, including that with his mistress, which had not previously been accessible. Bergengren produced a solid and well-balanced biography, still the best we have. The present executive director of the foundation, Stig Ramel, has given two thoughtful addresses, "Alfred Nobel and the Nobel: How a Dream Survived in a Changing World," in the *Proceedings of the Robert A. Welch Foundation Conferences on Chemical Research* 22, Chemistry of Future Energy Resources, 6–8 November, 1978, Houston, Texas, pp. 339–44; and the Fourth Israel Sieff Lecture in London, in the *British Association for Commercial and Industrial Education Journal* (November–December 1982):352–54.

Nobel's genius, the puzzling contradictions of his personality, and the dramas of his life have given rise to a number of popular biographies. Notable are Herta E. Pauli, *Alfred Nobel: Dynamite King, Architect of Peace* (New York: Fisher, 1942), well written but romantic; Nicholas Halasz, *Nobel* (New York: Orion Press, 1959), which also tells a good story but bases it on primary sources; and Michael Evlanoff and Marjorie Fluor, *Alfred Nobel: The Loneliest Millionaire* (n.p.: Ward Ritchie Press, 1969). Evlanoff was a friend of Nobel's relatives.

Bergengren gives a fairer account of the influence of Bertha von Suttner on Nobel, which had been played down by Sohlman-Schück. The Nobel-Suttner correspondence has been studied by me in 1962 and by Suttner's biographers, Kempf in 1964 and Hamann in 1986 (see the bibliography for Bertha von Suttner). See also Ursula Jorfald, *Bertha von Suttner og Nobels Fredspris* (Oslo: Forum, 1962), translated by Gerd de Mautort as *Le Prix Nobel de la Paix: Pourquoi? Comment?* (Angers: Forum, 1979).

Two recent studies of Nobel's ideas about peace are the essay by Professor S. Tägil in Gunnar Brandell et al., *Nobel och Hans Tid: Fem Essäer* (Stockholm: Atlantis, 1983), and the paper by Jakob Sverdrup, director of the Norwegian Nobel Institute, "Alfred Nobel and the Peace Movement," presented at the 150th anniversary of Nobel's birth in San Remo in 1983.

The story of Nobel's will and the struggle to implement it is told by Sohlman in *Nobel: The Man and His Prizes* and more fully in his *Ett Testamente* (Stockholm: Norstedt & Söner, 1950). A revised edition was also published in the year of Nobel's anniversary, with an important foreword by Stig Ramel and the full text of the will (Stockholm: Atlantis, 1983). The English translation by Elspeth H. Schubert is entitled *The Legacy of Alfred Nobel: The Story behind the Nobel Prizes* (London: Bodley Head, 1983). In this valuable memoir, written in his last years before he died in 1948, Sohlman supplemented what he had written earlier with intimate memories of Nobel and personal details about his own crucial role in the battle over the will.

The account of Carl Lindhagen, the lawyer who helped Sohlman, is in his *Memoarer,* 3 vols. (Stockholm: Bonnier, 1936–39), 1:246–79. Leonard Hwass and R. W. Strehlenert, witnesses to the will, published their recollections in "Nobels Testament" and "Nochmals Nobels Testament," *Die Woche* 16 (10 January and 28 March 1914):43–46, 512–13. Elisabeth T. Crawford deals with the implementation of the will in her study of the early years of the science prize, *The Beginnings of the Nobel Institution* (New Rochelle, N.Y.: Cambridge University Press, 1984).

The statutes of the Nobel Foundation and the prize-awarding institutions were printed in *Nobel: The Man and His Prizes* and are available, as amended, in a brochure published by the Nobel Foundation in 1984. The legal opinion on posthumous awards is in the foundation archives: Per Santesson and Wilhelm Pehrsson: "Översyn av Nobelstiftelsens Grundstadgar, September 30, 1968."

The foundation prints its annual reports, including an accounting of its financial management, in both Swedish and English and also issues the *Nobel Foundation Directory,* with complete information about the foundation, the prize-awarding institutions, and the laureates. The most recent edition is for the years 1987–88. The foundation's yearbook, *Les Prix Nobel,* with information about each year's prizes, laureates, and ceremonies and the texts of the Nobel addresses, has been published since 1901, since 1977 by Almqvist & Wiksell International, Stockholm.

The Nobel Foundation also authorized the Elsevier Publishing Company of Amsterdam to publish a series of volumes in English of all the Nobel lectures, with presentation speeches and short biographies of the laureates. Sixteen volumes were published in the series between 1964 and 1972. Those on peace, edited by Frederick W. Haberman, are referred to below.

There is an informative description of the Nobel Foundation by Stig Ramel in the beautifully illustrated book by Peter Wilhelm, *The Nobel Prize* (London: Springwood Books, 1982).

The Norwegian Nobel Committee and Its Prizes

The basic books on the committee and the institute are the account by Moe, referred to above, and the important work by Oscar J. Falnes, *Norway and the Nobel Peace Prize* (New York: Columbia University Press, 1938, reprint, New York: AMS Press, 1967), which covers the work of the committee for its four first decades and prints its special statutes. Jakob Sverdrup, the present director of the institute, has presented a more recent view from Oslo in "Norway and the Peace Prize," *Peace and Change* 10 (Fall–Winter 1984): 27–38. A few years ago the institute published a very informative booklet, *Alfred Nobel and the Peace Prize.*

The members of the Norwegian Nobel Committee have a remarkable record of observing their vow of silence, and practically nothing has been published about their discussions. The recent slim volume of recollections by Aase Lionaes, who served on the committee from 1948 to 1978, chairing it from 1969, *Tredveårskrigen for freden* ("Thirty years' war for peace") is subtitled "High points in the history of the Nobel Committee" (Oslo: Aschehoug, 1987). Although it contains interesting comments on individuals and on the public reaction to certain prizes, there are no revelations about how the decisions were reached.

It was most unusual when a former committee member, Einar Hovdhaugen, still unhappy about his brief experience on the committee before he resigned after the Kissinger award, wrote an article eleven years later purporting to reveal what actually happened in 1973: "Gjest i Nobelkomiten" ("Guest in the Nobel Committee"), *Syn og Segn* 91, no. 4 (1985):297–304.

Since the present work is not intended as a monograph, thoroughgoing research was not undertaken in the committee archives or in the official documents of the Storting, and only selective use was made of such materials. The Norwegian Nobel Committee does not keep minutes, and in accordance with the foundation's statutes, documents used for a decision are not to be made available to scholars for fifty years.

Now accessible in the committee archives under the fifty-year provision are the bundles of each year's nominations from 1901 to the 1930s, the printed reports of the advisers for these years (*Redegjørelse for Nobels Fredspris*), and the general registers of nominees. Some use was made of these as well as of the collection of scrapbooks and press releases on the awards, made regularly from 1975 on. Use was also made of the annual reports of the committee to the Storting in the published proceedings (*Stortingsforhandlinger*), mainly for statistics, but these reports have become thinner and thinner over the years. They were helpful in certain instances, especially in connection with the aftermath of the Ossietzky and Kissinger awards and for information about the committee during the Second World War.

Also available in the archives are copies of certain private papers of Halvdan Koht, committee member for almost two decades after 1919. As a historian, Koht could not refrain from making notes of some of the discussions, and Dr. Sverdrup kindly made available to me Koht's report of the disagreement in the committee over President Wilson.

In the Elsevier series referred to above, the Nobel lectures on peace through 1970 were edited by Frederick W. Haberman, professor of communication arts at the University of Wisconsin-Madison: *Nobel Lectures: Peace,* 3 vols. (Amsterdam: Elsevier, 1972). This is a most valuable collection. Professor Haberman could rely mainly on the official texts in *Les Prix Nobel,* but he supplemented these where necessary by resourcefully exploiting archive collections and newspaper reports. For close work the translations should be checked, but the biographical data are most helpful, and the bibliographies, although not annotated, are extensive. Unfortunately, these volumes were poorly promoted and are not as available in libraries as they should be.

The most important reference works for scholarly assessments of the majority of the peace laureates are the twin biographical dictionaries published by Greenwood Press: *Biographical Dictionary of Internationalists,* edited by Warren Kuehl (Westport, Conn.: Greenwood, 1983), and *Biographical Dictionary of Modern Peace Leaders,* edited by Harold Josephson (Westport, Conn.: Greenwood, 1985). The entries, each written by an authority, and the bibliographical references have greatly facilitated the present work.

The entries on the peace laureates in the *World Encyclopedia of Peace* (Oxford: Pergamon, 1986) are presented in the context of their prizes, using the addresses in *Les Prix Nobel.* The bibliographies are brief but do include periodical items. The entries are carefully done but cannot claim the authoritativeness of the Greenwood biographical dictionaries.

Articles on some laureates, especially statesmen, are to be found in the *Dictionary of National Biography* (Oxford: Oxford University Press, 1921–), and the *Dictionary of American Biography* (New York: Scribners, 1928–).

For the most recent prizewinners, and even for personal details about some of the earlier laureates, the annual volumes of *Current Biography Yearbook* (New York: H.W. Wilson, 1940–), are invaluable.

Part Two

The Laureates

1

The Peace Prize over the Years: 1901–18

In March 1901 the five members of the Nobel Committee assembled to consider the nominations for the first Peace Prize. The committee members were a distinguished group, clear evidence of the high importance the Storting had placed on the responsibility given it by Nobel. Included were Johannes Steen, the prime minister; Jørgen Løvland, who was to become Norway's first foreign minister; and John Lund, another top politician, all three from the bourgeois liberal party of the Left. With them was the great national poet Bjørnson. These four had elected as their chairman Bernhard Getz, Norway's leading jurist. When he died just before the peace award was decided, Hans J. Horst, another leading politician of the Left, joined the committee.

Let us try to imagine how the great questions of war and peace appeared to these men as they looked at the first list of nominees. Foremost in their minds would have been the uneasy relations among the Great Powers of Europe. Nobel himself in an early draft of his will had equated international peace with the "pacification of Europe."

True, Europe had been at peace for a generation, since the war between France and Prussia which led to the establishment of the German Empire in 1871. But it was an armed peace, with the major states of the Continent maintaining huge armies of conscripts and increasing their armaments every year. Diplomats spoke of a balance of power keeping the peace. The French Republic and the Russian Empire had formed a Dual Alliance in the 1890s to balance the Triple Alliance of Germany, Austria-Hungary, and Italy. England had remained aloof from Continental involvements, with a small army but a great fleet to protect its home island and its worldwide empire. It had fought colonial wars, however, and encountered conflict overseas with other great powers as the tide of European imperialism rose; now in 1901 England was at war in South Africa, seeking to subdue the Boers, descendants of Dutch settlers. Soon England would sense a threat in the new German fleet and in Germany's bid for colonies, and in 1907 would ally itself with France and Russia in the Triple Entente to balance the power of the Triple Alliance.

With benefit of hindsight, we know that these two alliances would stumble into war in 1914, and we tend to think of the years leading to that cataclysm with a sense of inevitability. Only fairly recently have historians been giving proper attention to the popular movement to prevent war that was growing in the 1890s and which marked its first political success in the International Peace Conference that met at The Hague in 1899. While great power politics had much to do with the call for the meeting by Tsar Nicholas II of Russia and did limit its achievements, the conference ended with international recognition of the principle of settling conflicts between states through arbitration, and with the establishment of the Permanent Court of Arbitration at The Hague.

This was but a small step away from the prevailing international anarchy, but it represented more than the hiring of a staff, the appointment by their governments of a panel of judges, and a professed willingness of the signatory states to resort to the court to arbitrate conflicts between them. It meant that for the first time in modern history, diplomats of the great powers and other sovereign states had assembled in a peace conference, not for the purpose of ending a war, but to adopt measures to keep the peace. Diplomatic historians can trace a direct line from the Franco-Prussian War of 1870–71 through the two world wars of our own century, but there is a more hopeful line that leads from the Hague Peace Conference to the League of Nations and the United Nations.

What the tsar had originally called for was a conference to discuss disarmament, an idea that his ministers had first conceived in order to maintain the balance of power with Austria-Hungary, which was arming faster than Russia was able to do. The other great powers were quite unwilling to reduce their armaments, but they could not refuse the invitation to the conference. At this juncture the leaders of the organized peace movement, internationally minded members of parliaments and heads of peace societies, helped persuade the diplomats to place on the conference agenda an item that might lead to a tangible result, and they set up at The Hague what was the first international peace lobby to pressure the governmental delegates to achieve it.

A few days after the Hague Conference ended, peace parliamentarians from eighteen countries assembled in the Norwegian capital of Christiana in the ninth annual Interparliamentary Conference. All the deputies of the Storting were enrolled as members of this body, and the members of the Nobel Committee were especially prominent. Prime Minister Steen officially welcomed the delegates, and Lund and Horst, as presidents of the Storting's two houses, presided over the sessions.

In the resolutions that were adopted, the members of the Interparliamentary Conference applauded what had just been achieved at The Hague and referred with satisfaction to the fact that in their own meeting in Brussels in 1895 they themselves had approved a proposal for an international tribunal of arbitration. They also noted that several of their members had been sent by their governments to participate in the Hague meeting.

A decade before, in 1889, deputies from nine national legislatures had gathered in Paris during the international exposition to discuss how they could unite their efforts to bring their governments to enter into agreements to arbitrate disputes, and they had resolved to meet annually in the Interparliamentary Conference. Now, ten years later at Christiana, with the largest number of countries ever represented in their meetings, and encouraged by the events at The Hague, the delegates resolved to give their association more permanent form, renaming it the Interparliamentary Union, the name it bears today, and giving more responsibilities to the Interparliamentary Bureau, which had been established in 1894.

The foundations for the gains made at The Hague by the peace movement had been laid in the previous three decades, not only by the parliamentarians, but by international jurists and by peace societies. Much of the inspiration had come from the successful arbitration of the *Alabama* case in 1871–72, when Britain and the United States agreed to submit to an international panel of judges a serious dispute over claims arising from damage done in the Civil War to northern shipping by a southern commerce raider fitted out in an English port. The judgment was accepted by both parties, demonstrating that international arbitration was practicable and practical.

The *Alabama* case, in giving priority to law over force, had given high encouragement to the jurists who were seeking to bring order out of the complicated relationships that stretched beyond the national borders, both in the public and private sectors of international life. In 1873 these savants founded the Institute of International Law, and many of them also worked with the more popular International Law Association that was formed at the same time with a similar motivation. From the very beginning the Institute of International Law had concerned itself with the procedures of arbitration, and a number of its members took an influential part in these discussions at the 1899 Hague Conference. They also contributed there to the agreements reached on the laws of war, another matter that had long been on the institute's agenda.

But much earlier in the nineteenth century, long before the concerned parliamentarians and the international lawyers had organized to join the cause, the peace activists were already at work, carrying on their propaganda and seeking to bring to bear upon governments the pressure of public opinion. Their message, originally religious, had become more rational and utilitarian as the century advanced.

In 1889, the same year that the deputies held their first interparliamentary conference, the civic peace leaders organized the first of their so-called "universal congresses," also in Paris. After 1892 these annual meetings were organized by their secretariat, the Permanent International Peace Bureau. While the practice of holding the annual meetings of both groups in the same city, one following the other, was discontinued, a number of deputies were also active in peace societies and took part in their congresses. Many of these peace leaders became as politically seasoned as career diplomats. By the end of the century there were reported to be over 400 peace organizations in the world, mainly in Europe and the United States, but also including Japan and Australia.

In 1901, in the light of this expansion of the peace movement and with the Hague Conference and the Christiana interparliamentary meeting still fresh in their minds, the members of the Nobel Committee had reason to be hopeful about the future of their prize. In formulating the rules for those eligible to submit nominations, they had given special recognition to the groups we have been discussing. Members of the Hague Court, the Institute of International Law, and the Commission of the Permanent International Peace Bureau were all specified.

We are handicapped in our efforts to understand how the Nobel Committee has reached award decisions. Following the statutes, committee members have kept no minutes of the meetings and have respected a vow of silence regarding their discussions. The committee, although not required to state the reasons for its choices, indicate them nevertheless in the speeches made at the ceremonies. And now, moreover, the confidential reports of the secretary and the committee advisers for the first three decades are available. These tell us who were nominated and by whom, which ones the committee selected for further consideration, and what the advisers wrote about them. As we follow the history of the prize into the 1930s, we shall make good use of these materials.

We know, for example, that by February 1901, only eighty-nine communications had been received regarding the first prize and that these yielded a total of thirty-six candidates, thirty individuals and six institutions. Of the thirty-six, Secretary Lange was asked to report on thirteen at the final meeting, when the decision was made to divide the prize equally between Frédéric Passy, doyen of the peace movement and cofounder of the Interparliamentary Union, and Henry Dunant, founder of the Red Cross.

The short list of thirteen is instructive in understanding the thinking of the first committee. Seven were to receive a prize within the decade. Four individuals on this list had been active in the Interparliamentary Union: Passy (1901) and cofounder Cremer (1903); Gobat (1902), the executive secretary; and Marquis Pandolfi, head of the Italian Interparliamentary group who had also presided over the Universal Peace Congress of 1891. The Interparliamentary Union itself was the fifth.

Also on the list were three nominees related to international law: the Institute of International Law (1904), and two noted jurists, Chevalier Descamps of Belgium and Fyodor Martens of Russia, who were both prominent at the First Hague Conference. Descamps and Martens were to make the short list in three other years, but neither received the prize. Another candidate given special consideration in 1901 and in two later years was the energetic English editor of the *Review of Reviews,* who had done so much to publicize the Hague Conference, W. T. Stead.

The more popular branch of the peace movement was represented in the short list of 1901 by Passy (1901); Élie Ducommun (1902), secretary of the Peace Bureau; and the bureau itself (1910). Passy had been everybody's candidate, uniting as he did both strands of the organized peace movement. He had founded a peace society as early as 1867 and later served the cause in the Chamber of Deputies for many years. He had been nominated not only by all the other leading peace workers but by French intellectuals, interparliamentary groups, and a leading international jurist.

The naming of Passy's colaureate, Henry Dunant, came as a surprise and, to the peace activists, a shock. Dunant had founded the Red Cross at about the same time as Passy had established his first peace society, in 1867. For many years he had been living in obscurity until discovered by an enterprising journalist shortly before the end of the century. Many belated honors were then bestowed upon him, and a campaign to win him the peace prize produced nominations by an array of distinguished parliamentarians, professors, and others, including the first chairman of the Nobel Committee. The chairman's death in November 1901 may have added weight to the consideration of his candidate.

Of the thirteen nominees who reached the final round, only Dunant had not engaged in peace activities recently. The statutes, however, had modified Nobel's intention of rewarding an achievement of the previous year, and all the awarding bodies were soon giving their prizes to graybeards.

The question raised by the peace activists was whether Dunant's achievement was work for peace at all. Was not his principal contribution the relief of the suffering of war rather than its prevention? Passy's position was: "You do not humanize war. You get rid of war by becoming more human." Bertha von Suttner said that in improving the laws of war, which was one of the results of the Hague Conference, was like regulating the temperature when boiling someone in oil. She had graphically described the horrors of the battlefield in her great pacifist novel in order to mobilize opinion against war; Dunant wrote about the horrors of the battlefield of Solferino to persuade governments to make agreements to take better care of the wounded.

Nobel had written in his will, however, not only about peace congresses and arms reduction; he had specified work for "fraternity between nations," and the committee apparently considered relief to the victims of war's violence and brutality as falling within that category. It is doubtful if the committee members realized at the time all the implications of this decision. What they were doing in giving such liberal interpretation to Nobel's "fraternity between nations" was to set a policy that would enable their successors to give recognition to every kind of distinguished effort that promoted or testified to *human* fraternity, to the unity of humanity. It was one of the most important decisions in the history of the prize.

One name on that short list of 1901 is yet to be mentioned, that of Leo Tolstoy, the great Russian novelist and the world's foremost advocate of Christian nonviolence. In Stockholm there was controversy when he was passed over that year for the literature prize. The secretary of the Swedish Academy maintained he had not been properly nominated, and in protest forty-two Swedish writers and artists signed a tribute to the novelist. Nor had he been properly nominated for the Peace Prize. Only one person had sent in his name to the Norwegian committee, a Swiss professor who had scribbled it on a visiting card. The proposal was accepted nevertheless, and the committee asked for a report. This proved to be not one of Secretary Lange's better efforts, an unusually brief summary of one-and-a-half pages, showing little acquaintance with Tolstoy's peace activities or his writings on the subject.

In 1902 when Tolstoy was properly nominated to the Swedish committee for the literary prize, the secretary of the Swedish Academy in an ill-tempered report wrote that the Russian writer had "denounced all forms of civilization . . . rewritten the New Testament . . . denied the right of both individuals and nations to self-defense." Besides, the secretary added, Tolstoy was opposed to prizes anyway and would not accept one.

The adviser of the Norwegian committee gave a much fairer appraisal when Tolstoy was nominated again for the Peace Prize in 1909, the year before his death, this time by five members of the Storting. The adviser wrote a strong positive report of thirteen pages, showing great familiarity with Tolstoy's writings and his doctrine of nonresistance. He discussed the attacks on patriotism, militarism, and the state and Tolstoy's advocacy of refusal to do military service; he summarized the hostile opinions and concluded that Tolstoy's inadequacies and exaggerations would be forgotten. What would be remembered was that he had placed humanity face-to-face with its own conscience.

The committee did not agree with its adviser, however, and gave the 1909 prize to two peace-minded politicians. It would take many years before the committee would feel comfortable in awarding the Peace Prize to outspoken advocates of nonviolence. But the day would come in Oslo when one of the greatest peace laureates of all would pay full tribute to Tolstoy. In 1954 in his Nobel lecture Albert Schweitzer spoke of Tolstoy as a moral teacher who had reached a *higher* level of civilization. The committee adviser of 1909 would have felt his prediction had come true.

After 1901 the committee in the great majority of its awards continued to recognize representatives of the three groups considered that first year. Of the twenty awards in the period ending in 1919, twelve went to two branches of the organized peace movement and four to international jurists. After the Dunant prize, another humanitarian award was not made until the war year of 1917, when it was bestowed upon the International Red Cross. A new departure, which was to become highly important in future years, was the first statesman award, made to President Theodore Roosevelt in 1906, followed by the 1912 prize for Elihu Root, former secretary of state.

The members of the Interparliamentary Union who became laureates in this period were usually active in the peace societies as well. Those not mentioned above as included on the short list of 1901 were Klas Pontus Arnoldson of Sweden and Fredrik Bajer of Denmark (1908) and Baron d'Estournelles de Constant of France (1909). The other representatives of the organized movement were writers and journalists: Bertha von Suttner, finally named in 1905; the Italian editor and peace leader Ernesto Moneta (1907); and Suttner's Austrian colleague Alfred Hermann Fried, prominent publicist and theoretician of the movement (1911).

Theodore Roosevelt was given the award in 1906 for his role in bringing to an end the Russo-Japanese War. For the first time the Peace Prize now enjoyed wide publicity in the world press. The *New York Times,* which had been reporting only the Stockholm awards, began to cover the Peace Prize too at this time. The Roosevelt award was the first to arouse public controversy. The peace leaders had been critical of the Dunant award, the long delay in recognizing Baroness von Suttner, and the divisions of the prize, but they had followed a policy of keeping their reservations to themselves. Now they made public their disappointment, and protests were published by social democrats and others. Although Roosevelt had also been a supporter of the Hague Court and of arbitration treaties and had even received peace activists in the White House, his foreign policy had been warlike and imperialistic, especially his seizure of the Panama Canal Zone from Colombia.

In 1905, 10 December had fallen on a Sunday when the Storting was not in session, so for the first time the announcement had been made outside the Storting, at the inauguration of the building of the Nobel Institute. In 1906 the committee's announcement was made in the Storting once again, but for the last time. The American ambassador was invited to accept for the president, and the prize and the insignia were presented to him, not by the chairman of the Nobel Committee, but by a leader of the Storting "in behalf of the Norwegian parliament." It is unfortunate that the integrity of the committee was not better preserved in this first award to a head of state. The occasion seemed to lend credence to the Swedish critics who charged that the real reason for the award was the desire of the government of newly independent Norway to win a useful friend.

There is, however, no reason to suspect that the major motive for the award was political. The report on which the committee based its decision, which happened to be written by Halvdan Koht, later a committee member and foreign minister, was a remarkably thorough and well-balanced account of thirty-seven pages. Koht carefully noted Roosevelt's imperialist and war policies as well as his contribution to peace, and concluded with an account of the successful mediation between Russia and Japan. Roosevelt had been nominated not by Norwegians but by professors, five from the United States and one from Germany. Moreover, the committee had actually considered rewarding a diplomatic effort to bring a war to an end several years before. In 1902 the committee gave special consideration to two British envoys in Latin America for their achievement in reconciling a dispute between the countries to which they were accredited.

A few figures throw light on the committee's activities in this period. The secretary send out about 500 announcements soliciting nominations, compared to over 5,000 today. The number of communications received in response is not always given in the reports, but it seems to have risen and fallen somewhat erratically. In 1902 there were 92, in 1906, 144. Today there are several hundred each year. In this first period the number of candidates proposed usually varied between 20 and 30; today the number is over 80. In the first decade a total of 50 nominees reached the final round; 15 became laureates. In the second decade, which included the war years, 91 were selected for further consideration; only 7 received the prize.

The list of "also rans" contains some interesting names: Ludwik Zamenhof, the inventor of Esperanto; Richard Bartholdt, the Missouri congressman who was very active in the Interparliamentary Union; Andrew Carnegie, for his munificent gifts to the Peace Palace at The Hague and the Carnegie Endowment for International Peace. Emperor William II of Germany was nominated by President Benjamin Ide Wheeler of the University of California, who had been exchange professor at the University of Berlin, but he did not reach the finals. The Germans who ran strongest in these years were the international jurists. In 1914 the German peace activist Pastor Umfrid had twenty-five nominations from peace workers, parliamentarians, and international lawyers, but the war prevented the consideration of his claims.

The committee did not close shop when the war broke out in August 1914, although it decided to make no award in that year, nor for 1915, 1916, and 1918; the 1919 decision was put off to 1920. There were strong candidates in those years, however: Norman Angell and Jane Addams, who were to be given the prize later; President David Starr Jordan of Stanford University, strong peace advocate and a biologist, one of the first scientists to be given consideration; and the international jurists Heinrich Lammasch of Vienna, who was considered every year from 1915 to 1919, and James Brown Scott of the United States, who was considered in 1917 and 1918. Some voices urged the committee to make awards particularly in wartime, when the banner of peace especially needed to be raised. But the committee decided otherwise and made only one award during these years, to the International Red Cross. Until the war, the committee had missed only one year, 1912, and it made that award the next year.

All in all, the Norwegian Nobel Committee had started out well in its first two decades, repaying Nobel's trust. It spent much of this time rewarding the pioneers, whose activities were known to Nobel who had had them in mind when composing his will. But the committee marked out new paths in its awards to humanitarians and statesmen, setting directions for the prize that would make of it something different than Nobel intended, but something far greater than he could ever have dreamed.

1901

Frédéric Passy (1822–1912)

France

Doyen of pre-1914 peace movement; active since 1867 as organizer of peace societies and later international congresses; as a member of Chamber of Deputies, cofounder of the Interparliamentary Union; lecturer and writer in economics.

Passy was a universal choice for the first Nobel Peace Prize. No one had worked so long and so hard for the cause, and no one enjoyed more respect from both branches of the organized movement, the parliamentarians and the peace society leaders. Their only criticism of the award was that Passy should have received the full prize, instead of having to share it with Henry Dunant, founder of the Red Cross.

Passy had publicly criticized war as early as 1856, during the Crimean War, and he was in touch with the English peace and free-trade leaders Richard Cobden and John Bright. It was not until 1867, however, that Passy, then forty-five years old, began his active crusade for peace. A conflict had arisen between France and Prussia that threatened to lead to war. On the same day Passy and two other public figures, independently of one another, wrote to the editor of the leading newspaper of Paris, urging him to speak out against war and to open his columns to voices calling for peace. This led to a flood of letters urging peace as well as other expressions from both sides of the Rhine, which helped calm the international situation. Passy's friends said to him, "You have stopped a war; now try to stop *war.*" So he set about organizing the first important peace society in France, with the imposing title the International League for Permanent and Universal Peace.

Frédéric Passy was born in Paris in 1822 into a propertied and well-connected family, and he married a young lady of means. He could have lived a life of ease, but he was also endowed with a social conscience that made him a lifelong servant of the public good.

The two causes to which he devoted his life were free trade and peace, which were intertwined in the social reform movements of the mid-nineteenth century. As a young man Passy had become an ardent adherent of the economic liberalism of Claude-Frédéric Bastiat and Edouard-René Laboulaye in France and Cobden in England and first made his reputation as a lecturer and writer on political economy. Such ideas were popular during the Second Empire of Napoléon III (1852–1870), and Passy would have been appointed as university professor had he not, as a convinced republican, refused to take the required oath to the emperor. After the fall of Napoléon III, free trade went out of favor, and the opportunity did not present itself again. This was the greatest disappointment of Passy's life.

With regard to peace, however, Passy was championing a cause that went from unpopularity to respectability. The apparent success of the peace forces in 1867 was not long-lasting. The Franco-Prussian War broke out in 1870, and after Prussia's victory and annexation of the French provinces of Alsace and Lorraine, peace propaganda seemed unpatriotic. Nevertheless, Passy was able to reconstitute the peace league on a less ambitious basis as the French Society of the Friends of Peace (later renamed the French Society for Arbitration between Nations), calling for renewal, not revenge, affirming the right of all peoples to self-determination, and advocating arbitration as the proper method for the settlement of international disputes.

In 1878 Passy joined the English pacifist Henry Richard in an unsuccessful effort to lobby for peace at the Congress of Berlin. That same year he managed to gain the approval of the French government for the Universal Peace Congress held in Paris at the time of the World Exposition.

Passy had already entered political life in 1874, when supporters of the new Third Republic, looking for "a good republican candidate," persuaded him to campaign for the General Council of the Department of Seine-et-Oise. He was elected and regularly reelected until he retired after serving for twenty-four years. A street in Saint-Germain-en-Laye still bears his name.

A similar situation brought Passy into national politics. In 1881 only one electoral district of Paris, the wealthy eighth arrondissement, was still represented in the Chamber of Deputies by a reactionary; republican politicians picked Passy to oppose him. Passy was a confirmed republican and moderate, known to the electorate through his six years in the provincial council, and he had recently been elected to membership in the prestigious Institute of France (Academy of Moral and Political Sciences). Passy won the election and was reelected in 1885; he was defeated in 1889, however, by a Bonapartist candidate who appealed to religious prejudice. As a liberal Catholic, in disagreement with such doctrines as papal infallibility, Passy had been vulnerable.

In his eight years in the Chamber, Passy, who stood somewhere left of center in his political beliefs, voted his convictions on every issue, whether this meant voting with the Left, the Center, or the Right. Ever the gentleman, an accomplished orator of the old school, he was respected for his character, even if not often for his ideas. It was especially difficult for him to gain a proper hearing for proposals for peace and arbitration. Moreover, few deputies agreed with his opposition to French colonialism, which derived from both his ethical convictions and his free-trade philosophy. He was never more eloquent than when he attacked the government's imperialist policy in Indochina in 1885 in the name of the same human rights his countrymen were invoking in asking for the return of Alsace-Lorraine. The government of France, claiming that the inhabitants were barbarians, could move to take the territory, but, Passy asserted, "It is their life. . . . It is their Alsace, to them; it is their Lorraine, to them. For them and before humanity as before God, it is worth as much as ours."

As international arbitration began to win support in the House of Commons and the American Congress, Passy was able to get some of his fellow deputies to endorse the idea of arbitration treaties with those countries. In 1888 he and his French colleagues hosted a meeting in Paris with English MPs led by Randal Cremer, and the next year these two organized in Paris a multinational meeting of deputies over which Passy presided and which laid the foundation for the Interparliamentary Union.

Cremer always insisted that he alone was the founder of this association. It is true that in 1888 Passy was responding to Cremer's initiative, but the idea of international cooperation among parliamentarians had been in the air for more than a decade. Passy deserved equal credit, but characteristically he would put forward Cremer's claims to the paternity, reserving for himself the title of "second father." It was Passy, moreover, who helped secure for Cremer the French decoration of the Legion of Honor that Cremer coveted (an honor Passy himself had been awarded some years earlier).

In 1889 Passy presided over yet another Universal Peace Congress in Paris that he helped organize, the first in the series that brought together almost every year the representatives of peace societies from many countries. Thus Passy had a most important part in the institutionalization of the two strands of the organized peace movement, the peace-minded politicians and the peace society leaders.

Passy was to remain active for peace for almost another quarter of a century, although he had to face growing blindness, failing health, and the deaths of his beloved wife of fifty-two years and other members of his closely knit family. He continued to attend international peace meetings; when no longer able to travel alone, he was accompanied by one or another of his many grandchildren. He made the great effort to attend the universal peace congress in Munich in 1907, when he was eighty-five, because of his abiding concern for Franco-German reconciliation.

As the grand old man of the peace movement, his counsel was sought in France and abroad by the younger leaders, and his appearance at an international congress was always an event. He would have to be helped to the podium, a frail octogenarian with flowing white beard, but once standing there, like Anteas touching Mother Earth, Passy somehow would retrieve his vigor and deliver an eloquent and moving speech. His speeches were all extemporaneous now. As he explained, "When I begin I don't know what I am going to say, but this is the best way to give a speech—if you have something in your head and on your heart."

Passy's physical infirmities never affected his active and alert mind nor his smoothly flowing prose, which now had to be dictated to a secretary, provided for with the Nobel Prize money. Reading through those of his private letters that have been preserved in the libraries of the Hague Peace Palace and the United Nations in Geneva, one appreciates the special qualities of this high-minded idealist—his dedication to the welfare of humanity, the utter absence of self-seeking in his nature, his tender thoughtfulness of others, his faith and hope for the future. When his health worsened and his powers began to fail as he approached his ninetieth birthday in 1912, his ever robust optimism weakened. In a letter to Bertha von Suttner he had to confess that the news of international tension and conflict made his physical condition worse. He could not refrain from asking himself if all the work of himself and others for peace had been in vain, "if this world was anything else but a melée of cupidity and violence." He said it was terrible to face such enigmas at such a moment in his life: "I'm trying to get hold of myself. I would not want to finish in discouragement and weakness." As he ends the letter, however, he sees a ray of hope in a recent speech in the Chamber of Deputies.

Passy was too weak to attend his birthday party in May 1912, and on 12 June, he died. Two years later the war came that seemed to confirm his worst fears about the world that he had expressed during his last illness. Yet even in his slough of despond toward the end, Passy had found some reason for hope. And the record of his own life, like those of the other Nobel Peace laureates of his stature, may point to a more positive answer to his enigmatic question about humanity.

BIBLIOGRAPHY

Primary Sources

Passy, Frédéric. *Feuilles éparsé (1840–1904).* Paris: Société Fr. d'Imprimerie et de Librairie, 1904. "Scattered leaves" of light verse, mostly personal.

———. *Pour la paix: Notes et documents.* Paris: Charpentier, 1909. Reprint. New York: Garland, 1972. With introduction by Adolf Wild. All too brief autobiography, with documentary appendix.

———. "Le Prix Nobel." *La paix par le droit* 36 (December 1926): 435–37. This criticism, written after he won the first Peace Prize, was intended for publication after his death.

Secondary Sources

"Passy, Frédéric." In *MPL.*

Passy, Paul. *Un Apôtre de la paix: La vie de Frédéric Passy.* Paris: La Renaissance du Livre, 1927. A brief memoir by his son.

Puech, Jules L. "Frédéric Passy." In *The Interparliamentary Union from 1889–1939.* Geneva: Interparliamentary Union, 1939, pp. 153–57. An excellent sketch by a younger French activist.

Wild, Adolf. "Frédéric Passy—der Gründer der internationalen Friedensbewegung." in *FNP* 1:126–35, documentation, 188–93.

1901

Henry Dunant (1828–1910)

Switzerland

Founder of the Red Cross.

In June 1859, a Swiss gentleman of thirty-one years of age turned up near the northern Italian town of Solferino, seeking an audience with Napoléon III who was with the French troops preparing, along with their Italian allies, to join battle with the Austrians. He had a plan to make a fortune that needed only the emperor's approval, and he had come all the way from Paris to secure it. The young man never met with the emperor, but what he saw of the Battle of Solferino and of the suffering it caused gave him a new mission in life and a different kind of fortune.

Jean Henri (later Henry) Dunant was born to a well-to-do Calvinist family in Geneva in 1828. As a child he was inspired with the spirit of Christian service, and in his early life he engaged in religious activities and was a member of the League of Alms, which cared for the poor and the sick. After working for a time with the Christian Union of Young People (antecedent to the YMCA), he decided at the age of twenty-six to take up a banking career, an occupation appropriate for one of his social standing in Geneva.

His banking firm sent him for long periods to North Africa, where European business interests were engaged in economic development. From this experience came his first publication, a travel book on Tunis that contained an interesting account of Muslim culture, with a chapter published separately on slavery among the Muslims and in the United States (the last prompted by his meeting in Geneva with Harriet Beecher Stowe). Abolition of slavery became one of his lifelong causes.

In both his humanitarian impulses and in his financial schemes Dunant dreamed great dreams. In Algeria he acquired rights to a promising tract of land that needed only the water from the adjacent land owned by the French government to make it highly profitable. Dunant raised capital in Geneva to form his own company and went to Paris to secure the grant of concessions from the emperor. Finding that Napoléon III had left with the army for Italy, young Dunant, nothing daunted, set out after him.

What he stumbled upon at Solferino was a bloody engagement that caused some forty thousand casualties in one day of fighting, with many wounded soldiers left lying on the battlefield to die miserably and needlessly in torrid heat without water and with no one to care for them. Dunant, his Calvinist conscience stirred, tried to do what he could personally. He established an extemporized field station in a church in the small town of Castiglione, pressing into service the women of the town and others to help succor all the wounded, friend and foe alike, with the motto *tutti fratelli,* "all are brothers."

In 1862 Dunant published his *Memoir of Solferino,* describing in detail the horrors he had seen, ending with the plea: "Could not the means be found in time of peace to organize relief societies whose aim would be to provide care for the wounded in time of war by volunteers of zeal and devotion, properly qualified for such work?" He proposed a plan of action and dispatched sixteen hundred copies of the *Memoir* to all the rulers and heads of government of Europe, and to all the cabinet ministers and other distinguished personages who might be helpful in realizing such a project.

The book was a sensation throughout Europe. Within a month a second edition was published, and soon there were translations in other languages. In Geneva itself the Society for Public Welfare appointed a committee of Dunant and four others to consider next steps. It was this committee, meeting on 7 February 1863, that issued the call for an international conference and, in effect, founded the Red Cross.

Dunant, traveling all over Europe to make his case, threw himself and all his resources into an effort to persuade governments to send representatives to this conference and to inspire the organization in each country of a voluntary society to provide relief on the battlefield. When the conference assembled in October, there were thirty-nine representatives present from sixteen countries. The main outcome was to arrange for a gathering of plenipotentiaries the following year, officially convened by the Swiss government to draft an international treaty. This agreement, the Geneva Convention for the Amelioration of the Wounded in Armies in the Field, was signed in August 1864 and then ratified by sixteen nations. They agreed to guarantee neutrality to medical and transit personnel working under the symbol of a banner showing a red cross on a white field.

Dunant was now a famous man, and he was able to promote other causes, such as international arbitration, the abolition of slavery, and especially better treatment of prisoners of war. This was a natural adjunct to the care of the wounded, and Dunant's proposals, first advanced in a meeting of the Red Cross at the Paris World Exposition in 1867, influenced later international conventions on the rules of warfare.

While working for humanity, however, Dunant had neglected his own business affairs. The water rights in Algeria were never secured and the company was poorly managed. In 1867 Dunant went bankrupt, and his friends and associates in Geneva who had invested in the venture incurred serious losses. Among the good bourgeoisie of Geneva this was an unpardonable sin. Dunant resigned as secretary of the Red Cross and left town as an outcast, never to return.

He stayed abroad until his funds were exhausted and then slipped back unnoticed to Switzerland, where he lived in Appenzell as a recluse, impoverished and forgotten by the world. There were times, he later recalled, when he dined on a crust of bread, blackened his coat with ink, whitened his collar with chalk, and filled out "a shabby, formless hat with papers" in the effort to maintain his self-respect; he even had to sleep outdoors.

Finally he fell ill in 1892 and entered a hospice in the village of Heiden, where he lived in Room 12 for the last eighteen years of his life. In 1895 his whereabouts were discovered by chance by a Swiss journalist, who published an interview with him. The world was surprised to learn that he was still alive and sought to make amends. Awards and honors were heaped upon him, and the Swiss government granted him a modest pension. Emerging from obscurity, Dunant contributed to peace efforts again, writing for Bertha von Suttner's journal and other peace periodicals.

Two of Dunant's admirers now set out to win for him the first Nobel Peace Prize, beginning their efforts even before the prize machinery was in place. Rudolf Müller was a German high school teacher who cooperated with Dunant in a book on the origins of the Red Cross, and Hans Daae was a Norwegian army doctor who had watched the Red Cross at work on a battlefield in the Balkans. Müller used the book to enlist supporters among Red Cross committees, university professors, and politicians, and he supplied Daae with copious documentation, which the doctor translated into Norwegian to be sent to the Norwegian Nobel Committee and which was also used as the basis for articles in the press. Most important, in December 1900 Dr. Daae visited Bjørnstjerne Bjørnson, who was a member of the committee; he reported to Müller that he had persuaded Bjørnson, who had already declared himself in favor of Passy, to agree that the first award should be shared between them.

When the committee met in November 1901 to decide on the first prize, Secretary Lange reported that there were more pages of documentation supporting Dunant than for any of the other thirteen candidates on the short list, even including Passy, who had provided through his nominators documents demonstrating his continual work for peace for over thirty years. Moreover, Daae had seen to it that Dunant was nominated by some prominent Norwegians, and Müller had secured nominations from university professors and parliamentary deputies.

Thus it was that on 10 December 1901 the committee dispatched telegrams to both Passy and Dunant, informing them that they were to share the award. The first campaign waged for the prize had been successful. And with the honoring of Dunant the committee served notice at the outset that its award would be more broadly conceived than Nobel had anticipated. Passy, as the dean of the organized peace movement, had worked for many years to prevent war; Dunant, on the other hand, had brought into being an organization that relieved war's suffering. The committee recognized that the humanitarian activities of the Red Cross carried on in the midst of war embodied "the fraternity of nations" to which Nobel had referred in his will. Moreover, Dunant had provided a remarkable demonstration of how a single individual could awaken the conscience of the world and bring governments to agree on higher levels of conduct.

Dunant owed yet another debt of gratitude to Dr. Daae. To forestall any attempt by Dunant's old creditors in Switzerland from applying for a court order to seize the prize money, the doctor secured a delay in its remittance until Dunant could send him a power of attorney. This was not done so that Dunant could spend the money on himself, however. He went on living simply in Room 12, saving the Nobel money and other grants he received for bequests in his will to those who had cared for him in the hospice and to endow a free bed for the poor people in the village who fell ill. The rest he left to charities in Norway and Switzerland.

Dunant could feel that the Nobel award had completed his rehabilitation in the eyes of the world, but he had lived too long neglected and unappreciated really to enjoy his new honors. When he died in 1910, Dunant, as he had directed, was carried to his grave "like a dog," and buried without a ceremony or funeral procession. His bitterness can be understood. Nevertheless, this did not diminish the memory of his great achievement. That grave in a Zurich cemetery is marked by a white marble monument of a man kneeling to offer water to a wounded soldier. And every year on Dunant's birthday, 8 May, we celebrate World Red Cross Day.

BIBLIOGRAPHY

Primary Sources

Dunant, Henry. *Mémoires.* Edited by Bernard Gagnebin for the Henry-Dunant Institute, Geneva. Lausanne: Editions l'Age de l'Homme, 1971. Written in his later years.

———. *A Memory of Solferino.* Washington: American Red Cross, 1959. The famous account published in 1862 as *Un souvenir de Solferino.* This edition also includes a short biography of Dunant and a sketch of the history of the Red Cross movement.

Secondary Sources

Boissier, Pierre. *History of the International Committee of the Red Cross: From Solferino to Tsushima.* Translated from the French edition published in 1963. Geneva: ICRC, 1985. The authoritative history.

Durand, André. "The Development of the Idea of Peace in the Thinking of Henry Dunant." *International Review of the Red Cross,* January–February 1986, pp. 16–51.

Gagnebin, Bernard. *Encounter with Henry Dunant.* Translated by Bernard C. Swift. Geneva: Georg, 1963. Texts and documents; illustrated.

Gigon, Fernand. *The Epic of the Red Cross or the Knight-errant of Charity.* Translated by Gerald Griffin. London: Jarrolds, 1946.

Gumpert, Martin. *Dunant: The Story of the Red Cross.* New York: Oxford University Press, 1938.

Hart, Ellen. *Man Born to Live: The Life and Work of Henry Dunant.* London: Gollancz, 1953.

Heudtlass, Willy. "J. Henry Dunant and the Events Leading to the Award of the First Nobel Peace Prize." *International Review of the Red Cross,* June 1964, pp. 283–96. Based on newly discovered documents.

Mercanton, Daisy C. *Henry Dunant: Essai bio-bibliographique.* Henry-Dunant Institute, Geneva. Lausanne: Editions l'Age de l'Homme, 1972.

Simson, Gerhard. "Henry Dunant—Die Tragödie eines Menschenfreundes." In *FNP* 1:50–125, documentation, 180–87.

1902

Élie Ducommun (1833–1906)

Switzerland

Veteran peace advocate, active from 1867. Editor, writer, legislator, railroad executive, first honorary secretary of the Permanent International Peace Bureau.

Élie Ducommun became cowinner of the second Nobel Peace Prize with Albert Gobat, secretary-general of the Interparliamentary Union, when the Norwegian Committee decided to endow in the persons of their executives the two major institutions of the international peace movement. Ducommun was the first secretary-general and organizing genius of the International Peace Bureau, but his contributions to peace went far back beyond the establishment of the bureau in 1891. He was one of the most sympathetic of all the pacifists of the heroic period, a man of universal talents and a gifted organizer, orator, editor, and poet.

Ducommun was born in Geneva in 1833, son of a skilled watchmaker from Neuchâtel. After completing his studies, he became a teacher of French and German, but, moved by liberal and progressive causes, he left the classroom, first for journalism and then for politics and public service. In Geneva he served on the Grand Council, becoming vice-chancellor and then chancellor of the canton. When he moved to Bern in 1865, he was a member of the Grand Council there and official translator for the Federal Council. In his forties, Ducommun turned to the private sector and began a career of thirty years with a Swiss railroad company as secretary-general, which he resigned early in 1903, to give his full time to peace.

Ducommun first became associated with the peace movement in 1867, when radical republicans from all over Europe came to Geneva for a peace congress that established the International League of Peace and Liberty. Ducommun helped write the manifesto and became vice president and editor of the French edition of the league's journal, the *United States of Europe.* The goal of the league was to establish peace by founding a European federation, following the political doctrines of Mazzini. Since true peace could be based only upon liberty, this meant that all the nationalities of Europe had first to become free and republican. Peace could come, therefore, only by revolution and the redrawing of the map of Europe along national lines. One day such ideas of national self-determination and peace based upon justice would be widely shared. Meanwhile, it was only in republican Switzerland that the league prospered, and Ducommun, with his connections with Swiss statesmen and Freemasons, became a leading spirit of the peace movement.

In 1891, however, when Ducommun was asked to organize the International Peace Bureau, he put his personal, relatively aggressive peace philosophy behind him. As he wrote to the French president of the league, "You are the advance guard of the left wing of the army of Peace and I am the rallying point of the different corps of the army. . . . As secretary of the Bureau I have no inclinations to make known, and I am not to impose on anyone, my point of view—political, religious, or social."

Ducommun's resolve to maintain official neutrality was particularly important because the different corps of his peace army were not all marching to the beat of the same drum. To the religious absolutists of the old London Peace Society, for example, the League of Peace and Liberty was advancing to war, not peace. Then there were the serious differences between German and French peace societies over Alsace-Lorraine, which Germany had annexed after the Franco-Prussian War. The Germans insisted that peace demanded the maintenance of the status quo, whereas the French insisted that peace could not be based upon conquest. To keep the peace in the Universal Peace Congresses, Alsace-Lorraine had to be kept off the agenda.

Ducommun not only resisted the demands of certain peace leaders that the bureau take stands on current political issues but opposed proposals that the bureau structure become a federation, recognizing that the young peace movement was not ready for such moves. It was, after all, no mean feat that Ducommun accomplished in keeping all the societies of the time working together in what remained a loose coalition. He had to use all his diplomatic skills, and he could not have succeeded had there not been such a general confidence in his fine integrity.

Ducommun took the job as honorary secretary of the bureau refusing any remuneration, with the understanding that he would remain only until the bureau was out of its swaddling clothes; then a paid secretary would be hired, and Ducommun would retire. Efforts to raise funds to endow the bureau properly were unsuccessful, however, so he remained, directing its destinies with a sure and steady hand until his death.

Until 1903 Ducommun could give only his evenings to the bureau, but he was a zealous and indefatigable worker. Nothing was left undone. No letter went unanswered; the most inconsequential request was attended to. The old records of the bureau, now at the UN Library in Geneva, can be seen today in the apple-pie order in which Ducommun left them.

Although Ducommun was given a paid helper, he virtually *was* the International Peace Bureau. He personally carried on all the correspondence with over two hundred peace societies and with individual peace advocates all over the world, kept them informed about developments, edited journals and pamphlets, wrote diplomatic notes to governments, and managed the office files and accounts. In preparing the agenda for the annual congresses Ducommun displayed the utmost tact and discretion. With his disposition to compromise and conciliate, he forestalled many a divisive debate.

When Ducommun died in harness in 1906, his coworkers felt that "the incomparable Ducommun" could not be replaced, that "the Bern Bureau has become an orphan, the heart of the whole peace movement has ceased to beat." Fortunately, his fellow laureate Gobat was prepared to add the duties of the Peace Bureau to those he was already performing for the Interparliamentary Bureau. Gobat built on the foundations Ducommun had laid, and the Peace Bureau was granted the Nobel Peace Prize in 1910.

After Ducommun's death a collection of his poetry was published, including tender love poems for his wife, Adele. They had been married in 1857, when he was twenty-four, and they had three children. A poem written in 1893 to the "Angel of Our Hearth" testifies to their happy life together; some of its lines express a conviction that inspired him throughout his life:

To live not for oneself,
  but for others
This is happiness here below.

BIBLIOGRAPHY

Primary Sources

Ducommun, Élie. *Derniers sourires.* Bern: Buchler, 1908. With a biographical introduction.

———. *A Key to the Deliberations of the Annual Peace Congresses.* Bern: International Peace Bureau, 1897.

———. *Précis historique du mouvement en favour de la paix.* Bern: Boneff, 1899.

Secondary Sources

Bajer, Frederick. *Les Origines du Bureau international de la paix.* Bern: Walchli, 1904.

Brassel-Moser, Ruedi. "Élie Ducommun—der unentbehrliche vermittler." In *FNP* 1:136–47, documentation, 194–97.

"Ducommun, Élie." In *MPL.*

Monnier, Victor. "Notes et documents pour servir à la biographie d'Élie Ducommun." *Revue européenne des sciences sociales* 22, no. 67 (1984):139–64. Includes a list of his publications.

Simon, Werner. "The International Peace Bureau, 1892–1917." In *Peace Movements and Political Cultures.* Edited by Charles Chatfield and Peter van Dungen. Knoxville: University of Tennessee Press, 1988.

1902

Albert Gobat (1843–1914)

Switzerland

Lawyer, legislator, first secretary-general of the Interparliamentary Bureau (1892–1909), secretary-general of International Peace Bureau (1906–14).

Albert Gobat was the leading international administrator in the peace movement, something of a forebear of the international civil servants of the League of Nations and the United Nations. He shared the Peace Prize of 1902 as the first secretary-general of the Interparliamentary Bureau, and in 1910 he was secretary-general of the International Peace Bureau when that institution was given an undivided prize. From 1906, when he assumed the responsibilities of the Peace Bureau on the death of Élie Ducommun, his corecipient of the earlier prize, Gobat directed both bureaus until 1909.

Born in Tramelan, Switzerland, in 1843, Gobat was the son of a Protestant pastor. He was a brilliant student, distinguishing himself in his studies at universities in his own country and in France and Germany, finally taking his doctorate in law, summa cum laude, at Heidelberg in 1867.

For the next fifteen years he practiced law in

Bern, where he became a well-known lawyer and lecturer on French civil law at the university. Thereafter he turned to education and politics. From 1882 until 1912 he held the office of superintendent of instruction for the canton of Bern, where he modernized the educational system, introducing along with the traditional classical curriculum the study of foreign languages and vocational and professional training.

At the same time he embarked upon a career as a liberal politician, first in cantonal politics and then as a member of the Swiss parliament from 1884 until his death. In the first six years he was a member of the Council of States and after 1890 a deputy in the other chamber, the National Council.

Gobat took part in the Interparliamentary Conferences from the beginning. He attended the first meeting in 1889 in Paris and presided over the fourth conference held in Bern, which asked him to organize the Interparliamentary Bureau as its first secretary-general. He agreed, refusing to take any salary, just as his fellow countryman Ducommun had in assuming the post of secretary of the International Peace Bureau in Bern.

The duties were not onerous, consisting mainly in making arrangements for the annual meetings and publishing the proceedings. Gobat was prepared to take more responsibility, but the English opposed a strong executive and most of the other national groups showed little interest in having the office serve as anything more than a weak link between them. Gobat started a monthly journal, declaring that it would be "the tribune of the parliaments of Europe." It became nothing of the sort. Few members submitted articles, and Gobat found himself writing most of the contents himself. In 1897 he asked and received permission to end publication.

Throughout its first decade the Interparliamentary Conference remained just that, a body having little independent life between its annual meetings. These, it is true, were usually carried off with éclat, with official welcomes from the governments of the host countries and red-carpet treatment for the delegates, most of whom were well practiced in the art of oratory.

Having originated in cooperation between French and English deputies to promote international arbitration, the organization continued to emphasize this function. Its major tangible accomplishment was the development of a set of rules for an arbitration tribunal, which became the basis for the Permanent Court of Arbitration established by the Hague Conference of 1899.

In the early 1900s the peace movement could point to the work of the Hague Conference as the cornerstone of the temple of peace, and in Gobat's last years as secretary-general the organization grew in membership and authority. Its name was changed from the Interparliamentary Conference to the Interparliamentary Union, which had the ring of a more substantial association. The annual meetings had long urged members to work for arbitration provisions in commercial treaties. Now that the Hague Court was established, Gobat was able in 1902 to carry through legislation obligating the Swiss government to include in all future treaties of commerce a clause that would require the two states to refer to the court any dispute arising under the treaty.

In 1904 the annual assembly of the Union, meeting at the international exhibition in Saint Louis, passed a resolution calling for the convening of the Second Hague Conference. Gobat as spokesman persuaded President Theodore Roosevelt to work toward this end. The conference actually met in 1907, with Tsar Nicholas of Russia, who convoked the first conference, being given the credit for reasons of protocol.

In 1906 Gobat delivered his Nobel lecture, which the committee had agreed to postpone. It was a careful analysis of the work of the First Hague Conference, highlighting those elements that Gobat recommended be developed further for settling international differences. He spoke as "a practical politician," he said, which is what he was, adding, "It is true that I am not one of those who laugh at utopias. The utopia of today can become reality tomorrow. . . . But though I take my place in the crowded ranks of the optimists, I draw a distinction between the aims which can be realized immediately and those for which we are not yet ready."

As secretary-general of the International Peace Bureau, Gobat was able to take stronger stands than was possible as director of the Interparliamentary Bureau. Indeed, he was far more frank and forceful in his initiatives than his predecessor at the Peace Bureau, Ducommun. He sent communications urging governments to submit disputes to arbitration, and in 1911 he strongly criticized both the Italian government for waging war against Turkey and the Italian peace societies who supported the war effort.

Gobat published widely on peace issues, and found time in his busy life for publications in his favorite field of history, including a well-received scholarly work on the history of Bern and a very successful popular history of Switzerland.

Gobat died at his post, at a meeting of the Council of the International Peace Bureau early in 1914. He was seventy-one years old.

BIBLIOGRAPHY

Primary Sources

Gobat, Albert. *Le cauchemar de l'Europe.* Paris: Soudier, 1911. The question of Alsace-Lorraine.

———. *Croquis et impressions d'Amerique.* Paris: Fischbacher, 1904. Drawings and impressions after a visit to the United States.

———. *Histoire de la Suisse racontée au peuple.* Neuchâtel: Zahn, 1899. History of Switzerland.

Secondary Sources

Böschenstein, Hermann. "Albert Gobat—der unfriedliche Friedensförderer." In *FNP* 1:148–57, documentation, 200–5.

"Gobat, Albert." In *MPL.*

Simon, Werner. "The International Peace Bureau (1892–1917)." In *Peace Movements and Political Cultures.* Edited by Charles Chatfield and Peter van Dungen. Knoxville: University of Tennessee Press, 1988.

1903
William Randal Cremer (1838–1908)

Great Britain

Only labor leader in the peace movement, organizer of the International Arbitration League, longtime member of the House of Commons, cofounder of the Interparliamentary Union.

William Cremer, one of the peace veterans recognized in the earliest awards, was the only labor leader among them. When he was granted the first undivided prize in 1903, his peace activities had spanned a period of over three decades. He had fought untiringly for international arbitration both inside and outside of Parliament, and with Frédéric Passy (1901) he had founded the Interparliamentary Union.

Cremer was born in 1828 in a small town near Portsmouth to working-class parents. In his infancy, the family was abandoned by the father, and the mother raised the three children. An ardent Methodist, she sent the boy to a church school, the only formal education he ever had. At fifteen he was apprenticed to his uncle, a carpenter, and at twenty-four, moved to London, where he became involved in trade union activities, soon showing leadership qualities. At the age of thirty he played a major role in a local campaign for the nine-hour day and other labor struggles and soon thereafter became a national leader of the carpenters' union.

In the 1860s Cremer was chosen secretary of the Workmen's Committee supporting the North in the American Civil War and then secretary of the International Workingmen's Association. He withdrew when the International came under the control of Karl Marx and his friends, whom Cremer regarded as "men who cared more for their isms than for the cause of real progress." Like other English labor leaders of the time, Cremer was closer to English liberalism than to the more radical labor movement of the Continent, and he worked with the Reform League to widen the franchise among Englishmen. His experience with the International, however, left him with a sense of the potential of cooperation across national borders in the efforts for world peace.

Cremer was first drawn into the peace movement in 1870, when he feared that England would intervene in the Franco-Prussian War. To arouse the workers to oppose intervention, Cremer and other labor leaders formed the Workmen's Peace Association, with Cremer once again the secretary. With financial assistance from the old religiously based Peace Society, the association agitated among the workers, advocating nonintervention and, for the longer term, the familiar Peace Society prescription of disarmament and arbitration.

Arbitration particularly took Cremer's fancy. Here was no utopian dream but a practical down-to-earth way for states to resolve their conflicts without war. When the United States and England did just this in 1871, agreeing to abide by an arbitral decision to settle a serious issue that had arisen between them during the American Civil War, Cremer was convinced that therein lay the only path to peace and that the rest of the world should follow their example. The Workmen's Peace Association became the International Arbitration League, with Cremer as permanent secretary of a membership that included

Liberals along with workers. Anglo-American cooperation in arbitration was declared to be the first step to peace.

It became clear to Cremer that to push his ideas effectively he needed to hold political office. He made two unsuccessful tries for a seat in Parliament before the Reform Act of 1884 gave the vote to the workers' district of Haggerston in the metropolitan London area. Cremer was elected to Parliament from this district in 1885 and reelected in 1886 and 1892. In 1895 he lost by a few votes, but Haggerston sent him back to Parliament in 1900 despite his opposition to the Boer War, and he served until his death eight years later.

In the House of Commons Cremer became known as "the member for arbitration." One year after entering Parliament he began to work on a memorial from members who pledged their support for any American initiative that would be forthcoming for an Anglo-American treaty of arbitration. He secured the signatures of one-third of the membership of the House, not only of his fellow Liberals, but of Liberal Unionists and even Conservatives. Following the advice of Andrew Carnegie, the American industrialist and peace advocate, Cremer led a delegation of English parliamentarians and trade unionists across the Atlantic to present the memorial to President Cleveland. Consequently, a resolution passed both Houses of Congress recommending that the president enter negotiations with other nations for arbitration treaties.

This effort did not bear fruit immediately, but the collaboration between representatives of the two legislatures was a method of peacemaking that had often been proposed by European parliamentarians but had never been put into action. Now it led to a meeting of English and French deputies in Paris in 1888, arranged by Cremer and Frédéric Passy, then a member of the French Chamber of Deputies. The following year ninety-six deputies from nine national parliaments gathered in Paris to establish the Interparliamentary Union. Cremer always maintained that he deserved the credit for this because his league paid the expenses of the Paris meeting of 1889 and the meeting in London in 1890. Passy, more modest and generous, publicly supported Cremer's claims of paternity, but the documents show they were in fact cofounders.

Cremer rose far beyond his humble origins and deserves full credit for the way he overcame the disadvantages of his background. Yet in class-conscious Victorian England such an achievement unfortunately was likely to leave psychological scars. Cremer could not forget his beginnings, and he was forever suspecting fellow workers of jealousy and others of class discrimination in their relations with him. Deprived of the advantages of a broad education, he was inclined to concern himself more with means than with ends. Once convinced that the secret of peace lay in the practical application of international arbitration, he never bothered to think further, and the rest of his life was spent in relentless pursuit of this particular goal.

Cremer had all the perseverance of a bulldog and the stubbornness as well. He was uncompromising and dogmatic and, as the years went on, more and more difficult to work with. Although he could organize men as few of his contemporaries could, he was better at persuading than inspiring, except by the example of his own selfless devotion to the peace cause.

He was capable of personal warmth toward a few close friends, yet he was a lonely man, especially in his last twenty years after the death of his second wife. There were no children. Cremer's work for arbitration was his life, and he gave himself to it unsparingly. So thoroughly did he identify with the cause of peace that he was incensed with his country for becoming embroiled in the Boer War. His last private secretary told me that after pondering what Cremer's reactions would have been to the outbreak of the First World War had he lived to see it, he had decided that Cremer would have taken it as a personal insult.

Cremer was seventy-five when he won the Peace Prize and seventy-seven when, ever conscious of his obligations, he finally made the long journey to Christiana (Oslo) in wintertime to deliver the laureate's lecture on 15 January 1905. He chose as his topic, as could have been anticipated, "The Progress and Advantages of International Arbitration." He told the audience that he had used his entire prize to establish an endowment for the International Arbitration League. Three years later he died, full of honors, including a knighthood and the French Legion of Honor, his lifetime crusade for social justice and world peace at an end.

BIBLIOGRAPHY

Primary Source

Cremer, William Randal. "Parliamentary and Interparliamentary Experiences." *Independent* 61 (30 August 1906): 508–13. An interview with Hayne Davis.

Secondary Sources

"Cremer, William Randal." In *DNB: Twentieth Century Supplement, 1901–1911.*

"Cremer, William Randal." In *MPL.*

Evans, Howard. *Sir Randal Cremer: His Life and Work.* Boston: Ginn, 1910. Reprint. New York: Garland, 1973. With a new introduction. By a longtime friend and colleague.

Schulz, Paul Otto. "Sir Randal Cremer." In *FNP* 1:158–67, documentation, 206–11.

1904

Institute of International Law

Founded in 1873 in Ghent.

In 1904 the Nobel Committee recognized the contribution to peacemaking of the international jurists and gave an undivided award to the Institute of International Law, the first to an institution.

During the previous three decades, great strides had been made in the study and practice of international law, moving from the province of the philosophers to the faculties of law and political science. When the first scholarly journal of international law appeared in 1869, the Belgian editor Rolin-Jacquemyns spoke of "the necessity of reconciling the juridical and historical spirit which takes into account *what has been* and *what is* with the philosophical spirit which is concerned with *what ought to be.*"

International law was just beginning to be recognized as a separate subject of study. The subject was not even offered in many leading universities, those of Italy being the outstanding exceptions. Germany lagged behind, despite the presence of some distinguished scholars, and in both France and England there was a tendency to couple international law with the study of diplomacy.

The public was not clear as to whether such a thing as a law of nations existed. The *Times* of London defined the international lawyer as "that amphibious being who works midway between law and morality." Prime Minister Lord Salisbury expressed a commonly held opinion when he said in the Commons, "International law has not any existence in the sense in which the term 'law' is usually understood. It depends generally upon the prejudices of writers of textbooks. It can be enforced by no tribunal, and therefore to apply to it the phrase 'law' is to some extent misleading." This was the doctrine of John Austin that law had to have both visible power to proclaim it and sanction to enforce it.

In the face of such thinking, ten savants came from nine different countries to the little town of Ghent in Belgium in September 1873, and another twenty-four sent in their adhesions, or agreements to join, in response to the call of Rolin-Jacquemyns. "The transformation of the society of fact which exists between nations into a veritable society of law," he wrote, had hitherto proceeded by diplomatic agreement, as in the Geneva Convention on the laws of war, or by "individual scientific action." Now Rolin proposed a third method, "collective scientific action," by a permanent scholarly institution that could aspire "to serve as the organ, in the realm of the law of nations, of the legal conscience of the civilized world."

The Institute of International Law was established, with Rolin as the first secretary-general, and with the objective rephrased less pretentiously a few years later: to attempt to formulate the general principles of the science of international law "in a way to respond to the juridical conscience of the civilized world."

It was decided that the official seat of the institute was to be at the residence of the secretary-general. Consequently the first seat was at Rolin's home in Ghent. (In 1987 Nicolas Valticos held this post, and his office was in Geneva.)

In 1912 the twenty-seventh session of the institute was held in Oslo, so that the president, Georg Hagerup—Norwegian statesman, jurist, diplomat, and at that time a member at the Nobel Committee—could give the opening address at the Nobel Institute, thus at the same time satisfying the statutory provision that the prizewinner should give a public lecture in the Norwegian capital on the work that had won the prize.

Hagerup summarized the work of the institute in the forty years since its establishment, attributing its influence to the competence of its members and its independence. According to its statutes it had remained "an exclusively scientific association, without any official character," and its membership had been restricted to those "who have rendered services to international law in the domain of theory or of practice."

The institute had helped the world move toward the rule of law slowly and gradually, Hagerup pointed out, in contradistinction to the utopianism of those pacifists who wanted universal peace all at once. As for the skeptics, who saw no such movement at all, Hagerup asked that they cast their eyes "upon the vast domains which are today regulated by international conventions or by generally recognized codes of law—domains which embrace political, economic, philanthropic, artistic and literary relations which lie at the very heart of the material interests and ideals of nations and which dominate their everyday life."

The way of the institute was quiet and inconspicuous, but effective. In the years before 1914 principles that were first discussed and defined in its meetings became part of international law. In the 1880s, for example, the proposals of the institute for the international protection of the Suez Canal and of the transatlantic and other submarine cables were incorporated into international treaties. The results achieved by the Hague Conferences in both public and private international law were largely due to preliminary work done by the institute, whose members took prominent roles at these meetings. Moreover, rules suggested by the institute for arbitration procedures were effectively followed in a number of cases.

Since the First World War the institute has continued its good work. Both the League of Nations and the United Nations have considered its proposals. Legislation on extradition is only one area where the institute's recommendations have been accepted. Recently the institute has worked on such timely subjects as human rights law and the problems of pollution of international waters and of the air.

Since the days when the Nobel Committee honored the pioneers of international law by awarding its prize to the institute and subsequent prizes to international jurists Renault, Beernaert, and Asser, lawyers in this field have found their regular place on faculties of law and even on international courts of justice. But the Institute of International Law still makes a unique contribution. Although appointments to intergovernmental judiciary and legal bodies cannot be altogether free from political considerations, the institute as an unofficial scientific body has retained its independence from politics. Bringing together the best international legal talent of the world, the institute speaks in the resolutions of its regular meetings with a scientific weight that is greater than any other body in the field.

The society of law among nations, toward which the founders of the institute aspired, has still not arrived, but the "collective scientific action" they initiated has played an important, if largely unheralded, part in the long march toward the twin goals expressed in the institute's motto, "Peace and Justice."

BIBLIOGRAPHY

Primary Source

Wehberg, Hans. *Institut de Droit International: Tableau général des resolutions, 1873–1956.* Basel: Editions Juridiques, 1957.

Secondary Sources

Abrams, Irwin. "Emergence of the International Law Societies." *Review of Politics* 19 (1957): 361–80.

Fitzmaurice, G. "Contribution of the Institute of International Law to the development of international law." Academy of International Law, The Hague, Recueil des Cours, vol. 1, 1973.

Harten, Marten van. "Institut de Droit International—Wirkung aus dem Hintergrund." In *FNP* 1:168–78, documentation, 212–16.

Institut de Droit International. *Livre de centenaire.* Basel: Karger, 1973. A centennial survey with biographical sketches of the founders.

Rolin, Alberic. *Les Origines de l'Institut de Droit International (1873–1923).* Brussels: Vromant, 1923. A personal memoir.

1905

Bertha von Suttner (1843–1914)

Austria

Friend of Alfred Nobel and inspirer of the Peace Prize, "generalissimo" of the organized peace movement in the early twentieth century, author of the antiwar novel, *Lay Down Your Arms,* first woman political journalist, one of the best-known women of her time.

When Baroness Bertha von Suttner first heard in early 1897 of the terms of her friend Alfred Nobel's will, she was so excited she could hardly sleep that night. He had actually done what he had told her he would do for the peace movement—surely the prize would come to her one day, perhaps the first one!

Almost nine years later, while she was on a lecture tour in Germany, the baroness was informed that a telegram had arrived, forwarded from Vienna. Would she please pay the extra charge? She almost refused but finally paid and found it was a message from Chairman Løvland that she was at last to receive the Peace Prize, an undivided award. Once more the baroness had a sleepless night, joyous at the recognition but also apprehensive about the prospect of uncomfortable travel to far-off Norway.

Four times the committee had passed Baroness von Suttner by. In 1901 half the prize had gone to the peace veteran Passy, whom she had loyally nominated, and in 1902 it was shared by the executives of the Peace Bureau and the Interparliamentary Union, a disappointment, but she could not quarrel with the choice. What she did not know was that in 1901 and 1902 the committee had not even placed her on the short list for special consideration.

In 1903 she was distressed to have been overlooked once more when Cremer was named. She recognized his merits, but she was not a little indignant at the way he distanced himself as a practical politician from the "utopians" of the peace societies. In 1904 she was appalled to have been displaced by the Institute of International Law. She had never reconciled herself to the compromise that permitted institutions to be named along with individuals. By this year peace leaders from many countries were not only nominating her—in 1903 she had had twenty-four nominations in all—but writing her personal notes of condolence at her failure to be given the prize, although they were careful to refrain from any public criticism of the committee.

After the award to the institute, Bjørnstjerne Bjørnson dissociated himself from the decision by giving the newspapers the text of the letter he had written to his fellow members of the committee when he could not be present for the final deliberations. He had written them what he had learned both from Emanuel Nobel, nephew of the donor, and from one of the witnesses to the will: Nobel had wanted the baroness to have the prize. This, he said, was an order. The baroness wondered whether Bjørnson's controversial public revelation would help or hinder her chances. A rumor reached her early in November 1905 that the committee was irritated because her German publisher had been advertising her novel with notices that she had already received the prize. Resignedly, she wrote in her diary, "Adieu therefore Nobel Prize." And she wondered whether it would be better perhaps if she did not receive it and would have to continue to work for her livelihood. Only three weeks later came the telegram from Løvland.

Even without the evidence of Nobel's wishes, the committee sooner or later would have had to recognize Baroness von Suttner's qualifications. In 1905 she received the highest number of nominations of all twenty-four candidates, and they came not just from peace activists but from parliamentarians and leading personages in many countries.

Bertha von Suttner's first contribution to the peace cause had been the widely read antiwar novel, *Lay Down Your Arms,* published in 1889. In writing it she had become so committed to peace ideals that she had thrown herself into the movement with all her talents and energies. She rose to leadership in the 1890s, taking a prominent part in the establishment of peace societies in Central Europe, editing the peace journal named after her novel, writing, lecturing, assuming a leading role in the universal peace congresses. When the world's diplomats met at The Hague in 1899 to discuss international peace, her salon was a center of influence. By 1901 she was considered by her colleagues in the movement to be their "general in chief." When she made a lecture tour in the United States in 1904, she had become one of the most famous women of her time, and President Theodore Roosevelt received her in the White House.

Not the least of her achievements was her break from her origins in a noble family with a military tradition. Born Countess Bertha Kinsky in Prague in 1843 after the death of her father, an Austrian field marshal, she was raised to take her place in the higher circles of an aristocratic society. Her education stressed foreign languages, music, and the social graces. But when her mother gambled away most of the family assets, Bertha showed her independent spirit by deciding to earn her own living. She took a position in the Suttner family as tutor to their four daughters. To the discomfiture of the parents, who hoped their son Arthur would make a brilliant marriage and repair the family fortunes, he and the beautiful and accomplished young governess fell in love. Arthur's mother then persuaded Bertha to leave her job and apply for the position of confidential secretary that was being advertised by an "elderly gentleman" in Paris.

The gentleman was Alfred Nobel, who was looking for someone to manage his household and his social affairs and perhaps become the companion who would temper his loneliness. When Bertha came to Paris in 1876 for the interview, Nobel was impressed with her qualifications, but their meeting was to have far different consequences than he envisaged. She found him witty and charming, but when Arthur telegraphed that he could not live without her, she immediately returned to Vienna to elope with him. To distance themselves from his disapproving parents, they fled to friends of hers in the Caucasus. There they remained for nine years, educating themselves in the works of Darwin and Spencer and other leading thinkers, and becoming successful writers.

In 1885 they were finally welcomed home by Arthur's parents and in the next years were familiar figures in Austrian literary and artistic circles. Inspired by the contemporary concepts of evolution, progress, and free thought, they became critics of their society and eventually reformers. Arthur founded an association in Vienna to oppose anti-Semitism, and when Bertha heard about the peace societies in London, she decided to write her next novel to propagate these ideas. As she studied the wars of the mid-century, she became convinced of the futility and folly of war, so out of step with the European civilization that seemed to be advancing on all other fronts.

It was through her highly acclaimed novel that she was drawn into the peace movement, and henceforth that cause would absorb all her creative talents. Her writings appeared in peace journals and in newspapers where she commented on international affairs from a pacifist point of view. She maintained her friendship with Nobel, informing him of developments in the peace movement and soliciting his support for the cause. The establishment of the Peace Prize in his will was one outcome of their mutual interest.

After winning the 1905 Peace Prize, she arranged to give her Nobel lecture in the spring of the following year. The crowd expected was too large for the assembly hall of the newly opened institute, so the baroness spoke in the Hals Brothers Concert Hall to a large audience. She was introduced in glowing terms by Bjørnson on behalf of the committee. Now in her sixties, still a handsome woman of commanding presence and dressed in black as she always was after the death of her beloved husband in 1902, the baroness spoke from deep conviction, but with controlled emotion. She held her audience to the end, using no oratorical flourishes but speaking directly and with great sincerity. What spoke to her hearers most of all was not so much what she said as what she was.

Her lecture, "The Evolution of the Peace Movement," testified to her unshakable faith in human progress, which was inevitably leading to an era of peace. She recognized the facts of violence, referring to the Russo-Japanese War of 1904–5 and the subsequent revolution in the Russian Empire, "an orgy of the Demon Violence." She spoke of the threatening situation in Central and Western Europe, where "we have distrust, threats, saber rattling, press baiting, feverish naval buildup, and rearming everywhere." Yet, she went on,

> We must also look for the new growth pushing up from the ground below. . . . Quite apart from the peace movement, which is a symptom rather than a cause of actual change, there is taking place in the world a process of internationalization and unification. . . . The instinct of self-preservation in human society . . . is rebelling against the constantly refined methods of annihilation and against the destruction of humanity.

Among the hopeful signs of this development, she said, was President Theodore Roosevelt's recent public support for arbitration, and she spoke of the hope for the peace movement that the United States represented, with its practical idealism. The movement toward peace was sure, but slow. As Roosevelt had said when he received her in the White House in 1904, "World peace is coming; it certainly is coming, but only step by step."

There were still many obstacles, however:

> We are dealing with a goal as yet not perceived by many millions or, if perceived, regarded as a utopian dream. Also, powerful interests are involved, interests trying to maintain the old order and to prevent the goal's being reached. . . . Thus pacifism faces no easy struggle. . . . The advocates of pacifism are well aware how meager are their resources of personal influence and power, . . . but when they realistically consider themselves and the ideal they serve, they see themselves as the servants of the greatest of all causes. On the solution of this problem depends whether our Europe will become a showpiece of ruins and failure, or whether we can avoid this danger and so enter sooner the coming era of secure peace and law in which a civilization of unimagined glory will develop.

For the struggle to prevent war, she had only eight more years left. Even with the prize money she was not able to support herself, as she was too generous in helping friends and good causes. The baroness was beginning to feel her age now, but she continued her peace activities unabated, lecturing, writing, lobbying at the Second Hague Conference, playing a leading role in the international peace congresses. In 1912 she made a second lecture tour in the United States and in 1913 attended her last peace congress at The Hague.

The next year's congress was to be held in Vienna, and it was planned to honor her at that time, including the showing of a Norwegian film version of *Lay Down Your Arms*. But it was not to be. In June the baroness died after a short illness, and a week later the archduke of Austria-Hungary was assassinated, setting off the series of events that culminated in August in the war she had tried so hard to prevent. The peace congress was called off, and the monument the movement had planned to honor her with was never built. Her monument lies rather in the achievements of her life, as an outstanding woman in a time when women were generally excluded from public life, and an outstanding leader in the service of what would one day be recognized as "the greatest of all causes."

BIBLIOGRAPHY

Primary Sources

Suttner, Bertha von. *Lay Down Your Arms.* Authorized translation of *Die Waffen Nieder* by T. Holmes, revised by the author. London: Longmans, Green, 1892. Reprint. New York: Garland, 1971. With a new introduction by Irwin Abrams.

———. *Memoirs.* Boston and London: Ginn, 1910. Reprint. New York: Garland, 1972. With an introduction by Irwin Abrams.

Secondary Sources

Abrams, Irwin. "Bertha von Suttner and the Nobel Peace Prize." *Journal of Central European Affairs* 22 (October 1962): 286–307. Based on her correspondence with Alfred Nobel.

Hamann, Brigitte. *Bertha von Suttner: Ein Leben für den Frieden.* Munich: Piper, 1986. Based on exhaustive research in the Suttner unpublished materials.

Kemp, Beatrix. *Woman for Peace: The Life of Bertha von Suttner.* Translated by R. W. Last. Park Ridge, N.J.: Noyes, 1973. Best short biography, with excerpts from her writings and a complete bibliography.

Lengyel, Emil. *And All Her Paths Were Peace: The Life of Bertha von Suttner.* Nashville and New York: Nelson, 1975.

Pauli, Hertha. *Cry of the Heart: The Story of Bertha von Suttner.* Translated by Richard and Clara Winston. New York: Washburn, 1957. A fictionalized account.

Playne, Carolene E. *Bertha von Suttner and the Struggle to Avert the World War.* London: Allen & Unwin, 1936.

1906
Theodore Roosevelt (1858–1919)

United States

Twenty-sixth president of the United States (1901–9); mediator in ending the Russo-Japanese War (1904–5).

The award of 1906 to President Theodore Roosevelt broke new ground in several ways. It was the first prize for a statesman and the first for a specific action for peace performed in the previous year, as Nobel had prescribed, rather than for service to peace over an extended period, as earlier awards had been. It was the first highly controversial prize, and it set a precedent in the circumstances of the presentation. Instead of the prizewinner's name merely being announced in the Storting on the traditional day of 10 December, the diploma and medal were presented to the American minister, representing the president, by the presiding officer of the Storting "on behalf of the Norwegian parliament."

The basis for the committee's decision was stated in the presentation address as "President Roosevelt's happy intervention to terminate the bloody war recently waged between two Great Powers, Japan and Russia." This war had begun in February 1904 with a series of spectacular Japanese victories that, however, left them overextended on the Asian continent and financially drained. For the Russians the situation was desperate. Their fleet was destroyed, their bastion of

Port Arthur captured, and their main army in Manchuria forced north of Mukden. At home was the threat of revolution.

Both sides, then, were eager for an end to hostilities, but neither could take the initiative for fear of loss of face. What was needed was an offer of mediation by an apparently disinterested third party. The European powers were involved in complicated relationships with the belligerents, but the United States was well situated to make a proposal. It had just emerged as a Great Power through its victory over Spain, and although it had some interests now in the Pacific, it was unentangled in alliances. Moreover, President Roosevelt, whose secretary of state, Elihu Root, was not well, was readily disposed to embark upon a venture of personal diplomacy. When the Japanese confidentially sounded him out in May 1905, the president first secured assurance that the Russians would accept a proposal and then invited them both to begin negotiations for peace, offering to make the arrangements for the meeting.

Roosevelt was better prepared for his "happy role" than many of the occupants of the White House before or since. Descendant of an old aristocratic Dutch family, he had been educated at Harvard and Columbia and had also studied in Germany. Blessed with abundant talent and extraordinary energy, he could have won success in a variety of fields. He became an accomplished man of letters whose writings in history and biography have endured. He chose, however, to devote his life mainly to public service.

Roosevelt served as civil service commissioner, police commissioner of New York City, and assistant secretary of the navy. In the war with Spain he led a regiment of volunteer cavalry, the "Rough Riders," to fight in Cuba. He served as governor of New York and in 1900 was elected vice president of the United States. When McKinley was assassinated in 1901, Roosevelt succeeded to the presidency. In 1904 he was elected to a full term.

Roosevelt offered his services as peacemaker as one who knew the world and understood international politics. His handling of the negotiations leading to acceptance of this offer by the belligerents and his later facilitation of discussions between them revealed a sure hand in the practice of diplomacy. With an excellent sense of timing, he knew just when to use the gentle nudge, and he could also employ the proper nuance of phrase to spare the sensibilities of his listeners.

There is no better example of Roosevelt's diplomatic skills than the way he managed the first critical encounter between the two delegations. It was vitally important that both sides be treated equally, that there be not the slightest indication of favoritism in word or action. Roosevelt decided to introduce the two delegations to each other at a luncheon aboard his yacht at Oyster Bay, where he was spending the summer of 1905. He arranged for each delegation to be brought there separately by an American warship and after the occasion to be conveyed in similar fashion to Portsmouth, New Hampshire, where the meetings were to be held in a more congenial clime than that of summertime Washington.

Roosevelt knew that the diplomats on each side would be greatly concerned with questions of protocol: Who would enter the dining salon first? Who would have the seat of honor next to the president? Who would be served first? Would the first toast be raised in honor of the tsar or of the mikado?

Roosevelt contrived to perform his welcome and the introductions adeptly and then to shuffle his guests into the salon, keeping up a stream of fractured French all the while, with no one noticing who entered first. Awaiting them was a round table with a luncheon buffet laid out. When the time came for the toast, the president raised his glass to both great nations and to a just and lasting peace between them.

During the subsequent negotiations at Portsmouth, Roosevelt kept closely in touch with the proceedings, urging appropriate concessions and compromises and employing personal appeals to the imperial rulers when needed, yet all the while keeping behind the scenes. The Peace Treaty of Portsmouth was signed in September 1905.

Congratulations poured in on Roosevelt from all over the world. An adviser to the Russian delegation later paid him perhaps the highest tribute:

> All through our conferences the personality of Roosevelt made itself felt, but this was done so artistically . . . that nobody could have been offended at the advice which he tendered with such consummate discretion. We Russians had come to Portsmouth without taking anything that he had said seriously, and yet when we left the United States it was with the knowledge that . . . we had been brought in close proximity with one of the most powerful personalities now alive in the whole of the world.

Although Roosevelt's main motive, as he later wrote, "was the disinterested one of putting an end to the bloodshed," he was no less influenced by the desire to stabilize the balance of power in the Far East between Russia and Japan "so that each may have a moderating action on the other." As for the Peace Prize, Roosevelt told the Nobel Committee that "there is no gift I could appreciate more," but in his memoirs, *An Autobiography,* he declared, "In my own judgment the most important service that I rendered to peace was the voyage of the battle fleet around the world." This was a demonstration of naval power in 1907 and was designed to impress the Japanese as well as the American public.

Much of the controversy over the Roosevelt award derived from the bellicose posture that had always been his stance on the public stage. The *Philadelphia Ledger* reported that most of the American press was saying how curious it was that "the preacher of the strenuous life, the disseminater of the doctrine that there are dangers to the moral fiber of a nation from the cankers of a long peace, the militant champion of a large army and navy and the wielder of the 'big stick' should be crowned as America's great pacificator." The *New York Times* commented later that "a broad smile illuminated the face of the globe when the prize was awarded . . . to the most warlike citizen of these United States, of whom a national poet had declared, 'His sword within its scabbard sleeps / But goodness, how it snores.' "

Yet Roosevelt was no warmonger. Although he frequently castigated advocates of "peace-at-any-price," a term he readily extended to cover opponents of large armament expenditures, he genuinely supported arbitration and the Hague Conferences. At the urging of peace forces, he had provided the Hague Court with its first case, and he was prepared to convene the Second Hague Conference but relinquished this role to the tsar.

Roosevelt gave his Nobel address in 1910, after he had left office and was making a tour of European capitals. He had not planned to accept the invitation of the Nobel Committee until Andrew Carnegie cabled him that his refusal could prejudice the committee against future candidates from the United States. His visit to Christiana (Oslo) was a great success. He quite charmed the royal family, especially the little crown prince Olaf, with whom he romped as he had with his own children. His lecture to an attentive audience of some twelve hundred remains the best expression of his ideas on internationalism.

He declared at the outset that since what he had done had been possible only because he was president, he felt the prize had been given to him in trust for the United States. He therefore intended to use it to start a foundation in his country for industrial peace. This plan did not materialize, however, and during the First World War the money was returned to him and distributed to various war charities.

Roosevelt emphasized in his lecture his conviction that "the great end is righteousness" and peace is not the highest good unless it comes "as the handmaiden of righteousness." Peace is an evil thing if it is only a mask for cowardice and sloth. "No nation deserves to exist if it permits itself to lose the stern and virile virtues whether due to materialism, indulgence or the deification of a warped and twisted sentimentality."

He held that peace could be advanced practically along several lines: first of all, by treaties of arbitration among civilized nations (not between them and backward countries); second, by the work of the Hague Conferences and the establishment of a world court; third, by an international agreement to check the growth of armaments, such as through limiting the size of battleships; and finally, by forming a league of peace to provide an executive or police power to enforce the decrees of an arbitral court. Roosevelt declared that the statesman who formed this league of peace would have earned "his title to the gratitude of all mankind."

Roosevelt did not think that Woodrow Wilson was going to be that statesman. Wilson became president when Roosevelt split the Republican party in the election of 1912, and Roosevelt opposed most of his policies. He condemned Wilson for not intervening immediately against Germany, and he did not forgive him for refusing to let Roosevelt raise an army division to fight with him in France.

In his last formal utterance before his death in 1919, Roosevelt once again assailed Wilson for the rhetoric of the Fourteen Points and declared that the best way to get the right kind of League of Nations that "all of us earnestly desire" would be to start with the league of the allies who had fought together to win the war and then extend membership to other nations "as rapidly as their conduct warrants it." Weaker nations would be admitted without "a guiding voice in the councils." Each state would retain its sovereignty over "questions which are non-justiciable." Finally, the United States would "make it perfectly clear that we do not intend to take a position of an international 'Meddlesome Matty.' " Americans, he said, do not want to go into an overseas war they do not approve of.

On 6 January 1919, Theodore Roosevelt died in his sleep of an embolism at his home in Oyster Bay, New York. He was only sixty years of age. Had he lived, he might well have been the standard-bearer of the Republican party in 1920 and president once again. For the United States this would not have been the "return to normalcy" that it was under President Warren G. Harding and certainly no retreat into isolationism. For Theodore Roosevelt had a sense of world politics that no American president had had before him, a disposition and a talent to lead his country in the international arena, and, by his own lights, a sincere commitment to the peace of the world.

BIBLIOGRAPHY

Primary Sources

Roosevelt, Theodore. *An Autobiography.* New York: Scribner's, 1913.

———. *The Writings of Theodore Roosevelt.* Edited by William H. Harbaugh. Indianapolis: Bobbs-Merrill, 1967.

Secondary Sources

Beale, Howard K. *Theodore Roosevelt and the Rise of America to World Power.* Baltimore: Johns Hopkins Press, 1956.

Bishop, Joseph B. *Theodore Roosevelt and His Time.* 2 vols. New York: Scribner's, 1920. Authorized and uncritical, but supplements the *Autobiography.*

Cooper, John Milton, Jr. *The Warrior and the Priest: Woodrow Wilson and Theodore Roosevelt.* Cambridge: Harvard University Press, 1983. A comparative study.

Dennett, Tyler. *Roosevelt and the Russo-Japanese War.* Reprint. Gloucester, Mass.: Peter Smith, 1959.

Harbaugh, William H. *Power and Responsibility: The Life and Times of Theodore Roosevelt.* New York: Straus & Cudahy, 1961. Best full-length biography, written for the general reader by a scholar.

Kuehl, Warren F. *Seeking World Order: The United States and World Organizations to 1920.* Nashville, Tenn.: Vanderbilt University Press, 1969.

Marks, Frederick W., III. *Velvet on Iron: The Diplomacy of Theodore Roosevelt.* Lincoln: University of Nebraska Press, 1979.

Trani, Eugene P. *The Treaty of Portsmouth: An Adventure in American Diplomacy.* Lexington: University of Kentucky Press, 1969.

1907
Louis Renault (1843–1918)

France

Foremost French international jurist, counselor to the Ministry of Foreign Affairs, representative to the Hague Peace Conferences, member of the Permanent Court of Arbitration at The Hague.

In the presentation speech in 1907 for the award that Louis Renault shared with Teodoro Moneta, Chairman Løvland of the Nobel Committee called him "the guiding genius in the teaching of international law in France." Renault not only was a distinguished scholar and teacher—he called himself "a professor at heart"—but had what Løvland called a "decisive influence" in the shaping of international law in intergovernmental conferences. The most important were the Hague Peace Conferences of 1899 and 1907. In 1907 the president of the conference had declared, as Løvland noted, "that his dictionary had run out of words of praise with which to describe Renault's share in the work of the conference." The Nobel Committee had had him on their short list since 1904, and clearly it was his stellar performance at the Hague Conference of 1907, which ended shortly before the committee met to make its decision, that brought him the prize in that year. Francis Hagerup, who had been elected to the Nobel Committee because of his competence in international jurisprudence, was one of Norway's delegates at The Hague and had watched Renault in action.

Louis Renault was born at Autun in France in 1843. Books were important to him from an early age, as his father was a bookseller who loved his work. The youth showed intellectual promise from the beginning. He was first in his class at the lycée, going on to win honors in his literature studies at the University of Dijon in Burgundy and then at Paris, where he took his doctorate in law in 1868.

He began his career in that year, when he was twenty-five, returning to Dijon to teach Roman and commercial law. Five years later he was invited to join the Faculty of Law in Paris as an acting professor of criminal law. In the next year occurred one of those happenstances that can give new direction to a life. There was a temporary opening in the Law Faculty in a subject that was not Renault's primary interest, but in order to stay on he decided to apply for the position. The field was international law, a subject still very new in the law faculties in 1874. The major scholarly journal had been founded only a few years before, in 1869, and the handful of scholars prominent in the field had just founded the Institute of International Law in 1873. Renault was taking something of a chance when he moved from more traditional subjects to this new field, but he found it more and more challenging. He achieved an impressive list of publications, the prerequisite for advancement and in 1881 was appointed to the chair of international law. He was then thirty-eight years of age. In the next thirty-seven years Renault, through his service to international law, both within and outside academe, did much to help make it a highly respected field of academic study.

These were the years in which economic and technological developments were multiplying international relationships of all kinds, necessitating cooperation between governments. In 1890 Renault was appointed counselor to the Foreign Ministry, eventually rising to the rank of minister plenipotentiary. He represented France in many conferences on international legal matters, including those dealing with international private law; he participated in the congress to revise the Geneva Convention on Red Cross activities; and he was his country's representative at both Hague Peace Conferences.

Renault had a clear logical mind, and he was especially skilled in sensing the areas of agreement between participants in international meetings and articulating them effectively. He knew that resolutions to be adopted had to express the compromises of the diplomat rather than the precision of the scholar. In his Nobel lecture he spoke of himself as "one who has often used the pen and who knows, better than anyone else, that the end result is not perfect. Had he been as uncompromising in the drafting of resolutions as he would be in the formulating of a purely scientific work, he would have achieved nothing."

He was often chosen as *rapporteur,* or summarizer, as in the Hague Peace Conference of 1899, when he performed this service for the commission on the laws of war and was mainly responsible for the drafting of the Final Act of the conference. In the 1907 Hague Conference Renault helped with the formulations of agreements on the actions of belligerents and neutrals in wartime, and he was the spokesman of the committee that drafted the Final Act. At both conferences he worked hard for arbitration.

After the Hague Tribunal was established by the 1899 conference, Renault was named to the panel of twenty-eight judges from which each party to a dispute selected the arbiters. In the first fourteen years of the tribunal Renault was asked to serve more often than any other member of the panel. So highly was he respected for his impartiality, that in one case involving England and France, both parties requested his services.

It was characteristic of Renault to arrange to give his May 1908 Nobel address to coincide with the celebration of Independence Day in the Norwegian capital. He won the hearts of his Norwegian auditors when he began his lecture by speaking of how he had been inspired to watch "all the gay young people in their varied and picturesque costumes, stepping so briskly and waving all their flags so joyously," making him think "of the springtime of life on its march toward the future." Renault was describing a feeling that the foreign observer may still experience today on 17 May in Oslo.

Renault's lecture, appropriately enough, was a careful review of "The Work at the Hague in 1899 and 1907" and its implications for the future. He said he had never approved the term *Peace Conference,* because this only misled the public to expect the result would be "everlasting peace." Moreover, critics were invited to mock at a Peace Conference so much concerned with resolutions about war. But was the term "entirely unjustified"?

> I do not believe so. Anything that contributes to extending the domain of law in international relations contributes to peace. Since the possibility of future war cannot be ignored, . . . it is a *humanitarian* policy that strives to reduce the evils of war in the relations between the belligerents themselves and to safeguard as far as possible the interests of noncombatants and of the sick and the wounded. . . . wars will not become rarer by becoming more barbarous.

Alfred Nobel had thought otherwise.

In "extending the domain of law," the Peace Conferences represented the beginnings of a slow but sure movement toward the *"juridical organization of international life."* At this early stage Renault identified a problem with which the League of Nations and the United Nations have since grappled, the implications of the principle of state sovereignty. Renault firmly believed in the rule of unanimity in intergovernmental conferences as no state should be forced to accept an agreement to which it was actually opposed. On the other hand, he did not believe in absolute democracy in international conferences like those at The Hague, because in a decision about maritime law, for example, Luxembourg's vote should not be given the same weight as Great Britain's. Yet small nations had an important role to play there: "they are most frequently the true representatives of justice, precisely because they do not have the strength to impose injustice."

Renault felt that the movement toward the rule of law was irresistible. It would take time, but "we must help it along." He ended on a personal note as he had begun: "I promise you to devote to the task I have described the years of work still left to me. I would like to try in this way to justify the distinguished honor you have conferred upon me."

In the next ten years Renault continued to labor in the vineyard of international law to fulfill this promise. He continued with his official duties and with his scholarly research and publication. He was much honored by his own and foreign governments and universities, and was named to the Legion of Honor and the Academy of Moral and Political Sciences of France. Unlike some distinguished professors, however, he never forgot his students. Over the years he directed some 252 doctoral theses. Along with his law courses at the University of Paris, he lectured in military schools and to students who were preparing for the foreign service. He was still teaching at seventy-five. On 6 February 1918, he gave a class, went to take a brief vacation at his Barbizon villa, fell ill, and died on 8 February.

BIBLIOGRAPHY

Primary Source

Renault, Louis. "War and the Law of Nations in the Twentieth Century." *American Journal of International Law* 9 (January 1915): 1–16.

Secondary Source

Fauchille, Paul. *Louis Renault (1843–1918): Sa vie—son oeuvre*. Paris: Pedone, 1918.

1907

Ernesto Teodoro Moneta (1833–1918)

Italy

Leader of the Italian peace movement, editor, journalist.

Ernesto Teodoro Moneta, who shared the 1907 prize with Louis Renault, was a leader of the Italian peace movement who had fought for his country's national unification in his youth. As a popular editor and journalist, he was a sturdy interpreter at home and abroad of the internationalism of the Italian republican tradition.

He was born to an impoverished aristocratic family in Milan in 1833, when Italy was a land of disunited principalities. Lombardy, the province where Moneta grew up, belonged to Austria, as did Venice. Italians who longed for a national state were stirred by the writings of Giuseppe Mazzini; he urged them to fight for a free and independent country that would be part of a federation of republics, when all other nationalities had also become free and united.

The uprising in Milan in 1848 against Austrian rule left an indelible mark on Moneta. As a youth of fifteen, he fought on the barricades alongside his father and his brothers. One day, as he told the story some sixty years later in his Nobel laureate lecture, he saw three Austrian soldiers fall in a hail of bullets. Later he watched one of them in the throes of death: "My blood turned to ice in my veins and a great compassion took possession of me. In these three soldiers I no longer saw enemies but men like myself. . . . In that instant I felt all the cruelty and inhumanity of war." The next day the victorious Milanese revolutionaries published a Mazzinian manifesto to the peoples of Europe:

> The day is probably not far distant when all nations will forget old quarrels and rally to the banner of international brotherhood, putting an end to all conflict and enjoying peace and friendship, strengthened by the bonds of commerce and industry. We look forward to that day. Italians! Free and independent we shall seal the peace of brotherhood with our own hands, not least with the nations which today constitute the Austrian Empire, if only they are willing.

Moneta went on to finish military school and to fight with the great hero Garibaldi and in other campaigns in the peninsula. After Italy was unified under King Victor Emmanuel, Moneta served in the national army as an officer and might have had a distinguished military career, had he not left the army, discouraged by a defeat Italy suffered in 1866.

He found his true métier in journalism, becoming editor of the Milan daily newspaper *Il secolo* in 1867 and remaining for almost thirty years, making it the most widely read newspaper in Italy. Moneta was dynamic, idealistic, and courageous, a gifted writer who had strong personal convictions but wielded his editorial power with good judgment and balance. On one subject there was no moderation, however. Whatever seemed to Moneta to harm or weaken his beloved Italy formed a target for stinging editorials, whether it was inefficiency in the army or clerical abuses that stood in the way of the country's social progress. Moneta was a practicing Catholic himself, but the anticlericalism of the *Secolo* affronted the church and led to an estrangement with his very devout wife.

In 1870 he became active in the peace movement and in 1878 helped establish the League of Liberty,

Brotherhood, and Peace in Milan. In 1887 he helped found two associations, the Society for International Peace and Justice, and the more political Lombard Union for International Peace and Arbitration, of which he became president. Well before the movement organized itself internationally, he came into touch with foreign peace leaders, such as Hodgson Pratt of England and Frédéric Passy of France. Thereafter Moneta was a regular attender of the international peace congresses, joining the Commission of the International Peace Bureau in 1895 and presiding over the fifteenth Universal Peace Congress held at Milan during the International Exhibition of 1906. For this exposition Moneta arranged for the construction of a Pavilion of Peace. Moneta supported the peace cause in *Il secolo* throughout his years as editor and thereafter in his fortnightly review *La vita internazionale* (International life), one of the leading periodicals of the peace movement.

As a liberal internationalist, Moneta distinguished between those nationalists who "would have liked to make modern Italy a military power of the first rank" and those like himself who wanted their fatherland to be "a nation outstanding for its great freedom and advancement." When the militant nationalists, angered in 1881 by the French occupation of Tunis across the Mediterranean from Italy, began to talk of a war to take Nice and Corsica away from France, Moneta roundly attacked this "Gallophobia," reminding Italians that France had helped them win their liberty from Austria in 1859. There were later occasions as well when he worked for better understanding between the two countries. His efforts were one of the influences leading to the Franco-Italian arbitration treaty of 1903.

Moneta also opposed designs militant nationalists had on the Ticino, an Italian-speaking canton of Switzerland, and on Trentino and Trieste, which belonged to Austria-Hungary. As a disciple of Mazzini and Garibaldi, Moneta believed firmly that one day all Italians should live under the same flag, but he did not advocate war to bring this about. He had faith in the advance of international peace and justice.

In 1911 when Italy went to war with Turkey over Tripoli, however, Moneta backed his government, to the puzzlement and dismay of his pacifist friends abroad who had been congratulating him so warmly on winning the Nobel Peace Prize just a few years before. They recalled his earlier opposition to the Italian attempt to establish a protectorate over Ethiopia and strongly criticized the now nearly blind old man for abandoning his principles. What he had never abandoned, however, was his fervent patriotism, and he felt that in this conflict his country's cause was just. Not long afterwards he enthusiastically supported Italy's entry into the First World War on the side of the Allies, more certain than ever that Italy was fighting for the right. The key to his actions throughout his life lies in the words he wrote at that time, "I, as an Italian, cannot put myself above the battle. I must participate in the life of my country, rejoice in her joys, and weep in her sorrows."

Moneta never saw any contradiction between the destiny of the country he so passionately loved and the highest good for humanity. He died in 1918 at the age of eighty-four, in the very act of conferring a patriotic benediction upon his soldier son.

BIBLIOGRAPHY

Primary Source

Moneta, Ernesto Teodoro. *La nostra pace.* Milan: Bellini, 1909.

Secondary Sources

Combi, Maria. *Ernesto Teodoro Moneta: Premio Nobel per la pace 1907.* Milan: Mursia, 1968.

Cooper, Sandi E., ed. *Internationalism in Nineteenth Century Europe.* New York: Garland, 1976.

"Moneta, Ernesto Teodoro." In *MPL.*

"Moneta, Ernesto Teodoro." In *WEP.*

Pinardi, Giuseppi. *La carrière d'un pacifiste: E. T. Moneta.* Le Havre: L'Universel, 1904.

1908
Fredrik Bajer (1837–1922)

Denmark

Scandinavia's foremost peace advocate, heading both popular and parliamentary peace forces in Denmark; prominent in Interparliamentary Union and international peace congresses; first president of the International Peace Bureau.

Fredrik Bajer was born in Denmark in 1837, the son of a clergyman. After attending military school, he became a lieutenant in the Dragoons at the age of nineteen. His military career lasted for nine years and included distinguished service in command of troops during the war with Austria and Prussia in 1864.

He then turned to a serious study of foreign languages and established himself in Copenhagen as a teacher, translator, and free-lance writer. In 1869 he established the first liberal association in the Danish capital, and in 1872, at the age of thirty-five, he was elected as an independent progressive to the Folketing, the lower house of the legislature. He served without interruption for the next twenty-three years, one of the longest terms as parliamentary representative of any of the early Nobel Peace Prize winners.

In the Folketing Bajer pressed peace issues and consistently opposed increases in the war budget and appropriations for the fortification of Copenhagen. In a series of travel letters he published in 1886, each one ended with the words, "Moreover, I am of the opinion that the fortifications of Copenhagen should be destroyed." Denmark's security could most effectively be ensured, he maintained, by international recognition of Scandinavian neutrality, on the models of Belgium and Switzerland. Bajer was convinced that Scandinavian unity could best be achieved if Denmark, Sweden, and Norway were all republican, and he founded a Society of Nordic Free States.

It was through his language study that Bajer first came into touch with Frédéric Passy and the peace movement in 1867, and he undertook to distribute the materials issued by Passy's Peace Society. He even attempted, but without success, to establish such an association in Denmark. Fifteen years later in 1882, however, he was one of the organizers of the first peace association in the country, the Society for the Promotion of Danish Neutrality, with twenty-six members of the Folketing as founding members. Peace and neutrality were closely related in his thinking and that of his colleagues. Bajer was president for the first ten years, and the organization was later renamed the Danish Peace Society.

Over the years Bajer kept up an active correspondence with other European peace advocates, and when the movement began to organize internationally in 1889, he was already well known. In that year he attended both the Peace Congress and the Interparliamentary Conference held in Paris and both meetings that were held the next year in London.

Bajer dreamed in the grand manner of one central office coordinating and directing all the worldwide activities of the peacemakers, both parliamentarians and peace societies, a central executive that would be officially recognized by governments. This would come only with time, however. For the moment Bajer proposed a common secretariat for both the Interparliamentary Conference and the popular peace societies, a bureau such as that of the Universal Postal Union. This was to be a sort of focus for the whole peace movement, forming a bond of association between all institutions and individuals who desired to cooperate for peace, and serving as a source of information. In promoting this idea during the course of 1890 and 1891, Bajer sent out 3,518 pieces of mail, without any other secretarial help than that of his wife, Mathilde.

At both the Peace Congress and the Interparliamentary Conference in London Bajer submitted his proposal for a single permanent bureau. The Peace Congress approved, but among the politicians of the Interparliamentary Conference there were those who insisted on keeping their distance from "impractical" peace activists. The upshot was that the Peace Congress of 1891 in Rome established the International Peace Bureau, and the Interparliamentary Conference of 1892 held in Bern established its own office, the Interparliamentary Bureau.

Neither bureau realized Bajer's hopes for strong coordination of peace activities, although the International Peace Bureau under Élie Ducommun had the better record in keeping its constituents informed and in preparing the annual congresses. Bajer himself provided liaison of a sort between the two bodies as first president of the board of the Peace Bureau and a member of the council of the Interparliamentary Union. He organized the Danish Interparliamentary Group in 1891, which came to include all the members of the Folketing, and he was its secretary for twenty-five years. He also was one of the organizers of the Scandinavian Interparliamentary Union.

Bajer also made his mark in Denmark in the struggle for the emancipation of women, working with his wife, and in the development of the educational system.

Bajer reached the Nobel Committee's short list every year beginning in 1905 before being named as cowinner with Arnoldson in 1908. In that year he was ill and unable to receive the award in person in December, but in the spring he came to Christiana (Oslo) to deliver his Nobel address, which appropriately surveyed "The Organization of the Peace Movement" to which he himself had contributed so much.

In his last years Bajer had to give up his peace activities because of ill health, but he lived to see the establishment of the League of Nations, whose constitution embodied many of the ideas for which he and the other peace pioneers had worked.

BIBLIOGRAPHY

Primary Sources

Bajer, Fredrik. *Fredrik Bajers Livserindringer: Udgivne af hans son.* Copenhagen: Gjellerup, 1909. Memoirs, published by his son.

———. *Acte Final de la Deuxième Conférence de la Paix, suivi d'un index alphabétique et analytique* (The Final Act of the Second Hague Peace Conference, with an alphabetical and analytical index). Monaco: Institut International de la Paix, 1908.

Secondary Source

"Bajer, Fredrik." In *MPL.*

1908

Klas Pontus Arnoldson (1844–1916)

Sweden

Liberal Christian advocate of peace as writer, organizer, orator and member of parliament.

Klas Pontus Arnoldson shared the all-Scandinavian award of 1908 with Fredrik Bajer of Denmark as Sweden's leading veteran pacifist, who had worked for the cause for over thirty years as politician, peace society leader, and influential orator and writer.

He was born in Göteborg in 1844, the son of a caretaker. He was sixteen when his father died, and he had to leave school and go to work. For the next twenty-one years he worked for the Swedish Railroad, becoming clerk and then station inspector. Through his omnivorous reading he became a staunch liberal in his political and religious thinking. The essence of Christianity, as he came to understand it, was a practical ethic, rational, undogmatic, and incompatible with war. These Christian pacifist convictions were deepened by what he learned of the wars that were being waged while he was in his twenties, especially when the Danes were fighting Austria and Prussia in 1864 and the French battled the Prussians in 1870–71.

When Arnoldson began to publish articles in the press on peace and other subjects close to his heart, he discovered that he had a talent for writing. At the age of thirty-seven he left the railroad to enter public life as a publicist and legislator. In 1882 he was elected on a peace platform to the Riksdag, the lower house of the Swedish parliament. Before he left office in 1887, Arnoldson had made a name for himself as an able proponent of peace and Swedish neutrality as well as of religious freedom and the extension of the franchise.

In 1883 he was one of the founders of the Swedish Peace and Arbitration Society and its first secretary; he edited its paper and later other peace publications. He carried on a vigorous campaign for arbitration in his writings and oratory. In 1888 he organized the circulation of a petition to the king, asking for the negotiation of arbitration treaties with other governments. Norway was at that time united with Sweden in a dynastic union, so Arnoldson carried his campaign into Norway, where his well-received speeches indirectly led to a Storting resolution addressed to the king in Stockholm.

When the Norwegians began their agitation for more equality with Sweden, Arnoldson supported their position. He influenced public opinion in both countries in favor of a peaceful resolution of the conflict, which ended in 1905 with the dissolution of the union. Arnoldson's role in the affair was not forgotten. Three years later his many friends in Norway were delighted with his peace award, but Swedish conservatives fulminated at the "outrage," which was even worse because the Norwegians were paying it in "Swedish money." Chairman Løvland of the Nobel Committee took special care in his presentation speech to point out that Arnoldson's candidacy had been unanimously supported by the Swedish Inter-parliamentary Group.

Arnoldson was a prolific writer, turning out a succession of articles, books, and didactic novels and plays. He produced substantial works on religion and peace. His most important contribution to the literature on peace was one of the first comprehensive surveys of the movement, translated into English two years after it was published in Stockholm in 1890 as *Pax Mundi: A Concise Account of the Progress of the Movement for Peace by means of Arbitration, Neutralization, International Law and Disarmament.*

Arnoldson's Nobel lecture was both eloquent and original. In a global expansion of his old method of petitioning for peace, he proposed that in all countries of the world an appeal should be issued for every adult man and woman to sign the following declaration:

> I, the undersigned, desire peace on earth. I want all armed forces to be abolished. I want a joint police force to be created, to which each nation should contribute according to the size of its population. I want that force to be subject to an International Supreme Court. I want all states to be in duty bound to refer any kind of international controversy to this court, and subject themselves to the judgment of the court.

In his conclusion Arnoldson said the prize would enable him to work more effectively for this world referendum and to serve the cause of peace with "even stronger perseverance." But his major work for peace had already been accomplished. Although never blessed with the best of health, he lived seven years longer, dying in Stockholm in 1916 at the age of seventy-one.

BIBLIOGRAPHY

Primary Source

Arnoldson, Klas Pontus. *Pax Mundi: A Concise Account of the Progress of the Movement for Peace by Means of Arbitration, Neutralization, International Law and Disarmament.* 1890. London: Sonnenschein, 1909. Translated from the Swedish.

Secondary Source

"Arnoldson, Klas Pontus." In *MPL.*

1909

Baron Paul Henri d'Estournelles de Constant (1852–1924)

France

Foremost internationalist leader in Europe, 1900–1914; diplomat, politician, author, delegate to Hague Peace Conferences, 1899, 1907; organized French parliamentary group for arbitration; founded Conciliation Internationale; member Permanent Court of Arbitration at The Hague; president, European Center of Carnegie Endowment for International Peace; promoted Franco-British and Franco-German understanding.

Baron Paul Henri d'Estournelles de Constant, who shared the prize of 1909 with the Belgian Auguste Beernaert, was his country's leading peace advocate in the years before the First World War. Bertha von Suttner called him "the most successful peace worker in France." His effectiveness stemmed from his wide-ranging background: as a former diplomat, he knew the world of international politics from the inside; as a prominent member of the French parliament, he was highly regarded by his country's political leaders and by parliamentarians elsewhere; as an aristocrat, he enjoyed the best social connections in France and abroad; as French delegate at both Hague

Peace Conferences, he could promote the cause of arbitration with some authority in his extensive public speaking and writing; and as a successful organizer of projects to promote Franco-British and Franco-German understanding, he was well qualified to work for the more distant objective of European union. When the Nobel Committee gave him the award in 1909, it was the fifth time he had been on the short list for special consideration.

Paul Henri Benjamin Balluet, Baron d'Estournelles de Constant de Rebecque was born in 1852 in the Sarthe district of the Loire to a noble family descended from Crusaders. He attended the famous lycée Louis le Grand in Paris and then studied law and received a diploma from the School for Oriental Languages. In 1876 at the age of twenty-four he entered the diplomatic service. After a series of assignments in the Balkans, North Africa, and Western Europe, he was appointed assistant director of the Near Eastern Bureau at the Foreign Ministry in Paris. His next post was a coveted position as counselor at the embassy in London with rank of minister. He was in charge of the embassy during a serious dispute with England over Siam, which he successfully resolved. With a bright future as a diplomat now assured, d'Estournelles decided to leave what he called "the gilded existence of the diplomatist" in order to work for peace through an active role in politics. In 1895 he won election to the Chamber of Deputies, and he used his parliamentary office as the base for his political activities from then on, serving after 1904 in the Senate.

In 1896 he began to publish a series of articles on "the precarious state of Europe." When Tsar Nicholas II issued his surprising call for a peace conference at The Hague, d'Estournelles was a natural choice for his country's delegation. France was as little interested as any of the other powers in disarmament, the tsar's original emphasis, but the French government could not be unresponsive to the support for arbitration that the peace movement had mobilized in public opinion. There was also good reason for France, as Russia's ally, to spare the tsar the embarrassment of a possible failure of the conference. France consequently sent a strong peace delegation, headed by Léon Bourgeois, who was to be a Nobel Peace Prize laureate, and assisted by d'Estournelles and the international jurist Louis Renault, also destined for the award, with instructions to help make the conference a success.

Under these favorable circumstances, d'Estournelles emerged as a leader in the international peace movement. At the conference he fought hard for the principle of arbitration and for the establishment of an arbitral tribunal which was finally agreed upon. Henceforth d'Estournelles made international understanding and peace the main objectives of his life.

The first task was to try to breathe life into the Hague Court. What was the use of a panel of arbiters if the sovereign states did not call upon their services? D'Estournelles thereupon decided to use a lecture tour in the United States in 1902 as the occasion to try to persuade President Theodore Roosevelt to make the first move. The French ambassador presented him to the president, to whom he boldly declared, "You are a danger or hope for the world. . . . It is believed you are inclined to the side of violence; prove the contrary." "How?" asked the president. "By giving life to the Hague Court," replied d'Estournelles, pointing out how Roosevelt could cover himself with glory if he would submit to the tribunal some question, no matter how insignificant, and thus give an example to the world.

This was just the right approach to use with Roosevelt, who liked to take a dare. The next day he instructed his secretary of state to look for something to arbitrate. The outcome was the first case to come before the Hague Court, a long-standing dispute between the United States and Mexico over Catholic church funds designated for use in California, but withheld by Mexico when the territory was ceded to the United States after the Mexican war.

In 1903 d'Estournelles organized French parliamentarians into an active section of the Interparliamentary Union and instituted visits to and from their foreign counterparts. The exchange of visits with British members of Parliament helped bring about the Anglo-French Entente Cordiale in 1904. D'Estournelles also took his French colleagues to Munich, and on another occasion he addressed the Prussian House of Peers, where in prophetic words he warned against war which "drives the republics into dictatorship, the monarchies into the grip of revolution." In 1907 he continued the good work for arbitration at the Second Hague Conference.

Through all these activities d'Estournelles built an international network which he used to found the Conciliation Internationale, an association favoring arbitration and arms reduction composed of many intellectual, political, and business leaders in Europe and the United States. He became an important link between the peace forces in Europe and those in the United States. As his wife, Daisy Sedgwick-Berend, was an American, he often traveled to the United States on lecture tours and had many friends there. One was Andrew Carnegie, whom he influenced to give funds to build the Peace Palace as a home for the Hague Court. Another was President Nicholas Murray Butler of Columbia University, head of the Carnegie Endowment for International Peace, who made d'Estournelles president of its European center. As a recognized authority on the United States, d'Estournelles told Europeans that Americans did not fear the European union he was advocating. On the contrary: "The Americans are businessmen, and they prefer well-organized and stable conditions to the armed peace which presents a constant menace to World Peace."

When he was named laureate in 1909, d'Estournelles was at fifty-seven the youngest peace activist to receive the prize. Five years later his world was shattered by the advent of the war he had given his best energies to prevent. Although he supported the war effort as a good Frenchman, he worked during its course for what came to be the League of Nations and afterward renewed his attempt at Franco-German reconciliation. In 1924, he died in Paris at the age of seventy-two. Two days later his son read at The Hague his last speech, prepared for the twenty-fifth anniversary of the conference of 1899, which had been the scene of his first public appearance as a champion of peace. Despite the setbacks of the world war he lived through and the second one that followed, the movement toward international organization that he helped inaugurate continued. Moreover, there would come a time when the leaders of the two great countries d'Estournelles had tried so hard to bring together would stand together, hand in hand, at a once bloody battlefield where their fathers had fought one another. That European union, of which he had dreamed, would not seem so far away.

BIBLIOGRAPHY

Primary Sources

Estournelles de Constant, Paul Henri d'. *America and Her Problems.* Translated by George A. Raper. New York: Macmillan, 1915.

———. "Women and the Cause of Peace." *International Conciliation* 40 (March 1911): 5–17.

Estournelles de Constant, Paul Henri d', and David Jayne Hill. *The Results of the Second Hague Conference.* New York: International Conciliation, 1907.

Secondary Sources

Chickering, Roger. *Imperial Germany and a World without War.* Princeton: Princeton University Press, 1975. This study of the German peace movement before 1914 includes a brief summary of the movement in France.

Cooper, Sandi E., ed. *Voices of French Pacifism.* New York: Garland, 1973.

Davis, Calvin D. *The United States and the Second Hague Peace Conference.* Durham, N.C.: Duke University Press, 1975.

Davis, Hayne, ed. *Among the World's Peacemakers.* New York: Progressive Publishing Co., 1907. Reprint. New York: Garland, 1972, with an introduction by Michael Lutzker. Chap. 28 is based on an interview with d'Estournelles at his chateau.

Hill, David Jayne, Paul Henri d'Estournelles de Constant, and James Brown Scott. *The Second Hague Conference.* Washington, D.C.: U.S. Government Printing Office, 1908.

Wild, Adolf. *Baron d'Estournelles de Constant (1852–1924).* Hamburg: Verlag Sasse, 1973. A biography emphasizing his work for German-French reconciliation and European unity.

1909
Auguste Beernaert (1829–1912)

Belgium

Statesman and international jurist, Belgian representative at Hague Conferences, member of the Permanent Court of Arbitration, president of the Council of Interparliamentary Union.

Auguste Marie François Beernaert was a Catholic jurist who took a prominent role in the politics of his country and later rendered significant service to the peace movement in the work of both Hague Conferences, in the development of international law, and as presiding officer of the Interparliamentary Union. In 1909, the first time that his candidacy was give special consideration by the Nobel Committee, he was made colaureate with Baron d'Estournelles of France, who had also served the peace cause in governmental capacities and as a leader of the organized movement.

Beernaert was born in Ostend, Belgium, in 1829, the son of a Catholic government official of Flemish origin. His mother was a strong, high-minded woman who taught him and his sister at home. At the age of seventeen he entered the University of Louvain and five years later took his doctorate of law with highest honors. He then spent two years studying legal education in the universities of France and Germany before being admitted to the bar at the age of twenty-four. In the next twenty years he made his reputation as a highly paid lawyer and as a legal scholar known for his contributions to law journals.

He then turned to politics and public life. He joined the cabinet of the Catholic party as minister of public works, serving for five years with distinction, and was elected to the Chamber of Representatives from the west Flanders town of Thielt, which reelected him as long as he lived. In 1884 he became prime minister and finance minister for the next ten years, presiding over the longest-lived ministry in the history of Belgium. Under his enlightened leadership the franchise was extended, reforms were adopted to improve the lot of the workers, including child labor laws, Flemish rights were protected, a public works program reduced unemployment, and the budget was kept balanced. The Congo, which King Leopold had been privately developing, was made the Congo Free State, with the king as its sovereign. Beernaert supported loans to the new state with high hopes that Belgium's influence would end the slave trade and raise the cultural level of the people, but he could not support King Leopold's policies of exploitation, and after he left office he actively opposed them.

In church matters, as a Catholic liberal, Beernaert urged conciliatory policies on the papacy. His government was finally defeated over the issue of proportional representation, which Beernaert wanted to introduce to guard the rights of minorities, and he left office in 1894. He remained in the government as advisory minister of state and contined in the Chamber, where he was elected president in 1895, seeing his proposal of proportional representation finally become law. His major energies for the last eighteen years of his life, however, were devoted to international peace as a leading advocate of international arbitration and disarmament.

In 1899 he was the obvious choice to represent his country at the First Hague Conference. He presided over the Commission on Arms Limitation, an important concern to Tsar Nicholas II, who issued the call for the conference, but arms limitation was opposed by the other Great Powers, and virtually nothing was accomplished. At the Second Hague Conference Beernaert chaired the Commission on Land Warfare, where he spoke for limitations on the military use of the air and helped write regulations on neutrality and the protection of prisoners of war. In the latter two areas Beernaert's efforts constituted an important contribution to the development of the law of nations. He had already played a role in the movement to unify international maritime law, and an international conference was held in Brussels in 1910 that led to new maritime treaties.

Beernaert was also a prominent figure in the progress of international arbitration. In the first case brought before the Permanent Court of Arbitration established by the First Hague Conference, he represented Mexico in a dispute with the United States. Beernaert was a strong proponent of obligatory arbitration in certain restricted cases, an idea he had supported in the Interparliamentary Union. As a delegate of Belgium at the Second Hague Conference, however, his government instructed him to oppose any such proposal, apparently because of concern that Belgium's freedom of action in the Congo might be restricted. Beernaert refused to vote against his principles and offered to resign. The government compromised by agreeing to leave him free to speak his mind, but not to participate in the vote.

Beernaert was recognized to be a man of high integrity who practiced his religious convictions. He was named president of two Catholic peace associations, the Catholic League for Peace and the International League of Catholic Pacifists. Both associations worked for international relationships based upon Christian morality.

For eighteen years after the end of his term as prime minister, Beernaert remained active in the Interparliamentary Union. He presided over several of its international conferences, was president of the council from 1899 and of the Executive Council when it was established in 1908. It was on returning home from the Geneva conference of 1912 that he fell ill and died in Lucerne.

BIBLIOGRAPHY

Secondary Sources

"Beernaert, Auguste." In *BDI.*

"Beernaert, Auguste." In *Biographie nationale.* Vol. 33. Brussels, 1965.

"Beernaert, Auguste." In *MPL.*

Carton de Wiart, Henry. *Beernaert et son temps.* Brussels: Renaissance du Livre, 1945.

Passelecq, Ferdinand. *Auguste Beernaert.* Brussels: Dewit, 1912. The emphasis is upon his role in the Belgian Catholic party.

Van der Smissen, Édouard. *Leopold II et Beernaert.* 2 vols. Brussels: Goemaere, 1920. Based on their unpublished correspondence of 1884–94.

1910

Permanent International Peace Bureau

FOUNDED IN 1891, BERN

Before 1914 the Permanent International Peace Bureau in Bern, Switzerland, was the headquarters of the popular peace movement. The bureau reached the committee's short list in seven of the first ten years of the prize. In the second award of 1902 the committee divided the prize between Élie Ducommun, director of the Peace Bureau, and Alfred Gobat, director of the Interparliamentary Bureau, also in Bern, presumably recognizing the value of the work of the two bureaus in the persons of their managers. The peace activists, however, continued to press for an award to the Peace Bureau itself since it was always in need of funds. In 1907 the World Peace Congress meeting in Munich requested all those eligible to make nominations, which included the members of the commission of the bureau itself, to propose the Peace Bureau. Its turn finally came in 1910, when Chairman Løvland of the Nobel Peace Prize Committee noted this support from those in the peace movement all over the world and declared that the selection was "entirely in the spirit of Alfred Nobel's plan; he wanted his money to be used to support, accelerate, and promote the peace movement."

The bureau was established by action of the third World Peace Congress in Rome in 1891, with Fredrik Bajer the chief proponent. The idea of coordinating the peace activities in the different countries through some kind of general office had already been urged by certain peace activists for over a decade, especially by the veterans Hodgson Pratt of England and Charles Lemonnier of France. Pratt was the Johnny Appleseed of the movement whose travels on the Continent left societies for peace and arbitration sprouting in his wake. Lemonnier headed the republican International League of Peace and Liberty which had given consideration in 1880 to the establishment of "an international bureau of arbitration and disarmament." Lemonnier recognized, however, that Pratt had been the first to give precise form to the idea of concentrating the affairs of peace in a single bureau.

A strong executive was in any case precluded by the many divisions in the ranks of the friends of peace. When they began to meet regularly in international congresses at the end of the 1880s, they were a variegated lot: Christians and freethinkers, republicans and royalists, absolute pacifists and advocates of wars of defense and national liberation, politicians who prided themselves on their practicality and utopian dreamers, businessmen and trade unionists, even a few socialists. All were agreed on the necessity of peace, but hardly on the ways to achieve it. Some of the peace societies were as jealous of their independence as the governments they hoped to unite. The measure of the cooperation they did attain through the International Peace Bureau was actually quite an accomplishment.

Bajer's "Plan of War for the Friends of Peace," in which he envisaged one general headquarters for the army of peace, went too far for the Interparliamentary Conference, which approved of unity only to the extent of agreeing to set up its own coordinating office. The Peace Congress of 1890 had already approved Bajer's idea in general, and before the next congress met in 1891 in Rome, Lemonnier helped Pratt round up support and the delegates of his league to the congress were instructed to vote for the project. One of them was Ducommun, who was to be the *rapporteur* on the question. The resolution at the congress consequently moved to adoption without difficulty: the Permanent International Peace Bureau was to be established in Bern, and Ducommun himself was to be the secretary-general.

The congress had no funds at its disposal, but Ducommun refused to accept a salary and a subscription was opened to cover other costs. Characteristically, it was Hodgson Pratt who gave the first check, and Bertha von Suttner contributed her royalties from the Italian edition of *Die Waffen Nieder* (*Lay Down Your Arms*). Eventually the bureau became empowered to accept gifts and legacies as the agency of the Society of the Permanent International Peace Bureau set up under Swiss law, and small subventions were received from the governments of Switzerland and later from Denmark, Norway, and Sweden. Ducommun had to start his work on a very modest scale, for his expenses could not exceed what was in those days about twenty-five dollars per month. By 1900 the annual income was about two thousand dollars, and even before the Nobel prize money was received in 1910, there was enough income from contributions and grants and the interest on a modest endowment to cover the office operations.

The work of the bureau consisted in serving as a

clearinghouse of information for the peace movement, in keeping the pacifists in touch with one another between the congresses, in making the preparations for these gatherings, and in implementing their resolutions. Later the bureau made arrangements for Peace Day, celebrated by peace societies as an international demonstration for peace. In 1892 all Ducommun could manage as a news sheet was a biweekly circular written by hand and duplicated. From 1895 on this was printed as *Correspondance Bi-Mensuelle.*

All this was progress, but a far cry from Bajer's original conception. In fact, the old London Peace Society, which had refrained from adhering to the bureau because it suspected Ducommun's republican politics and also feared federation, was so reassured by 1894 that it yielded to the entreaties of the other pacifists and sent the bureau as a peace offering a generous check.

The bureau's relations with governments were generally confined to the transmission of the resolutions of the congresses as well as all peace publications, and there was correspondence with foreign ministries recommending the conclusion of treaties of arbitration. When there was war or the threat of war, the bureau usually issued an appeal for a peaceful settlement. In 1895, for example, Ducommun appealed to the king of the Belgians to offer his services as mediator of the conflict between France and Madagascar. A courteous reply came back pointing out that Madagascar was a protectorate of France and mediation was therefore impossible. In 1899 Ducommun sent telegrams to Queen Victoria of England and the Boer leader Kruger urging arbitration. Kruger was willing, and Ducommun so notified the English Foreign Office, which promptly replied that arbitration was out of the question. Three days later the Boer War began.

The Peace Bureau was obviously not a power in the world, but at least it was recognized as an entity to be dealt with, and it gave the peace movement an authority that it had not enjoyed before. This increased after the Hague Conference of 1899, the first diplomatic conference called not to resolve a war or an international crisis but to promote peace. Ducommun, moreover, was universally respected, and the strong moral authority he exerted over all the pacifists had a unifying effect.

When Ducommun died in 1906, it was fortunate that another experienced and respected administrator (also unpaid), Albert Gobat, was prepared to take over the Peace Bureau duties along with his responsibilities as secretary-general of the Interparliamentary Union. In the three years that he directed both bureaus in Bern, there was perhaps some of that unity at the center of the peace movement that Bajer had hoped for. During his tenure of office at the Peace Bureau from 1906 until 1914, Gobat continued the initiatives Ducommun had taken in communications to governments and went even further. In 1911 he took a strong stand when Italy went to war with Turkey, criticizing both the Italian government and the Italian erstwhile pacifists who supported the war. He worked for Franco-German reconciliation, and in 1913 he made one last effort to reorganize the bureau as more of an executive authority. This was cut short by the war, and it turned out that international organization came to the governments with the League of Nations before it came to the peace societies.

The Peace Bureau proved entirely unable to cope with the peace movement born in the First World War, which grew up outside its influence. The proliferation of a much greater variety of peace societies and the development of the League of Nations and other intergovernmental bodies presented a very different situation from the days when the young international peace movement could concentrate its efforts on encouraging the use of arbitration and expanding the work of the Hague Conferences. The Peace Bureau moved to Geneva in 1924 to be closer to these new developments and to seek a new role for itself. It was no longer in position to attempt to coordinate the popular movement for peace, however, and its importance steadily declined until its activities were suspended during the Second World War and its assets were taken over for disposition by the Swiss government.

After the war there was a long drawn out legal process to decide about these assets, which included a valuable property in Geneva where the office had been situated. In 1959 the Swiss court declared that the International Peace Bureau had ceased to exist. Its assets were given to the International Liaison Committee of Organizations for Peace (ILCOP), which had been founded after World War II with aims similar to those of the former bureau and several of the same member organizations. The archives and book collection went to the UN Library in Geneva, a great boon for scholars.

The ILCOP then formally christened its new secretariat in Geneva the International Peace Bureau and proceeded to assume a continuity that does not in fact exist. The Norwegian Nobel Committee does, however, recognize the members of the board of the new bureau as entitled to submit nominations for the prize.

The new International Peace Bureau cannot speak for all the peace societies of the world, as Ducommun and Gobat once did, nor does it organize "universal peace congresses." It accepts as members only "independent non-aligned peace organizations" and excludes the government-sponsored peace associations of the Soviet bloc countries.

It has done good work in facilitating communications between organizations, intergovernmental and nongovernmental, that are working for peace, and it has organized working parties and seminars on various peace issues. It has made a contribution to the UN disarmament deliberations in Geneva and was particularly active under the presidency of Nobel laureate Sean MacBride.

Bolstered by a generous grant from Sweden, the new bureau has recently entered upon a serious effort to recruit more member organizations and to become a more important international center for the independent peace societies of the world.

BIBLIOGRAPHY

Secondary Sources

Ducommun, Élie. "The Permanent International Bureau of Peace." *Independent* 55 (19 March 1903): 660–61.

Simon, Werner. "The International Peace Bureau, 1892–1917." In *Peace Movements and Political Cultures.* Edited by Charles Chatfield and Peter van den Dungen. Knoxville: University of Tennessee Press, 1988.

See also Bibliographies for Élie Ducommun (1902) and Albert Gobat (1902).

1911
Alfred Hermann Fried (1864–1921)

Austria

Leading peace publisher, publicist, and theoretician, close collaborator of Bertha von Suttner, founder of German Peace Society.

When Alfred Hermann Fried was named cowinner of the prize in 1911, Chairman Løvland of the Nobel Committee noted that "he has probably been the most industrious literary pacifist in the past twenty years. . . . since 1891 he has devoted his whole life to work for peace, one of the few men to do so." Fried's periodical, *Die Friedenswarte* (Peace watch), was called "the best journal in the peace movement" by Løvland. Through this journal Fried had succeeded in winning to the peace movement distinguished German university professors in international law, history, and political science, whom Løvland identified as his nominators, adding that Fried had also been nominated by Swedish members of parliament. Løvland did not have to refer to the leading peace activists who had supported Fried, among whom were the laureates Bertha von Suttner and Fredrik Bajer.

This eminent writer, editor, and theoretician of peace had no formal schooling after his fourteenth year of age. Educationally, he was a self-made man. He was born in Vienna in 1864 to a Jewish family of simple origins. After trying his hand as a bookseller, he moved to Hamburg and then to Berlin, where he struggled to make ends meet, finally starting a publishing business. His political and social ideas, influenced by socialism, were slowly taking shape. He had begun to think about war when, still in Vienna, he had seen the antiwar canvasses of the Russian painter Verestschagin, and he had been moved by Bertha von Suttner's novel, *Lay Down Your Arms.* But he had always felt alone in his thinking about war and peace. One day in 1891 he was reading the newspapers in the Kaiserhof Café in Berlin when his eye fell upon a report that a peace society had just been founded by Bertha von Suttner in Vienna. Now he realized there were others who not only thought as he did about war but were organizing to work for peace.

On that same day Fried impulsively dashed off a note to the baroness, proposing the establishment of a peace journal which he would publish and of which she would be the editor. The novelist had never heard of the young publisher, but his earnestness and the enthusiasm quite won her, and she agreed. In January 1892, the monthly, named *Die Waffen Nieder* after her novel, began to appear. It was the beginning of a close cooperation between Fried and the baroness, which lasted twenty years until she died with Fried at her bedside.

Later in 1892 they collaborated on the founding of the German Peace Society in Berlin, with Fried doing all the organizing work on the spot, following the careful advice of the baroness, who wrote follow-up letters to all those he approached. Fried was a good organizer, but not an organization man. He was hard to work with, very sensitive and easily offended. It was not long before he withdrew from the society he had brought into being, and he never joined such a peace society again. In 1903 he returned to Vienna.

Fried continued to publish the monthly organ of the German Peace Society, however, and *Die Waffen Nieder* appeared until 1899 when it was succeeded by *Die Friedenswarte,* which Fried himself edited until his death. At the same time he sent reports on peace developments to any newspapers that would publish them, and he popularized the peace cause in numerous articles and books. His two-volume *Handbuch der Friedensbewegung* (Handbook of the peace movement) was the most comprehensive and authoritative work on that subject for the period before 1914.

In his peace theory Fried moved beyond the ethical appeal of earlier pacifists. In the early days of his cooperation with Baroness von Suttner, he wrote her about the value of a scholarly treatise on peace by a Dresden jurist which he had just read. This represented "the North," he said, "while you, gracious lady, with your style of attack, represent the South. Heart and Intellect, as if one or the other could work alone." Fried, although himself from the South, came more and more to see his own role as strengthening the intellectual foundations of pacifism.

It was wrong to emphasize disarmament, Fried insisted. War and armaments were only symptoms of the existing state of international anarchy. When there was organization in relations between states, disarmament would naturally follow. The organization of international life in all areas was proceeding apace, carried forward irresistibly by social forces. In his *Annuaire de la vie internationale,* another journal Fried founded, he tracked the many evidences of these growing international bonds, including the Pan-American movement and the Hague Conferences. He recommended the Pan-American Union as a model for Europe, to promote unification through the dissemination of information about all kinds of cultural and economic developments.

Fried christened this approach "scientific" and even "revolutionary" pacifism. As in Marx's socialist theory, the laws of development would inevitably bring about the new international order. The tasks of the peace advocates were to help their contemporaries become aware of where history was moving and to try to remove the obstacles to the march of progress. Fried had no ready-made international constitution to propose, and in accepting the sovereign state he was anything but a revolutionary. In matters of current politics, he could sometimes be naive.

The last years before 1914 were a time of success and recognition for Fried. The Nobel award in 1911 came the same year the Carnegie Endowment for International Peace began to grant an annual subsidy for *Die Friedenswarte,* finally stabilizing the journal's finances and making possible a distribution of some ten thousand copies of each issue. Two years later, in 1913, Fried received a high academic distinction, an honorary doctor's degree from the Dutch university of Leiden.

In the following year Fried could expect further triumph. He was in charge of arrangements for the Universal Peace Congress to be held in Vienna in September 1914, which was to pay homage to Baroness von Suttner in her home city and in which Fried would play a leading role. But these high hopes and all his hopes for the future came crashing down when in August 1914 the European war broke out. There was no place for peace advocates as war fever rose in Vienna. Fried was charged with high treason and had to move to neutral Switzerland to carry on his international activities and continue the publication of *Die Friedenswarte.* After the war he returned to a Vienna crushed by defeat and crippled by the effects of the war. Bitter and exhausted, he spent his remaining energies attacking the injustices of the peace treaties, which were a further disillusion for him, and trying to explain how the war had been proof of the validity of his analysis of international politics.

He had invested his savings in Austrian government bonds, which were now worthless. Impoverished and malnourished, despite the efforts of his pacifist friends abroad to get food to him, Fried succumbed in May 1921 to bronchial pneumonia. He was only fifty-seven, and he had had less than three years to enjoy his Nobel award before the war brought the period of trials and suffering that now came to an end.

BIBLIOGRAPHY

Primary Sources

Fried, Alfred Hermann. *Les bases du pacifisme.* Translated by Jean Lagorgette. Paris: Pedone, 1909. Reprint. New York: Garland, 1972. With an introduction by Sandi E. Cooper.

———. *The German Emperor and the Peace of the World.* Translated from the German edition of 1910. New York and London: Hodder & Stoughton, 1912. A hopeful view of the peace interests of William II of Germany.

———. *Handbuch der Friedensbewegung.* 2d rev. ed. Berlin and Leipzig: Friedenswarte, 1911–13. Reprint. New York: Garland, 1972. 2 vols. in 1, with an introduction by Daniel Gasman. The most complete compendium of information about the pre-1914 peace movement.

———. *Mein Kriegs-Tagebuch*. 4 vols. Zurich: Rascher, 1918–20. The journal Fried kept during the war.

———. *The Restoration of Europe*. Translated by Lewis S. Gannett from the Zurich edition of 1915. New York: Macmillan, 1916. Reprint. New York: Garland, 1971. With an introduction by Sandi E. Cooper. On postwar reconstruction.

Secondary Sources

Chickering, Roger. *Imperial Germany and a World without War: The Peace Movement and German Society 1892–1914*. Princeton: Princeton University Press, 1975. The only study in English. Recommended.

"Fried, Alfred Hermann." In *MPL*.

Hamann, Brigitte. *Bertha von Suttner*. Munich: Piper, 1986. Biography of Fried's close collaborator, with extensive use of their correspondence.

Scheer, Friedrich-Karl. *Die deutsche Friedensgesellschaft (1892–1933)*. Frankfurt: Harg & Herchen, 1981. A very thorough monographic study of the German Peace Society.

1911
Tobias Asser (1838–1913)

Netherlands

International jurist, counselor to Dutch Foreign Office, minister of state, delegate to Hague Peace Conferences, member of Permanent Court of Arbitration at The Hague, president of conferences on private international law.

In the presentation of the award to Tobias Asser that he shared in 1911 with Alfred H. Fried, Chairman Løvland of the Nobel Committee declared that "Asser has above all been a practical legal statesman. . . . As a pioneer in the field of international legal relations," he had made an important scholarly contribution "overshadowed" only by his public activity as negotiator of international legal treaties, delegate at the Hague Peace Conferences, arbiter of international disputes, and minister of state.

Tobias Michael Carel Asser was born in Amsterdam in 1838 into a Jewish family distinguished in the law. His intellectual promise was first recognized when at the age of nineteen he won a competition with a thesis on economics. After considering a career in business, he decided to follow in the family tradition, studying law at the Athenaeum in Amsterdam and taking his doctor's degree at the famous University of Leiden in 1860. In that same year, when he was only twenty-two, he was named to an international commission concerned with the tolls on the Rhine River, the first of many appointments by the Dutch government.

Asser entered upon the practice of law and then, after a few years, began teaching law at the Athenaeum. Through his relationships with the international jurists John Westlake of England and Rolin-Jacquemyns of Belgium he became interested in international private law, which deals with legal relationships between nationals of different states. In 1869 the three men founded the first important scholarly journal of international law. This led to contacts with other scholars, who came to Ghent in Belgium in 1873 to found the Institute of International Law. Asser, then thirty-five, was one of the youngest members of this group, but he impressed the others, most of whom were "grave elderly gentlemen," as a brilliant young man of great culture and facility in debate.

At that time international law was not widely recognized as an academic discipline in universities. Of the eleven savants who met at Ghent and were known to one another mainly through publications in the field, only four were actually university lecturers in international law and only one, James Lorimer from the University of Edinburgh, held a chair endowed especially for a professor of the law of nations.

When the Athenaeum afterwards became the University of Amsterdam, Asser was appointed as professor of international law, and he came to be recognized as one of the leading scholars in the field of international private law. At his urging, the Dutch government convened a series of international conferences at The Hague to work on codification in this field, beginning in 1893. Asser had long argued that the best way to achieve some uniformity was to secure agreements at such intergovernmental meetings, which could then be implemented by the actions of national legislatures, and so it came about. As a result of these conferences, presided over by Asser, a number of international conventions was concluded. In the field of family law, for example, laws of different states relating to marriage, divorce, and the guardianship of minors were brought into harmony.

Asser thus came to hold a position in international private law similar to that enjoyed by an earlier laureate, Louis Renault, in the sphere of international public law, which had to do with relations between sovereign states. In this field Asser also made an important contribution. Like Renault, he served as legal counselor to his government's Foreign Ministry, represented his country at the Hague Peace Conferences, and served as a member of the Permanent Court of Arbitration at The Hague. He was selected as a judge of the tribunal that heard the first case to come before that court, a dispute between Mexico and the United States in 1902.

Whereas Renault never gave up his teaching, Asser left the University of Amsterdam in 1893 to become a member of the Council of State, the highest administrative organ. From 1904 until his death he was minister of state without portfolio. As a skilled negotiator, Asser played a key role in many treaties that the Netherlands signed with other powers. His most noted diplomatic success was in the negotiations leading to the neutralization of the Suez Canal, when he obtained for his own country and for Spain seats on the Suez Canal Commission along with the Great Powers of Europe.

Asser did not live long after receiving his award. He died in 1913 at the age of seventy-five, his contribution to international law recognized throughout the world as a continuation of the pioneer work of the Dutchman Hugo Grotius in the seventeenth century.

BIBLIOGRAPHY

Primary Source

Asser, Tobias M. C. *La convention de La Haye du 14 Novembre 1896*. Haarlem: Bohn, 1901. On civil law.

Secondary Sources

Abrams, Irwin. "Emergence of the International Law Societies." *Review of Politics* 19 (1957): 361–80.

"Asser, Tobias." In *BDI*.

"T. M. C. Asser." *American Journal of International Law* 8 (1914): 343–44.

1912

Elihu Root (1845–1937)

United States

Statesman, jurist, prominent conservative; secretary of war, secretary of state, U.S. senator from New York; president, Carnegie Endowment for International Peace, American Society of International Law.

Elihu Root first reached the committee's short list in 1909, when he was considered for his services to peace as secretary of state (1905–9). In 1913 the committee gave him the reserved prize for 1912 in recognition of these achievements and of his accomplishments after he left office, when, in the words of the presentation address, Root "gave himself heart and soul to the cause of peace" as president of the "great Carnegie Peace Foundation" and as a member of the U.S. Senate.

Root was sixty-eight with most of his public career behind him when he won the prize. He lived for another twenty-four years, however, as a highly respected elder statesman, continuing to work for the development of a juridical order between states.

Root entered public service in 1899 as secretary of war in President McKinley's cabinet, known as a staunch Republican conservative and one of the leading corporation lawyers in the country. Son of a mathematics professor at Hamilton College, Root had graduated from there at nineteen, first in his class, studied law at New York University, and praticed successfully for some thirty years before joining the cabinet.

What McKinley wanted was a skilled lawyer who could sort out administrative relationships with the former Spanish possessions, Cuba, the Philippines, and Puerto Rico, the responsibility for which had been given to the War Department after the victory over Spain. Root proved to be such an able administrator that under McKinley's successor, Theodore Roosevelt, he moved to higher cabinet rank as secretary of state.

In this office what impressed the Nobel Committee most, as specified in the presentation address, was Root's "work in bringing about better understanding between the countries of North and South America." The republics south of the Rio Grande had long been accustomed to condescending treatment from the United States. More recently they had been alienated by President Roosevelt's aggressive policy in acquiring land for the Panama Canal from Colombia, and they feared an increasing disposition in Washington to intervene in their domestic affairs. As secretary of state, Root inaugurated what later came to be called the Good Neighbor policy. He cultivated the friendship of Latin American envoys in Washington, aligned the United States with Mexico in peace efforts in Central America, and arranged for greater representation of the Latin American states at the Second Hague Conference.

The active role taken by the U.S. delegation at this conference was a further demonstration of Root's peace policy. Following his instructions, the delegates worked both for making obligatory the submission of a certain limited class of international disputes to arbitration and for the establishment of a permanent Court of Arbitral Justice. Root felt that the First Hague Conference had established a new standard of international conduct by transforming arbitration from "an exceptional expedient" to a "recognized and customary method of diplomatic procedure." The Hague Court it had established, however, was only a panel of many members from which arbiters could be selected by states deciding to arbitrate a dispute, and many of these prospective judges were diplomats and statesmen, few of whom were ever chosen. Root hoped that the Second Hague Conference would take the next step and set up a small court with qualified full-time judges, to which states would be obligated to submit certain disputes.

The conference was not willing to go this far, but the World Court established after the First World War was modeled on Root's conception. As for mandatory arbitration, Root incorporated this principle in twenty-five bilateral treaties which he negotiated and then skillfully piloted through the Senate.

His arbitration treaty with Japan was one element in Root's policy of smoothing relations with that country, which had been troubled by discriminatory actions taken in California against unwelcome Japanese immigrants. The presentation speech referred to this issue as Root's "most difficult problem" and called his effort to resolve it "of great value." This was the so-called Gentlemen's Agreement, an exchange of notes in which Japan agreed to limit emigration of Japanese laborers to the West Coast.

The Nobel presentation also referred to Root's work for peace as senator from New York, specifying his support of an unconditional arbitration treaty with Great Britain and his speech on the Panama Canal tolls, opposing special privileges for American shipping as inconsistent with an earlier treaty with Great Britain. Root's main contributions as a senator were in foreign affairs, where his voice was always listened to, but his senatorial career as a whole was not marked by great achievement.

The presentation address, delivered by a spokesman of the Nobel Committee on 10 December 1913, declared that as president of the American Society of International Law and of the Carnegie Endowment for International Peace, "Root has been recognized as the leader of the peace movement in the United States." It would have been fairer to say that Root was head of two major branches of the peace movement in the United States, the international lawyers and the establishment-centered sector, which the Carnegie Endowment represented.

When the peace-minded steel magnate Andrew Carnegie established his Endowment for International Peace with a grant of $10 million in 1910, Root became president of the board of trustees. With Nicholas Murray Butler, president of Columbia University, he helped shape the endowment's course so that it became a peacemaking institution very different from what most pacifist leaders of the time had hoped for. What this was to be was reported at the outset by the well-informed correspondent of the London *Times*: the endowment would work "in the most practical spirit," rather than encouraging "pacifists of the sentimental order." The emphasis would be on "quiet educational work," not on "promiscuous preaching against war and armaments," and it would seek to be a "sober and steady" force for peace, avoiding any "propagation of useless sentimentalism." This was Root's chosen path to peace—practical, scholarly, eschewing popular agitation and controversy.

He never explained it more cogently than in the text of his Nobel lecture, which was canceled because of the onset of war in 1914 but published in Root's collected works. It is the expression of faith of an enlightened conservative, aware of the deeper causes of war in "man's savage nature," but feeling that popular passions can be controlled in a "long slow process," and noting hopeful signs in the progress of international law and its teaching, in the development of the Hague system, and in research on causes and effects of war.

Two quotations Root cites sum up his attitude toward peace. The first was an old English saying he was very fond of repeating, "Leg over leg the dog went to Dover." With the second he closed his address. After referring to certain troubling current international conflicts, he ended with "the apocryphal exclamation of Galileo, 'and still the world moves.' "

In his own efforts for peace Root was always conscious of what the traffic would bear. His sense of the possible accounted for his most successful negotiations as secretary of state, both with foreign powers and with the Senate. In his Nobel address Root stated his firm conviction that "under the present organization of civilization in independent nationalities" questions of vital interests cannot be submitted to arbitration "because that would be an abdication of independence and the placing of government *pro tanto* in the hands of others."

This concern for national sovereignty, and in particular the sovereign interests of the United States, led Root to oppose certain provisions of Woodrow Wilson's League of Nations, especially the one that committed member states to take action against an aggressor. In the controversy over the Versailles treaty Root recommended that the Senate give its consent, but with important reservations. Wilson refused to make any compromise, and the treaty with the League was defeated in the Senate.

As to the World Court, which Root had long advocated, he participated in drawing up the plans and urged adhesion by the United States. This continuing effort and his participation as a delegate in the successful Washington Conference on the Limitation of Armaments in 1921 were Root's last services to peace. The failure of the United States to join the World Court was a great disappointment to him. He died in 1937 just before his ninety-second birthday.

The achievements that won Root the Peace Prize in 1913 have been somewhat overshadowed in today's histories of internationalism by his reservations about Wilson's League and the part he played in its defeat, He is generally recognized, however, as one of the ablest secretaries of state who ever occupied that office. The Good Neighbor policy he inaugurated is one of the brighter elements in American foreign policy, and Root's sense of the meaning of the Hague movement and his support for the slow development of international law and a world court perhaps accorded more closely to the level of international consciousness his fellow countrymen had reached in the early twentieth century than did Woodrow Wilson's more ambitious hopes.

BIBLIOGRAPHY

Primary Source

Root, Elihu. *Addresses on International Subjects.* Edited by Robert Bacon and James Brown Scott. Cambridge: Harvard University Press, 1916. Reprint. Freeport, N.Y.: Books for Libraries, 1969. One of eight volumes of Root's speeches and papers edited by Bacon and Scott and published by Harvard University Press from 1916 to 1925.

Secondary Sources

Herman, Sondra R. *Eleven against War: Studies in American Internationalist Thought.* Stanford, Calif.: Hoover Institution Press, 1969, chap. 2.

Jessup, Philip C. *Elihu Root.* 2 vols. New York: Dodd, Mead, 1938. The authoritative biography by an international jurist who knew him well.

Leopold, Richard. *Elihu Root and the Conservative Tradition.* Boston: Little, Brown, 1954.

"Root, Elihu." In *DAB.* Supp. 2.

Scott, James Brown. "Elihu Root." In *American Secretaries of State and Their Diplomacy.* Vol. 9. Edited by Samuel F. Bemis. New York: Knopf, 1929, pp. 193–282.

Toth, Charles W. "Elihu Root." In *An Uncertain Tradition: American Secretaries of State in the Twentieth Century.* Edited by Norman Graebner. New York: McGraw-Hill, 1961, chap. 3.

1913
Henri La Fontaine (1854–1943)

Belgium

International lawyer, politician, president of the International Peace Bureau for thirty-six years, scholar of internationalism, founder of the Union of International Associations, delegate to the League of Nations Assembly, first socialist peace laureate.

In awarding Henri La Fontaine the Peace Prize of 1913, the representative of the Nobel Committee called him "the true leader of the popular peace movement in Europe." He was that and more—"the true international man." La Fontaine was not only a pioneer scholar of internationalism; in his own person he embodied many of the movements that were expressions of the growing interrelationships between the peoples of the world.

He was a professor of international law, a longtime member of the Belgian senate who played an active role in the Interparliamentary Union, a moderate representative of international socialism, the author of substantive works on arbitration and peace, the organizer of a center of world documentation, of the Union of International Associations, and of a variety of other efforts to track and coordinate the internationalization of world culture, and an activist who attended almost all the prewar peace congresses and succeeded Fredrik Bajer as the head of the Commission of the International Peace Bureau. All this he had achieved when awarded the prize at the age of fifty-nine. He went on to serve as a link between the old peace movement and both the League of Nations and the postwar peace movement, heading the Peace Bureau until his death in 1943.

Henri Marie La Fontaine was born in Brussels in 1854. He studied law at the Free University of Brussels, winning his doctorate after he had already begun his legal career at the age of twenty-three at the Brussels Court of Appeal. He practiced law for the next sixteen years with great success, at the same time beginning to give his attention to problems of peace and to social questions.

These concerns led him into politics. La Fontaine became an active socialist, making speeches and writing, and he was one of the founders of the socialist paper, *La justice.* In 1895 he was elected to the senate as a socialist and served for thirty-six years, with only two interruptions. For fourteen of these years his fellow senators chose La Fontaine as secretary of the senate; for thirteen years he was one of the vice presidents. From 1904 to 1908 he served concurrently as a socialist member of the City Council of Brussels.

In the senate La Fontaine occupied himself with legislation to improve labor conditions and to reform education. He was always active in foreign affairs. He pushed arbitration bills and espoused the other issues that the peace movement was endorsing. After the war these included the League of Nations, the Kellogg-Briand and Locarno pacts, disarmament, and economic union with Luxembourg.

La Fontaine entered the international peace movement in the 1880s, prompted by the ubiquitous English pacifist Hodgson Pratt to organize the Belgian Society of Arbitration and Peace in 1889 on the model of Pratt's London organization. La Fontaine began to take part in the world peace congresses in that same year, when the prewar series of such meetings began. In 1894 he organized the congress held in Antwerp and was recognized as one of the chieftains of the international peace movement. He joined the other peace leaders as a member of the Commission of the International Peace Bureau, and after his election to the Belgian legislature, he took leadership in the Interparliamentary Union. La Fontaine was the only socialist among the pacifist elite. He was a very moderate socialist, however, a social reformer, not a revolutionary, and he was concerned more with international solidarity on all fronts, not just among the workers. In the gradual evolution toward world government that La Fontaine envisaged, the gatherings of the elected representatives of the people in the Interparliamentary Union were one step toward what Tennyson called "the Parliament of Man." After the First World War La Fontaine chaired the Interparliamentary Union commission on preparing a model world parliament.

The Nobel Committee presentation referred to La Fontaine as "one of the best informed men working for peace," which was no exaggeration. To begin with, there was his outpouring of writings, chief among which was his monumental case history of arbitration, referred to in the Nobel presentation as his "great documentary work." Then there were his bibliographies of peace literature, published by the International Institute of Bibliography, which he founded with his friend Paul Otlet in 1895. This so-called House of Documentation was established to file, index, collate, and provide information on major scientific work in every language of the world, an ambitious project that could be realized only in an age of computers. All the same, La Fontaine and Otlet, with some government support, developed a universal classification scheme and issued several bibliographies. Today UNESCO's bibliographies provide something of what La Fontaine dreamed of doing.

La Fontaine was one of those singular dreamers with administrative talents. "There is no one," as the Nobel Committee recognized, "who has contributed more to the organization of peaceful internationalism." Another institution to spring from his fertile brain was the Union of International Associations, which still exists today. La Fontaine was one of the first to have such a clear sense of the international culture that was evolving in the world, to interpret this effectively, and to try to give it institutional form.

When the German army invaded Belgium in 1914, La Fontaine fled to England and then to the United States, where he lived in Washington, D.C. He looked beyond the war, insisting that at its end there should be a peace congress of all the nations to adopt an international charter. His robust optimism, however, had been tempered by the unhappy march of events. "I foresee the renewal of . . . the secret bargaining behind closed doors," he wrote a friend. "Peoples will be as before, the sheep sent to slaughterhouses or to the meadows, as it pleases the shepherds." Still he went on propagandizing for a brighter future. In 1915 he published a plan for a world supreme court, and in the next year, his *Great Solution: Magnissima Charter,* in which he proposed a set of principles for international organization—not for a world state, which he realized would come only in the distant future, but for some sort of society of nations with international courts and provision for military sanctions.

In recognition of La Fontaine's work on postwar organization, he was appointed as a technical adviser to the Belgian delegation to the Peace Conference in 1919 and then as a delegate to the First Assembly of the League of Nations in 1920–21, where he spoke with deep conviction in favor of obligatory armed sanctions against any would-be aggressor prepared to violate the covenant of the League.

La Fontaine was a many-sided man. He was an ardent mountain climber (and bibliographer of "Alpinism"); he translated librettos from Wagner's operas; his lectures at the Free University of Brussels dealt not only with international law and peace issues but with modern art; and he was an early champion of women's rights.

He lived to see the horrors of war come once more to his country and to the world. He died in 1943 at the age of eighty-nine, thirty years after receiving the Nobel Peace Prize. He had kept up his labors for peace almost to the end.

BIBLIOGRAPHY

Primary Sources

La Fontaine, Henri. *Bibliographie de la paix et de l'arbitrage internationale.* Vol. 1, *Mouvement pacifique.* Monaco: Institut International de Bibliographie, 1904. The first major bibliography on the peace movement.

———. "The Existing Elements of a Constitution of the United States of the World." *International Conciliation* 47 (October 1911): 3–13.

———. *The Great Solution: Magnissima Charta.* Boston: World Peace Foundation, 1916. A proposal for a postwar international organization.

———. *Pasicrisie internationale: Histoire documentaire des arbitrages internationaux, 1794–1900.* Bern: Stämpfli, 1902. A case history of international arbitration.

Secondary Sources

Davis, Hayne, ed. *Among the World's Peacemakers.* New York: Progressive Publishing Co., 1907. Reprint. New York: Garland, 1972. With an introduction by Michael Lutzker. Chapter 30 is based on an interview with Lafontaine.

"La Fontaine, Henri." In *Biographie nationale.* Vol. 38. Brussels, Cols. 213–21.

"La Fontaine, Henri." In *MPL.*

1917

International Committee of the Red Cross

Switzerland

The only Peace Prize awarded during the First World War was to the International Committee of the Red Cross (ICRC), whose founder, Henry Dunant, had shared the first prize of 1901. The work of the Red Cross has been honored by a Peace Prize more frequently than any other organization. After 1917 there was another award for wartime activities in 1944, and in 1963 the one hundredth anniversary of the founding of the Red Cross was marked by the prize shared by the ICRC and the League of Red Cross Societies.

In 1863, the year after Dunant had published his *Memoir of Solferino* in Geneva, the Society of Public Welfare in that city appointed a committee to consider his proposals (1) for the establishment of relief societies to care for wounded soldiers and (2) for governments to come to an international agreement that would form the basis for the wartime work of these societies. This Geneva committee was presided over by Gen. Guillaume Dufour, who had in his youth served as an officer under Napoleon. The vice president was Gustave Moynier, a young advocate who had graduated with highest honors in law in Paris and was president of the Society of Public Welfare. Dunant was secretary, and the other two members were prominent surgeons.

The Geneva committee met for the first time on

17 February 1863 and decided to constitute itself as a permanent International Committee for the Relief of the Wounded, which later became the International Committee of the Red Cross. Its mission has always been international, but it has remained, as it was in the beginning, a private independent institution composed exclusively of Swiss nationals.

Its first international initiative was to convene a meeting in Geneva in October 1863, which was attended by thirty-one persons from sixteen European countries, including representatives of governments and philanthropic societies, medical experts, and other important personalities, many of them recruited by Dunant on a tour of Europe after the invitations had been sent out.

The conference resolved that relief committees should be established in each country to assist the army medical services in time of war, that the volunteers should be distinguished by armbands and flags with a red cross on a white ground, and that governments should enter an international treaty to guarantee the neutrality of volunteers wearing this emblem in war zones. It was also recommended that governments extend their patronage to the relief committees and facilitate their work and that in time of war belligerents should proclaim the neutrality of all medical personnel and facilities. The Geneva committee was recognized as the intermediary through which the national committees would communicate.

The delegates returned home to establish these societies and to report to their governments, while Dunant went to Paris to persuade the French government to issue the call for an intergovernmental meeting to adopt the proposed international treaty. Switzerland joined with France to convene this meeting in Geneva in August 1864, which produced the Convention for the Amelioration of the Condition of the Wounded in Armies in the Field. Known henceforth as the Geneva Convention, this was signed by the plenipotentiaries of twelve countries on 22 August 1864, with the protocol remaining open for the signatures of all other states.

For the first time in history the neutrality of those bearing medical service to the wounded in wartime was recognized in international law, with an international symbol, the red cross, to accord them legal protection. Meanwhile, a network of relief societies was being established in many countries, prepared to send volunteers to care for the wounded on the battlefield without distinction of nationality. Only two years had elapsed since Dunant had published his book proposing governmental and private action to such an end.

Dunant's great work was done, and after a time of great popularity, his personal financial troubles would lead to his resignation from the International Committee. Moynier succeeded Dufour as its head, and for half a century it was he who dominated the Red Cross movement, his greatest moment coming in 1906, when he presided over another congress in Geneva, when delegates from thirty governments gathered to amend and expand the Geneva Convention of 1864.

Meanwhile, the International Committee under his leadership had, on the one hand, worked to bring the Geneva Convention to the attention of governments and to develop the laws of war, and on the other, nurtured the development of the national societies, granting new ones official recognition. The policy was to maintain the independence of each society, but to keep them all in touch with one another and in conformance with the basic principles of the founders of the movement.

The Dutch society was the first to call itself a Red Cross Society, and others soon followed. In 1875 the Geneva committee changed its name to the International Committee of the Red Cross, and the conference it convened in Geneva in 1884 was called the Third International Conference of the Red Cross.

Just before the outbreak of the First World War, at the Ninth International Conference held in Washington, the first outside Europe, the decision was made to include services for prisoners of war in Red Cross activities. When the war began, the national societies were prepared to care for the wounded and sick, but it was the neutral ICRC that was in the best position to help prisoners of war by serving as an intermediary between them and the country that had captured them and by providing communications across the battle lines between them and their families at home.

This became the major activity of the ICRC during the war. When it set up the International Prisoner-of-War Agency in the first month of the war, it had no administrative staff or secretarial services of its own, and the agency had to be run by the nine members of the ICRC, who took turns on duty. Volunteers began to turn up, and in the first report it was recorded that "routine errands are performed by two Boy Scouts." Telegrams were sent to the Red Cross Societies of the belligerents announcing the opening of the agency, and within a few weeks the flow of inquiries and letters reached two to three thousand every day.

Larger offices had to be found, more staff engaged, and a system developed to classify all inquiries and information received about prisoners and internees, including death notices, and record them on separate index cards, filed alphabetically according to the names of individuals. When an inquiry card on someone turned up next to an information card on the same person, the information could then be sent to the inquirer. This was a monumental task. By the end of the war the files contained 4,895,000 index cards. The German section alone had 1.5 million. This information service was a precious link between a prisoner cut off from all knowledge of his family, who might have heard at most that he was "missing." The ICRC workers would have read Dunant's description of the dying soldier who had beseeched him, "Oh! sir, if you could write to my father, so that he could comfort my mother" and would have known what a holy service they were rendering through their little cards.

During the war the ICRC also dispatched delegates to inspect conditions in the camps for prisoners of war and internees, and the agency sent relief supplies comprising some 2 million individual parcels and 1,813 wagonloads. The ICRC also tried to overcome the many obstacles and to help civilians who were detained, deported, or held hostage.

Along with this concentration of effort on helping prisoners of war, the ICRC maintained its traditional responsibility of keeping belligerents aware of their obligations under the Geneva Conventions. On the basis of reports from its own delegates and from the national societies, reminders and protests of violations were regularly sent to the governments, unfortunately with little effect. The Nobel Committee could not be unaware of these efforts, but it was obviously the relief work for the prisoners of war that the committee had mostly in mind in deciding to award the ICRC the 1917 prize.

BIBLIOGRAPHY

Secondary Sources

Boissier, Pierre. *History of the International Committee of the Red Cross: From Solferino to Tsushima.* 1963. Geneva: Henry-Dunant Institute, 1985. With Durand (below), the authoritative history from the beginnings.

Buckingham, Clyde E. *For Humanity's Sake: The Story of the Early Development of the League of Red Cross Societies.* Washington, D.C.: Public Affairs Press, 1964.

Dunning, Henry W. *Elements for the History of the League of Red Cross Societies.* Geneva: League of Red Cross Societies, 1969.

Durand, André. *History of the International Committee of the Red Cross: From Sarajevo to Hiroshima.* 1978. Geneva: Henry-Dunant Institute, 1985. With Boissier (above) the authoritative history to 1945.

Forsythe, David F. *Humanitarian Politics: The International Committee of the Red Cross.* Baltimore: Johns Hopkins Press, 1977. History since 1945.

Huber, Max. *The Red Cross, Principles and Problems,* Geneva: ICRC, 1945. By the first German-Swiss on the ICRC, who became its fourth president in 1928.

ICRC. *Catalogue of Publications (1864–1980).* Geneva, 1980. Comprehensive; serves as a bibliography.

ICRC. *Inter Arma Caritas: The Work of the International Committee of the Red Cross during the Second World War.* 2d ed. Geneva, 1973. Excellent brief summary by Frédéric Siordet.

ICRC. *International Review of the Red Cross.* Published in Geneva, since 1919 in French, since 1961 also in English. Important articles on historical and current activities of the ICRC.

Joyce, James A. *Red Cross International and the Strategy of Peace.* London: Hodder & Stoughton, 1959. A well-written popular account.

See also the bibliography for Henry Dunant (1901).

2

The Peace Prize over the Years: 1919–39

When the Nobel Committee met early in 1919, the hostilities of the First World War had ended the previous November but the peace treaty was still to be written. Between 10 million and 13 million men had perished and about 20 million had been wounded. The great empires of Russia, Austria-Hungary, and Germany had collapsed, and Europe would never be the same again. From the republic across the Atlantic had come the material resources to help the armies of the Allies overcome the Central Powers and the assurance of its president that they were fighting a war to end all wars. President Wilson had come to Paris to make sure the peace treaty would incorporate his idealistic Fourteen Points, the last of which was the establishment of a League of Nations to preserve the peace.

The secretary of the Nobel Committee reported that Woodrow Wilson was the leading candidate. He had eleven nominations, with wide support from Western parliamentarians, international lawyers, and peace society leaders. The committee put him on the short list, along with the French internationalist Léon Bourgeois, the international jurists Heinrich Lammasch of Austria and Walther Schücking of Germany, and the Dutch pacifist, Benjamin de Jong van Beek en Donk.

When the committee reassembled to consider the reports of the advisers on these candidates, the Treaty of Versailles had been signed, and it was clear that it was not the "peace without victory" of which Wilson had talked, but rather a classic victor's peace. The League of Nations was a part of the treaty, to be sure, but the government of the new German Republic was to lose territory in Europe and overseas, to remain disarmed, to accept responsibility for Germany's having started the war, and to pay reparations for war damage. Allied soldiers were to be stationed in the German Rhineland for fifteen years.

There had been much criticism of Wilson, not just in the defeated countries, but among peace advocates and liberals in the West who felt that he had betrayed their confidence in him and their hopes for a lasting peace. This feeling was expressed within the Nobel Committee, as we know from a member's confidential notes recently made available in the archives of the Norwegian Nobel Institute. Halvdan Koht wrote that one of his colleagues was so opposed to Wilson that he threatened to resign if the committee were to give him the prize. The committee finally decided to reserve the prize for 1919, postponing the decision until the following year.

In 1920 Wilson was once again nominated with strong support, one of his nominators being a member of the Norwegian government. Chairman Løvland proposed that the committee pay tribute to the League of Nations by sharing the honors: Wilson could be given the 1919 prize and Bourgeois the award for 1920. The members were still divided, but the decision for the 1919 prize was finally made in Wilson's favor by a vote of three to two.

The response to the Wilson award was mixed. In general, now that the League was in operation, the reaction was favorable. The strongest criticism came from the German press, where German pacifists also protested, and the Austrian press declared that the prize should have gone to Herbert Hoover, whose American Relief Administration had organized a great program of food relief for Central and Eastern Europe after the war.

A few months after the American minister to Norway accepted the prize in Wilson's behalf on 10 December 1920, the Senate repudiated the president by rejecting the Versailles treaty. Bitterly, Wilson predicted that within a generation the world again would be at war.

This prediction, of course, came true, and the failure of the United States to join the League was one of the reasons for the League's weakness. Yet there seemed reason for hope in the later 1920s, a brief period of Franco-German reconciliation. This ended, however, with the world economic collapse and the unbridled nationalist and racist policies of Adolf Hitler in the 1930s. Throughout this period between the wars the decisions of the Nobel Committee clearly reflected the international situation of the moment.

The awards of 1921 and 1922 were hopeful, both related to the new international organization that had come into being. In 1921, as with the prize for Bourgeois in 1920, the award recognized the link between the prewar internationalist movement and the League. In a second all-Scandinavian decision (the first was the prizes to Arnoldson of Sweden and Bajer of Denmark in 1908) the committee honored the Swedish socialist leader Hjalmar Branting and the Norwegian secretary-general of the Interparliamentary Union, Christian Lange, both longtime peace advocates and now active as their country's delegates in Geneva.

In 1922 the committee paid tribute to the relief work of the League's high commissioner for refugees, the great Norwegian explorer Fridtjof Nansen. Nansen was a strong supporter of the League who had accepted this responsibility because he wanted to demonstrate that only such an international body could deal with such a world problem. This was the first award to an individual for humanitarian endeavor since the Dunant prize of 1901.

Between 1922 and 1926 the committee awarded no prizes. Despite the efforts at the League of such staunch supporters as Branting, Lange, and Nansen, the war mentality persisted in the early 1920s. Allied soldiers continued to occupy the Rhineland, and German reparations payments were set so high that Germany was declared in default. In 1923 French and Belgian troops marched into the Ruhr Valley, the center of the German coal and steel industry. The Germans responded with a campaign of passive resistance that prevented the French from operating the Ruhr mines and railroads at any profit to themselves, but that threw the whole of German society and economy into disarray. Passions flared on both sides of the Rhine, and the entire European economy suffered.

Finally the German government called off the passive resistance, and the French government agreed to refer the question of reparation payments to a committee of financial experts. The committee's recommendations, named the Dawes Plan after the American chairman, were accepted by all parties involved and were implemented in 1924. This was the first step toward Franco-German reconciliation after the war. It was followed by the Locarno pacts of 1925, which stabilized the frontiers between the two countries, and then by the entry of Germany into the League of Nations in 1926.

It now appeared that a new era of peace and good feeling had begun. The Nobel Committee waited until 1926 so that it could give recognition at the same time to all these achievements for the pacification of Europe by making awards to Charles Dawes and the three foreign ministers responsible for the Locarno agreements. The 1925 prize, which had been reserved, was divided between Dawes and Austen Chamberlain of Britain, which neatly left the 1926 prize to be shared by Aristide Briand of France and Gustav Stresemann of Germany.

In 1927 the committee decided to highlight the Franco-German reconciliation in public opinion which it declared had made possible the Locarno pacts. It named the veteran French and German pacifists, Ferdinand Buisson and Ludwig Quidde, who had worked in the peace movement long before the war and more recently had been active in efforts for understanding between their two countries.

In the next years the committee was watching the hopeful developments in public opinion and diplomacy that led to a treaty renouncing war, which was signed by fifteen nations in Paris in 1928 and ratified by the U.S. Senate in early 1929. This was the Kellogg-Briand Pact, for which the committee gave the 1929 prize to Secretary of State Frank B. Kellogg in 1930 and named as corecipient of the 1931 prize Nicholas Murray Butler, president of Columbia University and of the Carnegie Endowment for International Peace, for his leadership in the popular movement.

The Kellogg prize was the last for the statesmen of this period of hopefulness. The 1930 award went to Archbishop Nathan Söderblom of Sweden, who worked for peace through ecumenical cooperation. It was the first Peace Prize for a churchman. In 1931 the great humanitarian and peace activist Jane Addams shared the prize with Butler. She was the only woman laureate since the award to Bertha von Suttner in 1905. It is difficult to explain this delay without suspecting some prejudice on the part of committee members. Addams had been frequently nominated and had reached the short list four times before the year of her award, three times in years when the committee found no one worthy of the prize.

The international events of the following years gave little ground for hope. In 1931, the year of the

Butler-Addams awards, Japan advanced in Manchuria, and the failure of the League of Nations to resist Japanese aggression marked the beginning of the League's decline. In 1932 the long-awaited disarmament conference of the League finally convened. Its covenant had been framed with the assumption that "the enforcement by common action of international obligations" would be the main purpose of national armaments, which could consequently be limited. Collective security would precede a reduction of armaments. But since the League had never become an instrument through which member states could find security, each state had to provide for its own security by its own arms. The French continued to advocate the establishment of an international force, which Britain opposed. The main object of Germany, as a disarmed nation, was to gain equality and rearm. Over this claim to equality Germany temporarily withdrew from the conference. Soon afterward the committee decided to reserve the prize for 1932.

In 1933 Hitler came to power in Germany and announced the nation's definitive withdrawal from the disarmament conference and from the League itself. For all intents and purposes, this ended the conference, although there was one general meeting in 1934 and the conference was never officially concluded. In 1933 the committee decided to withhold the 1932 prize and to reserve the prize for 1933. This was awarded the following year to Norman Angell, a prominent British publicist for peace, whose most influential book had been published more than two decades earlier. The prize for 1934 the committee gave in a gracious gesture to the British statesman Arthur Henderson, chairman of the disarmament conference who was still trying vainly to keep it alive.

The prize for 1935 was reserved. This was the year when Hitler announced German rearmament in violation of the Versailles treaty and Mussolini's Italy invaded Ethiopia. For once British and French interests seemed to coincide, and the League declared Italy an aggressor and voted economic sanctions. The sanctions were applied halfheartedly, however, and by May 1936, the Italians completed the conquest of Ethiopia. The next month the League Assembly voted the end of sanctions, and with this action any hope that the League of Nations could preserve peace came to an end. In the same year of 1936 Hitler remilitarized the Rhineland in abrogation of both Versailles and Locarno, intervened along with Italy on the side of General Franco in the Spanish civil war, and formed the Rome-Berlin Axis.

The last Peace Prizes of the 1930s were made in the shadow of war. In 1936, after a worldwide campaign in behalf of the German publicist Carl von Ossietzky, who had been incarcerated and brutally mistreated in a concentration camp for his antimilitarist writings, the committee courageously awarded him the price for 1935. As if to balance this unprecedented action, the committee at the same time awarded the 1936 prize to Saavedra Lamas, foreign minister of Argentina, who had been active in the League but was more successful as mediator of the dispute between Paraguay and Bolivia. At the request of Lamas, American secretary of state Cordell Hull had strongly supported his candidacy.

In 1937 the committee finally honored Britain's Robert Cecil, Viscount Cecil of Chelwood, who had done yeoman service for the League since its inception and who had been on the committee's short list four times before. Christian Lange, in his presentation speech for the committee, spoke of "the fearful winter which we are experiencing in our international life." He compared Lord Cecil's lifelong work for peace to the efforts of the mythological Sisyphus, doomed in Hades forever to push uphill a heavy stone which always rolled down again. Lange cited the words of a Danish poet extolling Sisyphus for "not the deed fulfilled, but tireless exertion." Lange's grim classical allusion speaks volumes for the mood of the committee that year.

In 1938 after Germany's annexation of Austria and diplomatic victory at Munich, the committee turned from political and pacifist candidates to make a humanitarian award to the International Nansen Office for Refugees in the last year of its mandate. This agency had been established in 1930 to carry on Nansen's refugee work after his death, with the optimistic expectation that it would be completed in 1938.

Looking at our second period as a whole, it was a troubled time for the prize. In 1919 when the period began, the prize was reserved because of questions about the peace treaty; in 1939 when it ended, the prize was withheld because the peace had failed. During this period the committee postponed a decision ten times, deciding after five of these to award no prize at all.

Yet there was no dearth of good candidates, even by the committee's own standards. No prize was given in 1923, for example, although two candidates who were on the short list, Jane Addams and Lord Cecil, were to be awarded the prize later and had already made major contributions to peace. President Tomáš Masaryk of Czechoslovakia and Secretary of State Charles Evans Hughes, both frequently nominated and given special consideration, were also on the short list for 1923. Masaryk had made it first in 1913 and was to be on it for the fifth time in 1936. The year 1924 was also skipped, with Addams and Cecil once again candidates, as well as Buisson, Quidde, and the Quakers, who all got later prizes, and Hughes and James Brown Scott, the American jurist, who made the short list four times between 1917 and 1937.

The individual record holder in the just-missed category was Count Coudenhove-Kalergi, the indomitable proponent of European unity. He was on the short list six times between 1931 and 1937. The all-time record holder for the first two periods of the prize was the Interparliamentary Union, which was on the short list eight times between 1901 and 1938.

Other distinguished candidates who were given special consideration in the second period three times or more were: Walther Schücking (five); President Giuseppe Motta of Switzerland (four); Carl Lindhagen, lord mayor of Stockholm (four); Cordell Hull (four); J. B. Scott (three); Ramsay MacDonald, the British statesman (three); Charles Evans Hughes (three); Professor Théodore Ruyssen, the French pacifist (three); Lord Baden-Powell, founder of the Boy Scouts (three); and Prince Carl of Sweden (three).

In 1933 when the Nobel Committee announced that the prize for that year would be reserved, the dispatch in the *New York Times* explained that "no statesman in the world had achieved anything worthy of the honor." And indeed, among statesmen was where the committee was looking for its laureates throughout the second period. Of the twenty individual awards, more than half went to men who were holding or who had held governmental positions. One third of them were in high office at the time. Wilson was still president, Branting was prime minister of Sweden, and the others were foreign ministers. In contrast, during the first period of the prize, only two major statesmen received awards, Theodore Roosevelt and Elihu Root.

The prizes to the statesmen of the Locarno and Kellogg pacts illustrate the problems involved in celebrating diplomatic achievements in the glow of the moment. These treaties have not stood the test of time very well nor the documentary investigations of later historians. It was the statesman awards, however, that brought a new prominence to the prize in the interwar years. Many of the earlier laureates had been little known or of little interest to the general public. Beginning in the 1920s the laureates made better newspaper copy. It was even newsworthy when the committee decided not to award the prize.

The clearest indication of the position in the world the prize had attained was provided by the Ossietzky award in 1936. Ossietzky's comrades in Paris who organized the campaign in his behalf saw the prize as a means of striking a blow at Hitler in world opinion, whether or not it would bring about Ossietzky's freedom. They understood that this was a way to speak to the conscience of the world more effectively than through general appeals against Nazi atrocities. In the outcome, the award to a pacifist who was a victim of the concentration camps gave the Peace Prize a new dimension that was to be fully understood by Nobel Committees only years later in their human rights awards. In 1936, because of understandable political reasons, Chairman Stang in his speech of presentation emphasized Ossietzky's struggle against militarism and war and did not even refer to how he had been made to suffer for these convictions. But never before had the Nobel Peace Prize so caught the attention of the world.

Even so, the number of nominations did not perceptibly increase. Throughout the 1930s the secretary of the committee sent out about eight hundred notices each year soliciting proposals. Less than two hundred communications would be received, which yielded about forty valid nominations. The organizers of the Ossietzky campaign found that with their appeals to likely nominators they needed to send full information about the procedure of submitting proposals, and they astutely included a sample letter of nomination, with directions for when and where to send it.

At this midpoint of our survey, a few figures may be of interest. Between 1901 and 1939 forty-one prizes were awarded, thirty-eight to individuals and three to institutions. In this period, the last for which the archives are open, we know that 159 individuals and 29 institutions were given special consideration by the committee.

1919
Woodrow Wilson (1856–1929)

United States

Wartime and peacemaking president of the United States, 1913–21, primary force in establishment of the League of Nations.

Of all the statesmen who have won the Peace Prize, Woodrow Wilson would seem among the strongest choices. Without him it is very doubtful that an international organization would have been established after the First World War. Wilson achieved this objective, however, by attaching the League of Nations to the Treaty of Versailles, which was not at all the "peace without victory" he had promised, nor was it consistent with the liberal spirit of his Fourteen Points, on the basis of which Germany had agreed to an armistice. By the terms of that treaty, not only did Germany lose territory in Europe and overseas, but foreign troops were stationed on German soil, and the nation was required to acknowledge responsibility for starting the war and agree to pay reparations. Wilson was accused of betrayal both by the Germans, including German pacifists, and by liberals on both sides of the Atlantic.

This criticism of Wilson was also voiced in the Nobel Committee. He was first nominated in 1918, before the war ended, but that year the committee decided there would be no prize. In 1919 the committee discussed his candidacy after the the Treaty of Versailles was signed. We know from notes made by one of the members that there was strong disagreement in the committee, which finally decided to reserve the prize for the next year. In 1920, when the committee took up his candidacy again, the League was now in existence and Wilson had sacrificed his health in a vain effort to secure his country's adhesion. He had worldwide support for the prize. Nominations had been made by members of the Norwegian government and of the Swedish Interparliamentary group and by French pacifists, Mexican senators, and Balkan diplomats. Nevertheless, it was only by a majority of one that the committee decided to give the 1919 prize to Woodrow Wilson.

We do not know details of the discussion among the members of the committee, but we can assume that they considered the two major areas in which their adviser supplemented his report of the previous year: Wilson's personal diplomacy in the peace negotiations in Paris, which had been severely criticized in a book just published by an expert attached to the British delegation, and his struggle with the Senate to get the treaty approved. The two main questions that must be raised in any evaluation of Wilson as a peacemaker are, in fact, these: did he make too many compromises at Paris, and did he make too few compromises at home?

Historians have naturally been divided in their assessments, but they are generally kinder to Wilson in considering his performance at Paris. In negotiating with the war leaders of France and Great Britain, Clemenceau and Lloyd George, Wilson was dealing with wily politicians of far more experience with European realities than he had, and more important, he was confronting age-old passions and hatreds that had been refired in the furnace of war. Lloyd George had just won an election promising to squeeze the Germans like an orange "until the pips squeaked," and Clemenceau, who himself had seen Germany invade his country twice in his lifetime, represented a national determination to impose such terms on Germany that it would never happen again.

In the face of such currents of national feeling, Wilson reluctantly compromised his principles in order to secure within the treaty an agreement to establish an international organization to preserve the peace. The Covenant of the League, as adopted, included provisions for united action against an aggressor state, for reduction of armaments, and, most important of all in the light of the harsh terms imposed upon Germany, for revision of treaties.

Wilson cannot be faulted for the unwillingness of other statesmen to make use of the peace machinery of the League. On the other hand, his failure to bring the United States into the League deprived the peace forces at Geneva of an influence that would most likely have been exerted on the side of moderation and reconciliation. To understand Wilson's responsibility for this outcome, reference must be made to his background and personality.

Thomas Woodrow Wilson was born in Staunton, Virginia, in 1856, son and grandson of Presbyterian ministers, and was brought up as a firm believer in that faith. He graduated from Princeton University in 1879 and took a law degree at the University of Virginia; but he found the practice of law (and lawyers) not to his liking, so he entered upon graduate study in history and political science at Johns Hopkins. After receiving a doctorate, he taught at Bryn Mawr and Wesleyan colleges and was then appointed professor of jurisprudence and political economy at Princeton. His scholarship was highly regarded, and he was a very effective lecturer, having trained himself in oratory since boyhood.

In 1902 Wilson became president of Princeton and made a national reputation as an educational reformer. A controversy arose over his policies, in which Wilson first demonstrated that inflexible unwillingness to compromise that was such a deep part of his nature. He was already prepared to resign from Princeton when New Jersey Democratic politicians, seeing him as a likely reform candidate, asked him to run for governor. Because Wilson had always been interested in participating in politics, he accepted and was elected governor of New Jersey in 1910. Two years later similar circumstances propelled him into national politics, and he was nominated as the Democratic candidate for the presidency. William H. Taft, the incumbent, and Theodore Roosevelt split the Republican vote, and Wilson won the election.

After two years of implementing important domestic reforms, Wilson directed his major attention to foreign affairs when war broke out in Europe. At first he tried to maintain American neutrality and offered mediation to the belligerents, but in vain. In 1916 he was reelected on the slogan, "He kept us out of war." Forces of sentiment, economics, and geopolitics were drawing the United States to the side of the Allies, however, and when Germany embarked on a policy of unrestricted submarine warfare, in what appeared to be a clear violation of international law, Wilson asked Congress for a declaration of war, which was issued in April 1917.

Wilson proved himself an able war leader. He presided over an effective mobilization of the country's resources for the war effort, and his eloquent pronouncements on world peace gave the Americans a worthy cause to fight for and provided new inspiration for the war-weary Allies.

In January 1918, Wilson presented to Congress his Fourteen Points, declaring that "the program of the world's peace . . . is our . . . only possible program." The first five points were general: "open covenants of peace, openly arrived at," freedom of the seas, removal of economic barriers, limitation of armaments, recognition of the interests of native populations in the adjustment of colonial claims. The greatest number of points referred to the evacuation of occupied territories and to territorial settlements, where the principle of self-determination was to be applied. The fourteenth point called for the establishment of "a general association of nations . . . under specific covenants for the purpose of affording mutual guarantees of political independence and territorial integrity to great and small states alike."

It was principally to secure this fourteenth point that Wilson went to Paris, the first president to leave the country, and it was for this that he was willing to modify certain of the other thirteen. In the United States certain Republican senators led the opposition to elements of Wilson's League. When the president left Paris for home, one of his closest advisers urged him "to meet the Senate in a conciliatory spirit" and to treat the senators "with the same consideration he had used with his foreign colleagues." Wilson's reply was succinct: "I have found one never gets anything in this life that is worthwhile without fighting for it."

Wilson was far more prepared to meet foreign statesmen, whom he had to treat as equals, with a conciliatory spirit than he was with American politicians, toward whom he was inclined to act condescendingly, thinking they served an aim less noble than his own. His relatively short path to the presidency had not given him much experience with the rough-and-tumble of political life. He had a religious conviction that he was on the high road of morality, and once his mind was made up on an issue as to where the right lay, he stood fast. In the matter of the League of Nations there could be no question as to what was right. It was "the main object of the peace . . . the hope of the world." Moreover, Wilson's enthusiastic reception by the crowds in the Allied capitals he visited before the meetings in Paris began further convinced him that the peoples of the world were with him in his crusade.

Wilson was probably correct in his feeling that at the end of the war the majority of thinking Americans favored some kind of League of Nations. But they were never to vote on it as a single issue. What Wilson failed to take sufficiently into account was that the votes he needed were those of two-thirds of the Senate, which was required to approve a treaty. It was a major error not to include among his peace commissioners for Paris one eminent Republican who could have eased his relations with the Senate. An obvious choice would have been the Nobel laureate Elihu Root, former secretary of state and senator, head of the American movement for international law and closely associated with the effort to build a juridical order on the basis of the work of the Hague Conferences. Wilson did not like lawyers, he scoffed at the Hague efforts, and he dismissed Root as a "reactionary."

A second major error was Wilson's making his peace policies a partisan issue in the congressional election of 1918, which returned a Republican-controlled Congress to Washington. In a parliamentary form of government, such a vote would have turned Wilson out of office. As it was, the election results alienated possible Republican supporters of the League in Congress and weakened Wilson's hand in Paris.

When he finally presented the finished treaty to the Senate in July 1919, Wilson was confident that he had so intertwined the League with the treaty that the Senate would have no other choice but to accept it if peace with Germany was to be concluded. He disregarded the possiblity that the Senate could accomplish this by a separate resolution, which is what eventually happened.

In the Senate a small number of "Irreconcilables" were absolutely opposed to any kind of League. A majority of Republican senators, however, were prepared to vote for the League, but only with certain reservations, which Root had helped work out and which were designed to preserve the United States' independence of action, rejecting any obligation to join in armed action against an aggressor. To Wilson this obligation was the heart of the Covenant, and he refused the reservations.

In order to bring the pressure of public opinion to bear upon the Senate, Wilson decided to make a speaking tour across America. He had been ill in Paris, he was under great stress, and his physician warned him that such a tour could endanger his life. Wilson was determined, however. He said that he had sent young men to die for this great cause, and he must do his duty. In twenty-two days he covered eight thousand miles, making thirty-two major addresses and eight minor ones. His spirit was strong, his eloquence was resounding, but his body could not bear the strain. In Pueblo, Colorado, on 25 September 1919, Wilson gave what was to be his last public speech. His final words were an affirmation of his faith: "There is one thing that the American people always rise to . . . and that is the truth of justice and of liberty and of peace. We have accepted that truth and we are going to be led by it, and it is going to lead us, and through us the world, out into pastures of quietness and peace."

Afterwards on the train he collapsed and had to be brought back to Washington, where he suffered a stroke that left him an invalid for the rest of his life. His mind was still clear, however, and when the votes were taken in the Senate on the League, he ordered the Democrats to oppose any reservations. There could be no compromise. Consequently, the Democrats and the Irreconcilables voted together against those in favor of joining the League with reservations, and the United States remained outside the new international organization.

Wilson's illness prevented him from properly exercising the powers of the presidency during his remaining months in office. Thereafter he lingered on in retirement until February 1924, certain until the end that he had acted correctly in his struggle for the League and that eventually that which was right would triumph.

Wilson recognized that what he had achieved at Paris was no final answer to the problem of war. His telegram of acceptance to the Nobel Committee referred to Nobel's "far-sighted wisdom" in arranging for continuing awards:

> If there were but one such prize, or if this were to be the last, I could not of course accept it. For mankind has not yet been rid of the unspeakable horror of war. . . . it is the better part of wisdom to consider our work as only begun. It will be a continuing labor. . . . There is indeed a peculiar fitness in the grouping of these Nobel rewards. The cause of peace and the cause of truth are of one family. Even as those who love science and devote their lives to physics or chemistry, even as those who would create new and higher ideals for mankind in literature, even so with those who love peace, there is no limit set. Whatever has been accomplished in the past is petty compared to the glory and promise of the future.

In this great work for peace Wilson had wanted his country to take the lead. But the United States was not yet prepared to take the moral leadership that he envisioned. Only after a second terrible war was the nation prepared not only to help build an international organization but this time to become a major participant in its work.

BIBLIOGRAPHY

Primary Sources

Wilson, Woodrow. *The Public Papers of Woodrow Wilson.* Edited by Ray Stannard Baker and William E. Dodd. 6 vols. New York: Harper, 1925–26.

———. *The Papers of Woodrow Wilson.* Edited by Arthur S. Link and others. 53 vols. Princeton: Princeton University Press, 1966–. In progress.

Secondary Sources

Bailey, Thomas A. *Woodrow Wilson and the Peacemakers.* New York: Macmillan, 1947. Two of his earlier books combined. Well written and provocative.

Cooper, John Milton, Jr. *The Warrior and the Priest: Woodrow Wilson and Theodore Roosevelt.* Cambridge: Harvard University Press, 1983. Comparative biography.

Ferrell, Robert H. *Woodrow Wilson and World War I, 1917–21.* New York: Harper, 1985. Highly recommended.

Gardner, Lloyd G. *Safe for Democracy: The Anglo-American Response to Revolution 1913–1923.* Oxford: Oxford University Press, 1984.

Keynes, John Maynard. *The Economic Consequences of the Peace.* New York: Harcourt, Brace, 1920. Highly critical of Wilson and of the treaty, by an economist with the British delegation. Used by the Nobel Committee's adviser in his report on Wilson.

Kuehl, Warren. F. *Seeking World Organization: The United States and International Organization to 1920.* Nashville, Tenn.: Vanderbilt University Press, 1969.

Levin, N. Gordon. *Woodrow Wilson and World Politics.* New York: Oxford University Press, 1968.

Link, Arthur S., ed. *Woodrow Wilson and a Revolutionary World 1913–1921.* Chapel Hill: University of North Carolina Press, 1982. Link is the leading Wilson scholar; he has worked for years on the publication of his papers and a multivolume authoritative bibliography. This book presents papers from a symposium at Princeton.

———. *Woodrow Wilson: Revolution, War and Peace.* Arlington Heights, Ill.: Harlan Davidson, 1979.

Seymour, Charles. "Wilson, Woodrow." In *DAB.* Vol. 20.

Walworth, Arthur. *Wilson and His Peacemakers.* New York: Norton, 1986.

———. *Woodrow Wilson.* 2d rev. ed. Boston: Houghton Mifflin, 1965. Pulitzer Prize–winning biography.

1920

Léon Bourgeois (1851–1925)

France

Spiritual father of League of Nations, lawyer, legislator, cabinet minister, prime minister, statesman, scholar; represented France at both Hague Conferences, at 1919 peace conference, and at Council of League of Nations; member, Permanent Court of Arbitration.

Léon Bourgeois, who has been called the spiritual father of the League of Nations, represented the continuity between the League and the pre-1914 movement for an international order, centering around the Hague Conferences. As chairman of the French delegation to both Hague Conferences, he was a leading spirit in the effort to extend the practice of international arbitration by progressing from a panel of arbiters to a court of judges. He was one of the few government officials of high rank with a clear sense of the evolution toward international order that was taking place in the midst of the anarchy of the period. He entitled his collected speeches, published in 1910, *Pour la Société des Nations* (the French term for the League of Nations). During the war he worked for the establishment of a league, and at the peace conference he represented France on the commission, chaired by Woodrow Wilson, that was charged with writing the Covenant. In 1920 he was unanimously elected the first president of the Council of the League, and in the same year he presided over the Advisory Committee of jurists that planned the World Court. That was also the year in which he became president of the French Senate and received the Nobel Peace Prize.

In his own country Bourgeois's remarkable public career spanned almost half a century, in the course of which he occupied almost every important office except the presidency of the Republic, which he probably could have held as well if he had not twice declined to run.

Bourgeois was born in Paris in 1851, the son of a clockmaker, and he lived there most of his life. As a twenty-year-old he interrupted his schooling to serve in the artillery during the Franco-Prussian War and then returned to take his law degree at the University of Paris. His extraordinary talents equipped him for a variety of careers. He studied Hinduism and Sanskrit and could have become a distinguished scholar. He loved the arts, knew music well, practiced sculpture, and liked to draw amusing caricatures of his friends and colleagues. His ambition and social conscience, however, directed him toward public life, for which he was especially well fitted by his oratorical skills and his administrative capacities. After briefly practicing law, he entered government service when he was twenty-five, moved up through a series of bureaucratic posts, and finally was appointed chief commissioner of the Paris police in 1887, at the age of thirty-six.

The next year he was elected to the Chamber of Deputies, defeating a leading candidate of the Right. He remained in the legislature until shortly before his death, as deputy from 1888 to 1905 (he became president of the chamber in 1902) and as senator from 1905 to 1923 (he was president of the Senate from 1920 to 1923). For many years he was the leading orator of his party, the middle-class Radical Socialists.

Bourgeois frequently served in the cabinet. At various times he held the portfolios of justice, education, public works, and foreign affairs, and he was briefly premier, refusing repeated invitations to form a government. In these positions he effected social reform, accomplishing major improvements in the educational system and working for labor and health legislation. Always an intellectual as well as an administrator, Bourgeois developed a social philosophy that he sought to implement as a government minister and a legislator. This was formulated in his book *Solidarité,* published in 1897, in which Bourgeois stressed the evolving conception of solidarity in the family, the nation, and the international community. The volume went through a number of editions before the war and is considered to have been the most influential work of its kind among French social thinkers of the time.

In 1899 Bourgeois emerged as a leader in the international peace movement, when, as the head of the French delegation, he chaired the Commission on Arbitration at the First Hague Conference, which produced the Convention for the Pacific Settlement of International Disputes. When the Permanent Court of Arbitration was organized, he was named a member of the tribunal.

Bourgeois also led the French delegation at the Second Hague Conference and chaired the working group on arbitration, this time attempting to secure an agreement to make submission of certain cases to the Hague Court mandatory. So strenuously did he labor for this objective that another participant called Bourgeois the "living embodiment of obligatory arbitration." The most that could be achieved at the conference, however, was a resolution endorsing the principle that differences over the intepretation and application of treaties should be submitted to arbitral procedures. The conference did agree that a third meeting should be convened in the future. Bourgeois was firmly convinced that the Hague system of regular international peace conferences and a developing arbitral tribunal meant that the sovereign states were moving in the direction of peaceful association, toward what he called "La Société des Nations," the society or community of nations, in keeping with his solidarist social philosophy.

For Bourgeois the coming of the war in 1914 was a violent interruption in this process. Just as Germany had opposed arbitration at The Hague, now that country had begun another war and started off with the violation of an international treaty by invading neutral Belgium. Germany was clearly on the side of international lawlessness; France had to be on the side of international law. The German attack on France, the second Bourgeois had experienced in his lifetime, was convincing evidence that France's security could be achieved only through an international community based on justice. "We must see things as they are," he wrote in 1916. "We, in France, are not from the point of view of birth rate and material strength, at the same stage of development as, for example, our enemies." A balance of power policy could result only in the triumph "of the greatest number, and the most brutal . . . not in the triumph of the noblest." Only a policy of justice could give France peace and security, but "there will be no policy of justice if the League of Nations is not set up."

During the war Bourgeois was minister of state. In January 1918, he chaired an official commission on proposals for a postwar association of nations, which had its counterpart in the United States and Britain. With d'Estournelles de Constant he presented a plan to the French government, which differed in important respects from the conceptions of Wilson and the British. In the commission that drafted the Covenant of the League, Bourgeois urged building on the work of the Hague Conferences by providing for a system of obligatory arbitration and an international court of justice with power to enforce decisions through sanctions, which could be diplomatic, juridical, economic, or even military.

France wanted an international organization that could serve as the instrument of French security. But military sanctions went far beyond what the Anglo-Saxon powers could accept. Nor could Bourgeois persuade Wilson or Lord Cecil, the British delegate, to make any reference in the preamble of the Covenant to the work of the Hague Conferences as the forerunner of the League. Wilson firmly resisted any association of his League with what he regarded as the great failure of the Hague Conferences to preserve the peace. He privately referred to Bourgeois as "the leader of the talkfest at The Hague in 1899." To Wilson "the whole business was wishy-washy." After Wilson prevailed upon the commission to vote down Bourgeois's last attempt to give any recognition to the Hague Conferences, Bourgeois was heard to say, almost in tears, "My life's work is wiped out!"

The British did persuade Wilson to include in the Covenant a provision for a world court, and here the Hague precedent was clear. The Council of the League appropriately asked Bourgeois to preside over the sessions of the Advisory Committee of international jurists that in 1920 drew up the plan for the new court. In December of that year the Nobel Committee gave prizes to both Wilson (for 1919) and Bourgeois. It was an interesting juxtaposition, for Bourgeois was the "living embodiment" of the continuity with the internationalist movement of the past, which Wilson, convinced that he was charting new seas, denied.

Bourgeois was ill and unable to travel to Norway

to give his Nobel address, but in December 1922, he sent a carefully considered "Communication," developing at length his ideas on peace. Although the war appeared to be a negation of hopes for peace, the victory of free nations "had been, above all, a victory for law and order, and for civilization itself." Above all, the League of Nations, "heralded in 1899 and 1907 by the Hague Peace Conferences" became in 1919 "a living reality." The question was whether this could "furnish us at last with a stable instrument of peace." Drawing upon his theory of solidarity and extolling reason, which had led men upward from barbarism, Bourgeois answered positively.

He then attempted to clear up certain misconceptions, declaring that the concept of patriotism is not incompatible with that of humanity and that "the nation is and can be no more than the vital basic unit of any international league." Such an institution would have to be based upon the sovereignty of each nation. It would not be a "superstate" imposing its will on member states or an organization that would involve a state in military operations to which it had not given its consent, as "our American friends" feared.

Bourgeois recognized that basic to the success of an international organization is "a community of thought and feeling . . . among the associated states" that shares "a common understanding of the principles of international order." To help create this community of understanding there must be intellectual cooperation. To this end Bourgeois proposed to the League of Nations Assembly of 1921 a resolution for the establishment of a Commission of Mutual Intellectual Cooperation, which the Assembly adopted, foreshadowing the development of UNESCO later.

Bourgeois concluded that the path to peace was still long, but with the League of Nations the road toward the final goal was clearly marked. "If we consider how far we have come since the dawn of history, then our hope will gather strength enough to become a true and unshakable faith."

In 1923, ailing and growing blind, Bourgeois retired from the Senate; he died two years later at the age of seventy-four. France honored him with a public funeral, and in 1933 in the presence of the president of the Republic a monument was raised to the memory of Léon Bourgeois, "the apostle of solidarity and peace."

BIBLIOGRAPHY

Primary Sources

Bourgeois, Léon. *Pour la Société des Nations.* Paris: Charpentier, 1910. On the Hague Peace Conferences of 1899 and 1907 and their implications.

———. *Solidarité.* Paris: Colin, 1896. The important book on his social philosophy, amplified in later editions. The eleventh edition appeared posthumously in 1926.

Secondary Sources

"Bourgeois, Léon." In *BDI.*

Davis, Calvin, D. *The United States and the Second Hague Peace Conference.* Durham, N.C.: Duke University Press, 1975. Discusses the Hague movement for international law and arbitration, in which Bourgeois played a major role.

Hamburger, Maurice. *Léon Bourgeois, 1851–1925.* Paris: Librairie des Sciences Politiques, 1932.

Scott, James Brown. "Léon Bourgeois, 1851–1925." *American Journal of International Law* 19 (October 1925): 774–76.

1921
Hjalmar Branting (1860–1925)

Sweden

Founder and leader of Swedish Socialist party; legislator, cabinet minister, and premier; longtime peace advocate; as Swedish delegate at League of Nations, a strong supporter of disarmament; chairman of International Labor Organization, 1924.

The award of 1921, which Hjalmar Branting shared with Christian Lange, gave recognition to Branting's long service for peace and his more recent contributions at the League of Nations. Branting had been on the committee's short list twice before 1914. As early as 1885 he had helped organize one of the first peace societies in Sweden. Later, as the founding father of Swedish socialism, international peace was a central part of his platform. Norwegians were grateful for the role he played in their peaceful secession from the union with Sweden in 1905. It was in the following year, in fact, that the Nobel Committee first gave him special consideration for the prize. Branting was also a force for peace in the international socialist movement before and during the war. He worked for Swedish neutrality and then for Sweden's entrance into the League of Nations. Thereafter, as Swedish delegate he took significant leadership in the disarmament effort and in the resolution of a number of international conflicts.

Karl Hjalmar Branting was born in Stockholm in 1860, the son of one of the founders of the Swedish school of gymnastics. He made a brilliant record in his science courses at the University of Uppsala, and after completing his studies in 1882 he became assistant to the director of the Stockholm Observatory.

His priorities changed, however, as he became more and more concerned about social conditions. As a result of his reading and contacts with prominent Marxists during his European travels, Branting decided to abandon his scientific career and work for socialism. He became editor of the *Social-Demokraten* and kept up his association with this newspaper for over three decades, using it to educate the Swedish working class in socialism.

In 1889 Branting was the chief organizer of the Social Democratic Labor party, which adopted a program looking toward peaceful evolution toward socialism. The party's demands for universal suffrage, freedom of the press, an eight-hour day, free education, and social security were radical for the time but have long since become ordinary features of Swedish society. Other demands were never met: a single-chamber parliament and the elimination of the state church and the standing army. Branting always supported national defense, but he opposed large appropriations for defense at the expense of social services. What he wanted was a citizen militia on the Swiss model, such as the French socialist leader Jean Jaurès advocated. Branting pointed out that the workers would most strongly defend a country in which they shared political and economic benefits. Therefore, the most sensible defense policy meant social and political reform.

Branting was not only the publicist and theorist of Swedish socialism but its organizer and foremost orator. He formed workers' clubs, organized unions, and formulated strike strategy. In 1896 he was elected to the lower house of parliament from a working-class constituency, and he held his seat as long as he lived. For six years he was the only Social Democrat deputy. The party grew under his leadership until in 1917 it was strong enough to form a coalition with the Liberals, and Branting became a cabinet minister for the first time. Thereafter the Socialists came to replace the Liberals as the second major party, and finally, after Branting's death, they were dominant in the country for many years. Between 1920 and 1925 Branting was prime minister three times.

In the international socialist movement Branting firmly opposed the revolutionary socialists who held that the worker has no fatherland. His conviction that national self-determination is a prerequisite for the liberation of the working class led him to support Norwegian independence from Sweden. For a speech opposing the use of military force against Norway he was sentenced to three years in prison, although the sentence was later commuted to a fine. In 1905, with a growing workers' movement behind him, Branting was a major influence in the peaceful outcome of the conflict.

During the war Branting resisted upper-class militarists who pressed for intervention on the side of Germany. Although his sympathies were clearly with the Allies, he called for Sweden to remain neutral and to use that position to work for a democratic peace. He took a major role in the international socialist congress that met in Stockholm in 1917 to consider ways to bring the war to an end.

Branting severely criticized the Treaty of Versailles for its punitive provisions against Germany, but he took comfort from the many instances where the principle of national self-determination had been observed, and he threw all his weight into bringing Sweden into the League of Nations. He then represented his country in both the Assembly and the Council and played an outstanding role in attempting to make the League live up to the best hopes of its founders. In the first international conflict of importance submitted to the Council, Branting set an impressive example by loyally accepting the decision in favor of Finland over his own country. This strengthened his hand in his continuing effort to get the Council to act as mediator in other disputes. Branting's major disappointment with the League was its failure to take any action for disarmament, for which he, as a leading representative of the smaller powers, worked very hard.

Despite such disappointments and despite the terrible catastrophe of the recent war, Branting still was hopeful. In his Nobel address of 1922, Branting had to deal with the fundamental question: "As a result of the World War and of a peace whose imperfections and risks are no longer denied by anyone, are we not even further away from the great aspirations and hopes for peace and fraternity than we were one or two decades ago?"

His view was positive: "The signs of renewal are far too numerous and promising to allow of despair." He pointed to "the birthpangs of a new Europe," with the appearance of "new, free nations" and "the beginning development of a League of Nations"—despite its faults, not the least of which was it did not comprise all states, only a few. To remedy these faults Branting thought that the small states should work as a bloc. He envisaged such a coalition as a safeguard against domination of the League by the Great Powers. There were other forces in the world also working for peace, he reminded his hearers, of which the international trade union movement could be the most important.

In the last analysis, however, Branting pinned his hopes on the League. He recognized that "to create an organization which is in position to protect peace in this world of conflicting interests and egoistic wills is a frighteningly difficult task. But the difficulties must not hold us back." He concluded in the words of James Bryce that whatever the obstacles may be, we must go forward: "If the nations do not try to annihilate war, then war will annihilate them."

Branting died in Stockholm in 1925 at the age of sixty-five, his robust constitution worn out by a lifetime of labor for the welfare of his country and of the world.

BIBLIOGRAPHY

Secondary Sources

"Branting, Hjalmar." In *BDI.*

Höglund, Zeth. *Hjalmar Branting.* Stockholm: Tidens, 1949. Condensation of the standard two-volume biography published in 1928–29.

Jones, Shepherd. *The Scandinavian States and the League of Nations.* Princeton: Princeton University Press, 1939.

Tingsten, Herbert L. *The Swedish Social Democrats: Their Ideological Development.* 1941. Totowa, N.J.: Bedminister Press, 1973.

Verney, Douglas. *Parliamentary Reform in Sweden 1866–1921.* Oxford: Oxford University Press, 1957.

1921
Christian Lange (1869–1938)

Norway

Internationalist scholar and executive; secretary-general of the Interparliamentary Union, 1909–33; member of and adviser to the Norwegian delegation to the Assembly of the League of Nations, 1920–38.

The award to Christian Lange as corecipient with Hjalmar Branting in 1921 was the second prize for the chief executive of the Interparliamentary Union. In 1902 the committee had wanted to honor the union in the person of its first secretary-general, Albert Gobat; the award to his successor two decades later was for Lange himself. The committee, however, had to tread carefully in giving the prize to one of its own; he was not only a fellow countryman but the Nobel Committee's first secretary, the first director of its institute, and after 1909 its honorary adviser on the history of the international peace movement. But the committee members knew Lange's qualifications so well that after he was nominated by Danish and Swedish Interparliamentary Union members, they considered it unnecessary to call for a report on him by another adviser. Lange enjoyed a distinguished reputation among the world's peace advocates as a leading scholar on internationalism and more especially as the one who single-handedly had kept the Interparliamentary Union alive during the war years. When the committee met in 1921 to discuss the prize for that year, fresh in their minds would have been Lange's success in convening the first postwar conference of the union, as well as his outspoken speeches for disarmament as Norway's delegate to the League of Nations Assembly.

Christian Lous Lange was born in 1869 in the coastal city of Stavanger, son of an army engineer and grandson of a distinguished historian and archivist. He studied history and languages at the University of Christiana (Oslo) and also in universities in France and England, and started out as a teacher in secondary schools. His special competence in foreign languages led to a temporary assignment helping prepare the arrangements for the interparliamentary conference to be held in Christiana in 1899. He so impressed the Norwegian members with his administrative abilities that the next year he was appointed the first secretary of the newly formed Nobel Committee. He was then thirty-one, and it was the beginning of his internationalist career.

Lange set up procedures for the committee that are still in use. At first he wrote all the advisory reports himself. He organized the Norwegian Nobel Institute, putting together one of the best libraries in the world at the time on the peace movement and international politics. He wrote the annual reports to the parliament and assigned the reports on the candidates to all the advisers when others were later added to the committee's staff. Lange dreamed great dreams for the institute, and had there been interest in the committee and more resources available, he would have made the institute the first world center for peace research.

In 1907 Lange served as a technical adviser to the Norwegian delegation at the Second Hague Peace Conference. In 1909 he took his administrative talents to the Bureau of the Interparliamentary Union. Gobat, a deputy himself, had been volunteering his time since the establishment of the bureau in Bern in 1894 and since 1906 had also been serving as secretary-general of the International Peace Bureau. Now the Interparliamentary Bureau had outgrown Gobat's office in Bern, and Lange was engaged as a full-time salaried executive, his first assignment being to move the bureau to Brussels and reorganize its secretariat.

The union worked for peace and international understanding by strengthening relationships among the members of the parliaments of the world. Since the beginning the major emphasis had been upon promoting the use of international arbitration and, after 1899, in supporting the work of the Hague Conferences. Lange's responsibilities were to keep all the national groups in touch with one another through visits and publications and to arrange for the annual meetings and the reports of their proceedings. Relations with governments were restricted to sending official communications and to correspondence about the subsidies that some of them contributed to help maintain the bureau.

When Germany invaded Belgium in 1914, Lange moved the bureau to his own home in Christiana. The funds in Brussels were impounded by the Germans, and subsidies from most governments and national groups were halted. Lange was able to borrow from the Carnegie Endowment for International Peace, but he carried on much of the work of the union with his own resources. He continued most of the correspondence in his own hand, keeping up what international connections were possible. Since the Scandinavian countries were neutral, Lange was able to arrange for their parliamentary groups to meet together annually during the war, and they worked out proposals for postwar international organization. After the war ended, Lange convened the Council of the union in Geneva in 1919, arranged for the first postwar general meeting there in 1921, and moved the seat of the union to that city to be closer to the League of Nations.

Lange remained until 1933 as secretary-general of the union, whose major emphasis now was the support of the League. For almost a quarter of a century he had been the guiding spirit of this international body. He was a superb administrator with a seemingly infinite capacity for work, but what made him particularly effective were his personal qualities. Lange was a man of integrity, sensitivity, and discretion, who inspired the greatest of confidence in all who knew him. I remember well with what graciousness, kindness, and understanding Lange once took time out from his official duties on the floor of the League's Assembly to receive me as a student from the United States and assist me with my researches.

During the war years Lange was asked by the Carnegie Endowment of International Peace to send reports on conditions in the warring countries. His account of his trip to Russia after the fall of the tsar was given almost two pages in the *New York Times*. He participated in the international meetings of the Central Organization for a Durable Peace held in neutral Holland, where he chaired the committee working on plans for postwar development of the international institutions that had been in existence before 1914. He was already a leading expert on this subject through his work with the Nobel Institute and the union, and he now found time to investigate the antecedents of this development. His masterful work on the early history of internationalism earned him a doctorate at the University of Christiana in 1919.

Lange's Nobel address remains one of the best succinct expositions ever published on "Internationalism," which he himself had lived as well as studied as no one else had done. He drew an important distinction between pacifism, which he considered "a moral protest against the use of violence and war in international relations," and internationalism, "a *social* and *political* theory, a certain concept of how human society ought to be organized, and in particular a concept of how the nations ought to organize their mutual relations."

Lange saw no conflict of internationalism with nationalism, only with one-sided nationalism. Through the development of international interdependence technically, economically, and intellectually, the territorial state, which "in our epoch likes to justify itself by national sentiment," has been outgrown. "If the territorial state remains as the last word in the development of society, war is inevitable. For the state according to its very essence claims *sovereignty,* the right to employ its power without limit, inspired only by self-interest. Basically the state is anarchistic."

Therefore, we must work for a higher form of organization, "an all-embracing human community." The "unity of the human species" has been an idea since ancient times, but now the science of biology has given it a scientific basis. "If humanity forms a physiological entity, then war, international and civil, is suicide."

Lange's internationalism, then, is

> a social theory based on economic, spiritual, and biological facts. . . . Nationalities must form the constituent elements in a great world federation; they must be assured an independent life in the realm of the spiritual and for delimited tasks of a local order, while economic and political questions must be submitted to an international organization in a spirit of peaceful cooperation for the promotion of the common interests of the human species.

Lange concludes on a high note:

> The idea of eternity lives in all of us. We would like to base our life on a belief which raises our small personality to a higher coherence—a coherence which is human and yet superhuman absolute and yet steadily growing and evolving, ideal and yet real. Can these aspirations be realized? It seems to be a contradiction in terms. And yet there is a belief which satisfied these aspirations and resolves the contradictions. It is the belief in the unity of humanity.

It was this belief that sustained Christian Lange throughout a lifetime of effort to help move the anarchy of sovereign states to that higher plane. He died in Oslo in December 1938 at the age of sixty-nine.

BIBLIOGRAPHY

Primary Sources

Lange, Christian L. *The Conditions of a Lasting Peace.* Christiana: Interparliamentary Union, 1917. A summary of the work of the union as a contribution to wartime discussions of the organization of peace.

———. "Histoire de la doctrine pacifique." In Academy of International Law, The Hague, *Recueil des Cours 1926.* Vol. 3. Paris: Librairie Hachette, 1927, pp. 170–426. Lectures on the doctrine of peace from antiquity to the League of Nations. Includes a list of his major publications up to 1925.

———. *Histoire de l'internationalisme.* 2 vols. Christiania: Aschenhoug, 1919–54. A publication of the Norwegian Nobel Institute. Lange completed the first volume, which covers the history of internationalism to 1648, and part of the second, which ends with 1815. August Schou finished the second and wrote a third volume, published in 1963, which covers the period to 1914. Lange's chapters represent his major scholarly work.

———. *Histoire documentaire de l'Union Interparlementaire.* Brussels, Guyot, 1915.

———. "The Inter-Parliamentary Union and Reduction of Armaments." In Inter-Parliamentary Union, *The Inter-Parliamentary Union from 1889–1939.* Lausanne: Payot, 1939, pp. 61–83.

———. "Preparation de la Société des Nations pendant la guerre" and "La Société des Nations et le problème des armements." In *L'origine et l'oeuvre de la Société des Nations.* 2 vols. Edited by Peter Munch. Copenhagen, 1923–24, 1:1–61 (the movement of ideas among peace organizations during the war) and 2:416–52 (the League of Nations and the armament problem).

———. *Russia, the Revolution and the War: An Account of a Visit to Petrograd and Helsingfors in March 1917.* Publication no. 12. Washington, D.C.: Carnegie Endowment for International Peace, 1917. Lange's report to the endowment, which was also published in the *New York Times.*

———. *Union Interparlementaire: Résolutions des conférences.* 2d ed. Brussels: Misch & Thron, 1911. With an introduction and bibliography.

Secondary Sources

Douglas, James. *Parliaments across Frontiers: A Short History of the Interparliamentary Union.* 2d ed. London: H.M. Stationery Office, 1976. Written by a former assistant secretary-general to celebrate the London meeting of the Union in 1975.

Falnes, Oscar. "Christian L. Lange and His Work for Peace." *American Scandinavian Review* 57 (1969): 266–74.

———. *Norway and the Nobel Peace Prize.* New York: Columbia University Press, 1938. Reprint. New York: AMS Press, 1967. Includes an account of Lange as the first secretary of the Norwegian Nobel Committee.

Jones, Shepherd S. *The Scandinavian States and the League of Nations.* Princeton: Princeton University Press, 1939.

Koht, Halvdan. "Christian Lous Lange." In *Norsk Biografisk Leksikon.* Vol. 7. Oslo: Aschehoug, 1938, pp. 172–74.

1922

Fridtjof Nansen (1861–1930)

Norway

Arctic explorer, scientist, diplomat, and foremost figure in international relief work after First World War; high commissioner for refugees of League of Nations, 1921–30.

Fridtjof Nansen was awarded the prize in 1922 for his humanitarian work after 1920, organizing large-scale programs for the repatriation of prisoners of war, for the care of refugees, and for Russian famine relief. Chairman Stang of the committee declared in his presentation speech that although the human mind can grasp the need of one starving person, of one homeless refugee, it is staggered by "a program whose aim is to rescue a continent's millions from misery and death." The ultimate significance of Nansen's work was that it "delved deep into the primordial roots of human fellow-feeling which lie buried in all of us, the feeling that the human race is one, however much it may split itself up into States and societies."

Nansen was already a famous man when he responded to this cry of human need. Before the turn of the century his Arctic expeditions had made him a national hero in Norway with a world reputation as explorer and scientist. He was born near Christiana (Oslo) in 1861, the son of a well-to-do lawyer of firm religious principles. Like all Norwegian children, Nansen grew up to love the outdoor life, and he became highly skilled as a horseman, hunter, fisherman, and athlete. Before he was seventeen he won the national distance skating championship and a year later broke a world speed skating record. The following year he won the cross-country skiing race in his first attempt, and he continued to win it for the next eleven years until he retired.

Nansen entered the university at the age of twenty to study zoology. In the following year he joined a sealing ship on a voyage of several months to the east coast of Greenland, and he knew he would return to the North. As he later explained in an address at St. Andrew's University: "We all have a Land of Beyond to seek in life—what more can we ask? Our part is to find the trail that leads to it. . . . Rooted deep in the nature of every one of us is the spirit of adventure, the call of the wild—vibrating under all our actions, making life deeper and higher and nobler."

Nansen's spirit of adventure called him not just to venture forth but to set out for the unknown on a scientific quest, and he spent the next six years continuing his university training and completing his doctorate in 1888. Now he was prepared for scientific exploration, and in the same year he led a party across the interior of Greenland amid great hardships, a feat that had never been accomplished before. During the next four years he published the scientific results and planned a new more venturesome expedition into the Arctic. This time he proved his revolutionary hypothesis that his specially designed ship, the *Fram* (Forward), could drift with the ice floes from east to west. Starting out in June 1893, the expedition did not return until August 1896; Nansen with a companion had come closer to the North Pole than any one else before. Nansen and his party met with an enthusiastic welcome as the *Fram* journeyed down the Norwegian coast. He wrote later, "I realized for the first time how near this land and this people lay to my heart."

Now Nansen became research professor at the University of Christiana, freed from teaching until he had completed working on the mass of scientific data he had collected. His publications, both scholarly and popular, illustrated by his own hand, further established his reputation as the most famous explorer in the world. He was only thirty-five when he returned from the Far North, his major explorations now accomplished.

In 1905 Nansen for the first time took a political role, contributing to the peaceful dissolution of Norway's union with Sweden. With his great prestige in the world, he was most effective in interpreting his country's case abroad. When Norway became independent, it was said that Nansen could have chosen to be king or president or premier. He would agree, however, to serve only as Norway's first diplomatic representative in London until 1908, then returning to the chair in oceanography especially created for him at the university.

During the First World War Norway called upon Nansen again, sending him to the United States in 1917–18 to work out a trade agreement to bring more American food to neutral Norway and permit some Norwegian export of fish to Germany despite the blockade. Nansen was to remain on the international stage as a central figure for the rest of his life. To him the war was "a nightmare of insanity," and he worked for the establishment of a postwar international organization as president of the Norwegian Union for the League of Nations. He went to Paris in 1919 during the peace conference to lobby for the adoption of the League of Nation's Covenant and for the inclusion of small neutral nations as members. Thereafter he was influential in persuading the Scandinavian nations to join, and he became Norway's first delegate in 1920.

Nansen saw the League as a new ship sailing "a new course with the future hopes of mankind on board." He was a familiar figure in Geneva, tall and lean, his weather-beaten countenance with its flowing mustache crowned by his fair hair and his ever-present broad-brimmed hat. One journalist called him "one of the sights of Geneva—the proudest after Mont Blanc."

While urging disarmament, Nansen recognized the prior need for "the disarmament of the mind." He advocated the development of a world court and the entrance of Germany into the League. He defended the small nations so ardently that the delegates when reassembling for a new session would joke, "Let's hope that Nansen hasn't discovered another little nation since last we met."

It was because of his devotion to the League that Nansen reluctantly left his scientific work when the League Council in 1920 asked him to organize the repatriation of the great number of prisoners of war who had not been able to return home after hostilities ended. At first he declined, but when Philip Noel-Baker of the League secretariat came to Norway to describe the suffering of these war victims and to ask for just a few months of his time, Nansen finally agreed, feeling that it was important to show skeptics that the League could achieve practical projects.

More than half a million men were languishing in prison camps, nearly half of them from the armies of Germany and its allies in Russia and Siberia, where first revolution and then civil war had thrown the country into turmoil. The new Soviet government, ostracized by the West, would not recognize the League but was willing to work with Nansen himself. He raised money, organized transport, and made agreements with governments, and in eighteen months he succeeded in returning almost all the men to their homelands. Noel-Baker, who assisted Nansen, said afterward, "There is not a country on the continent of Europe where wives and mothers have not wept in gratitude for the work which Nansen did."

The few months for which the League asked lengthened into ten years. Before the program for the war prisoners had ended, the League had another request. A million and a half refugees had fled from the Russian Revolution and were scattered throughout Europe and Asia. Relief societies were trying to cope, but there were so many countries and organizations involved that a single director was needed to coordinate all the efforts, one with official standing so as to be able to treat with all the governments involved. Would Nansen become the League's high commissioner for refugees? He could hardly refuse. Through the repatriation program Nansen had demonstrated that the world needed the League, and here was another opportunity to show that only such an international body could tackle the problem of resettling the masses of people made homeless by war and civil strife.

Unfortunately, the refugee problem has persisted and even intensified since the Second World War. But Nansen set the precedents for work for refugees that continued after his death, sponsored first by the League and then by the United Nations; this work was to be honored three times through the years by the award of the Peace Prize. Of great importance was his invention of the "Nansen passport," a certificate recognized by many governments that provided stateless refugees with documentation for international travel.

Nansen's last important program as high commissioner was the exchange and resettling of Greek and Turkish populations after the Greco-Turkish War. He also developed a plan for the establishment of a homeland for Armenians. It is estimated that in the course of these refugee programs Nansen assisted and resettled 1.25 million Greeks, 1 million Russians, 300,000 Armenians, and tens of thousands of others.

In one great work of humanitarian relief Nansen had to proceed without the League. In the summer of 1921 famine struck the Soviet Union, still not recovered from the dislocations of war and revolution, and millions were threatened by starvation and disease. The International Red Cross appealed to Nansen, but so strong was anti-Bolshevik feeling in the West that his eloquent pleas in the League's Assembly were unavailing. He declared that "less than half of the cost of one battleship, the cost of maintaining only half a battalion of soldiers, would feed the starving of Russia." When it was objected that this would help the Bolsheviks, Nansen answered, "I do not think we shall strengthen the Soviet Government by showing the Russian people that there are hearts in Europe."

Finally he had to organize a relief program outside the League, assisted by Herbert Hoover's American Relief Administration, the Quakers, and others. The program saved perhaps 20 million people, but Nansen always thought that another 7 million had needlessly died.

In his Nobel address Nansen did not spare those he held responsible for this tragedy: "In all probability their motives were political. They epitomize sterile self-importance and the lack of will to understand people who think differently. . . . They call us romantics, weak, stupid, sentimental idealists, perhaps because we have some faith in the good which exists even in our opponents and because we believe that kindness achieves more than cruelty." Having come face to face with human misery in the aftermath of war as few men had, Nansen spoke bitterly of "the lust for power, the imperialism, the militarism, that have run amok across the earth," and declared, "The soul of the world is mortally sick." How is confidence in peace, in the future, to be inspired? Not by politicians or diplomats. "I believe that the only road to this goal lies through the League of Nations," undergirded by "a new spirit in a new generation" imbuing men with "love of their fellowmen and an honest desire for peace" and bringing "back the will to work and the joy of work . . . faith in the dawn of a new day."

Nansen's last ten years of unceasing toil, lived in an endless and frustrating struggle with boundless human suffering, finally wore down even his splendid physical constitution. On 13 May 1930, in his beloved Norway, he died at the age of sixty-nine. He was to have spoken on Constitution Day, as he had twenty-five years before on the eve of his country's independence. Instead, on that day he was laid to rest, as his nation mourned. Nansen's life had shown how a great patriot could be at the same time a great humanitarian. He had written of Norway: "I see valleys and mountains, woods and green meadows, fields where the golden grain stands ready to be cut. This glorious land is mine. I want to live, to give it my best powers. . . . I see farther ahead a new world to be built and I want to help build it."

BIBLIOGRAPHY

Primary Sources

Nansen, Fridtjof. *Adventure and Other Papers.* London: Hogarth Press, 1927. Includes his address at St. Andrews University in 1926 and his Nobel lecture.

———. *Norway and the Union with Sweden.* London: Macmillan, 1905.

———. *Russia and Peace.* London: Allen & Unwin, 1923.

Secondary Sources

Greve, Tim. *Fridtjof Nansen.* 2 vols. Oslo: Gylendal, 1973–74. Authoritative biography by a family member who used Nansen's papers. With a complete bibliography.

Marrus, Michael R. *The Unwanted: European Refugees in the Twentieth Century.* New York: Oxford University Press, 1985. Excellent study of refugee movements since 1880, including Nansen's era.

Møyer, Liv [Nansen]. *Nansen: A Family Portrait.* Translated by Maurice Michael. London: Longmans, Green, 1957. By his daughter.

Noel-Baker, Philip. *Nansen's Place in History.* Oslo: Universitetsforlaget, 1962. A memorial lecture by the Nobel laureate who had worked with him.

Reynolds, E. E. *Nansen.* London: Penguin, 1949. First published in 1932.

Scott, James Maurice. *Fridtjof Nansen.* London: Heron Books, 1971.

Sörensen, Jon. *The Saga of Fridtjof Nansen.* Translated by J. B. C. Watkins. New York: American-Scandinavian Foundation, Norton, 1932. One of the best biographies available in English, by a

Norwegian educator who knew Nansen and had full access to his unpublished papers. With bibliography and illustrations.

Vogt, Per, ed. *Fridtjof Nansen: Explorer, Scientist, Humanitarian.* Oslo: Dreyers, 1961. With illustrations. Excellent collection of essays.

1925
Charles Gates Dawes (1865–1951)

United States

Coauthor of Dawes Plan for payment of German reparations; financier, U.S. comptroller of the currency; as brigadier general, purchasing agent for American Expeditionary Forces in France; first U.S. director of the budget; vice president of United States, 1925–29; ambassador to Great Britain 1929–32; chairman, Reconstruction Finance Corporation.

Since the Nobel Committee could not, by the statutes, give the prize to all members of a committee, the prize for 1925 was given in 1926 to the chairman of the commission on German reparations, Charles G. Dawes, in recognition of the achievement of the ten financial experts who worked under his leadership in 1924 to produce the Dawes Plan for Germany's payment of reparations.

The vexed question of reparations was a major destabilizing factor in European relationships after World War I. By the terms of the Treaty of Versailles Germany had had to acknowledge her responsibility for starting the war and to agree to pay reparations for the damage done to civilian populations. An Allied Reparations Commission was established to set the amount to be paid and to oversee the payment. The figure arrived at was about $32 billion, more than thirty-two times the indemnity France had to pay after the Franco-Prussian War and a sum far beyond Germany's capacity to pay. After Germany was declared in default, France and Belgium occupied the highly industrialized area of the Ruhr, and the inhabitants began a campaign of passive resistance. Coal miners, factory workers, and railwaymen all stopped work, frustrating the occupying forces but also throwing the German economy into chaos, with run-away inflation. The old wartime hatreds burned fiercely again. The occupation became a fiasco when the French and Belgians found that they could not "dig coal with foreign bayonets." The whole economic structure of Europe was threatened with disruption, and American business interests began to be concerned as well. The German government called off the passive resistance, but the situation was desperate.

At this point a suggestion was taken up that had been made by American secretary of state Charles Evans Hughes that the reparations problem be referred to an international committee of experts, "men of such prestige, experience, and honor" that their recommendations "would be accepted throughout the world as the most authoritative expression obtainable." The United States was officially holding itself aloof from European affairs, but Hughes promised that American experts would be willing to serve without government appointment.

The Reparations Commission decided late in 1923 to appoint the First Committee of Experts, composed of representatives from Belgium, Great Britain, France, Italy, and the United States. The British representative was the distinguished economist Sir Josiah Stamp. From the United States came the New York industrialist Owen D. Young and General Dawes, who was appointed as chairman.

Charles Gates Dawes was an excellent choice to head the committee. A native of Marietta, Ohio, he had graduated from Marietta College and taken his law degree at the University of Cincinnati; he then made his fortune in business and banking in the Midwest. As an active Republican, he was appointed by President William McKinley in 1893 as comptroller of the currency, his first governmental position. His service in the First World War gave Dawes extensive experience in Europe. He volunteered as a major but became a brigadier general as Gen. John J. Pershing's purchasing agent for the American army in France and then a member of the Military Board of Allied Supply. After the war he remained in France as a member of the commission that disposed of surplus war materials. In 1919 he was one Republican who strongly urged approval of the Treaty of Versailles and entry into the League of Nations. Back home he became the first director of the budget under President Warren Harding.

The Committee of Experts convened in Paris in January 1924 and submitted its report in April. The approach was "business, not politics." The Dawes Plan called for a sliding schedule of annual payments based upon Germany's ability to pay and outlined measures to stabilize the country's monetary system and balance its budget. The installments were to be raised partly in the budget and partly from state railway bonds, assessments against industry, and a transport tax. The transfer of funds, a thorny problem, was to be handled through extensive foreign investment in Germany so that foreign currencies would not have to be purchased. There was to be a foreign loan of $200 million. The plan assumed the evacuation of the Ruhr by foreign troops.

A fifteen-power conference convened in London in the summer of 1924 to discuss the plan. The United States, preserving the fiction of its noninvolvement with Europe, was not officially represented, but Secretary Hughes arranged to be in London then for a meeting of the American Bar Association, and he unofficially urged adoption of the recommendations. The conference approved and directed that the plan be implemented beginning in September 1924.

The Dawes Plan led to the easing of the conflicts and anxieties that had plagued Europe since the end of the war. As Nansen declared in his speech at the award ceremonies held in the Nobel Institute on 10 December 1926, "It marked the beginning of the policy of reconciliation and peace which led to the Locarno agreements. This was the first dawning of the day after the long darkness."

In his telegram of acceptance of the Peace Prize, Dawes, now vice president of the United States, declared, "It was the endeavor of the experts to found their plan upon the principles of justice, fairness, and mutual interest." In this they largely succeeded. To what extent Dawes himself was responsible for the committee's achievement, we can only surmise. He always paid tribute to his colleagues, especially to Sir Josiah Stamp. What Dawes himself brought to the committee was significant practical experience, a no-nonsense approach to problems, and, with Young, a more objective perspective perhaps than the others. There is no doubt that his leadership was most effective.

Dawes was fifty-nine when the Committee of Experts did its work. He continued an active and productive life for another two decades as financier, politician, diplomat, author, philanthropist, and musician. He made several other appearances on the international stage. As vice president presiding over the Senate, he gave strong support to the Kellogg-Briand Pact of 1928. As ambassador to Britain, he made an important contribution to Anglo-American understanding and took part in the London Naval Conference of 1930. In the next year he was involved in efforts to deal with the Japanese advance in Manchuria and with the developing economic crisis. In 1932 he was appointed chairman of the American delegation to the disarmament conference in Geneva, but resigned to become head of the Reconstruction Finance Corporation, established after the onset of the Great Depression.

Dawes gave his prize money to the Walter Hines Page School of International Relations at Johns Hopkins University. He died at his home in Evanston, Illinois, in 1951.

BIBLIOGRAPHY

Primary Source

Dawes, Charles G. *A Journal of Reparations.* London: Macmillan, 1939. The diary covers the work of the Reparations Commission. Dawes was accustomed to keeping a journal while in public office, and four such volumes have been published, covering the McKinley years, the First World War, his ambassadorship to Great Britain, and his last year as vice president.

Secondary Sources

Auld, George P. *The Dawes Plan and the New Economics.* London: Allen & Unwin, 1927.

Bergmann, Karl. *The History of Reparations.* 1926. Boston: Houghton Mifflin, 1927. A German view.

"Dawes, Charles G." In *BDI.*

Dawes, Rufus C. *The Dawes Plan in the Making.* Indianapolis: Bobbs-Merrill, 1925. Largely in diary form, by Dawes's brother, who was the commission's chief of staff.

Leach, Paul R. *That Man Dawes.* Chicago: Reilly, 1930. A friendly biography.

Leffler, Melvyn P. *The Elusive Quest: America's Pursuit of European Stability and French Security, 1919–1933.* Chapel Hill: University of North Carolina Press, 1979.

Schuker, Stephen A. *The End of French Predominance in Europe: The Financial Crisis of 1924 and the*

Adoption of the Dawes Plan. Chapel Hill: University of North Carolina Press, 1976.

Timmons, Bascom N. *Portrait of an American: Charles G. Dawes.* New York: Holt, 1953. Extensive but not scholarly.

Trachtenberg, Marc. *Reparations in World Politics: France and European Economic Diplomacy 1916–1923.* New York: Columbia University Press, 1980. An examination of the traditional view that France was unreasonable and Germany unable to pay.

1925
Austen Chamberlain (1863–1937)

Great Britain

Prominent Conservative politician and statesman; frequently cabinet minister; foreign secretary, 1924–29.

1926
Aristide Briand (1862–1932)

France

Politician and statesman; lawyer; journalist; frequently prime minister; foreign minister.

1926
Gustav Stresemann (1878–1929)

Germany

Politician and statesman; National Liberal delegate in Reichstag before and during World War I; founder German People's party; Reichstag deputy; chancellor and foreign minister, 1923; foreign minister, 1923–29.

After all the papers had been signed in the little Swiss town of Locarno by the foreign ministers of Great Britain, France, and Germany, and the representatives of the other states, church bells were rung, bands played, and there was dancing in the village square. The next day's headline in the *New York Times* announced, "France and Germany Ban War Forever," and the *Times* of London declared, "Peace at Last."

These events in October 1925, preceded the year before by the adoption of the Dawes Plan, were followed in 1926 by the entry of Germany into the League of Nations, and hopes were running high that peace had finally been assured. It was not surprising that the Nobel Committee, meeting in October 1926, recognized in their awards the principal figures responsible for these international developments: Charles Dawes, for the Dawes Plan, which lessened the Franco-German conflict over reparations and made Locarno possible, and the three foreign ministers who were the chief architects of the Locarno agreements. The reserved prize of 1925 was shared with Dawes by Austen Chamberlain, the British foreign secretary, and the 1926 prize was divided between Aristide Briand of France and Gustav Stresemann of Germany.

None of the laureates was able to come to Oslo for the award ceremonies, so Fridtjof Nansen, the earlier winner, was invited to give the major speech at the Nobel Institute. In his own Nobel lecture in 1922, Nansen had castigated the diplomats. They were, he said, "a barren race in these days and have done humanity more harm than good of late." At that time Nansen was thinking of the governmental representatives who had blocked his efforts to induce the League of Nations to help the famine victims in Soviet Russia. Now, however, he was glad to pay tribute to the achievements of diplomat laureates. Calling the Locarno pacts "a complete reconstruction of European policy as a whole, between the antagonists of the war," Nansen said that "a new spirit" had been instilled in their mutual relations. All the same, he warned, there was still a long way to go. Civilization had by no means recovered from the rude shock suffered in the war. A new war could be averted only if the great powers would adopt what he called "the policy of the League of Nations" and throw themselves into building up the influence and the strength of the League.

This, however, was not the way Austen Chamberlain saw it. He once said of the League, "Being temperamentally inclined to moderate and unsensational ways, I do not suppose if I had had anything to do with the League's foundation that I should have aimed at anything so ambitious. However, there it was when I came into office as Foreign Minister."

In his maiden speech at Geneva, Chamberlain reversed the League policy of the previous Labour government and rejected the Geneva Protocol, which the Assembly had unanimously recommended for adoption by the member states. By the terms of the Protocol, signatory states agreed to compulsory arbitration for the settlement of disputes. A state refusing arbitration would be deemed an aggressor, and sanctions would then be applied as called for under the Covenant. This Protocol was to go into effect only after a plan for disarmament had been adopted. But the British Conservatives did not want a strong League and disapproved of sanctions.

The Labour party looked upon the Protocol as a means of deterring an aggressor by making more explicit and strengthening the obligations already assumed under the Covenant. They did not like the prospect of actually employing sanctions and at most envisaged using only those of an economic nature. To the Conservatives this was still too radical a course. As Chamberlain explained to the League Council, the new emphasis upon sanctions suggested that "the vital business of the League is not so much to promote friendly cooperation and reasoned harmony in the management of international affairs as to preserve peace by organizing war." He thought it would be better "to deal with specific situations as they arose and to supplement the Covenant by making special arrangements in order to meet special needs." This was the path that led to the regional arrangements of the Locarno treaties.

The French had warmly supported the Geneva Protocol, continuing to demand a strong League that would provide them with security against a revived Germany. Chamberlain understood France's need for security, but he was clear that Britain could not provide for this either through a military alliance with France or through the Geneva Protocol. He therefore picked up on the Germany initiative for a regional security treaty. Negotiations led to the meeting in Locarno in October 1925 of the foreign ministers of Britain, France, and Germany, and representatives of Italy, Belgium, Poland, and Czechoslovakia.

The most important agreement reached was the Rhineland Pact in which the western frontiers of Germany established by the Versailles treaty and including the demilitarization of the Rhineland were reaffirmed by France and Belgium and guaranteed by Britain and Italy. Any differences between Germany and France or Belgium were to be settled by arbitration, as were any between Germany and Poland or Czechoslovakia, although there was no equivalent of the Rhineland Pact covering Germany's eastern frontiers. With Poland and Czechoslovakia France entered into bilateral treaties of mutual assistance in case of German attack. It was also understood that Germany would be admitted to the League of Nations.

For Chamberlain the Locarno agreements meant a happy return to the old concert of the Great Powers, providing for French security through a multilateral guarantee of the Versailles frontiers that did not single out Germany as the potential aggressor. He considered Germany's western borders with France and Belgium to be an area "on which, as our history shows, our national existence depends." As for Germany's eastern frontiers, this was a region "for which no British government ever will or ever can risk the bones of a British grenadier." Nevertheless it was Hitler's attack on Poland in 1939 that brought the British government, then headed by Austen's half brother, Neville Chamberlain, to declare war on Germany.

Chamberlain's policy can be explained in the context of Britain's traditional effort to maintain the balance of power on the Continent. The motives of Briand and Stresemann have been subject to varying interpretations. Briand was charged by his nationalist critics with naively neglecting the interests of French security and becoming the dupe of the wily Stresemann. Some observers thought he was a sincere internationalist; others felt he was consumed by personal ambition. The most generous interpretation of his motives was that he realized that French security would best be served through reconciliation with Germany. In time Germany's greater strength in population and industrial development would reassert itself and one day a resurgent Germany might belligerently overthrow the terms of Versailles. If gradual concessions were made, the peace-minded forces in Germany could be strengthened and that country brought into constructive participation in the League of Nations. Moreover, it was thought, the Locarno agreements represented Britain's limits in guaranteeing French security against Germany. A harsh policy, like the occupation of the Ruhr, would only alienate Britain as well as the United States, the two powers France needed if war with Germany ever did come.

Like Briand, Stresemann was attacked by the ultranationalists in his own country for his policy of conciliation with the traditional enemy. They were adamant in refusing to admit the defeat of 1918 and in resisting compliance with the *Diktat,* the "dictated peace" of Versailles. Stresemann was just as intent on the revision of the treaty, but he realized this could be achieved only through peaceful means and international cooperation. Thus at Locarno he was prepared to abandon any claim to Alsace-Lorraine in the West and to renounce the use of force to recover the lost territory in the East; the nationalist extremists would not forgive him for either of these concessions. Stresemann succeeded, however, in moving his country a considerable distance on the road to international reacceptance. As to other peace terms imposed upon Germany, Stresemann secured the withdrawal of the inter-Allied military commission which monitored Germany's observance of the disarmament clauses, an early departure of foreign troops from the Rhineland, and reduction of German reparations payments.

Historians still debate whether Stresemann, who had been annexationist in his war aims during the war, was misleading his Locarno partners as to his ultimate objectives. On the international stage he was the good European, but domestically he had to profess certain nationalist positions in order to get his policies approved by the Reichstag. It is clear that he wanted to free Germany from the restraints of Versailles and to restore the country to the status of a great power. He wanted Germany to be strong again, but was he planning German hegemony in Europe? Certainly he left Chamberlain and Briand under no illusions as to his unwillingness to accept Germany's eastern boundaries as determined at Versailles, yet he appears to have been entirely committed to achieving this change peacefully.

Locarno did represent a "new spirit" in European politics, as Nansen called it, as France and Germany moved from the confrontations of the years after the war to conciliation and cooperation. But it did nothing to change the basic relationships among European states, which continued to be based upon power. Neverthless, Nansen called the three foreign ministers "realistic and responsible statesmen" who had come to realize the necessity of working together. Each was endeavoring to further the national interest of his own sovereign state, and the arrangements they made to keep the peace reflected the political realities at that particular moment: Germany reviving after the war, France needing to be reassured, Britain holding the balance.

A period of stability and prosperity now followed, which gave Europe a breathing space, a chance to set out on the long road to a lasting peace, which, as Nansen pointed out, led by way of Geneva and the League. Although Locarno brought Germany into the League, nothing was done to strengthen the League's machinery to keep the peace. In a few short years Stresemann died, and in the same week in October 1929 the stock market crash on Wall Street precipitated a world economic crisis that brought Hitler and the ultranationalists to power in Germany. The chance for peace was lost.

With the coming of the war in 1939, it was easy to write off the Locarno agreements as the "Magic House of Paper" and the years 1925–29, which also saw the Kellogg-Briand Pact, as "years of illusion." This is especially unfair to Briand and Stresemann, whose policies lessened the chances for Franco-German conflict in their time. They spoke of being a Frenchman and a German first, but they said this did not prevent either of them from being a European. To what extent each of them consistently followed this higher vision expressed in their oratory is debatable, but their personal cooperation symbolized the reconciliation of age-old foes, and in pursuing the policy of conciliation each met with violent criticism in his own country. Chamberlain returned from Locarno to an ovation in Britain, and he was made a Knight of the Garter, a distinction rarely accorded a commoner. Briand continued his peace policies and became the personal embodiment of the ideals of reconciliation and peace. Stresemann wore himself out defending his peaceful policies and died at the age of fifty-one.

Austen Chamberlain

Of the three statesmen of Locarno, Chamberlain seems the most unlikely candidate for the Nobel pantheon of peace. It is not surprising that he is conspicuously missing from the authoritative *Biographical Dictionary of Internationalists,* where Briand, Stresemann, and Dawes each has a place.

The full realization of what Locarno meant became apparent only later in Britain. In 1936 a Labour critic commented that "The Locarno Pact took a very big step in giving the League a twist out of its right course." Chamberlain's defenders have maintained that Britain was not ready for a strong League policy, that the political commitments of Locarno were as far as his fellow countrymen were willing to go.

Born in 1863, he was the eldest son of the doughty imperialist politician Joseph Chamberlain of Birmingham. He was educated for a public career, studying at Cambridge and in Paris and Berlin. When he was twenty-four years old, he became his father's assistant and two years later entered the House of Commons, holding his seat there for forty-five years. Chamberlain served in many ministerial posts in Conservative and coalition governments, but he first came to the Foreign Office in 1924, when he was sixty-one years old.

At Geneva Chamberlain won respect for his integrity and diplomatic skills, but never popularity among the diplomats at the League of Nations, who sensed his distrust of that organization. Tall and spare in figure, his speech precise, his manner cold and reserved, with the monocle fixed in his eye he seemed the quintessential English patrician, a conservative of the old order. It was said of Chamberlain that just as he never got rid of his strong English accent in speaking French, so he never shed his basic English suspicion of the European continent and the people who lived there.

That he spoke French easily was a credit to him, and it meant that he got on well with Briand, although the two were very different personalities. They came to develop a real appreciation for one another, which greatly facilitated the negotiations. His German was rusty, although he could understand most of a conversation, and he did not have the same relationship with Stresemann.

Chamberlain left office in 1929, but his voice was still heard in the House of Commons. He died on 17 March 1937, at the age of seventy-four, the year before Hitler reoccupied the Rhineland and completed the destruction of the Locarno agreements.

Aristide Briand

Aristide Briand was born in Nantes in Brittany in 1862, the year before the birth of Chamberlain. Trained in the law, he started a practice but soon turned to journalism. He found his true métier, however, when he was elected to the Chamber of Deputies in 1902. He became one of France's leading politicians, frequently serving as premier or cabinet minister. He had begun his career on the extreme Left, but after being expelled from the Socialist party for joining a bourgeois government, he became progressively more conservative and remained independent of party affiliation. Once a proponent of the general strike, as premier he broke a railwaymen's strike by threatening to mobilize the strikers. In the First World War he headed the government for eighteen months.

Briand was foreign minister several times before his long tenure of five and a half years beginning in 1925, which corresponded with the terms of Stresemann (1923–29) and Chamberlain (1924–29). Briand was in charge of French foreign affairs longer than anyone else since the time of Talleyrand in the early nineteenth century.

As a politician he was a master of compromise, ever sensitive to the directions in which the winds of politics were blowing. He spent little time in writing and even less in reading, but in listening and speaking he excelled. His associates marveled at how quickly he could grasp the substance of an issue and then speak eloquently, without a note, as though he had been giving the matter long study. When addressing an audience he could listen with some sixth sense to the response of his auditors and adjust his shafts of oratory so that they would go directly to the mark.

He delivered his greatest speech at the League Assembly in 1926 where, in consequence of the Locarno pacts, the German delegation appeared for the first time. Stresemann spoke first, bullet-headed and stocky, standing stiffly, naturally ill at ease, reading his speech in German. It was a positive statement, free of any complaints about Versailles, firmly committing the German Republic to cooperation and peace. Then Briand slowly moved to the tribune, short, shoulders bowed, his leonine head crowned with a straggling mane of graying hair. He spoke extemporaneously as was his custom, starting slowly and quietly and then, his voice rising in volume and power, holding his listeners spellbound. In his peroration he asked,

> Is it not a reassuring spectacle to think that a few years after the most terrible of all wars, the same nations that fought so hard should meet in this Assembly and express their common desire to collaborate in the work of universal peace? Peace for Germany and for France. This means an end to all those sanguinary encounters which have tarnished the pages of all our past history. It is ended, that long war between us. Ended, those long veils of mourning for the pains that will never be assuaged. Henceforth we will settle our differences by peaceful procedure. Away with the rifles, the machine-guns and the cannon! Here come conciliation, arbitration, and peace!

This memorable speech may stand as the finest expression of the new spirit of Locarno. Briand never rose to such oratorical heights again on the international stage, although he was one statesman laureate who continued with significant peacemaking policies after receiving his award. He negotiated with American secretary of state Frank B. Kellogg a pact for the renunciation of war, which arose from Briand's effort to draw the United States out of its isolation and closer to France in a bilateral agreement. The result, however, was a multilateral treaty, the Kellogg-Briand Pact, signed by fifteen nations in Paris on 27 August 1928.

Briand's last peace venture was his proposal for a European union, which he presented to the League's Assembly in 1930. The original concept had featured economic cooperation, but the final proposal called for a political committee, which appeared to other statesmen to be just another form of the familiar French pursuit of security. In 1931 Briand lost his bid for the French presidency and left the Foreign Office some months later. In March 1932, he died at his cherished farm in the country, where he had used his Nobel prize money. Stresemann had died in 1929, and the hopes for strengthening the forces for peace in Germany were already dim. Briand was spared witnessing the end of such hopes with the coming to power of Adolf Hitler less than a year after his death.

Gustav Stresemann

Born in Berlin in 1878, Gustav Stresemann was the son of an innkeeper and brewer's agent. He was some fifteen years younger than Briand and Chamberlain. Stresemann took his doctorate in economics at the University of Leipzig, and his first jobs were with associations of industrialists as executive officer. At the age of twenty-five, Stresemann married the intelligent and charming daughter of a prosperous Berlin family, who was to be a rock of support for him throughout his career. At twenty-eight he brought his organizing talents and skills in personal relations to the field of politics, becoming town councilor of Dresden. The next year he was elected to the Reichstag as a National Liberal, and by 1917 he had become the leader of that party.

During the First World War Stresemann supported a strong military policy and territorial annexations after the expected victory. Disillusioned with the imperial government because of Germany's defeat, he founded the German People's party after the armistice and was one of its delegates at Weimar in the framing of the republican constitution. In 1923 as chancellor of a short-lived coalition government, he courageously ended the passive resistance to the French occupation of the Ruhr in the face of nationalist opposition to his policy, and he dealt effectively with an insurrection in Saxony and the unrest surrounding Hitler's putsch in Bavaria. He also took strong measures to stabilize the disastrously inflated currency. He described later the "courage to be unpopular," which he demonstrated in these days and was to have occasion to call upon all too often in the future: "To know that one is right, that one could not have acted otherwise—and then to find oneself suddenly quite alone, hated, despised, calumniated—to ask oneself how one is going to hold out against the error of a whole nation—how one is to prove, unaided, that one was not wrong . . . is the hardest test that fate can impose."

In 1924 in the next government Stresemann became secretary of foreign affairs and retained this portfolio in four cabinets until his death in 1929. His first success was securing Reichstag approval of the Dawes Plan, after which he took the initiative that led to the Locarno negotiations. While waiting for Germany's formal admission to the League, Stresemann signed a neutrality treaty with the Soviet Union, renewing ties first established in 1922. The Western powers were still worried about the Bolsheviks, and Stresemann's move no doubt hastened Germany's entry into the League, which gave the Weimar Republic a Westward rather than Eastward orientation.

Of the four peace laureates crowned in 1926 for the 1925 and 1926 prizes Stresemann was the only one to come to Oslo to present a Nobel lecture. Chamberlain and Briand pleaded the pressures of office, as did Dawes, who was now vice president of the United States. Stresemann, however, recognized the opportunity to interpret "The Way of the New Germany" to a foreign audience. His address was delivered in the Aula of the university in June 1927 and broadcast throughout Scandinavia.

Stresemann declared that the Germany he represented was trying to achieve a synthesis of the best of the old and the new. There were, however, some great difficulties. First, "it is easier for the victor than for the one who has suffered defeat to express thoughts of peace." Then referring to the old Germany, which had once been "a symbol of greatness" to the leaders today who had spent the greater part of their lives in that country, he asked his audience to try to understand how painful it had been "to believe that the work of half a century had brought one to the summit, and then to plunge down from that summit."

The most serious loss suffered from the war was the collapse of the intellectual and professional middle class, which had been proletarianized by inflation. "The best cargo in the middle of the German ship which had preserved it from heavy rolling, that infinitely valuable middle class group of citizens no longer exists," he said, adding, "A great wave of Bolshevism also surged over the German wall, appearing on the Left as Communism and on the Right as National Socialism." It was members of the uprooted class who in their bitterness opposed the Locarno policies as "weak resignation and the politics of renunciation."

Stresemann's struggle with the nationalists to secure approval for the Locarno policies demanded even more of his political skill and physical energies than his efforts abroad. His heart had never been strong, and toward the end of his life it was only by a tremendous effort of will that he managed, against his doctor's orders, to make his last appearances abroad in 1929: the meeting at The Hague on Germany reparations, where, on his urgent plea, the date for the evacuation of the Rhineland was decided upon; and his last speech at the League Assembly, where he gave the appearance of a man under sentence of death as he made his final plea for the League. A few weeks later he was dead.

Stresemann had closed his Nobel address with a quotation from his beloved Goethe: "We acknowledge that we belong to the generation which is struggling out of the darkness to the light," and he expressed the hope that these words would be true of his own times. But the threat to the Weimar Republic that he had diagnosed so clearly was to grow with the economic crisis he could not foresee, and the forces of darkness with which he had had to contend were to shape a "New Germany" in another image. Only many years later, after a new German state more in keeping with Stresemann's spirit, was there unveiled in the Foreign Office in Bonn a tablet in his honor: "to the memory of a Great European."

BIBLIOGRAPHY

Secondary Sources

Jacobson, Jon. *Locarno Diplomacy: Germany and the West.* Princeton: Princeton University Press, 1972.

Stern-Rubarth, Edgar. *Three Men Tried: Austen Chamberlain, Stresemann, Briand and Their Fight for a New Europe.* London: Duckworth, 1939.

Aristide Briand

Primary Sources

Briand, Aristide. *Discours et écrits de politique etrangère.* Paris: Plon, 1965. Speeches and writings on peace, European unity, and the League of Nations.

———. "Memorandum on the Organization of a Regime of European Federal Union." *International Conciliation* (Special edition), June 1930. The memo of 17 May 1930 that was addressed to twenty-six European governments.

Secondary Sources

Ludwig, Emil. "Briand, the French European." In *Nine Etched from Life.* New York: McBride, 1934, pp. 99–131. A sympathetic portrait by the well-known biographer.

Suarez, Georges. *Briand: Sa vie—son oeuvre.* 6 vols. Paris: Plon, 1939–41. A comprehensive biography, using his private papers.

Austen Chamberlain

Primary Source

Chamberlain, Sir Austen. *Down the Years.* London: Cassell, 1935. Autobiography. Chapters on the Locarno pacts and on Stresemann and Briand.

Secondary Sources

"Chamberlain, Sir (Joseph) Austen," by Charles Petrie. *DNB,* 1931–40.

Petrie, Charles. *The Life and Letters of the Right Hon. Sir Austen Chamberlain.* 2 vols. London: Cassell, 1940. Emphasis on his political life, with full use of correspondence as well as public documents.

Gustav Stresemann

Primary Sources

Stresemann, Gustav. *Essays and Speeches on Various Subjects.* Selected and translated by C. R. Turner. London: Butterworth, 1930.

———. *Gustav Stresemann: His Diaries, Letters and Papers.* 3 vols. Edited and translated by Eric Sutton. New York: Macmillan, 1935.

Secondary Sources

Bretton, Henry L. *Stresemann and the Revision of Versailles: A Fight for Reason.* Stanford, Calif.: Stanford University Press, 1953.

Gatzke, Hans W. *Stresemann and the Rearmament of Germany.* Baltimore: Johns Hopkins Press, 1954. New light on Stresemann's nationalism from his unpublished papers.

Grathwol, Robert P. *Stresemann and the DNVP: Reconciliation or Revenge in German Foreign Policy, 1924–1928.* Lawrence, Kansas: Regents Press, 1980. Stresemann's problems with domestic politics in conducting his foreign policy.

Kimmich, Charles. *Germany and the League of Nations.* Chicago: University of Chicago Press. 1976.

Turner, Henry Ashby. *Stesemann and the Politics of the Weimar Republic.* Princeton: Princeton University Press, 1963. Emphasizes domestic politics.

Walsdorff, Martin. *Bibliographie Gustav Stresemann.* Düsseldorf: Droste, 1972.

1927

Ludwig Quidde (1858–1941)

Germany

Veteran peace leader, historian, journalist, liberal politician.

In jointly awarding the 1927 prize to two longtime peace leaders of France and Germany, Ferdinand Buisson and Ludwig Quidde, it was the committee's intention to acknowledge the Franco-German rapprochement in public opinion that had made possible the achievements of the Locarno statesmen honored the year before.

For the German cowinner, the committee could not have made a better choice than Quidde, who had already made its short list in the two preceding years. Although Buisson had joined his first peace society as early as 1867, a quarter of a century before Quidde became a member of the newly formed German Peace Society in 1892, Quidde had a much more substantial record of leadership in peace activities in his own country and internationally throughout the succeeding years. Moreover, Quidde's efforts to promote understanding with France went back before 1914. His celebrated handshake with Frédéric Passy, the French pacifist leader, at the 1905 World Peace Congress in Lucerne, Switzerland, was a high point of Franco-German reconciliation in the prewar peace movement. Years later on his deathbed Passy spoke of this moment as "the first really honorable and loyal handshake exchanged between Germany and France." Even on the eve of war, Quidde was active in meetings between German and French parliamentarians seeking avenues of reconciliation between the two countries.

Ludwig Quidde was born in 1858 in Bremen, the son of a wealthy merchant. He took his doctorate in history at the University of Göttingen at the age of twenty-three. He had already in his student days been a critic of the conservative prejudices of the time. He published a tract attacking anti-Semitism among the students, which brought him half a dozen challenges to a duel. To Quidde this was a barbaric practice, but he felt he could not let the anti-Semites call their opponents cowards, so he accepted one. Fortunately, "honor" was satisfied by an exchange of pistol shots that injured neither of the combatants. There would be other such occasions when Quidde would be called upon to demonstrate the courage of his convictions.

Next came a confrontation with authority that had serious consequences for Quidde. After he finished his studies with distinction, he married and was starting on a promising career as a historian. He became an editor of the great collection of Reichstag documents of the Middle Ages, served two years as the director of the Prussian Historical Institute in Rome, and founded an important historical journal. After resettling in Munich, Quidde wrote an anonymous pamphlet criticizing German militarism, and in 1894, under his own name, he published the satirical essay "Caligula, a Study of Imperial Insanity," a thinly veiled attack on William II under the guise of a study of the mad Roman emperor. The publication caused a sensation in the country, eventually going through thirty editions. Quidde's lawyer advised him to take the next train to Switzerland, but Quidde refused, saying that flight would be used against him as evidence of guilt. The state's attorney finally decided not to prosecute because of the embarrassment for William II, but he bided his time and two years later convicted Quidde on a charge of lèse-majesté for something he said in a political speech and sent him to prison for three months.

"Caligula" closed the door to a university career for Quidde, since professorships were state appointments. He had to withdraw from his historical journal, although he managed to remain as editor of a documentary series for which remuneration was nominal (he kept this post for many years until finally dismissed by the Nazis). But Quidde was a marked man. He and his wife found many social connections broken off, and thirteen years after the publication of "Caligula" when Quidde was a municipal councillor of Munich and had organized the World Peace Congress there, he had to absent himself from certain formal occasions in which officials of the imperial government were participating. Even in 1914, when Quidde was an obvious choice for president of the German Peace Society, objections were raised that "Caligula" might cause difficulties with the government. After all other possibilities were exhausted, however, Quidde was finally elected, and he served for fifteen years.

Possessed of private means, Quidde could turn his energies to the peace movement and to politics, where he was active in left-liberal parties. He served nine years on the Munich Municipal Council, and he was a deputy in the Bavarian legislature from 1907 until 1918. This qualified him to join the German group of the Interparliamentary Union and take an active role in its international conferences. He was a member of the executive council of the German Peace Society after the turn of the century, represented it on the Commission of the International Peace Bureau, and headed the German delegation to world peace congresses, where his command of French and English made him especially effective.

Immediately after the war broke out in 1914, Quidde went to The Hague to try to establish relationships with French, English, and Belgian pacifists. The attempt failed, and he went home to face charges of treason. He defended himself successfully, but he continued to have difficulties with the authorities throughout the war, and it was all he could do to hold the German peace movement together. In 1915 Quidde published a pamphlet setting forth carefully reasoned arguments against the popular demand for territorial annexations after the war. The government confiscated copies of the pamphlet and began to censor Quidde's mail.

After the war Quidde was elected to the National Assembly at Weimar, where, speaking without notes as always, he vigorously attacked the Versailles treaty in probably his most memorable speech. He declared that the treaty destroyed any chance of peace and would only push the world into hatred and war. The speech was greeted with resounding applause, but it was not popular with many German pacifists, who also disagreed with Quidde's position on Germany's war guilt. They approved the clause in the treaty that laid the blame on Germany for starting the war, whereas Quidde opposed the clause. As a historian, he declared that it was necessary to distinguish between the longtime underlying causes and the actions of the statesmen in the crisis of 1914.

There were other differences of opinion in the German peace movement after the war. Quidde's pacifism was inspired by the moral philosophy of Immanuel Kant, and he was committed to democracy as a middle-class liberal, but more radical elements were coming to the fore, insisting upon making appeals to the masses. Quidde's talents as a mediator and his organizational abilities were much appreciated, however, and he remained as president of the German Peace Society until 1929 and even headed the German Peace Cartel, a loose organization within which all the peace organizations tried to cooperate.

Skilled as Quidde was at finding compromises within the movement, his peace principles were too dear to him to make the compromises that might have ensured him a successful political career in the Weimar Republic. After the National Assembly he did not again hold an elective public office. In 1924 he was briefly imprisoned again for his convictions, this time for publishing an article about Germany's secret rearmament in violation of the Versailles Treaty. The treason charges against Quidde were dropped, but a few years later in a similar situation Carl von Ossietzky, who was also to win a Nobel Peace Prize, was convicted.

In 1933, after Hitler came to power, Quidde finally took the train to Switzerland and exile. The only alternative would have been a concentration camp. In Geneva Quidde lived in straitened circumstances, his personal fortune having been lost in the inflation of the 1920s. Some support came from pacifists abroad, but it was the Nobel prize money that in Quidde's case fulfilled, at least to some extent, Nobel's original intention to enable a laureate to devote major efforts on behalf of peace. In his years of exile Quidde depended upon the monthly subsidy the Norwegian Nobel Committee gave him to work on a history of the German peace movement in the First World War. When Quidde's friends made up a substantial purse for him on the occasion of his eightieth birthday in 1938, he gave much of it away to the committee he had established for assistance to refugee German pacifists.

In Geneva Quidde continued his international peace activities, but he had to be careful not to provoke the Nazi government, since his wife, whose father was Jewish, had remained in Munich. It was only with some difficulty that fellow German pacifists in exile were finally able to persuade him to nominate Ossietzky, then in a concentration camp, for the Peace Prize.

I remember Quidde in his Geneva days as a kindly old patrician with a trim white beard, every inch the gentleman, as so many others had found him. His reminiscences were peppered with touches of good humor. He could not be optimistic about the immediate future, and he lived to see the conflagration break out again in 1939. But he could feel that he had done his best throughout his long life to prevent it. Quidde died in Geneva in 1941. On his tombstone it is appropriately written, "I have loved justice."

BIBLIOGRAPHY

Primary Sources

Quidde, Ludwig. *Der deutsche Pazifismus während des Weltkrieges 1914–1918: Aus dem Nachlass Ludwig Quiddes.* Edited by Karl Holl. Schriften des Bundesarchivs, 23. Boppard-am-Rhein: Boldt, 1979. In Quidde's papers the editor found the manuscript of his history of German pacifism during World War I, on which Quidde was working in his last years, and prepared this edition, with a biographical introduction.

———. "The Future of Germany." *Living Age* 328 (5 April 1924): 635–38.

Secondary Sources

Chickering, Roger. *Imperial Germany and a World without War: The Peace Movement and German Society 1892–1914.* Princeton: Princeton University Press, 1975.

Goldstein, Brigitte M. "Ludwig Quidde and the Struggle for Democratic Pacifism in Germany, 1914–1930." Ph.D. diss., New York University. Ann Arbor, Mich.: University Microfilms International, 1984.

"Quidde, Ludwig." In *MPL.*

Taube, Utz-Friedebert. *Ludwig Quidde: Ein Beitrag zur Geschichte des Demokratischen Gedanken in Deutschland.* Kallmunz: Lassleben, 1963. Quidde in the perspective of the history of German democratic thought.

Wehberg, Hans. *Ludwig Quidde, ein deutscher Demokrat und Vorkämpfer der Völkerverständigung.* Offenbach am Main: Bollwerk, 1948. A short admiring biographical sketch.

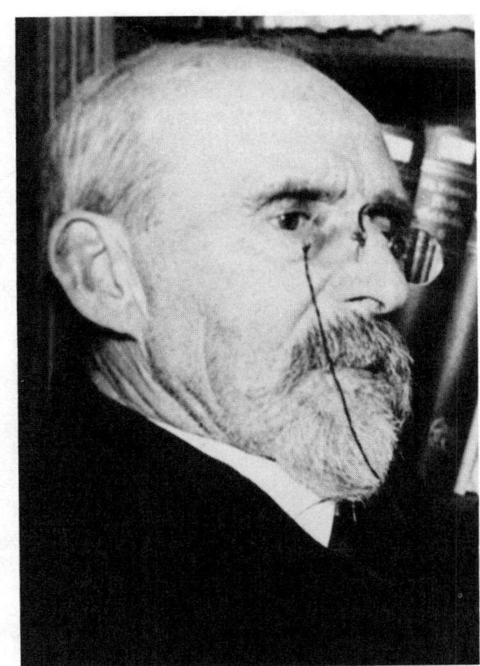

1927
Ferdinand Buisson (1841–1932)

France

Education administrator and professor, legislator, lifelong champion of human rights and peace.

Ferdinand Buisson of France and Ludwig Quidde of Germany shared the prize of 1927 for their contributions to the movement of opinion for Franco-German reconciliation, which the Nobel Committee felt had made possible the achievement of the statesmen of Locarno honored the year before. Quidde had been a leader of the organized peace movement in Germany for many years. Buisson had been notably active in peace societies only at the beginning and toward the end of a long life devoted to many liberal causes. He was twenty-six when he attended his first peace congress. A half century later he joined in the movement for the League of Nations and took a prominent role in French national peace congresses. What especially impressed the committee were his efforts for Franco-German understanding after the First World War. The committee first gave his candidacy special consideration in 1925, the year after he had, at the age of eighty-three, made a speaking tour for peace in Germany, and two years later it gave him the award.

Ferdinand Buisson was born in Paris in 1841, the son of a Protestant judge. He studied to be a teacher, but because he refused to take the oath of allegiance to Emperor Napoléon III, he had to take a teaching position in Switzerland. With other French political exiles and republicans from all over Europe, he attended the Peace Congress of 1867 in Geneva that founded the International League of Peace and Liberty, which aimed to establish the United States of Europe. Buisson published an article in the organization's journal, entitled "Abolishing War through Education," which emphasized the importance of his chosen profession in the work for peace. This was a concern that he never forgot during his career as an educator and a topic to which he returned in his Nobel essay written in 1928 in place of the laureate lecture.

After the fall of Napoléon III, Buisson came back to Paris to take a series of posts in educational administration, culminating in his appointment as national director of primary education, a position he held for seventeen years until 1896, when he became professor of pedagogy at the Sorbonne. In these years he was a leader in the establishment of a system of primary education that was free, compulsory, and secular. Buisson was a critic of organized religion; he based his liberal Christianity on personal morality. His anticlericalism brought him under heavy attack from conservatives.

In the 1890s France was divided between conservative clerical-army forces and liberal defenders of individual rights when the army captain Alfred Dreyfus, an Alsatian of Jewish background, was falsely accused and convicted of espionage. Buisson was one of the first to speak out for Dreyfus. He campaigned vigorously to get the conviction reversed and helped found the French League of the Rights of Man, of which he later was president for many years. These events led Buisson into politics. In 1902 he was elected as a Radical Socialist to the Chamber of Deputies, where he continued to work for liberal causes, such as educational reform, women's suffrage, and social security. He held his seat until 1914 and again from 1919 to 1924, thereafter serving as municipal councillor in his home community.

It was the war that brought Buisson once more into significant engagement with the organized peace movement. He supported the war effort, convinced that France's cause was just, but he wanted victory to lead to a new international order based on justice. He was a leading member of the French Association for the League of Nations, along with men like d'Estournelles de Constant and Léon Bourgeois.

Disappointed in the Treaty of Versailles, Buisson attacked its punitive terms in an open letter and criticized the League of Nations as a league of victors. Nevertheless, it must be supported, he wrote, and by the pressure of public opinion transformed into a true instrument of international solidarity. In a eulogy on Woodrow Wilson in 1924, he expressed his conviction that the League would one day realize Wilson's hopes, but before there could be the disarmament of nations there had to be the disarmament of hatred.

When the French occupied the Ruhr and passions on both sides of the Rhine were inflamed, Buisson and other French peace leaders, putting words into deeds, invited German pacifists to Paris and then returned the visit. Buisson sounded the keynote of this effort in one of his addresses in Germany: "A force exists which is far greater than France, far greater than Germany, far greater than any nation, and that is mankind. But above mankind itself stands justice, which finds its most perfect expression in human brotherhood."

Buisson was eighty-six years of age when he received the award, the oldest peace laureate on record. Most of those who received the prize toward the end of their lives were honored for long years of service to the cause. Buisson did not lack for such qualifications, but in his case it was his most recent work for peace that won him the prize. He died at his home at the age of ninety-one, having given away his share of the prize money to various peace causes.

BIBLIOGRAPHY

Primary Source

Buisson, Ferdinand E., and Fred. E. Farrington, eds. *French Educational Ideals of Today.* Yonkers-on-Hudson, N.Y.: World, 1919. An anthology selected to explain French education to Americans.

———. *Un moralistic laïque. Pages choisi.* Paris: Alcan, 1933. A selection of his writings, including chapters on his souvenirs and on the organization of peace.

Secondary Sources

"Buisson, Ferdinand." In *MPL.*

Roussel, B. E. *La Vie et l'oeuvre de Ferdinand Buisson.* Montpelier: 1931.

Talbott, John E. *The Politics of Educational Reform in France.* Princeton: Princeton University Press, 1969.

1929
Frank B. Kellogg (1856–1937)

United States

Coauthor of Kellogg-Briand Pact; attorney; senator, ambassador to Great Britain, secretary of state; judge, Permanent Court of International Justice.

The 1929 prize awarded to Frank B. Kellogg in 1930 was the last of the statesmen awards of the late 1920s that seemed well deserved at the time but have not stood up in the light of later events and the investigations of historians. Kellogg was recognized for his role as American secretary of state in the formulation of a multilateral antiwar treaty. It, however, not only did nothing to maintain the peace but has been shown to have originated in a diplomatic game of chess in which Kellogg's moves were in the beginning prompted more by the pressures of American public opinion than by any faith in the efficacy of such a treaty. But once the pact was on its way to realization, Kellogg himself became a convert. He regarded it as the "crown and consummation of all his labors" and expressed the hope that it would win him the Nobel Peace Prize, which it did.

Frank Billings Kellogg was an American success story—"farm boy to world statesman." Of humble origins, he was born in Potsdam, New York, in 1856, and grew up in Minnesota, where he went to school only until the age of fourteen and then worked on the family farm. At nineteen he went to Rochester, Minnesota, where he found an unsalaried job in a law office and supported himself as a handyman for a local farmer while studying law, history, Latin, and German on his own. At twenty-one he passed the state bar examination, which he later called "a life line to rescue me from a desperate struggle for a livelihood."

He now entered upon a successful career in the law which brought him a national reputation as a trust-busting attorney, the presidency of the American Bar Association, and important political connections in the Republican party. In 1917 he was elected to the Senate from Minnesota. He was one of those Republican senators who would have approved the entry of the United States into the League of Nations with provision for very mild reservations. World War I had made him an internationalist, one who preferred moral sanctions, however, to the use of any stronger collective force in keeping the peace.

Kellogg was not a skillful politician—he refused to call himself a politician, in fact—and he lost his bid for reelection after one term in the Senate. Thereafter he was given two diplomatic missions, first as a delegate to the Pan-American Conference in Chile and then, a prize political plum, appointment as ambassador to Great Britain. These assignments helped prepare him for the post of secretary of state, to which he was appointed by President Calvin Coolidge, serving from 1925 to 1929.

Kellogg is not generally rated among our best secretaries of state. He was not one to take imaginative initiatives, although, to be fair, it is unlikely that Coolidge, who knew little and cared less about foreign affairs, would have given him much support if he had. The comment of Elihu Root, the last American secretary of state to have won the Nobel award and one in a position to judge, was that Kellogg "had a permanent alibi against missing opportunities, because as a matter of fact he never sought them or saw them, and his whole policy as Secretary of State was to take the easiest way and do nothing which he could avoid doing." Of all his accomplishments, aside from the Pact of Paris, Kellogg seems to have been proudest that he had signed more treaties (eighty-one) than any other secretary of state in the history of the country. Over a third of these were bilateral arbitration and conciliation agreements, which testified to his concern for international peace but had little if any effect on international relations.

Kellogg did bring an abundance of energy to the position and a good measure of intelligence and common sense. He was hard-working and conscientious, but he was not particularly sensitive to others, he was uneven in temperament, and his hestitations and vacillations earned him the unkind sobriquet of "Nervous Nellie."

His policy toward Latin America did represent movement away from interventionism. Toward China he maintained the traditional policy of goodwill. With regard to Europe, which was enjoying brief years of prosperity and peace, Kellogg's policy was isolationist—to leave well enough alone. The League was a dead issue, and despite his previous support, Kellogg left it there. He did show interest in the United States joining the World Court, but he had no desire to try to see the matter through an obstructionist Senate. Kellogg's only major effort involving Europe was the sponsoring of the three-power Geneva Conference of 1927 with Great Britain and Japan to limit naval armaments, which was poorly conceived, inadequately prepared for, and an outright failure. If anything, this experience intensified Kellogg's isolationism toward Europe and disposed him to reject the proposal Foreign Minister Briand of France was making to the United States for a treaty between the two countries renouncing war as an instrument of national policy.

The concept of outlawing war had first been popularized by Salmon Levinson, a wealthy Chicago lawyer, who maintained that if states were to agree that war was illegal, they would follow international law and no longer go to war. Levinson lobbied for this idea in Washington and the capitals of Europe and was joined by prominent Americans such as Senator William Borah and the philosopher John Dewey as well as leading clergymen and peace activists.

A parallel movement was led by Nicholas Murray Butler and Prof. James T. Shotwell of the Carnegie Endowment for International Peace. Apparently it was Shotwell who gave Briand the idea of renouncing war as "an instrument of policy," a phrase taken from the classic work on war by Gen. Carl von Clausewitz, although Butler sought to take this credit for himself. It was Shotwell who was asked by Briand to draft the message to the American people that the French statesman published on 6 April 1927, the tenth anniversary of the American declaration of war on Germany, which proposed a Treaty of Perpetual Friendship between the two Allies, outlawing and renouncing war between them forever.

What motivated Briand was not a new formula for peace but the prospect of drawing the United States into a special visible relationship with France, thus complementing the system of alliances in Europe through which that country was seeking to guarantee its security. Kellogg and his colleagues at the State Department were under no illusions as to what Briand was up to. They delayed answering him, but the two groups of peace leaders mounted a powerful propaganda campaign that became irresistible when Charles Lindbergh's solo flight across the Atlantic to Paris produced an outburst of pro-French feeling. Kellogg finally found the way to satisfy the popular movement and at the same time avoid a European entanglement. After shrewdly consulting with the Foreign Relations Committee of the Senate, he countered Briand's offer with the proposal that the treaty for the renunciation of war be not just Franco-American but multilateral.

"We now have Briand out on a limb," declared a State Department official—and not only Briand, for to all the diplomats a treaty renouncing war made as little sense as Tsar Alexander's proposal once to other European sovereigns that their foreign policies henceforth should conform to Christian principle. Yet to refuse to sign the pledge Kellogg was proposing meant refusing to line up against sin, and public opinion in many countries was becoming inspired with the highest expectations from such a treaty. British foreign minister and Nobel laureate Chamberlain felt that Kellogg had given them all "a knotty problem." He was convinced that Kellogg's motives had mostly to do with the fact that it was election year in the United States, but how could he and Nobel laureates Briand and Stresemann refuse to go along with a treaty renouncing war? Moreover, there was always the possibility that the result might bring the United States out of its isolationism.

All the same, the other statesmen were not prepared to sign until Kellogg assured them that the treaty did not abrogate the right of self-defense or any commitments assumed under the Covenant of the League of Nations, the Locarno treaties, or the French alliances. The British added a reservation that there were "certain regions," the defense of which was vital to their security, where the treaty would not be applicable.

Kellogg himself began to see the treaty in a new light as "the greatest accomplishment of my administration." He sent his wife a news report that he had been nominated for the Nobel Peace Prize and told her that if he could get the treaty through, "I think it quite likely I would get that prize." Kellogg's change of heart—he now seemed "to take it all with profound seriousness"—was incomprehensible to a close colleague at the State Department. "The political trick has been turned," he wrote in his diary, and now he felt it was time to call things off.

In the end, plenipotentiaries of fifteen nations signed the document in Paris on 27 August 1928. Stresemann came from his sickbed. Chamberlain, also ill, sent a representative. Briand, the only speaker on the occasion, announced, "Peace is proclaimed. That is well; that is much; but it still remains necessary to organize it."

By the first article of the treaty the signatories condemned recourse to war for the solution of international controversies and renounced it as an instrument of national policy in their relations with one another. In the second they agreed that the settlement of all conflicts between them "shall never be sought except by pacific means."

Eventually sixty-four states in all adhered to the pact, only Argentina, Bolivia, El Salvador, and Uruguay failing to sign. Mussolini called it "sublime," even "transcendental," and the Japanese praised "this sublime and magnanimous treaty." The Senate ratified it almost unanimously, but one senator said he would vote for it as "worthless but perfectly harmless," while another referred to the pact as an "international kiss."

When the original fifteen signatories had all ratified the treaty and President Hoover proclaimed it in force in a solemn ceremony in Washington on 24 July 1929, war was already brewing between two of the states, Russia and China. Secretary of State Henry Stimson, Kellogg's successor, appealed to them in vain, invoking the antiwar pact. When Japan then advanced in Manchuria, Stimson announced that territorial changes made in violation of the treaty would not be recognized by the United States. This was the so-called Stimson Doctrine, later used by the League Assembly.

Kellogg, who spent his last active years as a judge on the World Court, took the position that this Japanese violation and then the Italian violation of the pact in Ethiopia should have been met by representations from all the other signatories, but his treaty did not explicitly call for any commitment to consult in the face of a violation, let alone any sanction against the violator. Moreover, only wars that were not wars of defense were outlawed, with the war-making state free to make the distinction. In the Nuremberg trials of Nazi leaders after the Second World War, a court of the victors convicted them of the crime of waging war in violation of the Pact of Paris, but international lawyers are far from agreed that this procedure was just.

President Coolidge in his farewell note to his secretary of state told Kellogg that what he had achieved with the peace treaty was "revolutionary." But it was true that peace had been proclaimed, not organized. As an instrument of practical peacemaking, the Pact of Paris was futile. It was not exactly harmless, as the senator thought, since it nurtured the illusion that the demon of war could be exorcised by the magic spell of renunciation. What the episode did represent, perhaps, was another step in the evolution in the conscience of humankind of the realization that war must be brought to an end—but unmatched as yet by the realization that this necessitated a reordering of international society that would indeed be revolutionary.

BIBLIOGRAPHY

Primary Sources

Kellogg, Frank B. "The Renunciation of War." *Review of Reviews* 78 (December 1928): 595–601.

———. "The War Prevention Policy of the United States." *American Journal of International Law* 22 (1928): 253–61.

Secondary Sources

Bryn-Jones, David. *Frank B. Kellogg: A Biography.* New York: Putnam, 1937.

Ellis, L. Ethan. *Frank B. Kellogg and American Foreign Relations, 1925–1929.* New Brunswick, N.J.: Rutgers University Press, 1961.

Ferrell, Robert H. *Frank B. Kellogg—Henry L. Stimson.* Vol. 11 of *American Secretaries of State and Their Diplomacy.* Edited by Samuel F. Bemis. New York: Cooper Square, 1963, pp. 1–135.

———. *Peace in Their Time: The Origins of the Kellogg-Briand Pact.* New Haven: Yale University Press, 1952. A revealing diplomatic study.

"Kellogg, Frank B." In *BDI.*

"Kellogg, Frank B." In *DAB,* supp. 2.

Miller, David Hunter. *The Peace Pact of Paris: A Study of the Briand-Kellogg Treaty.* New York: Putnam, 1928. A close examination of the documents available at the time.

Myers, Denis P. *The Origin and Conclusion of the Paris Pact.* Boston: World Peace Foundation, 1929. Reprint. New York: Garland, 1972. With an introduction by Charles DeBenedetti. A factual analysis using the official documents.

1930
Nathan Söderblom (1866–1931)

Sweden

Leader of ecumenical movement, working for world peace through Christian unity; archbishop of Uppsala, theologian, scholar.

Nathan Söderblom was the first representative of religion to receive the prize. The Nobel Committee spokesman declared that his "great achievement is that he has thrown the power of the spirit into the fight for peace." As a champion of unity among Christian churches, Söderblom also called upon Christians to work for world peace. As primate of the Lutheran state church of Sweden, he attempted to bring Christian churchmen together during the First World War to speak out for brotherhood and peace. His major achievement was the international conference on Christian unity held in Stockholm in 1925. Here and in subsequent ecumenical meetings Söderblom strove to keep the Christian churches aware of their responsibility to help create peace on earth. Söderblom was a man of deep spirituality, vast learning, and great personal charm. Even as the young pastor of the Swedish Church in Paris, he had impressed Alfred Nobel, who was no friend of organized religion, but who discussed his unorthodox religious ideas with Söderblom and contributed funds for his parish work. Söderblom conducted Nobel's memorial service.

Nathan Söderblom was born in Tränö, Sweden, in 1866, the son of a Lutheran minister. He attended Uppsala University, where he studied Greek, Hebrew, Arabic, and Latin, and then went on the School of Theology. Here at the age of twenty-two he published his first papers as editor of the review of the Student Missionary Association. In 1890 he traveled to a Student Christian Conference in New England, where after listening to a lecture he was moved to write in his diary, "Lord, give me humility and wisdom to serve the great cause of the free unity of Thy church." He was then twenty-four, and he was to render this cause distinguished service during the rest of his life.

Söderblom was ordained in 1893 and decided to accept a call from the Swedish Church in Paris. With him went his bride, the accomplished Anna Forsell, who had been one of twenty women students among the seventeen hundred men at the university. She was to become the mother of thirteen children, and also Söderblom's collaborator in many of his prolific publications. His seven years in Paris broadened his intercultural understanding and helped prepare him to work for unity among Christian churches. He was further equipped for this through his studies at the Protestant Faculty of the Sorbonne, where he was the first foreigner to be granted the doctorate.

In 1901 he returned to Uppsala to teach theology. His wide range of publications, which included history of religion, comparative religion, and the psychology of religion, gained him a national reputation and led to something of a theological revival in the country. In 1914 he was elected archbishop of Uppsala, surprisingly, since he had not been a bishop. This meant that he was the top prelate of the country, and as head of Sweden's ecclesiastical establishment, he had to undertake extensive administrative duties along with his continued research and writing.

With this position Söderblom could take international leadership in the work for church unity and for peace. In 1914 he helped found the General World Union of Churches for International Understanding, whose activities were abruptly terminated by the war. Despite wartime dislocations, Söderblom managed to keep some lines of communication open among the Christian churches, working primarily with churchmen in neutral Scandinavia. In 1917 he tried to arrange an international church congress with participants from the belligerent countries, but the Allied governments refused to grant passports to Western representatives. Consequently, a Neutral Church Conference was held in Uppsala, which issued a manifesto in December 1917 that was largely Söderblom's handiwork. It was an impressive reaffirmation of Christian unity addressed to a war-torn world in which churchmen were all too prone to see God on the side of their own nation's battalions.

The manifesto declared: "The church should represent the waking conscience of mankind. Together with the Christians in all nations at war, we are deeply aware of the incompatibility between war and the spirit of Christ." The church must "fully participate in efforts to remove the causes of war, whether these are of a social, economic, or political nature." Christians "should try to understand others, their thoughts, languages, and behavior," and "the church must work for international understanding and for the settlement of international disputes through mediation and arbitration." The church must preach that "nations and communities, like individuals, must act according to ethical principles, basing their hopes for coexistence on the principles of truth, justice, and love."

Once the war ended Söderblom arranged for a conference in Geneva which laid the foundations for the great ecumenical assembly in 1925 in Stockholm, which is considered his triumph. More than six hundred delegates came to this Universal Christian Conference on Life and Work, representing Protestant and Orthodox communities in thirty-seven countries. Only the Roman Catholic church abstained. Under Söderblom's influence, a major topic of discussion was "The Church and International Relations," and this remained on the agenda in future meetings.

In his Nobel address, delivered on 11 December 1930, Söderblom discussed at length "The Role of the Church in Promoting Peace." He started out by declaring, "Peace can be reached only through fighting against the ancient Adam in ourselves and in others." He continued, "All people and all nations must participate in the construction of a supranational legal system, which, according to our Christian doctrine, is a continuation of God's creation." He concluded, "The noble and practical measures for world peace will be realized only to the extent to which the supremacy of God conquers the hearts of the people."

Another great honor came to the distinguished theologian with an invitation to deliver the famous Gifford Lectures at Edinburgh five months after receiving the peace award. He planned a major undertaking; he would deliver the first ten lectures in 1931 and the others in 1932 and publish them in two volumes. But his first lecture series, which he presented in May and June 1931, turned out to be his last scholarly contribution to an understanding of the Divine. Söderblom died on 12 July, the day he decided on the title for the book: *The Living God.* He was sixty-five years old.

BIBLIOGRAPHY

Primary Sources

Söderblom, Nathan. *The Church and Peace.* Oxford: Clarendon, 1929. The Burge Memorial Lecture.

———. *The Living God: Basal Forms of Personal Religion.* London: Oxford University Press, 1933. The Gifford Lectures delivered at the University of Edinburgh in 1931.

Secondary Sources

Curtis, Charles J. *Nathan Söderblom: Theologian of Revelation.* Chicago: Covenant Press, 1966.

———. *Söderblom: Ecumenical Pioneer.* Minneapolis, Minn.: Augsburg Publishing House, 1967.

Idleman, Finis. "Archbishop Söderblom." *Christian Century* 40 (18 October 1923): 1337–38. Soderblom is presented as "the most powerful single influence in European Protestantism."

Mott, John. "Archibishop Nathan Söderblom." In *Addresses and Papers* 6 vols. New York: Association Press, 1946–47, 6:442–46. Warm appreciation from a longtime friend.

Simons, Walter. *The Religious Basis of World Peace.* London: Williams & Norgate, 1929.

"Söderblom, Nathan." In *BDI.*

Sundkler, Bengt. *Nathan Söderblom: His Life and Work.* London: Butterworth, 1968. Emphasizes his ecumenical leadership. With a bibliography by and about Söderblom.

1931
Jane Addams (1860–1935)

United States

Social reformer, advocate of peace and women's rights, author and lecturer, leader of American settlement house movement, cofounder of Women's International League for Peace and Freedom.

The Nobel Committee divided the 1931 prize between Nicholas Murray Butler and Jane Addams, considering them two of the finest representatives of American practical idealism. "In honoring Jane Addams," Prof. Halvdan Koht, the committee spokesman declared, "we also render homage to the work which women can do for peace and human brotherhood."

It was high time. Twenty-six prizes had been awarded since the last one to a woman, Bertha von Suttner, in 1905. Beginning in 1916 the committee had Addams on its short list six times before finally giving her a divided prize. The most appropriate moment for the award would have been in 1916, when she was leading a spectacular movement to promote mediation between the belligerents of the First World War. The year she received the greatest support was 1923, when her admirers in England and the United States generated thirty nominations from among the most eminent personages of the time, a list headed by Woodrow Wilson and including the philosopher John Dewey, Supreme Court Justice Felix Frankfurter, Senator Robert La Follette, Stanford University president David Starr Jordan, and the English social thinkers Graham Wallas and Sidney Webb. The committee adviser gave her a strong recommendation in his report, but again Addams was passed over, and, as in 1916, no prize was awarded. She was on the short list again in 1924 and 1928, years in which the committee made no award, and in 1929 and 1930, when the prize was given to others.

To be sure, there were no doubt special reasons for each negative decision. Committee members have generally been chary of awarding the Peace Prize in wartime, for example, and 1923 was the year of the Franco-German conflict over the Ruhr. Still, it is not to the credit of the members of the Nobel Committee that they could not agree to honor Jane Addams until close to the end of her life, and then with only half of the prize. Many of the letters of congratulation she received deplored her having to share the award, and especially with Butler. Although Jane Addams never expressed her feelings publicly about her Nobel partner, she must have remembered all too well how, after the United States entered the war and she was made to suffer for her pacifist convictions, the august president of Columbia University was busily harrying the pacifists on his faculty.

In a way her frequent appearance on the short list before final recognition by the Nobel Committee is a testament to the magnitude of her personal achievement. She rose to national and international prominence at a time when most professions were closed to women and they were excluded from political life. Moreover, the ancient prejudice to which Koht referred in his presentation speech, "that woman was the source of nearly all the sins and of all the conflicts on earth," persisted. Today, Koht declared, we see women in a different light, and they are showing a new independence that will constitute a new force in the work for peace. The feminine will which revolts against war can be seen wherever women are organized, and "we can say that Jane Addams combines in herself all the best feminine qualities which will help us to organize peace on earth."

Jane Addams herself saw femininity as central to woman's role as peacemaker, but this was something positive, not negative. Peace was not "the absence of war but the unfolding of world-wide processes making for the nurture of human life." Woman, by nature a life-giver and life-nurturer, was a basic part of these processes. The maternity instinct imposed a special obligation, for

> quite as an artist in an artillery crops commanded to fire on the *duomo* at Florence would be deterred by a compunction unknown to the man who had never given himself to creating beauty and did not know the intimate cost of it, so women, who have brought men into the world and nurtured them until they reach the age for fighting, must experience a peculiar revulsion when they see them destroyed, irrespective of the country in which these men may have been born.

On her tombstone, as she had asked, there is engraved "Jane Addams of Hull House and the Women's International League for Peace and Freedom." These were the two achievements for which she wanted to be remembered, and the one grew out of the other. Her vision of the international community was based on her experiences with the community around Hull House, her settlement house in the slums of Chicago, where she helped immigrants of many nationalities and watched them working together to meet one another's needs. Her "newer ideals of peace," as she explained in the book of that title published in 1907, were "aggressive and dynamic," as compared with the older "dovelike" ideals, which had been based more upon sentiment and calculations of the costs of war. She had seen the new ideals at work in her immigrant neighborhood, the "impulse toward compassionate conduct" of the humble, which in the age of industrialization would produce a sort of internationalism of goodwill.

Jane Addams was born in Cedarville, Illinois, in 1860, the daughter of a well-to-do miller and politician who was a friend of Abraham Lincoln. At twenty-one she graduated from the Rockford Female Seminary, where the religious atmosphere inspired the students with the desire to do good works. The death of her beloved father precipitated a long period of intermittent depression and illness, interspersed with study and travel abroad, from which she emerged with a clearer idea of how she wanted to spend her life.

In 1889, when she was not yet thirty, Jane Addams and a friend rented the Hull mansion in Chicago, with the plan of developing a social center along the lines of Toynbee Hall, the first settlement house, which she had visited in London. The crowded tenements nearby were thronged with poor immigrants living in squalor, nineteen nationalities in all, including Italians, Poles, Irish, Germans, and Czechs. Hull House offered them a variety of recreational and educational programs. Addams was the esteemed head resident, friend, counselor, and nurse, providing all manner of assistance to people in need, and at the same time the able administrator, skillful public relations director, and fund-raiser.

Her experience of the appalling conditions in which the immigrants lived and worked propelled her into the movement for social legislation and reform. She became a well-known figure in Chicago and then, as Koht declared, "the leading woman in the nation, one might almost say its leading citizen." Her autobiographical account, *Thirty Years at Hull House,* became a classic. Visitors came from near and far to observe her work, including a young Norwegian historian named Halvdan Koht.

In 1914 the news of the war gave Jane Addams "a basic sense of desolation, of suicide, of anachronism." With suffragist Carrie Chapman Catt, she issued a call for a meeting of women's organizations, which convened in Washington early in 1915 and formed the Women's Peace party, with Addams as chair. Proposals were adopted for ending the war by "continuous mediation," for liberal peace terms and permanent international peace agencies after the war, and for the representation of women in national and international life. Suffragists in Europe invited this organization to send delegates to an international peace congress of women to be held in the Netherlands. Jane Addams set sail on the Dutch ship, the *Noordam,* with her friend Emily Greene Balch and over forty other delegates. Peace laureate Theodore Roosevelt called them "silly and base," and other bellicose opponents named the ship "The Palace of Doves" and its passengers "Pro-Hun Peacettes." The British government stopped the vessel en route but finally permitted it to continue.

Eventually almost fifteen hundred delegates from twelve countries reached The Hague in April 1915 for the meeting. Jane Addams presided over this International Congress of Women, which adopted resolutions on peace and mediation, formed a continuing International Committee with Addams as president, and sent two delegations to make the rounds of European capitals to explore the possibilities of mediation with such statesmen as would receive them. Addams herself went with two colleagues to London, Berlin, Vienna, Rome, and Paris. Such a citizen peace mission in wartime was unprecedented, but the delegations reported that many statesmen had welcomed them and that the idea of a conference of neutral powers for mediation was under serious discussion. Addams returned home to urge President Woodrow Wilson to accept the presidency of such a conference, but in vain. She then secured the support of Henry Ford for a conference of private individuals to be held in Stockholm for the same purpose. Although Addams fell ill and was unable to sail with Ford's mercilessly ridiculed "Peace Ship," the conference went off as planned.

Addams saw Wilson again in January 1916 and was encouraged to find that he had read the Hague resolutions she had left with him six months earlier. Apparently this report of the women's initiative confirmed his feeling that the great masses of the world were yearning for peace. When Wilson made his "peace without victory" speech in January 1917, Addams was convinced he was repeating many of the Hague resolutions. To her dismay, however, in April 1917, the president asked Congress to declare war against the Central Powers, and most of her liberal and progressive friends supported the move.

Jane Addams, following her deepest convictions, publicly opposed the war. This was the most difficult period of her public life. Hull House had been a popular cause, but pacifism in wartime to many loyal patriots was nothing short of treason. Addams was reviled in the press and felt lonely and depressed. After the war during the Red Scare she was again to be denounced as a dangerous radical and Hull House charged with being a hotbed of communism.

Meanwhile, the international network formed by the women at The Hague continued to function. Some months after the armistice, in July 1919, the Hague delegates reconvened in Zurich, where they formed a permanent organization, the Women's International League for Peace and Freedom (WILPF). Jane Addams, as the group's international president, went to Paris to present their criticisms of the peace treaty that was being written as a punitive document. Later the WILPF formally denounced the Treaty of Versailles. Addams, as international president of the WILPF until 1929 and thereafter honorary president, helped develop the organization's procedures, presided over its four international congresses in the 1920s, interpreted its work, and attended meetings when she could. She helped raise funds, contributed five hundred dollars monthly herself to the American section, and gave the WILPF her share of the Nobel Peace Prize.

Addams's last connection with the prize was her nomination of Carl von Ossietzky for the 1935 award, in response to a request from Albert Einstein. The prestige of her name gave a crucial boost to the campaign which was ultimately successful. She died in 1935, having, as Koht said, "regained the place of honor she had had before in the hearts of her people." The Chicago City Council passed a resolution declaring that she was "the greatest woman who ever lived." In the words of philosopher William James of Harvard, "she inhabited reality." The commentator Walter Lippman put it most succinctly, "She was not only good, but great."

BIBLIOGRAPHY

Primary Sources

Addams, Jane. *A Centennial Reader.* Edited by Emily C. Johnson. New York: Macmillan, 1960.

———. *Jane Addams on Peace and Freedom, 1914–1935.* Edited by Blanche Cook. New York: Garland, 1972. Essays and unpublished correspondence, with an introductory essay by the editor.

———. *Newer Ideals of Peace.* New York: Macmillan, 1907.

———. *Peace and Bread in Time of War.* With an introduction by John Dewey. Anniversary ed. New York: King's Crown, 1945. Reprint. New York: Garland, 1972.

———. *The Second Twenty Years at Hull House.* New York: Macmillan, 1930.

———. *The Social Thought of Jane Addams.* Edited by Christopher Lasch. Indianapolis: Bobbs Merrill, 1965.

———. *Twenty Years at Hull House.* New York: Macmillan, 1910.

Addams, Jane, Emily G. Balch, and Alice Hamilton. *Women at The Hague.* New York: 1915. Reprint. New York: Garland, 1972. With an introduction by Mercedes Randall.

Secondary Sources

Davis, Allen F. *American Heroine: The Life and Legend of Jane Addams.* New York: Oxford University Press, 1973. Scholarly and well written.

Farrell, John G. *Beloved Lady: A History of Jane Addams' Ideas on Reform and Peace.* Baltimore: Johns

Hopkins Press, 1967. With excellent critical bibliographies.

Herman, Sondra R. *Eleven against War.* Stanford, Calif.: Hoover Institution Press, 1969, Chap. 5.

Levine, Daniel. *Jane Addams and the Liberal Tradition.* Madison: State Historical Society of Wisconsin, 1971. Her place in American social reform thought.

Linn, James W. *Jane Addams: A Biography.* New York: Appleton-Century, 1935. An authoritative account by her nephew, who discussed the first chapters with her before her death.

Tims, Margaret. *Jane Addams of Hull House, 1860–1935: A Centennial Study.* London: Allen & Unwin, 1961.

1931

Nicholas Murray Butler (1862–1947)

United States

Educator; internationalist; Republican party leader; president, Columbia University, Carnegie Endowment for International Peace.

Sharing the 1931 prize with Jane Addams was Nicholas Murray Butler, longtime president of Columbia University, a major figure in the national and international life of his times, and leader of the establishment sector of the American peace movement. The Nobel Committee had been impressed not only by his long work for peace for over twenty-five years but by the role he had played in the development of the Kellogg-Briand Pact and by the quality of his nominators, who included laureates Aristide Briand, Sir Austen Chamberlain, and Elihu Root. Butler had been nominated before, but this was the first year he made the short list.

Butler was the son of an Elizabeth, New Jersey, importer and manufacturer. He made a brilliant record at Columbia, where he earned his B.A., M.A., and Ph.D. degrees. Then he studied for a year at universities in Paris and Berlin and returned in 1885 to take a position in the Department of Philosophy at his alma mater. His exceptional organizational talents soon brought him administrative responsibilities, and he rose rapidly through the ranks to become president of the institution in 1902, a position he held almost until the end of his long life.

Butler built Columbia into one of the greatest universities of the world, in size, in faculty distinction, and in endowment. He cultivated connections with the corporation lawyers and investment bankers of New York City and proved a phenomenal moneyraiser. Since his study year abroad, on which he embarked well armed with introductions to famous people in Europe, he had always pursued the great and the powerful. Reflecting later on his successes, he wrote in *Across the Busy Years,* "It is literally true, I think, that beginning with Mr. Gladstone, Cardinal Newman, and Pope Leo III, it has been my happy fortune to meet, to talk with and often to know in warm friendship almost every man of light and leading who has lived in the world during the past halfcentury."

As a prominent member of the Republican party, Butler took a leading part in the national conventions and sought, unsuccessfully, the presidential nomination. He was a respected adviser of presidents Theodore Roosevelt, William Howard Taft, and Warren Harding, and on occasion he served an unofficial presidential envoy to foreign governments. He became accustomed to being well received in the chancelleries of Europe, and he even spoke on invitation to foreign parliaments.

Butler traveled to Europe more than a hundred times, an unusual feat in the days of steamboats. On his return from his trips abroad, he would grant the press an interview in which he reported what the political and cultural leaders of Europe had told him about the issues of the day. Often he could also report on some new honor he had received. H. G. Wells called him "the champion international visitor and retriever of foreign orders and degrees."

It is probable that Butler was more highly

regarded in Europe than in his own country, however. Here in his interviews and in his innumerable speeches, he was prone to pontificate, and he was considered pompous. Indeed, pomp and ceremony were dear to him—once he spoke critically of King Haakon of Norway for not being regal enough. Butler's few intimates reported that he could be convivial on occasion, but even in most of his personal relationships he maintained his dignity and seldom would unbend. His was a commanding presence in bearing, if not in size: of medium height, round-faced, and balding, he always stood straight and tall. Butler published some twenty books, but no significant work of scholarship. Most are collections of his addresses and articles and betray little sign of originality. Public speaking came so easily to him that as time went on, he spent less and less time in preparation.

Butler first became interested in peace at the time of the First Hague Conference. He became friendly with Baron d'Estournelles de Constant, who had represented France at the conference and who was to win a Nobel Peace Prize for his work promoting international arbitration and understanding. D'Estournelles founded the Association for International Conciliation, which encouraged exchanges between prominent parliamentarians and intellectuals from different countries. This was the kind of peacemaking that appealed to Butler, who organized and led the American section of the association. Together with d'Estournelles, Butler founded the well-regarded pamphlet series, *International Conciliation.* Butler was well situated at Columbia for ventures in international education, and it was at the same time that he arranged with the German government for one of the earliest exchange professorships between American and European scholars.

In 1910 Butler helped persuade Andrew Carnegie, the peace-minded industrialist, to give his spectacular gift of $10 million to establish the Carnegie Endowment for International Peace "to hasten the abolition of international war." With Elihu Root, Butler was largely responsible for setting the direction of the new foundation. From the beginning Butler directed the Division of Intercourse and Education, and in 1925 he succeeded Root as the president of the endowment.

Although Carnegie had generously supported previously existing peace organizations, Butler and Root shared a distrust of traditional peace propaganda, which they dismissed as "sentimental." Neither had any faith in public opinion, which they felt was too vulnerable to demagogery. What was needed was rather the proper instruction of the masses by an enlightened elite, who would preside over a gradual evolution toward peace through the advance of judicial settlement of international disputes and the extension of international law. After the war Root and Butler were proponents of the World Court, but had reservations about the United States joining the League of Nations. The emphasis of the endowment was consequently placed upon scientific and academic endeavors, targeted at the "intelligent citizenship of the world." The intention was to further what Butler called the "International Mind," which was "nothing else than that habit of thinking of foreign relations and business, and that habit of dealing with them, which regard the several nations of the civilized world as friendly and cooperating equals in aiding the progress of civilization, in developing commerce and industry and in spreading enlightenment and culture throughout the world." To this end the endowment organized conferences, issued publications, stocked "international alcoves" in libraries, promoted international relations clubs, and subsidized research, including a monumental series of monographs on the social and economic results of the First World War.

The governing board of the endowment was made up of pillars of society, a different breed than the nonconformists and dissenters who had provided much of the drive for the older peace societies. Butler tried to centralize and control these organizations through the channeling of endowment funds. After this attempt failed, little if any support from the endowment reached peace societies that were not favored by Butler.

Butler did have an influence on the negotiations leading to the Kellogg-Briand Pact, not by giving the idea to Briand as he claims in his memoirs, but rather by the part he played in winning American public opinion for such a treaty, which pressured a reluctant State Department to respond to Briand's initiative. In gratitude Briand wrote Butler on the day the multilateral pact was signed in Paris, acknowledging "the effective part you have played in the vast movement of ideas which have paved the way and assured the success of the pact signed today."

Butler called himself a "liberal," in the sense of his opposing any government encroachment upon the freedom of the individual. He was, for example, an outspoken opponent of Prohibition, and he criticized high tariffs as restrictions on international trade. But in other regards, he was out of step with the liberal and progressive ideas of his time. He had long admired the German monarchy and had made much of his personal relations with William II, but once the United States declared war on Germany in 1917, he became an ardent patriot and refused to tolerate any dissent on the Columbia faculty.

In the 1920s and 1930s he continued his staunch support of international understanding, but his positions on various international issues were not always consistent. He visited Mussolini and had good words to say about fascism. Later he refrained from public criticism when Hitler began his persecutions. In 1938 he applauded the Munich agreement that France and Britain made with Germany. In the United States he opposed the neutrality legislation and roundly condemned isolationists. In the fall of 1940 he declared in a special convocation at Columbia that the struggle in Europe was a "war between beasts and human beings" and any students or faculty whose convictions were otherwise should leave the university.

By the end of the war in 1945, Butler, now eighty-three and almost blind, resigned from the university and the endowment. Two years later, in December 1947, he died. Butler will be remembered best as the builder of Columbia University, which was always his highest priority. He was also the very embodiment of the "International Mind." But whether he used Carnegie's millions efficaciously "to hasten the abolition of international war" continues to be a matter of debate.

BIBLIOGRAPHY

Primary Sources

Butler, Nicholas Murray. *Across the Busy Years: Recollections and Reflections.* 2 vols. New York: Scribner, 1939–40. Best single source, although not always reliable. Many anecdotes.

———. *The Basis of Durable Peace.* New York: Scribner, 1917.

———. *The Family of Nations.* New York: Scribner, 1939.

———. *The International Mind: An Argument for the Judicial Settlement of International Disputes.* New York: Scribner, 1912. Reprinted in *Before the War: Last Voices of Arbitration.* New York: Garland, 1972. With an introduction by Charles Chatfield.

Secondary Sources

Abrams, Irwin. "John W. Burgess, Theodore Roosevelt Professor in Berlin, 1906–1907: A Case Study in Educational Exchange." *Vitae Scholasticae* 2 (Fall 1983): 327–37. Describes Butler's role in this early program of exchange professors.

Burgess, John W. *Reminiscences of an American Scholar: The Beginnings of Columbia University.* New York: Columbia University Press, 1934. By Butler's mentor who became his close associate.

De Benedetti, Charles. *Origins of the Modern American Peace Movement, 1915–1929.* Millwood, N.Y.: KTO Press, 1978.

Herman, Sondra R. *Eleven against War: Studies in American Internationalist Thought.* Stanford, Calif.: Hoover Institution Press, 1969, chap. 2.

Kuehl, Warren F. *Seeking World Order: The United States and World Organization to 1920.* Nashville, Tenn.: Vanderbilt University Press, 1969.

Lutzker, Michael A. "The Formation of the Carnegie Endowment for International Peace." In *Building the Organizational Society.* Edited by Jerry Israel. New York: Free Press, 1972, pp. 143–62.

Marrin, Albert. *Nicholas Murray Butler.* Boston: Twayne, 1976. Scholarly interpretation of his thought in interaction with his environment.

1933

Norman Angell (1872–1967)

Great Britain

Journalist, author, lecturer, peace propagandist.

In 1934 the Nobel Committee spokesman declared that the awards recognized a division of labor between technicians of peace and educators. The prize for that year went to a technician, the statesman

Arthur Henderson, and the deferred prize of 1933 was given to Norman Angell, one of the educators. Angell was, in fact, one of the most influential publicists for peace who ever set pen to paper. His book, *The Great Illusion,* published in 1910, became a peace classic. When in 1912 Angell was nominated for the Peace Prize, one of his supporters wrote the committee that the book had "done more to destroy the modern justification for war than has been done by all the advocates of peace combined."

In the next two decades Angell was a tireless propagandist for peace in a succession of books, articles, and speaking tours. As he declared in his memoirs, others were also doing this kind of work for peace, "while what I was doing in 1912 did break new ground, in a new way, for peace; in a way that had secured for the peace problem a worldwide attention." Consequently, he felt that it would have been more logical to have given him the prize then. Angell may well have been correct that the committee's timing was off, but this did not prevent him from making a great effort to win the 1933 prize through a campaign that he himself orchestrated. Such a personal effort on the part of a laureate may not be unique in the annals of the Peace Prize, but no other case has been so well documented by scholarly study of the laureate's private correspondence.

Angell was the editor of the Paris edition of the *Daily Mail* when he published *The Great Illusion.* He had been born Ralph Norman Angell Lane to a well-to-do family in Lincolnshire, England, thirty-eight years before, had attended schools in England, France, and Switzerland, and had held a variety of jobs in the American West before settling down as a journalist in Paris when he was twenty-six. Five years later he published his first book, which was not a success.

Then in 1909 he published a pamphlet called *Europe's Optical Illusion,* using the name Norman Angell, and expanded it as *The Great Illusion* the following year. The book made Angell famous. It was translated into twenty-five foreign languages, sold more than two million copies, and produced a peace movement called "Norman Angellism." The illusion, which Angell maintained was moving Europe to war, was that war could be profitable to a nation. This was a belief that had been exposed many years before by Richard Cobden and the free-trade movement. The leaders of the established peace societies claimed that Angell was not saying anything they had not said before, but they could not deny that he was saying it better, in a clear, logical, hard-hitting, and witty style that at least sounded new and certainly was reaching a new audience.

Angell distanced himself from the peace societies, which he dismissed as utopian, and made a nonpartisan appeal to the Conservative, Liberal, and Labour parties. A wealthy industrialist established a foundation to fund Angell's efforts and the propagation of his doctrines. In England "Norman Angellism" stirred the minds of university youth and convinced many of their elders; in the United States the Carnegie Endowment for International Peace promoted Angell and his ideas, and the movement spread to both Germany and France.

Unfortunately, as Angell laments in his autobiography, the book was a publishing success but a political failure, for, of course, it failed to stop the drift to war. Moreover, a myth was generated that Angell had proclaimed not that war did not pay but that war was impossible. So when war came in 1914, despite his call to reason, it was claimed that his ideas were discredited. But in fact, the war and its aftermath demonstrated the validity of his doctrines. The disastrous experience of heavy Germany reparations proved what he had been saying all along about the futility of a victor's hopes to profit from a war indemnity.

In wartime Angell was one of the founders of the Union of Democratic Control, which called for public discussion of foreign policy and a negotiated peace with Germany. This lost him his Conservative connections and drew him into cooperation with the Labour party. He became an adviser to its leader, Ramsay MacDonald, and helped move Labour to a pro–League of Nations position. In the Labour victory in 1929 Angell was elected to the House of Commons as a Labour candidate. He was disappointed not to obtain a cabinet post, but he was given responsibility in important Labour committees.

When MacDonald formed the national government in 1931, Angell resigned to turn his attention to propaganda for peace and disarmament. Angell endorsed League sanctions against Japan when that nation invaded Manchuria, and after Hitler came to power he increasingly backed League policies of collective security. When the League failed to stop Italian aggression against Ethiopia, however, Angell began to support British rearmament, and he was a strong opponent of the policies of appeasement.

Throughout most of the period between the wars Angell had been a champion of the League of Nations. In more than forty books, he consistently sought to dispel illusions about international politics, as he saw them, by appealing to reason and common sense. It has been said that Angell wrote one book over and over again. It is true that like every great pamphleteer he would seek to drive home a truth by constant repetition, always phrased in new ways, which he knew how to buttress with colorful illustrations. His writings were stock items in every peace library, and as a talented debater, he was much in demand on the lecture circuit and often toured the United States.

In Chicago, in November 1932, Angell found that Jane Addams, who had won her Peace Prize the year before, was interested in supporting his candidacy for the award. She agreed to nominate Angell for the 1933 prize and prevailed upon one of her friends to solicit other American nominations. She also wrote to Angell's good friend Harold Wright, formerly editor of the London *Nation,* asking him to organize the campaign in England. To make sure, Angell wasted no time in cabling Wright himself, and when he returned to London in January, Wright's campaign was in full swing.

In the middle of January, with little more than a fortnight until the 1 February deadline for nominations, Angell was shocked to discover that Ragnvald Moe, director of the Nobel Institute and secretary to the committee, had just published a book on the Peace Prize in which he had sharply criticized *The Great Illusion.* Moe called Angell an "eloquent popular propagandist," but said that he was not a scholar and his theories were scientifically weak. Angell immediately devised a new strategy. He shifted the emphasis from *The Great Illusion* to a book he had just published in 1932, *The Unseen Assassins,* which had the further advantage of representing a more recent achievement. Within a week Angell had an eleven-page document ready to be sent to Oslo, along with six copies of the Swedish edition of his new book. The document included a summary of laudatory comments on the book and a memorandum answering Moe's criticisms. From a close reading of Moe's publication, Angell thought he knew just what kind of credentials would be most likely to impress him, and these were all included: his knighthood, his election to Parliament, and his membership in the Royal Institute of International Affairs. There was also much name-dropping of eminent personalities with whom Angell had been associated in various endeavors. A covering note declared that the sending was made at the request of Jane Addams, Viscount Snowden, a member of the House of Lords, and Seymour Cocks, a member of the House of Commons, who had nominated Angell.

Angell and Wright now thought that Moe's criticisms had been blunted and that a large number of nominations had been secured. Actually, committee records show only nine valid nominations—the three above, Arthur Henderson from England, and from the United States a member of the Commission of the International Peace Bureau and four professors. The committee put Angell on the short list for the 1933 prize, which also included Henderson and Carl Lindhagen, the mayor of Stockholm, but it finally decided to reserve the prize for the following year.

Beginning in January 1934, Angell drafted a new nominating letter for himself, and the campaign was started up again. This time the publication emphasized was Angell's latest work, *The Great Illusion 1933,* an update in the light of postwar developments. On 11 November 1934, Chairman Stang of the committee cabled Angell that he had won the deferred 1933 prize. Angell declares in his memoirs, "The award was genuinely a surprise to me," a statement open to question.

Angell used the bulk of his prize money of about $41,000 as Alfred Nobel had intended the recipients to do—to relieve himself of financial difficulties so that he could "do the work I want to do, instead of the work I have to do." After paying off his debts and purchasing an annuity to provide security for the future, Angell used the remainder to send a modest check to each of those who had helped most with his campaign, to make several contributions to peace organizations, and to establish an Emergency Peace Fund, with the intention of making small grants in the next few years to young peace activists, for whom a ten-pound note could solve some urgent need in their work.

Angell was unable to be present in Oslo for the award ceremony, but he came to deliver his lecture in June 1935. The sixty-three-year-old Angell, slight of build and short of stature, treated his audience in the university Aula to a distillation of the theories of peacemaking that he had been preaching for over thirty years. Peacemaking should not be based on intensifying the fear of war, he declared. The will to peace already exists. War does not spring from our evil or aggressive nature. "It is the outcome of policies pursued by good men usually passionately convinced that they are right." Right thinking, then, was the road to peace. Angell's mission, as he conceived it, was to expose the fallacies, to clear away the mists that prevented the public mind from seeing clearly, and simply to induce people to apply to foreign policy the knowledge that was "inherent in the commonplaces of daily life." He concluded the lecture with his testament of faith: it was only by the application of intelligence in the management of human relations that civilization could be saved. "There is no refuge but in truth, in human intelligence, in the unconquerable mind of man."

Angell lived another thirty years and continued to be active as author and lecturer. In the war years, which he spent in the United States, and thereafter, he became less concerned with internationalism and more of a nationalist and imperialist and a strong proponent of Anglo-American power. At the age of ninety he was putting forward such ideas on a two-month lecture tour in the United States. He died at the age of ninety-four in England. In 1983 the newspapers carried a brief note that his Nobel medal was being auctioned at Sotheby's in London.

BIBLIOGRAPHY

Primary Sources

Angell, Norman. *After All: The Autobiography of Norman Angell.* New York: Farrar, Straus & Young, 1952. Includes a complete list of his books.

———. *The Fruits of Victory.* 1921. Reprint. New York: Garland, 1972.

———. *The Great Illusion.* 1910. Reprint. New York: Garland, 1972.

———. *The Great Illusion 1933.* London: Heinemann, 1933.

———. "Pacifism" and "Peace Movements." In *Encyclopedia of the Social Sciences.* New York, 1930–35.

———. *The Unseen Assassins.* London: Hamilton, 1932.

Secondary Sources

Bisceglia, Louis. *Norman Angell and Liberal Internationalism in Britain, 1931–1935.* New York: Garland, 1982. A critical interpretation. Based on the Angell papers at Ball State University.

———. "The Politics of a Peace Prize." *Journal of Contemporary History* 7 (July–October 1972): 263–73. Angell's campaign for the prize.

Ceadel, Martin. *Pacifism in Britain, 1914–1945.* New York: Oxford University Press, 1980.

Marrin, Albert. *Sir Norman Angell.* Boston: Twayne, 1979.

Moe, Ragnvald. *Le Prix Nobel de la Paix.* 2 vols. Oslo: Aschehoug, 1932, 1:169–71.

Weinroth, Howard. "Norman Angell and *The Great Illusion.*" *Historical Journal* 17 (September 1974): 551–74.

1934
Arthur Henderson (1863–1935)

Great Britain

President, World Disarmament Conference, 1932–35; labor leader, parliamentarian, cabinet officer, foreign secretary.

Arthur Henderson is one of the most tragic figures among the peace laureates. When the Nobel Committee first placed him on its short list early in 1931, he was British foreign secretary with a record of solid accomplishment in peaceful policies and support of the League of Nations. In May 1931 he was unanimously elected at the League to preside over the Disarmament Conference he had worked so hard to prepare. When Henderson came to Oslo to receive the Peace Prize in December 1934, however, Germany under Hitler had withdrawn from both the League and the conference, rearming rather than disarming was the order of the day, and the conference, although still formally in existence, was generally regarded as moribund. Henderson himself was in poor health, and within a year he would be dead.

Premier Johan Mowinckel, who gave the presentation address in behalf of his fellow Nobel Committee members, paid tribute to Henderson's unflagging efforts for peace. He spoke of him as "a man who stands firm and faithful . . . of indestructible endurance and never-ending patience. Despite indifferent health, despite adversity and disappointments, he never tires. . . . If the Conference is still alive and if there is still a thin thread of hope, it is primarily because of Arthur Henderson."

After Henderson died in 1935, Clement Attlee in his eulogy in the House of Commons spoke of how this ironworker had had the qualities to "rise to preside over the Assembly of the nations." Henderson's origins were simple. He was born in Glasgow, the son of a manual worker whose early death left the family in poverty. When the boy was nine, he had to leave school to go to work in a photographer's shop. When his mother remarried and the family moved to Newcastle-on-Tyne, he was able to return to school for three more years, but at the age of twelve his formal education was finished and he became an apprentice at an iron foundry. Six years later he was a journeyman and could join the Ironfounders Union. He was soon elected secretary of the local lodge, and his career in the labor movement was begun. He was also a lay preacher in the Methodist church, where he met Eleanor Watson, whom he married when he was twenty-five. His organizing and speaking abilities led him into full-time work with the union and then into local politics. In Darlington Henderson became the first Labour mayor.

In the early 1900s Henderson played a prominent role in the organizing of the new Labour party. Elected to Parliament as a Liberal in 1903, he chaired the 1906 conference that formed the Labour party and became its leader in Parliament. From 1911 to 1934 he served as party secretary and occupied other top positions.

With the coming of the war, he turned his attention to international affairs. A supporter of the war, he served in Lloyd George's war cabinet and in 1917 was sent to Russia to strengthen the determination of the Provisional Government to remain in the war. In 1918, however, he broke with Lloyd George over the government's refusal to permit British delegates to go to Sweden to attend the international socialist peace conference that Hjalmar Branting was attempting to convene. In the same year Henderson published a pamphlet on the postwar aims of the Labour party, which included a system of international security.

During the 1920s Henderson increased his knowledge of international affairs through extensive travel and participation in international socialist meetings, and he came to be recognized as the Labour party expert on foreign policy. In 1924 he was home secretary in Ramsay MacDonald's first Labour government, and he served as a British delegate to the League Assembly and worked on the implementation of the Dawes Plan and the Geneva Protocol. When the next Labour government was formed in 1929, Henderson insisted on the post of foreign secretary, despite the reservations of MacDonald, who never concealed his dislike for his colleague and frequently treated him quite unfairly.

At the Foreign Office Henderson was surprisingly successful in winning the respect and even affection of the permanent staff. Despite his limited education and his lack of foreign languages, he impressed them with his honesty and forthrightness, his ability to understand the basic problems without being burdened by detail, and his courage and decisiveness. He was equally well regarded by the other foreign ministers who came to know him in Geneva, where he represented Britain as first delegate to the League Assembly and Council. The journalists in Geneva fondly referred to him as "Uncle Arthur."

The Labour party had at first been critical of both the Versailles Treaty and the League of Nations, which were viewed as instruments of the victors in the war. Henderson took the position that the only connection between the Covenant of the League and the peace treaties was "purely mechanical," that the Covenant was in no sense based upon the treaties. On the one hand, he helped ease Germany's reparations burden and facilitate an early evacuation of Allied occupation troops from the Rhineland. On the other, he worked to strengthen the League of Nations as the most hopeful road to international security, the prelude to disarmament. He was successful in bringing his party and much of British public opinion to a pro–League of Nations position. He was ahead of them, however, in countenancing the use of military as well as economic sanctions. But he was not willing to go as far with explicit military commitments as the French wanted, although he was more symphetic with their concern for security than many of his Labour colleagues, and he worked closely with the French in developing the Geneva Protocol. Moreover, it was in the interest of bringing the Soviet Union into the effort for world peace and disarmament that Henderson reestablished relations with the Soviet government in 1929.

When it was decided that Henderson would be the president of the Disarmament Conference that was to begin early in 1932, the growing popular movement looking forward to it felt great encouragement, not only because there was so much confidence in him personally, but also because he would be representing an influential state. In the autumn of 1931, however, the Labour party suffered a crushing election defeat, and Henderson lost not only his office but his seat in Parliament. At the same time Japan marched into Manchuria, the first of a series of events that marked the decline of the League of Nations.

Despite pressure from the new British government, Henderson returned to Geneva to open the conference, convinced that he had been chosen in his own right, not as a representative of his government. The conference convened in inauspicious circumstances. The opening session was delayed so that the Council of the League could discuss the news just arrived that the Japanese were shelling Shanghai.

Henderson was universally respected as a man of utter integrity, completely devoted to the purpose of the conference, but he lacked a power base and was not even a member of the British delegation, which rudely ignored him in its own deliberations. He managed to keep the conference going by the force of his own pesonality, but nothing much came of the meetings. Germany's withdrawal in October 1933 was the death blow, although the conference dragged on for several more years.

If Mowinckel really saw a "thin ray of hope" when he presented the Peace Prize to Henderson in December 1934, it was very thin indeed. This was something, however, that Henderson could not bring himself to admit. In responding to Mowinckel's presentation address, Henderson agreed that the conference had been "a period of difficulty and delay and disappointment—of hopes deferred. . . . But if success is yet to be achieved, at least that decisive and heartbreaking word 'failure' has not been written. And I cannot conceive that it will be allowed to be written."

In his Nobel lecture Henderson speculated on what might have been. As a member of the first Labour government in 1924, he had helped to formulate the Geneva Protocol, which provided for compulsory arbitration as part of a system of collective security that was to be the basis for reduction of armaments. There was much support for the Protocol at the League, but when Labour lost the next election, the Conservatives rejected it, substituting the regional agreements of Locarno. Had the Protocol been accepted, Henderson declared wistfully, the Disarmament Conference would have been held some years before the onset of the economic crisis and the consequent intensification of nationalism. The course of history, then, would have been very different.

Despite Henderson's dogged determination, disarmament in December 1934 was already a lost cause. The members of the Norwegian Nobel Committee no doubt realized this. They were giving a compassionate award to the man who had become the embodiment of the cause of disarmament, and in so doing they were hearkening to Alfred Nobel's original directive to endow those who made great achievements in this area of peacemaking. The Disarmament Conference was to go down in the history books as a failure, but Henderson's great achievement lay in no one accomplishment, such as has brought the Peace Prize to a number of statesmen, but in dedicated service to the cause of peace and disarmament, both in and out of office, in a period that spanned two decades.

BIBLIOGRAPHY

Primary Source

Henderson, Arthur. *Labour's Way to Peace.* London: Methuen, 1935.

Secondary Sources

Carlton, David. *MacDonald versus Henderson: The Foreign Policy of the Second Labour Government.* New York: Humanities Press, 1970.

Hamilton, Mary Agnes. *Arthur Henderson, a Biography.* London, Heinemann, 1938. By a colleague.

"Henderson, Arthur." In *BDI.*

"Henderson, Arthur." In *DNB.*

Slocombe, George. *A Mirror to Geneva.* New York: Holt, 1938, chap. 17.

Winkler, Henry R. "Arthur Henderson." In *The Diplomats, 1919–1939.* Edited by Gordon A. Craig and Felix Gilbert. Princeton: Princeton University Press, 1953. Competent analysis.

1935
Carl von Ossietzky (1889–1938)

Germany

Pacifist journalist, who opposed militarism and secret rearmament in Weimar Republic; imprisoned by Nazis in concentration camp.

"The Nobel Committee for the Peace Prize has never before had the opportunity to crown an apostle of peace who has remained true to his cause till his martyrdom." So wrote Nobel literature laureate Romain Rolland in urging the award for Carl von Ossietzky, the antimilitarist German journalist, who was being held in a Nazi concentration camp, the object of the most brutal mistreatment by his jailers.

The Ossietzky prize still stands today as a supreme recognition that peace has its heroes no less than war. Ossietzky refused to escape abroad when Hitler was about to take power, but remained at his editorial desk and was immediately imprisoned. Tortured by the Nazis in the camp, he rejected again and again their offer of freedom if he would only sign a statement abandoning his principles. In a Berlin hospital after the announcement of the prize, he declared in an interview with foreign correspondents, "I was and remain a pacifist," and it was this statement that decided the Nazis against letting him go to Oslo to receive the prize in person. A few weeks before he died in a Berlin sanatorium, he told two Norwegian visitors that he was still a pacifist.

The award to this peace martyr was largely the work of a small band of German refugees, who enlisted in Ossietzky's behalf some of the most eminent men and women of the time. Their hope that the prize would bring freedom for Ossietzky was not realized, but they succeeded in inflicting a moral defeat upon Hitler by drawing the attention of the world to the inhumanity of Nazism. At the same time, there was demonstrated to the world the existence of "another Germany," as personified by Ossietzky, a Germany committed to ideals of true peace and freedom.

When Ossietzky was first proposed for the prize in 1934, he was little known outside Germany. Only in 1931 had he appeared briefly in the pages of the world press, when, as editor of the radical weekly *Die Weltbühne* (The world stage), he was brought to trial at the instance of the army chiefs and their conservative allies for publishing information about Germany's secret rearmament in violation of the Versailles peace treaty and the laws of the country.

It was a trumped-up charge, for the information was actually to be found in published sources, but the prosecution called him a traitor and the high court convicted Ossietzky of "betraying military secrets," sentencing him to eighteen months in prison. Ossietzky was in fact a staunch defender of the German Republic that had been founded when the German Empire collapsed in the First World War. He saw the greatest threat to the republic coming from the reactionaries of the Right, who dreamed of restoring German power and militarism, and he attacked every sign of reviving militarism with an eloquent and ironic pen that the generals were determined to silence.

Carl von Ossietzky had been born in Hamburg in 1889 into a Catholic lower-class family. The "von" did not mean noble lineage; Carl's father, who died when the boy was two years old, was only a minor government official. But with the help of his father's former superior in the bureaucracy, Carl was able to enter a school attended mostly by children of well-to-do parents and to receive a good elementary school education. His record there gave little promise of future intellectual attainments, and after leaving school, he became a minor bureaucrat himself. On the eve of the war, at the age of twenty-four, he married Maude Woods, an Englishwoman whom he met when she was visiting in Hamburg.

Even before the First World War Ossietzky had published articles critical of militarism, perhaps influenced by his socialist stepfather. His service as a soldier in that war confirmed his antiwar convictions, and after it ended he became active in peace societies, becoming for a time the secretary of the old German Peace Society and helping organize the *Nie Wieder Krieg* (never again war) movement. It was in journalism, however, that he finally found his niche, as a writer for republican and progressive journals and finally, in 1927, as editor-in-chief of *Die Weltbühne,* the organ of the leftist intellectuals of the Weimar Republic.

Ossietzky was a free thinker and a free spirit. Never a party man, he criticized the socialists and communists on the Left as well as the conservatives and reactionaries on the Right. He censured the peace societies for what he felt were their unrealistic policies, but his was the most influential voice in Germany speaking out against war and militarism and for international understanding and peace. Gustav Stresemann, who won the Nobel Peace Prize for his policy of reconciliation with France, later told a friend of Ossietzky that he could not have carried out this policy without Ossietzky's editorial help.

Ossietzky's conviction produced a storm of protest among liberals and leftists in Germany and widespread sympathetic editorials appeared abroad. All appeals for leniency were denied, however, and on 10 May 1932, he began to serve his sentence. He was accompanied to the prison gates by an automobile procession of the leading intellectuals of Berlin. The friend who was driving with him suggested that they keep on going across the frontier. But Ossietzky absolutely refused to flee the country, as his codefendant in the trial had done. He was convinced that as a political journalist, his place was in his own country—his voice would sound hollow from across the border.

After serving seven months he was freed by a general amnesty on 22 December 1932. He immediately returned to his desk at *Die Weltbühne* to attack the Nazis, again rejecting the appeals of his friends to leave the country. On 30 January 1933, Hitler became chancellor, and on 28 February Ossietzky was arrested along with all the leading enemies of the Nazis who could be found.

Thus began Ossietzky's calvary, three terrible years of mental and physical torture in concentration camps, followed by two years of painful illness in hospitals until his death. In October 1935, a representative of the International Red Cross was allowed to visit him in the concentration camp. He described later what he had found: "a trembling deadly pale something, a creature that appeared to be without feeling, an eye swollen, teeth apparently smashed, it dragged a broken, badly healed leg . . . a human being that had reached the uttermost limits of what can be borne."

Long before this, word had reached Ossietzky's friends in exile of his suffering and the deterioration of his health, and they had been desperately seeking ways to secure his release. They finally hit upon the idea of securing world attention for Ossietzky's tragic situation by nominating him for the Nobel Peace Prize. How a handful of refugees in Paris, without funds or any official standing and opposed by the German government with its high-powered propaganda and all its diplomats abroad, managed to mobilize liberal world opinion and to deluge the Nobel Committee with such a multitude of nominations and appeals that could not be denied is an exciting story.

Carefully keeping themselves in the background, the Paris organizers of the campaign worked through a network of fellow émigrés in other capitals to recruit intellectuals and parliamentarians for the cause. Albert Einstein, now at Princeton, a Nobel laureate in physics but ineligible to nominate for the Peace Prize, asked Jane Addams, the peace laureate, to propose Ossietzky to Oslo, while in London the network enlisted Prof. Harold Laski of the London School of Economics as another prominent nominator. Einstein himself wrote directly to the Nobel Committee, as did literature laureates Romain Rolland of France and Thomas Mann, now an émigré from Germany himself.

In Oslo a young German émigré named Willy Brandt wrote articles on Ossietzky for the newspapers, lobbied members of the Norwegian parliament, and kept the Paris group informed about developments in Norway. In Prague the network's representative worked with Czech contacts to win the support of President Tomáš Masaryk, who was considered the most serious rival of Ossietzky for the prize. In 1935 the committee received six nominations for Ossietzky, and their adviser who wrote the report on him submitted a strong recommendation. None of the committee members favored Ossietzky, however, and the prize for 1935 was reserved.

The Paris organizers now redoubled their efforts for the 1936 prize, widely circulating an impressive memorandum on Ossietzky to prospective nominators. The campaign produced a record number of nominations, eighty-six in all from eleven countries, many of them coming not just from one individual but from groups of university professors and parliamentarians of different legislatures. Many other individuals and groups publicly expressed their support, and the tide of pro-Ossietzky public opinion swelled. In London a brochure in support of the candidacy was published over the names of such distinguished public figures as Bertrand Russell, H. G. Wells, Aldous Huxley, Leonard and Virginia Woolf, Gilbert Murray, and Norman Angell.

To the Nazi authorities, this public attention directed to their prisoner became a serious cause of concern. For one thing, in the summer of 1936 the Olympic Games were to be in Berlin, and a propaganda show was being planned on the New Germany which had no place for concentration camps and their inmates. Ossietzky's health was worsening, and, fearful of the effect on world opinion if he died in the camp, they transferred him to a prison hospital in Berlin.

At the same time, the Nazi authorities took a number of steps to counter the Ossietzky candidacy. They disseminated anti-Ossietzky materials through both their propaganda channels and their diplomats abroad, who were instructed to support the candidacy of Baron de Coubertin of France, founder of the modern Olympic Games. The propaganda ministry fabricated an interview that Ossietzky was said to have terminated by saying "Heil Hitler!" And the German minister in Oslo was told to let the Norwegian government know that a Peace Prize for Ossietzky could bring unfortunate consequences. At the Norwegian Foreign Office the German minister was reminded that the Nobel Committee was entirely independent. Lest there be any question of government involvement in the eventuality of a decision for Ossietzky, however, two members of the committee withdrew, the foreign minister and another political leader.

The committee adviser who wrote the report on Ossietzky solicited from the Paris group documentary evidence that Ossietzky had not changed his mind about Nazism and that he was not a communist. Communist propagandists had been seeking to take credit for the campaign and coupling Ossietzky's name with those of communist prisoners in the concentration camps. Reassured on both counts, the adviser submitted to the committee a most favorable report on Ossietzky.

The Oslo committee was now faced with a difficult decision. On the one hand, liberal world opinion had resoundingly declared its support for Ossietzky. On the other hand, Nazi Germany had warned of the fateful consequences of an Ossietzky award. Moreover, it was a time when ruling circles in Europe were either denying that the Nazis were committing atrocities or else looking the other way. Moreover, conservatives in Norway were mostly opposed to a prize for Ossietzky, influenced by the Nazi propaganda that he was a traitor. They maintained that he was being considered because his supporters did not like Nazism, not because of his work for peace.

Nevertheless, on 23 November the Nobel Committee took its courage in its hands and made the unprecedented decision to award the 1935 prize to a man considered an enemy of the state by his own government. The committee members were not without some misgivings and reservations. They balanced their daring action by announcing at the same time the more conventional award of the 1936 prize to Foreign Minister Carlos Saavedra Lamas of Argentina. In no way did they want their decision to be seen as simply a political gesture. The chairman of the committee in his official statement made no reference to Ossietzky's treatment by the Nazis, and he insisted, "Ossietzky is not just a symbol. He is something quite different and something much more. He is a deed; and he is a man." The chairman protested that Ossietzky's candidacy had been "examined in the same manner as that of all others," and he concluded, "In awarding this year's Nobel Peace Prize to Carl von Ossietzky we are therefore recognizing his valuable contribution to the cause of peace—nothing more, and certainly nothing less."

To the Nazis the award was a brazen insult to Germany. A formal protest was made to the Norwegian government, and Hitler forbade any citizen of the Reich henceforth to accept any of the Nobel prizes. Ossietzky was not allowed to leave Germany to accept the prize in Oslo, and most of the money was embezzled by a crooked lawyer who was later convicted in a show trial designed to demonstrate to the foreign press how the Nazis protected all German citizens, even traitors.

Ossietzky was permitted to move to a private sanatorium in Berlin, where he lived on in a sort of half-life for another seventeen months, ever weaker and in pain, but with his wife now constantly at his side in their tiny room. The surveillance by the secret police continued, mail was controlled, and visits were forbidden or discouraged. When a Norwegian pacifist couple did manage to make their way to his sick room at Easter time in 1938, Ossietzky told them that he had had only three or four visitors there in all that time. He rejoiced to be in touch with the outside world again, and he went on talking for several hours about ideas and affairs to the limit of his strength.

A few weeks after the visit, on 4 May 1938, his sufferings ended. Steadfast to the last, his great deed for peace was done. The secret police, ever vigilant, saw to it that the cremation and placement of the burial urn were done in secret, and only a brief notice appeared in the German newspapers.

In other countries news of Ossietzky's death brought lead editorials and sorrowing farewells from his friends and the supporters of the ideals for which he had fought and died. Thomas Mann wrote that the respect Ossietzky's fate inspired in him was deepened and forever fortified. He thought that "the unforgettable figure of this brave and pure minded journalist could grow with time into that of a fighter for humanity and martyr of almost legendary proportions."

Ossietzky's story is tragic, yet triumphant. The inhumanity that was visited upon him evidences the depths to which human beings can descend. But his heroism, his integrity, his endurance of suffering, and his forgiveness attest to the heights to which the human spirit can rise.

BIBLIOGRAPHY

Primary Sources

Ossietzky, Carl von. *Rechenschaft: Publizistik aus den Jahren 1913–1933.* Edited by Bruno Frei. [East] Berlin: Aufbau, 1970. Translated by John Peet as *The Stolen Republic: Selected Writings of Carl von Ossietzky.* London: Lawrence & Wishart, 1971. *Rechenschaft* was published in paperback in Frankfurt-am-Main: Fischer, 1984.

———. *Schriften.* 2 vols. Edited by Bruno Frei. [East] Berlin: Aufbau, 1966. A more complete edition.

Secondary Sources

Deak, Istvan. *Weimar Germany's Left-Wing Intellectuals.* Berkeley: University of California Press, 1968. A history of the *Weltbühne* circle.

Grossmann, Kurt. *Ossietzky: Ein deutscher Patriot.* Munich: Kindler, 1963. Standard biography, by the former head of the German League for Human Rights, who helped in the campaign for the prize from Prague, where he had fled from the Nazis.

Leber, Annedore, ed. *Conscience in Revolt.* Translated by Rosemary O'Neill. Westport, Conn.: Associated Booksellers, 1957. Biographical sketches of anti-Nazis, including Ossietzky.

Nathan, Otto, and Heinz Norden, eds. *Einstein on Peace.* New York: Simon & Schuster, 1960, pp. 264–67. Includes Einstein's letter to the Norwegian Nobel Committee.

Suhr, Elke. *Carl von Ossietzky. Eine Biographie.* Cologne: Kiepenheuer & Witsch, 1988. Scholarly account which makes good use of the Ossietzky papers now at the University of Oldenburg.

Vinke, Hermann. *Carl von Ossietzky.* Hamburg: Dressler, 1978. A popular account, well illustrated.

Walter, Hilde. "Aus der Chronik der Nobelpreises für Carl von Ossietzky." *Das Parlament.* Supplement, 9 October 1969. The most detailed account of the campaign, by its coordinator in Paris.

What Was His Crime? The Case of Carl von Ossietzky. London: Camelot Press, 1936. The pro-Ossietzky brochure.

Wild, Adolf and Helmut Donat, eds. *Carl von Ossietzky: Republikaner ohne Republik.* Bremen: Temmen Verlag, 1986.

1936

Carlos Saavedra Lamas (1878–1959)

Argentina

Statesman who mediated Paraguay-Bolivia War; parliamentarian, foreign minister, professor of international and labor law, university rector.

Foreign Minister Saavedra Lamas of Argentina was the first laureate from outside Europe and the United States. He was honored for his practical statesmanship in bringing to an end the war between his country's neighbors, Paraguay and Bolivia, which had broken out over the Gran Chaco region in 1932, the year he entered office. As in other statesman awards, the Nobel Committee was paying tribute for recent achievement. Saavedra Lamas first reached the committee's short list in 1935, the year when his mediation efforts led to an armistice between the belligerents. He was given the prize in 1936, the year he presided over the Assembly of the League of Nations and the Inter-American Peace Congress, which was held in Buenos Aires. With this award to Saavedra Lamas the committee balanced its unconventional prize for Carl von Ossietzky, who in the same year received the reserved prize for 1935.

Carlos Saavedra Lamas was born in Buenos Aires in 1878 into one of Argentina's leading families. He made a distinguished record as a student, took his doctorate in law in 1903, and married the daughter of a president of the republic. As a university professor he made notable contributions in labor law and international law. In 1908 he was elected as a Conservative to the first of two terms in parliament, becoming minister of justice and education in 1915. In 1932 he entered upon six years service as foreign minister, which brought a new international prestige to his country.

Saavedra Lamas first made his mark on the international stage as leader of his country's delegation to the Conference of the International Labor Organization. In 1928 he was elected president of the conference. This was Argentina's major connection with the international establishment in Geneva, since it had left the League of Nations over a disagreement in its first year. When Saavedra Lamas became foreign minister, he brought his country back into active participation in the League, where Argentina was warmly welcomed and elected to one of the three-year seats on the Council.

Two members of the Nobel Committee, Christian Lange and Halvdan Koht, were members of Norway's delegation to the League and could report to their colleagues on their firsthand observations of the contributions of Saavedra Lamas in Geneva and the high regard in which he was held. Lange's presentation speech at the award ceremony is an excellent account of his skillful diplomacy in ending the Gran Chaco War.

Lange points out how Saavedra Lamas was able

to coordinate three factors: first, he was a scholar of international law; second, he was experienced in the international organizations of the League and the Pan-American Union; and third, he knew how to take account of the foreign policy of the United States. Saavedra Lamas was consistently opposed to what he called "Monroeism," Washington's use of the Monroe Doctrine to intervene in Latin America and to dominate its states. Lange noted that in Latin America there was speculation as to whether the Pan-American Union was basically "a clever camouflage for American imperialism." Under President Franklin Roosevelt and Secretary of State Cordell Hull, however, the United States had begun a Good Neighbor policy which gave the Argentinian foreign minister more freedom to take a primary role in Latin American affairs and at the same time to make use of the Pan-American Union. It has been suggested that Saavedra Lamas was really more interested in reducing the influence of the United States in the hemisphere than in ending the war on Argentina's borders. Lange did not agree with this view, nor, apparently, did Cordell Hull, who on the request of Saavedra Lamas himself, instructed the American minister to Norway to support his candidacy for the prize.

In setting out to end the Gran Chaco War, Saavedra Lamas began by formulating a theoretical expression of his ideas. This was the Antiwar Pact, the first two articles of which were clearly conceived with an eye on the United States: all forms of aggressive war were condemned, the basis of the Kellogg-Briand Pact; and any territorial change not effected by peaceful means was not to be recognized, the Stimson Doctrine, which was formulated by President Hoover's secretary of state when Japan invaded Manchuria in 1932.

After these declarations of principle, the Antiwar Pact sets forth a procedure by which states not involved in a conflict would work together using conciliation and other political, legal, and economic means to put an end to the conflict. Intervention, diplomatic or armed, is excluded, subject to any engagements assumed by the parties under other agreements. This last clause refers to sanctions that member states of the League of Nations were to take under the Covenant. The genius of this Antiwar Pact was the way it provided for collaboration between members of the League and nonmembers, especially the United States.

To secure the acceptance of his pact, Saavedra Lamas now made some shrewd moves. First he obtained the signatures of six Latin American states at a ceremony in Rio de Janeiro in October 1933, thus assuring the support of Brazil. Two months later he gained the approval of all the American states at a Pan-American Conference at Montevideo, with Cordell Hull in attendance. Early in the next year he submitted the pact to the Council of the League, where it was warmly received and subsequently signed and ratified by a number of member states, including Norway.

Meanwhile, the Gran Chaco War had reached a stalemate. Although Paraguay and Bolivia had not ratified the pact and it could not be invoked officially, Saavedra Lamas nevertheless followed the procedure prescribed in the treaty and formed a conciliation commission under his own chairmanship, with representatives from Argentina, Chile, Peru, and Uruguay, which were members of the League, and the United States and Brazil, which were not. He persuaded the foreign ministers of both Bolivia and Paraguay to participate in the sessions of the commission, and within weeks after his first initiative, protocols were signed on 12 June 1935, ending the hostilities. Through his personal leadership Saavedra Lamas had demonstrated the usefulness of his Antiwar Pact and brought peace.

Although the prize for Saavedra Lamas may have been one of the most deserved of the statesman awards, it received little notice in the world press because of the more dramatic prize for Ossietzky at the same time. In Buenos Aires, of course, there was great rejoicing, and in the United States the National Broadcasting Company arranged for the laureate to speak over a national hook-up on the significance of the prize. He was unable to be present in Oslo for the ceremony on 10 December because he was then presiding at the Inter-American Conference for the Maintenance of Peace in Buenos Aires.

After Saavedra Lamas retired from the foreign ministry in 1938, he returned to the University of Buenos Aires, where he served as rector for two years and as professor until 1946. He died in 1959 at the age of eighty, full of honors.

BIBLIOGRAPHY

Primary Sources

Saavedra Lamas, Carlos. *La conception Argentine de l'arbitrage et de l'intervention à l'ouverture de la conference de Washington* (The Argentine conception of arbitration and intervention at the opening of the Washington Conference). Paris: Les Editions Internationales, 1928.

———. *La crise de la codification et la doctrine Argentine du droit international* (The crisis of codification and the Argentine doctrine of international law). 2 vols. Paris: Les Editions Internationales, 1931.

———. *Traité general pour developper les moyens de conserver la paix.* Paris: Pedone, 1936.

Secondary Sources

Jessup, Philip C. "The Saavedra Lamas Anti-war Draft Treaty." *American Journal of International Law* 27 (January 1933): 109–14.

Meyer-Lindenberg, Hermann. "Saavedra Lamas Treaty (1933)." *Encyclopedia of Public International Law,* vol 1 (1981), 189–91.

"Saavedra Lamas, Carlos." In *MPL.*

1937
Viscount Cecil of Chelwood (1864–1958)

Great Britain

Cofounder of League of Nations; lawyer, parliamentarian, cabinet minister, delegate to League; president, League of Nations Union, International Federation of League of Nations Unions; copresident, International Peace Campaign.

No one was more closely identified with the League of Nations than Viscount Cecil. He was responsible for the planning from the British side during World War I and took a leading role in the drafting of the Covenant at the peace conference. As a delegate to the League from the beginning, he helped shape its institutions and took a leading role in its activities for many years. Thereafter, outside the League, he organized a popular movement in its support. In 1946 when the time came to transfer the League's responsibilities to a new international organization, it was Cecil who at its last session pronounced a final farewell: "The League is dead. Long live the United Nations!"

It is ironic that the Nobel Committee waited to give Cecil the prize until the League was practically on its deathbed. It would have come more appropriately in 1923, when the committee first had him on its short list. Fridtjof Nansen, who worked closely with Cecil in Geneva, nominated him immediately after he received his own prize in 1922, but 1923 was the year of the Ruhr conflict, and the committee decided to make no award. Nansen and others continued to put his name forward, and Cecil was again on the short list in 1924 and 1925 and then in 1935 and 1937, the year when the committee finally granted him the prize.

In the presentation speech Christian Lange, an old friend of Cecil's from his Geneva days, spoke with deep appreciation of his lifelong work for peace, but in the light of "the terrible winter now prevailing in our international life," Lange felt that he had to address to Viscount Cecil some lines from a Danish poet dedicated to the mythological figure Sisyphus—heroic not for "the great feat achieved, but for the tireless exertion."

That Cecil should become the champion of a "Great Experiment," as he called the League in his memoirs, was most unlikely for a member of the old landed aristocracy whose career had followed traditional Conservative lines until he was in his fifties. Edgar Algernon Robert Gascogne Cecil was born in London in 1864, third son of the marquess of Salisbury, who had served under Disraeli and later led the Conservative party for nearly twenty years. Young Lord Cecil took the usual route through Eton and Oxford, where he studied law. In his early twenties he served as private secretary to his father, who was then prime minister and foreign secretary. Cecil thereafter embarked on his own legal career and won a reputation practicing at the parliamentary bar. In 1889 he married Lady Eleanor Lambton, which he later claimed was the cleverest thing he had ever done. Over the long years of their happy marriage she was his greatest source of both moral encouragement and intellectual support.

In 1906 Cecil entered the House of Commons as a Conservative and served with one interruption until 1923. When war came in 1914, being over age for military service, he undertook administrative work with the Red Cross. He was soon asked to join the government and served as parliamentary undersecretary for foreign affairs 1915–18, as minister of blockade, 1916–18, and as assistant secretary of foreign affairs, 1918–19.

Cecil was so appalled by the horrors of the war and its incalculable damage to civilization that he became convinced that a way must be found to stop it. To this end he devoted his major energies for the rest of his life. In 1916 he circulated a memorandum within the cabinet, making proposals for an international organization, which he later described as the "first document from which sprang British official advocacy of the League of Nations." There was already a League of Nations Society in Britain, but it was Cecil who secured the inclusion of the League in the government's peace aims, and it was his ideas, along with those of President Woodrow Wilson and General Jan Smuts of South Africa, that were basic to the original plans for the League. At the Paris peace conference Cecil was the British representative on the commission to draft the Covenant, serving as chairman in Wilson's absence. Wilson's personal authority was decisive for including the Covenant in the peace treaty, but Cecil's leadership in the commission was critical, and it has been said that without him there might not have been any Covenant at all.

Only in his proposal to have the League comprise all nations, including Germany, was Cecil balked. His ideas dominated the discussion of the League machinery; he drew up the plan for the League secretariat; he added to the League's authority responsibility for international humanitarian, social, and economic activities; and, over Wilson's resistance, he succeeded in laying the basis for a world court.

When the League began operations in Geneva, General Smuts appointed Cecil as a delegate from South Africa. This gave him a measure of freedom in the first three critical years of the League's existence that he no longer enjoyed when he became official representative of the British government. In 1923 he was made Viscount Cecil of Chelwood, accepting a seat in the House of Lords so that he could withdraw from the political responsibilities in the House of Commons and give full time to the League. From 1923 he was responsible for League affairs in Conservative cabinets. That party, however, never gave wholehearted support to the League, and in 1927 Cecil resigned from the cabinet. He continued as delegate to the League Council and Assembly, with some interruptions, until 1932, when he finally moved in the House of Lords to the nonparty benches and became once more, as he said, a free man.

In his first speech at the League Assembly in 1920 Cecil declared, "Publicity is the very lifeblood of the League of Nations." With the help of Nansen and other Nordic delegates, he put through a resolution that the Assembly should meet annually and that its sessions were to be held in public. Moreover, each annual session was to begin with a general debate on the report of the secretary-general, in which delegates were to be free to bring up any international issues they chose.

In the same speech Cecil challenged the Assembly to take as its motto, "Be just and fear not." "Let us go on from strength to strength," he declared. "The one danger that threatens the League is that it may gradually sink down into a position of respectable mediocrity and useless complication with the diplomatic machinery of the world."

Unfortunately, Cecil had to watch the League ultimately go from weakness to weakness. He strove in vain to strengthen its peacemaking components and to work for disarmament. After 1932 he turned his attention to mobilizing public opinion, convinced that it was not the League that was failing, but the governments, and public pressure could force them to follow a League policy. When asked to sign a guest book at this time with his occupation, he put down "agitator."

As president of the League of Nations Union he organized a peace ballot on the League. Eleven and a half million responses were sent in, with more than 11 million in favor of Britain remaining in the League, more than 10 million approving economic sanctions against an aggressor, and nearly 7 million voting for the use of military sanctions. These results helped move the Conservative government to take up a League policy of collective action when Italy began the war against Ethiopia in 1935, but, to Cecil's dismay, this turned into a policy of appeasement, first of Mussolini and then of Hitler. Cecil's appeal for the use of the League against the aggressors resulted only in his being called a warmonger.

When the Second World War broke out in 1939, as he had expected, Cecil still did not despair. In 1941 he wrote on the title page of a copy of his book on the League, "*Le jour viendra*" (The day will come). In 1944 he was comforted by a message from Churchill that the war could have been prevented if, as Cecil had pleaded, the League had been been used with courage and loyalty.

Cecil lived to see the first years of the United Nations, dying in 1958 at the great age of ninety-four. Lady Eleanor survived him by only a few months.

BIBLIOGRAPHY

Primary Sources

Cecil, Viscount. *All the Way.* London: Hodder & Stoughton, 1949. Autobiography.

———. *A Great Experiment: An Autobiography.* London: Cape, 1941. His experiences with the League of Nations.

———. *Peace and Pacifism.* Oxford: Clarendon Press, 1938. The Romanes Lecture.

———. *The Way of Peace: Essays and Addresses.* London: Allen, 1928. Reprint. Port Washington, N.Y.: Kennikat Press, 1968.

Secondary Sources

Birn, Donald S. *The League of Nations Union 1918–45.* New York: Oxford University Press, 1981.

Carlton, David. "Disarmament with Guarantees: Lord Cecil, 1922–1927." *Disarmament and Arms Control* 3, no. 2 (1965): 143–64.

"Cecil, Viscount." In *BDI.*

Egerton, George W. *Great Britain and the Creation of the League of Nations.* Chapel Hill: University of North Carolina Press, 1978.

Noel-Baker, Philip. "Viscount Cecil." In *DNB, 1951–1960.*

Thompson, J. A. "Lord Cecil and the Historians." *Historical Journal* 23, no. 3 (1981): 709–15.

1938

Nansen International Office for Refugees

Authorized by League of Nations, September 1930; opened 1 April 1931, closed 31 December 1938.

In 1938, with the League of Nations in full decline, the committee decided to give its special recognition to the League's Nansen International Office for Refugees. Not only was this activity an impressive affirmation of human solidarity, but, whatever the political failures of the world's first international organization of states for peace, the committee wanted to call attention to how effective it had been in carrying out a great humanitarian work of worldwide dimensions. Chairman Stang declared that perhaps it was precisely in this kind of activity that the true road lay to the "more stable organization of which we have dreamed and to which we have attached our hopes."

The award was timely because at the end of 1938 the office was to be officially closed. When Fridtjof Nansen was named high commissioner for refugees of the League of Nations in 1921, he had estimated that the refugee problem would be solved in ten years. When he died in 1930, however, the need was still pressing, and the League set up the office named after him, with the mandate to complete its work in eight more years. Once again the problem only worsened, especially as a result of the Nazi persecution of Jews and political opponents in Germany and Austria, and the League decided to set up a new agency to continue the refugee work.

At the award ceremony the president of the Nansen Office, Norwegian international jurist Michael Hansson, described its work. Despite Nansen's great achievements, at his death there were still over a million refugees in need of assistance. These were mainly Russians who had fled the revolution and civil war and several hundred thousand Armenians who had been uprooted as a result of the postwar massacres and deportations. In addition there were Assyrian, Assyro-Chaldean, and Turkish refugees, and then in 1935 the Germans who left the Saar region after the plebiscite brought it into Hitler's dominion.

The funds available to the Nansen Office were minimal, even when augmented by a contribution from the British government and the donation of the bulk of the Nobel prize money from Nansen's estate, which had been matched by a gift from a Danish admirer of Nansen. The remainder of the Nansen prize had been used for model farms in Russia after the famine and to assist new Greek settlements. The most important source of revenue for the office came from the fee for the Nansen Passport, the identity document for the stateless, which many governments now recognized. This meant that the greater part of the expenses for the work of the office were covered by the refugees themselves. Some money was earned also by the sale of special stamps in France and Norway, and voluntary donations were received. Each year the office made grants to the ill and the aged. Loans were extended to encourage self-help, and the annual repayments represented a significant item in the budget.

Along with this material assistance, the central office in Geneva and its representatives throughout the world intervened to help refugees secure documentation, work and residence permits, and any social benefits for which they were eligible. The office also sought to protect them from expulsion and other injustices. Hansson calculated that in its eight years of existence the office had interceded in more than 800,000 instances. Just the very fact that it existed, he said, had given "the homeless the hope and confidence without which men are condemned to despair." Despite the impact of the depression, which in 1929 began to bring new immigration barriers and restrictions on work permits for refugees, Hansson was able to report that the number of refugees under the care of the office had fallen to under half a million.

In 1933 the establishment of Nazism in Germany gave rise to a new wave of refugees, and the League acted to establish in London a High Commission for Refugees Coming from Germany. It was clear that the needs for international assistance were increasing, and Norway, which as a legacy from Nansen has always felt a special responsibility for refugees, proposed that the League merge the two organizations in a new agency to begin operations in January 1939 under a high commissioner in London.

There was some opposition at first because of concern that the agency might exercise its mandate too broadly with regard to political refugees, but finally in 1938 there was unanimous approval to establish the Office of the High Commissioner for All Refugees under League of Nations Protection. Sir Herbert William Emerson became high commissioner, and in February 1939, he also became director of the Intergovernmental Committee on Refugees, which was established on the initiative of President Franklin Roosevelt to negotiate with the Third Reich to ease the problems of refugees from Germany and Austria.

Hansson had hoped that the new League refugee agency would continue to bear the name of Nansen, but he said that for "political reasons" this had proved impossible. He was certain, however, that Nansen's name would continue to be blessed in millions of homes all over the world. He told a moving story of once simply mentioning Nansen's name when he was speaking at an Armenian affair in Aleppo, whereupon the whole company had risen to stand in silent prayer. Hansson was told, "We Armenians believe that Nansen sits at our Lord's side watching over the destiny of the Armenian people."

With the impact of World War II and subsequent political dislocations all over the world, the number of those who have been forced to leave their homes and their homelands has risen to unheard of proportions. In recognition of the international work to aid them begun by Nansen and carried out in his spirit by his successors, the committee has given the prize twice to the Office of the United Nations High Commissioner for Refugees, in 1955 and 1981.

BIBLIOGRAPHY

Secondary Sources

Chandler, Edgar H. S. *High Tower of Refuge: The Inspiring Story of Refugee Relief throughout the World.* London: Odhams, 1959.

Holborn, Louise W. "The League of Nations and the Refugee Problem." *Annals of the American Academy of Political and Social Science* 203 (May 1939): 124–35.

McDonald, James G. "Refugees." In *Pioneers in World Order: An American Appraisal of the League of Nations.* Edited by Harriet E. Davis. New York: Columbia University Press, 1944, pp. 208–28.

See also bibliographies for Fridtjof Nansen (1922) and the Office of the United Nations High Commissioner for Refugees (1954).

3

The Peace Prize over the Years: 1940–59

The advent of the Second World War brought a suspension of the awards for six years until the war ended, the longest period when no prizes were granted. During the First World War the Norwegian Nobel Committee had continued to meet, although during those years it made only one award, to the International Red Cross in 1917. In the Second World War Norway itself was invaded by Germany, and only the connection with the Nobel Foundation in neutral Sweden enabled the committee to maintain its continuity.

In January 1940, a few months after the war began, the well-known Swedish explorer Sven Hedin published a widely noted article calling for the abolition of the committee. Hedin, a staunch supporter of Hitler, had never forgiven the committee for its award to Carl von Ossietzky in 1936. In an extensive review of the history of the prize, he maintained that in all its thirty-nine years the committee had made no contribution to peace in the world. According to Hedin, except for the awards to Dunant and the Red Cross, the committee's selections had been a disappointment and even harmful, as in the Ossietzky prize, and the decisions of the Norwegian committee had had unfortunate effects on the other four "nonpolitical" Nobel committees.

Since the Peace Prize had become a "mockery," Hedin proposed that the funds be returned to Sweden and money given to the Red Cross of Finland, which would help that country defend itself in the war begun by the Soviet Union in November. In asking the Norwegian committee to disband, he pointed out that ending the peace committee would be easier now that it was no longer under the same crown as the other committees. Hedin's article made the Norwegians indignant and found little support in Sweden. In May 1940, however, the committee's work was disrupted when the Germans occupied the country and set up the puppet government of Vidkun Quisling, which lasted until liberation in 1945.

There is no truth to the widely believed story that the Germans arrested the members of the committee in revenge for the Ossietzky prize. Of the five who had participated in that decision, only two were still on the committee when the Germans invaded, Chairman Stang and Martin Tranmael. It is true that Tranmael and another member of the 1940 committee, Carl J. Hambro, fled the country, but Tranmael would have been in danger in any case as a leader of the Labor party and Hambro was also one of Norway's political leaders.

The committee members who remained in the country were not disturbed in their persons, but it was the Nobel Foundation in Stockholm that took action to ensure the continuity of the Norwegian prize. The foundation asked the members in Norway to extend their appointments and also asked that the Peace Prize of 1939, which had been reserved, and that of 1940 both be reserved for 1941. At that time the prizes of 1939, 1940, and 1941 were all canceled, as were the prizes of 1942 and 1943 in the following years. Similar action was taken for the prizes awarded in Sweden.

In January 1944, the Quisling government, maintaining that the appointments of the committee members had now expired, attempted to take over the committee's functions. To forestall this move, the Swedish consul general asked the three committee members to inform him officially that they were unable to carry out their mandates for 1944. The Nobel Foundation then asked the Swedish consul general to take over the Norwegian Nobel Institute and any other foundation assets in Norway. To denote Swedish possession, the Swedish diplomat used one of the rooms of the institute for passport and visa matters. As for the 1944 prize, the foundation asked the king of Sweden in October to agree that it should be reserved until the following year.

When Carl Hambro, then in the United States, read a report about this last action in the *New York Times,* he sent a letter to the editor to correct the "misunderstanding," saying that the Swedish government had nothing to do with the Peace Prize and that, in any case, no candidates had been proposed since 1940. It is understandable that Hambro should want jealously to preserve the committee's prerogatives, but he did not realize that the Swedish intervention was intended actually to save the independence of the committee. He was quite right that the Swedish government had nothing to do with the Peace Prize, but legally the highest authority in connection with all the prizes was the Swedish Crown. The Nobel Foundation had been set up with the approval of the king, and royal approval was needed for any amendment of the original statutes. In the present circumstances, with the Norwegians unable to act freely for themselves, it was not inappropriate that the Swedish government should take the action it did. Hambro was also out of touch with regard to nominations during the war. In fact, three institutions, including the International Red Cross Committee, had been proposed for the 1944 prize, which was, however, reserved for 1945 in accordance with the action of the king of Sweden.

After liberation in 1945, the Storting formally reconstituted the committee. Gunnar Jahn, director of the Bank of Norway, had become chairman after Stang's death in 1941. He withdrew from the committee briefly while he served as a cabinet minister but rejoined before the decisions were taken in 1945.

Only four valid nominations had been received for the 1945 prize, although, of course, the committee members themselves could have added to the list. The nominations were for one individual, U.S. secretary of state Cordell Hull, and three institutions. The committee decided to award the 1944 prize to the International Red Cross Committee and the prize for 1945 to Cordell Hull for his contribution to the establishment of the United Nations. Once again after a great war the Peace Prize started out on a note of hope, and again it was with a grant to an American statesman for his part in the formation of a new international organization to preserve the peace, as had been the case with the 1919 prize to Woodrow Wilson. Of the fifteen postwar awards through 1959, six were given to individuals or institutions significantly involved with the activities of the United Nations.

The nations that united to win the war, however, did not remain united very long after their victory. The United States and the Soviet Union soon became competing superpowers, each with a group of associated states, and the military forces of the two blocs, the countries of the North Atlantic Treaty Organization and those of the Warsaw Pact, came to face one another across a line that divided Germany into the Federal Republic in the West and the German Democratic Republic in the Soviet sphere.

The uneasy relationship between the two superpowers, moving between periods of cold war and periods of détente, dominated international politics and largely determined how the UN machinery would be used. In this major conflict the Western European states took subordinate roles. They retained their longtime cultural importance, but their political power was further diminished by the loss of their colonial empires. Former colonies and other developing countries came to represent a new factor in international diplomacy and an increasingly important force in the General Assembly of the United Nations, where all states had representation. The privileges of the Great Powers were preserved through their membership in the more exclusive Security Council. Another new factor on the postwar international scene was the People's Republic of China, established on the mainland by the Chinese Communists, first allied with Soviet Russia, but then following an independent policy.

European hegemony had vanished, and international politics were becoming more and more global, but the institution of the sovereign state remained as strongly entrenched as ever, and the new developments represented no basic break with the diplomatic history of the past. What was new under the sun and what made the pursuit of peace now urgent as never before was the invention of the atomic bomb, first employed by the United States in the war against Japan with a devastating effect that was unimaginable. The Soviet Union soon had its own atomic bomb, and as the two superpowers built their nuclear arsenals, ever increasing the lethal effect of their weapons, it became clear that the prevention of nuclear war was the new imperative for the survival of civilization.

In the immediate postwar years the Norwegian Nobel Committee found no statesman to honor for directly tackling this most vital problem of all. After the Hull award, in fact, there were in this period few awards to statesmen. Gunnar Jahn, the committee's chairman, was known to view with disfavor the kind of statesman awards that had been prominent in the interwar period. Those that the committee made were to Gen. George Marshall, responsible as secretary of state for the Marshall Plan for the postwar reconstruction of Europe; to Lester Pearson, Canadian secretary of state for external affairs, for his leadership in the establishment of an international UN force in a regional conflict; and to Ralph Bunche for a new kind of statesmanship, his role as a mediator in the Middle East conflict, where he replaced Prince Bernadotte.

In the next two years after Cordell Hull's award it became evident that there was to be a new emphasis upon humanitarian and religious candidates. In 1946 the award was shared by the second religious leader after Söderblom, John Mott of the United States, noted for his lifelong international service for Christian youth, and by another American, Emily Greene Balch, a scholar and leader in the world's organized peace movement.

In 1947 the candidates proposed to the committee included Mohandas Gandhi; former president Edvard Beneš of Czechoslovakia; Governor Herbert Lehmann, the head of the UN Relief and Rehabilitation Agency; and the American and British Quaker service agencies. There was also an interesting proposal intended to reconcile the cold war adversaries by sharing the prize between Eleanor Roosevelt, for her work as U.S. representative to the UN Commission on Human Rights, and Alexandra Kollontai, Soviet ambassador to Sweden, for her role in the ending of the war between Finland and the Soviet Union.

This was the year when Gandhi, whose absence from the Nobel Peace Prize rolls seems so inexplicable, might have won the prize. He had been nominated several times before the war and had made the short list, but in 1947 he won his great nonviolent victory in securing India's independence from the British Empire. This triumph was followed, however, by the bloody war between India and Pakistan, and during the time when the committee would have been making its decision about the 1947 prize, there was much confusion in the press reports as to whether Gandhi was approving of military action against Pakistan. It would have been logical for the committee to postpone its decision on Gandhi until his position was clarified. Meanwhile, the committee decided unanimously to give the prize for 1947 to the American Friends Service Committee and the British Friends Service Council, whose relief efforts during the war and afterward had brought these Quaker bodies international recognition.

The next year it was too late for Gandhi. Both Quaker groups had immediately nominated him for 1948, as had many others, but in January of that year he was assassinated by a Hindu who opposed his efforts for reconciliation with Pakistan. Ironically, these efforts would have stilled any doubts the committee might have had as to just where he stood. There is evidence, in fact, that the committee considered a posthumous award, possibly to be shared with Prince Bernadotte of Sweden, who had also given his life for peace. Bernadotte was on a UN mediation mission when he was assassinated by Israeli terrorists who did not want any peaceful settlement with the Arabs. There had been only one posthumous Nobel prize, however, that to the Swedish poet Erik Karlfeldt in 1931. When the Norwegian committee queried the Swedish committees about their policy, the advice from Stockholm was not encouraging. The Nobel prizes were, after all, intended for the laureates, not for their heirs. Consequently, the committee finally decided to make no award for 1948, declaring that "there was no suitable living candidate"—a final gesture, perhaps, to the uncrowned Gandhi and Bernadotte.

The next three prizes went to persons active with the United Nations and its associated agencies. In 1949 the committee honored Lord Boyd-Orr, who had been director of the Food and Agriculture Organization, making the connection between the struggle against hunger and the establishment of peace. In 1950 Ralph Bunche received his prize, the first black to be so honored. The next year the committee named Léon Jouhaux, head of the French labor movement, who had worked for peace through the International Labor Organization, the major Geneva agency that had survived the war.

The 1952 prize was reserved and then given in 1953 to Albert Schweitzer, the theologian and philosopher who was putting his beliefs into practice as a medical missionary in Africa. With this prize the Norwegian committee made a new statement about peace: the prize was not to be restricted to those engaged in international activities, whether a statesman like Hull, an international civil servant like Bunche, a leader of the world peace movement like Balch, an international labor chieftain like Jouhaux, an international religious figure like Mott, or those engaged in global humanitarian endeavors like the Quakers and the Red Cross. To the Nobel committee Schweitzer was demonstrating the meaning of human brotherhood just as powerfully in his modest hospital in the African jungle.

In the same year the committee made its statesman award to General Marshall. He was honored for his Marshall Plan, which Chairman Jahn called "the greatest example the world has seen of help given from one country to others and a true expression of brotherhood between nations."

In 1955 there was another UN award when the

reserved prize of 1954 was given to the Office of the UN High Commissioner for Refugees. In his speech of acceptance the high commissioner paid tribute to Fridtjof Nansen, who had begun the work the office was continuing. Ever since Nansen's day the Norwegians have never forgotten the plight of the refugees. In 1981 the committee was to honor the Office of the UN High Commissioner once again.

After two years of no awards, Lester Pearson received the prize in 1957 for his work for peace through the United Nations during the Middle East conflict of 1956. This was one of the infrequent occasions in the history of the prize when the committee gave recognition to an achievement of the previous year, as Nobel had originally intended.

In 1958 the committee recognized both religious inspiration and work for refugees in its award to Father Pire, a Belgian priest who was founding villages in different parts of Europe for the resettlement of families displaced by the war and its aftermath. Through such activity he was seeking to strengthen European unity, to create a "Europe of the Heart."

The 1959 award went to Philip Noel-Baker, a Quaker who had served the cause of peace in his long career as an international civil servant in the League of Nations, as a Labour member of Parliament and cabinet member, and as a publicist. Of all the laureates of this period, he and Emily Greene Balch most resembled the earliest recipients, Balch as the leader of an unofficial peace organization and Noel-Baker as a worker for peace in the corridors of government. He came to be identified particularly with the cause of disarmament, and in choosing him the committee was following one of the specifications in Nobel's will.

In the early years after the war, the Nobel Committee started releasing the official list of nominees, so we know whom they were considering. A number of candidates had been on the committee's short list before the war—the Quakers, Léon Jouhaux, and Cordell Hull, all of whom won the prize in this period, and some other good candidates who did not, including Gandhi; former president Beneš of Czechoslovakia; J. F. Shotwell, the American scholar; Hans Wehberg, the German international lawyer; Wilhelm Foerster, the German pacifist; Salvador de Maderiaga, the Spanish diplomat and disarmament advocate; and the perennial candidates Coudenhove-Kalergi and the Interparliamentary Union.

Although the total number of nominees was relatively small, something under forty, there was no lack of well-qualified candidates. Within the first decade after the war, there were no less than eight who were later to be granted the prize. Others included Prime Minister Jawaharlal Nehru of India, who was repeatedly nominated; Presidents Harry Truman and Dwight D. Eisenhower; Eleanor Roosevelt; Frank Buchman of Moral Disarmament; Clarence Streit, head of the federalist Union Now movement; UN secretary-general Trygve Lie; the French pacifist André Trocmé; the Swiss pacifist Elisabeth Rotten; and the International Olympic Committee.

In general, the committee's record in this period was a good one. Its laureates were worthy additions to the rolls, and in only two years did it withhold the prize. The committee also made some progress in broadening its vision. The first black laureate was chosen in the person of Ralph Bunche, and Emily Greene Balch became the third—but only the third—woman laureate.

Norway was now a staunch member of NATO, and it was not surprising that the committee found no laureates east of the Iron Curtain. Consequently, in these years the Soviet Union established its own world peace prize, first named after Stalin and then after Lenin.

Most serious, however, was the committee's persistent shortsightedness with regard to all the regions of the world outside Europe and the Americas, which in the first six decades of the prize was never represented by a laureate. In the period under consideration, Gandhi was missed, Nehru overlooked, and no other Asian or African apparently considered. It would be left to future Nobel Committees to move toward a better balance.

1944

International Committee of the Red Cross

Switzerland

The 1944 prize, which had been reserved until the Norwegian Nobel Committee was reconstituted after the end of the war, was awarded in 1945 to the International Committee of the Red Cross (ICRC) for its humanitarian activities during World War II, its second wartime prize since 1917. At the award ceremony Chairman Jahn cited the words of Philip Noel-Baker (who was to win the prize later himself). Noel-Baker had proposed the ICRC for the award because it "has held aloft the fundamental conceptions of the solidarity of the human race." Jahn said that in so doing the ICRC had promoted "the fraternity among nations" referred to in Nobel's testament.

In accepting the prize, Max Huber, former ICRC president, carried this thought further by speaking of how, as the ICRC gives aid, "it serves another purpose no less important, that of rescuing in the dark storm of war the idea of human solidarity and respect for the dignity of every human being—precisely at a time when the real or alleged necessities of war push moral values into the background."

Serving this high purpose was even more difficult in the Second World War than in the first, when, despite all the efforts of the ICRC, the regulations agreed to at the Hague Conferences and other international meetings had been mostly disregarded by the belligerents. This happened once more, and the second world conflict was a far greater cataclysm than the first. The weapons of destruction were developed to the highest level of efficiency ever, culminating in the atom bomb, total war recognized no distinctions between soldiers at the front and civilians far behind the battle lines, invasions and bombardments generated floods of refugees, and Nazi policies of exterminating and enslaving certain categories of human beings involved the deportation and destruction of whole populations.

The national societies were authorized and organized to try to deal with injured civilians and those wounded in battle, but internationally the ICRC was limited both in means and in legal authority. It now had a small secretariat of fifty working with the score of Swiss citizens serving voluntarily on the committee. It had no regular income, although a grant from the Swiss government covered about half the budget and the rest came from voluntary contributions from the national Red Cross societies and some governments.

The ICRC's one new intergovernmental mandate, deriving from a convention adopted in 1929, was to set up a Central Information Agency for Prisoners of War, as it had done without such authority in 1914, and to provide other aid to POWs subject to the consent of the belligerents. The ICRC's Central Agency, building on the experience of the First World War but far more sophisticated and greatly expanded, was a major achievement. By October 1946, the agency had filed 39 million index cards, as many as 45,000 a day, and 13 million letters and postals had been forwarded for prisoners of war.

The Red Cross movement had been urging an international convention to cover wartime aid to civilians and had even prepared a draft, but the outbreak of the war in 1939 had cut short this development. Now without any legal authority, but recognizing the tremendous need, the ICRC attempted where it could to aid civilian war victims. In Geneva it set up a Civilian Message Section and a Dispersed Families Section and cooperated with the national societies in an effort to reconnect the millions of displaced persons and families. In the first month of the war about a thousand civilian messages daily passed through the agency. By the end of 1940, after the German attack on France, almost a million had passed through, and by the end of 1945, a total of 33.5 million messages had been received, and they were still coming.

To maintain this huge operation the agency had a staff of several thousand persons, mainly volunteers, centered in Geneva, but with branches in twenty-seven towns and cities in Switzerland. Everywhere people wanted to help, if only for a day or a few hours or evenings. At the Geneva office there was a special Evening Section, where persons helped who were employed at regular jobs during the day. This section filled out 250,000 index cards, filed 5 million cards, and worked on 200,000 messages. Part of the process could be automated, and Thomas J. Watson, president of the International Business Machines Corporation, loaned a number of machines to the ICRC for use, which speeded up the work considerably. The ICRC sent to the prisoner-of-war camps 36 million parcels and arranged for food and clothing to be sent on forty-five thousand freight cars, at a time when all transport was needed for military use. Its Intellectual Relief Service distributed over 1.3 million books in the camps.

Throughout the war the ICRC attempted to aid the inmates of the Nazi concentration camps. It became possible to send in some parcels, but requests for visits of inspection were rejected, with a few exceptions. In 1935 an ICRC representative was permitted to enter the Esterwegen camp and talk with Carl von Ossietzky. Toward the end of the war ICRC delegates began to receive permission for visits, and their presence in certain camps prevented the guards from executing prisoners who had not been evacuated. The other outstanding failure was the refusal of the Soviet Union and the Axis powers to permit the ICRC to aid each other's war prisoners. The Soviet Union had not ratified the 1929 convention on prisoners of war, so neither side was bound.

Despite such reversals and many other frustrations, the ICRC actually accomplished more during the war than has often been realized. Still, as its representative declared in Oslo at the Peace Prize ceremonies:

> What has been given it to do was, in the final analysis, of little significance when compared to the sum total of suffering it encountered in the course of its work. It strove to alleviate what misery it could; it tried to raise its flag above the ruins of the world to show that human hope should never falter.

BIBLIOGRAPHY

See bibliographies for Henry Dunant (1901) and International Committee of the Red Cross (1917).

1945
Cordell Hull (1871–1955)

United States

Democratic congressman and senator from Tennessee; secretary of state, 1933–44; played an important role in establishing the United Nations.

Cordell Hull was given the prize in 1945 chiefly for his contribution to the establishment of the United Nations, but Chairman Jahn in his presentation speech also emphasized Hull's long efforts to lower tariffs and cited his policy of maintaining peaceful relations in the Americas as an example and an inspiration to the world.

It was this Pan-American policy that brought Hull to the attention of the committee when he was first nominated in 1934. Hull supported in 1936 the successful candidacy of Saavedra Lamas, foreign minister of Argentina, responding to that candidate's request. Hull himself made the committee's short list that year and the next three years as well. In 1937 his nominators included members of the governments of Argentina and seven other Latin American states. But Hull considered President Franklin D. Roosevelt better qualified and wrote to the committee in support of the president, asking that his own name be withdrawn. At the same time, however, Roosevelt sent word to the committee that his choice was Hull. It was only in 1939 that Hull learned that the president had been recommending him for several years. In the archives of the committee is a copy of a letter from Roosevelt to the American minister to Oslo, asking the diplomat to let the committee know informally that he did not feel it was appropriate to push the candidacy of his own secretary of state, but that in his opinion Hull stood "far above any other individual" he could think of and had been "the guiding spirit of the great Inter-American contribution to world peace."

There is no question that Roosevelt held Hull in high esteem, but it is also true that the president liked to practice personal diplomacy, as had Theodore Roosevelt and Woodrow Wilson. He often bypassed Hull in affairs of state, and during the war years Hull was not invited to the summit conferences with Churchill and Stalin nor was he always kept adequately informed of what had transpired there. What saved the situation was Hull's loyalty to the president and the fact that there were no differences between them in the areas of the secretary's greatest interests: tariffs, the Good Neighbor policy in Latin America, and the postwar international organization. In these matters Roosevelt, often otherwise occupied, was content to have Hull take a leading role.

Cordell Hull came from the rural South. He was born on a farm in the Cumberland foothills of Tennessee, and he learned his ABCs at his mother's knee and in a one-room schoolhouse. When his father left farming and began to prosper in the lumber business, Hull was able to continue his education at institutions elsewhere in Tennessee and in Kentucky and Ohio. During vacations he worked for his father rafting logs down the Cumberland River to Nashville, an experience that was the source of many of the homely stories he liked to tell in later years.

Hull studied law on his own and then completed the ten-month course at the Cumberland Law School in Lebanon, Tennessee, in five months, securing his law degree in 1891 at the age of twenty. Politics attracted him early. When he was only nineteen, he was elected chairman of the Democratic Committee of his county, and when he was twenty-two, he was elected to the lower house of the state legislature. After four years in the legislature, Hull volunteered for the Spanish-American War, serving as a captain. His company arrived in Cuba after the fighting was over, but for Hull it was his first foreign experience and a chance to pick up a little Spanish.

Hull returned to his law practice afterward and in 1903 became a judge of the circuit court. In 1906, at the age of thirty-six, he was elected to Congress, beginning a career that, except for two years, was to last until 1933, ending with a term in the Senate. Hull considered himself a Jeffersonian Democrat and a liberal, but by nature he was circumspect and cautious, and he was to be on the conservative side of Roosevelt's cabinet. In Congress the lean, courtly, white-thatched Hull became a familiar figure. His straightforward unaffected ways won him many friends, and his integrity and trustworthiness gained him much respect in Washington and in the South. He became an influential member of the Ways and Means Committee, where he was the acknowledged authority on tariff and income tax matters, and a party leader in the Democratic National Committee.

Hull was an early supporter of Franklin Roosevelt in the nominating convention of 1932. After the elections, Roosevelt, needing a political link with the South, appointed Hull as secretary of state. Hull, however, had had little experience with international affairs. As a congressman he had supported Wilson and the League of Nations and was one of those who gave Wilson the unheeded advice to take along a prominent Republican on the peace delegation to Paris. Hull agreed with Wilson that high tariffs were barriers to peaceful economic intercourse and made for international conflict and war. In Congress Hull had sought to keep the Democratic party faithful to its low-tariff tradition, and when he became secretary of state during the depression, his idea of "world commercial rehabilitation" emphasized reduction of tariffs.

Hull served almost twelve years in that position, longer than anyone else before or since. Looking back, he felt that his major accomplishments for which he hoped to be remembered were the reciprocal trade program, which lowered tariffs through bilateral agreements and presidential action; the Good Neighbor policy, which Roosevelt had announced, but which Hull had implemented through inter-American meetings at which he won for the United States a new confidence from the other governments; the nonpartisan support for the government's foreign policy during the war, which owed much to his adept handling of relations with Congress; and the establishment of the United Nations.

Although President Roosevelt announced directly on the outbreak of war that the United States would use its influence in working for the peace, it was Hull who on 1 January 1940 spoke explicitly of "creating a stable and enduring world order under law." A week later he appointed the first of a series of State Department committees charged with planning for the postwar world. From this time, as he says in his *Memoirs,* he did everything he could to persuade the American people that they would have to take some responsibility for the maintenance of world peace.

In August 1943 a State Department group drafted a "Charter of the United Nations." In October Hull took his first airplane ride as part of a journey to Moscow to meet with Foreign Ministers Molotov of the Soviet Union and Eden of Great Britain. Here he made a personal impression upon Stalin and, among other agreements, secured Soviet adherence to the Four-Power Declaration, committing those three states and China under Chiang Kai-shek to work for the establishment of an international organization to keep the peace. On his return Hull addressed a joint session of Congress, enthusiastically reporting the Moscow agreements and speaking with anticipation of the postwar international organization, which would eliminate the need for "spheres of influence, for alliances, for balance of power." Of course, he said, the four powers of the declaration had to agree to work together, and the organization would have to be prepared to use force, if necessary.

The four governments then sent representatives to meetings at Dumbarton Oaks, a Harvard estate in Washington, D.C., where the international organization took further shape. Hull opened the conference in August 1944. Although not a delegate, he had much to do with the successful outcome, which laid the groundwork for the founding conference of the United Nations a few months later in San Francisco.

But Hull had worn himself out. He had labored tirelessly for almost twelve years, avoiding social occasions, permitting himself only the entertainment of an occasional game of croquet, taking his work home from the office, and even working on Sundays until his doctor forbade this. Before the end of the Dumbarton Oaks Conference, Hull had to take to his bed and then to enter the hospital in a state of exhaustion. He resigned his position in November 1944. In accepting the resignation "with deep regret," Roosevelt wrote, "When the organization of the United Nations is set up, I shall continue to pray that you, as the father of the United Nations, may preside over its first sessions."

At Yalta, Roosevelt, Churchill, and Stalin agreed that the conference to approve the United Nations Charter would be held in San Francisco in April 1945. Roosevelt immediately wrote Hull to tell him that he was his first choice to head the U.S. delegation, but in view of the state of Hull's health, he would be appointed only as a member of the delegation, although its senior adviser. During the organizing meeting of the United Nations, Hull was actually a delegate in absentia, but daily he was kept in touch with developments and his advice was sought.

Hull recovered sufficiently from his illness to work with a colleague for two years on his *Memoirs,* published in 1948. Although not a personal story, it is a valuable and dispassionate account of his tenure as secretary of state and indispensable as an official documentation of the foreign policies of the Roosevelt years. He never recovered completely and often had to be hospitalized, but he remained active until March 1954, when the death of his wife seemed to break his spirit. In July 1955, he suffered a stroke and succumbed at the age of eighty-four. Hull was buried in the crypt beneath the National Cathedral "reserved for those who have given service of an outstanding nature to God and mankind."

BIBLIOGRAPHY

Primary Source

Hull, Cordell. *The Memoirs of Cordell Hull.* 2 vols. New York: Macmillan, 1948.

Secondary Sources

Hinton, Harold B. *Cordell Hull: A Biography.* Garden City, N.Y.: Doubleday Doran, 1942.

"Hull, Cordell." In *BDI.*

"Hull, Cordell." In *DAB,* supp. 5.

Pratt, Julius. *Cordell Hull, 1933–44.* 2 vols. Vol. 13 of *The American Secretaries of State and Their Diplomacy.* Edited by Robert H. Ferrell. New York: Cooper Square, 1964. The first scholarly assessment. An important work.

Russell, Ruth B. *A History of the United Nations Charter: The Role of the United States, 1940–1945.* Washington, D.C.: Brookings Institution, 1958.

1946
Emily Greene Balch (1867–1961)

United States

Social worker and reformer, professor of economics and sociology, cofounder and longtime leader of Women's International League for Peace and Freedom, international scholar, acknowledged dean and intellectual leader of the American peace movement.

In speaking of Emily Greene Balch's "lifelong, indefatigable work for peace" in his presentation address, Chairman Jahn declared, "She has shown us that the reality we seek must be won through hard work in the world in which we live, but she has shown us more than this: that one does not become exhausted and that defeat gives new courage for the struggle to those who have within them the holy fire."

Indeed, her indomitable spirit had sustained Balch through two great wars, one that she had entered the peace movement to try to stop and the second that she had labored long years to prevent. At seventy-nine she was still staying the course. But along with her high hopes for humanity in the long run, she had a strong sense of realism that spared her false expectations. She told the audience at her Nobel lecture that the world society was being organized, but slowly, step by step: "We are not asked to subscribe to any utopia or to believe in a perfect world just around the corner; we are asked to be patient . . . and to be ready for each step ahead as it becomes practicable." This pragmatism was the hallmark of Balch's peacemaking.

Balch was born of New England stock, her father a distinguished Boston lawyer who had been secretary to Charles Sumner, the Massachusetts senator and peace leader. She attended the women's college of Bryn Mawr near Philadelphia, newly founded by Quakers, where her concern to work for a better society was quickened. When the faculty, impressed not only by her brilliance of intellect but by her "extraordinary beauty of moral character," awarded her on graduation Bryn Mawr's highest honor, the European Fellowship, she used it to study economics for a year at the Sorbonne in Paris, doing research on public relief for the poor.

On her return to Boston in 1891 at the age of twenty-four, she turned to social work. She helped found Denison House, one of America's first settlement houses, and became head worker. In helping the poor and unemployed, she came into close contact with the labor movement and joined the American Federation of Labor, on one occasion representing the cigarmakers' union at a convention.

Gradually Balch came to realize that perhaps she could make a greater contribution in college teaching, where she could try to "awaken the desire of women students to work for social betterment" and help them find the best methods to use. To qualify herself to teach about economics and society, Balch took courses at the Harvard Annex (later to become Radcliffe) and the University of Chicago, and then set out to study for a year at the famous University of Berlin, which was then attracting some of the most promising American scholars. Balch was one of the few women students.

Back in Boston, now twenty-nine, she took a half-time job at Wellesley College correcting student papers in economics. Her career in academe, which was to last two decades, had begun. In the second semester she taught a class, and four years later, in 1900, she was asked to organize Wellesley's first course in sociology. Balch was a demanding teacher, who insisted that her students go beyond the library to do fieldwork in real-life situations. She herself was often asked to serve on state and municipal commissions dealing with industrial relations, and she chaired the state commission that drafted the first minimum wage law in the United States.

Such off-campus activities led Balch to a special concern with immigration. She offered the first college course in the subject, and when she was on sabbatical leave she investigated the immigration of the Slav peoples to the United States. The inquiry took Balch to firsthand study of Slav centers in different parts of this country and then to the Austro-Hungarian Empire, their place of origin, in the process learning some of their languages. In 1910 she published *Our Slavic Fellow-Citizens,* an original, thoroughly researched study that was much acclaimed and remains a basic work in the field. Her earlier writings on the economic role of women and other social problems had also been well received, and Balch's reputation as a social scientist was firmly established. In 1913 at the age of forty-six, she was appointed to chair Wellesley's Department of Economics and Sociology.

The next year the war began that was to take her from the classroom and into the front lines of the peace movement for her third career. Her first reaction to the news was "largely a sense of tragic interruption of what seemed to me the real business of our times—the realization of a more satisfactory economic order." This had been her own preoccupation as social worker and professor. But now she came to see that "the way of war is not the way of Christianity" and was convinced that "resort to war can and must come to an end."

Balch joined the Woman's Peace party after it was founded in January 1915, and when the invitation came from Europe to attend an international peace congress of women at The Hague, Balch obtained a leave of absence from Wellesley to participate along with Jane Addams and forty other American delegates. The story of the congress and its aftermath is recounted in the entry on Jane Addams (1931). Of the two delegations the congress sent to call on European statesmen with the proposal for a conference of neutral states to offer mediation, Balch was chosen for the group that went to Scandinavia and Russia; she also participated in interviews in The Hague and London. In the Norwegian capital the delegates were received by King Haakon, who talked with them for almost two hours. The women found some receptiveness to their proposal among the statesmen, but the key to success, they knew, was that President Wilson summon the conference. This Addams and Balch and others who called on him on various occasions failed to persuade him to do. Balch believed that Wilson thought he himself had a better plan for mediation. But when he did make a move, it was too late.

One consequence was the unofficial conference held in Stockholm in January 1916, supported by Henry Ford, who sent his Peace Ship there with an assortment of peace leaders and other people of goodwill on board. The voyage, badly managed, was pilloried in the American press, but the conference itself was a serious affair, with able representatives from peace organizations in six neutral countries in attendance. Balch did not sail on the Peace Ship, nor did Addams, who was ill, but Balch served as Addams's replacement for several months in Stockholm as one of the two American delegates. She wrote two original proposals for the conference, one suggesting an internationalization of war reparations and the other calling for international administration of colonies, with aspects that resembled the later mandate system of the League of Nations.

In July 1916 Balch returned and arranged an unpaid leave from Wellesley so that she could work in New York opposing American intervention in the war. She worked with the American Union against Militarism, sat on the council of the religious pacifist Fellowship of Reconciliation, and supported the People's Council of America, which after the United States entered the war came under particular attack by patriotic groups.

Like Jane Addams and the minority in the peace movement who remained faithful to pacifist principles, Balch suffered abuse and ridicule. For the Wellesley trustees, who had been willing to put up with her as a declared socialist (which she no longer was), disloyalty in wartime was too much, and they decided not to renew her appointment, ending her teaching career of twenty years. Balch reflected philosophically that she had "overstrained Wellesley's liberality" and refrained from bitterness or recrimination, which made it easier for the college in later years to try to make amends.

All the same, as Balch wrote later, "This left me at 52 with my professional life cut short and no particular prospects." She thankfully accepted an invitation from the liberal New York *Nation* to join their staff. Then, in May 1919, the women of The Hague reassembled after the war, as they had agreed to do, denounced the inequities of the Treaty of Versailles, which had just been signed, formed a continuing association, the Women's International League for Peace and Freedom (WILPF), and elected Jane Addams president and Emily Balch secretary-treasurer.

Balch set up the headquarters of the association in Geneva "in that early springtime of the League of Nations," and in the following years she spent most of her time there, even after she relinquished her office in 1922 because of ill health and established her home in Wellesley. She put the WILPF on a firm footing, developed branches in more than fifty countries, and served as the association's chief representative at the League of Nations. She resumed the office for a time in 1934, and in 1937, after the death of Jane Addams, she was elected honorary international president.

Balch's gradualist conception of the League of Nations was the basis of the policy toward that body that was adopted by Jane Addams and the WILPF. In her view it was primarily a mechanism for working on nonpolitical problems, such as social and economic issues; these experiences of international cooperation could then one day be extended to political matters. On behalf of the WILPF Balch worked with League delegates and members of the secretariat, and her scholarly knowledge, her astute judgment, and her sense of tact gave her an important behind-the-scenes influence. She was thin and somewhat austere in appearance—she referred to herself as "the plainest of New England spinsters"—but kindness radiated from her gray-blue eyes, her dry wit saved many a tense situation, and her friendships were warm and deep.

Early in these Geneva years she formally joined the Quakers, explaining to Addams that she was "as remote from orthodox Christian theology as ever," but "what is central to Friends is central to me—the wish to listen, as it were, to understand and receive as much as we can and to try to live out, as far as we can, all that one has of enlightenment—no creed, no pretending to honor what we don't know."

In Geneva Balch worked on such matters as drug control, the internationalization of aviation, and, above all, disarmament. She developed proposals on economic questions, revision of treaties, reform of the League of Nations, mediation in the Spanish civil war, and neutrality. In 1926 she organized a WILPF mission to investigate conditions in Haiti, then occupied by the U.S. Marines. The report she wrote and her subsequent campaign helped bring about the withdrawal of the marines and the adoption of many of her recommendations.

When war broke out in 1939, and especially after the Japanese attack on Pearl Harbor in 1941, Balch, in her own words, "went through a long and painful mental struggle, and never felt that I had reached a clear and consistent conclusion." She had taken a prominent role in helping Jewish refugees, and she knew all too well the evil that Hitlerism represented. She reluctantly concluded that this evil had to be vanquished. "I am not an absolute pacifist," she said, "though I have retained my membership in organizations like the Fellowship of Reconciliation and the War Resisters' International." She felt that conscientious objectors performed "an enormous service to the cause both of peace and of freedom of conscience, and in protest against the State worship of the present day. It is the dread of exaggerated political power and its intrusion into fields where its heavy and clumsy methods violate human personality that gave me pause in my attitude toward socialism."

In 1942 the American section of the WILPF, which she had served as president, gave her a public luncheon in Philadelphia for her seventy-fifth birthday. It was wartime, and her lifetime of efforts for peace might have seemed in vain. Yet she could declare in an address to the group:

> In looking back over the years, I have not the feeling that our efforts have been unreasonable. On the contrary, I have the impression that although the world was not ready to realize them, the trend of developments runs obviously and unmistakably toward the end that we have sought—a planetary civilization. Our planetary barbarism, is, I have faith to believe, the forerunner of this.

The holy fire was still burning brightly. In her conclusion she said that it did not matter how fast or in what form this international unity came:

> International unity is not in itself a solution. Unless this international unity has a moral quality, unless it accepts the discipline of moral standards and possesses the quality of humanity, it will not be the unity we are interested in. . . . It will be imperfect, of course. But instead of being largely concerned with so-called political issues and notably with questions of power and prestige its interest will center on human beings in their everyday living, with their sufferings and their aspirations and it will be permeated by a warm personal desire to serve the common good.

To the audience this sounded like a final message, and there was a momentary silence. Sensing the emotion, Balch quickly added, "But this is not my swan-song. I intend to live quite a while longer. My grandfather used to say, 'An old woman is as tough as a boiled owl.' "

She lived on, in fact, for almost twenty more productive years, traveling, speaking, writing for peace. She continued to develop proposals for slow international progress through functional cooperation, calling for international authorities to administer seas and waterways, the polar regions, the air, and strategic bases, and she proposed an international reconstruction corps, with volunteers from all countries rebuilding the countries shattered by war.

In the fall of 1946 the WILPF asked Mercedes Randall to organize a campaign to secure the Nobel Peace Prize for Balch. In the six weeks that she had before everything had to be mailed to Oslo, Mrs. Randall did a remarkable job. Through the pages of the Balch papers in the Swarthmore College Peace Collection, we see her working night and day, compiling materials and generating nominations, keeping four typists busy. She enlisted the noted philosopher John Dewey, who was an admirer of Balch, and he sent some ninety-two personal letters to possible nominators in the United States and abroad. Mrs. Randall sent another hundred letters to national organizations and influential persons who were not eligible to nominate, asking for letters of support, and she wrote to the twenty-one European branches of the WILPF asking for their help.

The prestige of Dewey's name and the universal regard for Balch produced a stream of letters from a distinguished list of American scholars and public figures. Prof. John Herman Randall, Jr., of Columbia, Mrs. Randall's husband, was an eligible nominator as a professor of philosophy, and he sent with his own nomination these letters and the other materials collected, along with the biographical sketch he had put together from notes Balch supplied. This was an eloquent and compelling essay, and the WILPF published it in revised form and sent copies to its Norwegian branch for distribution to each member of the Nobel Committee. As Mrs. Randall bundles up all the documents to send them to Oslo on 15 January 1946, we can practically hear her sigh of relief.

The weight of all this evidence was persuasive. Even though, as Jahn was to say at the award ceremony, "the name of Emily Balch may not be familiar to many of us here," the committee decided to divide the prize between Balch and the ecumenical leader, John Mott. It is clear from Jahn's account of Balch in his presentation address that he had carefully read Professor Randall's biographical essay. The cable from Oslo reached Balch in the hospital, where she was suffering from an attack of bronchitis. She could not attend the ceremony in December but said she would come later to give her Nobel address. When Mrs. Randall sent her copies of what had been mailed to Oslo, Balch wrote that she was both "flattered and abased. . . . It is as good as going to one's funeral without having to die first."

It was not until April 1948 that Balch could go to Norway. Once again she was received by King Haakon, and they talked of their first meeting over three decades earlier. Her lecture, "Toward Human Unity or Beyond Nationalism," showed the marks of the extra time she had had to prepare it. From the height of her years she thoughtfully surveyed the trends of the period she had lived through and the efforts undertaken to organize world society.

Balch turned most of her prize money over to the WILPF, as Addams had done. She continued her own efforts for peace, less energetic now, but always dedicated. In 1955 she sought to bridge the gulf that had widened between the United States and the communist Chinese People's Republic by sending a poem to "Dear People of China." It began, "This is a letter of love I am sending you," and concluded, "Groping we may find one another's hands in the dark." A response came from the Chinese minister of health, inviting Balch to China as her personal guest, but she declined, not because she was too old to travel—she was then eighty-eight—but because she felt that she was too old to be of any use.

When she was ninety-two, Balch wrote, "I have had a long and happy and I should like to think not wholly useless life to look back on." In 1961, the day after her ninety-fourth birthday, her life came to a close.

BIBLIOGRAPHY

Primary Sources

Balch, Emily Greene. *Approaches to the Great Settlement.* New York: Huebsch, 1918.

———. *Beyond Nationalism: The Social Thought of Emily Greene Balch.* Edited by Mercedes Randall. New York: Twayne, 1972. An important collection of documents, published and unpublished, with a comprehensive list of her publications.

———. *Our Slavic Fellow-Citizens.* New York: Charities Publication Committee, 1910.

Balch, Emily Greene, with Jane Addams and Alice Hamilton. *Women at The Hague.* New York: Macmillan, 1915. Reprint. New York: Garland, 1972. With an introduction by Mercedes Randall.

Secondary Sources

"Balch, Emily Greene." In *MPL.*

Bussey, Gertrude, and Margaret Tims. *Women's International League for Peace and Freedom, 1915–1965.* London: Allen & Unwin, 1965.

Randall, John Herman, Jr. *Emily Greene Balch of New England: Citizen of the World.* Washington, D.C.: Women's International League for Peace and Freedom, 1946. A revised version of Professor Randall's eloquent statement in support of his Nobel nomination of Balch, published as a brochure.

Randall, Mercedes. *Improper Bostonian: Emily Greene Balch*. New York: Twayne, 1964. The standard biography. Based on Balch's papers, now in the Swarthmore College Peace Collection, where Mrs. Randall has also deposited her records of the campaign she directed for Balch's prize.

1946
John R. Mott (1865–1955)

United States

World ecumenical leader and evangelist, who held top positions in international Protestant organizations, and as its longtime executive led the YMCA in works of humanitarian service and peace.

John Mott shared the prize of 1946 with Emily Greene Balch "because he has created worldwide organizations which have united millions of young people in work for the Christian ideals of peace and tolerance among nations." Mott was the second Christian leader to become a laureate. In 1930 Archbishop Söderblom had been recognized for his work for world understanding and peace through his leadership in unifying the Christian churches. He and Mott were both inspired by the central message of peace in their Christian faith, but Mott was never ordained and worked as a layman to spread the Gospel and to promote understanding through globe-girdling speaking tours and projects of Christian service.

Mott was a product of the missionary movement that aroused the generation of American youth in the late nineteenth century and sent so many of them to distant lands to serve the Lord. He was a college student at Cornell University in his twentieth year when he first heard the call that was to give his life direction.

He had come to Cornell from Postville, Iowa, where his parents had moved from Livingston Manor, New York, after he was born. The family was Methodist, and he had first enrolled in a small Methodist institution, where he read avidly in history and literature and won prizes in debating. By 1885, however, he needed greater challenge and transferred to the young university at Ithaca, New York, which was already gaining renown.

Mott was trying to decide whether to become a lawyer or to prepare to enter the parental lumber business, as his father was hoping he would do. Then, on 14 January 1886, not very far into his first year at Cornell, a lecturer pronounced the words that touched his soul: "Seekest thou great things for thyself? Seek them not. Seek ye first the Kingdom of God." Mott never forgot that moment. The young man felt that God was calling him to a life in Christian work, and the law and lumbering were forgotten. A second experience, a few months later, gave him further direction. In the summer Mott represented the Cornell YMCA at the first interdenominational student Christian conference held in the United States. The evangelist Dwight Moody spoke so compellingly that one hundred of the young men present took the pledge to work in foreign missions, Mott among them.

More immediately, however, there were the needs of Cornell's YMCA, to which Mott began to devote his abundant energies. In his junior year he became president, tripled the membership, raised money for a YMCA building on campus, and made it the largest and most active student Y in the world. Mott had found himself a career. When he graduated in 1888 with a degree in history and a Phi Beta Kappa key, the national YMCA invited this promising young man who had demonstrated such remarkable gifts for organizing and fund-raising to join its staff, and he remained with the YMCA and its associated agencies for the rest of his life.

His first task was to visit colleges and universities for the Intercollegiate YMCA of the United States and Canada, and he was so successful that in 1890 he was appointed senior student secretary. Tall and handsome, with a commanding presence, he spoke simply and directly out of a deep personal faith, stressing Christian commitment, the social gospel, and missionary service. He felt a special vocation to work with young people, and the students flocked to hear him. In these early years he developed his great love for travel, logging some forty thousand miles on the train. By 1895, largely owing to Mott's efforts, the Intercollegiate YMCA had practically doubled its membership, and at the same time he integrated with the Y the work of the Student Volunteer Movement for Foreign Missions.

In 1891 he married Leila Ada White, an English teacher, who edited the stream of publications he began to produce. They had four children, but their home life was limited by Mott's long absences on his travels. It was also in 1891 that he crossed the Atlantic to study the British student movement, the first of a hundred crossings.

Mott had long dreamed of a world association of Christian students, and in 1895, with the support of wealthy industrialists John D. Rockefeller, Jr., and Cyrus McCormick, he was able to organize the World's Student Christian Federation at an international meeting held at a castle in Sweden. As general secretary he started off on a series of journeys during the next two years that ended with seventy national affiliates organized in India, Japan, China, Australia, New Zealand, and countries in Europe and elsewhere. For three decades this federation was to be his major concern. Out of its activities grew the strong ecumenical movement that has characterized twentieth-century Christianity, and Mott's role in organizing and leading the federation has been considered his outstanding achievement.

Through his activities throughout the world in behalf of the federation, the YMCA, and the missionary movement, Mott became a well-known and respected figure in his own country and abroad. So committed was he to this worldwide Christian work that he declined college presidencies and political appointments and even President Woodrow Wilson's invitation to send him as ambassador to China, much to Wilson's disappointment. He did agree to Wilson's request that he serve on a commission to deal with a conflict with Mexico in 1916, and in the next year he was an influential member of Elihu Root's mission to Russia.

When the First World War began in 1914, Mott mobilized the resources of the international YMCA to provide services for soldiers at the front and then for prisoners of war. Although Mott regarded war as un-Christian, when the United States intervened he did not hesitate to support the war effort, offering to President Wilson the services of the national YMCA, of which he was then chief executive. For his contribution as general secretary of the YMCA National War Council Mott received the Distinguished Service Medal.

After the war the international YMCA under Mott's leadership helped with reconstruction in many countries in Eastern Europe, and then he turned his efforts again to the development of international Christian cooperation. In 1926 Mott became president of the World's Alliance of YMCAs, which represented 2 million young men and boys from fifty countries, a far broader membership than the Student Federation he had founded. He was also chairman of the International Missionary Council, and he was called the father of the World Council of Churches.

In the Second World War the YMCA under Mott again took up its work to aid prisoners of war. At its conclusion, Mott, now eighty, set out once again on his world travels to rebuild the links between the national YMCA organizations, and he convened at Geneva their first international congress. Mott had been brought to the attention of the Nobel Committee during his long years of work for international understanding, and in 1938 the committee had had him on its short list. Now, when he was nominated again after the war, the committee had decided to honor him.

Although the youth who took the pledge that summer day in 1886 never worked in a foreign mission, he did become something of a missionary to the world. His biographers have suggested his significance in the sobriquets they have chosen in their titles: "World Citizen," "Architect of Cooperation and Unity," and "Layman Extraordinary." It has been estimated that for over half a century Mott averaged thirty-four days a year on the ocean during his missionary journeys. He was much decorated by nations all over the world and presented with honorary degrees by universities from Edinburgh to Upper Iowa. One honor in which he delighted came from the Russian Orthodox church of Paris.

In his Nobel address, "The Leadership Demanded in these Momentous Times," Mott declared that the leaders the world needed should be comprehending, vividly aware of the world situation, creative, "thinkers, not mechanical workers." They should be statesmanlike—"the genuinely Christian statesman must be a man of vision." The most trustworthy leader, Mott declared, follows his principles no matter what. Of greatest importance is "spotless character." In conclusion, Mott returned to the one whose words had changed his life sixty years before. He said that Jesus Christ had summed up the "outstanding, unfailing and abiding secret of all truly great and enduring leadership" in saying, "He who would be greatest among you shall be the servant of all." In listing these qualities, which he felt were so urgently needed in the world's leaders, Mott was, of course, describing the ideals he himself had tried to live by. His record of achievement stands as the measure of his success in this effort.

Nine years after receiving the prize, John Mott died at his home in Orlando, Florida, a few months before his ninetieth birthday.

BIBLIOGRAPHY

Primary Source

Mott, John Raleigh. *Addresses and Papers.* 6 vols. New York: Association Press, 1946–47.

Secondary Sources

Fisher, Galen M. *John R. Mott: Architect of Co-operation and Unity.* New York: Association Press, 1952.

Hopkins, C. Howard. *John R. Mott 1865–1955: A Biography.* Grand Rapids: Erdman's, 1979. The best biography, fifteen years in the researching and writing. With a Mott bibliography.

Mackie, Robert C., and others. *Layman Extraordinary: John R. Mott, 1865–1955.* New York: Association Press, 1965. Centenary volume sponsored by World Council of Churches, including excerpts from Mott's writings and colleagues' reminiscences.

Matthews, Basil. *John R. Mott, World Citizen.* New York: Harper, 1934. Authorized by Mott, who gave extensive interviews. The purpose: to present an example to youth.

1947

Friends Service Council

Great Britain

American Friends Service Committee

United States

The two most important Quaker organizations engaged in relief and reconstruction during and after the Second World War.

When the Norwegian committee announced that the prize for 1947 was to be awarded to the Quakers, an Oslo newspaper applauded the decision and commented that the Quaker religion consisted of good deeds. The Quakers were indeed best known for their works. They had first been nominated for the Peace Prize after the First World War for their relief efforts and then again in the 1930s for their assistance to refugees from Hitlerism.

During the Second World War and afterward Quaker volunteers had administered relief on more than one continent, and it can be assumed that it was these well-known activities that led a member of the Norwegian Nobel Committee, Christian Oftedal, a liberal newspaper editor, to ask a Norwegian Quaker whom he knew to send information for "a possible prize . . . to go to the head church." Oftedal was informed that the Quakers had no central organization and that "a possible prize" should be divided between the Friends Service Council (FSC) and the American Friends Service Committee (AFSC). The FSC represented British and Irish Quakers and had been formed in 1927 by the amalgamation of several committees engaged in foreign work. The AFSC had been established in 1917 to provide overseas work for Quaker and other conscientious objectors and still remains the major agency of American Quakers for peace and humanitarian activities. The Norwegian Friends explained this and saw to it that the committee was abundantly supplied with literature on Quaker history and activities.

The sect was formed in the seventeenth century as the Society of Friends, influenced by the words of Jesus "I have called you friends." Because these early Friends "trembled in the spirit of the Lord," they were given the name of Quakers, and it has come into common use. George Fox, the English weaver who founded the society, and his followers were persuaded that they were reviving "primitive Christianity," and in their meetings for worship, which were based on waiting silence, they felt that they were stirred by the Spirit just as the first Christians had been. They knew from this direct experience that there was "that of God in every person"—they called this variously the "Christ Within" and the "Inward Light"—and they felt no need of minister or church ritual for the worship group to enter into communion with God.

They knew the Scriptures well and cherished them, but they were convinced that God had not spoken his last word there. They were certain, however, that what the Spirit had inspired to be written in the Holy Book was not likely to be at variance with what they knew through the Inward Christ in their hearts. Thus the roots of Quaker pacifism were to be found in inward experience, not scriptural authority. The Friends felt that such sayings of Jesus as "Blessed are the peacemakers," "Resist not evil," and "All they that take the sword shall perish by the sword" were in accordance with their inward knowledge of Truth, whereas such sayings as "I came not to bring peace but a sword" were not to be understood literally.

Friends often refer to how Fox described in his journal his answer to those who offered him release from prison in 1650 if he would accept a commission in the army: "I told them that I lived in the virtue of that life and power that took away the occasion of all war." The first declaration against war made by the Society was in 1660 in response to a charge that they were plotting against the king: "We do testify to the world that the Spirit of Christ which leads us into all truth, will never move us to fight and war against any man with outward weapons, neither for the kingdom of Christ, nor for the kingdoms of this world." Quaker pacifism has never been a mere refusal to join the armed services; to Quakers it is a way of life with which war is incompatible, an outward expression of the Inward Spirit of Truth and Love and Goodness, with which every person is endowed and which is to be nurtured and translated into action.

Quakers consider their humanitarian activities as a natural consequence of the workings of the Inward Spirit. They are fond of quoting the words of William Penn, one of their early leaders and the founder of Pennsylvania: "True Godliness does not take men out of the world, but leads them into it, to mend it." Penn also advised, "Let us then try what love can do," and this Quakers have attempted in a variety of social causes, such as prison reform, care of the mentally ill, and the struggle against slavery. In the early nineteenth century they helped found the first peace societies.

Chairman Jahn in his presentation speech referred to Quaker efforts for social justice and peace, and then he spoke of war relief work. The Friends Service Council stood in the line of descent from the Friends War Victims Relief Committee, which had sent help to France after the Franco-Prussian War of 1870–71, when the Quaker workers had first adopted the red and black eight-pointed star as their emblem. At the outset of the First World War in 1914, this organization was revived. Many Quaker conscientious objectors were thrown into prison, but others found their way to ambulance and relief units in France and elsewhere in Europe. In 1917 the AFSC sent American conscientious objectors to join them.

After the war Quaker volunteers brought food and clothing and medical care to Eastern Europe and worked in the famine districts of Russia. At the request of Herbert Hoover, who had a Quaker background and headed first the U.S. Food Administration and then the American Relief Administration, the AFSC undertook the distribution of food to 1 million undernourished German and Austrian children.

Emergency relief gave way to efforts for reconstruction in Europe, until the 1930s when the Depression devastated America itself and there were many needs to be met at home. With the coming to power of Hitler AFSC was involved in helping refugees to leave their homeland and resettle abroad, and during the Spanish civil war, 1936–39, Quakers helped distribute food to both sides. Wherever possible, the effort was made to preserve the self-respect of the recipient of aid and to help people help themselves. Unemployed coal miners in West Virginia were assisted to build homes for themselves and others, for example, and in southern France injured war veterans from Republican Spain were given a workshop to make artificial limbs.

In the Second World War conscientious objectors were legally recognized in both England and America, but American COs who were drafted had to do their "work of national importance" at home, where they served in forestry camps, hospital wards, as guinea pigs for medical experiments, and in assignments in social work. When the war ended, many of them joined Quaker relief units in Europe, India, China, and Japan. The AFSC volunteers often worked together with volunteers from the official British FSC, as well as with the unofficial Friends Ambulance Unit, which took on more dangerous work, such as its transport service on the Burma Road.

Chairman Jahn's speech showed that he had studied the Quaker literature carefully. He quoted the antiwar declaration of 1660 and said it was much more than a simple refusal to take part in war: "It is better to suffer injustice than to commit injustice. It is from within man himself that victory must in the end be gained." Jahn declared, "It is through silent assistance from the nameless to the nameless that they have worked to promote 'the fraternity among nations,' to use the phrase in the will of Alfred Nobel." And again: "It is not in the extent of their work or its practical form that the Quakers have given most to the people they have met. It is in the spirit in which this work is performed." Jahn recognized that this was the Quaker religion being translated into positive action, that this was the spirit that must form the basis for lasting peace. "For this reason alone the Quakers deserve to receive the Nobel Peace Prize today. But they have given us something more: they have shown us the strength to be derived from faith in the victory of the spirit over force."

The Quaker representatives of the two organizations, Margaret Backhouse of FSC and Henry Cadbury of AFSC, in their acceptance speeches emphasized that the Quaker work had been made possible by the support of thousands who were not members of the small Society of Friends, whose total membership, most of which was in the United States and Britain, numbered perhaps 200,000. Backhouse pointed out that the Quakers were ordinary people. Cadbury declared that the committee was saying "that common folk, not statesmen, not generals, but just simple plain men and women like the few thousand Quakers and their friends, if they devote themselves to resolute insistence on goodwill in place of force, even in the face of great disaster past or threatened, can do something to build a better world."

In their Nobel lectures both Quaker representatives stressed the religious basis of Quaker work for humanity and peace. It was the first prize for advocates of nonviolence, and they used the occasion to explain absolute Christian pacifism. Few in their audience would themselves have taken such a stand, but the Norwegians had used methods of nonviolence to resist the German authorities during the occupation, and they had reason to believe that, as Jahn had said in his address, quoting a Norwegian poet:

> Only the unarmed
> Can draw on sources eternal
> To the Spirit alone will be the victory.

When the cable had come from Oslo announcing the prize, Clarence Pickett, executive secretary of the AFSC, in opening a staff meeting, asked for a moment of silence and for consideration of the text "Beware when men think well of you." For their peace testimony Quakers have more often had to face what their poet John Greenleaf Whittier called "the public frown." When the AFSC used its share of the prize money in efforts of reconciliation between the Soviet Union and the United States, American public opinion in this time of cold war treated such activities with suspicion and hostility. Later, in its early opposition to the Vietnam War, the AFSC was to feel the "public frown" in no small measure.

Although the Quaker prize was well received by world opinion, the editorial writers had much more to say about Quaker good works than about the Quaker path to peace. The Quakers themselves were properly humble about their prize, seeing its significance in the inspiration it could give the common people of the world, as Henry Cadbury had explained. Clarence Pickett declared that "in an age when increasingly the state was held to be supreme and the individual only a tool, the prize has gone, in a basic sense, to that way of life which holds each individual to be a child of God and therefore of supreme value." What the Quaker prize meant, he said, was "a striking vote of confidence" in "people all over the world and of various creeds, who were of this fundamental faith."

BIBLIOGRAPHY

Secondary Sources

Bacon, Margaret. *Let This Life Speak: The Legacy of Henry Cadbury*. Philadelphia: University of Pennsylvania Press, 1987. Biography of the longtime chairman of the AFSC, who received the award in Oslo.

Forbes, John V. *The Quaker Star under Seven Flags, 1917–1927*. Philadelphia: University of Pennsylvania Press, 1962. Wartime and postwar relief work.

Greenwood, John O. *Friends and Relief*. Vol. 1 of *Quaker Encounters*. 3 vols. York, England: Sessions, 1975–78. Two centuries of the relief work of British Quakers.

Hall, Willis. *Quaker International Work in Europe since 1914*. Chambéry [Savoie]: Imprimeries Réunies, 1938. A doctoral thesis at the University of Geneva. Surveys both relief work and efforts for international understanding.

Hirst, Margaret. *Quakers in Peace and War: an Account of Their Peace Principles and Practice*. 1923. Reprint. New York: Garland, 1972. With an introduction by Edwin B. Bronner. The first comprehensive study of Quaker pacifism through World War I.

Jones, Mary Hoxie. *Swords into Plowshares: An Account of the American Friends Sevice Committee, 1917–1937*. New York: Macmillan, 1937.

Pickett, Clarence. *For More than Bread: An Autobiographical Account of Twenty-Two Years' Work with the American Friends Service Committee*. Boston: Little, Brown, 1953. Pickett was AFSC executive secretary.

Wilson, Roger. *Quaker Relief: An Account of the Relief Work of the Society of Friends, 1940–1948*. London: Allen & Unwin, 1952. The experience of British Quakers, by a top administrator.

1949

Lord Boyd-Orr of Brechin (1880–1971)

Great Britain

Medical doctor and nutritional scientist, responsible for Britain's food policy during World War II; founding director-general of UN Food and Agricultural Organization, 1945–48; founder, International Emergency Food Council, 1946; president, National Peace Council, World Union of Peace Organizations.

Lord Boyd-Orr was the first scientist to win the Peace Prize not for his scientific discoveries but for the way they were employed "to promote cooperation between nations." Chairman Jahn declared in presenting the prize, "The purpose of his scientific work is to find ways of making men healthier and happier so as to secure peace," believing as he does that "healthy and happy men have no need to resort to arms in order to expand and acquire living space." He went on, "Few can claim to have planned and carried through a work as important to the human race as his, a work which clearly paves the way for peace."

His beginnings were simple. John Boyd-Orr was born on a farm in Scotland and went to the village school, where he became a student teacher at the age of eighteen. As a scholarship student he was able to attend Glasgow University where, after an interruption to teach in a secondary school, he won university degrees in medicine and biological sciences. He tried the practice of medicine but soon decided on research, and by 1914 he had been appointed director of a new institute for research in animal nutrition in Aberdeen.

The war soon took him off, and he served in the Royal Army Medical Corps and then the navy, winning medals for bravery under fire. After the war he returned to the institute at Aberdeen, and under his leadership it gained national and international renown for its studies in crop production and animal nutrition. He developed the skill of fund-raising and attracted to the institute the money for new buildings and an experimental farm.

Researchers in nutrition at the time were concerned only with animals. It was Orr who led the way to the investigation of human diets. His institute was looking into the effect of poor pasture land on the herds of two tribes in East Africa. Orr sent out doctors to make a comparative study of the tribes as well, since one was meat-eating and blood-drinking and the other ate cereals and drank milk. In 1935 Orr turned his attention to schoolchildren in Scotland, showing how the addition of milk to their diet accelerated growth and improved health. It startles us to realize that something we now take for granted had to be demonstrated experimentally sixty years ago.

Orr was surprised to discover that he could readily induce farmers to improve the food of their animals because it paid off at market, but they were uninterested in using his scientific findings to improve the nutrition of their children. To bring the matter to the attention of the public, he made a nationwide survey of the relationships among income, diet, and health, which showed that half the British people did not earn enough money to afford an adequate diet. The report made health and diet a national issue. Other nations became interested, and the League of Nations appointed committees to inquire into world food needs and their relationship to agriculture, health, and economics. Orr, now Sir John (he was knighted in 1935), took a leading role in these developments. The coming of the war in 1939 ended the work of the League's committees, but in Britain Sir John's researches and his leadership brought food policies that actually improved the standards of health, despite the impact of the war economy and the cutting off of all dairy products from the Continent.

While carrying heavy wartime responsibilities, Sir John began to plan for the postwar years. In 1942 he visited the United States on a private mission to secure support for international coordination of food supplies, and in the next year he published a little book, *Food and People,* in which he argued for a postwar effort to achieve a major goal of the Atlantic Charter—freedom from want. "Food is the first want or need of all men," he declared and outlined how enough could be produced to feed the world.

In that same year of 1943 a conference was held in Hot Springs, Virginia, which, influenced by Sir John although he was not present, laid the groundwork for the postwar Food and Agriculture Organization (FAO). In October 1945, the FAO was formally established as the first specialized agency of the evolving United Nations Organization. The natural choice for director-general was Sir John. Equally concerned for world peace, especially after his only son was killed in action with the Royal Air Force, Sir John also found time in that year to preside over the National Peace Council of Britain, with its fifty cooperating organizations, and the World Union of Peace Organizations.

As director-general of the FAO, Sir John met the urgent need to revive agricultural production in order to avert the famine with which a number of countries were threatened, while at the same time planning for long-term food needs, especially in developing countries. The emergency needs were met through the International Emergency Food Council, which Sir John also headed. For the long term, he proposed a World Food Board with authority and funding to stockpile food stores, stabilize world food prices, and make grants of surplus food to the neediest countries. The United States and Britain, however, were unwilling to give such power to a central organization and were apprehensive about the cost, and the plan failed. A World Food Council with powers to advise and encourage national governments was then established within the framework of the FAO.

The rejection of his proposal confirmed Sir John's conviction that only a world government could take the necessary action to free the world from hunger. He resigned from the FAO at the end of his first term in 1948 to go into private business and devote much of his new income and energies to the movement for world government. On the occasion of his retirement from FAO, he said that it was something of a miracle that that organization had succeeded as well as it had. It was difficult to prevail upon nations to cooperate on the political level. But at the council table of the FAO, he said, "representatives of governments are not talking about war, not thinking about war. They are planning for the greatest movement that will make for peace—increased food production, the strengthening of agriculture, and food for the people of the world."

After his retirement he was made Baron Boyd-Orr of Brechin, and in 1949, the year after his resignation, the Nobel Committee chose to recognize his achievements with the Peace Prize.

Boyd-Orr's Nobel address was considered one of the best speeches he had ever given. It was a testament to his faith in science and in humanity. He described the changes that science had brought in the past, as humanity had had to adjust to such inventions as gunpowder, printing, and the steam engine. Now science and technology had made the whole world one and at the same time had produced a bomb that was so destructive that "the only alternative to war is the United States of the world."

He gave the prize money for the building of a Peace Center in London to house the National Peace Council and other peace organizations. He himself became president of the World Movement for a World Government.

In June 1971, Lord Boyd-Orr died at his home in Scotland, a few months before his ninety-first birthday.

BIBLIOGRAPHY

Primary Sources

Boyd-Orr, John. *As I Recall.* Garden City, N.Y.: Doubleday, 1967. Autobiography.

———. *Food and the People.* London: Pilot Press, 1943.

———. *Housing and Health.* London: Dent, 1944. The effect of inadequate housing.

———. *The Wonderful World of Food: The Substance of Life.* Garden City, N.Y.: Garden City Books, 1958. Illustrated book for young readers.

Boyd-Orr, John, and David Lubbock. *The White Man's Dilemma.* Rev. ed. London: Allen & Unwin, 1964. Food for needy nations as the basis for world peace.

Secondary Sources

"Boyd-Orr, John." In *BDI.*

Hambridge, Gove. *The Story of the FAO.* New York: Van Nostrand, 1955.

Kenworthy, Leonard S. "John Boyd-Orr: World Hunger Fighter." In *Twelve Citizens of the World.* Garden City, N.Y.: Doubleday, 1953.

Vries, Egbert de. *Life and Work of Sir John Boyd-Orr.* Wageningen, The Netherlands: Veenman, 1948. Brief summary.

1950

Ralph J. Bunche (1904–71)

United States

Social scientist, university professor, State Department official, international civil servant with United Nations as mediator and administrator of trusteeships and peacekeeping.

Ralph Bunche was awarded the prize the year after his success as UN mediator in ending Arab-Jewish hostilities over Palestine in 1949. When asked how he had achieved this, he replied:

Like every Negro in America, I've been buffeted about a great deal. I've suffered many disillusioning experiences. Inevitably, I've become allergic to prejudice. On the other hand, from my earliest years I was taught the virtues of tolerance, militancy in fighting for rights—but not bitterness. And as a social scientist I've always cultivated a coolness of temper, and attitude of objectivity when dealing with human sensitivities and irrationalities, which has always proved invaluable—never more so than in the Palestine negotiations. Success there was dependent upon maintaining complete objectivity. Throughout the endless weeks of negotiations I was bolstered by an unfailing sense of optimism. Somehow, I knew we had to succeed. I am an incurable optimist, as a matter of fact.

Chairman Jahn quoted this statement in his presentation because it was such an excellent self-description and tells so much of what went into the making of Ralph Bunche.

His grandfather was a slave who came north after Emancipation and raised a family in a Detroit slum, where Ralph's father later eked out a living as a barber. After the grandfather died, Grandmother Johnson became the head of the family, and they all lived together in one shanty dwelling. She was an extraordinary woman, teaching them all, as Bunche never forgot, "to stand up for our rights, to suffer no indignity, but to harbor no bitterness toward anyone, as this would only warp our personalities." She would say, "Go out into the world with your head high, and keep it high at all times."

Little Ralph helped support the family at an early age as a newspaper boy, but he showed promise in school, and his grandmother was determined that he would not drop out as so many black children were forced to do for economic reasons. The barber shop failed when Ralph was ten, and the family moved to Toledo, Ohio, and then to Albuquerque when his parents fell ill and needed a better climate. But after a short time there, when Ralph was only eleven, they both died.

Grandmother Johnson now moved Ralph, his little sister and their two aunts to Los Angeles, where their struggles to make a living continued. But she kept him in school, where he was doing well, and in 1918 he was one of the few blacks to enter Jefferson High School, working at odd jobs after school and during vacations. He somehow found time to star in basketball and football, so that when he graduated, with honors, he was able to attend the University of California at Los Angeles with an athletic scholarship and a job as janitor in the women's gymnasium. He did brilliantly in his studies and played guard on three conference-winning basketball teams. In 1927, one of only two black graduates, he received his degree summa cum laude and was a member of Phi Beta Kappa, the national scholastic honor society.

Then he won a scholarship to Harvard for graduate work, and the proud black community of Los Angeles raised a thousand dollars to send him to Cambridge and help with his expenses. Proudest of all was Grandmother Johnson, but her job was now done. Not long afterward, Grandmother Johnson died peacefully in her sleep.

In Cambridge he worked in a bookshop while studying for his M.A. degree, which he received in 1928. Turning down offers from white institutions, he accepted an appointment at Howard University in Washington, D.C., the most famous black university in the country, where he established the Department of Political Science. He was soon a popular teacher. He was a good lecturer, held his students to high academic standards, and was always felt to be fair. One of his brighter and more attractive students was Ruth Harris, to whom he became engaged, although they had to wait to be married because he had a scholarship to spend another year at Harvard starting on his doctorate. After the first year of their marriage, they were separated again when Bunche went off to Europe and Africa with a Rosenwald Fellowship to do research for his dissertation. In 1934 he was the first black to earn a doctorate in political science.

His teaching at Howard was interrupted once more when he was a awarded a Social Science Research Council postdoctoral fellowship in anthropology and colonial policy. He studied at Northwestern University, the London School of Economics, and Capetown University in South Africa, where he was admitted only after convincing the authorities he was not planning any subversive activities. He lived three months with the Kikuyu in East Africa, who made him an honorary member. His fellowship also made possible a trip around the world.

Now a recognized authority on race relations, with a well-regarded book on *A World View of Race,* Bunche was invited to join Gunnar Myrdal, the Swedish social scientist, in a two-year study of blacks in America, leading to the publication of Myrdal's landmark survey, *An American Dilemma.* After each of these assignments Bunche would return to Howard, but his next departure marked the beginning of a new career altogether.

He left Howard in 1941 to make a contribution to the war effort by joining the staff of what was to become the Office of Strategic Services. As a senior social science analyst, his job was to provide information about colonial areas where American armed forces were operating. His knowledge was exhaustive, his memorandums models of exposition, and he moved up through positions of higher responsibility until in January 1944 he was brought into the State Department to deal with colonial problems. Race prejudice in the department had held up his appointment until Secretary of State Cordell Hull, after reading Bunche's personnel file, told his subordinates to delay no longer, but to appoint the person who was obviously best qualified.

Bunche rose steadily in the department until he was finally appointed to the Office of Political Affairs as acting chief in the division concerned with trusteeships, the first black to hold such a high desk job at State. He was often sent to international conferences, serving as delegate or adviser at nine such meetings within four years. On one assignment he helped draft the sections of the UN Charter relating to non-self-governing territories and trusteeships.

In 1946 Secretary-General Trygve Lie asked Bunche to join the UN Secretariat to organize and direct the Trusteeship Division. The next year, when Britain was preparing to give up its mandate in Palestine, Lie sent Bunche to Palestine to assist the UN committee that was studying the situation, and he drafted much of the committee's report recommending partition between Arabs and Jews. Despite his desire to stay with his trusteeship work, Bunche was drawn more and more to the Palestine problem, and when the fighting broke out in 1948 he was the logical member of the Secretariat to assist Count Folke Bernadotte as UN mediator.

They were an unusual pair. Bernadotte was the nephew of the king of Sweden and as the head of the Swedish Red Cross had successfully negotiated the release of Scandinavian prisoners from the Nazis. He had been seriously considered for the Nobel Peace Prize. Bunche had risen far above his origins in the Detroit slums, but he was still little known outside university and UN circles. Both men had the qualities Bunche once prescribed for mediators: "They should be biased against war and for peace. They should have a bias which would lead them to believe in the essential goodness of their fellowman and that no problem of human relations is insoluble. They should be biased against suspicion, intolerance, hate, religious and racial bigotry."

Almost immediately Bernadotte obtained a truce, but it was broken, and on 17 September he was assassinated by Jewish terrorists who opposed his mission. They also killed the French officer in the car with him; it was only a matter of chance that Bunche was not with Bernadotte at the time. Shocked and grieved as he was, Bunche did not hesitate to accept Trygve Lie's telephoned request that he succeed Bernadotte and carry on the mediation effort.

The negotiations dragged on for eleven months in all. Even after they were moved to the island of Rhodes for a better atmosphere, both Arabs and Jews so distrusted one another that they refused to sit around the same table. Bunche had to see the delegations separately and then wait until each sent off for instructions. The Arab delegation included Egyptians, Jordanians, and Syrians, who did not always agree among themselves. Bunche needed infinite patience, an iron will, and a rugged constitution. By needling, cajoling, and bluffing, using all the arts of conflict resolution as well as his anthropological understanding of the two cultures, and often going without food and sleep, Bunche finally got the two sides to agree to an armistice.

The American press had been filled with reports of the ongoing negotiations, and now Bunche returned home as a hero to a ticker-tape parade in New York City and a "Ralph Bunche Day" in Los Angeles. President Truman received him in the White House, and the United Nations, wishing to capitalize on his success, sent him on a speaking tour around the country. A record number of universities bestowed upon him honorary degrees, and President Truman offered him the position of assistant secretary of state. Bunche declined; Washington was segregated, and he remembered "when I was working in Washington how I had to drive my daughters many miles to school because they were Negroes." Bunche preferred to live near New York City.

Throughout all the hero-worship, Bunche retained his customary modesty. When he received the cable from Oslo that he had won the prize, he said he was "flabbergasted." He had heard rumors that he was the leading candidate, but he had refused to take them seriously. He tried to turn away the praise that was being heaped upon him, saying: "I am one man, working for the United Nations. Without the UN, I am nothing."

In his Nobel address Bunche spoke of the United Nations as "the greatest peace effort in human history," declaring, "Peace and the United Nations have become inseparable. If the United Nations cannot ensure peace, there will be none." But "peace is no mere matter of man fighting or not fighting." Peace "must be translated into bread or rice, shelter, health, and education, as well as freedom and human dignity." Bunche insisted that the West become fully aware of "the massive and restive millions of Asia and Africa. . . . Their vast numbers will prove a dominant factor in the future world pattern of life. They provide virgin soil for the growth of democracy, but the West must first learn how to approach them understandingly and how to win their trust and friendship." He emphasized that the United Nations "exists not merely to preserve the peace but also to make change—even radical change—possible without violent upheaval. . . . In the dynamic world society which is the objective of the United Nations, all peoples must have equality and equal rights."

Bunche remained as director of the Trusteeship Division until 1955, then became under secretary-general, with special responsibility for peacekeeping operations. In his last years at the United Nations he suffered from diabetes and heart disease, but he held out until he finally resigned on 1 October 1971. He died two months later, on 9 December.

The official positions he held kept Ralph Bunche from sharing leadership in the civil rights movement of the 1960s, although he participated in freedom marches, and there was never any question of his support for Martin Luther King, Jr., and others on the front line. What he achieved in his life, however, was not only a source of pride and inspiration for those leaders; it represented a supreme demonstration of the capacities of the human spirit, clothed in whatever color, to surmount obstacles of social circumstance and rise to the height of human endeavor. The life of a Ralph Bunche is the best argument for the cause for which he labored—equal rights and opportunities for all.

BIBLIOGRAPHY

Primary Sources

Bunche, Ralph. "My Most Unforgettable Character." *Reader's Digest* 95 (September 1969): 45–69. A loving portrait of his remarkable grandmother.

———. *Peace and the United Nations.* Leeds: University of Leeds Press, 1952. A lecture.

———. *The Political Status of the Negro in the Age of FDR.* Chicago: University of Chicago Press, 1973. Based on field work in the South for Gunnar Myrdal's study of race relations, *An American Dilemma.*

———. *A World View of Race.* 1936. Reprint. Port Washington, N.Y.: Kennikat Press, 1968.

Secondary Sources

"Bunche, Ralph." In *BDI.*

Haskins, Jim. *Ralph Bunche, A Most Reluctant Hero.* New York: Hawthorn, 1974. For youthful readers.

Kenworthy, Leonard S. "Ralph Bunche: Champion of Colonial Peoples." In *Twelve Citizens of the World.* Garden City, N.Y.: Doubleday, 1953.

Kugelmass, J. Alvin. *Ralph J. Bunche, Fighter for Peace.* New York: Messner, 1952. A popular account.

Myrdal, Gunnar. *An American Dilemma.* New York: Harper, 1944.

Pearson, Lester B. "Unforgettable Ralph Bunche." *Reader's Digest* 102 (March 1973): 89–93. An appreciation by the Nobel laureate, who knew Bunche well at the United Nations.

Urquhart, Brian. *Hammarskjöld.* New York: Knopf, 1972. Biography of Bunche's chief, with whom he worked closely.

1951
Léon Jouhaux (1879–1954)

France

Veteran international labor leader, who worked for peace through the International Federation of Trade Unions, the International Labor Organization, which he helped found, the League of Nations, the United Nations, and the European Movement, of which he was president.

In granting the prize to Léon Jouhaux, the Nobel Committee not only honored an individual for his long-term leadership of the trade union movement in the fight for peace but gave recognition to the principle he represented—that enduring peace can be based only upon social justice.

Léon Jouhaux was a child of the working classes and knew social injustice from personal experience. His father was a worker in a match factory who had participated in the uprising of the radical Paris commune in 1871, and his grandfather had fought in the republican revolution of 1848. Jouhaux had shown intellectual promise in his boyhood, and his parents had cherished the hope that he might become an engineer, but before he was twelve he had to leave elementary school to help support the family when his father was on strike. Twice he tried to continue his schooling, but the family needed his wages, and at the age of fourteen he resigned himself to the life of an industrial worker.

When he was sixteen, he joined the trade union at the match factory where his father worked. In his Nobel address he said:

> I did so without question. My father's vigorous example and my own experience led me quite naturally to participate in the worker's movement. I had suffered personally from the social order. My school work, my intellectual gifts, my eagerness to study, had all come to nothing. I had been brutally compelled to leave the upper primary school and even the vocational training school and to become a wage earner of the humblest order.

When Jouhaux was doing his military service in Algeria, he was called home. His father had gone blind from working with white phosphorus in the factory, and he had to return to his job there to support the family. In 1900, at the age of twenty-one, he took part in his first strike, serving as secretary in the union's meeting because, brief as his schooling had been, it was more than his comrades had had. His interest in this strike was personal, for it was aimed at prohibiting the use of white phosphorus in the manufacturing process. The strikers won, and eventually an international conference adopted a convention against the use of the dangerous chemical.

This success showed Jouhaux how effective the trade union could be in the struggle to improve the lot of the worker. Soon afterward, as he explained in his lecture, he came to see trade unionism also as a means of freeing the world from war.

In 1906 his union sent him as representative to the *Confédération générale du travail* (the general confederation of labor, called by its initials in French, the CGT), which had been established in 1895 to unite the trade unions of France. By 1909 Jouhaux's talents as organizer and speaker had brought him to the post of secretary-general of the CGT, which he held until 1947. In this position he took a prominent part in the efforts of European trade unions to prevent the First World War, speaking in England, Germany, Switzerland, and Belgium, and urging their trade unions to join together for peace. The CGT took a more radical antimilitarist position than most other national unions, vowing to call a general strike if war were declared.

As war approached in July 1914, Jouhaux sent one last desperate appeal to the international secretariat to exert pressure on the governments, but a few weeks later the war began, and the trade unionists of each of the belligerent countries were soon trooping behind the national colors, along with members of the Marxist parties on their political left.

Jouhaux now put his antimilitarism behind him for good. In the Nobel lecture he explained it away as the product of the enthusiasm of youth. From this time Jouhaux led the CGT to take a more moderate line. He himself worked for the war on several government committees, and he was able to get a hearing for the CGT program for the future peace, which called for disarmament, compulsory international arbitration, an end to secret treaties, and a peace treaty that would lay the groundwork for a United States of Europe. In an Inter-Allied Labor and Socialist conference in 1918, the CGT submitted a far-reaching proposal for a supranational authority, with an international legislature whose decisions would be binding on all member states.

These were ideas that other peace forces were also putting forward, and some of them were to find their way into the Treaty of Versailles. Another proposal from Jouhaux and other trade union leaders was for the establishment of an international labor organization. They also joined with the socialists to demand socialist and labor representation at the peace conference negotiations. This led to Jouhaux and Samuel Gompers of the American Federation of Labor serving as technical advisers to the delegations of France and the United States, and the two worked together to get the constitution of the International Labor Organization written into the Versailles Treaty. In this document two of the most important principles of Jouhaux and the trade union movement were internationally agreed to: (1) that universal peace could be established only if the new international order was based upon social justice; and (2) world peace was imperiled by inhumane conditions of labor, and an improvement of those conditions was urgently required.

Jouhaux became one of the leading figures in the new organization, serving on the governing body as the workers' representative from France for over three decades, including the years after World War II. Jouhaux also represented his country in the Assembly of the League of Nations, and his voice was always heard for disarmament, collective security, and international economic cooperation. In 1936 he organized the French peace forces in the international peace campaign inaugurated by Lord Cecil and the British League of Nations Union. Also in the interwar years, Jouhaux supported peace issues as vice president of the World Federation of Trade Unions.

In World War II, after the German invasion of France, Jouhaux worked with the Resistance until he was arrested by the Germans. He was first confined to his home, then sent to the concentration camp at Buchenwald in Germany, and finally interned in Austria. With his rugged constitution he managed to survive his incarceration of twenty-five months still in good health. At the age of sixty-five Jouhaux returned to France after liberation to take up once again the causes that were dear to his heart.

His beloved CGT, which he had kept free of involvement in intraparty struggles for so long, now fell under the domination of the Communist party, with which he had disagreed from the time of its establishment in France after the First World War. After an attempt to cooperate, he finally had to withdraw from the CGT and to form a new organization, the non-Communist *CGT-Force ouvrière* (Workers' force). At the same time he helped form a new non-Communist international trade union association, since the old World Federation of Trade Unions was also taken over by the Communists. Among other objectives, the CGT-FO stood for the establishment of the United States of Europe.

In France Jouhaux became president of the National Economic Council, an agency he had long been working toward, whose purpose was to coordinate the economic forces of the country. He was elected six times to this body, the last time on the eve of his death. In this council and elsewhere Jouhaux worked for European economic cooperation, becoming president of the European Movement in 1949. He formulated its aim in these words: "We want Europe to be a peaceable community, united, despite and within its diversity, in a constant and ardent struggle against human misery and all the suffering and dangers that it engenders. We have no desire to make Europe into a larger, better entrenched armed fortress."

On another occasion he spoke out for civil liberties: "But democracy is not, nor can it be merely a theoretical respect for these rights. It must give every man effective opportunities to enjoy them, and it must do so under the kind of moral and material conditions that will encourage him to exercise such rights. One who must be constantly preoccupied with his own subsistence cannot be an alert citizen."

In concluding his Nobel lecture, Jouhaux said the prize, which he accepted on behalf of the trade union movement of the world, would strengthen its will "to work ceaselessly to develop a society free of injustice and violence. . . . We know well, alas, that men and civilizations are mortal. We wish to leave to indifferent nature the responsibility for their demise and to free mankind at last from its remorse for having begotten Cain."

Four years after receiving the prize, still active on all fronts, Léon Jouhaux died of a heart attack at the age of seventy-five.

BIBLIOGRAPHY

Primary Sources

Jouhaux, Léon. *Le Désarmement.* Paris: Alcan, 1927.

———. *Le Syndicalisme: Ce qu'Il est, ce qu'Il doit être.* Paris: Flammarion, 1937. Unionism and its future.

Secondary Sources

Georges, Bernard, and Denise Tintant. *Léon Jouhaux: Cinquante ans de syndicalisme.* 2 vols. Paris: Presses Universitaires de France, 1962.

"Jouhaux, Léon." In *BDI.*

"Léon Jouhaux, 1879–1954." *International Labour Review* 70 (September–October 1954): 241–57. Selections from tributes to Jouhaux after his death.

Léon-Jouhaux, Augusta. *Prison pour hommes d'etat.* Paris: Denoël-Gontier, 1973. Mme. Jouhaux tells of the internment of her husband and a diverse group of French leaders in a castle in Austria during World War II.

Lorwin, Val. "The Struggle for Control of the French Trade-Union Movement 1945–49." In *Modern France: Problems of the Third and Fourth Republics.* Edited by Edward M. Earle. Princeton: Princeton University Press, 1951, pp. 200–18.

1952
Albert Schweitzer (1875–1965)

France

Philosopher and theologian, minister and teacher, musicologist and organist, medical missionary in Africa.

In 1932 a group of distinguished German scholars began an international campaign to win the prize for Albert Schweitzer, urging the Nobel Committee in Oslo not to restrict the award to statesmen and leaders of peace societies, but to recognize an outstanding contribution that far transcended what could be achieved through an organization or an office. What Schweitzer was trying to do, they said, was no less than to awaken humanity to a new ethos of brotherly love. He had written cultural-philosophical works to expound this ethos, and he could have founded an organization to promote it. Instead, he was embodying this ethos in his personal life and thereby giving the world an example of "sacrifice for humanity."

It took the committee twenty years to reinterpret its mandate and to recognize what a contribution to peacemaking Albert Schweitzer's personal example represented. In awarding the 1952 prize to Schweitzer, Chairman Jahn was only repeating what the German scholars had said when he declared: "His whole life and all his work are a message. . . . He has made the concept of brotherhood a living one."

Albert Schweitzer was the son of a Protestant pastor in the village of Günsbach in Alsace, born a few years after Alsace-Lorraine had passed from French to German rule as a consequence of the Franco-Prussian War. He grew up in a harmonious and religious home, learning to play the organ in his father's church when his feet could hardly reach the pedals. Very early in his life he began to feel uncomfortable that he was so privileged while many of his schoolmates lived in miserable peasant huts, were ill clad, and did not have enough to eat.

When he went off to the University of Strasbourg at eighteen, he rejoiced in his theological studies and his music, but he still could not help thinking of those who were less fortunate. Then, as he tells in his autobiography, one brilliant summer morning when he was twenty-one and home at Günsbach for the Whitsuntide holidays:

> there came to me, as I awoke, the thought that I must not accept this happiness as a matter of course, but must give something in return for it. Proceeding to think the matter out at once with calm deliberation, while the birds were singing outside, I settled with myself before I got up, that I would consider myself justified in living till I was thirty for science and art, in order to devote myself from that time forward to the direct service of humanity.

Schweitzer felt that he now understood the words of Jesus that "whosoever shall lose his life for my sake shall save it": "in addition to the outward, I now found inward happiness."

Just how he would serve was not yet clear to him. He continued with his studies, earning his first doctorate, in philosophy, at the age of twenty-four with a dissertation on the religious philosophy of Immanuel Kant, and his second, in theology, with a treatise on the Synoptic Gospels. At the age of thirty he received a doctorate in music for his definitive work on J. S. Bach. Meanwhile, he had become ordained and served as professor and preacher at the theological College of St. Thomas at the University of Strasbourg and at the same time managed to commute to Paris to study organ and to become a celebrated concert organist.

In 1904, several months before his thirtieth birthday, Schweitzer happened upon an appeal of the Paris Missionary Society for missionaries to go to French Equatorial Africa. He felt immediately that this was the work for humanity he had been seeking. He decided that first he should train as a doctor so that he could serve the Africans in the capacity for which there was clearly the greatest need.

His friends and relatives expostulated with him, arguing that he was on the verge of a brilliant career and that he would be wasting his gifts in the jungle. Could he not help the Africans more by raising money with organ concerts? Schweitzer only deplored that "people who passed for Christians" could oppose his desire to "serve the love preached by Jesus." One university student at Strasbourg agreed with his plan—Helene Bresslau, who became his wife and trained as a nurse while he was doing his medical studies.

Schweitzer was a man of inexhaustible energy. He had to give up his preaching, but during his seven years as a medical student he continued his writing and published a book on organ-building and two works of Biblical scholarship, including the brilliant and provocative *Quest for the Historical Jesus.* To the members of the Paris Missionary Society, his unorthodox writings raised the question whether they could accept someone who, as Schweitzer put it, "had only Christian love," but did not "hold also the correct Christian belief." Schweitzer reassured them by agreeing not to preach when he got to Africa.

After completing his medical studies, Schweitzer set out in 1913 with his wife for the missionary station of Lambaréné, on the banks of the Ogawé River in the Gabon, two days by river steamer from the coast. The site was well chosen for the tiny hospital he built, since patients could come with their canoes on hundreds of waterways that stretched into the jungle. They came with all kinds of diseases—malaria, dysentery, leprosy, elephantiasis—and with sores and ulcers and animal bites. Schweitzer had to treat them in primitive conditions after first winning their confidence. He toiled from morning to night in the torrid heat, his only relaxation the time he could find to play on the special piano-organ the Bach Society of Paris sent to him. In the late night hours he worked on a philosophy of civilization.

The First World War reached even into Schweitzer's jungle, however. He and his wife first were subjected to restrictions as German citizens in French territory; then they were taken to France in 1917 and interned as enemy aliens. Schweitzer emerged from this experience in 1918 depressed and ailing, but Archbishop Söderblom, who was to become the first religious peace laureate, arranged for him to lecture at the University of Uppsala in Sweden, where he regained his health and spirits.

Schweitzer spent the next years supporting his family and raising money for Lambaréné by presenting concerts and lectures throughout Europe and writing major autobiographical, religious, and philosophical works. When he returned to Lambaréné in 1924, after an absence of seven years, he spent the first months repairing and rebuilding the old structures. Now that he and his work were well known in Europe, however, contributions and gifts began to arrive, as well as doctors and nurses to help with the increasing numbers of patients.

After 1927 Schweitzer returned a number of times to Europe, where he could lecture, give concerts, and write at Günsbach, but his base remained the hospital at Lambaréné. On a trip to Europe in 1939, he got as far as Bordeaux, where he learned of the worsening international situation. Fearing that the coming war would prevent his return to Lambaréné, he ordered supplies for the hospital and went back immediately. During the conflict he received supplies from the United States, where the Albert Schweitzer Fellowship had been formed to support his work. He finally visited America in 1949 to speak at the two-hundredth anniversary celebration of the birth of Goethe, held in Aspen, Colorado.

One day late in 1953 at Lambaréné, Schweitzer's nephew, Dr. Guy Schweitzer, burst into his room to congratulate his uncle. "For what?" Albert Schweitzer asked. "Has my black cat finally had her kittens?" Dr. Guy told him that the radio station in Brazzaville had just announced that Schweitzer had been awarded the Nobel Peace Prize. Schweitzer was delighted to learn that he would receive about $33,000, enough to build and equip the hospital for lepers that he had dreamed of.

He postponed his appearance in Oslo until he was in Europe again, delivering his Nobel lecture on 4 November 1954. Schweitzer was now almost eighty, but he stood straight and tall, with a bushy mustache and a crown of unruly white hair, dressed in the black frock coat an Alsatian tailor had made for him many years before and which he had worn on every great occasion since. Schweitzer had worked on his address over a period of six months. It had been, he said, the hardest written work he had ever had to do. At Oslo he was asked to reduce the length, but the lecture still lasted almost an hour. He read his French text quietly and slowly and almost in a monotone, but the audience, knowing they were in the presence of a great thinker toward the end of his long life, listened intently.

Man had become superman with his scientific and technological advances, Schweitzer declared, but "we are becoming inhuman to the extent that we become supermen. We have learned to tolerate the facts of war: that men are killed en masse—some twenty million in the Second World War—that whole cities and their inhabitants are annihilated by the atomic bomb, that men are turned into living torches by incendiary bombs.

"We learn of these things from the radio or newspapers and we judge them according to whether they signify success for the group of people to which we belong, or for our enemies. We should all of us realize that we are guilty of inhumanity."

The League of Nations and the United Nations had failed because "there was no prevailing spirit directed toward peace. And being only legal institutions, they were unable to create such a spirit." This spirit "can find no home other than in the basic nature of man. . . . compassion, in which ethics takes root, does not assume its true proportions until it embraces not only man but every living being. To the old ethics, which lacked this depth and force of conviction, has been added the ethics of reverence for life."

The greatest obstacle to mutual understanding between peoples was "spurious nationalism," which could be overcome "only when the spirit becomes a living force within us and leads to a civilization based on the humanitarian ideal. . . . All men, even the semicivilized and the primitive, are, as beings capable of compassion, able to develop a humanitarian spirit. It abides within them like tinder ready to be lit, waiting only for a spark.

"It is my profound conviction that the solution lies in our rejecting war for an ethical reason; namely that war makes us guilty of the crime of inhumanity. . . . The only originality I claim is that for me this truth goes hand in hand with the intellectual certainty that the human spirit is capable of creating in our time a new mentality, an ethical mentality." May the world's leaders, Schweitzer concluded, avoid actions that would make the present situation even more dangerous; may they "do their utmost to give the spirit time to grow and to act."

In this address Schweitzer referred only very generally to the threat of nuclear war. He had been urged to use the occasion to speak out, but he had always wanted to keep aloof from political questions; besides, this was a subject on which he felt he had little scientific knowledge. But Schweitzer did feel that now that he had been given the Nobel Peace Prize, he "should do something to earn it." He began to consider carefully the suggestions he received from world leaders like Bertrand Russell and Pablo Casals that he take a public stand, and characteristically, he set out to acquire technical information about radiation and its effects upon health.

It was Norman Cousins, the American editor, who finally convinced Schweitzer that he had the responsibility to give a message to the world. In January 1957 Cousins traveled to Lambaréné to discuss the matter with Schweitzer, and he persuaded him to make a public statement opposing nuclear tests. Schweitzer decided that this should be read over Radio Oslo "of the city of the Nobel Peace Prize," and the Norwegian Nobel Committee agreed to sponsor the broadcast.

On 24 April 1957, Chairman Jahn read in Norwegian the text of what has become known as Schweitzer's Declaration of Conscience, and later that evening it was broadcast in the major European languages. "I raise my voice," Schweitzer had written, to warn of the catastrophe for the human race which increasing radioactive fallout represents and to appeal for an international agreement to stop atomic testing: "The end of further experiments with atom bombs would be like the sunrays of hope which suffering humanity is longing for."

Schweitzer's declaration was broadcast from 150 transmitters all over the world. It contributed to the movement among scientists to oppose atomic testing, which Linus Pauling coordinated in 1957 and which eventually led in 1963 to the international agreement to ban atomic tests in the atmosphere. Schweitzer took an active part in this crusade and had come so far from his earlier position of avoiding political issues that in his last public statement, made shortly before his death, he supported an appeal for a cease-fire in Vietnam.

He died in Lambaréné in 1965 at the age of ninety and was buried there. He had said once that it would not matter whether his grave was in Günsbach or Lambaréné—it is "God's earth."

BIBLIOGRAPHY

Primary Sources

Schweitzer, Albert. *Goethe: Four Studies.* Translated by Charles R. Joy. Boston: Beacon, 1949.

———. *J. S. Bach.* 2 vols. Translated by Ernest Newman. London: Black, 1947.

———. *Memoirs of Childhood and Youth.* Translated by C. T. Campion. New York: Macmillan, 1949.

———. *On the Edge of the Primeval Forest: Experiences and Observations of a Doctor in Equatorial Africa.* Translated by C. T. Campion. New York: Macmillan, 1948. Two books republished as one; the first covers his first mission, the second the period 1924–27.

———. *Out of My Life and Thought, an Autobiography.* Translated by C. T. Campion. New York: Holt, 1949. Through 1931. A postscript by Everett Skillings covers the years 1932–49.

———. *Philosophy of Civilization.* Translated by C. T. Campion. New York: Macmillan, 1950.

———. *The Quest of the Historical Jesus.* New York: Macmillan, 1948.

———. *Reverence for Life.* Translated by R. H. Fuller. New York: Harper & Row, 1969.

Secondary Sources

Barbazon, James. *Albert Schweitzer, a Biography.* New York: Putnam's, 1975.

Cousins, Norman. *Doctor Schweitzer of Lambaréné.* New York: Harper, 1960.

———. *Albert Schweitzer's Mission: Healing and Peace.* New York: Norton, 1985.

Griffith, Nancy Snell, and Laura Persons. *Albert Schweitzer: An International Bibliography.* Boston: G. K. Hall, 1981. The first international comprehensive bibliography of works by and about Schweitzer.

Jack, Homer, ed. *From One Human Being to Another: Albert Schweitzer on Nuclear War and Peace.* Elgin, Ill.: Brethren Press, 1988. Includes the radio appeals, "A Declaration of Conscience" and "Peace or Atomic War," and many letters. With an important introduction by the editor.

1953
George Catlett Marshall (1880–1959)

United States

U.S. Army officer, 1901–45; chief of staff and "organizer of victory" in World War II; secretary of state, 1947–49; head, American Red Cross, 1949–50; secretary of defense, 1950–51.

When the 1953 prizewinner was announced as George C. Marshall, the first career military man to be so honored, there was comment in the press as to the appropriateness of the Peace Prize being awarded to a soldier. The general responded to this in his Nobel address, declaring that he knew a great deal about "the horrors and tragedies of war." As chairman of the American Battle Monument Commission, with oversight of military ceremonies, he said, "The cost of war in human lives is constantly spread before me, written neatly in many ledgers whose columns are gravestones. I am deeply moved to find some means or method of avoiding another calamity of war."

The prize was given to General Marshall for what has been called the Marshall Plan, his policy as secretary of state to restore the war-shattered economy of Europe. From 1948 to 1952 the United States spent about $13 billion to rebuild the economies of sixteen Western European countries in what Chairman Jahn referred to as an unprecedented act of altruism. The motives were actually as complex as those behind any foreign policy, and naturally considerations of the national interest are the overriding concern of a secretary of state. But it is only fair to credit General Marshall with a high degree of idealism and certainly with a major contribution in securing congressional approval for the policy of reconstructing Europe.

As the only representative of the military in the Nobel pantheon of peace, General Marshall not only exhibited the very best of the soldierly virtues but was an outstanding human being in many ways. To President Truman, he was "the greatest general since Robert E. Lee," but also "the man of honor, the man of truth, the man of greatest ability. He was the greatest of the great in our time."

George Catlett Marshall was born in Uniontown, Pennsylvania, to a well-to-do merchant family of Virginia and Kentucky stock that went back to Chief Justice Marshall. His mother inspired him with the values of integrity and fairness, and he early developed a strong desire to excel. This resolve resulted from his brother's objection to having George follow him as a student at the Virginia Military Institute. George did not have a distinguished school record, and when he overheard his brother tell their parents that the younger brother would be a disgrace to the family, he determined that he would show them. Thereafter he never ceased to try to be the very best at whatever he set out to do.

He was sixteen when he went off to VMI at Lexington, Virginia, tall, gangling, and shy. He did not impress his teachers as a student, but he soon showed prowess in the field. He seems to have been a born leader, with a natural talent for managing men. He graduated as a leading cadet and then received his commission as second lieutenant in the regular army. At twenty-one he married the beautiful Elizabeth Coles, but then had to leave his bride of a few weeks for a lonely post in the Philippines.

Despite the clear evidence of his superior talents in every position he held, Marshall's rise in the army was very slow. When the United States entered the First World War in 1917, he was still a junior officer, and despite a brilliant performance as aide to Gen. John Pershing, the American commander, after the war he had to wait years for advancement because of the rigid seniority rules. Finally, in 1939 President Roosevelt reached over twenty major generals and fourteen brigadier generals to make him chief of staff just as World War II began with Germany's invasion of Poland.

Churchill called Marshall "the organizer of victory." He built and trained an army that reached more than 8 million, planned general strategy, and selflessly gave the command of the invasion forces to Gen.

Dwight Eisenhower when Roosevelt told him he could not sleep if Marshall were not nearby.

He retired from the army after the victory over Japan, hoping to cultivate his garden, only to answer the call of duty again when President Truman asked him to go to China to settle the conflict between Chiang Kai-shek and the Communists. Truman finally realized that this was an impossible mission and in 1947 called Marshall home to become secretary of state.

Marshall was now sixty-five, universally respected and well equipped through his wartime international experiences to handle foreign relations. Dean Acheson, his under secretary, wrote later that when Marshall came into a room, everyone felt his presence: "His figure conveyed intensity, which his voice, low, staccato, and incisive, reinforced." He did not fancy military glamor, and he was firmly committed to the subordination of the military to civilian authorities.

His watchwords were *honor* and *self-sacrifice,* which he emphasized in a commencement address at VMI. As a soldier and as a public servant, Marshall was utterly selfless, possessed of an overwhelming sense of duty. He expected respect from his associates, and he gave it to them, keenly conscious of rank and office, yet with an abiding concern for the individuals under his command and on his staff. He was well disciplined, thoroughly in control of himself, and rather aloof. Nobody except his wife called him "George"; he was always "General Marshall." His only vice was said to be a weakness for maple sugar candy.

Marshall ran the State Department as he had his military commands, picking talented subordinates, expecting good staff work from them, delegating much responsibility, and reserving top decisions for himself. He put Dean Acheson in charge of administration and told him, "I shall expect of you the most complete frankness, particularly about myself. I have no feelings except those I reserve for Mrs. Marshall." This was Katherine Tupper Marshall, whom he had married after his first wife died.

When Marshall took office President Truman was moving toward supporting the governments of Greece and Turkey against the communists, a policy that became known as the Truman Doctrine. Marshall was critical of anticommunist rhetoric, but he was told that it was necessary to get congressional approval. His own first international venture as secretary was a Council of Foreign Ministers meeting in Moscow, where Marshall became convinced that the Soviets intended to let the war-torn European economy deteriorate further, after which they would move in and pick up the pieces. In both France and Italy the Communist parties were strong.

Marshall returned from Moscow at the end of April 1947 and made a radio broadcast emphasizing Europe's desperate need for assistance. He then appointed George Kennan chief of the Policy Planning Staff, with top priority to be aid to Europe, telling him, "Avoid trivia." Acheson and others also played a part in the evolution of the policy to provide mammoth economic support to Europe, which Marshall enunciated in a famous speech at the Harvard commencement in June 1947. There he declared, "Our policy is directed not against any country or doctrine but against hunger, poverty, desperation, and chaos. Its purpose should be the revival of a working economy in the world so as to permit the emergence of political and social conditions in which free institutions can exist."

The idea was certainly not the monopoly of any one person, but it was Marshall under whose leadership it became a policy, and it was his influence that helped convince Congress and the country to support it. It was his decision not to impose an American plan. There never actually was a Marshall Plan. Rather, there was a Marshall policy that European governments should draw up their requests for aid cooperatively; from this developed a far-reaching movement for European unity.

It was also Marshall's decision that the aid should be offered to *all* Europe, including the Soviet Union and its neighbors, a position on which he had to overrule some of his subordinates, who claimed that the Kremlin would sabotage the whole undertaking. But Marshall maintained that if Europe was to be divided, let the Soviet Union do it. The Russians soon obliged, withdrawing from the European consultations and forcing Poland and Czechoslovakia to withdraw as well, claiming that American aid was being used to secure European markets and subject the Europeans to economic imperialism. Subsequent Soviet actions, such as the sending of troops into Czechoslovakia in August 1948, underlined the importance of the Marshall Plan in erecting a barrier in Western Europe against further Soviet expansion.

Whatever the humanitarian motives involved, after the Truman Doctrine the Marshall Plan was a further development in the policy of containment that was to continue long after Marshall left office. Revisionist historians have blamed such policies for the cold war, while Marshall's defenders have maintained that containment was the only proper answer to Soviet initiatives. Meanwhile, Marshall became the target of Sen. Joseph McCarthy, who leveled at him the baseless charge of being "soft on communism." Marshall later resigned after European reconstruction was well along, only to be called back into harness when President Truman asked him to serve as secretary of defense during the Korean War.

The cable from Oslo about the prize came when Marshall, then seventy-three, was in the Walter Reed Army Hospital with a persistent case of influenza. He was still not well when he boarded the *Andrea Doria* in December for Europe. Other laureates under such circumstances had asked to be excused, but Marshall felt duty-bound to make the trip. After a rough crossing, he staggered ashore when the ship reached Italy and flew from Paris to Oslo.

On 10 December in the university Aula, just as Marshall was accepting the prize from Dr. Hambro, vice-chairman of the committee, some communist journalists interrupted the ceremony, dropping leaflets from the balcony and shouting, "We protest!" King Haakon VII indignantly rose to his feet and led the audience in applause for Marshall. The general turned to Hambro and commented drily that in his own country he was more accustomed to such treatment from anticommunists.

The next day he returned to deliver his Nobel lecture. He had not been able to work on it on shipboard as he had wanted to do, and the speech was not one of his best. He declared that the audience might have anticipated an argument that the maintenance of world peace depended largely upon military strength. This was true "in the present hazardous world situation," where Allied cohesion was also imperative, but "the maintenance of large armies for an indefinite period is not a practical or a promising basis for policy.

"The guarantee for a long continued peace," he said, "will depend on other factors in addition to a moderated military strength, and no less important. Perhaps the most important single factor will be a spiritual regeneration to develop goodwill, faith, and understanding among nations."

Marshall, although offered $1 million, refused to write his memoirs because he could write only the truth, and this might do injury to persons still living. He did approve an authoritative biography to be written by Forrest C. Pogue, the military historian, and he gave Pogue a valuable series of interviews. He left his papers to the George C. Marshall Research Foundation, which constructed a library to house them in Lexington, Virginia, next to VMI.

In 1959, after a long illness, Marshall died in Walter Reed Hospital at the age of seventy-eight. As he had requested, there was only a short funeral service, which was attended by his former subordinate, now President Eisenhower, and his former commander in chief, now former president Truman. He was buried in Arlington Cemetery.

BIBLIOGRAPHY

Primary Source

Marshall, George Catlett. *The Papers of George Catlett Marshall.* 2 vols. Edited by Larry I. Bland. Baltimore: Johns Hopkins University Press, 1981–86. In progress.

Secondary Sources

Acheson, Dean. *Sketches from Life.* New York: Harper, 1961, pp. 147–66. On Marshall.

Ferrell, Robert H. *George C. Marshall.* Vol. 15 of *American Secretaries of State and Their Diplomacy.* New York: Cooper Square, 1966.

Gimbel, John. *The Origins of the Marshall Plan.* Stanford, Calif.: Stanford University Press, 1976. A well-documented revisionist interpretation.

"Marshall, George Catlett." In *BDI.*

"Marshall, George Catlett." In *DAB,* supp. 6.

Marshall, Katherine Tupper. *Together: Annals of an Army Wife.* Atlanta: Tupper & Love, 1946. The second Mrs. Marshall's reminiscences.

Mee, Charles L., Jr. *The Marshall Plan: The Launching of the Pax Americana.* New York: Simon & Schuster, 1984.

Mosely, Leonard: *Marshall: Hero for Our Times.* New York: Hearst Books, 1982.

Pogue, Forrest C. *George C. Marshall.* 4 vols. New York: Viking, 1963–87. The definitive biography.

1954
Office of the United Nations High Commissioner for Refugees

Established by the UN General Assembly to provide legal and political protection for world's refugees; began activities in 1951.

Ever since the 1922 award to Fridtjhof Nansen, the committee has continued to recognize work for refugees in its awards. Sixteen years later, in 1938, the Nansen Office received the prize, and after another sixteen years, the Office of the United Nations High Commissioner for Refugees (UNHCR) received the 1954 prize in 1955. In 1981 UNHCR would win a second prize.

At the 1955 ceremony Chairman Jahn explained the basis of such awards: "This work teaches us that the unfortunate foreigner is one of us, and it makes us understand that the solidarity extending equally to human beings beyond the frontiers constitutes the very foundation on which any lasting peace must be built." There were many public and private organizations assisting refugees, Jahn said, but the office of the UNHCR was the focus of the effort, and its staff, led by Dr. G. J. van Heuven Goedhart of the Netherlands, the editor and writer and former Dutch delegate to the United Nations, was serving as "the watchful conscience of the world."

As Jahn pointed out, there had been refugees since time immemorial, but it was not until the twentieth century that international institutions were established to deal with the problem, first under the League of Nations and later in connection with the United Nations. In the midst of World War II the Allies set up the UN Relief and Rehabilitation Administration (UNRRA) to deal with postwar problems. At the end of the war there were at least 30 to 50 million people who had lost their homes because they either had been deported or had fled, and UNRRA was faced with the monumental task of repatriation. By the autumn of 1945, some 6 million had been repatriated. In 1947 UNRRA was succeeded by the International Refugee Organization (IRO), which had responsibility for 1.7 million people; IRO spent some $470 million before it was disbanded in 1949, having helped over a million refugees to emigrate.

Large numbers still remained in camps, but there was a reluctance to continue to use UN funds for their care and resettlement. The General Assembly therefore set up UNHCR, which began activity in 1951, providing financial support only for its administrative expenses and giving it a mandate to act as protector of the refugees, not to engage in fieldwork. Such protection was to be provided by working with governments, intergovernmental bodies, and private agencies, promoting international conventions and special agreements with governments on behalf of refugees, monitoring their implementation, and facilitating cooperation among all those working to assist the refugees. The UNHCR was to be concerned with all refugees except Palestinian Arabs and Koreans, for whom special organizations existed.

A refugee was defined as a person who, because of racial, political, or religious persecution, has left his homeland and no longer wishes to avail himself of the protection of the authorities of that country. The UNHCR provides protection under international conventions on the status of refugees and territorial asylum, which declare that refugees should enjoy the same privileges as the citizens of their host country such as the right to work, social security, and freedom of travel.

As was the case in the League of Nations, expectations about the time needed for the work were too optimistic. The UNHCR was first established for three years, which was then extended to five years and subsequently regularly renewed every five years. Nor did it prove practical for the office not to have funds at its own disposal; the General Assembly had to give the UNHCR permission to raise money from governments and private organizations. The Ford Foundation, for example, made an early grant of nearly $3 million and subsequently considerably increased its contribution. The staff remained small, however, supervising but not administering the relief projects. In 1955 the number at headquarters and in the fourteen branches did not much exceed a hundred, so that when Dr. van Heuven Goedhart gave a staff party after the Nobel prize announcement, he could tell them that each was responsible for about 1 percent of the award.

In his Nobel lecture at Oslo he skillfully explained the deeper meaning of the refugee problem with reference to Alfred Nobel and Fridtjof Nansen. Nobel's villa in San Remo, where he died, was named "Mio Nido" (My Nest). But this was just what Nobel never had. Van Heuven Goedhart quoted the comment of Nobel's associate, Henrik Schück, that he was "a lonely man and with his sensitive nature he suffered keenly from the misfortune of being without a home." Nobel lived most of his life as a "homeless foreigner," far away from his native Sweden, infrequently speaking his mother tongue, often in travel from place to place, and living in hotels and attended by paid servants.

Nansen, on the other hand, was deeply rooted in Norway. Whereas Nobel could appreciate a refugee's longing for a home because he himself had none, Nansen, cherishing his own, was moved to provide homes for hundreds of thousands of uprooted people. The essence of the refugee problem, said van Heuven Goedhart, was to find a "Mio Nido" for people who for reasons of persecution have left their country and become homeless:

> "*Mio Nido*" is not just a roof over one's head, not just a place to live in. It is the all-embracing term for a series of elements which together constitute a man's independence, and therefore his freedom and dignity.
>
> The refugee problem has nothing to do with charity. It is not the problem of people to be pitied, but far more the problem of people to be admired. It is the problem of people who somewhere, somehow, sometime, had the courage to give up the feeling of belonging, which they possessed, rather than abandon the human freedom which they valued more highly.

The high commissioner emphasized the magnitude of the problem his office faced. Under its mandate there were about 2.2 million refugees, more than 50 percent in Europe, of whom seventy thousand were still living in camps. The days of repatriation were over. Resettlement was still the dream of most refugees, but the process was a gradual one, being a sort of

Darwinism in reverse, "the exodus of the fittest." The major answer to the refugee problem was integration within the country of the refugee's residence, which did not necessarily mean assimilation, but the possibility of receiving a house and a job. Only when the refugee was able to put down roots in a new community might that house become a "Mio Nido." The first step, however, was the recognition of the legal status of the refugee, and it was a major task of UNHCR to persuade individual governments to follow reasonable policies of eligibility for refugee status.

The problem *could* be solved, Dr. van Heuven Goedhart concluded, but only if the world heeded the words of Nansen that "love of man is practical policy." These words in the original Norwegian, NESTEKJAERLIGHETER REALPOLITIK, are inscribed on the Nansen Medal, which Dr. van Heuven Goedhart instituted in 1954 as an annual award for outstanding service in the cause of refugees. When Dr. van Heuven Goedhart died in 1956, the year after accepting the Peace Prize in Oslo, the Nansen Medal was awarded to him posthumously.

BIBLIOGRAPHY

Secondary Sources

UNHCR. *Refugee.* Geneva. A monthly journal on refugees.

UNHCR. "A Bibliography on Refugees." Supplement to *Refugee,* no. 4 (October–November 1980). Selected and annotated by Barry N. Stein. The most comprehensive bibliography.

Heuven Goedhart, G. J. van. "The Problem of Refugees." In Academy of International Law, The Hague, *Receuil des Cours,* vol. 82. Leyden: Sijthoff, 1954, pp. 265–369. Five lectures by the high commissioner.

Holborn, Louise W. *Refugees, a Problem of Our Time: The Work of the United Nations High Commissioner for Refugees, 1951–1972.* 2 vols. Metuchen, N.J.: Scarecrow Press, 1975.

Marrus, Michael R. *The Unwanted: European Refugees in the Twentieth Century.* New York: Oxford University Press, 1985. Excellent survey.

Stoessinger, John G. *The Refugee and the World Community.* Minneapolis: University of Minnesota Press, 1956.

United Nations Yearbook. Each year the yearbook offers a summary of the work of the UNHCR.

Vernant, Jacques. *The Refugee in the Post-War World.* New Haven: Yale University Press, 1953.

See also the bibliography for the Nansen International Office for Refugees (1938).

1957
Lester Bowles Pearson (1897–1972)

Canada

Civil servant, diplomat, Liberal party politician, secretary of state for external affairs, prime minister; "father" of UN Emergency Force in Suez crisis of 1956.

Lester Pearson, former foreign minister of Canada, was given the 1957 prize principally for the role he had played the previous year in resolving the Middle East conflict through the United Nations. At the award ceremony Chairman Jahn went so far as to call him "the man who contributed more than anyone else to save the world at that time." Jahn emphasized his personal qualities: "the powerful initiative, strength, and perseverance he has displayed in attempting to prevent or limit war operations and to restore peace in situations where quick, tactful, and wise action has been necessary." During the years when Pearson was in charge of his country's foreign relations, 1948–57, he had become one of the few outstanding UN statesmen of the day, and Canada enjoyed an unprecedented influence in international affairs.

Lester Bowles Pearson came from Protestant

Irish stock, both his father and grandfather having been Methodist ministers. He was born in Toronto, went to the local schools, and entered the University of Toronto in 1913 at the age of sixteen. When Canada entered the European war in the next year, he volunteered to serve with a medical unit sponsored by the university. He saw service in England, Egypt, and Greece, and then transferred to the Royal Flying Corps. During training, his squadron commander decided that Lester was not a proper name for a fighter pilot and that he should be called "Mike." Pearson was Mike from then on, and that was the title he chose for his memoirs.

Unfortunately, Mike's first solo flight ended in a crash, and he had to be invalided home, where he served as a training instructor for the rest of the war, at the same time resuming his university studies. He graduated in 1919 and went to work for Armour and Company of Chicago, the meat-packers, but after two years he decided against a career in business and returned to academe. He attended Oxford University on a two-year scholarship to study history, making a good record in his studies and an excellent record in sports.

In 1924, now twenty-seven, he returned to the University of Toronto as an instructor in history. He enjoyed his teaching and his coaching of athletics on the side; he married one of his students, started a family, and seemed to have found his life work. But just at that time Canada was taking control of its own foreign affairs, and Pearson was urged to enter the competition for positions in the new Department of External Affairs. He passed the examination at the head of the list, was offered more salary and opportunity than the university could match, and accepted a position.

In 1928, then, Pearson became a civil servant and remained one for twenty years, moving up through the ranks and gaining wide experience in a variety of assignments in Geneva, London, and Washington, and at international conferences. After serving as ambassador to the United States, he returned to Ottawa as the top professional in the department. Pearson said of these years that they had given him "a fine view of the stage and its major actors." He was now prepared to become one of the major actors himself on the international stage. In 1948 Pearson accepted an invitation from the Liberal party to take over the department in which he had worked so long. This meant resigning from the civil service, winning a safe seat as a parliamentary deputy of the Liberal party, and joining the cabinet.

Pearson was a champion of the United Nations, but he felt that it could not provide security against Soviet expansionism. For this the North Atlantic Treaty Organization (NATO) was needed. Pearson drafted the speech in 1949 in which his prime minister proposed the establishment of NATO, and he led the Canadian delegation to NATO until 1957, urging that it be made more of a cultural and economic community.

Pearson had already made his mark during the war in the preparatory work for postwar international organizations, helping establish both the United Nations Relief and Rehabilitation Administration and the Food and Agricultural Organization. In the formation of the United Nations he was a spokesman for the medium-size and smaller powers, opposing the Great-Power veto in the Security Council and upholding the autonomy of the smaller nations. From 1946 to 1956 Pearson headed Canada's delegation to the United Nations. In 1947 as chairman of the General Assembly's Special Committee on Palestine, Pearson strongly urged the ending of the British Mandate and division into a Jewish and an Arab state. During the Korean conflict, when he was chairman of the General Assembly, he opposed the bombing of China and advocated the limiting of hostilities and negotiations to end them.

The Suez conflict, of course, was the occasion for his major achievement. In 1956 Egypt nationalized the Suez Canal, provoking first an invasion of Egyptian territory by Israel and then an attack on Egypt by Great Britain and France. The majority in the Security Council called on the aggressors to withdraw, but action was blocked by British and French vetoes. The matter then came before the General Assembly, which passed a resolution against the aggressors but provided for no action to deal with the problem.

At this critical juncture Pearson introduced another resolution proposing that the secretary-general set up an international UN force to bring about and supervise the end of hostilities. In the corridors of the United Nations, in informal talks and conferences, Pearson worked tirelessly in behalf of his proposal, which allowed Britain and France, opposed by the United States and confronting worldwide condemnation, to withdraw without loss of face. Pearson's efforts not only helped bring peace, but served to heal the serious rift that was widening between the United States and Britain as well as within the British Commonwealth. The outcome meant a great moral boost to the United Nations, which was also given a new instrument for peacekeeping in the United Nations Emergency Force.

Pearson, in his Nobel address, warned against exaggerating the significance of what had been accomplished. A step had been taken "in the direction of putting international force behind an international decision," and a small conflict had been ended and prevented from becoming larger. But it was a ceasefire that had been secured: "there is no peace in the area." Moreover, the new force "would be futile in a quarrel between, or in opposition to, big powers."

Indeed, Pearson had become very aware of the inability of the United Nations to confront one of the superpowers, when during the Suez crisis the Soviet Union suppressed a popular uprising in Hungary. At the General Assembly Pearson had vainly called for support for the Hungarian people: "Why should we not now establish a suitable United Nations mission for Hungary when it has been agreed to form a United Nations authority in the Middle East?"

In his Nobel lecture, "The Four Faces of Peace," Pearson explained the implications for peace of prosperity, power, policy, and people. He had not enjoyed lecturing when he was a university teacher, but he was an able and effective speaker, and this was a good effort—literate, carefully considered, challenging, and moving. He declared that "we prepare for war like precocious giants and for peace like retarded pygmies," and urged renewed efforts to reduce tension between Moscow and Washington, not in summit meetings, "where the footing is precarious and the winds blow hard," but in "frank, serious and complete exchanges of views" through diplomatic channels.

It was ironic that in December 1957 when he received the Nobel prize, Pearson was no longer foreign minister, the Liberal party having been defeated in the spring election. Pearson was now leader of the opposition. Six years later his party would regain power and Pearson would be prime minister for five years. In 1968 he resigned from the leadership, and in 1972 he died at the age of seventy-five. He had completed only the first part of his memoirs, which give an engaging picture of a warm and witty personality.

BIBLIOGRAPHY

Primary Sources

Pearson, Lester B. *Democracy in World Politics.* Princeton: Princeton University Press, 1955.

———. *Diplomacy in the Nuclear Age.* Cambridge: Harvard University Press, 1959.

———. "Keeping the Peace." In *The Quest for Peace: The Dag Hammarskjöld Memorial Lectures.* Edited by Andrew Cordier and Wilder Foote. New York: Columbia University Press, 1965.

———. *Mike: The Memoirs of the Right Honorable Lester B. Pearson.* 3 vols. New York: Quadrangle, 1972–75. Only the first volume was completed before his death. Volumes 2 and 3 were edited by John A. Munro and Alex I. Inglis.

———. *Words and Occasions.* Cambridge: Harvard University Press, 1970. Selected essays, speeches, and lectures, mostly on Canadian politics.

Secondary Sources

Bothwell, Robert. *Pearson, His Life and World.* Toronto: McGraw-Hill, 1978.

"Pearson, Lester B." In *BDI.*

Thordarson, Bruce. *Lester Pearson, Diplomat and Politician.* Toronto: Oxford, 1974.

1958
Father Dominique Pire (1910–69)

Belgium

Dominican priest, doctor of theology and professor of Christian ethics, founder of relief organization for refugees.

When the committee gave the 1958 prize to Father Pire "for his efforts to help refugees to leave their camps and return to a life of freedom and dignity," there were those who questioned whether his achievements deserved such a high honor. To be sure, the committee had shown its concern for the uprooted in three awards, the first to Fridtjof Nansen, then to the Nansen Office, and most recently to the

Office of the UN High Commissioner for Refugees, but these were in recognition of major efforts to grapple with the problem. The numbers of refugees Father Pire had helped leave their camps were few. As Chairman Jahn said in his presentation address, however, "It would be dangerous to judge on the basis of numbers alone. Of far greater importance are the spirit which has animated Georges Pire in his mission and the seed he has sown in the hearts of men, for they give us hope of a harvest to come."

Father Pire was little known, even in his own country. The telegram from Oslo was sent to the wrong town in Belgium, where it was marked "Unknown" and returned to the Central Office in Brussels. And when the *New York Times* asked the Belgian embassy and the Belgian mission to the United Nations for information about the new laureate, no one had heard of him. The story of how this relatively unknown Dominican came to win the prize is unusual, even in the annals of the Norwegian Nobel Committee.

Georges Charles Clement Ghislain Pire, who became Brother Henri Dominique when he joined the Dominican Order, was the son of a schoolmaster in the suburbs of Dinant. His father was a methodical man, mindful of his social position, and it was his pretty young wife, with her zest for life, who had the greater influence on their first son. Father Pire said appreciatively of his mother, "She has sailed along with all canvas spread, like a frigate in fine weather."

In 1914, when little Georges was only four and a half, the Germans marched into his country, quickly defeating the Belgian army and brutally putting down any resistance encountered or suspected from civilians. His grandfather was shot in front of his own house, which was then set afire, as was much of the city. The rest of the family escaped to France, where they lived as refugees until they could return to their liberated but devastated Dinant in 1918. When Georges grew up, he could understand very well the feelings of those whom war had driven from their homes.

Madame Pire brought up her three children to be good Catholics. Georges was devout as a boy—his mother recalled later that she "was almost envious of his inner devotional life"—and it was not surprising when at the age of sixteen he announced to his parents that he wanted to be a religious. An exploratory visit to a nearby Dominican monastery in the town of Huy convinced him that it was this preaching order that he must join: its "irradiating intellectual magnanimity" was for him "the lasso of God."

He entered the monastery at the age of eighteen, and four years later he took his final vows. He was then chosen to study at the Dominican University in Rome, where his contact with Christians from all over the world first gave him an international perspective. He studied theology and also prepared for the priesthood: "I longed to save souls, to communicate joy and warmth." In July 1934 he was ordained as a priest at Rome and then prepared his doctoral dissertation, which criticized the opinion of certain second-century theologians that the height of moral perfection is the entire mastery of reason over the emotions, a position that Father Pire was to disprove even more through his life than his logic. After defending his thesis, he was awarded his doctorate in theology in 1936: "After having vowed before the High Altar to be faithful to Thomist theology, I was declared 'wedded to truth' and capped with the three-cornered biretta."

He was then twenty-six, pleased to be finished with moral philosophy after nine years of study. He returned to the monastery of Huy, eager to enter upon a life of active dedication, only to find that he was expected to lecture to the brothers—on moral philosophy. Obediently, he spent another year in study at the Belgian University of Louvain to acquaint himself with sociology, and then began teaching.

But a more active life was not far ahead. First he began offering theology classes to some interested Girl Guides in return for instruction in Scouting, and then in 1938 he enlisted his Girl Guide theologians in service projects, open air camps for children of the poor and a family mutual aid service.

In 1939 the war broke out, and again Belgium was invaded and occupied. Father Pire's open air missions became feeding stations for children, and secretly he served as chaplain to resistance forces, as head of a small intelligence unit, and with an escape network for downed Allied flyers. He never talked much afterward about these war experiences, but the medals for valor with which he was decorated spoke for him.

After the war he again asked his superiors for more active duties, and he was appointed as priest of the church of the parish where the monastery stood, an unusual office for a Dominican, but one to which he brought his organizing ability and his concern for people in need, serving from 1946 to 1953. He also continued with his other activities, including the theological discussion group with the Girl Guides. One evening someone suggested inviting a young American who had worked in refugee camps in Austria to speak with them. That discussion, which took place on 27 February 1949, when Father Pire was thirty-nine years old, changed the direction of the rest of his life.

Edward Squadrille had left the refugee work convinced that the refugee organizations were selecting for emigration only the able-bodied and the skilled, leaving the rest—the old, the infirm, the sick, the families without a breadwinner—to live out their lives in the camps. Father Pire, deeply moved, asked what could be done for this "Hard Core," as they came to be known. Squadrille could offer no suggestions, so Father Pire decided to go to Austria to see for himself.

He found the situation even more appalling than he had anticipated: thousands of men, women, and children in dire circumstances, provided with minimal food and shelter, but living utterly without hope,"sitting on their suit-cases, waiting for the train that never came." His first idea was at least to provide these homeless people with human contacts from outside the camps. He founded a "sponsorship service," collecting the names of individuals who would serve as "godparents," or sponsors for those in the camps and send them letters and parcels. By the end of 1949 he had enrolled one thousand sponsors. In the next two decades the list grew to eighteen thousand people from twenty countries, who were in correspondence with the refugees.

Next Father Pire established four homes for the aged in Belgium, to which he brought old refugees so that they could "dream of their homeland in peace." But his most ambitious plan was to build small villages of 150 persons, where the refugees could make new lives, regaining their self-respect and independence. He established seven in all, in Belgium, West Germany, and Austria. The sites selected were just outside towns where there were factories or other firms hiring workers; thus the formation of refugee enclaves within the inner city was avoided. In 1957 his organization became known as Aid to Displaced Persons and European Villages, and Father Pire had to spend a great deal of time in fund-raising.

After the suppression of the uprising in Hungary by Soviet tanks in 1956, a new wave of refugees fled to the West. Father Pire had no resources to help them, so he dispatched begging letters to the large foundations he had heard about, Ford, Rockefeller, and Nobel. The replies were all negative, but the Nobel Foundation pointed out that although it made no grants, the Norwegian Nobel Committee had given prizes for refugee work.

Father Pire promptly send off a booklet to Oslo describing his refugee projects, and a friend who was president of the Council of Europe sent a covering letter. The 1957 prize went to Pearson, but Pire was encouraged by his friends to try again. In December 1957, he compiled another report, mistakenly routing it by way of the Belgian government, where it was filed by some bureaucrat and not located until the middle of January when it was finally sent to Oslo. Some qualified nominator had obviously also made a proposal to the committee, however, since the statutes forbid anyone submitting his own name.

In March 1958, Father Pire laid the foundation stone of his new refugee village in Belgium, which he named after Fridtjof Nansen, and, of course, Ambassador Otto Kildal of Norway was invited to the ceremonies. It appears that Kildal now took a personal interest in Father Pire's candidacy, and so did the Belgian ambassador in Oslo. One evening in Brussels the Dominican monk was invited to the Norwegian embassy, where among the guests who listened to him talk about his work was a representative of the Nobel Committee.

Pire's friends now secured an invitation for him from the Norwegian branch of the European Movement (for Unity) to speak in Oslo on the evening of 21 October, shortly before the final meeting of the Nobel Committee was to take place. In the afternoon he was received by King Olav, who also did him the special honor of attending his lecture in the evening. It was arranged for the lecture to be given in the large auditorium of the university, where the Peace Prize ceremonies are held. The audience filled the hall, and Father Pire did not disappoint them. Standing tall and straight in his white Dominican robes, he spoke simply, but movingly, about what he was doing for refugees and why he was doing it. He told of his five villages and his hope for the sixth, which was to be named after Anne Frank, the Jewish girl who had died at the concentration camp at Belsen. He wanted both Germans and Europeans whose countries had fought the Germans to contribute funds to build this "village of the outstretched Hand, the Village of Peace." He said his work went beyond the nation and the church: "I therefore hold no hidden mysterious mandate from a church or a country. I am bound by no border, belong to no political party and have my name on no list. I do not even take time to be anti-communistic. I am simply pro-human."

The applause was loud and long, and as he left Oslo, Father Pire could not help but wonder if members of the committee had been present and how they had judged him. It was not long before he found out. On 10 November, when he was holding a retreat in the guest house of his monastery, he was interrupted with word that the press was trying to reach him because he had been awarded the Nobel Peace Prize. He had heard nothing himself because of the missent telegram; all Belgium was talking about its laureate before he himself received official word. Henceforth, a communication marked simply "Pire, Belgium" or addressed to "The Reverend Father of the Hard Core Refugees" would be promptly delivered.

When Father Pire returned to the University of Oslo to accept the prize, he declared that the joy he felt was not because he was being rewarded: "I am not an old admiral receiving the last and most magnificent decoration of his life. It is a profound joy, a joy of the soul, like that of a mountaineer who, half way up, has just had a sudden glimpse of the path which will allow him to climb farther and better." Father Pire noted that he was one of only five laureates who were not yet fifty when they received the prize. "Fifty years, the half of life—I offer you the second half."

But he was given only ten years more of life; he died after an operation just before his fifty-ninth birthday. He climbed higher, nevertheless. The prize money, which came to about $45,000, helped him complete Nansen Village and build Anne Frank Village in West Germany. His organization, Europe of the Heart, now became The Heart Open to the World. Through "fraternal dialogue" four separate agencies pursued world brotherhood: the University of Peace, founded at Huy in 1960; World Friendships, to promote international exchange of letters; World Sponsorships, expanded to refugee families in Africa and Asia; and Islands of Peace, a program to encourage intervillage cooperation and local initiative in Pakistan and India. Pire also became something of a consultant to governments, visiting a number of countries to investigate their refugee problems.

In his work for refugees of so many countries and backgrounds, working along with Christians and non-Christians and persons of goodwill who belonged to no church, Father Pire said he was ever more certain that God was one, that all humanity was one, and that Satan rejoiced in divisions. His vocation, as he conceived of it, was not only to bring material and moral assistance to the homeless and the uprooted but to be a builder of bridges. In such a labor, as Chairman Jahn recognized, the results were not to be calculated in numbers.

BIBLIOGRAPHY

Primary Source

Pire, Father Dominique-Georges. *Building Peace.* In collaboration with Doctor Charles Dricot. Translated by G. M. Ogg. London: Corgi, 1967. Includes the speeches at the Oslo award ceremony.

Secondary Sources

Houart, Victor. *The Open Heart: The Inspiring Story of Father Pire and the Europe of the Heart.* Translated by Mervyn Savill. London: Souvenir, 1959.

"Pire, Father Dominique-Georges." In *MPL.*

"Pire, Father Dominique-Georges." In *CB,* 1959.

Vehenne, Hugues. *The Story of Father Dominique Pire.* Translated by John L. Skeffington. New York: Dutton, 1960.

1959
Philip Noel-Baker (1889–1982)

Great Britain

Quaker politician, cabinet minister, scholar, athlete; helped found League of Nations and United Nations; apostle of disarmament.

In presenting the Peace Prize to Philip Noel-Baker for a lifetime of work for peace and disarmament, Chairman Jahn declared, "I do not think it an exaggeration to say that he has had some share in practically all the work that has been carried out to promote international understanding in its widest sense, and this is true of him both as a private individual and as a representative of his country."

As if to document such a claim, Noel-Baker began his Nobel address by telling of how he had worked closely with three previous laureates, Nansen, Cecil, and Henderson. Certainly there was no one else who had been present at the creation of the League of Nations and the United Nations and had also participated in the Disarmament Conference in 1932, playing an important role on each occasion. Moreover, Noel-Baker was one of the world's leading authorities on disarmament, the major cause with which he was associated during his life.

The source of the drive that carried him through almost seven decades of peacemaking lay in his

Quaker background. His family had been Quakers almost since the beginning of the Society of Friends in the seventeenth century. His father, Joseph Baker, was a well-to-do businessman, whose social concern took him into politics. In Parliament Joseph Baker was a staunch advocate of peace, and the outbreak of the war in 1914 found him in Germany at an international peace congress he had helped organize through the churches.

Philip Alan Baker grew up in an atmosphere of Quakerism, Liberal politics, and peacemaking. So many foreign guests were entertained at his home that it was called the "International Hotel." He went to Quaker schools and spent a year at the Quaker college of Haverford near Philadelphia. He returned to take his degree at Cambridge University, where he excelled in history and economics, as well as in debating and athletics. He captained the Cambridge track team and in 1912 ran in the Olympics, despite a taped dislocated foot.

After Cambridge he was appointed vice-principal at Ruskin College, Oxford, but after a few months the war began. With his Quaker convictions he could not join the army, so with the support of his father and other Friends, he helped organize the Friends Ambulance Unit and became its first commandant in France, where the unit was loosely attached to the Red Cross and provided medical services at the front. One of the ambulance drivers was a pretty English girl named Irene Noel whom Philip married in 1915, later adding her name to his to become Noel-Baker. In 1916 the army decided to tighten its control over the Friends Ambulance Unit and requested that its leader be commissioned as an officer. This Philip could not conscientiously do, so he left to organize the British Ambulance Unit to work on the Italian front, where he spent the remainder of the war.

At war's end Philip had a collection of medals for valor from both France and Italy and a burning desire to do something to prevent war from happening again. At Cambridge he had twice been named Whewell Scholar in international law and had also briefly studied in both Paris and Munich. Thus he was qualified for an appointment with Lord Robert Cecil, who was looking for a bright young man to help him draw up plans for postwar peace machinery. Philip went with Cecil to Paris to work on the Covenant of the League of Nations and the charter of the International Labor Organization and was then appointed to the secretariat of the League. He was thirty-one.

There is a story that Lloyd George got the idea that the new League should take on the job of repatriating prisoners of war and asked the young man in the secretariat who could do it. Philip replied, "Fridtjof Nansen," and Lloyd George said, "Get him." However it all began, Philip was indeed the messenger sent to Norway to persuade the famous explorer to take the job, and Nansen accepted. In the following years Philip continued to assist and advise Nansen in his work for refugees and as Norway's delegate in the Assembly. Philip himself was principal adviser to Sir Eric Drummond, the first secretary-general of the League, from 1920 to 1922, and then secretary to the British delegation. In 1927 Nansen wrote to Noel-Baker, "All I have done in the League has been done with you, and could not have been done without you. . . . Oh, dear friend, how much you have done for me and for the League during many years."

Noel-Baker kept up his League connections even after leaving Geneva in 1924 for a major academic appointment as the first Sir Edward Cassel Professor of International Relations at the University of London, only the second such chair in the British Isles. In his five years in that position Noel-Baker firmly established the Department of International Relations and published his first scholarly works, including *Disarmament* in 1926, which became a peace classic.

The preparatory work was under way for the League's Disarmament Conference, and the book was written "to show the complexity of the problems to those who think them simple; and to suggest solutions to those who think them insoluble." He based his account on his "personal experience of debates among soldiers, sailors and other experts who have had to consider at Paris, Geneva, and elsewhere the practical realization of disarmament policy." As in all his books, he devoted much space to the arguments against disarmament, which he sought to answer with ample documentation and careful reasoning. He did not claim that disarmament would be a panacea in itself, but regarded it as a vital component in the development of intergovernmental cooperation: "When a general treaty of disarmament is signed, the central bastion of the enemy defences will be captured." He foresaw a slow, painful "struggle against the age-long misery of war," and he felt victory had to be won first "in the minds and hearts of men." Of this he remained hopeful, and for the rest of his life he remained a major force in the movement for disarmament, never abandoning this hope until perhaps at the very end of his life.

It was a great setback to his hopes when the League Disarmament Conference, which was finally convened in 1932, was a failure almost from the start. Noel-Baker always blamed this on the Conservatives, who had replaced the more pro-League Labour government just before the conference began. Noel-Baker was now a Labour politician himself, having left the university in 1929 to win a seat in the House of Commons and to become parliamentary secretary to the foreign secretary, Arthur Henderson. At the Disarmament Conference he was principal assistant to Henderson, who was chairman, and he worked hard to support him in what was a losing cause.

In 1933 he came to America again to lecture at Yale and to receive the Howland Prize for "distinguished work in the sphere of government." In 1936 Noel-Baker helped his old friend Cecil organize the Peace Ballot of the League of Nations Union, which showed strong backing for the League. In the same year Noel-Baker was elected to Parliament from Derby, which he continued to represent until he retired in 1970, after almost forty years in the House of Commons and having become a leader of his party.

During World War II Noel-Baker served as a top government official in the Ministry of Transport. When Labour returned to power, he held a number of posts, including cabinet rank, but the position of foreign secretary always eluded him. Perhaps his unyielding peace position disturbed some of his Labour colleagues. On the other hand, his fellow Quakers were very uncomfortable when he was appointed secretary of state for air, but pleased when he moved to the Commonwealth Relations Office, where he served for three years and made a significant contribution in the transition from empire to commonwealth.

At the formal closing session of the League of Nations, Noel-Baker had declared, "Geneva has been the first Parliament of the World. Our work has not ended; it has only begun." When the UN Preparatory Commission was formed in 1944, he was sent as the British delegate, for he was singularly fitted to share his unparalleled experience with the League. He was at San Francisco in 1945 to help draft the charter of the United Nations and then became a member of the British delegation to the General Assembly. He helped develop policies for the UN Secretariat and also lent a hand at meetings of the Food and Agricultural Organization and the Economic and Social Council.

With the introduction of nuclear weapons, disarmament became more imperative than ever. In 1958 Noel-Baker brought out a new book, *The Arms Race: A Programme for World Disarmament,* updating his *Disarmament* of 1926 for the nuclear age, although with a preface that was very much the same. Once again, Noel-Baker's book became something of a basic primer on the subject, and it won the Albert Schweitzer Book Award. It certainly strengthened his candidacy for the Nobel Peace Prize, which was awarded to him in the year following its publication, although Chairman Jahn declared, "It is not through his writings but in his personal activities that Noel-Baker has made his greatest contribution."

For his Nobel lecture Noel-Baker appropriately chose as his theme the arms race, recalling Nansen's words in his lecture in 1926 that this was the supreme issue of the age. Now, Noel-Baker asked, "In the age when the atom has been split, the moon encircled, diseases conquered, is disarmament so difficult a matter that it must remain a distant dream? To answer 'Yes' is to despair of the future of mankind."

Another honor came to Noel-Baker in 1960, when he was made president of UNESCO's International Council of Sport and Physical Recreation. He was the only winner of a Nobel medal who had also won a medal in that other international competition, the Olympic Games, having won the silver in the 1500 meters event at Antwerp in 1920. He had captained the British team again at the 1924 Olympics, and he always kept up with athletics. He played tennis most of his life and took long walks until arthritis stiffened his legs and he had to use a cane.

In his old age many honors came: in 1976, the French awarded him the Legion of Honor; in 1977 he was made a life peer, Baron Noel-Baker of Derby, his longtime constituency; and in the same year he became a Papal Knight of Sylvester, an unusual honor for a Quaker. When he retired from the House of Commons in 1970 at the age of eighty-one, he declared, "While I have the health and strength, I shall give all my time to the work of breaking the dogmatic sleep of those who allow the nuclear, chemical, biological, and conventional arms race to go on."

This he did, traveling, speaking, and writing for peace and disarmament, and working with the British UN Association, to which he gave the Nobel prize money. In 1978 he was a member of the British delegation to the first Special Session on Disarmament of the UN General Assembly. His experience there persuaded him that only the pressure of public opinion could force the Great Powers to implement the final document, which he called "the greatest state paper in human history," that was approved in the second session. He thereupon helped organize in Britain a great campaign for disarmament.

In 1982 Noel-Baker made his final effort for the cause of disarmament. He was then almost ninety-three, frail, almost blind, in need of help to walk, but nothing could prevent him from traveling to New York to be present for the second Special Session. It was, however, a great disappointment, amounting mostly to a repetition of the recommendations of the first meeting.

A few months later, in October 1982, Noel-Baker died at his home in London, shortly before his ninety-third birthday. There are those who believe that the disappointment he had suffered in New York broke his heart.

BIBLIOGRAPHY

Primary Sources

Noel-Baker, Philip. *The Arms Race: A Programme for*

World Disarmament. London: Atlantic Books, 1958. Considered his most important work.

———. *Disarmament.* London: Hogarth, 1926. Reprint. New York: Garland, 1971. With introduction by Richard D. Burns. His landmark study.

———. *The First World Disarmament Conference 1932–1933 and Why It Failed.* Oxford: Pergamon, 1979. Reflections on this failure and its implications for the continuing failure of efforts for disarmament.

———. *The Private Manufacture of Armaments.* 2 vols. New York: Oxford University Press, 1937. Comprehensive study of a major obstacle to disarmament.

Secondary Sources

"Noel-Baker, Philip." In *CB,* 1946.

"Noel-Baker, Philip." In *MPL.*

Noel-Baker, Philip, and Elizabeth Balmer Baker. *J. Allen Baker, Member of Parliament, a Memoir.* London: Swarthmore, 1927. A biography of Philip's father, who also worked for peace.

4

The Peace Prize over the Years: 1960–87

As the Norwegian Nobel Committee entered its seventh decade, world peace seemed as distant as ever. And in the next quarter century the committee was to watch international and civil wars erupt all over the globe. The United States, home of the largest number of peace laureates, would fight a long war in Vietnam and would be judged by the International Court of Justice in The Hague to have violated international law in its covert operations against Nicaragua. Hostilities would break out in the Middle East, once again between Israel and her neighbors, and between Iraq and Iran. The Soviet Union would send its armed forces into Czechoslovakia and Afghanistan, and Great Britain would fight a naval war with Argentina.

During this period there would be confrontations and periods of détente between the superpowers. In 1960 a projected summit between Premier Nikita Khrushchev and President Dwight Eisenhower was called off when an American spy plane was shot down deep in the Soviet Union. In 1961 the crisis over the erection of the Berlin Wall by East Germany evoked an unprecedented Declaration of Peace to world leaders signed by all the members of the Norwegian Nobel Committee and by seven peace laureates. The next year the two superpowers narrowly avoided war over the Soviet attempt to install missiles in Cuba. On the other hand, while distrust between the two powers would persist, there would be summit meetings, agreement to limit nuclear tests, some progress on strategic arms limitation, and an understanding about the boundaries in Eastern Europe that had emerged from World War II.

The Peace Prizes of this period reflected two new departures of the committee, both evident in the selection in 1961 of the recipient of the postponed prize for 1960: Albert John Lutuli, the South African Zulu chieftain who led a nonviolent movement for equal rights for blacks. For sixty years the committees had restricted their choices to Europeans and Americans, only once including South America, with the award in 1936 to Saavedra Lamas of Argentina. Now other regions of the world would be within their ken, although it would take another twelve years before the first Asian was named. In the following years, however, prizes were given to persons from the Soviet Union, the Middle East, India, Argentina, Mexico, South Africa again, and Costa Rica, and committee members have declared their intention to continue this geographical distribution.

The Lutuli award also marked the committee's broadening of its concept of peace to include human rights. As Chairman Egil Aarvik told me, "Nobel's will does not state this, but it was made in another time. Today we realize that peace cannot be established without a full respect for freedom." In this period ten champions of human rights have won prizes, the largest number in any category, including four of the last eight awards (see appendix A, table 1).

This conception is in keeping with that of peace scholars today, who do not think of peace as concerned only with relations between states or as something negative, merely the absence of war. There is no real peace, they point out, where the enforcement of the status quo involves the suppression of individual freedoms, whether internationally or within a state. In this sense peacemaking means not only efforts to resolve international conflicts but attempts to build harmonious personal relationships within which human dignity can be maintained and human potential can flower.

The human rights awards have been diverse. Since Lutuli, they have gone to Martin Luther King, Jr. (1964), for his leadership of the nonviolent movement for civil rights in the United States, to René Cassin of France (1968), for his role in the adoption by the United Nations of the Declaration of Human Rights; to Andrei Sakharov (1975), for his struggle for human rights in the Soviet Union; to Amnesty International (1977), which mobilizes world public opinion in behalf of prisoners of conscience all over the world; to Pérez Esquivel (1980), Argentinian leader of the nonviolent Peace and Justice Service in Latin America; to Lech Wałesa (1983), for his nonviolent struggle for workers' rights in Poland; to Bishop Tutu (1984), for his nonviolent crusade against apartheid in South Africa; and to Elie Wiesel (1986), the survivor of the Holocaust who fights against its recurrence in any form and had become a defender of human rights in many parts of the world. Another laureate, Sean MacBride (1974), has been prominent in the work of Amnesty International and other campaigns for human rights.

A precedent for these awards, as we saw earlier, was the prize awarded in 1936 to the German antimilitarist journalist, Carl von Ossietzky. On that occasion, the Nazi government formally protested to Oslo and even threatened reprisals. But more recently the independence of the Nobel Committee from the Norwegian government has been clearly recognized, and that government has not been held responsible for the committee's decisions. Of course, the press of a dissident laureate's government may well denounce the award and claim that the committee is playing politics with its prize. Committee members, however, have insisted that this is not the case, that their awards should be judged by their conception of peace, which goes far beyond the politics of the moment. They have affirmed in their announcements and speeches of presentation that peace involves a fraternity among peoples that must rest upon justice and human rights. Moreover, that peace must be peacefully sought. In the awards to dissidents in conflict with their governments, the committee has always been explicit about the use of nonviolent methods. And although the committee has in no way wanted to make of the prize a political instrument, the human rights awards have certainly rendered major assistance to the dissidents.

When the committee broadened its vistas in 1961, Gunnar Jahn was still chairman, having served since 1941. His long tenure followed the pattern set by the first two chairmen. After Jahn died in 1966, however, this changed. In the last two decades, four persons have presided, the longest tenure being that of Mrs. Aase Lionaes, who chaired for ten years. Prof. John Sanness served for four years, and Nils Langhelle for two.

The present chairman, Egil Aarvik, joined the committee in 1973 and has chaired it since 1982. He has been an active politician with the Christian People's party, a former member of the Storting who once was a cabinet member. Aarvik is a deeply devout man, whose addresses at the award ceremonies have raised these occasions to a high level of the spirit. His present term on the committee will end in 1990.

Jahn was known to have been critical of many of the earlier statesman awards. The only statesman honored for a national policy was George Marshall (1953). Hull (1945) and Pearson (1957) were recognized for their association with the United Nations Organization, and Bunche and Hammarskjöld were UN statesmen.

Hammarskjöld was named posthumously in 1961 for his efforts as UN secretary-general to strengthen that organization's peacemaking capacities and especially for his personal attempt to end the conflict in the Congo, where he lost his life in a plane crash. The fact that in the next twenty-five years no other UN statesman has received the prize is indicative of the reduced powers of his successors and of the international organization itself. Hammarskjöld was also the last laureate to be designated for the prize posthumously, the statutes of the Nobel Foundation having been changed to permit such an award only to someone who dies after the announcement has been made.

During the ten-year term of Aase Lionaes as chair of the committee, eight national statesmen were named, one of whom refused the prize. The first was Willy Brandt (1971), honored for his policy of reconciliation with Germany's wartime enemies, the Soviet Union and Poland, which significantly reduced East-West tensions.

The subsequent statesman awards were less felicitous, however. Two double awards were made for negotiators of peace agreements—in 1973, Henry Kissinger and Le Duc Tho for the armistice of that year in the war between the United States and North Vietnam, and in 1978, Menachem Begin and Anwar el-Sadat for the Camp David Accords to bring an end to the war between Israel and Egypt.

Le Duc Tho would have been the first Asian to receive an award, but he rejected it outright, charging that the United States and its ally, South Vietnam, were not observing the agreement. Kissinger too tried to return the prize later, after South Vietnam fell to the North Vietnamese. The war policy of the United States had found little favor in world public opinion, and the prize for Kissinger was seen by many as a prize for a war maker, not a peacemaker. Critics also regarded a prize for so shaky an armistice as premature.

Similar criticism was leveled against the 1978 award. After the committee's announcement, there were still disagreements between the two states. Sadat chose not to attend the Oslo ceremonies, which were held in the most unpeaceful surroundings, having to be shifted to a fortress for reasons of security. Sadat later was assassinated by Egyptian religious fanatics, who were angered by his approach to Israel as well as by his suppression of their activities. Begin was soon to involve Israel in an ill-conceived war in Lebanon, which provoked a demand by some in the Norwegian legislature that he return his prize.

The 1974 award was made to former premier Sato of Japan for his policies of antinuclear proliferation and peace in Asia, but critics questioned his credentials and charged, apparently with some justice, that the committee had been unduly influenced by the campaign his rich supporters had waged for his prize. At least the Sato award did mean that an Asian had entered the Nobel honor rolls of peace.

The next statesman award of the period has held up better than the previous ones. In 1982 former foreign minister García Robles was honored for the Latin American antinuclear treaty, of which he had been the prime mover. Since leaving office, he has headed the Mexican delegation to the UN Disarmament Committee in Geneva, where he has continued to work actively for arms control.

The 1987 award was for a statesman and came as a surprise to many. The committee named President Arias of Costa Rica, the architect of the Central American peace plan that had been signed by the five presidents of that troubled region only some weeks before the committee reached its decision. They agreed to provisions that would end the armed struggles between governments and rebel forces in the area. Chairman Aarvik declared that the committee wanted to throw the prestige of the prize behind the Arias plan, and the announcement did brighten the prospects for success, although there were still many obstacles in the way of a peace settlement. The committee's award was one of the most daring—and certainly one of the most political—in its history.

The seven awards for national statesmen (omitting Le Duc Tho) were second in number to the ten human rights prizes. Humanitarian laureates included Norman Borlaug (1970), an American scientist whose discoveries brought food to hungry millions, and Mother Teresa (1979), the saint of the Calcutta slums. Also honored for humanitarian endeavors were two Red Cross organizations—the International Committee of the Red Cross for the third time and the League of Red Cross Societies (both in 1963)—and three agencies associated with the United Nations—UNICEF (1965), the International Labor Organization (1969), and the Office of the High Commissioner for Refugees (1981), which had already won the 1954 prize.

Laureates of the organized peace movement in this period were Linus Pauling (1962), for mobilizing the scientists of the world to press for a nuclear test ban; Betty Williams and Mairead Corrigan (1976), leaders of the grass-roots movement for reconciliation between Catholics and Protestants in war-torn Northern Ireland; and International Physicians for the Prevention of Nuclear War (1985). Alva Myrdal, who shared the 1982 disarmament prize with García Robles, had been Sweden's minister for disarmament and a prominent advocate of this cause at the United Nations. After leaving office, she continued her efforts unofficially and her prize came shortly after she published a widely acclaimed book on the subject.

In the last twenty-five years, the total number of individual candidates considered by the committee each year rose from about fifty in the 1960s to over ninety in the 1980s, the highest number being ninety-nine in 1985, including sixty individuals and thirty-nine institutions. In 1986 there were eighty-one candidates, fifty-seven individuals and twenty-four institutions, in 1987, there were ninety-three, sixty-two of them individuals; and in 1988 there are ninety-seven, including seventy-four individuals.

The committee has continued to keep confidential the official lists of candidates considered, but according to what nominators told the press, we know that in this period a number of presidents and former presidents were nominated: Harry Truman and Richard Nixon of the United States; Tito of Yugoslavia; Kekkonen of Finland; and Echeverra Alvarez of Mexico. Other nominees in the news were Bishop Helder Camara of Brazil; Pope John Paul II; Caesar Chavez, leader of the California farm workers; Danilo Dolce, the Italian pacifist activist; and the American diplomat, Philip Habib.

In 1987 the newspapers reported that the nominees included President Corazon Aquino of the Philippines, Brian Urquhart, who during a long UN career was responsible for peacekeeping efforts; Terry Waite, the Anglican Church representative who was taken hostage himself while working for the release of others; Bob Geldof, the organizer of the Live Aid program for African relief; the Dalai Lama, the Tibetan spiritual leader; the South African leaders, Nelson and Winnie Mandela; and the World Health Organization.

On several occasions the committee used anniversaries in deciding on its awards: René Cassin was honored twenty years to the day after the adoption by the UN General Assembly of the Declaration of Human Rights; the two Red Cross agencies received their prizes on the one hundredth anniversary of the founding of the Red Cross in 1863; and the International Labor Organization was given the prize on its fiftieth birthday. Special occasions were also observed when Amnesty International was named in the Year of the Prisoners of Conscience, and when Alva Myrdal and García Robles were recognized for their efforts for disarmament in the year the UN Special Session on Disarmament was held in New York City.

The period that began with the angry canceling of a summit meeting between leaders of the superpowers ended with the revival of summits, an agreement for arms control signed, and bright prospects for another to follow.

1960
Albert John Lutuli (1898–1967)

South Africa

Teacher, Zulu tribal chief, leader of African National Congress and nonviolent struggle for equal rights in South Africa.

Albert John Lutuli received the prize for 1960, which had been reserved, at the same ceremony in 1961 at which Dag Hammarskjöld was recognized posthumously. Chairman Jahn remarked that despite the differences between the two men, they had in common their fight "for the ideals expressed in the Declaration of Human Rights embodied in the Charter of the United Nations." The late secretary-general of the United Nations had other qualifications for the prize as well, and Lutuli's was the first in a series of grants to leaders of nonviolent movements for human rights. His prize also marked the first occasion on which the committee went beyond the Western community in its choice.

Albert John Lutuli (this is the spelling he preferred; the name is frequently spelled "Luthuli") descended from a line of Zulu leaders. His grandfather and his uncle had both been tribal chiefs in Natal, a province of the Republic of South Africa. His grandparents were the first Christian converts in the community, and their younger son, Lutuli's father, became a missionary in what was then Rhodesia, where Lutuli was born. After his father's death, his mother returned with her eight-year-old son to Groutville, a small town near Durban on the east coast of South Africa, where she sent him to a Congregationalist mission school and took in washing to pay for his school books.

Lutuli continued his education in missionary schools with the help of scholarships, graduating at twenty-three from Adams College in Natal, trained as a teacher. He was offered another scholarship to do graduate work, but he chose to accept a teaching position at Adams College in order to support his mother. He was one of the first two black teachers hired at Adams, and he remained there for fifteen years, teaching Zulu history and literature. In 1927 he married a fellow teacher, and in 1929 the first of their seven children was born. During this period Lutuli rose to positions of leadership among African teachers, becoming president of the African Association of Teachers in 1933. He was also active in church organizations, which led to a trip to India to attend a Christian conference and a lecture tour in the United States, sponsored by missionary societies.

In 1935 the elders of his tribe asked him to become the chief, which was an elective position subject to approval by the South African government, which paid the salary. Lutuli, who was committed to his teaching, hesitated, but finally in 1936 he accepted, and his life took a new turn. Lutuli was then thirty-eight, and he had never occupied himself with political issues. Nor did these concern him in his early years as chief of the community of five thousand Zulus in the Groutville area, where he was kept busy by his duties as civil administrator, judge, and presiding figure at tribal ceremonies. His policy was to preserve the best of the tribal culture, while fostering Christian values and giving his people the benefits of modern civilization. He also tried to improve the conditions of laborers on the sugar-cane plantations.

Meanwhile, the government of the ruling white minority had begun imposing restrictions on nonwhites. In 1936 the government disenfranchised the only Africans who had the vote, in Cape Province. In

1948 the Nationalist government adopted the policy of apartheid to keep the races apart. The Pass Laws limited where nonwhites could live and work, and their educational opportunities were reduced.

These measures brought Lutuli into active opposition. In 1944 he joined the African National Congress (ANC), which had been founded in South Africa in 1912 to secure civil rights for Africans in that country, including the vote. Members of other racial groups were invited to join the struggle. In 1945 Lutuli was elected to a position in the Natal division of the ANC, and in 1951 he became its president and helped organize nonviolent measures of resistance, such as boycotts, strikes, and noncompliance, to discriminatory policies.

The government demanded that he withdraw either from the ANC or from his office as tribal chief. Lutuli refused to do either, and in 1952 the government deposed him. He issued a declaration, "The Chief Speaks," asking, "What have been the fruits of my many years of moderation?" Only more laws limiting rights, he said, "an intensification of our subjection to ensure and protect white supremacy." Lutuli defended the ANC, whose nonviolent passive resistance campaign was not subversive and did not seek to overthrow the state. Any chief worthy of his position, he said, had no choice but to fight fearlessly against laws and conditions that tend to debase human personality, a God-given force. He concluded, "It is inevitable that in working for Freedom some individuals and some families must take the lead and suffer: the Road to Freedom Is via the Cross."

One month after the government dismissed him as chief, Lutuli was elected to the presidency of the ANC and became the national leader of the struggle for racial equality in South Africa. Determined to fight only with nonviolent means, he opposed extremists on the left who wanted to use violence and establish an all-black state, as well as those conservatives who wanted to compromise with the government.

The government now began a succession of bans against Lutuli to limit his freedom of expression and his movements beyond the limits of his home district. In 1956 when he attended an ANC congress, he was arrested, along with 155 others, and charged with treason. After spending a year in jail, he was released and the charges dropped. He testified at the trials of the remaining defendants, who were all acquitted in 1961 with a verdict acknowledging that the ANC was neither plotting violent revolution nor dominated by communists.

In 1960 a mass demonstration at Sharpeville against the pass regulations was fired on by the police, and 69 people were killed and 180 wounded. Lutuli publicly burned his pass in solidarity with the victims, for which he was given a jail sentence that was suspended because of his health, and he was returned to Groutville. The ANC was then outlawed by Parliament.

Lutuli was living in Groutville under restrictions when word came that he was to receive the Peace Prize. The government newspaper condemned the award as "an inexplicable pathological phenomenon," but Lutuli said later that he never knew he had so many friends in South Africa, as congratulations came pouring in from people of all racial groups. Yielding to pressure, the government finally agreed to grant Lutuli a passport to go to Oslo for the ceremony, but it was good only for ten days, and he could not go anywhere else, not even to Stockholm to meet the other prize winners. Wherever his plane landed, however, Lutuli was met by enthusiastic ovations.

In presenting him with the prize, Chairman Jahn quoted Lutuli's letter to the prime minister of South Africa: "We believe in a community where the white and the non-white in South Africa can live in harmony and work for our common fatherland. . . . We believe in the brotherhood of peoples and in respect for the value of the individual. My congress has never given expression to hatred for any race in South Africa." Lutuli, said Jahn, "brings a message to all who work and strive to establish respect for human rights both within nations and between nations. Well might we ask: will the non-whites of South Africa, by their suffering, their humiliation, and their patience, show the other nations of the world that human rights can be won without violence?"

As Lutuli mounted the stage, a handsome regal presence in tribal dress, the audience that filled the auditorium rose to its feet and cheered him loud and long. When the cheering ended, he said, "This is the greatest occasion in my life and in that of my wife. She has not only encouraged but has also actively supported me." He said that for once he found himself in agreement with the foreign minister of South Africa, who had said that Lutuli did not deserve the prize. The award, he said, was for the people of South Africa, and he accepted it in their behalf.

The next evening when Lutuli returned to the auditorium to give his Nobel lecture, in an unprecedented move he was asked to bring his wife to the stage. His command of English surprised many in the audience. He was not tied to his manuscript, but made many extemporaneous comments as he went along.

He spoke of how moved he was "to be plucked from banishment in a rural backwater" and placed where so many great men had stood before. He told of how he, "a Christian and patriot, could not look on while systematic attempts were made . . . to debase the God-factor in man or to set a limit beyond which the human being in his black form might not strive to serve his Creator to the best of his ability. To remain neutral in a situation where the laws of the land virtually criticized God for having created men of color was the sort of thing I could not, as a Christian, tolerate."

How strange it was that with Africa torn with strife and racial conflict, "a man of Africa should be here to receive an award given for service to the cause of peace and brotherhood between men." What a paradox that such an award "should come to one who is citizen of a country where the brotherhood of man is an illegal doctrine, outlawed, banned, censured, proscribed and prohibited." Lutuli paid tribute to the Christian missions in Africa: "a shaft of light to which we owe our initial enlightenment." Even the church in South Africa seemed to be awakening to its true mission. He noted the march of the rest of Africa to independence, with South Africa "a museum piece in our time, a hangover from the dark past of mankind." But the refusal of his people to be silenced by force was "a living testimony to the unconquerable spirit of mankind."

He closed by calling upon Africa, as "an emergent continent, bursting to freedom through the shell of centuries of serfdom," to cease "bemoaning her past, with its humiliation and sufferings" and to "see her destiny as being that of making a distinctive contribution to human progress and human relationships with a particular new Africa flavor enriched by the diversity of cultures she enjoys . . . building a non-racial democracy that shall be a monumental brotherhood."

A free and independent Africa, Lutuli declared, might be "man's last hope for a mediator between the East and the West, and is qualified to demand of the great powers to 'turn the swords into ploughshares' because two-thirds of mankind is hungry and illiterate." After concluding, Lutuli burst into song, singing in Zulu the African national song, and was joined by Africans in the audience.

He returned to the isolation to which his government had condemned him, but he was not forgotten. The South African Colored People's Congress nominated him for president, the National Union of South African Students elected him honorary president, and the students of Glasgow University voted to name him rector, although he declined.

Lutuli's autobiography, *Let My People Go,* appeared in 1962. Its concluding words reaffirmed his hope for Africa: "Somewhere ahead there beckons a civilization, a culture, which will take its place in the parade of God's history beside other great syntheses, Chinese, Egyptian, Jewish, European. It will not necessarily be all black; but it will be African."

He remained restricted to his home during his last years, his powers declining, no doubt saddened by the continued intransigence of the government and the turn away from nonviolence among many of his former followers. In 1967, while walking on a trestle near his home, he was struck by a train and killed.

BIBLIOGRAPHY

Primary Source

Lutuli, Albert John. *Let My People Go.* New York: McGraw-Hill, 1962. Autobiography.

Secondary Sources

Benson, Mary. *Chief Albert Lutuli of South Africa.* London: Oxford University Press, 1963. A brief biography.

Callan, Edward. *Albert John Lutuli and the South African Race Conflict.* Kalamazoo: Western Michigan University Monograph Series on Cultural Change no. 1, 1965. A study of Lutuli's life up to 1961.

Legum, Colin and Margaret. *The Bitter Choice: Eight South Africans' Resistance to Tyranny.* New York: World, 1968.

"Luthuli, Albert John." in *BDI.*

"Luthuli, Albert John." in *CB,* 1962.

"Luthuli, Albert John." in *MPL.*

1961

Dag Hammarskjöld (1905–61)

Sweden

Civil servant in finance and foreign ministries, chairman of Bank of Sweden, representative of Sweden in European economic affairs and in United Nations, second secretary-general of United Nations.

Dag Hammarskjöld was rumored to be the leading candidate for the Peace Prize in 1960, but his policies as UN secretary-general came under attack by the Soviet Union, and the Nobel Committee, apparently wishing to avoid controversy, reserved the prize for decision the following year. Once again he was nominated, by Norwegian parliamentarians and his UN colleague, Ralph Bunche. Shortly before the committee met in October to make its decisions, there occurred Hammarskjöld's tragic death on a UN mission in Africa. Whereas in 1948 the committee had finally decided not to give posthumous awards to Gandhi and Prince Bernadotte, this time the members had no hesitation in granting Hammarskjöld the 1961 award, at the same time giving the 1960 award to Lutuli.

Dag Hammarskjöld came from a high-born family with a long tradition of serving the Swedish state. His father was prime minister, and two of his three older brothers had distinguished public careers. In explaining the forces that had shaped him, he gave first place to his heritage:

> From generations of soldiers and government officials on my father's side I inherited a belief that no life was more satisfactory than one of selfless service to your country—or humanity.
>
> From scholars and clergymen on my mother's side I inherited a belief that, in the very radical sense of the Gospels, all men were equals as children of God, and should be met and treated by us as our masters in God.

These two ideals, he wrote, were harmonized for him in the service ethic of Albert Schweitzer, based on the Gospels, and the strength for this service came from the example of the medieval mystics, who, through "self-surrender," "singleness of mind," and "inwardness" had been able "to say yes to every fate life had in store for them when they followed the call of duty, as they understood it."

Hammarskjöld's call had led him not to withdrawal from the world but to the very center of international life. So busily was he occupied with the world's affairs that there was general astonishment after his death when *Markings* was published, "notes along the way" of his inner pilgrimage, which he called, in diplomatic parlance, "a sort of *white book* concerning my negotiations with myself—and with God." He had remodeled the UN Meditation Room as "a room of stillness," Hammarskjöld said, because "when we come to our own deepest feelings and urgings we have to be alone, we have to feel the sky and the earth and hear the voice that speaks within us."

Dag Hammarskjöld grew up in Uppsala, the site of Sweden's famous old university and the seat of the primate of the national church. Nathan Söderblom, the last Swedish peace laureate before Hammarskjöld, was archbishop of Uppsala when Hammarskjöld's father was governor of the province, and the two families were very close.

The senior Hammarskjöld was often away from home on government commissions in Sweden and abroad; he was premier for three years and was also a member of the Swedish Academy and chairman of the Nobel Foundation. He was a stern authoritarian man, whereas the mother was warm and "as open to life as a child," in her son's words.

Dag distinguished himself at the University of Uppsala, where at nineteen he took his first degree, having studied literature, philosophy, and French. Three years later he took a degree in economics and finally a degree in law when he was twenty-five, having become fluent in English and German as well as French. He loved literature, music, and art and the Swedish outdoors, where he often went with his friends to ski, hike, and climb mountains.

In 1930 Hammarskjöld moved to Stockholm, where he continued his studies in economics at the University of Stockholm, taught for a year, and received his doctorate in 1934. He turned naturally to public service, and at the young age of thirty he was given a responsible position in the Ministry of Finance, where he became the top civil official and served concurrently as chairman of the Governors of the Bank of Sweden.

At the Ministry of Finance he cooperated with his elder brother Bo, his counterpart as under secretary of the Ministry of Social Welfare, in drafting the legislation through which the Social Democrats made Sweden a welfare state. He remained a non–party man, however, and he retained this independence when he shifted his base to the Ministry of Foreign Affairs. He had already advised this ministry on economic questions, and in 1947 he became under secretary responsible for all economic questions. In 1949, at forty-four, he was appointed secretary-general of the ministry, sitting in the cabinet after 1951 as a nonpolitical deputy foreign minister.

In this position Hammarskjöld first became known abroad. He represented Sweden in financial negotiations with the United States and Britain and took a leading role in the European discussions leading to the Marshall Plan and in the Organization of European Economic Cooperation. He was a member of Sweden's delegation to the UN General Assembly in 1949 and again in 1951–53.

On the evening of 31 March 1953, Hammarskjöld was dining with two friends in his Stockholm apartment when a reporter phoned to ask him if he was going to be the secretary-general of the United Nations. Hammarskjöld had had no intimation that his name had been proposed, and he told the reporter that his watch was fast and it was not yet time for April Fool pranks. Official word from the United Nations soon followed, and Hammarskjöld cabled back expressing his "strong feeling of insufficiency," but saying yes to the call of duty. He was then forty-seven.

The post had become vacant on the resignation of Trygve Lie of Norway, the first secretary-general, who had run into difficulties with the Soviet Union, which had also vetoed the candidacy of Lester Pearson of Canada. What little was known of Hammarskjöld was that he was an able civil servant, and it was expected that he would concern himself chiefly with administrative affairs and refrain from a public role. Since Sweden was a neutral state, he was acceptable to the Soviet Union.

On Hammarskjöld's arrival in New York, Lie welcomed him to "the most impossible job in the world." Hammarskjöld was quite aware of the difficulties ahead. The high hopes of the founders of the United Nations had seemed to founder on the shoals of superpower conflict, and disillusionment and cynicism were rampant. The new secretary-general had faith in the long-term future but was realistic about the present. "When trying to change the world," he said, "we have to face it as it is." He saw his role in the perspective of history:

> Working at the edge of the development of human society is to work on the brink of the unknown. Much of what is done will one day prove to have been of little avail. That is no excuse for the failure to act in accordance with our best understanding, in recognition of its limits but with faith in the ultimate result of the creative evolution in which it is our privilege to cooperate.

His first task was to reorganize the Secretariat and to try to infuse this staff of more than five thousand persons from sixty-seven countries with his own spirit of the international civil servant—impartial, objective, independent, and owing first allegiance to the UN Charter. Then he began to broaden his functions.

The first opportunity came when the General Assembly passed a resolution asking him to seek the release of the American fliers who had been captured by the People's Republic of China during the Korean conflict. In a spectacular venture of personal diplomacy, Hammarskjöld flew to Peking for direct talks with Foreign Minister Chou En-lai. He won his confidence, and Chou En-lai listened carefully to the humanitarian and practical arguments he presented. Some months later, on Hammarskjöld's birthday, the fliers were freed as a present for him.

Hammarskjöld's greatest success was his handling of the Suez crisis of 1956, when France, Great Britain, and Israel were embroiled in war with Egypt. It was Lester Pearson who first proposed the UN Emergency Force to replace the invading troops, but it was Hammarskjöld who organized the UNEF in forty-eight hours and was mainly responsible for bringing the conflict to a conclusion.

In this conflict and others, he displayed an unusual ability as a negotiator to convince each party that he deeply understood its position. As he explained, "You can only hope to find a lasting solution to a conflict if you have learned to see the other objectively, but at the same time, to experience the other person's difficulties subjectively."

The episode demonstrated the potential of the secretary-general as an independent factor in international conflicts, dealing quietly with both sides in ways that were impossible for the states themselves or even the Security Council. The limits to his possibilities when a matter involved the vital interests of a superpower, however, were just as clearly displayed during the Hungarian uprising, which occurred at the same time. The secretary-general was not even permitted to go to Budapest, and the movement was suppressed by Soviet tanks.

Hammarskjöld's indefatigable work habits were the marvel of his staff. His desk was never cluttered, and a memo that reached him at the end of the working day was generally acted upon the next morning. In crises he seemed to be able to banish sleep and yet be fresh and effective each morning. He loved his job and was exhilarated by its challenges. He never succumbed for very long to discouragement, and he drew strength from his "inwardness."

He once said that the UN Charter should have included an article stating that the secretary-general "should have an iron constitution and not be married." He was fortunate to enjoy good health throughout his life, and he was filled with abundant energies. When the queen of Sweden once asked him why he never married, he replied that he had watched the effect of his father's public obligations upon his mother, and he had not wanted to impose such a life upon any woman. He avoided social functions, but he found time for evenings with his friends, discussing books and the arts in his Manhattan apartment or at his favorite restaurants. He relaxed in his weekend hideaway in the woods near Brewster, New York, and during the summer at his farmhouse on Sweden's southern coast, where he hoped one day to retire.

In his last annual report, Hammarskjöld set down his conception of the United Nations. Either it could be a conference machinery for sovereign states, with the Secretariat reflecting their competing interests in its staff members, or it could become an organic body, moving beyond national sovereignties, with member states faithfully carrying out their obligations and with a truly international Secretariat, whose staff would not be subjected to pressures from their own national governments. In this conception the secretary-general would be above the conflicts, free to act for the safeguarding of peace even in the absence of specific directions from the Security Council and the Assembly.

When Hammarskjöld was reelected for a second term, he hoped to move the United Nations along these lines. Unfortunately, in the crisis that developed in the Congo, the cold war rivalries of the United States and the Soviet Union became involved, and the Soviet Union accused the secretary-general of becoming an "agent of the imperialists" and exceeding his constitutional powers.

In dramatic scenes at the General Assembly, Premier Nikita Khrushchev of the Soviet Union pounded the desk with his shoe and demanded that Hammarskjöld resign and that he be replaced by a committee of three. Hammarskjöld replied in what was his greatest speech that if it were only a matter of his having lost the confidence of the Soviet Union, he would resign, but then the Soviets would insist on an arrangement for the executive that would destroy the United Nations: "It is not the Soviet Union or, indeed, any other big powers who need the United Nations for their protection; it is all the others. . . . I shall remain in my post during the term of my office as a servant of the Organization in the interests of all those other nations, as long as *they* wish me to do so."

The ovation that greeted this speech showed what the wishes of the great majority of the member states were. Unfortunately, Hammarskjöld was to remain in his post for only one more year. On 17 September 1961, he perished in a plane crash in the Congo during his attempt to settle the conflict there.

He left behind in the room where he spent his last night the book he had been reading, *The Imitation of Christ* by Thomas à Kempis, a classic of Christian mysticism, for which he was using as a bookmark a copy of the secretary-general's oath of office. Also there was the typed copy of an article about his youth in Uppsala and the typed first pages of the Swedish translation he was doing of *I and Thou,* by the Jewish philosopher Martin Buber.

At the Nobel Peace Prize ceremonies, the Swedish ambassador to Norway accepted the award for the Hammarskjöld family, who planned to use it for the works of peace that were dear to Dag Hammarskjöld's heart. "My fellow countryman became a citizen of the world," the ambassador said, "but on that cool autumn day of falling leaves when he was brought back to the Uppsala of his youth, he was ours again; he was back home. Shyly he had guarded his inner world, but at that moment the distance disappeared and we felt that he came very close to us."

Hammarskjöld was a universal man, and he rose to greatness at the principal civil servant of the world, but he never lost touch with his beloved homeland and its people. When his little essay on Uppsala was published, they could see how he had kept to the end the most tender living memories of his birthplace.

BIBLIOGRAPHY

Primary Sources

Hammarskjöld, Dag. *Castle Hill.* Translated by Alan Blair. Uppsala, Sweden: Dag Hammarskjöld Foundation 1977. The essay on Uppsala.

———. *Markings.* Translated by Leif Sjoberg and W. H. Auden. New York: Knopf, 1964. His spiritual diary, originally published in Swedish.

———. *Public Papers.* In *Public Papers of the Secretaries-General of the United Nations.* Edited by Andrew Cordier and Wilder Foote. Vols. 2–5. New York: Columbia University Press, 1972–75.

Secondary Sources

Cordier, Andrew, and Wilder Foote, eds. *The Quest for Peace: The Dag Hammarskjöld Memorial Lectures.* New York: Columbia University Press, 1965. Essays by Alva Myrdal, Ralph Bunche, and others.

Lash, Joseph P. *Dag Hammarskjöld: Custodian of the Brushfire Peace.* Garden City, N.Y.: Doubleday, 1961. Well informed, well written.

Smith, Bradford. *Men of Peace.* Philadelphia: Lippincott, 1964, pp. 310–45.

Snow, C. P. *Variety of Men.* London: Macmillan, 1967, pp. 151–68.

Svolpe, Sven. *Dag Hammarskjöld: A Spiritual Portrait.* Translated by Naomi Walford. New York: Scribner, 1966. By a longtime friend.

Trachtenberg, B. L. S. "A Bibliographical Essay on Dag Hammarskjöld." In *Dag Hammarskjöld Revisited.* Edited by Robert S. Jordan. Durham: University of North Carolina Press, 1982.

Urquhart, Brian. *Hammarskjöld.* New York: Knopf, 1972. Definitive account of his secretary-generalship by a UN associate who used the best sources.

Van Dusen, Henry P. *Dag Hammarskjöld: The Statesman and His Faith.* New York: Harper, 1964. Relates *Markings* to his public life.

1962

Linus Pauling (1901–)

United States

One of the leading scientists of his time; only winner of two undivided Nobel prizes, chemistry and peace; mobilized world scientists to help achieve the partial Test Ban Treaty of 1963.

In presenting the postponed 1962 prize to Linus Pauling at the ceremony in 1963, Chairman Jahn referred to the part Pauling played in bringing about the treaty banning nuclear tests in the atmosphere, which had been concluded on 23 July 1963, between the United States, the Soviet Union, and Great Britain: "Does anyone believe that this treaty would have been concluded now if there had been no responsible scientist who, tirelessly, unflinchingly, year in and year out, had impressed on the authorities and on the general public the real menace of nuclear tests?" Moreover, said Jahn, "through his campaign, Linus Pauling has manifested the ethical responsibility which he believes science should bear for the fate of mankind, today and in the future."

It was the dropping of the atomic bombs on Japan in 1945 that first awakened in Pauling what became a compelling sense of social concern. Up to that time Pauling had been a distinguished scientist, enjoying a happy family life, whose driving force was his insatiable curiosity about the world of nature.

He remembers a critical incident when he was a high school freshman in Portland, Oregon. One afternoon a schoolmate took him home to show off a brand new chemistry set. Pauling watched in amazement as his friend mixed colored powders in solutions that fizzed and smelled and then combined something with some table sugar, added a drop of acid, and the sugar burst into flame. It was not long before Pauling was putting together his own chemistry set to try experiments himself. This was the beginning of a long road he was to travel. As he wrote years later, "I was simply entranced by chemical phenomena, by the reactions in which substances, often with strikingly different properties, appear; and I hoped to learn more and more about this aspect of the world."

His desire to learn about the world had shown up in Pauling very early. When he was only nine years old, his father had written to the Portland newspaper to say that his son had read everything about history and natural sciences that could be found for him, and he was now seeking advice as to what to give the boy next. Only a few months after writing this letter, Herman Pauling died. The family lost the drugstore he had owned, and the mother moved with Linus and his two sisters into a smaller house, where she took in boarders. Money worries were a constant concern, and Pauling held a variety of jobs after school. He made few friends, but he kept devouring all the books he could find.

At high school he took all available science and mathematics courses. When he was refused permission to finish his requirements quickly so that he could enter college early, he dropped out before the last term and went off to college anyway. Many years later the high school was proud to award its most famous alumnus his missing diploma.

Pauling entered Oregon Agricultural College (now Oregon State University) when he was sixteen and worked his way through. His last and best summer job was as state inspector of paved roads. While still an undergraduate he was made an instructor of quantitative chemistry, and it was in his classroom that he encountered an intelligent and attractive student named Ava Helen Miller. A romance quickly developed that soon led to an engagement and a wedding the following year, when Pauling was twenty-two. It was a happy marriage that was to produce four children and to last for fifty-eight years until Ava Helen died in 1981.

By 1923 Pauling had finished his first year of graduate work at the California Institute of Technology and had published his first scientific paper on molecular structure of crystals. He published four more in his second year and was awarded his Ph.D. in 1925. This was followed by a Guggenheim grant to study in Europe, and when he returned in 1927,

Caltech made him assistant professor, at twenty-six the youngest member of the faculty.

When he was thirty, Pauling published a paper, "The Nature of the Chemical Bond," that became a classic. In this and subsequent papers he explained for the first time the structure of molecules in terms of quantum mechanics. For this he was given the Nobel Prize for chemistry in 1954. Meanwhile he had gone on to a succession of important discoveries, making connections among physical sciences, biology, and medicine.

During the Second World War, Pauling directed a number of programs, including research in explosives and the production of a blood substitute for field hospitals, and he was given the Presidential Medal of Merit for his contribution to the war effort. He declined an invitation to work on the atomic bomb project because he was too busy. This meant that when Pauling later began to speak out about the dangers of the bomb, he could speak freely because he had not been working with classified materials.

After his first public lecture on the bomb soon after the Hiroshima blast, Pauling was visited by an agent from the Federal Bureau of Investigation, who wanted to know where he had gotten his information. Pauling had simply been making inferences from the scientific knowledge he already had. He was appalled by his realization of the bomb's destructive potential, but he felt that he could not speak as authoritatively about questions of war and peace as he could about science. Admiring his wife's seriousness about the cause of peace, he later recalled, "I began to devote half my time to catching up with Ava on social, political, and economic matters. It changed my life."

Pauling now joined Albert Einstein's Emergency Committee of Atomic Scientists and began to speak out against war and nuclear testing. In the cold war mood of the time, a supporter of a policy of peace was all too readily suspected of being pro-Communist, and Pauling suffered such indignities as having the State Department refuse him a passport and having to face congressional committees and declare that he was not a Communist. On one such occasion he tried to explain why he was independent of any political line: "Nobody tells me what to think—except Mrs. Pauling." Despite such harassment and vilification by the press, Pauling refused to be silent. "I kept on going to keep the respect of my wife," he says today.

In April 1957, Albert Schweitzer issued his Declaration of Conscience from Oslo, describing the human damage done by radioactive fallout and asking for the cessation of nuclear tests. On 15 May, Pauling echoed this appeal in a speech at Washington University in Saint Louis, and the response was so enthusiastic that that very evening Pauling, encouraged by several colleagues, wrote the Scientists' Bomb-Test Appeal, calling for a test-ban treaty, and sent it out to the scientific community. Within two weeks two thousand American scientists had signed the appeal, and Pauling began to solicit signatures from other countries. Eventually over eleven thousand scientists from forty-nine countries signed the document, and Pauling and his wife were able to present the petition to the United Nations in January 1958 as the opinion of the great majority of the world's scientists.

In 1958 Pauling published *No More War!,* an exposition of the scientific facts of nuclear weapons in clear and simple language and an appeal to prevent their use in war. (It was reprinted twenty-five years later, with little need to revise its basic explanation and message.) In 1959 at a conference on nuclear weapons in Hiroshima, Pauling wrote the resolution calling for a ban on their testing and development.

The Paulings then circulated an appeal against the proliferation of nuclear weapons and convened an international conference on the subject in Oslo in May 1961. Among the sponsors were Albert Schweitzer, Philip Noel-Baker, Lord Bertrand Russell, and other notables. Sixty distinguished scientists from fifteen countries attended the conference, which was financed by funds from Pauling's Nobel Prize in chemistry and private contributions.

In September 1961, Pauling sent telegrams to both President Kennedy and Premier Khrushchev, urging them to sign a ban on testing. In November he was invited to Moscow to attend the second centenary celebration of the Soviet Academy of Science, and he used the occasion to speak against new nuclear tests by the Soviet Union. He sent Khrushchev two letters and the draft of a test-ban treaty, which was strikingly similar to the form of the treaty that was finally signed in 1963. The treaty went into effect on 10 October 1963, the day Pauling was notified that he was to receive the Peace Prize.

In accepting the prize in Oslo, Pauling said that it should have been shared with Ava Pauling. Chairman Jahn pointed out that she had not been nominated, and he also told Pauling privately that he had had a hard time getting Pauling's candidacy through the committee. Apparently Pauling was also a controversial figure in Oslo.

In his laureate's address, "Science and Peace," Pauling referred to Nobel's prediction that once war's destructive power became too terrible, wars would cease. Now that the new bombs had an explosive energy ten to fifty million times that of Nobel's nitroglycerine, "war has been made impossible forever." Science and peace were closely related, Pauling declared. Scientific advance "now provides the possibility of eliminating poverty and starvation, of decreasing significantly the suffering caused by disease, of using the resources of the world effectively for the benefit of humanity." He quoted, however, the words of Albert Einstein, "There is no defense in science against the weapon which can destroy civilization."

Pauling presented scientific estimates of the genetic damage caused by fallout from atmospheric testing and calculated some of the devastating effects of a nuclear war. He hoped that the recent test-ban treaty would be only a first step in a general program of disarmament, not only of nuclear bombs, but of biological and chemical weapons as well.

In conclusion, Pauling reiterated his belief that war, "this curse to the human race," would be eliminated. With his customary exuberance, he declared:

> We, you and I, are privileged to be alive during this extraordinary age, this unique epoch in the history of the world, the epoch of demarcation between the past millennia of war and suffering and the future, the great future of peace, justice, morality, and human well-being. I am confident . . . that we shall in the course of time be enabled to build a world characterized by economic, political, and social justice for all human beings, and a culture worthy of man's intelligence.

With the prize money of about fifty thousand dollars, Pauling was now able to resign from Caltech, where the Board of Trustees, uncomfortable with his peacemaking, had already had him removed from the chairmanship of the Division of Chemistry and where he still felt limited in his work for peace. He spent several years at the Center for the Study of Democratic Institutions at Santa Barbara and then returned to academe, first at the University of California in San Diego and then at Stanford University. In 1973 he founded the Linus Pauling Institute of Science and Medicine in Palo Alto, where he now centers his activities.

In his offices there, dressed in jacket and baggy trousers, with the characteristic floppy beret on his desk, his blue eyes in his mobile face alight, Pauling told how he divides his time into three parts: one-third in thinking about pure science, which he loves to do most of all; the other two-thirds, out of his sense of social obligation, devoted to peace efforts and his more recent concern with nutrition and human health. Again in controversy, this time with much of the medical profession, Pauling is advocating vitamin C in treatment of ills from the common cold to cancer. His most recent book is entitled *How to Live Longer and Feel Better* (1986).

Is he still confident about the future? "If I weren't," Pauling answers, "I would not be working on improving the human condition, but I would be spending all my time on science." In his mid-eighties, that insatiable curiosity about the universe is still a driving force, but it has long been matched by his determination to place his extraordinary gifts and scientific knowledge at the service of humanity.

BIBLIOGRAPHY

Primary Sources

Pauling, Linus. *How to Live Longer and Feel Better.* New York: W. H. Freeman, 1986. With a short biography by Robert J. Paradowski. Pauling's regimen for good health through vitamin C and good nutrition.

———. *No More War!* Anniversary ed. New York: Dodd, Mead, 1983. Updates the 1958 edition with addenda to each chapter and documents on the opposition of scientists to nuclear weapons.

———. *Vitamin C, the Common Cold and the Flu.* New York: Berkley, 1981. A revised edition of *Vitamin C and the Common Cold.* San Francisco: Freeman, 1970. Named Phi Beta Kappa's "best book on science of the year."

Secondary Sources

Bendiner, Elmer. "The Passions and Perils of Pauling." *Hospital Practice* 18, no. 4 (April 1983): 210–43. Best biographical article.

Grodzins, Morton, and Eugene Rabinowitch, eds. *The Atomic Age: Scientists in National and World Affairs.* New York: Basic Books, 1963. A collection of articles from the *Bulletin of the Atomic Scientists,* including two by Harry Kalven, Jr., on Pauling's appearances before the Senate Internal Security Committee.

Jacobson, Harold K., and Eric Stein. *Diplomats, Scientists, and Politicians: The United States and the Nuclear Test Ban Negotiations.* Ann Arbor: University of Michigan Press, 1966.

"Pauling, Linus." in *CB.*

"Pauling Prize: A Welcome Honor from Norway." *Bulletin of the Atomic Scientists* 19 (December 1963): 18. An editorial.

"Weird Insult from Norway." *LIFE* 55, no. 17 (25 October 1963): 4. An editorial.

1963

International Committee of the Red Cross

Switzerland

League of Red Cross Societies

On the hundredth anniversary of the founding of the Red Cross, the 1963 prize was divided between the International Committee of the Red Cross (ICRC), and the League of Red Cross Societies, representing the two major elements of the Red Cross movement.

Since its founding in 1863 the ICRC had been the only international Red Cross organization, guarding the original principles, serving as the link between the national societies, and granting formal recognition to the new ones. The extensive activities of the national societies in the First World War and its aftermath, however, led them in 1919, under the inspiration of the American banker and Red Cross leader, Henry P. Davison, to form an international federation, the League of Red Cross Societies, with twenty-eight members.

What would be the relationships of this new international organization with the ICRC? The league resisted proposals of fusion, wanting to retain its independence because of its separate character and the new emphasis on the societies' peacetime activities. The earliest national societies had been formed to relieve wartime sufferings, but now they were dealing with the victims of epidemics, disasters, and natural catastrophes.

The matter was happily resolved in 1928 by the institution of a unified structure, the International Red Cross, composed of the ICRC, retaining its traditional character; the League of Red Cross Societies, with its own statutes, Board of Governors, and secretary-general; and the National Red Cross Societies. The supreme deliberative body was to be the International Conference, composed of delegations from each of these groups and delegates from the states that had signed the Geneva Conventions. This "Red Cross Parliament" was to meet every four years, and between meetings continuity was to be provided by a Standing Commission, formed of representatives from the ICRC, the league, and the national societies.

The International Red Cross has substantially kept this form ever since, although in 1986 the International Conference decided to change its name to the International Movement of the Red Cross and the Red Crescent. It was in 1877 that Turkey, which had signed the Geneva Convention, adopted the name and emblem of the Red Crescent for its aid society because of the feeling of Muslims that the cross was a religious symbol. This had not actually been the case. At the founding conference in 1863 it was first proposed simply to use a white armband, but the red cross seems to have been added to avoid confusion with the white cloth of truce. The traditional explanation, which is not substantiated by the minutes of the meeting, holds that the symbol was chosen to honor Switzerland, since it is the reverse of the Swiss flag of a white cross on a red ground. Nevertheless, Muslim nations have continued to use the red crescent, and in 1929 a diplomatic conference in Geneva officially decided to give this emblem equal recognition with the cross. Eventually the League of Red Cross Societies became the League of Red Cross and Red Crescent Societies, and it was a natural move ultimately to make a similar addition to the International Red Cross. This did not cover the Israeli society, which uses a red star of David.

Despite differences about organizational form and symbols, the international movement has always been in harmony on basic purposes. In 1965 the twentieth International Conference, meeting in Vienna, adopted seven fundamental principles:

Humanity: "Its purpose is to protect life and health and to ensure respect for the human being. It promotes mutual understanding, friendship, cooperation and lasting peace amongst all peoples."

Impartiality: "It makes no discrimination as to nationality, race, religious beliefs, class or political opinions."

Neutrality: "The Movement may not take sides in hostilities or engage any time in controversies of a political, racial, religious, or ideological nature."

Independence: "The National Societies . . . must always maintain their autonomy, so that they may be able at all times to act in accordance with the principles of the Movement."

Voluntary Service.

Unity: "There may be only one . . . Society in any one country."

Universality: The movement, in which all Societies have equal status and responsibilities, is worldwide.

The league, which in 1963 included 102 and by the 1986 International Conference was to include 144 member societies, has continued to stress peacetime activities, coordinating the relief operations of these societies for victims of natural disasters and for refugees outside areas of conflict, the province of the ICRC. Ever since the assistance in 1923 to the victims of the great Japanese earthquake, there has not been one year or scarcely any part of the world where the league has not responded to a call for help. In 1986, for example, there were thirty-three such appeals. The league's representatives were called to seven countries of Africa to meet the problems of drought, to four Latin American countries to aid flood victims, to Fiji and the Solomon Islands to deal with the aftermath of cyclones, to El Salvador and Greece to assist in earthquake relief, and to nine countries to help with refugees.

The league has aided in the creation of new societies, and it has worked closely with its member societies in their ongoing relief actions, medical and nursing care, social welfare, training of volunteers, information activities, and youth work. National societies in the developing countries have had much help from their sister organizations in the more developed world. In all its efforts the league, like the ICRC, has cooperated with the appropriate UN and international agencies.

The league and the ICRC have also worked together on many occasions, but the ICRC has a different mandate and, as a completely neutral and independent body recognized under international law, it has sent its delegates where the league's representatives may not go. The ICRC has consistently expanded its sphere of activity. Beginning with aid to those wounded in battle, it came to serve war prisoners, and by the 1930s it was extending its relief to victims of civil war as well as international war. In World War II it rendered service to civilian victims of war.

In 1949, on ICRC initiative, four new Geneva Conventions were signed, strengthening and supplementing the earlier treaties, and these conventions were in turn to be supplemented, again under ICRC inspiration, by two protocols signed in 1977. With the benefit of these extensions of humanitarian law and in the exercise of its own moral authority, the ICRC has been able to render aid not only to military and civilian victims of international armed conflicts but to those suffering from the violence of internal disturbances, civil wars, colonial wars, and wars of liberation; moreover, its delegates have been permitted to visit political prisoners without witnesses. The ICRC has, in fact, moved to extend its work to all areas of civil strife in which human rights are threatened.

After the Hungarian uprising of 1956, while the league moved to help care for the flood of refugees who fled abroad, it was the ICRC that was asked to distribute relief supplies to Hungary itself. Similarly, after the Second World War, the ICRC, on the invitation of the Japanese Red Cross, repatriated North Koreans from Japan to their homeland, and managed the delicate matter of Japanese compensation grants to Japan's former prisoners of war. In 1985 it was the ICRC representatives who escorted American hostages to Syria after their release by their Lebanese captors.

In his Nobel lecture of 1963, Leopold Boissier, speaking for the ICRC, pointed out that the Red Cross principle of promoting "a lasting peace amongst all peoples" had first been promulgated in 1961. The next year, when war threatened between the United States and the Soviet Union over the building of missile sites in Cuba, the United Nations asked the ICRC if it would send thirty inspectors to make sure no ships carrying atomic weapons reached Cuban ports. Mindful of the 1961 declaration, Boissier declared, the ICRC was prepared "to step beyond the limits of its traditional mission" and to accept the assignment. In the end, the conflict was resolved by other means. The incident showed, however, that the ICRC is always ready to take an unprecedented humanitarian initiative. It has, of course, not neglected its old functions. For example, in the Iran-Iraq War, the ICRC has visited prisoners of war in both countries; in 1986 there was an exchange of almost 2 million Red Cross family messages between the two sides. Moreover, the Central Tracing Agency, the successor to the Central Prisoner of War Agency of World War II, is still collecting information on prisoners, internees, and displaced persons, reestablishing links with their families, tracing missing people, and providing documents and travel papers.

In days of heightening international tensions and conflicts, with the United Nations divided on political and ideological lines, such a body as the ICRC of proven impartiality and integrity may well have some unusual opportunities for peacemaking. Whatever new challenge may come its way, the ICRC can stand on its long and distinguished record of demonstrating in the most trying circumstances the bonds of our common humanity.

BIBLIOGRAPHY

See bibliographies for Henry Dunant (1901) and International Committee of the Red Cross (1917).

1964
Martin Luther King, Jr. (1929–68)

United States

Baptist minister; leader of nonviolent movement for civil rights.

The 1964 prize was given to Martin Luther King, Jr., who was, after Ralph Bunche, the second black American to win the award. He was, said Chairman Jahn of the committee, "the first person in the Western world to have shown us that a struggle can be waged without violence. He is the first to make the message of brotherly love a reality in the course of his struggle, and he has brought this message to all men, to all nations and races."

King was born Michael Luther King, Jr., the second child and first son of a Baptist minister in Atlanta, Georgia. When the boy was six years old, two white playmates were told not to play with him, and his mother had to explain about segregation: it was a social condition, and he was as good as anyone else. The father lifted the boy's vision higher: he told him about Martin Luther, the great leader of the Reformation, and said that from now on they would both be named after him.

Martin Luther King, Jr., a very bright student, began to show his oratorical ability as early as his high school years. At fifteen he entered Morehouse College in Atlanta, the distinguished black institution, and decided to become a minister. As he said later, "I'm the son of a preacher . . . my grandfather was a preacher, my great-grandfather was a preacher, my only brother is a preacher, my daddy's brother is a preacher, so I didn't have much choice." During his senior year, when he was eighteen, King was ordained and elected assistant pastor of the Ebenezer Baptist Church, which had been established by his grandfather and where his father was then the minister.

He graduated at nineteen in sociology and went on to Crozier Theological Seminary in Chester, Pennsylvania, where he was one of only six black students in a student body of about one hundred. In three years he received the degree of bachelor of divinity, having been president of the senior class and valedictorian. With a Crozier fellowship, he entered Boston University in 1951 to study for the doctorate.

While at Crozier he first heard of Gandhi's nonviolent movement that had won independence for India, and he began to think of how such methods might be used by the black people in America. It appeared to him that Gandhi "was probably the first person to lift the love ethic of Jesus above mere interaction between individuals to a powerful effective social force on a large scale."

In his studies at Boston University, King was introduced to the leading theological ideas of the day, and he also had the opportunity to follow philosophy courses at Harvard. In Boston he met the beautiful and talented Coretta Scott, who was studying to be a concert singer at the New England Conservatory of Music, but who gave up her career to become his wife. They were married in 1953 and were to have four children. Coretta was always a great support for him, and after his death she carried on his work, becoming a national leader in her own right.

In 1954, after King had completed the course work for his Ph.D., he had job offers from colleges and churches in the North, but he felt that his place was in the South, where he could do more for his people. When he decided to answer the call from Dexter Avenue Baptist Church in Montgomery, Alabama, however, Coretta had reservations. She had grown up in Alabama only eighty miles from there, and she knew that Montgomery was still living in hallowed memories of its past as the first capital of the Confederacy and that they would encounter deep racial prejudices. Later she came to feel that the choice of Montgomery "was an inevitable part of a greater plan for our lives."

King officially entered upon his pastor's duties in Montgomery in September 1954. The next year he received his Ph.D. from Boston University, in November their first child was born, and a few weeks later the series of events began in Montgomery that propelled him into a greater role than he could ever have foreseen.

On 1 December 1955, Rosa Parks, a forty-year-old seamstress, refused to give up her seat in a bus to a white man as she was ordered to do by the driver. "I was just plain tired, and my feet hurt," she explained later. For this she was arrested and charged with disobeying the city's segregation ordinance.

The black community was outraged, and their pastors quickly organized a one-day boycott of the buses in protest. This was so successful that it was decided to continue the boycott until demands to desegregate the buses were met. For leadership the pastors turned to their young colleague of the Dexter Avenue Church, who had already won a reputation among them for his powerful preaching. They felt that he had not been in town long enough to make enemies and could easily relocate to another city if things went wrong. Consequently, Martin Luther King, Jr., became president of the committee to conduct the boycott, which was hopefully called the Montgomery Improvement Association. He was then not quite twenty-seven.

In his first speech, to a mass meeting on 5 December, King announced the nonviolent principles that were to guide the civil rights movement from then on. In the struggle for freedom and justice to which they were called, he said, "Our actions must be guided by the deepest principles of the Christian faith." He concluded: "If you will protest courageously, and yet with dignity and Christian love, future historians will say, 'There lived a great people—a black people—who injected new meaning and dignity into the veins of civilization.' This is our challenge and our overwhelming responsibility."

In this spirit the boycott effort persisted, despite bitter efforts to break it through all kinds of harassment, abuse, and persecution. For over a year the black community of Montgomery stayed out of the public buses, walking, car-pooling, and using all possible means of transit, until finally the United States Supreme Court ruled that segregation on the buses was unconstitutional. King was the target for arrests, constant anonymous death threats, and a night-bombing of his home.

The Montgomery bus boycott drew worldwide attention to the racial struggle in the South and to King. The movement for racial justice spread beyond Montgomery, and King became the leader of the Southern Christian Leadership Conference, which coordinated the major civil rights activities. Throughout the South blacks rallied at King's call, fighting segregation through marches, demonstrations, sit-ins, and other nonviolent methods. King was always at the forefront, and he was beaten, arrested, and jailed. In one prison cell he wrote his moving "Letter from a Birmingham Jail," explaining to some white ministers who counseled patience "why we can't wait."

He traveled thousands of miles, in the North as well as in the South, making speeches, raising money, appealing for support from political, labor, and business leaders. In 1963, when 250,000 persons, 75,000 of them white, took part in a march in Washington to urge Congress to pass civil rights legislation, King addressed them from the Lincoln Memorial in his most famous speech, "I Have a Dream," presenting his vision of an America living out the true meaning of its egalitarian creed. Great steps forward were taken when Congress passed the Civil Rights Act of 1964 and the Voting Rights Act of 1965, but realization of the dream was still far off.

King had not sought the leadership in Montgomery, but felt that God had directed him to take it on, and in the following years he continued to feel that he had no choice, despite the pain and suffering he endured. He sometimes thought wistfully of a peaceful life in a teaching post somewhere, but he put such thoughts aside. The public commendation that he received only drove him to devote more of his energies to the cause he served. He lived with danger and had premonitions of an early death, but he carried on, firm in the faith that he was meant to.

Early in 1964 King learned that he had been nominated for the Nobel Peace Prize by Swedish parliamentary deputies, and in the summer a request came from Oslo for documentation, indicating that his candidacy was being seriously considered. Possibly with an eye on the prize, arrangements were made for King to have an audience with Pope Paul VI and to visit West Berlin in September. But King expected that the award would be given to someone who was involved with international peace activities.

He returned from Berlin exhausted and checked into a hospital for a physical examination, mainly for a few days rest. The next morning Coretta telephoned to wake him up with the news that he had won the prize. Sleepily, he thought he was still dreaming. Once awake, he called a press conference at the hospital, but first met with his wife and closest associates, explaining to them that the prize represented the international moral recognition of their whole movement, not his personal part in it. He asked them to join him in prayer for strength to work harder for their goal. At the press conference he announced that he would give the prize money of approximately fifty-four thousand dollars to the movement, which he arranged to do on his return from Oslo.

Feeling that the award had been won by them all, King took with him to Oslo a number of the other leaders, and the party of thirty represented the largest group that had ever accompanied a prizewinner. Coretta remembers that they had quite a time getting her husband into his formal dress for the ceremony. He bridled especially at the "ridiculous" ascot tie, vowing "never to wear one of these things again." He never did.

All the same, King cut a handsome figure when he stepped to the rostrum to deliver his speech of acceptance, at thirty-five the youngest of all those who had received the prize. He was shorter than the audience had imagined, but as his rich baritone filled the hall with its throbbing cadences, he grew taller in their eyes.

He declared that he was accepting the award on behalf of the civil rights movement, considering it "a profound recognition that nonviolence is the answer to the crucial political and racial questions of our time—the need for man to overcome oppression without resorting to violence and oppression." He continued:

> Civilization and violence are antithetical concepts. Negroes of the United States, following the people of India, have demonstrated that nonviolence is not sterile passivity, but a powerful moral force which makes for social transformation. Sooner or later all the peoples of the world will have to discover a way to live together in peace, and thereby transform this pending cosmic elegy into a creative psalm of brotherhood. If this is to be achieved man must evolve for all human conflict a method which rejects revenge, aggression and retaliation. The foundation of such a method is love. . . .
>
> I accept this award today with an abiding faith in America and an audacious faith in the future of mankind.

In his Nobel lecture King said that the most pressing problem confronting humanity today was "the poverty of the spirit which stands in glaring contrast to our scientific and technological abundance." This was apparent in the three evils that had grown out of man's "ethical infantilism," racial injustice, poverty, and war, which were all intertwined. Nonviolence "seeks to redeem the spiritual and moral lag . . . to secure moral ends through moral means." It was a "weapon unique in history, which cuts without wounding and ennobles the man who wields it."

Jahn had already cited King's earlier statement that "the choice is either nonviolence or nonexistence." Now King emphasized that peace was a positive concept and called for "an all-embracing and unconditional love for all men. When I speak of love, I am speaking of that force which all of the great religions have seen as the supreme unifying principle of life. Love is somehow the key that unlocks the door which leads to ultimate reality."

King left Oslo with a new and overwhelming sense of what the world was expecting of him. At his hero's welcome in New York he expressed his own intensified feeling of personal responsibility in speaking of individuals who "will hold the torch firmly for others because they have overcome the threat of jail and death. They will hold this torch high without faltering because they have weathered the battering storms of persecution and withstood the temptation to retreat to a more quiet and serene life."

After Oslo, King attacked more vigorously all three of the evils of which he had spoken. He took a public stand against the American war in Vietnam, antagonizing political leaders who had helped with civil rights legislation and alienating former associates who thought he should keep to the one issue. He lobbied for federal assistance to the poor, insisting that the misery of poverty knows no racial distinctions, and he planned a "Poor People's March" on Washington for 20 April 1968. He was not to live to see it. On 4 April, while in Memphis, Tennessee, helping striking garbage workers, Martin Luther King, Jr., was assassinated.

Only a few months before, in a sermon at Ebenezer Baptist Church, he had spoken of his own death and funeral. He wanted no long eulogy:

> Say that I was a drum major for justice. Say that I was a drum major for peace. That I was a drum major for righteousness. And all of the other shallow things will not matter. I won't have any money to leave behind. I won't have the fine and luxurious things of life to leave behind. But I just want to leave a committed life behind.

In 1986, by act of Congress, the United States began the annual celebration of the birthday of Martin Luther King, Jr., in January as a national holiday.

BIBLIOGRAPHY

Primary Sources

King, Martin Luther, Jr. *Stride Toward Freedom: The Montgomery Story.* New York: Perennial Library, Harper, 1958. A graphic account, including the first speech to the mass meeting.

———. *A Testament of Hope: The Essential Writings of Martin Luther King, Jr.* Edited by James Melvin Washington. San Francisco: Harper, 1986. Organized by topic and chronologically. Includes famous sermons and speeches and a bibliography.

———. *The Trumpet of Conscience.* New York: Harper & Row, 1967. Five lectures broadcast in Canada; topics include peace and nonviolence.

———. *Why We Can't Wait.* New York: Harper & Row, 1963. Includes the "Letter from Birmingham Jail."

Secondary Sources

Garrow, David J. *Bearing the Cross: Martin Luther King, Jr., and the Southern Leadership Conference.* New York: Morrow, 1986. Pulitzer Prize–winning biography. Includes a perceptive discussion of King and the Nobel Peace Prize.

King, Coretta Scott. *My Life with Martin Luther King, Jr.* New York: Holt, Rinehart & Winston, 1969. An important memoir by King's widow.

Levering, Ralph. "Martin Luther King, Jr.: The Challenge of Inclusive Peacemaking." In *Peace Heroes in Twentieth-Century America.* Edited by Charles DeBenedetti. Bloomington: Indiana University Press, 1986, pp. 198–226.

"King, Martin Luther, Jr." In *MPL.*

Lewis, David L. *King, a Critical Biography.* 2d ed. Urbana: University of Illinois Press, 1978.

Lokos, Lionel. *House Divided; The Life and Legacy of Martin Luther King.* New Rochelle, N.Y.: Arlington House, 1968. By a critic of nonviolence.

Oates, Stephen B. *Let the Trumpet Sound.* New York: Harper & Row, 1982. Sympathetic biography. Well recommended.

Pyatt, Sherman E. *Martin Luther King, Jr.: An Annotated Bibliography.* New York: Greenwood, 1986. Most comprehensive bibliography of works by and about King. Lists articles on King and the Peace Prize on pp. 62–64.

1965
United Nations Children's Fund

Established by the United Nations in 1946.

The 1965 prize went to the United Nations Children's Fund (UNICEF), the UN organization charged with care for the world's children, for its "promotion of brotherhood among the nations." The United Nations Children's Emergency Fund was established by the UN General Assembly on 11 December 1946 to meet the desperate needs of children in postwar Europe for food, clothing, and medicine. Up to 1950 this was the focus of its operations. Clothing was distributed to 5 million children in twelve countries, 8 million were vaccinated against tuberculosis, and millions received a daily supplemental meal.

As the emergency in Europe ended, it became clear that the needs of children in the developing countries were not only very serious but likely to persist for a long time. In 1950 the General Assembly directed UNICEF to use its resources "particularly in undeveloped countries," and in 1953 the United Nations dropped the *Emergency* from its name and made the Children's Fund a permanent organization.

In 1959 the United Nations further clarified the purposes of UNICEF when it adopted the Declaration of the Rights of the Child, which stressed children's right to maternal protection, health, adequate food, shelter, and education. Moreover, the declaration stated that "the child shall be brought up in a spirit of understanding, tolerance, friendship among peoples and universal brotherhood, and in the full consciousness that his energy and talents should be devoted to the service of his fellow men."

Accepting the prize for UNICEF in 1965 was Henry R. Labouisse, the former American diplomat and UN relief official who had succeeded the first executive director, Maurice Pate. Labouisse used some very human statistics to describe the needs of children in the developing countries, explaining the odds that confront the *average* child in such regions:

> They are four to one against his receiving any medical attention, at birth or afterwards. Even if he survives until school age, the chances are two to one that he will get no education at all; if he does get into school, the chances are about four to one that he will not complete the elementary grades. Almost certainly he will have to work for a living by the time he is twelve. He will work to eat—to eat badly and not enough. And his life will, on the average, end in about forty years.

To meet these needs, Labouisse declared, UNICEF was helping governments with their own services to children, contributing such things as "medicines and medical equipment, jeeps and bicycles for public health and community development workers, science kits and other equipment for pilot schools, tools for vocational training, pipes and pumps for village sanitation, the stipends to pay for the training of teachers—or of teachers' teachers." The governments, expected to match UNICEF's contribution, were actually contributing more than two and a half times as much as their UNICEF grant.

The most important meaning of the Nobel award, said Labouisse, was "the solemn recognition that the welfare of today's children is inseparably linked with the peace of tomorrow's world. The sufferings and privations to which I have referred do not ennoble; they frustrate and embitter. The longer the world tolerates the slow war of attrition which poverty and ignorance now wage against 800 million children in the developing countries, the more likely it becomes that our hope for lasting peace will be the ultimate casualty."

The Nobel lecture was delivered by Zena Harman of Israel, who chaired UNICEF's executive board. She said that the prize money would be used to help set up a scholarship fund in honor of Maurice Pate, the first executive director, who had been UNICEF's guiding spirit during its first eighteen years: "A man of compassion, he was imbued with the love of people; he had infinite faith in them and saw good in everyone." He selected his staff not only for their professional qualifications but for "special qualities of heart, a willingness to subordinate self to a labor of love," and a sense that they were "entrusted with a task of sacred dimension."

Mrs. Harman underlined the financial needs of UNICEF. In 1964 121 member governments of the United Nations were contributing regularly to the budget, and private groups and individuals were raising some $6 million. Yet that year's total came to no more than $35 million, and UNICEF could not undertake viable new projects and had to put a ceiling on allocations. "It is an agonizing predicament," she said, "to know that millions of children will die each year, who might have lived were it not for lack of funds." She contrasted this parsimoniousness to the vast sums the nations of the world were spending on armaments. Could they not agree to spend a fraction of their arms budget for the children? "Perhaps each abortive disarmament conference would set itself a penalty—a contribution to UNICEF, the equivalent cost of one submarine or a dozen fighter planes."

Although this was not to be, in the years subsequent to the prize UNICEF has made important progress. In 1982 it began predicting that a "child survival revolution" in the third world was a possibility, and three years later in its annual report on the

"State of the World's Children," UNICEF could declare that in some forty countries the revolution was well under way, and child mortality rates had decreased.

This has been due to the willingness of governments to follow UNICEF's proposals. Basic to this progress has been the development of a simple and cheap salt-and-sugar packet that parents can administer to children suffering from dehydration caused by diarrhea, the single largest cause of child deaths in the third world. In 1985 200 million packets were distributed. The three other chief measures UNICEF has promoted have been breast-feeding of babies, regular checking of weight to detect malnutrition, and immunization against measles, diphtheria, tetanus, whooping cough, polio, and tuberculosis. The organization recognizes that childhood malnutrition cannot be conquered without long-term changes, such as land redistribution and fuller employment, but short-term measures have already brought significant improvements.

There has also been an important rise in UNICEF's income, which must derive from voluntary contributions from governments, organizations, and individuals. By the 1980s UNICEF was receiving a total of almost $400 million. Over $16 million of this came from the sale of greeting cards and calendars, to which leading artists of the world contributed their talents and which were sold through UNICEF's national committees in more than thirty countries.

The plight of disadvantaged and suffering children has always been an appealing cause. Many special benefits have been held for UNICEF, including an all-star soccer game at Giants Stadium in New Jersey in 1982, which was attended by almost seventy-seven thousand and watched on television by an estimated audience of one billion. Many celebrities have also volunteered their efforts, foremost among them the late Danny Kaye and Liv Ullmann.

But the unmet needs of the children of the developing countries are still staggering, and there are always the unexpected emergencies, such as the famine of the early eighties in Africa. In 1982 the UNICEF Executive Board made a formal appeal to the second Special Session on disarmament to do what it could to reduce armaments so that a part of the savings could be used to meet the minimum requirements of adequate nutrition, safe water, primary health care, and suitable education for all children.

The Maurice Pate Memorial Fund has long since exhausted the Nobel prize money, but it has been replenished from other sources, and each year a grant is made to an institution in the developing world that has done an outstanding job in training personnel to work with children and mothers. Even more important, in the years since Maurice Pate's death, the UNICEF administration has continued to give priority to those "special qualities of heart" and to remain faithful to what he called its sacred mission.

BIBLIOGRAPHY

Primary Sources

UNICEF. *The State of the World's Children 1988.* New York: Oxford University Press, 1988.

———. *UNICEF for All the World's Children: A Pictorial Record.* New York: UNICEF, 1952.

Secondary Sources

Heilbroner, Robert L. *Mankind's Children: The Story of UNICEF.* New York: Public Affairs Committee, 1959.

"The Peace Prize." *New Yorker* 4 (6 November 1965): 44–47. A visit to the UNICEF offices after the announcement of the prize.

Sicault, Georges, ed. *The Needs of Children: A Survey of the Needs of Children in the Developing Countries.* Glencoe, Ill.: Free Press, 1963. UNICEF reports, published for UNICEF.

Yates, Elizabeth. *Rainbow Round the World: A Story of UNICEF.* Indianapolis: Bobbs-Merrill, 1954.

1968
René-Samuel Cassin
(1887–1976)

France

Champion of universal human rights; lawyer, law professor and scholar; educational administrator; founder of national and international associations of disabled war veterans; French delegate to League of Nations, UN General Assembly, and UNESCO; member of high judicial bodies in France, president of Court of Arbitration at The Hague and of the European Court of Human Rights.

In the UN International Human Rights Year, twenty years to the day after the approval by the UN General Assembly of the Declaration of Human Rights on 10 December 1948, the Nobel Committee gave the prize to René-Samuel Cassin for his contribution to that landmark international development and for his continuing efforts for the protection of human rights. Cassin took a leading role in the collective effort that produced the declaration and subsequently contributed to its implementation in the Council of Europe, the one regional organization in the world where the principles of the declaration became the basis of an international judicial institution, the European Court of Human Rights.

Cassin was born in Bayonne in southern France, the son of a Jewish merchant. As a schoolboy he showed great academic promise, and made a brilliant record at the University of Aix-en-Provence and the Faculty of Law at Paris, where in 1914, at the age of twenty-seven, he received his doctorate in juridical, political, and economic sciences.

He began to practice law in Paris, but with the coming of the war in August 1914, Cassin had to leave his law books for the army. In 1916 he was severely wounded when a piece of shrapnel pierced his abdomen and was taken to the ward of hopeless cases in the hospital. By an extraordinary coincidence, his mother was serving as a nurse in that hospital, and she persuaded a surgeon to attempt the operation that saved her son's life.

Invalided home, Cassin married and became professor of law at his old University of Aix. His career in the law was distinguished. From Aix he moved to Lille in 1920, and then in 1929 he was appointed to the chair of fiscal and civil law at the University of Paris, where he taught until retirement in 1960 at the age of seventy-three. Through his writings and lectures in France and abroad, he enjoyed an international reputation among legal scholars.

The impact of Cassin's war experiences turned him toward international and humanitarian activities. Almost immediately after the Armistice, he took up the cause of victims of the war—disabled soldiers, war orphans, war widows—working for legislation that would provide adequate government care for them. In 1918 he founded the French Federation of Disabled War Veterans, serving as president and then honorary president until 1940. Beginning in 1921 he arranged conferences with war veterans of other nations, including former enemy countries, and in 1926 he established an international organization of disabled veterans. These associations of former combatants were strong supporters of peace and disarmament, and Cassin himself worked for disarmament as a delegate of France to the Assembly of the League of Nations and its conference on disarmament.

When Germany invaded France in 1940, Cassin was one of the first prominent civilians to join Gen. Charles de Gaulle in London in the effort to free France from its German invaders and their French collaborators of Vichy. Cassin became minister of justice in the government-in-exile, and he drew up the agreement with Winston Churchill according to which the French forces were to be independent and not under British orders. He next became commissioner of public instruction and represented France in the wartime meetings of the Allied ministers of education. He was also in position to make sure that the principle of human rights was included in the Atlantic Charter. For his services to the Free French, Cassin was deprived of his French citizenship by the Vichy government and sentenced to death in absentia.

After the war Cassin was given high positions in educational administration and in the judiciary of France, and he made his international contribution as delegate to the UN General Assembly and as a founding delegate to UNESCO and one of the authors of its charter. It was, however, in the UN Commission on Human Rights that Cassin made his most important contribution. The UN Charter had declared one of the purposes of the organization to be the respect for and promotion of human rights. This marked a new development in international relations, since up to this time a state's treatment of its nationals was considered its own business and any interference an encroachment upon its sovereignty. The war against Hitlerism, however, was not only to resist German armed aggression but to free the world from Nazi atrocities and brutal violations of human rights. Especially after the facts of the Holocaust became known, it was only natural that the international organization that emerged from this war would create a Commission on Human Rights. Thus when the UN General Assembly met in 1946, it asked the commission to prepare a Declaration of Human Rights and an international convention by which states would be obligated to respect these rights.

Eleanor Roosevelt was the first chair of the commission and Cassin was the vice-chairman. Mrs. Aase Lionaes, who made the presentation to Cassin in behalf of the Nobel Committee, had been a Norwegian delegate to the UN General Assembly when it discussed the document proposed by the commission, and she told how Cassin had held a key position in formulating the concepts of the declaration. She said he had served as mediator between the Western emphasis upon civil and political rights and the Eastern European concern for economic, social, and cultural rights. She felt that the bridging of "many minds, many religions, many ideologies, and many hearts . . . was primarily the engineering feat of René Cassin."

Cassin is often spoken of as "the principle author" of the declaration, but historians are not agreed that he deserves top billing since so many others made important contributions. There is no denying the fact, however, that he had been one of the world's most tireless and authoritative champions of human rights, and the Nobel Committee could not have found a more appropriate recipient of the prize in International Human Rights Year.

In his Nobel lecture, Cassin declared that the declaration

> constituted a historical event of the first magnitude. It is the first document of an ethical sort that organized humanity has ever adopted. . . . It proclaims as principles the whole body of rights and options without whose exercise man cannot fully realize his physical, moral, and intellectual individuality.
>
> The other salient characteristic of the Declaration is its universality: it applies to all human beings without any discrimination whatever; it also applies to all territories, whatever their economic or political regime.

Cassin recounted how it took the commission six more years before it could submit to the General Assembly the conventions for implementation of the declaration—the two covenants, one covering civil and political rights, the other concerning economic, social, and cultural rights. Then the General Assembly in turn took another thirteen years to consider these, since some member states resisted implementation measures that they regarded as encroachments upon their sovereignty.

Finally in 1966 the covenants were unanimously approved, with provisions for enforcement somewhat weakened. In his speech, Cassin deplored the fact, however, that they had not yet been ratified, and he appealed to the peoples of Europe to give a "magnificent example" to the world by acting in concert to ratify the covenants. But in spite of his plea, ratification by all 121 member nations of the United Nations was to take twelve more years. The last original member of the Council to ratify the European convention was Cassin's own country of France, in 1974.

After his term as vice-chairman of the UN Commission on Human Rights expired, Cassin served as vice-president and then president of the European Court of Human Rights. He had always conceived of the principles of the declaration as universal, but his experience with the European Court convinced him of the efficacy of regional agreements in applying these principles.

Cassin used the prize money to establish the International Institute of Human Rights at Strasbourg. It was with this objective in mind that he had actively promoted his own candidacy for the prize. He died in 1976 in Paris at the age of eighty-nine.

BIBLIOGRAPHY

Primary Sources

Cassin, René. "La Declaration universelle et la mise en oeuvre des droits de l'homme." In Academy of International Law, The Hague, *Receuil des Cours 1951*. Vol. 79. Leyden: Sijthoff, 1952, 2:239–367.

———. "How the Charter on Human Rights Was Born." *UNESCO Courier* 21 (January 1968): 4–6.

———. *René Cassin Amicorum Discipulorumque Liber*. 3 vols. Paris: Pedone, 1969–72. The first volume contains a bibliography of Cassin's writings after 1940 on human rights.

Secondary Sources

Agi, Mark. *De l'idée d'universalité comme fondatrice du concept des droits de l'homme, d'après la vie et l'oeuvre de René Cassin*. Antibes: Editions Alp'Azur, 1980. Originally a doctoral dissertation at the University of Nice, this work relates Cassin to political developments.

———. *René Cassin: Fantassin des droits de l'homme*. Paris: Plon, 1979.

"Cassin, René." In *BDI*.

Kiss, Alexandre. "L'Institut international des droits de l'homme." *Revue internationale de la Croix-rouge* 69, no. 768 (November-December 1987): 689–95.

1969
International Labor Organization

Established in 1919 by the Treaty of Versailles; became a specialized agency of the United Nations in 1946.

The Nobel Committee named the International Labor Organization (ILO) for the prize in 1969, the year of its fiftieth birthday. It was the only international organization associated with the League of Nations that outlived it. In fact, it was established in Geneva before the League. The ILO set up its secretariat in Geneva in July 1920, moving into its own building in 1926, whereas the League transferred its secretariat from London to Geneva in November 1920.

Aase Lionaes, in making the presentation as chair of the committee, recalled its founding principle that peace must be based upon social justice and declared, "There are few organizations that have succeeded to the extent that the ILO has, in translating into action the fundamental moral idea on which it is based."

The ILO was founded in 1919 as a consequence of pressures from the trade union and socialist movements. The Allied leaders who convened in Paris to make the peace settlement after the First World War faced a Europe in turmoil, with a great revolution having occurred in Russia and threatening to spread westward. The diplomats agreed it was important to satisfy the more moderate leaders of the workers, lest the extremists took over.

At the same time, the creators of the ILO invented an international technique whereby the workers' demands for social changes were balanced by forces more representative of the status quo. This was the principle of tripartism, according to which each member state sent to the annual conference of the ILO one representative of its workers, one representative of the employers, and two government representatives. The same principle was followed in the elections of delegates from the conference to the governing body, the Executive Council, which appointed the secretary-general and oversaw the implementation of the policies adopted by the conferences.

Another international novelty enabled the ILO to take initiatives that bypassed conventional diplomatic channels: conventions and recommendations agreed to by a two-thirds vote in the conference were to be directly submitted to the appropriate bodies of the member states for ratification. In the fifty years from 1919 to 1969, 128 conventions and 132 recommendations were so submitted. Of the 128, Norway had ratified 63, which placed her seventh highest among the 121 members.

In the first twenty-five years these agreements dealt mostly with improving the conditions of labor by setting standards in important areas: reduction of the length of the working day, equal pay for equal work, safety provisions in the workplace, health insurance, and the like.

In the second twenty-five years there was a new emphasis, heralded in the so-called Declaration of Philadelphia, approved at the wartime conference held in that city in 1944, which declared "poverty anywhere is a danger to prosperity everywhere." Whereas the previous effort had been mainly to set international labor standards that would protect workers in industrialized states, the new thrust was to promote economic development in the third world. In this effort the ILO cooperated with other UN agencies, principally the UN Development Program. In 1969 it launched the World Employment Program, to attack the causes of poverty by helping to generate remunerative employment.

This new direction reflected the changing membership of the ILO. In 1919, there were 29 member states, mostly European. On its fiftieth anniversary, its membership had grown to 121 states, with the balance having shifted to the new states that emerged in former colonial areas.

Receiving the prize for the ILO was Director-General David A. Morse, the American lawyer and former government official who had assumed that office in 1948 and was to remain until 1970. Morse declared that the goal of social justice had "proved to be a dynamic concept," and the ILO would continue "to seek to promote social evolution by peaceful means, to identify emerging social needs and problems and threats to social peace, and to stimulate action to deal with such problems."

Morse stated that the ultimate objective of the ILO was "the elimination of poverty, hardship and privation which weigh so heavily upon the dispossessed peoples of this earth." The ILO was "central to the international effort to raise their standards of living, to improve their living and working conditions, and to secure to them fundamental human rights, to the end that they may take their place in society as free, dignified and self-governing people." This would lay the basis for world peace. "But," said Morse, "we have no illusions about the difficulties which stand in our way. . . . We are only at the beginning of our task."

In the years subsequent to its receiving the prize, the ILO has continued along the same lines. Although its formal structure has remained the same, it has expanded far beyond its original form in membership and activities. By the 1980s there were 150 member states, and its major program areas, global in scope, included not only the improvement of working conditions and the strengthening of industrial relations among governments, employers, and workers but also the promotion of world employment and the advancement of human rights in social and labor fields. To its original instruments of action—standard setting and research and publishing—has been added a vast new dimension of technical cooperation with the developing world. The number of international labor conventions and recommendations adopted by ILO conferences is now over 300, including more than 150 conventions and more than 160 recommendations. Since 1919 over 5,000 ratifications of conventions have been registered.

The ILO has further developed its unique international machinery to monitor these agreements. The procedure involves three steps: first, the signatory governments submit regular reports as to how they are carrying out the provisions they have signed; then these reports are examined by independent committees composed of such eminent jurists as Chief Justice Earl Warren of the U.S. Supreme Court; and finally there is a more general review at the annual conference by a tripartite Committee on the Application of Conventions and Recommendations. This session is held in public, with the participation of representatives of the states concerned in each case selected for consideration.

No government can be compelled to comply, but the pressure of world public opinion has proven an effective spur to action. Since 1964 the observations of the ILO's supervisory bodies have resulted in more than fifteen hundred changes in national laws and practices to bring them into conformity with ratified conventions.

The ILO has paid special attention to complaints about workers' freedom of association, which have unfortunately become more frequent in recent years. On receiving a complaint, the ILO may send a representative to investigate, on the invitation or with the permission of the government. Israel, for example, has invited ILO representatives to make a number of visits to the occupied area of the West Bank, asking them only to "report fairly." And the Polish government even permitted an ILO representative to visit Lech Wałesa in 1982, when he was being held in detention after the suppression of the Solidarity trade union movement.

The ILO followed an unusual course with its prize money of $72,000. Instead of expending the funds for some project, it placed them in a special fund, making a few small grants, but letting the bulk of the money accumulate until the amount was large enough to make possible significant grants from the annual income. By 1987 the fund had reached $300,000, and discussions were proceeding on how the interest could be used to support efforts of disadvantaged groups to achieve economic independence and social progress.

In the early 1980s the small secretariat of 1920, which had grown to five hundred officials after World War II, now comprised a staff of nearly eighteen hundred people, plus some eight hundred experts in technical assistance scattered over the world. The International Labor Office outgrew the modest building on the shore of Lake Geneva that had been its headquarters since 1926 and is now housed in a grand edifice not far from the buildings of the European offices of the United Nations.

It has changed in other ways as well—in the composition of its membership, in having raised its sights far beyond the European horizon, in its varied programs and projects—but it has never wavered in its basic commitment to social justice as the foundation of international peace.

BIBLIOGRAPHY

Secondary Sources

Alcock, Antony. *History of the International Labor Organization.* New York: Octagon, 1971.

Blanchard, Francis. "Improving Worker Rights through Global Pressure." *Christian Science Monitor,* 27 April 1987.

Butler, Harold. *The Lost Peace.* New York: Harcourt, 1942. Memoirs of the top ILO official who was director, 1932 to 1938.

Galenson, Walter. *The International Labor Organization: An American View.* Madison: University of Wisconsin Press, 1981.

Haas, Ernst B. *Beyond the Nation-State: Functionalism and International Organization.* Stanford, Calif.: Stanford University Press, 1964. The ILO as a test case of the theory of integration.

———. *Human Rights and International Action: The Case of Freedom of Association.* Stanford, Calif.: Stanford University Press, 1970.

Jenks, Wilfred. *Social Justice in the Law of Nations: The ILO Impact after Fifty Years.* London: Oxford University Press, 1970.

———. *Social Policy in a Changing World: The ILO Response.* Geneva: ILO, 1976. Selected speeches. Jenks was director general 1970–73.

Johnston, G. A. *The International Labour Organisation: Its Work for Social and Economic Progress.* London: Europa, 1970.

Landy, E. A. *The Effectiveness of International Supervision: Thirty Years of ILO Experience.* Dobbs Ferry, N.Y.: Oceana, 1966.

Morse, David A. *The Origin and Evolution of the ILO and Its Role in the World Community.* Ithaca, N.Y.: New York State School of Industrial and

Labor Relations, 1969. Lectures. Morse was director general 1948–70.

Shotwell, James T., ed. *The Origins of the International Labor Organization.* 2 vols. New York: Columbia University Press, 1934. The standard work. The history is in vol. 1 and the basic documents in vol. 2.

1970

Norman Borlaug (1914–)

United States

Agricultural scientist; "father of the Green Revolution."

The 1970 award went to Norman Borlaug, the third scientist to win the prize, after Lord Boyd-Orr and Linus Pauling. Like Boyd-Orr, the nutritionist and first head of the UN Food and Agriculture Organization, Borlaug has been concerned with the great human right of freedom from hunger. In applying his scientific talents to increase agricultural production, he had had such impressive successes that Aase Lionaes could declare in her presentation speech that the committee was giving him the award because, "more than any other single person in this age, he has helped to provide bread for a hungry world. We have made this choice in the hope that providing bread will also give the world peace."

To the critics who felt that the committee might be stretching its mandate in giving the prize to a scientist who could be considered to be working for peace only indirectly. Mrs. Lionaes quoted Nobel's words. His prizes, he had said, should go to those who "shall have conferred the greatest benefit on mankind," and she asked if anyone could be more qualified than one whose work had made such a difference in the meeting of a basic human need.

The committee obviously took satisfaction in recognizing a son of Norway. Borlaug's parents were Norwegian immigrants, and he had been born in the little town of Cresco, Iowa, in what was known as the state's "little Norway." His father farmed fifty-six acres outside the town, and Borlaug grew up among neighbors who believed in hard work and virtuous living. Later he said of them, "Whatever I have become, these people are a part of it. They taught me to give the best that is within me."

Borlaug graduated from the local high school at the age of eighteen as captain of the football team. He might have stayed on the family farm had his grandfather not insisted that he go to college. He worked his way through the University of Minnesota, distinguishing himself both in academics and as a champion wrestler, graduating with a B.S. degree in forestry. He then entered graduate studies, supporting himself with forestry jobs on the way to his Ph.D. in plant pathology, which he received in 1941, when he was twenty-seven. He had by then married the former Margaret G. Gibson, and they were to have two children.

Borlaug's first job in his field was with the E. I. du Pont de Nemours chemical company, studying the effects of new chemicals on plants. He could have settled down in a comfortable life, but in 1944 he was invited by the Rockefeller Foundation to join a team of agricultural scientists to be sent "to export the United States agricultural revolution to Mexico," at the request of the Mexican Ministry of Agriculture. Borlaug accepted, and he had found his life's work.

At that time corn was still the staple bread grain in Mexico, having been cultivated by the Indians long before the Spaniards arrived. The Spaniards had brought wheat, but it was still being cultivated by primitive methods, and the yield was small. There was only one Mexican agronomist who was spending any time in wheat research, and there was no research going on to control diseases, insects, and weeds.

Borlaug found that even when improved methods of fertilization and irrigation were introduced, the tall, thin-stemmed varieties of Mexican wheat would become top-heavy and break. He thereupon set about developing a stockier, short-stemmed dwarf wheat, highly adaptable to varying conditions and producing a rich yield. It was characteristic of him that instead of growing only one experimental crop a year, he grew two, a summer crop just south of the border and a winter crop near Mexico City.

He was no mere theoretical or laboratory scientist "chasing irrelevant academic butterflies," as he called it. All his research was production-oriented, and he worked in the fields along with his staff. At first his Mexican assistants had protested that educated men did not work with their hands. "It's the only way I know how to work," Borlaug retorted. "This wheat will talk to you if you listen, but you can't hear it if you sit under a tree and watch other people doing the work."

It was while he was working in one of his experimental wheat fields that he first heard about his Nobel Peace Prize. Margaret Borlaug had to drive some fifty miles from their home in Mexico City to tell him the news. He was sure that there had been some mistake. Finally convinced, he said, "That's just fine, but I still have a day's work to do here. After that we'll celebrate."

Borlaug's success in Mexico brought him an international reputation. Young scientists were sent to train with him from all over the world, and he was invited to consult with agricultural authorities in many countries, including West Pakistan, India, Turkey, Afghanistan, Tunisia, and Morocco. The results were extraordinary: in some cases wheat production increased as much as 50 percent in two years. At the time of his prize it was estimated that in more than thirty countries all over the world, 25 million acres were planted to Borlaug's cereals, feeding 500 million people. Borlaug's impact on the production of wheat and other significant developments in the growing of maize and rice have been called the "Green Revolution."

The Peace Prize came to Borlaugh after a string of other honors and awards, including the naming of a street after him in the Mexican city that is the wheat capital. Through it all he remained humble and unassuming, as he was when he delivered his Nobel lecture, a tall and trim figure, bronzed from his work in the fields. He reminded his audience that he was "but one member of a vast team," comprising officials, scientists, and millions of small farmers.

Even the term *Green Revolution,* he said, exaggerated what had been achieved so far: "It is still modest in terms of total needs. Recalling that 50 percent of the present world population is undernourished and that an even larger percentage, perhaps 65 percent, is malnourished, no room is left for complacency. . . . Our aim must be to produce enough food to eradicate all present hunger while at the same time striving to correct malnutrition." Even if world food production were to be significantly increased, there would still be the "unsolved social-economic problem of finding effective ways to distribute the needed additional food to the vast underprivileged masses who have little or no purchasing power."

Moreover, there was the imperative necessity to control population growth: "The Green Revolution has won a temporary success in man's war against hunger and deprivation; it has given man a breathing space. If fully implemented, the revolution can provide sufficient food for sustenance during the next three decades. But the frightening power of human reproduction must also be curbed; otherwise the success of the Green Revolution will be ephemeral only." Still, Borlaug concluded, "I am optimistic for the future of mankind . . . since man is potentially a rational being . . . and will adjust the growth rate to levels which will permit a decent standard of living for all mankind."

Borlaug has continued with his scientific work, but his concern for the world's hungry has led him into other efforts as well. In 1988 he helped the Rockefeller Foundation and the Rockefeller Brothers Fund set up a foundation in Poland to alleviate economic hardships. The Foundation for the Development of Polish Agriculture, with Borlaug and a Polish agricultural scientist as cochairmen, uses Rockefeller grants to help Polish farmers and to increase agricultural production. The foundation is designed to be a self-supporting entity, engaging in commercial food and agricultural activities, but as might be expected from any Borlaug venture, research is a prominent part of the program. One of the first projects has been research to control potato blight and improve apple orchards.

BIBLIOGRAPHY

Secondary Sources

"Borlaug, Norman." In *CB,* 1971.

Brown, Lester R. *Seeds of Change: The Green Revolution and Development in the 1970s.* London: Pall Mall Press, 1970. Published for the Overseas Development Council. A general view, which helps put Borlaug's work in perspective.

Stakman, E. C., Richard Bradfield, and Paul C. Mangelsdorf. *Campaign against Hunger.* Cambridge: Harvard University Press, 1967. The "Three Musketeers of Agriculture," who were the original consultants for the Rockefeller Mexican project, here assess the state of the world effort.

1971
Willy Brandt (1913–)

West Germany

Governing mayor of West Berlin (1957–66); foreign minister (1966–69) and chancellor (1969–74) of the Federal Republic of Germany; chairman, Social Democratic party (1964–87); president, Socialist International (1976–); chairman, North-South Commission of World Bank.

Willy Brandt was the second German statesman to receive the prize. Like Gustav Stresemann he was honored for a policy of peace and reconciliation after a war in which Germany had invaded other countries. In naming him, the committee declared, "As leader of the Federal Republic of Germany and in the name of the German People, Willy Brandt has stretched out his hand to reconcile peoples who were enemies for a long time." Moreover, he had taken significant steps to achieve political and military détente between East and West Europe.

The committee's statement referred specifically to West Germany's signing of the agreement on the nonproliferation of nuclear weapons and of the agreements with Poland and the Soviet Union to renounce the use of force in their relations. It also spoke of Brandt's efforts "to guarantee the basic rights of personal security and freedom of movement for the population of West Berlin," when he was governing mayor.

In his acceptance speech in Oslo, Brandt called the prize "the highest honor, but also the most demanding to a man with political responsibility." He considered it "an encouragement to my political endeavors, not as a final judgment upon them," and he promised to "do everything I can in my future work to bring nearer to realization what many expect of me."

Willy Brandt was born in the old Hanseatic seaport of Lübeck to Martha Frahm, an unmarried nineteen-year-old shop assistant, who christened him Herbert Ernst Karl Frahm. He has said that he was "born into socialism." His mother was an active trade unionist, and the place of his father, whom he never knew, was taken by his maternal grandfather, a truck driver and veteran socialist, who talked to the boy enthusiastically about the founders of the German Social Democratic party (SPD) and taught him workers' songs.

At fourteen, with the help of a scholarship, he entered an excellent secondary school, where his classmates were mainly children of middle-class parents. He began early to write articles for the Lübeck socialist newspapers, and at seventeen he became a full member of the party, one year earlier than was usually the rule. He graduated at eighteen and became a clerk with a ship brokerage firm, continuing to write for the socialist press, where he first used the name Willy Brandt as a pen name.

These were the years when the Nazis were rising to power, and Brandt fought them "with words and fists." When he came to feel that the SPD was not effectively opposing them, Brandt joined a more radical socialist party. After Hitler became chancellor in January 1933, the young socialist activist was no longer safe from arrest. In April he secretly left the country, escaping on a fishing boat that took him across the Baltic to the coast of Denmark, where he arrived with a few shirts, a volume of Karl Marx, and a little money. He was only nineteen years old.

From Denmark he made his way to Oslo, where his party wanted him to be its representative. There, befriended by members of the Norwegian Labor party, Willy Brandt, as everyone now called him, quickly learned the Norwegian language and began writing for the Labor party newspaper. He also became chairman of an association formed to help other refugees from Germany.

In 1934 Brandt won a scholarship to study history and philosophy at the University of Oslo, but his political activities prevented him from continuing with his studies for very long. From his base in Oslo Brandt traveled widely in Western Europe to confer with party colleagues in organizing the leftist international opposition to Hitler. In 1936 he was the contact in Oslo for the group of German émigrés who campaigned successfully for the Nobel Peace Prize for

Carl von Ossietzky. When the prize was announced, Brandt was in Berlin, disguised as a Norwegian student and helping with underground activities. In 1937 he covered the Spanish civil war as correspondent for Scandinavian newspapers, continuing his party activities and vigorously supporting the cause of the republican government.

When the German army invaded Norway in the spring of 1940, Brandt's friends spirited him away from Oslo and fitted him out in a Norwegian uniform to elude the Nazi secret police. He was captured and interned briefly as a Norwegian soldier without his identity being discovered. Norway had become too dangerous for him, however, and in 1942 he fled to neutral Sweden, where he spent the rest of the war years as a well-regarded political journalist. Brandt was one of the circle of refugee socialists who gathered around Gunnar and Alva Myrdal to formulate the peace aims of what was called the "little Socialist International."

After the war ended, Brandt covered the Nuremberg trials of German war criminals as a Norwegian journalist, and then he was appointed press attaché with the Norwegian Military Mission in Berlin. In 1947, almost overwhelmed by the human tragedy and physical destruction he found in defeated Germany, but encouraged by his talks with surviving Social Democratic leaders, Brandt made the momentous decision to remain in his native country and help rebuild it. He gave up the bright promise of a Norwegian diplomatic career and applied for the restoration of the German citizenship of which he had been formally deprived by the Nazi government in 1938.

Now thirty-four, Brandt began a new career in Berlin as an SPD official. In 1949 he was elected as one of Berlin's nonvoting representatives in the Bundestag, the lower house of the legislature of the newly established Federal Republic of Germany. In 1957 he was elected governing mayor by the West Berlin parliament, and in 1959, as one of the national leaders of the SPD, Brandt helped formulate the new party program, which abandoned doctrinaire Marxist opposition to private property, a free market economy, and organized religion.

West Berlin had become an enclave, formed from the sectors of the city occupied by the Western Allies after the war, and surrounded by the territory of the German Democratic Republic, formerly the Soviet zone of occupation. It served as an escape hatch for a flood of East Germans seeking political freedom and economic opportunity in West Germany, and eventually the East German government sealed all the exit points by building a wall along the boundary with West Berlin. Brandt worked with the Western powers in resisting Soviet and East German threats and efforts to detach West Berlin from the Federal Republic. West Berlin was an outpost of the West in the cold war, and Brandt became a symbol of the courageous determination of its people to remain free.

As a world figure, Brandt was the logical Social Democratic candidate for federal chancellor in the national election of 1961. Konrad Adenauer, the Christian Democratic leader, stooped to making allusions to Brandt's illegitimate birth, and Brandt was criticized for going into exile and even accused of having shot Germans as a Norwegian soldier. He defended himself ably against these attacks, but the SPD lost this election and also the election of 1965, when he was again the standard-bearer. On each occasion the socialists increased their share of the vote, but the Christian Democrats remained in power in coalition with the liberal Free Democrats.

In 1966 this coalition collapsed, and the SPD agreed to form a national coalition with the Christian Democrats, with Willy Brandt becoming vice-chancellor and minister of foreign affairs. In the next three years he inaugurated a new policy of strengthening ties with France and at the same time seeking reconciliation with Germany's wartime enemies in the East.

In Brandt's conception, this so-called *Ostpolitik,* or East policy, was actually based upon furthering closer relationships in the West between the European powers and between them and the United States. Reconciliation with the East did not please the Christian Democrats, but it was approved by the voters in the national election of 1969, which produced a coalition government of the SPD and the Free Democrats and made Willy Brandt the fourth chancellor of the Federal Republic. Before the end of the year this new government had signed a multilateral treaty prohibiting the proliferation of nuclear arms, taken steps to bring Britain into the European Economic Community, and begun negotiations with Poland and the Soviet Union.

In August 1970 Brandt and Soviet premier Alexei Kosygin signed in Moscow a nonaggression treaty that renounced the use of force and territorial claims and recognized the inviolability of existing boundaries, including the line dividing the Federal Republic from the German Democratic Republic, and the western border of Poland, which extended that state into former German territory. In December Brandt signed a treaty with the premier of Poland recognizing the existing boundary between West Germany and Poland. These pacts represented for the first time a peace settlement between these former belligerents of the Second World War, recognizing the status quo in Eastern Europe. Brandt's Ostpolitik disavowed the claims of West Germany's nationalist revisionists, many of whom had been expelled or had fled from the districts lost to Poland at the end of the war.

In Warsaw Brandt performed the consummate act of reconciliation with the Jewish victims of Germany's war crimes when he knelt in contrition before the monument to the ghetto. Ultrapatriots in West Germany could not accept the spectacle of a German chancellor on his knees, but the news photo of this incident which went around the world did much to correct the image of the German that Adolf Hitler had projected.

In his acceptance speech at Oslo, Brandt declared how much the award had meant to him as an acknowledgment of the will for peace of the German people "after the unforgettable horrors of the past." If Hitler had twice driven him from his home, once from Germany and once from Norway, twice he had won over Hitler, first in 1936 when he had helped Ossietzky, the concentration camp victim, receive the Peace Prize, and now in receiving the award himself. Among the many messages of congratulation he had received from all over the world, a recurring theme had been that his prize represented a defeat for Hitler. Now an honored representative of the "other Germany," Brandt recalled "the young man who in his time was persecuted, driven into exile in Norway and deprived of his rights as a citizen." He identified himself not only with persecuted Germans but with "all those from whom the past has exacted a harsh toll."

Oslo gave Brandt a heartwarming welcome. He said that Norway had not been just an asylum for him, but a second homeland. His days in Oslo were a time of renewal of his many friendships with Labor politicians and others. His first wife, Carlota, was a Norwegian, and their daughter came to the ceremonies. Rut, his second wife, was also a Norwegian who had worked in the resistance during the war and then fled to Stockholm, where they had met. They had three sons, one of whom was with them in Oslo. Brandt said that Rut did not know whether she was on a visit away from home or actually coming home, and he might well have been speaking for himself.

Brandt's Nobel lecture, "Peace Policy in Our Time," explained the general principles of his policy and how he was attempting to implement them. "War must not be a means of achieving political ends," he said, thus contradicting the German general Clausewitz, who had called war "the continuation of policy by other means." Brandt called for the elimination of wars: "No national interest can today be isolated from collective responsibility for peace." He was working for "the prevalence of reason in my own country and in the world." Realpolitik, or realistic policy, today had to mean a policy for peace. If he had helped develop "this new sense of reality in Germany, then one of the greatest hopes of my life would have been fulfilled." Brandt declared, "A good German cannot be a nationalist"; he must be a European. Coexistence was realism: "An active policy of coexistence should be based neither on fear nor on blind confidence." And he continued, "That unimaginative principle that nations with different social and economic systems cannot live side by side without being in grave conflict" must be discarded. We have to "speak more of interests than of ideology."

After Oslo Brandt continued with his "realistic policies" toward the East. In 1972 he secured ratification of the treaties with the Soviet Union and Poland by the Bundestag and a vote of confidence by the electorate in a national election that gave the SPD the greatest victory in its history. In December Brandt became chancellor for a second term.

When he spoke at the UN General Assembly in 1973 after the two German states had been admitted to this body, Brandt was at the zenith of his political power. In May 1974, however, it was discovered that a close associate who had had access to secret documents was actually an agent of East Germany. Although the scandal raised no questions about Brandt's own integrity, as head of the government he took responsibility for the breach of national security and abruptly resigned. Many of his friends had tried to dissuade him, but apparently he felt that suspicion, even though unfounded, would persist and that he could no longer count on the full confidence of the German people. Some observers thought that he also wanted to avoid letting the espionage revelations become an election issue, especially at a time when the SPD was already losing some support.

Brandt retained the party chairmanship, however, and from this position he made a surprising comeback. In the party he continued to be regarded with affection and even veneration. Abroad he was elected president of the Socialist International, he played a role in the reestablishment of democratic governments in Portugal and Spain, and he served as chairman of the World Bank's Independent Commission on International Development Issues. This was the so-called North-South Commission, which produced the important report, "North-South—A Program for Survival," urging the industrialized countries to assist the developing world. For these and other endeavors for peace Brandt received a number of distinguished awards.

In the spring of 1985 Brandt impressed me when we talked in his spacious party chairman's office in Bonn with his charm and graciousness, his determination to pursue his work for peace, and the good humor with which he reported the unwillingness of President Ronald Reagan to receive him to accept a message on peace and disarmament from a group of world leaders. Brandt was thinner and grayer now than he had been in his prime, but he was still alert, very frank and responsive, and quick to smile.

Brandt's foreign successes were not paralleled with good fortune at home. The SPD fell upon hard times, with internal dissension and indecision as to how to deal with the new environmental party of the Greens. In January 1987, the SPD suffered a resounding defeat at the polls in the national election, and this was followed by losses in regional elections. Some of the other party leaders held Chairman Brandt responsible for the setbacks, and their difference with him over a minor party appointment led him to resign as chairman, lest these dissensions jeopardize the SPD's chances in the next regional elections. He had served as chairman for twenty-three years, and now he declared he was leaving the bridge, but not the ship.

It marked the end of an era in West German politics. Brandt had made great achievements, and he had become the very embodiment of the Social Democratic party. Among West German commentators there was a general sense of regret at the manner of his going, but most of them felt that perhaps he should have left the bridge earlier. In any case, they believed that his political career in West Germany was at an end. Visibly disheartened at the turn of events, but not without vigor at seventy-three, Willy Brandt was still a respected and experienced statesman on the world stage and in position to keep his Oslo promise to continue working for international peace.

BIBLIOGRAPHY

Primary Sources

Brandt, Willy. *In Exile: Essays, Reflections and Letters 1933–1947.* Philadelphia: University of Pennsylvania Press, 1971.

———. *My Road to Berlin.* As told to Leo Lania. Garden City, N.Y.: Doubleday, 1960.

———. *Peace: Writings and Speeches.* Bonn: Verlag Neue Gesellschaft, 1971. Includes Oslo speeches.

———. *People and Politics: The Years 1960–1975.* Boston: Little, Brown, 1978. First volume of his memoirs, revised from German edition.

Secondary Sources

Binder, David. *The Other German: Willy Brandt's Life and Times.* Washington, D.C.: New Republic Book Co., 1975.

Drath, Viola H. *Willy Brandt: Prisoner of His Past.* Radnor, Pa.: Chilton, 1975. Well informed; highly critical.

Fallaci, Oriana. *Interview with History.* Boston: Houghton Mifflin, 1976, pp. 210–34.

Harpprecht, Klaus. *Willy Brandt: Portrait and Self-Portrait.* Los Angeles: Nash, 1971. By Brandt's speech writer; carefully edited.

Prittie, Terence. *Willy Brandt: Portrait of a Statesman.* New York: Schocken, 1974. Very favorable.

Wechsberg, Joseph. "The Outsider." *New Yorker* 49 (14 January 1974): 35ff. A profile.

1973

Henry A. Kissinger (1923–)

United States

Political scientist, statesman; Harvard University professor; National Security adviser (1969–75); secretary of state (1973–77).

Le Duc Tho (1911–)

(declined the prize)

North Vietnam

Communist revolutionary in struggle for independence from France; North Vietnamese government leader.

The naming of Henry A. Kissinger and Le Duc Tho by the committee in 1973 was not only the most controversial in the history of the prize; it had two unprecedented consequences: division in the committee led to the resignations of two members, and the recipients themselves disagreed with the decision: one refused it, and the other tried to give it back.

The committee announcement in October declared that the prize was to be given to Le Duc Tho and Henry Kissinger for negotiating the cease-fire agreement in January 1973 between North Vietnam and the United States. But it was then nine months after the agreement had been initialed, and the hostilities were still continuing. Both sides claimed that the other was not carrying out the terms of the agreement. Le Duc Tho wrote the committee that he could not accept the award so long as peace was not established. Kissinger accepted it, but after the fall of South Vietnam to the North Vietnamese in 1975, he sent a letter to the committee declaring that the settlement he had reached with Le Duc Tho had been wrecked and he wanted to return his prize. The committee refused, explaining that the prize had been awarded for the *efforts* of the two negotiators. Besides, there was no provision in the statutes for the award's being returned.

The committee's announcement in 1973 met with a generally negative reaction, both in Norway and throughout the world. Critical comments in the press ranged from disbelief and cynicism to dismay and outright protest. Conservatives objected to the prize for a Communist who was committed to revolutionary violence. Far more widespread, however, were the denunciations of the Kissinger award by the peace movement in the United States and other countries, which had been opposing the American war in Vietnam. To these critics, Kissinger was no peacemaker, but a war maker, responsible along with President Richard Nixon for the widening of the war, the secret air bombing of North Vietnamese forces in neutral Cambodia, and the terror bombing of Hanoi at Christmas, 1972. Demonstrators at the White House held aloft placards mocking the "Ignobel Prize." American and English Quakers, who had won the prize in 1947, sent a joint delegation to Oslo that tried, in vain, to meet with committee members to remind them not to disregard in the future the moral and humanitarian bases of peacemaking that had given the prize such world stature in the past.

Meanwhile, Aase Lionaes, who chaired the committee, stated to the press that the decision had been "very easy." Two of the five members, however, had voted for Archbishop Helder Camara of Brazil, and they now felt that as a matter of integrity they had to resign. But critics claimed their real reason for resigning was the outcry against the award. Many years later, to set the record straight, one of the two broke the vow of silence and declared in an article that if the committee decision had been "easy," it was because three members had come to the meeting with their minds made up; there had been no discussion. Camara was the popular favorite in Norway, and a youth group raised a large sum of money for an alternative prize, which he came to Oslo to receive.

In her speech of presentation at the December ceremony, Mrs. Lionaes defended the decision. She said that the committee had been fully aware that it had been a cease-fire and not a peace settlement. This was "only the first but a tremendously important step." The committee had hoped that the award would encourage the recipients to take further steps. The committee had also hoped that in sharing the prize between Le Duc Tho and Kissinger, the point would be made that "nations with different systems of government must be able to live together in peace and solve their controversies by negotiation."

Le Duc Tho

Le Duc Tho was, of course, not present at the ceremony. Nor did he report to the committee any change of mind before, according to the statutes, time ran out for his award in October 1974. If he had accepted, he would have been the first Communist and the first Asian to receive the prize.

Because his life has been like that of many other revolutionaries who have conspired against the established order and led lives in underground resistance, there is much of his story we do not know. But even after his revolution succeeded and he became a member of the government of Communist North Vietnam, not very much has become known about him in the West.

He was born in a village of what later became North Vietnam, then a part of French Indochina. His father was a civil service official in the French colonial administration, but Le Duc Tho early entered the movement for national liberation, organizing anti-French demonstrations when he was working in the post office. In 1930, when he was only nineteen, he helped Ho Chi Minh found the Indochinese Communist party.

His activities led to arrest by the government and a sentence of ten years on a notorious prison island. After six years he was released and immediately took up his party work again. On the outbreak of war in 1939, the government sent him back to prison, where he wrote a poem, "Cell of Hatred," telling of his rage against the "barbaric imperialists" who had oppressed his country for so long.

Before the war ended either he was released or he escaped and may have helped Ho Chi Minh organize the nationalist resistance movement against the Japanese, which was directed against the French after the Japanese were defeated. In 1945, when Ho Chi Minh declared Vietnam independent, Le Duc Tho, at thirty-two, was a high-ranking member of the Viet Minh, the Indochinese Communist party. He was sent to the South to organize guerrilla warfare against the French, who were defeated finally in 1954. The country was then divided between the Communist North and the anti-Communist South.

At the capital of Hanoi in the North, Le Duc Tho was a member of the ruling politburo, with special responsibilities for party organization and ideology, and he remained in the government for many years. When conflict first broke out in South Vietnam between the government and the Communist guerrillas, Le Duc Tho was reported to be one of the top guerrilla leaders. It is unclear what his role was when the United States intervened on the side of South Vietnam and North Vietnam formally entered the fighting, but soon after Washington and Hanoi decided to open secret negotiations, Le Duc Tho appeared in Paris as the chief negotiator for North Vietnam.

It was in this capacity that he first met Kissinger in August 1969. They represented a striking contrast, having in common mainly their height, Le Duc Tho being tall for a Vietnamese at five feet eight, and Kissinger rather short for an American male at five feet nine. Le Duc Tho was always in his well-cut black Mao suit; Kissinger dressed according to the fashions of the West. Kissinger was twelve years younger than his gray-haired, austere, and single-minded counterpart, and, although both men were capable of working around the clock, the American somehow found time for some social life in the City of Light, whereas the Vietnamese kept pretty much to the North Vietnamese compound.

Over the four years of their negotiating, the owlish, bespectacled Kissinger and the "dour, dedicated revolutionary," as Kissinger wrote of him, developed a measure of mutual respect for each other. The American could not help but admire his partner's "subtlety, his acumen, his iron-discipline," although at the same time finding Le Duc Tho's party-line intransigence and his debating stance frustrating. On his side, Le Duc Tho, although capable of a warm smile on occasion, probably found Kissinger's play of wit frequently irrelevant.

After the two had been told of their award, Kissinger sent a friendly cable of congratulations to his negotiating partner, but Le Duc Tho apparently thought the time for politeness was past. He responded by charging that the agreement they had signed had been violated and declaring that until the agreement was carried out, peace could not be restored. Le Duc Tho kept his place among the Communist ruling group until 1986, when he and other members of the old guard resigned to make way for others.

Henry A. Kissinger

Henry Alfred Kissinger was born in southern Germany of Jewish parents. His father was a teacher who lost his position after Hitler came to power. Henry and his younger brother were sometimes set upon by the other children at school and were forced to transfer to an all-Jewish institution. In 1938, when Henry was fifteen, the family emigrated to the United States, settling in a neighborhood in Upper Manhattan. The youth attended a New York City high school for four years but always kept his German accent and his deep appreciation of German and European culture.

After graduation he entered the City University of New York, studying accounting in the evening and working during the day. In 1943, at the age of twenty, he was drafted into the army and became a U.S. citizen. His high intelligence and linguistic ability qualified him to become interpreter for the commanding general of his division in Europe and then an interrogator with counterintelligence. After the war ended, he was assigned as administrator of a small German town. Still in his early twenties, Kissinger was unusually mature. Seventeen of his relatives who had remained in Germany had been killed under the Nazis, but he announced to the population, "We have not come to take our revenge."

In 1946 he returned to the United States and took a well-paying job in an army training school, but hungering for an education, he gave this up and entered Harvard College in September, with the help of a New York State scholarship. As a major in political science, he graduated in 1950 with the highest honors and went on to graduate studies, receiving the M.A. in 1952 and the Ph.D. in 1954.

His doctoral dissertation, later published as *A World Restored,* dealt with European international relations in the early nineteenth century. He chose this topic to discover how the statesmen of that era developed a system that survived for a century without a general European war, and what relevance this could have for the management of foreign policy in his own day.

He concluded that stability, not peace, is the proper objective of statecraft and that to achieve it, the successful statesman will skillfully manipulate the balance of power between the sovereign states. Recognizing that international stability is a higher good than justice, the statesman must be realistic and pragmatic, avoiding ideological objectives and always ready for accommodations and compromises. A revolutionary state must be opposed by force, not because its ideology is evil, but because it will not play by the established rules. Conflicts between states that keep within the balance-of-power system can usually be handled by the arts of negotiation to prevent war. On the other hand, where peace becomes a primary objective, then the international system is at the mercy of the most ruthless member of the international community. Such were the lessons the graduate student drew from his doctoral research, which were to serve him as guidelines when he became a statesman himself.

Kissinger next addressed the question of *Nuclear Weapons and Foreign Policy,* the title of the book that won him national prominence. This was the product of his serving as *rapporteur* of a high-powered seminar conducted over many months by the Council on Foreign Relations in New York City. Here Kissinger argued against the official policy of massive retaliation, or meeting a Soviet attack on the West with an all-out nuclear response. He pointed out that this doctrine of the Great Deterrent had neither flexibility nor credibility, since it was unlikely that any Soviet advance anywhere in the world would provoke the United States to respond by unleashing a suicidal nuclear war. Far more effective would be a policy of graduated deterrence, giving the Soviet Union to understand that in case of Soviet aggression, tactical, not unlimited, nuclear war would be one of the options the United States would consider.

Critics pointed out that *any* use of nuclear weapons would inevitably lead to unlimited use by both sides and probably mutual extinction, and Kissinger was later to change his mind. Nevertheless, the book made his political fortune. He was now considered one of America's leading thinkers on nuclear strategy. Nelson Rockefeller sought him out as adviser on foreign policy, and President Dwight D. Eisenhower and Vice President Richard Nixon were reported as having been much impressed by the book.

In 1957 Kissinger returned to Harvard and was soon appointed professor with tenure. He was frequently called to Washington to consult on questions of defense and foreign policy, and in 1968 Governor Rockefeller had him write his foreign policy platform during his campaign for the presidential nomination.

It was Richard Nixon who won the nomination and the election of 1968, and he invited Kissinger to become his principal adviser on foreign policy. In 1969 Kissinger was appointed as assistant to the president for national security affairs and executive secretary of the National Security Council. Nixon liked to control his own foreign policy, and he used Kissinger as his personal envoy on foreign missions, circumventing the normal channels of the Department of State.

In this capacity Kissinger conducted the secret negotiations with Le Duc Tho in Paris, and he was also Nixon's emissary on clandestine missions to Peking and Moscow to prepare for the president's own visits to these capitals. Kissinger therefore had a part in the two most significant foreign policy achievements of the Nixon administration, the opening to the People's Republic of China after many years of hostility and the normalization of relations with the Soviet Union, with which state the first Strategic Arms Limitation Treaty (SALT I) was negotiated and the groundwork laid for the policy of détente.

These policies toward communist states followed by the Republican president who had been known for so long as anticommunist followed Kissinger's principles that foreign policy should be pragmatic, not ideological. Kissinger had made himself indispensable in the White House, and in October 1973 he received the reward he had long worked toward and was appointed by President Nixon as secretary of state.

The relationships between the two men were always uneasy. There was respect but also distrust. Nixon was jealous of the good press that Kissinger achieved for himself by charming and manipulating otherwise sophisticated reporters. More than once Nixon was on the point of sending Kissinger back to Harvard, but Kissinger was adept at maneuvers to keep his position. Moreover, when the Watergate scandal broke out, with revelations about Nixon's abuse of power, Nixon needed Kissinger to prevent further erosion of his respectability.

When Nixon left the White House in disgrace, Kissinger was able to remain as secretary of state under President Gerald Ford. He had managed to keep some distance from the darker schemes in which Nixon was involved, and he had emerged seemingly untouched by his association with the tarnished presidency.

In October 1973, when Kissinger received word of his Peace Prize, he issued a formal statement declaring, "Nothing that has happened to me in public life has moved me more than this Award." To mollify President Nixon, who had been hoping for the prize for himself, he twice gave him credit in the statement. In his memoirs Kissinger admitted that he deserved the prize more for his shuttle diplomacy in the Middle East that helped end hostilities between Israel and Egypt than for the Vietnam negotiations.

Kissinger became secretary of state shortly before the prize ceremonies in Oslo, and when the Oslo embassy advised him that his presence would set off massive demonstrations against the United States because of its war in Vietnam, Kissinger could excuse himself on the pretext of the pressure of state business. He did tell the committee, however, that he would consider it a privilege to deliver the Nobel lecture at a future time. The American ambassador was consequently the one who had to avoid the snowballs of the demonstrators as he entered the hall to represent his chief.

In his message Kissinger acknowledged that "the Nobel Peace Prize is as much an award to a purpose as to a person. More than the achievement of peace, it symbolizes the quest for peace." In words reminiscent of his doctoral dissertation, he went on to say: "To the realist, peace represents a stable arrangement of power; to the idealist, a goal so pre-eminent that it conceals the difficulty of finding the means to its achievement." About Vietnam, the basis of his prize, he said only, "Certain war has yielded to an uncertain peace," and that "there is hope, however frail." He declared that America's goal was "a stable world, not as an end in itself but as a bridge to the realization of man's noble aspirations of tranquility and community."

Kissinger used his prize money to establish a scholarship fund for children of American servicemen killed or missing in Vietnam. He never did go to Oslo to give the promised lecture, nor did he accept the invitation to contribute to an anthology of essays by laureates, which the Norwegian Nobel Institute published.

In 1974 Kissinger remarried, ending his status as the most eligible bachelor in Washington. He is the father of two children by a previous marriage. On leaving the Department of State the next year, he accepted a professorship at Georgetown University, but he has devoted his time to a variety of pursuits. He has served as consultant to multinational corporations, written his memoirs, and become one of the most highly paid lecturers in the country and familiar to millions of television viewers as the expert always called in to give his views on each new international crisis. He was appointed by President Ronald Reagan to chair a commission on Central America.

Henry Kissinger is a very complex man. He is said to be insecure, which might have helped produce his overgrown sense of self-esteem. Once someone came up to thank him for saving the world. Kissinger replied, "You're welcome"—and meant it. He can be charming with his friends—but treat lesser mortals rudely and his subordinates with contempt. Through sheer intellect and driving ambition, he deftly used propitious circumstances to rise close to the very top in Washington. He enjoyed wielding authority, but not for the sake of power alone. In his own way, which he believed "realistic," he worked to bring peace and stability to an unruly world, and there can be no question that he was an able negotiator, patient, hard-working, exceptionally knowledgeable, with a mind that could cut to the heart of an issue. He knew what he wanted, but he was understanding of the positions of others, and he could meet them with flexibility.

If the Nobel Peace Prize awarded to Henry Kissinger provoked controversy when it was announced, his historical role as a statesman has continued to be warmly debated. Some historians regard him as one of the ten best secretaries of state the United States has ever had; other scholars charge him with duplicity and deceit in his exercise of power and offer documents to prove it. Whatever the verdict of history will be, the American public, with its fondness for superstars in whatever field, is likely to continue to regard Henry Kissinger as one of its supreme interpreters in matters international.

BIBLIOGRAPHY

Henry A. Kissinger

Primary Sources

Kissinger, Henry A. *Nuclear Weapons and Foreign Policy.* New York: Harper, 1957. Paperback reprint. Garden City, N.Y.: Doubleday, 1958.

———. *The White House Years.* Boston: Little, Brown, 1979. Memoirs, covering November 1968–January 1973.

———. *A World Restored: Metternich, Castlereagh and the Problems of Peace 1812–22.* Boston: Houghton Mifflin, 1957. Kissinger's doctoral dissertation.

———. *Years of Upheaval.* Boston: Little, Brown, 1982. Memoirs covering January 1973 to the end of the Nixon administration.

Secondary Sources

Fallaci, Oriana. *Interview with History.* New York: Liveright, 1976, pp. 1–44. A revealing 1972 interview with Kissinger.

Hersh, Seymour M. *The Price of Power: Kissinger in the Nixon White House.* New York: Summit Books, 1983. An indictment by the Pulitzer Prize–winning journalist, based on extensive research. Should be read along with the memoirs.

Hovdaugen, Einar. "Gjest i Nobelkomiteen," *Syn og segn* 4 (1985): 297–304. Explains his resignation in 1973: he had been only "a guest in the Nobel Committee."

Kalb, Marvin, and Bernard Kalb. *Kissinger.* Boston: Little, Brown, 1974. A positive view of his diplomacy by two correspondents who covered it.

Landau, David. *Kissinger: The Uses of Power.* Boston: Houghton Mifflin, 1972.

Shawcross, William. *Sideshow: Kissinger, Nixon and the Destruction of Cambodia.* New York: Simon & Schuster, 1979. Highly critical.

Stoessinger, John G. *Kissinger: The Anguish of Power.* New York: Norton, 1976. An interpretation by a fellow scholar and friend.

Szulc, Tad. *The Illusion of Peace: Foreign Policy in the Nixon Years.* New York: Viking, 1978. Carefully researched.

Le Duc Tho

Secondary Source

"Le Duc Tho." In *CB,* 1975.

1974
Seán MacBride (1904–88)

Ireland

Irish revolutionary, journalist, lawyer, politician; foreign minister who piloted European Convention on Human Rights through Council of Europe; government consultant in Ghana; UN official; head of international human rights and peace organizations.

In 1974 the Nobel Committee divided the prize between former premier Sato of Japan, a much criticized selection, and Seán MacBride, a choice that was generally acclaimed. MacBride was recognized for his great contribution to the cause of human rights. He was a fervent Irish nationalist who, after fighting for Ireland's independence in his youth, became one of the leading internationalists of his time.

MacBride was born in Paris, the son of Major John MacBride, who had led the Irish Brigade against the British in the Boer War, and the beautiful Maude Gonne MacBride, who was active both in the movement for Irish independence and the struggle for women's rights. The parents became separated shortly after their son's birth, Major MacBride returning to Dublin to join the revolutionary forces and his wife and son remaining in Paris, where the boy attended a Jesuit school until he was twelve.

In that year, 1916, Major MacBride was executed by the British after taking part in the abortive Easter Rebellion, and Seán and his mother secretly returned to Ireland. The next year the thirteen-year-old joined the Irish Republican Army (IRA) as a junior volunteer, and for the next twenty years he worked in the underground against British rule. Three times jailed, the first time when he was only fourteen, MacBride rose in the ranks, receiving the Military Service Medal for Irish Independence in 1935 and becoming commander in chief of the IRA in 1936. In 1937 he withdrew from the IRA shortly before its leaders declared their intention of aiding Adolf Hitler.

During these years he had worked as a journalist, married Catalina Bulford, an Irish woman from Argentina, and visited the United States to secure support for the IRA. He had enrolled at Dublin University, but was arrested on the second day of classes. Through intermittent study over a period of seven years, however, he managed to complete the three-year lecture course for his law degree, and in 1937 he was admitted to the Irish bar. He soon became the most successful trial lawyer in Dublin, effectively defending, among others, former IRA comrades with whose policies he had disagreed.

After the Second World War, MacBride entered politics, founding the Republican party, which stood for the establishment of the Irish Republic, the end of the partition of Ireland between North and South, and a program of social welfare. In 1947 he was elected to the Irish parliament and continued to hold his seat until 1958.

From 1948 until 1951 he was foreign minister. During his tenure MacBride helped negotiate the Republic of Ireland Act, which finally established Ireland's complete independence of Britain, and he made his first appearance on the international stage, taking a leading role in the Council of Europe. He was mainly responsible for the European Convention for the Protection of Human Rights and Fundamental Freedoms, which he signed in 1950 along with the other foreign ministers of the member states. This represented the most important implementation of the UN Universal Declaration of Human Rights, with binding provisions for the signatories and setting up the European Court of Human Rights. MacBride always regarded this as his most satisfying accomplishment in law. From this moment on he was to devote his major energies to the protection of human rights, not only in Western Europe, but throughout the world.

He helped found and became president of Amnesty International, the organization that defends prisoners of conscience, and after this was well established, he served as secretary-general of the International Commission of Jurists from 1963 to 1970. This association had been founded in West Berlin to publicize acts of governmental injustice in Eastern Europe, but it expanded its work to take up violations of human rights all over the world, with jurists from over fifty countries participating. In 1968 during the UN Human Rights Year, MacBride led a coalition of nongovernmental organizations concerned about these matters. He was also a central figure in various international peace organizations, such as the World Federation of UN Associations and the International Peace Bureau.

MacBride's practical work with these organizations was accompanied by a profusion of speeches and articles, in which he developed legal and theoretical foundations for the protection of the individual. He took the position that no state could maintain that how it treated its citizens was a matter of concern to itself alone, since human rights are the common property of all mankind and cannot be violated. In all his activities, Mrs. Lionaes said in her speech of presentation, "he mobilized the conscience of the world."

MacBride was already in his sixties when he entered a new area of activity. He became the legal adviser to Kwame Nkrumah in newly independent Ghana and helped him establish the Organization of African States. Then, with strong support from the African countries, the UN General Assembly unanimously elected him as high commissioner for Namibia, a difficult assignment, since South Africa insisted on retaining its control. He was also assistant secretary-general of the United Nations.

MacBride's Nobel lecture, "The Imperatives of Survival," was a carefully considered, eloquent, and hard-hitting exposition of his ideas on peace. He began on a sobering note, saying he came before them "nearly with a feeling of despair . . . partly because we are living in a world where war, violence, brutality and ever increasing armaments dominate the thinking of humanity; but, more so, because humanity itself gives the appearance of having become numbed or terrified by its own impotence in the face of disaster."

He spoke of the "stupendous scientific and material revolution" that had fundamentally changed the world. Along with it, and perhaps because of it, "there has taken place a near total collapse of public and private morality in practically every sector of human relationships." Evidence of this was the acceptance by our political and religious leaders of the nuclear bomb, treating as normal "the most cruel, terrible, and indiscriminate weapon of all time," which, in violation of accepted international law and canons of morality, makes no distinction between combatants and noncombatants. Halfhearted efforts toward controlling those awful weapons had represented not really disarmament but "phased armament."

To the military-industrial complex and the financial interests that support it, MacBride said, "the arms race is a boon." The socialist countries, which do not have such profit-seeking forces, could only gain by disarmament, since it would mean turning resources into industrial development and production of consumer goods. Moreover, the military leaders on both sides, whose professional objective was the building of the most effective engines of destruction possible, resist any reduction of the means at their disposal or limitation of their use. There is the constant peril that in any crisis the general staff of one side or the other would advise its government in the name of national security that this is the time to strike, since in six months the other side might have the superiority.

The moment had come for "WE THE PEOPLE," referred to in the UN Charter, to demand the outlawing of nuclear weapons and a general disarmament. Public opinion had become more influential than ever before through the development of communication technology and the spread of literacy.

MacBride emphasized the fundamental relationship between peace and human rights and called the Universal Declaration of Human Rights "the most important declaration ever adopted by mankind." Only he would add one more right, one that had been urged by religious leaders: "the right of an individual to refuse to kill, to torture or to participate in the preparation for the nuclear destruction of humanity." He concluded, "The signpost just ahead of us is 'Oblivion.' Can the march on this road be stopped? Yes, if public opinion uses the power it now has."

In the ensuing years MacBride continued his efforts for peace and human rights and was also active in the ecumenical movement and the search for new sources of energy to replace nuclear energy. His talents as an international diplomat and mediator were drawn upon as chairman of the controversial UNESCO committee for the study of international communications and as a respected intermediary in the early days of the American hostage crisis in Iran, when he tried to get the matter moved from the political arena to the realm of international law.

In 1984, at the age of eighty, he was in the news for his MacBride principles, an antidiscrimination code aimed at requiring American companies in Northern Ireland to employ Roman Catholics on an equal basis with Protestants. In 1987 he was still active with the International Peace Bureau as president emeritus.

He probably received as many honors as any individual in our time; after the Nobel Peace Prize came the Lenin Peace Prize, recognition by the American legal profession with the American Medal of Justice, and the Silver Medal of UNESCO.

The diversity of his awards testify to his remarkable ability to gain the trust and respect of representatives of very different positions. He even quietly served as an intermediary between Irish extremists and the British government in the troubled question of Northern Ireland. Much as MacBride traveled the world in the service of humanity, he never lost his deep-felt love for his homeland. He died in Dublin in January 1988, at the age of eighty-three.

BIBLIOGRAPHY

Primary Sources

MacBride, Seán. "Anglo-Irish Relationships: The Overwhelming Majority of People Want a United Ireland." *Vital Speeches* 48 (1 November 1981): 40–44.

———. "Namibia Moves towards Independence." *UNESCO Courier,* November 1977, pp. 16–20. Written after serving as UN commissioner for Namibia, 1973–76.

———. *The Right to Refuse to Kill: A New Guide to Conscientious Objection and Service Refusal.* Geneva: International Peace Bureau, 1971.

Secondary Sources

Cogan, Timothy Patrick. *The I.R.A.* New York: Praeger, 1970. Historical account by a leading Irish journalist.

MacBride, Maud Gonne. *A Servant of the Queen.* Dublin: Golden & Eagle, 1950. Autobiography of Seán MacBride's mother.

"MacBride, Seán." In *CB,* 1949.

"Seán MacBride of Ireland Is Dead at 83" *New York Times,* 16 January 1988.

Travers, Herbert F., III, and others. "Seán MacBride: 20th Century Lawyer." *Suffolk University Law School Journal* 11, no. 2 (Spring 1980): 2–28. A very informative interview, conducted by the editors of the *Journal.*

Weil, Gordon L. *The European Convention on Human Rights: Background, Development and Prospects.* Leyden: Sijthoff, 1962. Well researched.

See also the bibliography for Amnesty International (1977).

1974
Eisaku Sato (1901–75)

Japan

Civil servant; politician; premier for almost eight years.

Former premier Sato of Japan, who shared the 1974 award with Seán MacBride, was the first Asiatic to receive the Peace Prize and only the fifth Japanese to win any Nobel prize. Aase Lionaes, chair of the Norwegian Nobel Committee, declared in her presentation that the committee wished "to emphasize the important role the Japanese people have played in promoting close and friendly cooperation with other nations" and that Sato had made a major contribution to peace "by countering the tendency towards a nationalistic policy in Japan after the war" and by conducting a peaceful foreign policy. She said that the committee attached considerable importance to Sato's opposition to nuclear arms for Japan and his bringing Japan into the pact on the nonproliferation of nuclear arms, signed in February 1970.

Welcome as it was that the committee was finally extending recognition to the continent of Asia, its choice of Sato has not generally been regarded very highly. The news of the prize was greeted by the Tokyo press with laughter and even a sense of outrage. Sato's political record was mercilessly dissected, and the Nobel Commitee was offered the "best black humor award." It was pointed out that Sato's rigid anticommunist policy and refusal to enter diplomatic relations with mainland China had produced international tensions, and that his support of the American war in Vietnam was hardly a peace policy.

Nor was Sato's personal life above reproach. He had been indicted for bribery, and his marital difficulties had found their way into the newspapers. His critics had nicknamed him "Haraguro," which means "Black Belly," the derisive Japanese term for "schemer." A kinder sobriquet was "Sato Quick-Ears," referring to his facility in picking up useful political information.

Public revelations about the efforts to win Sato the prize also caused a stir in the Japanese press. A leading Japanese industrialist proudly admitted that he had financed a fourteen-month campaign on behalf of the candidacy, which included flying Japan's former ambassador at the United Nations to Oslo to lobby for Sato and arranging for a collection of his speeches to be translated into English and published in a book in order to impress the committee.

Sato had been aware of all this, and for his part he had used his governmental and diplomatic connections to generate recommendations to Oslo from Japan and other countries (a not unusual practice in statesman nominations). Tim Greve, secretary of the Nobel Committee, admitted to the press that there had been a high amount of activity for Sato, "but not abnormally high," and he maintained that it had made no difference in the decision.

Sato was one of ten children born in southern Honshu to a family descended from a long line of nobles and government officials. He was named Eisaku, which means "Prosperity Maker." His father was of gentle disposition, and it was his strong-minded mother who saw to the rearing of the children. She would constantly remind her three sons, "Never forget that we are of samurai lineage; that the Sato family can never suffer a failure." The eldest grew up to be a vice admiral in the navy, and each of his brothers became prime minister.

Eisaku, the youngest son, graduated from the Japanese Imperial University in 1924 and two years later married the daughter of an uncle. He entered the civil service and served with the Ministry of Railways for twenty-four years, rising from the position of stationmaster to become chief of the national railroads in 1945 and then vice-minister of transportation.

In 1948, when he was forty-seven, he decided to enter politics, resigning from the ministry and joining the conservative Democratic-Liberal party. In the next year he won the first of a series of elections to the lower house of the Japanese parliament, and he entered upon a succession of high party and government posts, including positions in the cabinet.

In 1954, when he was secretary-general of his party, he and other politicians were accused of accepting a bribe from a shipbuilding association. Sato avoided arrest with the help of the minister of justice, a party colleague, and the charge was later withdrawn. He was indicted on the lesser charge of failing to register large donations to the party from the shipbuilding association. Sato admitted taking the money but thought this had been properly reported, as the law required. Eventually he won acquittal when the government issued a general amnesty to celebrate Japan's readmission to the international committee as a member of the United Nations.

For the next few years Sato kept a low profile, emerging to become finance minister when his brother was premier. He resigned with the rest of the cabinet in 1960 because of opposition to the security treaty with the United States in that year. But soon Sato was back in the government when a lifelong friend became premier. This was the office that he wanted for himself, however. "Friendship," he once observed, "should not be permitted to interfere with a person's decision when it has any bearing on his course of action in public life." Sato criticized his friend for weakness, resigned, and rejoined the cabinet in a series of maneuvers and finally reached his goal, becoming premier in November 1964.

Sato held this post for almost eight years, longer than any other Japanese premier. He was a consummate politician, content to operate behind the scenes rather than to become a popular leader. He kept to the middle of the road in his policies, moving slowly and with caution. It was said that Premier Sato would tap his way across a stone bridge to be sure that it was safe. Domestically, he fostered the economic development that made Japan one of the industrial giants of the world. Abroad, he gave strong backing to the policies of the United States, following Washington in opposition to the People's Republic of China and supporting the American bombing of North Vietnam.

The next month after taking office Sato went to Washington for talks with President Lyndon Johnson. He told reporters there, "Better to be the head of a chicken than the south end of an ox," but he declared that he intended for Japan to take a greater role in Asia and in the world.

Sato's one popular achievement was persuading President Richard Nixon in 1969 to return to Japan Okinawa and the other islands of the Ryukyu chain which the United States had captured toward the end of World War II and still administered. To the Japanese this meant that a million of their fellow countrymen were under foreign domination. In 1965 Sato had been the first postwar Japanese premier to visit Okinawa. When he visited the war memorials and watched schoolchildren waving Japanese flags and pleading, "Don't forget us, we are Japanese too," Sato, generally perceived as an unemotional man, had openly wept. He often said that "until Okinawa returns to the fatherland, Japan will not have completely emerged from her postwar period."

After the United States formally returned Okinawa to Japan in 1972 (although maintaining its military bases there), Sato announced his retirement from office. He had achieved his great aim, but just a few months earlier Sato's government had been shaken by the turn-around in United States policy toward the People's Republic of China, signaled by President Nixon's dramatic visit. Sato had maintained close relations with Taiwan, and the mainland government made it clear that there would be no diplomatic relations with Tokyo so long as Sato was premier.

The Peace Prize came to Sato two years after he left office. In his Nobel lecture, "The Pursuit of Peace and Japan in the Nuclear Age," Sato acknowledged that "the attainment of peace is the ultimate objective of all statesmen," and discussed his own efforts toward that end. He spoke of his achievement in securing Japan's adherence to the nuclear nonproliferation treaty, and he also highlighted his three principles on nuclear arms: "Never to produce arms of this nature, never to own them, and never to introduce them into Japan." His critics pointed out that Sato had opposed this treaty at the outset, claiming that it was unfair to nonnuclear powers, and that after Japan finally signed, Sato had made no effort to secure his government's ratification. Moreover, he had quietly permitted the berthing in Japanese harbors of American warships carrying nuclear warheads.

Sato also referred in his speech to his good neighbor policy toward other Asiatic nations, where it is true that he had worked to restore the relationships that had been broken by Japan's earlier imperialist and war policies. In particular, he emphasized the normalization of relations with South Korea. Finally, Sato spoke of the peaceful use of nuclear energy, of which he strongly approved, subject to the setting of international safety standards, the international control of nuclear fuel, and the pursuing of international research and development on nuclear fusion.

Sato announced that he would use his half of the prize money, sixty-two thousand dollars, for the United Nations University that was to be established in Japan. The year after receiving the prize he suffered a severe stroke while dining in a restaurant in Tokyo and never regained consciousness, dying at the age of seventy-four.

BIBLIOGRAPHY

Primary Source

Sato, Eisaku. *In Quest of Peace and Freedom.* Tokyo: *Japan Times,* 1973. Speeches collected and translated to support his candidacy for the prize.

Secondary Sources

Nakamura, Koji. "Sato: A Prize Choice for the Sniggers." *Far Eastern Economic Review* 86 (1 November 1974): 14. A highly critical view.

Obituary. *New York Times,* 3 June 1975, 1:36.

Reischauer, adv. ed. *Japan.* The Great Contemporary Issues series. New York: Arno Press, 1974. Articles from the *New York Times.* See especially pp. 358–62 and passim.

"Sato, Eisaku." In *CB,* 1965.

1975
Andrei Sakharov

Soviet Union

Outstanding physicist and codeveloper of the Soviet hydrogen bomb; leading human rights activist in the Soviet Union.

The Nobel Committee gave the 1975 prize to Andrei Sakharov, the first Soviet citizen so honored, calling him "one of the great champions of human rights in our age." Once again the committee recognized that peace must be based upon the respect for human rights, as it had done in such prizes as those for Albert Lutuli, René Cassin, and Martin Luther King, Jr. The October announcement declared, "Sakharov's fearless personal commitment in upholding the fundamental principles for peace between men is a powerful inspiration for all true work for peace. Uncompromisingly and with unflagging strength Sakharov has fought against the abuse of power and all forms of violation of human dignity."

In the summer of 1975 Sakharov had published his second major essay on world peace, linking it clearly with the end of repression in his own country. Shortly afterward Western and socialist states, including the Soviet Union, had signed at Helsinki an agreement on security and cooperation that included a section on the observance of human rights. These developments had to be in the minds of the committee members when they chose Sakharov from among the fifty or more candidates proposed.

An Oslo newspaper cartoonist suggested another motive, picturing Aase Lionaes, committee chair, delivering a swift kick to the posterior of Soviet leader Leonid Brezhnev. It was clear at least to the Soviet press agency, Tass, that those who made the award "were guided by other interests than interests of peace." The Soviet press declared that the prize was being given to "an enemy of détente," a man who was against his own country and its peace policy, a "Judas for whom the Nobel Prize was thirty pieces of silver from the West." Seventy-two members of the Soviet Academy of Sciences signed a statement viewing the award with "perplexity and indignation," charging that it contradicted the principles of the prize itself.

In November the Soviet government refused to grant Sakharov a visa to go to Oslo to receive the prize, declaring that he possessed state secrets. Sakharov had, of course, worked on nuclear weapons and had played a major role in the development of the Soviet hydrogen bomb, but his security clearance had been withdrawn seven years before. Even if granted permission to leave the Soviet Union, however, he would have insisted upon an ironclad guarantee that he could return.

The award created problems for the Norwegian Foreign Ministry, which had started discussions with the Soviet Union on increasing economic and cultural cooperation. The Soviets could hardly believe that the Norwegian Nobel Committee was entirely separate from the Norwegian government. Mrs. Lionaes made a special point in her speech at the award ceremony of emphasizing the complete independence of the committee. At the same time, however, she needled Moscow further by recalling that, like Sakharov, Carl von Ossietzsky had been prevented from coming to Oslo to accept his prize in person because the Nazi government refused to permit it.

Sakharov's wife, Elena Bonner Sakharova, happened to be in Italy for medical treatment, and it was she who received his prize for him and read his speech of acceptance and his Nobel lecture. "I am here today," she explained, "because, due to certain strange characteristics of the country whose citizens my husband and I are, my husband's presence at the ceremony . . . turned out to be impossible." She said that at that very moment Sakharov was standing in the cold outside the courtroom building in Vilnius, Soviet Lithuania, where his closest friend was being tried for anti-Sovietism.

In his speech of thanks, Sakharov shared the honor with all prisoners of conscience and those who defended them, and he repeated his call for a general amnesty. He commended the committee for its courage in giving the prize to one who disagreed with the leadership of a powerful state, and he was especially appreciative that his award symbolized the relationship of human rights to peace.

Andrei Dimitriyevich Sakharov was born in Moscow a few years after the Bolshevik Revolution to a family of the Russian intelligentsia. His father was a physicist who taught and wrote textbooks and popular books on science. The family lived in a large communal apartment building, where most of the other tenants were relatives who shared a love for science, literature, and music. Sakharov's father was an excellent pianist and had once supported himself by playing the piano accompaniment to silent films. His grandmother, who had taught herself English when she was fifty, used to read aloud English novels and plays in the original to her little grandchildren. In this setting Sakharov had his first lessons at home, and when he went to school, he found some difficulty in adjusting to the other children.

In his studies Sakharov always performed brilliantly. In 1938, when he was seventeen, he graduated with distinction from secondary school and entered the Faculty of Physics in Moscow University. When Germany attacked the Soviet Union in 1941, Sakharov was evacuated with others from Moscow. His extraordinary intellectual gifts were recognized, and he was spared military duty and enabled to continue his courses by correspondence and to pass his final examinations with distinction in 1942. Afterward he spent some weeks as a lumberjack, but in September he was assigned to a large munitions plant on the Volga River, where he worked as an engineer until the end of the war. Here he made a number of inventions that improved the process of production, and in 1944 he found time to write his first papers on theoretical physics.

When the war ended in 1945, Sakharov, now twenty-four, entered the Physics Institute of the Academy of Sciences, where he studied under the great theoretical physicist Igor Tamm, who was later to win the Nobel Prize for physics. In two years Sakharov was ready to defend his thesis, attaining the equivalent of an American Ph.D.

In 1948 Sakharov joined Tamm's team of nuclear scientists, working first in Moscow and later at a secret research center, and for the next twenty years he was occupied with the development of nuclear weapons. He worked under conditions of highest security, and he enjoyed all the special privileges the Soviet Union accords its top scientists.

Another group of scientists developed the Soviet atomic bomb by 1949, four years after the completion of the American bomb. Tamm, Sakharov, and their colleagues had the task of inventing the hydrogen bomb before American scientists did, which they accomplished in 1953. Sakharov has been called the "father" of the Soviet hydrogen bomb, but he has always protested that this was a collaborative effort. He was, however, awarded the coveted Stalin Prize, after having been decorated several times with the Order of Socialist Labor; in that same year of 1953 he was made a full member of the Soviet Academy of Sciences at the unprecedented early age of thirty-two. His mentor Tamm was granted full membership at the same time after twenty years of association with the academy in an associate capacity, which was the normal procedure.

Throughout most of this work on nuclear weapons, Sakharov had no moral reservations, since he and his colleagues felt they were only striving for parity with the West so that there would be less chance of war. By the end of the 1950s Sakharov could feel reassured: the Soviet Union had the hydrogen bomb and the intercontinental ballistic missile and was even leading the United States in space research.

In 1957 Sakharov was influenced by the public statements of Albert Schweitzer and Linus Pauling about the dangers of radioactive fallout from nuclear bomb testing, for which he came to feel that he bore some responsibility. In 1958 he tried in vain to persuade the Soviet government to call off a series of tests, and in 1961 he tried again, approaching the Soviet leader, Nikita Khrushchev, personally. Sakharov was again rebuffed, Khrushchev declaring: "Sakharov is a good scientist. But leave it to us, who are specialists in this tricky business, to make foreign policy." Sakharov, however, did not give up, and he feels that he may have had some influence on the conclusion of the partial Test Ban Treaty of 1963.

What he accomplished had been done quietly through his personal connections with the Kremlin. At the same time, however, Sakharov began to take a public role on certain issues. Stalin had died in 1953, and under Khrushchev there was at least some opportunity for highly placed scientists like Sakharov to take issue with the government in their own area of competence. In 1958 Sakharov and a colleague successfully protested an educational reform that would have compelled gifted science students to interrupt their studies with a period of practical work. A few years later Sakharov took a public stand in the field of biology, attacking an unscientific doctrine and helping correct it.

In 1966 Sakharov moved in his criticism beyond the sphere of science, signing a collective letter opposing measures rehabilitating Stalin and Stalinism. In the same year he protested a new law against dissenters then being drafted, and he sent Leonid Brezhnev, now the Soviet leader, the first of a series of letters on behalf of individuals who were being unjustly dealt with. The minister in charge of his research project said that he was an outstanding scientist, but "stupid as a politician."

Sakharov continued to develop his ideas, and early in 1968 he wrote a tract entitled, *Thoughts on Progress, Coexistence, and Intellectual Freedom.* Here he formulated the thesis that the only alternative to general nuclear destruction was the cooperation of the socialist and capitalist systems, which he saw as converging, in the control of nuclear arms, technological and scientific development, and assistance to the third world. Along with this international program, he called for a liberalization of Soviet society.

This manifesto was circulated in the Soviet Union through copies passed from hand to hand; it was then published in translation abroad and widely commented upon. As a result, Sakharov was barred from secret research in 1968, and the following year he was sent back to the Physics Institute, with reduced salary and privileges. Not long afterward he suffered a personal loss when his wife died.

From 1970 on Sakharov directed more and more of his attention to the defense of human rights and the support of individual dissidents who were facing political trials. He founded with two colleagues the Committee for Human Rights and began to attend the trials, standing outside in moral support when no longer permitted in the courtroom.

In his association with dissident circles, Sakharov met Elena Bonner, whom he married in 1971. He was then fifty, and she was two years younger, the daughter of an Armenian Old Bolshevik who had been arrested along with his Jewish wife in Stalin's purges and who had died in prison. Elena's mother survived, and her father was officially rehabilitated after Stalin's death. Elena served in the war as a nurse and was demobilized in 1945 as a lieutenant, with a condition of progressive blindness as a result of war wounds. This did not prevent her from becoming a doctor and pediatrician, and she was on one occasion selected for a special assignment in Iraq by the Soviet Ministry of Health. She was also active as a writer, journalist, and editor. She waited to join the Communist party until her parents were no longer listed as traitors, but later resigned when she became increasingly critical of the government's policies. She had two children at the time of her marriage to Sakharov.

Sakharov remained a member of the Academy of Sciences, even though attacked by the press and harassed by the secret police. Because of his scientific accomplishments and his reputation abroad, however, the government was reluctant to take punitive action against him. Instead, an effort was made to break him by persecuting his wife. The press denounced Bonner as a Zionist CIA agent who had ensnared "this spiritually unbalanced man" and was responsible for his "misguided" activities. Measures were also taken against Bonner's children, of whom Sakharov had become very fond. His own children had been encouraged to distance themselves from him.

In the summer of 1975 Bonner, after twice being refused, was finally given permission to travel to Italy for medical treatment of her eye condition. At the same time, Sakharov finished his second essay, *My Country and the World,* which was soon published abroad. He urged the Western powers to unite in their dealings with the USSR and to bring pressure on its leaders for a greater openness in Soviet society. So long as the Soviet Union was a totalitarian form of state capitalism, with a party-state monopoly of economic affairs and all other aspects of life, any détente with the West could be only a "false détente," and the Soviet leaders would exploit disarmament agreements for their own purposes.

Sakharov returned to such themes in his Nobel lecture, "Peace, Progress, and Human Rights," insisting that international peace and disarmament were conceivable only between open societies based on human rights. Such rights were also the basis for scientific progress and guaranteed that scientific advances would be used for economic and social purposes and not to "despoil mankind." He declared that "progress is possible and innocuous only when it is subject to the control of reason."

Sakharov's lecture referred at length to the many thousands of prisoners of conscience in the Soviet Union and listed over one hundred whose names he knew. He said that there must be liberation on the basis of international agreements of all prisoners of conscience in prisons, camps, and psychiatric clinics.

In conclusion Sakharov declared that although there may be infinite worlds and civilizations in infinite space, "this should not minimize our sacred endeavors in this world of ours, where, like faint glimmers of light in the dark, we have emerged for a moment from the nothingness of material existence. We must make good the demands of reason and create a life worthy of ourselves and of the goals we only dimly perceive."

After receiving the prize Sakharov continued to work for human rights in the Soviet Union, making statements to the West through Western reporters in Moscow. For the Soviet government, Sakharov's public opposition to the Soviet invasion of Afghanistan was the last straw. Early in 1980, without any charges or trial, he was sent into internal exile in Gorki, a closed city 250 miles east of Moscow, where he was isolated from all contacts. Bonner served as courier for a time, bringing his messages to Moscow, but in 1984 she was convicted of slander against the Soviet state and sentenced also to exile in Gorki.

In 1981 the couple went on a hunger strike for seventeen days to secure a permit for Bonner's daughter-in-law to join her husband in the United States. As Bonner's health deteriorated, Sakharov repeated such hunger strikes several times before Bonner was given permission to leave the Soviet Union in 1985 for heart surgery in Boston, close to her family.

After Mikhail Gorbachev came to power, he announced a policy of limited liberalization. In December 1986, a hitherto forbidden telephone was suddenly installed in the Sakharov apartment in Gorki, and the next day a personal call came from Gorbachev himself. He informed Sakharov that he and Bonner could go back to Moscow and that Sakharov was to return to the Physics Institute "to work for the public good." Sakharov used the occasion to remind Gorbachev of the letter he had sent him some months before, asking amnesty for prisoners of conscience. He made no agreement to abandon his work for human rights when he returned to Moscow.

In his autobiographical statement prepared for the Nobel Committee, Sakharov had referred to the "large measure of tragedy in my life at present," and then declared, "Yet, even so, both now and for always, I intend to hold fast to my belief in the hidden strength of the human spirit." The kind of courage he has shown has been rooted in just such an unshakable faith in humanity.

BIBLIOGRAPHY

Primary Sources

Sakharov, Andrei D. *Alarm and Hope.* Edited by E. Yankelevich and Alfred Friendly, Jr. New York: Knopf, 1978. Public statements of 1976–77, with an afterword by Sakharov and his Nobel lecture of 1975. The title essay was written for the anthology published by the Norwegian Nobel Committee in 1978 in Norwegian.

———. "The First Priority: Disarmament." *Bulletin of the Atomic Scientists* 35 (May 1979): 9. A letter from Sakharov.

———. *My Country and the World.* Translated by Guy V. Daniels. New York: Knopf, 1976. The second essay to be published in the West.

———. *Progress, Coexistence and Intellectual Freedom.* Translated by *New York Times* staff. His first manifesto.

———. "The Responsibility of Scientists." *New York Review of Books* 28 (25 June 1981): 12, 14.

———. "Tomorrow: The View from Red Square." *Saturday Review World,* 24 August 1974, pp. 12–14, 108–10. The problems facing mankind and some models for their solution.

Secondary Sources

Bonner, Yelena. *Alone Together.* Translated by Alexander Cook. New York: Knopf, 1986. Written by Sakharov's wife during her six-month leave from their Gorki exile to undergo medical treatment in the United States. Includes Sakharov documents.

Dornan, Peter. "Andrei Sakharov: The Conscience of a Liberal Scientist." In *Dissent in the USSR: Politics, Ideology and People.* Edited by Rudolf L. Tolkes. Baltimore: Johns Hopkins University Press, 1975, pp. 354–417.

Salisbury, Harrison E., ed. *Sakharov Speaks.* New York: Vintage, 1974.

1976
Mairead Corrigan {Maguire} (1944–)

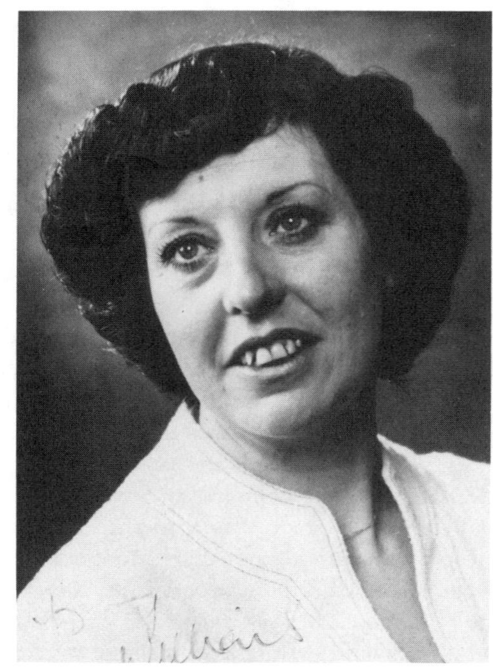

Betty Williams {Perkins} (1943–)

Northern Ireland, Great Britain

Cofounders of the Community of the Peace People.

The reserved prize for 1976 was divided the following year between Mairead Corrigan and Betty Williams for their "courageous acts of peace" in founding a movement "to put an end to the violence that has characterized the unfortunate division in Northern Ireland and taken so many innocent lives."

Their actions had been inspired by a tragic incident that occurred during the summer of 1976 in Belfast, capital of the province ruled by the British. The city, divided between the Protestant majority and the Catholic minority, for seven years had been the scene of unbridled violence. The Provisional Irish Republican Army (IRA) wanted to drive out the British and unite with the Republic of Ireland to the south. Their bombings, murders, and other acts of violence were directed not only against British soldiers but against Protestant and Catholic civilians. On the other side were Protestant extremists, who had formed their own paramilitary units and returned violence for violence.

On a sunny day in August of 1976, a mother was going for a stroll with her three children, the eldest pushing her six-week-old baby brother in his carriage. Suddenly they heard a shot, and a car came careening into them, killing two of the children outright, mortally injuring the third, and leaving the mother in critical condition. Following a shoot-out, British soldiers pursuing IRA gunmen had shot dead the driver of the car, which had gone out of control and smashed the little family against an iron railing. This senseless killing of innocent children evoked a wave of revulsion against the violence that had held the city so long in its grip, and a spontaneous movement for peace began that brought together Protestants and Catholics. It was led by two young women, Mairead Corrigan and Mrs. Betty Williams.

Betty Williams

Both had been born in Catholic sectors of Belfast, but Betty Smyth was the first child of a mixed marriage between a Catholic mother and a Protestant father, something that Belfast Catholics decried, and her maternal grandfather, whom she dearly loved as a child, was a Polish Jew whose relatives had been killed in World War II. She attended Catholic schools, but her father, a butcher, tried to keep her free of the religious prejudices she found all around her. It was not surprising that she herself married a non-Catholic, Ralph Williams, an engineer in the merchant marine. She saw something of the world with her seaman husband, but they came back to Belfast, where she continued working after they had their two children. In 1976, when she was thirty-four, she held a secretarial job in a casualty firm and also worked as a waitress.

She had originally sympathized with the Northern Irish revolutionaries, but she had come to realize that violence only breeds violence and makes victims of the innocent. In 1972 she had joined a movement started by a Protestant clergyman to try to end the violence. In 1973, when a young British soldier was shot before her eyes and lay dying on the sidewalk, she tried to comfort him, only to meet with insults from Catholic women who watched. "I learned that people had obviously lost their sense of value of human life," she said when relating this story in later years.

Mairead Corrigan

Mairead Corrigan was the second of seven children of a working-class family. Her father, who worked as a window cleaner, could not pay for her high school tuition, so after completing the primary grades, she left school at fourteen and earned money as a baby-sitter in order to enroll in business courses. At sixteen she was an assistant bookkeeper in a textile factory, and at twenty-one she was hired as secretary in a brewery. She stayed with the firm, and in 1976, when she was thirty-three, she had become private secretary to one of the directors.

Her religion has always meant much to her. After leaving her Catholic school, she joined the Legion of Mary, a Catholic lay welfare organization, in which she worked with children and adolescents and organized recreational activities for the disadvantaged. The legion sent her as a youth leader to a meeting of the World Council of Churches in Thailand when she was twenty-eight, and the next year to the Soviet Union, to help make a film on the life of religious believers. On her return she showed the film and lectured at Catholic centers.

Mairead Corrigan grew up hating the British soldiers and fearing the Irish Revolutionary Army, but she never felt herself to be a revolutionary and she watched the increasing violence with dismay. She sympathized with the British-held political prisoners of both sides, whom she visited in her work with the legion, but she felt that the acts of violence of which they were accused were not consistent with the way of Christ, and she told them so.

The tragedy on the Belfast street changed her life. It was her sister, Anne Maguire, whose children had been killed by the car. The next evening Mairead Corrigan was interviewed on a television program. She burst out sobbing: "It's not violence that people want. Only 1 percent of the people of this province want this slaughter." With courage, she condemned those who encouraged young people to join the paramilitary groups.

Betty Williams had actually witnessed the accident, and she had immediately set about walking the streets of her neighborhood, collecting signatures to a petition demanding peace and a stop to the violence. In two days she announced over television that she had six thousand signatures. She asked all women, both Catholic and Protestant, to help "rid our community of this riffraff." She admitted, "I've always been afraid of the IRA. I am afraid of it at this very moment. But after such a tragedy, we must and will have peace."

Corrigan joined Williams in leading a peace march of ten thousand women to the new graves of the Maguire children. Protestants marched with Catholics and persisted when IRA supporters physically assaulted them. The next week thirty-five thousand marched from a Catholic to a Protestant area of Belfast.

The two women were joined by Ciaran McKeown, a newspaper reporter, who helped them give more lasting direction to the movement. He suggested that an organization be established to be called "Community of the Peace People," rather than "Women for Peace," since men should be included as well. He wrote a "Declaration of Peace," a simple statement of aims, and gave the movement its nonviolent ideology, founding its journal, *Peace by Peace.* It was also McKeown who planned the strategy of the marches that were staged during the following months in cities both in Northern Ireland and in Great Britain.

The IRA claimed that the Peace People were dupes of the British and wanted "peace at any price" instead of "peace with justice." They continued to harass the marchers, but the thousands who joined these occasions testified to a deep yearning for peace in the land.

The movement captured the imagination of the world and was given wide publicity. In Norway, where it was too late for a nomination for the Nobel Peace Prize, a campaign organized by newspapers and civic organizations raised $340,000, which was presented to Corrigan and Williams at a mass meeting at Oslo's city hall. The two visited other countries in Europe and across the seas to raise more funds. In October 1976 they came to the United States to appeal to Irish-Americans to stop sending the money that was buying the guns and bombs for IRA terrorism.

The Peace People used the contributions to arrange nonsectarian activities, to repair damaged factories and schools, and to make loans for small businesses. It was clear that poverty and unemployment was giving rise to violence, and on their trips abroad Williams and Corrigan tried to generate foreign investments in Northern Ireland.

The Nobel Committee considered fifty nominations for the 1976 prize and then reserved it, presumably feeling that none of the candidates was as well qualified as the two Irish peace leaders. In 1977 Williams and Corrigan were properly nominated and duly presented with the 1976 prize at the same ceremony at which Amnesty International was given the prize for 1977.

The two women were a study in contrast: Williams, tall and imposing and the more aggressive, Corrigan, a small and slight brunette, ever smiling and deemed the more photogenic. Corrigan was more emotional and spiritual, Williams, more down-to-earth. "I drink, and I swear," she told an interviewer, "but I have profound faith in God."

It was Williams who delivered the Nobel lecture. She spoke of the tragedy that had led them "to make that initial call, a call which unlocked the massive desire for peace within the hearts of the Northern Irish people, and as we soon discovered, in the hearts of people around the world." It had been the "sheer needlessness of this awful loss of life" that had stirred thousands to march that week: "As far as we are concerned, every single death in the last eight years, and every death in every war that was ever fought represents life needlessly wasted, a mother's labor spurned."

Williams was, in fact, the first mother to receive the prize. In three-quarters of a century, there had been only three women laureates. Now Williams declared that she and Corrigan felt a special sense of honor for women:

> The voice of women has a special role and a special soul-force in the struggle for a nonviolent world. We do not wish to replace religous sectarianism, or ideological division with sexism or any kind of militant feminism. But we do believe . . . that women have a leading role to play in this great struggle.

Williams called on women everywhere to encourage men to have the courage to say no to war. Real courage was needed to breach the barriers that divided people: "The only force which can break down those barriers is the force of love, the force of truth, soul-force." To this force, she said, and to the cause of nonviolence, "we are deeply, passionately dedicated":

> To those who say that we are naive, utopian idealists, we say that we are the only realists, and that those who continue to support militarism in our time are supporting the progress towards the total self-destruction of the human race, when the only right and left, will be dead to the right and dead to the left, and death and destruction right, left, and center, east and west, north and south.

The subsequent history of the Peace People was something of an anticlimax. The number of violent deaths declined in 1977, but the movement was already losing its momentum in that year, perhaps as early as the end of the marches in the previous December and certainly with the move to less dramatic projects of reconciliation. Williams and Corrigan, who had given up their jobs to work full-time for the movement, were criticized for keeping most of the prize money so they could go off the Peace People's payroll and handle their own expenses, as well as continue their worldwide travel for interpretation and fund-raising. But Alfred Nobel had intended his prize to be used for just such a purpose—to free the laureate to be able to work harder for peace.

In 1978 Williams, Corrigan, and McKeown democratically stepped down from their leadership positions to give others the chance. Then McKeown's political ideas became a source of controversy, and a rift developed between Corrigan and Williams, who resigned from the organization. Williams was divorced, and eventually she emigrated to the United States and married Jim Perkins, an electrical engineer.

In 1980 Anne Maguire, after vainly seeking peace of mind through a brief emigration with her husband to New Zealand, succumbed to her insurmountable grief and took her own life. Mairead helped her brother-in-law take care of the three other children her sister had left, and in 1981, they were married. They moved to a home twenty miles southeast of Belfast, where Mairead was fully occupied with the growing Maguire family and had little time for the Peace People.

The organization has continued in existence but with a modest program and a membership that by 1988 had fallen to about fifty regular members. In reflecting on it all, Betty Perkins concluded, "Somewhere along the line, we lost sight of the basic simplicity of our message. We got organized, which is perhaps the worst thing we could have done."

Mairead agrees that they made mistakes, but she wrote in a letter to me, "The message of the Peace People is just as relevant today as in 1976 that nonviolence is the only way forward for the human family and it has not failed, it has just not been tried with enough determination by enough people."

The violence continues in Northern Ireland, but a number of small peace groups have been started with various kinds of projects to reconcile Catholics and Protestants. The great days of 1976, when so many overcame their fears, found their self-confidence and self-respect, and began to reach out to one another across the barriers, have not been forgotten.

The enduring quality of the service to peace of Mairead Corrigan and Betty Williams was highlighted in the words of Egil Aarvik, vice-chairman of the Nobel Committee, in his presentation speech:

> Love of one's neighbor is one of the foundation stones of the humanism on which our western civilization is built. But it is vital that we should have the courage to sustain this love of our neighbor in the very circumstances when the pressure to abandon it is at its greatest—otherwise it is of little worth. This is why it should shine forth when hatred and revenge threaten to dominate. . . .
>
> Betty Williams and Mairead Corrigan have shown us what ordinary people can do to promote the cause of peace.

BIBLIOGRAPHY

Secondary Sources

"Corrigan, Mairead." In *CB,* 1978.

Deutsch, Richard. *Mairead Corrigan, Betty Williams.* New York: Woodberry, 1977. Best account of events to 1977, but uncritical.

Deutsch, Richard, and Vivien Magowan. *Northern Ireland, 1968–1974: A Chronology of Events.* 3 vols. Belfast: Blackstaff, 1973–75.

Fairmichael, Rob. "The Peace People Experience." *Dawn Train,* no. 5 (1987). A careful account, bringing the story up to date. With a good bibliography.

"Williams, Betty." In *CB,* 1979.

Willis, David K. "Belfast Citizens Pursue Peacemaking in Shadow of Nobel Prize Winners." *Christian Science Monitor,* 8 February 1984, p. 1.

1977
Amnesty International

Worldwide organization established in 1961 to protect the human rights of prisoners of conscience.

The announcement of the prize for 1977 declared, "The Nobel Committee in the year of 1977—the Year of Prisoners of Conscience—has wished to honor Amnesty International for the contribution the organization has made to protect this group of prisoners against treatment which ignores human rights. With its work for the protection of human rights against degradation, violence, and torture, Amnesty International has contributed to securing a foundation for peace, for dignity, and thereby, also for peace in the world."

Amnesty International had proclaimed 1977 as Prisoners of Conscience Year and collected signatures for an appeal addressed to the UN General Assembly in behalf of this group, defined as "men and women detained anywhere in the world for their beliefs, color, ethnic origin, religion, or language, provided they have neither used nor advocated violence."

Amnesty International began when an incident of such injustice came to the notice of Peter Benenson, a wealthy London lawyer, as he sat in a London train reading his newspaper in the fall of 1960. The news item reported that two Portuguese students had been sentenced to seven years in jail by the dictatorial government, simply because they had dared to drink a toast to freedom in public. Profoundly shocked, Benenson decided on the spot that he had to do something to help the young men. His first thought was to organize a campaign of letters to the Portuguese government, asking for amnesty. But then he thought of all the other victims of such treatment throughout the world.

The upshot was that Benenson enlisted other sponsors and placed an article in the London *Observer* on 28 May 1961, entitled "The Forgotten Prisoners," which was reprinted in major newspapers in other countries, launching an "Appeal for Amnesty 1961." It was noted that this year marked the centennial anniversary of the emancipation of the slaves in the United States and of the serfs in Russia.

The article began with these words: "Open your newspaper any day of the week and you will find a report from somewhere in the world of someone being imprisoned, tortured or executed because his opinions or religion are unacceptable to his government." Such a report, the article continued, leaves the reader with "a sickening sense of impotence," but if "these feelings of disgust all over the world could be united into common action, something effective could be done." The cases of eight prisoners in different countries were then presented for individual action.

The appeal produced such a flood of letters and donations that the sponsors soon decided to make the campaign permanent, and Amnesty International was born. Not only was it evident from the response how widespread was the abuse of human rights all over the world, but the need to collect detailed documentation on every case made imperative the establishment of a research bureau.

The organization's growth was rapid. By 1963 it had expanded beyond its English origins, and an international secretariat and executive council, with Seán MacBride as chairman, had been established. After the first ten years the organization comprised more than 1,000 groups in 28 countries; by 1977 it had more than 168,000 active members from 107 countries. When Amnesty International celebrated its twenty-fifth birthday in 1986, it had grown to almost half a million members and supporters in over 150 countries, with a network of 3,600 groups. The staff at the London headquarters now numbered over 200, half of them working in the Research Department. The United States section alone had over 500 groups in communities and on campuses.

The statutes adopted in 1974 declared Amnesty International to be "independent of any government, political grouping, ideology, economic interest or religious creed. The activities of the organization focus strictly on prisoners." Its major objectives were the release of all prisoners of conscience, "fair and early trials for all political prisoners," and the abolition of torture and the death penalty.

The organization has scrupulously followed its basic commitment to remain neutral, impartial, and independent. A prisoner's politics or religion never enters into the decision to work for him or her, and the countries of the prisoners selected for special efforts are balanced geographically and politically to ensure impartiality. Moreover, Amnesty International has been very careful not to accept contributions from any source that might call into question its independence.

It has continued to press for international machinery to implement the UN Declaration of Human Rights, opposing the principle of noninterference in internal affairs and urging governments to sign and observe the international covenants on human rights, which by 1976 had been ratified by the requisite number of states and had come into force. Amnesty began a Campaign for the Abolition of Torture in 1972, publicized evidence of its use in over sixty countries, and secured more than a million signatures from all over the world in support of an antitorture resolution in the General Assembly, which was passed unanimously.

The heart of Amnesty International's effort, however, has been the work of the small groups, which, on the basis of authoritative information supplied by the secretariat, "adopt" individual prisoners and write letters to the authorities asking for their release and, where possible, to the prisoners themselves. A group will adopt two or three prisoners at a time—if three, in the interest of impartiality one is likely to be in the West, one in a communist-bloc country, and one in the third world. Amnesty also sends information to members about emergency cases that require immediate dispatch of telegrams and airmail letters.

Have the letter-writing campaigns been effective? The Nobel Committee thought so. Mrs. Lionaes noted in her presentation speech that between 1972 and 1975 Amnesty was working for six thousand prisoners, of whom three thousand had been released. She recognized that other factors may have led to this result, but noted that in any case, exact statistics were not important. What had impressed the committee was the indication the numbers gave of the scope of Amnesty's work; it was clear that its activities were an important part of the larger movement for human rights.

Since 1977 the numbers have further increased. Over the twenty-five years since it was founded, Amnesty has worked for over thirty thousand prisoners, and more than twenty-five thousand of these cases are now closed. It is the organization's policy not to take credit for a prisoner's release. But testimonials and letters of thanks have come from many of the former prisoners themselves. A labor organizer in the Dominican Republic wrote:

> When the first two hundred letters came, the guards gave me back my clothes. Then the next two hundred letters came, and the prison director came to see me. When the next pile of letters arrived, the director got in touch with his superior. The letters kept coming and coming: three thousand of them. The President was informed. The letters still kept arriving, and the President called the prison and told them to let me go.

Even some of the most oppressive governments have not been immune to letter campaigns. Apparently they have responded to the pressure because of their concern for their international image. Amnesty itself has earned such a reputation for integrity and accuracy that its public statements, the findings of its investigative missions, and its annual reports are widely respected.

The annual report in 1986 gave a grim picture. Violations of human rights in 128 countries were cited, the United States for its capital punishment, the Soviet Union for abuses in prisons, labor camps, and psychiatric hospitals, and South Africa (subject of the longest section in the report) for "torture and ill-treatment of uncharged political detainees." There is, the report declared, "a gulf between commitments and reality."

Yet the story of Amnesty International itself gives reason for hope. In the face of the dark record of inhumanity that the pages of its reports document, its work is carried out through the efforts of individuals concerned about human suffering who act in the faith that an ordinary individual can make a difference. As Mümtaz Soysal of Turkey, Amnesty International's vice-chairman, who with Chairman Thomas Hammarberg of Sweden represented the organization at the ceremony, declared in the Nobel lecture:

> It was upon this commitment of individual human beings to each other's welfare that Amnesty International was founded. . . . It began with the outrage of one man who, when confronted with the plight of unjustly detained individuals, called on others to join with him to rouse international public opinion, to do something concrete, and, where human beings are at stake, to break down all barriers.

He concluded with the words of a woman who had managed to send a letter from her prison cell:

> They are envious of us. They will envy us all.
> For it is an enviable but very difficult task to live through history as a human being, to complete a life as a human being.
> Soon the night will fall and they will close the doors of the cell.
> I feel lonely.
> No . . . I am with the whole of mankind
> And the whole of mankind is with me.

BIBLIOGRAPHY

Primary Sources

Amnesty International 1987. London: Amnesty International Publications, 1987.

Amnesty International. *A Major Collection of Published and Unpublished Research Material on Microfiche.* New York: Clearwater, updated annually.

———. *Report on Torture.* New York: Farrar, Straus & Giroux, 1975. Amnesty's first world survey.

Secondary Sources

Larsen, Egon. *A Flame in Barbed Wire.* New York: Norton, 1979.

Power, Jonathan. *Amnesty International: The Human Rights Story.* New York: McGraw-Hill, 1981. A journalistic account, well illustrated.

1978

Mohamed Anwar el Sadat (1918–81)

Egypt

President, Arab Republic of Egypt

Menachem Begin (1913–)

Israel

Prime minister, Israel.

On 27 October 1978 the Nobel Committee announced that the prize for that year would be shared by President Anwar Sadat of Egypt and Prime Minister Menachem Begin of Israel. It was six weeks after the momentous meeting of the two statesmen at Camp David with President Jimmy Carter produced the framework agreements for a peace treaty to end the state of war that had lasted for three decades. On 12 October the negotiations to draft the specific terms of the treaty had begun, and it was hoped that it would be ready to be signed on 19 November. This was the anniversary of Sadat's dramatic trip to Jerusalem that had made possible new relationships between the two countries.

By the time the committee announcement was made, however, these negotiations were at an impasse. On the morning of 27 October Secretary of State Cyrus Vance was vainly trying to move Foreign Minister Moishe Dayan to compromise, and the Egyptian representative was packing his bags to return to Cairo. Vance finally called off the negotiating session planned for the afternoon.

The committee's announcement did take note of the unfinished business. It said that in awarding the prize to Sadat and Begin, the committee wanted "not only to honor actions already performed in the service of peace, but also to encourage further efforts to work out practical solutions which can give reality to those hopes of lasting peace."

In Cairo the news of the joint prize was received with mixed feelings. Hopes had been high for a single award for Sadat, since, after all, it had been his courageous visit to Jerusalem that had opened the way to peace. Moreover, in extending the olive branch to Israel, Sadat had alienated other Arab states, and sharing the award with Begin only complicated his problems. He finally decided not to attend the Oslo ceremony and appear side-by-side with the Israeli premier; he sent instead his long-term counselor, Sayed Marei, to represent him.

In Oslo the prize was much criticized. Five years after the Kissinger–Le Duc Tho decision, Nobel Committee Chair Aase Lionaes once again had to defend an award for a peace that was not a peace. A newspaper poll in Oslo showed that only about 25 percent of the sample approved the award, while 30 percent disapproved. More revealing was the finding that 30 percent thought that Sadat should have been the sole laureate, while less than 1 percent thought that Begin should have been named alone. A rumor circulated in Olso that the members of the Nobel Committee had not been in complete agreement on the selection of Begin.

The arrangements for the ceremony were hardly in keeping with the spirit of peace. Out of consideration for the safety of the Israeli prime minister, the ceremony was moved from the great hall of the university to the old Akershus fortress overlooking the Oslo fjord, where police and soldiers with submachine guns patrolled the snow-covered grounds. Outside the gates Palestinian flags flew from balloons and demonstrators chanted "Begin—terrorist!" displaying signs calling for Palestinian self-determination.

For extra security Begin was taken by helicopter from the airport to the royal palace where he stayed, and from there to the fortress on the day of the award. Only a third of the number usually attending could crowd into the small Hall of the Knights to watch the ceremony. The ambassadors of most Arab and Soviet bloc states were conspicuously absent. Afterward, the torchlight procession usually held to honor the laureate was a protest march.

Mrs. Lionaes in her presentation speech briefly reviewed the history of Middle East conflict, carefully avoiding the points in contention, and credited the two laureates with actions that could "usher in a new era" in the whole region. She declared that they had a great deal in common: "From their earliest years they have identified themselves with the fate of their countries, they have fought and suffered, in prison and in labor camp, for the sovereignty of their native land and for the freedom of man."

Menachem Begin

Menachem Begin was born in 1913 in Poland in the city of Brest-Litovsk (now part of the Soviet Union). A Jewish state existed then only in the dreams and hopes of the Zionists, which Begin shared from his early youth. He followed his father, a prominent member of the local Jewish community, in supporting the militant Zionist Zeev Jabotinsky, who called for immediate direct action to establish a Jewish state in Palestine, then a British Mandate. As a law student in Warsaw, Begin was a leader in the Jabotinsky Zionist organization.

When the Germans invaded Poland in 1939, Begin and his wife, Aliza, fled to Lithuania in hopes of making their way to Palestine. They thus escaped the fate of most of the other Polish Jews, including Begin's parents and his brother, who died in the Holocaust. Lithuania, however, came under Soviet domination, and in September 1940, Begin, as a well-known Zionist, was arrested and sentenced to eight years in a Siberian labor camp. When Germany attacked the Soviet Union in 1941, he and other Polish citizens were released so that a Free Polish Army could be organized to fight against the Germans. Begin enlisted and was sent to the Middle East for training. In May 1942, Private Begin finally reached Palestine, assigned to the Polish town marshal's office in Jerusalem.

He was reunited with Aliza, and his friends soon secured his release from the Free Polish Army so that he could join them in the *Irgun Zvai Leumi* (IZL; National Military Organization), of which he was made commander in December 1943. Now thirty years old, Begin was the head of an underground paramilitary organization determined to use terrorism to force the British to recognize the establishment of an independent Jewish state. The larger Jewish organizations expected that this could come about peacefully in cooperation with the British. As chief of the IZL, Begin conducted such a ruthless terrorist campaign that the British placed a thirty-thousand-dollar price on his head. Such acts as the bombing of the King David Hotel in 1946, which killed many members of the British Mandate staff, brought a public condemnation of Begin as a fascist by leaders of the Jewish community.

In 1947, when the British relinquished their mandate and the United Nations Organization decided to partition Palestine between Jews and Arabs, fighting immediately broke out between them. Begin reorganized the IZL as an autonomous formation fighting along with the other Jewish forces. In 1948 the IZL was responsible for the massacre of over two hundred Arab civilians, including women and children, in the village of Dir Yassin, which Begin has always claimed was a legitimate military target.

When the state of Israel was founded, Begin disbanded the IZL and formed a political party, which was dedicated to the ideals of Jabotinsky, opposing the socialism of David Ben-Gurion's ruling party and insisting that all the lands that had once been part of the ancient Jewish kingdom should be annexed. In the Israeli parliament, the Knesset, Begin was a leader of the hard-liners. Short, bespectacled, intense, his integrity never in question, he was a fiery orator, at times a demagogue, but he had courtly manners, and in time his extremism was tempered.

Begin achieved political legitimacy at the time of the war of 1967, when he became a minister in the government of national unity. He resigned over the government's willingness to make territorial concessions to the Arabs to secure peace and forged the *Likud* (Unity) coalition of rightist parties, which finally broke the long dominance of the Labor party in the elections of May 1977. Begin then became prime minister.

Anwar el-Sadat

Just as Begin had identified himself from his earliest years with the ideal of a Jewish state, so had Sadat always dreamed of a free and independent Egypt. Anwar el-Sadat grew up in the village of Mit Abul-Kum in the Nile Delta, one of thirteen children of a poor government clerk. Throughout his life he never forgot the words of his grandmother, "You are a child of this earth." "I shall never go astray," he wrote in his memoirs, "because I know with such certainty that I have my roots in the village, deep down in the soil from which I, like the trees and other growing things, have sprung." Sadat gave his village the royalties from his autobiography and his Nobel prize money.

The family moved to Cairo, where the father's salary was stretched to the limit to support them. Sadat was able to complete secondary school and then to enter the Royal Military Academy, which had just been opened to others than sons of the aristocracy. He wanted to be an army officer and help oust the British from their domination of his country. At the academy he met Gamal Abdel Nasser and other cadets who shared his sentiments. After graduation in 1938, Sadat, then twenty years old, formed with Nasser and ten other officers a secret society to work for Egyptian independence.

When the Second World War began in 1939, Egypt was neutral, but Sadat cooperated with German spies to work against British interests. In 1942 he was court-martialed and spent two years in prison, while his fellow conspirators supported his wife and children. In 1944 they helped him escape from prison, and he went into hiding. He was all for direct action—"My idea was to blow up the British Embassy and everybody in it"—but Nasser, now the head of the Free Officers' Association, restrained him. In 1946, however, Sadat was arrested again after assassinations of pro-British officials, and although he maintained his innocence, he went back to prison for almost three more years—"the most terrible years of my life."

Finally released in 1949 with his officer's commission restored, he rejoined his comrades in the Free Officers' Association, who were now plotting to overthrow the feudal monarchy of King Farouk. Sadat's responsibility was liaison with civilian terrorist groups. In 1952 Nasser led the military coup that forced the king to abdicate. Sadat made the public announcement on the radio and supervised the departure of Farouk from the country.

When Nasser became premier and president of the Egyptian Republic, Sadat, as his most trusted aide, was given a number of posts both in Egypt and abroad. Tall and erect, with dark eyes and dark skin, he developed a relaxed and gracious manner that charmed foreign government leaders. His second wife, the beautiful and articulate Jihan, who was half-English, gave him good support. Sadat, who was vice president when Nasser died in 1970, was overwhelmingly elected to the presidency in a national vote. His political adversaries had underestimated him, and they were soon removed from their offices.

Sadat took the position that there could never be peace with Israel until that country gave up "every inch" of the territory it had taken from Egypt in the 1967 war. In 1973 he launched a surprise attack across the Suez Canal and Egyptian troops advanced into the Sinai Peninsula. With American assistance, the Israelis recovered and counterattacked across the canal, and then a cease-fire was concluded. The initial Egyptian advance against the hitherto invincible Israeli army, however, meant a return of Arab self-respect and left Sadat in a stronger position from which he could embark upon a peace initiative.

In 1977 Sadat announced to the Egyptian People's Assembly that he was prepared to go to the ends of the earth, even to Israel, in the cause of peace. Begin, who had just come to power calling for direct peace talks with Arab states, then sent Sadat on 17 November an official invitation to address the Knesset on 20 November. Sadat immediately accepted, rightly calculating that this "would break the vicious circle within which we had been caught up for years." It took great courage to appear before his country's enemies and speak frankly of the differences between them, perhaps even more to drive in an open car on his return to Cairo, although he met with a mass welcome.

Begin made his return visit to Sadat in December, when he came to the canal town of Ismailia in Egypt. There Begin made his own significant peace move, telling Sadat that he recognized Egypt's sovereignty over the whole of the Sinai Peninsula and going even further, announcing that he would not annex the West Bank of the Jordan River, which had been occupied by Israel since 1967, but instead would offer self-rule to the Arab inhabitants. This marked a fundamental change from his previous position. The stage was now set for Camp David.

At the ceremony in Oslo the messages of acceptance, delivered in person by Begin and read by Sadat's representative, both in English, were treated as the expected Nobel lectures. Each laureate accepted the prize in the name of his people and each described his people's age-old tradition of peace. Sadat referred to the first recorded peace treaty three thousand years ago between the Egyptians and the Hittites, and Begin cited the vision of the Hebrew prophets. Both laureates were devout believers, and their statements reflected their religious faith.

Each asserted his own commitment to peace and described the nature of true peace with reference to the Universal Declaration of Human Rights, the day of the ceremony being the anniversary of its adoption by the United Nations. Begin stressed the right "to go home," referring to Jews unable to leave the Soviet Union; Sadat emphasized the need to restore to the Palestinians their right to "a life of liberty and dignity."

Both paid tribute to President Jimmy Carter for what had been achieved, as had the Nobel Committee. If the statutes had permitted it, he might well have shared the prize with them. Perhaps the committee itself also deserves credit for strengthening the determination of Begin and Sadat to complete the peace process. The treaty was finally signed on 26 March 1979. It provided for the normalization of relations between Egypt and Israel, for trade and cultural exchanges, for Israel's withdrawal from the Sinai by 1982, and for further negotiations on Palestinian autonomy.

The consequences for Sadat were tragic. Muslim religious extremists in Egypt never forgave him for making peace with Israel, and he took dictatorial measures to curb them and other opponents of his policies. In 1981 he was cut down in a hail of assassin's bullets while reviewing a military parade.

Begin, on the other hand, became a war maker. In 1982 his government sent Israeli armed forces across the border into Lebanon with the aim of assuring Israel's security by driving out the Palestine Liberation Organization and establishing a government there friendly to Israel. Begin's war policy provoked opposition at home and condemnation abroad. In the Norwegian parliament voices were even raised calling for the return of his Peace Prize. In September 1983 Begin suddenly announced his resignation and withdrew from public life. He was depressed by the failure of the war to accomplish the objectives sought and by the toll it was taking in Jewish lives, and he was shattered by the death of his beloved Aliza. He went into seclusion in Jerusalem, receiving few visitors beyond his immediate family, keeping up with the news of political developments, but no longer desiring to have any part in them.

We cannot know how the peace agreement reached by Begin and Sadat will be assessed by future historians who will have the benefit of a longer perspective and adequate documents about actions and motives. Certainly, both had been men of violence, not of peace, during most of their lives before they were honored by the Nobel Committee, and Begin betrayed the honor a few years afterward. Sadat had little time after the prize to demonstrate the depth of his own peace commitment. Although he died something of a martyr to his peace policy, in his memoirs, written just after the trip to Jerusalem, he speaks of peace rhapsodically, but it is his military advance against Israel in 1973 about which he writes with the greatest satisfaction.

Whatever the verdict of historians might be, there is no question but that the episode of the 1978 prize highlighted once again the problems that are likely to arise in honoring political leaders for a single peace achievement.

BIBLIOGRAPHY

The Camp David Accords

Primary Sources

Carter, Jimmy. *Keeping Faith: Memoirs of a President.* New York: Bantam, 1982.

Kamel, Mohammed Ibrahim. *The Camp David Accords: A Testimony.* London: KPI, 1986. By the Egyptian foreign minister, who disagreed with Sadat and resigned.

U.S. Congress, House Committee on Foreign Affairs. *The Search for Peace in the Middle East: Documents and Statements, 1967–79.* Washington, D.C.: U.S. Government Printing Office, 1979.

Secondary Sources

"Camp David Accords" and "Arab-Israeli Conflict." In *WEP,* vol. 1.

Fredland, Melvin A. *Sadat and Begin: The Domestic Politics of Peacemaking.* Boulder, Colo.: Westview, 1983.

Quandt, William B. *Camp David: Peacemaking and Politics.* Washington, D.C.: Brookings Institution, 1986. Authoritative.

Menachem Begin

Primary Sources

Begin, Menachem. *The Revolt.* Rev. ed. New York: Nash, 1977. The struggle against the British, 1944–48.

———. *White Nights: The Story of a Prisoner in Russia.* Translated by Katie Kaplan. New York: Harper & Row, 1979.

Secondary Sources

"Begin, Menachem." In *CB,* 1971.

Gervassi, Frank. *The Life and Times of Menahem Begin: Rebel to Statesman.* New York: Putnam, 1979.

Haber, Eitan. *Menahem Begin: The Legend and the Man.* Translated by Louis Williams. New York: Delacorte, 1978. An admiring biography.

Reich, Bernhard. *The United States and Israel: Influence in the Special Relationship.* New York: Praeger, 1984.

Silver, Eric. *Begin, the Haunted Prophet.* New York: Random, 1984. "An unrepentant terrorist who won the Nobel Peace Prize, then launched another war."

Temko, Ned. *To Win or to Die: A Personal Portrait of Menachem Begin.* New York: Morrow, 1987. A vivid account by a journalist striving for objectivity. Concludes that Begin outnegotiated both Sadat and Carter at Camp David.

Anwar el-Sadat

Primary Sources

Sadat, Anwar el-. *Revolt on the Nile.* New York: Day, 1957. The revolt of the army officers.

———. *In Search of Identity: An Autobiography.* New York: Harper & Row, 1978. The story of his life and of his country after 1918.

Secondary Sources

Heikal, Muhammad Hasanayn. *Autumn of Fury.* New York: Random, 1983. Highly critical of Sadat. By a leading Egyptian journalist.

Hennebusch, Raymond A. *Egyptian Politics under Sadat.* New York: Columbia University Press, 1985.

Hirst, David, and Irene Beeson. *Sadat.* Winchester, Mass.: Faber & Faber, 1982. Highly critical.

Israeli, Raphael, with Carol Bardenstein. *Man of Defiance: A Political Biography of Anwar Sadat.* Totowa, N.J.: Barnes & Noble, 1985. A scholarly account, favorable to Sadat.

"Sadat, Anwar el-." In *CB,* 1971.

1979

Mother Teresa (1910–)

India

Founder and head of Roman Catholic order, Missionaries of Charity.

In presenting the prize to Mother Teresa, Chairman John Sanness reviewed the various categories of peacemaking that had been given recognition by the Nobel Committee over the years and asked, "Can any political, social, or intellectual feat of engineering, . . . however idealistic and principled its protagonists may be, give us anything but a house built on a foundation of sand, unless the spirit of Mother Teresa inspires the builder and takes its dwelling in the building?" Sanness said that in this award the committee wanted to recall the words of Fridjtof Nansen, "Love of one's neighbor is realistic policy," and Albert Schweitzer's "reverence for life."

Mother Teresa was born Agnes Gonxha Bojaxhiu to a family of Catholic Albanians in Uskup, a town in the Turkish Empire which is now Skopje, capital of Yugoslav Macedonia. Her father, of peasant stock, was a prosperous partner in a construction firm and a staunch supporter of the cause of independence for Albania, then also under Turkish rule. Their large home near the old stone bridge over the River Vardar was often filled with Albanian patriots discussing their nationalist aims.

Lazar, the son of the family, followed his father's political interests, but the mother and the two daughters were devoted to the Catholic church, to which the family had belonged for generations. The father died suddenly when Agnes was only nine, and from politics the center of attention at home now shifted to the affairs of the church. Lazar remembers that his mother and his two sisters practically lived in their parish church. The mother's piety was expressed in many acts of benevolence for people in town who were in need, and it was not surprising that at the age of twelve Agnes was already talking of becoming a missionary to help the poor.

Life was harder for the family after the father's death and the sale of his business, but by doing embroidery the mother managed to keep their home and even to send Agnes to secondary school after she left the Catholic elementary school, an unusual privilege for an Albanian girl in Skopje at that time. At the church Agnes heard reports of Catholic missionaries in Bengal and dreamed of going to India herself. Growing up in Skopje, with its many different cultural and religious groups, was in its way a good preparation for India.

At eighteen Agnes decided to join the Sisters of Loretto, a teaching order with a missionary school in Calcutta. Lazar, who had left home to enter the military academy in the Kingdom of Albania and was just then proudly receiving his officer's commission, wrote to her protesting that his attractive and vivacious sister would be throwing her life away. She replied, "You think you are so important as an officer in the service of the king of two million souls. Well, I'm an officer too, but I serve the king of the world. Which of us is right?"

It took courage and conviction for Agnes to leave her childhood home and say farewell to her mother and sister, whom she was never to see again, but she firmly believed that this was what God wanted her to do. She went first to the mother house of the order in Dublin to work on her English for several months, which was a struggle. Then she sailed for India to enter the novitiate in Darjeeling in the mountains of Bengal, three hundred miles north of Calcutta. She took her first vows in 1931 and her final vows in 1937, choosing the name Teresa, after St. Theresa of Avila, the Spanish nun and mystic.

Meanwhile, she had begun teaching geography and history in St. Mary's High School in Calcutta, where during the following years she also served as principal. She is remembered as a fine teacher and a devoted nun, but not for any extraordinary spiritual gifts. It was a happy life, but as she taught the daughters of well-to-do families, she could not be indifferent to the scenes ouside the convent, where the streets of Calcutta's slums were filled with the poor and the sick, for whom nobody seemed to care.

On 10 September 1946, she was riding on a train en route to her annual retreat when she received what she speaks of as a "call within my vocation. . . . The message was clear. I was to leave the convent and help the poor, while living among them." She asked her superiors for permission to follow this call, and after almost two years the Vatican gave its consent: she could live as an "unenclosed nun," subject to the archbishop of Calcultta. So on 16 August 1948, Teresa laid aside the Loretto habit and left the convent.

She went first to a religious institution for three months of nursing training, and then, with no program and only a few rupees, she went into the slums of Calcutta to see what she could do. Her first project was an open-air school for homeless children. Soon contributions were offered, facilities were found, volunteers from among her former students joined her, and she could take food to the hungry, minister to the sick, and care for the dying. Most of all, she brought a caring love to assuage what she refers to as the worst disease, the sense of being unwanted. Wearing a sari, the national dress, and speaking Bengali, she lived among the poor as one of them, insisting that they were giving more to her than she to them.

In 1950 she and her helpers were recognized as the Missionaries of Charity within the Archdiocese of Calcutta, and as their community grew and its activities expanded beyond Calcutta and beyond India, the Vatican placed the order under its own jurisdiction. Along with the three customary vows of poverty, chastity, and obedience, there is a fourth: to give "whole-hearted free service to the poorest of the poor—to Christ in his distressing disguise."

The order had a phenomenal growth. More women volunteered, an increasing number from many countries outside India. It was decided to accept brothers as well, and then for the laity there was formed the International Association of Cooperators with Mother Teresa—she rejected the more passive title Friends of Mother Teresa. Among the projects of the Missionaries of Charity have been homes for orphaned children, schools, mobile clinics, leprosy centers, food kitchens, and hostels for the dying. To perform these services members of the order undergo medical and social work training, and they have been called upon to help in natural catastrophes like floods and earthquakes, in epidemics, and in refugee relief. By 1986 the small community of the Missionaries of Charity of Calcutta had become a worldwide order with more than sixteen hundred sisters, some hundreds in training, and 230 houses in more than sixty countries on all the continents.

Mother Teresa, as everybody, even her older brother who now lives in Italy, calls her, has a fine disregard for such statistics. "It is not how much we do," she says, "but how much love we put into it. The moment we have given it to God, it becomes infinite." As the chief officer in this army serving her Divine King, she has shown a remarkable organizing ability. She has set up a strict discipline, to which she subjects herself first of all. Every morning at five she rises to hear mass before setting forth on her work. No one knows when she finds time to answer so many of the flood of letters that come to her, let alone when she sleeps.

It was in 1967 that Mother Teresa first came to the notice of the world, when she was interviewed on the BBC by the Catholic writer Malcolm Muggeridge. Letters and contributions for her work poured in, articles about her were written in many countries, honors came to her from many quarters, including the Vatican and Harvard University, and she became known as a "living saint," as *Time* magazine called her in its cover story in 1975.

Throughout all this acclaim, Mother Teresa remained herself, natural and unaffected, open and direct, ever humble and modest in her person—to each new honor she responded with the words "I am not worthy"—but unswerving in her decisions once she had made up her mind. When she was to receive the prize at Oslo and heard about the traditional banquet to be offered by the committee on the evening of the ceremony, she insisted it should be canceled and the money given to her to feed the hungry of Calcutta. This created problems for the committee because of the rules, but in the end a way was found to give her what she wanted. Officialdom in other places has also yielded to the determination of this little nun in the white sari trimmed in blue with the cross on her shoulder.

For her Nobel lecture Mother Teresa prepared a paper, but she was used to speaking without notes, simply saying what was in her heart, and she did not stick to her text on this occasion. She began, as she often did, leading the audience in the prayer for peace of St. Francis. Then she spoke simply of her religious beliefs, of how she and her sisters and brothers were trying to follow Christ's teachings about sharing our love with others, and telling of her experiences that confirmed these truths.

We may be thought of as social workers, she declared, "but we are really contemplatives in the heart of the world. For we are touching the body of Christ twenty-four hours. . . . Christ in our hearts, Christ in the poor that we meet, Christ in the smile that we give and the smile that we receive." Remember to smile at one another, she said, "for the smile is the beginning of love, and once we begin to love each other, naturally we want to do something."

Mother Teresa did not please the feminists in her audience, who had been rejoicing that at last the committee had named another woman (only the sixth), by her strong words about abortion. She felt it was "the greatest destroyer of peace today" because "it is a direct war, a direct killing—direct murder by the mother herself." No child should be unwanted, she said, and the Missionaries were fighting abortion by a large-scale adoption program, sending out word over India that they would find a home for every child brought to them.

Mother Teresa concluded with words of thanks and challenge to the Norwegian people: "If we could only remember that God loves me, and I have an opportunity to love others as he loves me, not in big things, but in small things with great love, then Norway becomes a nest of love. . . . If you become a burning light in the world of peace, then really the Nobel Peace Prize is a gift of the Norwegian people." And she ended as she always does, "God bless you!"

In the years following the Peace Prize, Mother Teresa has expanded the international scope of her work, although Calcutta has always remained her home. A remarkable documentary film released in 1986 shows her at work over a period of five years, not only in the slums of Calcutta, but taking help to spastic children across the dividing line in war-torn Beirut, aiding earthquake victims in Guatemala, famine victims in Africa, and the poor in San Francisco and the South Bronx, distributing everywhere her inspiring message of love and joy.

BIBLIOGRAPHY

Primary Sources

Mother Teresa. "This Gift of Peace: Smile at Each Other." *Vital Speeches* 46 (1 June 1980): 510–12. Her Nobel lecture.

Mother Teresa Treasury. 3 vols. San Francisco: Harper & Row, 1985.

Secondary Sources

Craig, Mary. *Mother Teresa*. London: Hamish Hamilton, 1983.

Doig, Desmond. *Mother Teresa: Her People and Her Work*. New York: Harper & Row, 1976. By an Indian journalist very familiar with her work. Illustrated by the renowned photographer Raghu Rai.

Egan, Eileen. *Such a Vision of the Street: Mother Teresa*. New York: Doubleday, 1985.

Gorrée, Georges, and Jean Barbier. *Love without Boundaries*. Translated by Paula Speakman. Huntington, Ind.: Our Sunday Visitor, 1976.

Le Joly, Edward. *Servant of Love*. San Francisco: Harper & Row, 1977. An account by the priest who was her spiritual director, mainly told in her own words.

"Mother Teresa." In *CB*, 1973.

Muggeridge, Malcolm. *Something Beautiful for God: Mother Teresa of Calcutta*. New York: Harper & Row, 1971. Based on the interview and conversations with her in Calcutta for the BBC-TV film of the same title. The author first brought her to the attention of the West.

Rae, Daphne. *Love until It Hurts: The Work of Mother Teresa and Her Missionaries of Charity*. San Francisco: Harper & Row, 1981.

Scolozzi, Brother Angelo Devananda. *Mother Teresa: Contemplative in the Heart of the World*. Ann Arbor, Mich.: Servant Books, 1985.

Spink, Kathryn. *The Miracle of Love: Mother Teresa of Calcutta, Her Missionaries of Charity, and Her Co-Workers*. San Francisco: Harper & Row, 1981.

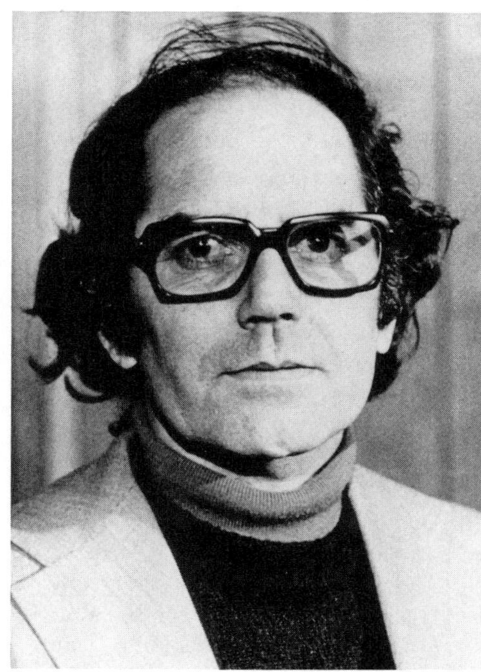

1980

Adolfo Pérez Esquivel (1931–)

Argentina

Secretary-general of Service for Peace and Justice, the Latin-American nonviolent human rights organization.

When the Nobel Committee made the surprise announcement that the prizewinner for 1980 was to be Adolfo Pérez Esquivel, he was so little known in Norway that the press services called him a Brazilian. Nor was he much better known in his own country of Argentina, where the press had been silent about his courageous opposition to the excessive acts of repression of the military government. In granting Pérez Esquivel the prize, the committee gave him an instant international reputation that did far more to support his efforts than the money he received.

In the presentation ceremony, Chairman John Sanness of the committee referred to the laureate's untiring and consistent championing of the principle of nonviolence in the struggle for social and political liberty. "He has lit a light in the dark," Sanness declared, "a light which, in the opinion of our Committee, should never be allowed to be extinguished." The committee recognized in Pérez Esquivel the same spirit that inspired Mother Teresa, his coreligionist who had won the prize the year before, and similar aims to those of the 1975 prizewinner, Andrei Sakharov.

His message of nonviolence, said Sanness, "is valid for the whole of Latin America—and not only for that part of the world." Others had proclaimed such principles in other countries, "but the reason his voice reached all the way from Latin America to the Norwegian Nobel Committee was not because of its strength but because of its purity and clarity."

Adolfo Pérez Esquivel was the son of a Spanish fisherman who had emigrated to Argentina. His mother died when he was three. Despite the family's modest circumstances, he was sent to Catholic boarding schools and then worked his way through the National School of Fine Arts in Buenos Aires. At the age of twenty-five, he received his degree of master of arts and became an art teacher and sculptor. His work won prizes and is on view in art museums and in the plazas of Argentinian cities. In 1956, the year he received his first teaching appointment, he married Amanda Itati, a pianist and composer, and they have three sons.

Pérez Esquivel was a successful sculptor and art teacher for fifteen years before he became an activist. Many influences contributed to his decision. He was always a devout Catholic who took the message of the Gospels seriously. He was inspired by the writings of the Catholic monk Thomas Merton and by the example of Charles de Foucauld, founder of the Little Brothers of Jesus, who said that one must "cry out the Gospel with all one's life." Through his professional interest in pre-Columbian art, he had become aware of the Indian peoples of Latin America and the conditions of poverty and oppression in which they were living. Around this time, also, the concept of liberation theology was spreading throughout the Catholic church in Latin America, awakening priests and laity to social and economic injustices. And a final factor was his lifelong interest in the principle of nonviolence. Pérez Esquivel had read about Gandhi when he was a teenager and had been much impressed with him and later with Martin Luther King, Jr.. In the late 1960s, then, Pérez Esquivel became associated with a Gandhian religious communitarian group.

The escalating violence in Argentina had a deep effect upon him. In 1972 he took part in a public fast to protest the violence on the part of both leftist and rightist guerrilla groups, and the next year he started the periodical *Paz y Justicia* (Peace and Justice). As he traveled outside Argentina to meet with other peace groups, he came into contact with a growing Christian nonviolent movement in Latin America.

In 1968 representatives of church, student, labor, and communitarian groups had first met in Montevideo, Uruguay, to discuss nonviolent liberation. In 1971, at a second conference in Costa Rica, the Servicio de Paz y Justicia en America Latina (Service for Peace and Justice in Latin America) was formally founded. At the next meeting, held in Medellin, Colombia, in 1974, Pérez Esquivel was named secretary-general and his periodical was made the official organ of the group.

He gave up his teaching duties to become the general coordinator of the loosely structured association. Based in a small office in Buenos Aires, he traveled throughout Central and South America to visit isolated groups of rural and urban workers and the indigenous population, working with economic development programs, organizing meetings, and promoting solidarity among the disparate groups in behalf of victims of oppression and injustice wherever they were to be found. At one moment he might be involved in nonviolent actions to support the land claims of a group of Indians in Ecuador, at another, protesting the persecution of Christian communities in Paraguay or helping the cement workers' union in Brazil. On two such missions, in Brazil and Ecuador, he was arrested and expelled from the country.

In Argentina itself, civil strife was increasing, and in 1975 Pérez Esquivel helped found two human rights organizations. In 1976 a military junta took power and embarked upon a vicious campaign of repression of alleged left-wing elements and those suspected of sharing their sentiments. Thousands of victims were jailed and tortured with no legal charge or simply abducted and murdered by death squads and never heard of again. Pérez Esquivel denounced these crimes and helped organize the weekly demonstrations of the mothers who came to the Plaza de Mayo in the center of Buenos Aires to demand information about their sons and daughters, the "disappeared ones."

In April 1977, when he went to the police office to renew his passport, he was detained and then imprisoned for fourteen months. The government never lodged any charges but let it be known that he was considered a subversive. They tried to break him by torture, but he stood up under the ordeal through constant praying and yoga exercises. As had happened once before in the case of Carl von Ossietzky, friends abroad urged his nomination for the Nobel Peace Prize to bring international attention to his situation. The 1976 laureates, Betty Williams and Mairead Corrigan, proposed him in 1978 while he was still in prison, and in 1979 and 1980 as well. Amnesty International adopted him as a prisoner of conscience, religious leaders protested his imprisonment, and the U.S. government interceded in his behalf. In May 1978, he was released, but was required to report to the police through much of 1979. He was finally able to resume his work with the Service for Peace and Justice.

While he was in prison the indigenous peasants of Ecuador, with whom he had worked, wrote to the government of Argentina to request his release. As he later reported, "Many of these Indians are illiterate and they signed with their fingerprints. Beside the fingerprints those who knew how to write put 'This finger is so-and-so's.' That is what is beautiful: the solidarity, the brotherhood of the simple people." Pérez Esquivel regards this as one of the highest honors he has ever received.

The Nobel Peace Prize, on the other hand, he did not accept "as a personal title." He received it, as he said at Oslo, "in the name of the people of Latin America . . . in the name of my indigenous brothers and sisters, the peasants, workers, and young people—in the name of the thousands of members of religious orders and of men and women of goodwill who relinquish their privileges to share the life and path of the poor, and who struggle to build a new society."

The award was a great embarrassment to the government of Argentina, which took thirty-six hours after the announcement to draft the lame explanation that Pérez Esquivel's activity had been "against his own intentions, put to use by others to secure the impunity of members of various terrorist groups. Hence he had to be arrested and placed at the disposal of the national executive power—in conformity with the norms in effect during a state of siege."

Pérez Esquivel's activity, of course, had been to oppose terrorism whoever used it. As he said, "We have denounced the killing of generals, colonels and innocent relatives of military officials. We have no connections with political parties of any sort, much less armed groups. We act by means of evangelical nonviolence, which we see as a force for liberation."

The controlled Argentinian press was critical of the award, declaring that it "maligned" Argentina, but congratulations poured in from abroad—from laureates Willy Brandt and Andrei Sakharov, from Senator Edward Kennedy and other political figures, from Joan Baez, the American folk singer, and from many others.

In Oslo Pérez Esquivel won the hearts of the Norwegians with his sweet spirit that needed no interpreter. He is small and slim, with thick brown hair always somewhat tousled above a receding hairline, his brown eyes looking out with a penetrating gaze through black-rimmed glasses. Soft-spoken and humble, his speeches were simple and forthright, moving the audiences not by oratory but by their genuine sincerity and his evident commitment.

Mother Teresa had begun her address the year before with the prayer of St Francis; Pérez Esquivel closed his acceptance speech with the Sermon on the Mount. He spoke of hope, as he had once done even in letters from his prison cell. "My voice," he said, "would like to have the strength of the voice of the humble and lowly. It is a voice that denounces injustice and proclaims hope in God and humanity. . . . For me it is essential to have the inward peace and serenity of prayer in order to listen to the silence of God, which speaks to us, in our personal lives and in the history of our times, about power of love."

"I come from a continent," he said, "that lives between anguish and hope." In his Nobel lecture the next day, Pérez Esquivel was more specific about the anguish. He cited the instances of injustice and oppression, country by country, not forgetting the political prisoners of Cuba. He also had a word of reproach for the great powers: the rules of the game they have inflicted upon the world permit "the biggest crime of our time, the arms race."

When he returned to Argentina, Pérez Esquivel went unnoticed by the press, and for months he and his family lived under constant threats of violence. Bombs were found in his office; he received death threats over the telephone and once had to escape from gunmen lying in wait for him. But he kept up his work with Peace and Justice, and helped the Mothers of the Plaza de Mayo organize an association. Word about him gradually circulated, eroding the government's credibility. Pérez Esquivel believes that his Nobel Peace Prize marked the beginning of the decline of the military government and strengthened the democratic forces that were ready to take over the country after its defeat in the Malvinas/Falkland War against Great Britain.

The prize also gave Pérez Esquivel a world forum in which to publicize human rights abuses and other peace causes. His writings are widely published in the Latin American press, he has been welcomed in many countries on speaking tours, including the United States, and his fasts and protests are always newsworthy. Because of his many activities, as well as the growth of Service for Peace and Justice, he has had to leave its leadership to others, and the central secretariat has moved from Buenos Aires to Rio de Janeiro.

Pérez Esquivel is still closely identified with the organization and gives it financial support, not only from the Peace Prize funds of $212,000, but from his monthly check of $5,000 from the Argentinian government. In accordance with a law passed some years ago, every Nobel laureate from Argentina receives a life pension equivalent to the salary of a judge of the Supreme Court. Even the military junta had grudgingly to comply with this law. In today's freer Argentina, Pérez Esquivel is properly honored.

BIBLIOGRAPHY

Primary Source

Pérez Esquivel, Adolfo. *Christ in a Poncho.* Edited by Charles Antoine. Translated by Robert R. Barr. Maryknoll, N.Y.: Orbis, 1983. Includes a brief essay by Pérez Esquivel, his Oslo acceptance speech, a reproduction of his painting that gives the book its title, and documents of the nonviolent struggles with which he has been associated.

Secondary Sources

Frank, Rosa. "Nobel Prize for Peace and Nonviolence." *Peace and Change* 8 (Spring 1982): 1–5. Translation of an interview with Pérez Esquivel originally published in *Mensaje Magazine,* Santiago, Chile, in December 1980.

Lundy, Michael [pseud.]. "An Interview: Adolfo Pérez Esquivel." *America* 143 (27 December 1980): 427–30.

Paz y Justicia 79 (October–December 1980). Special issue of the organ of the Service for Peace and Justice in Latin America on his Nobel Peace Prize. Includes a biography of Pérez Esquivel, his acceptance speech, and many pictures.

"Pérez Esquivel, Adolfo." In *CB,* 1981.

Priest, Dana. "Four Years Late: Argentina Honors Its Nobel Winner." *Washington Post*, 5 July 1984, p. A17.

1981

Office of the United Nations High Commissioner for Refugees

Established in 1951.

In 1981, on the thirtieth anniversary of the Office of the United Nations High Commissioner for Refugees (UNHCR), the Nobel Committee awarded it a second prize, a distinction exceeded only by the three prizes to the International Committee of the Red Cross. That the committee has honored work for refugees on five occasions (including the prizes to Fridtjof Nansen, the Nansen Office, and Father Pire) has reflected the feelings of the Norwegian people as a whole; Norway long made the largest per capita contribution of any country to the UN refugee office.

Nor has Norway been as reluctant as other governments to prolong the life of the agency. Under both the League of Nations and the United Nations, extensions of terms for refugee relief offices have always been limited. The UNHCR was originally established for a period of three years, from 1951 to 1954. In 1953, however, the UN General Assembly voted an extension until 1 January 1959, and five-year extensions became the rule.

In the beginning the UNHCR, like the Nansen Office, was mainly concerned with European refugees, and in 1953 it was felt that the problem was decreasing. In 1956, however, an uprising in Hungary sent 200,000 refugees fleeing westward. At the same time another refugee crisis was developing in northern Africa as a result of the war in Algeria. Similar situations in other parts of Africa and in Asia led the UN General Assembly to name 1960 World Refugee Year, thus acknowledging the global nature of the problem.

The primary function of the UNHCR was to provide the refugees with legal protection. Article 14 of the Universal Declaration of Human Rights declared, "Everyone has the right to seek and enjoy in other countries asylum from persecution," and this was implemented by the 1951 UN Convention Relating to the Status of Refugees and its 1967 Protocol, to which ninety countries had acceded by 1981.

These international agreements set down specific principles for the treatment of refugees, including protection against forced repatriation, physical harm, and unjustified detention, and assurances of adequate supplies of food, clothing, shelter, and medical care.

The Algerian experience was regularly repeated as over a hundred new countries became independent, many of them through violent struggles that drove hundreds of thousands from their homes. Regional conflicts exacerbated the problem. The UNHCR had to adapt to these new circumstances, expanding its services geographically and carrying out new programs of voluntary repatriation and rehabilitation.

The first large-scale repatriation program took place in 1962, when the UNHCR returned to their homeland 250,000 Algerians who had fled to neighboring Morocco and Tunis to escape the violence. In 1972 a massive effort returned 10 million refugees to newly independent Bangladesh from their camps in India, and in the next year the UNHCR organized a great airlift exchange of peoples between Bangladesh and Pakistan.

Then began the repatriation of other African refugees after their countries became independent, and in the late 1970s UNHCR officials were engaged in repatriating and assisting Nicaraguans on one continent and peoples of Southeast Asia on another. By the end of 1981 UNHCR representatives had resettled 700,000 refugees, including 400,000 "boat people."

Reviewing these achievements in his Nobel lecture, Poul Hartling of Denmark, the high commissioner, pointed out that although the office had carried out some of the most extensive population movements in history, there were still 10 million refugees waiting for a home. Addressing them directly, Hartling assured the refugees of the world that the Nobel Peace Prize bore witness to the fact that their voices were being heard: "Today the world is focusing on your plight and today it renews its commitment to help. This gives us reason to send you a message of hope for the future."

Hartling announced that because 1981 had been declared the UN International Year for Disabled Persons, the prize money of about $180,000 would be used to set up a trust fund for handicapped refugees. The fund, which would welcome other donations, would finance rehabilitative treatment and the purchase of such equipment as artificial limbs and wheelchairs.

Hartling left office in 1985. At that time, the UNHCR staff, which had numbered one hundred when it received the prize in 1954, had risen to sixteen hundred people working in ninety offices around the world. During Hartling's eight-year tenure, the budget had increased from $50 million to $500 million.

Elected by the General Assembly to succeed him was Jean-Pierre Hocké of Switzerland, former high official of the International Committee of the Red Cross. (Although Switzerland does not belong to the UN, it contributes to the budget of the UNHCR.) Hocké had been vigorously supported by the United States, which provided 25 percent of the budget and favored a proven administrator rather than the four career diplomats who were competing for the post.

As the new high commissioner took office on 1 January 1986, there were still at least 10 million refugees in the world, with little prospect that their numbers would diminish. As Hartling had said in Oslo, the refugee agency is one of those organizations that "year after year observe their anniversaries with a certain feeling of regret." Each new birthday is "nothing to be proud of—rather, it is a sad reflection of our times: without persecution, without violation of human rights, without armed conflicts there would be no need for UNHCR." Unfortunately, there is little hope the refugee office will not have many more anniversaries to mark.

BIBLIOGRAPHY

UNHCR. *Nobel Peace Prize 1981* Geneva: UNHCR, [1982]. Documents, newsclippings, and letters of congratulation.

See also bibliography for Office of the United Nations High Commissioner for Refugees (1954).

1982

Alva Reimer Myrdal (1902–86)

Sweden

Sociologist and social reformer, author, diplomat, parliamentarian, cabinet minister, Sweden's international disarmament negotiator.

Alfonso García Robles (1911–)

Mexico

Diplomat, UN official, foreign minister chiefly responsible for treaty banning nuclear weapons in Latin America, champion of disarmament in United Nations.

In 1982 the Nobel Committee made a joint award, dividing the prize between Alva Myrdal of Sweden and Alfonso García Robles of Mexico for their efforts to promote disarmament, one of the areas of peacemaking that Alfred Nobel had explicitly mentioned in his will. Arms control was a major concern in 1982. The UN second Special Session on disarmament was convened in New York City—the first disarmament session had been held there in 1978—and there was a widespread popular demand in the United States and other countries to halt the building of nuclear weapons—to declare a nuclear freeze.

The UN session of 1982 accomplished very little, but it may have been this very disappointment that led the committee to try to strengthen the disarmament movement by selecting two of its leaders over such candidates as Pope John Paul II, Philip C. Habib, the American diplomat, and Lech Wałesa, who would be named the following year. Chairman Aarvik in his presentation speech declared that the committee wanted the 1982 prize "to be interpreted as a helping hand" to the disarmament movement.

The committee had selected two candidates, Aarvik explained, who, in the face of "ample grounds for pessimism," had refused to give up. They were outstanding candidates for two reasons: "In the first place owing to their magnificent work in the disarmament negotiations in the United Nations, . . . and secondly, because, too, they have made such a notable contribution to the task of informing world opinion on the problems of armaments."

Alva Myrdal

Alva Myrdal had often been nominated for the prize. In 1981 her many supporters had included members of the Storting, but she was passed over again. It is even possible that the campaign for Alva Myrdal had led the committee to reassert its independence of the Storting. The news that the Office of the United Nations High Commissioner for Refugees was to be given a prize for the second time produced a storm of criticism in Norway, and a popular movement raised some sixty thousand dollars to present the Norwegian People's Peace Prize to Alva Myrdal in a moving ceremony at the Oslo city hall in February 1982.

In October, to her great surprise, the secretary of the committee phoned from Oslo to inform her that she was to be a Nobel laureate. Alva Myrdal had already received more than a dozen awards for her peace and humanitarian work, including prizes from West Germany, the Netherlands, India, the Food and Agricultural Organization, the Swedish Royal Academy of Sciences, and the first Albert Einstein Peace Prize, but receiving the Nobel, she told me, was for her "the peak." Nevertheless, the Norwegian People's Prize, she added, "is dearer to my heart."

The announcement of the 1982 prize was well received by world public opinion. The only criticism, expressed by some Myrdal backers, was that she should have been the sole winner. But hers was a generous spirit, and she was genuinely pleased that García Robles, whom she knew well and admired, was her cowinner.

The list of Alva Myrdal's accomplishments over her long life is all the more remarkable because her record of achievement was made in a man's world. She pointed out to me: "I had not held my first important position until I was almost forty years old." Thereafter she had carried on two careers of distinction, one in her own country and one abroad, before she took up the cause of disarmament at the age of fifty-nine.

She and her husband first won acclaim as scholars and social reformers. She was a sociologist and educator, and Gunnar Myrdal was an economist who later won the Nobel Memorial Prize in Economics (they are the only married couple who won Nobel prizes in different fields). Together the Myrdals played an important role in the shaping of the Swedish welfare state. Later their individual work made it necessary for them to live apart for some periods, but they tried to make these as short as possible.

Alva Reimer was born in Uppsala in 1902, the daughter of a self-taught building contractor who was a Social Democrat and active in social welfare matters and the cooperative movement. She grew up in the little town of Eskilstuna, where very early her qualities of mind and spirit became apparent. She developed a passion for reading, and a friendly second-hand book dealer let her read anything she chose. Girls in Eskilstuna were supposed to finish the seventh grade at age fourteen and then prepare themselves to be farmer's wives. The high school was only for boys. But Alva was determined to continue her education. She learned office skills in a commercial school and when she was fifteen, she took a job in the local tax office, operating an adding machine. For two years she saved her earnings, spending money only for books and to contribute to the family income. Then she persuaded her father to talk the local school board into setting up classes for a group of girls, the same courses that the boys were taking, but for a tuition fee, and the girls were not allowed in the school buildings.

On one summer day three university students on a bicycling trip stopped at the Reimer farm and asked to sleep in the hayloft. One was a law student named Gunnar Myrdal, who was much taken with this highly intelligent and beautiful young woman, as was she with him, so much so that she did something unheard of. Not telling her parents, she accepted his invitation to join the bicycle tour.

With Gunnar's encouragement, Alva made her way to Stockholm University. She received her degree in 1924, when she was twenty-two, and in the same year she and Gunnar were married. They were to be parents of a son and two daughters.

In the following years they pursued advanced studies in Stockholm, London, Leipzig, Geneva, and the United States, before settling down in Sweden in 1932. In 1934 they published *The Crisis of the Population Question,* which had an important influence on social policies throughout Scandinavia and led to Alva Myrdal's participation in government commissions on population and housing.

In 1936 Alva Myrdal founded the Training College for Nursery and Kindergarten Teachers and directed its work until 1948, gaining a reputation as an expert in early childhood education. A member of the Social Democratic party, she served on its program planning committee and also on a number of government commissions. At the same time she was prominent in the struggle for equal rights for women.

From 1938 to 1940 she accompanied her husband to the United States, where Gunnar Myrdal was engaged in research for his classic study of American race relations, *An American Dilemma.* She was busy with her own projects, lecturing, writing, and investigating American education and social problems. In 1939 the Swedish government appointed her to the board responsible for Swedish participation in the New York World's Fair.

During the Second World War, in which Sweden remained neutral, Alva Myrdal became concerned with the plight of refugees both in her own country and elsewhere in Europe. For her war work she was later decorated by both Finland and Norway.

After the war Alva Myrdal entered upon a second career, in international relations. She was an early supporter of the United Nations Organization and served on the board of the World Federation of United Nations Associations. In 1949 she was appointed director of the UN Department of Social Affairs and was the highest ranking woman in the UN Secretariat. In 1951 she moved to UNESCO as the director of the Department of Social Sciences.

In the councils of these world bodies Alva Myrdal showed such unusual skill in dealing with people in international relationships that in 1955 the Swedish government appointed her as ambassador to India, with responsibilities for the neighboring countries as well. Swedish businessmen were at first apprehensive because of her socialist background, but they were soon applauding her expertise in trade matters. She achieved a special relationship with Prime Minister Jawaharlal Nehru and cultivated wide acquaintanceships throughout Indian society. Her diplomatic reports on India were considered models.

It was in March 1961, after her service in India had ended, that Alva Myrdal was "drafted" into disarmament, as she put it. She was then at the disposal of the Foreign Office, with the title of ambassador-at-large, and the foreign minister, who was looking toward his final appearance at the UN General Assembly, asked her to serve as his special assistant on disarmament and to draft a speech on that subject for him. She replied that she had no detailed knowledge of disarmament and asked for two weeks to study the subject before the appointment became public. Her inventive mind came up with four proposals, of which he selected one on nuclear-free zones. She emerged from the exercise so engaged with the problem that she declared, "Disarmament is my main preoccupation for the foreseeable future."

In 1962 she became a member of the upper chamber of the Swedish parliament and was invited to join the cabinet, first without portfolio and then as minister both for disarmament and for church affairs. Prime Minister Olof Palme asked her to take the latter responsibility because she was the only member of the Social Democrat cabinet who had not gotten around to resigning formally from the state church. She agreed on condition that she would not have to make any election speeches on Sundays. She was a member of the cabinet for twelve years in all and was fondly called the "Grand Old Lady of Swedish Politics." In the cabinet and in the parliament she had an important influence upon Sweden's unilateral renunciation in 1968 of nuclear weapons and shortly thereafter all chemical and biological means of warfare. In 1973, at the age of seventy-one, she resigned from all her government positions.

From 1962 to 1973 she was a member of the Swedish delegation to the UN General Assembly, serving on the Political Committee, where disarmament matters were dealt with. Also during these years she headed the Swedish delegation to the UN Disarmament Committee in Geneva, where she became the leader of the representatives from nonaligned nations. Now in her sixties, she cut a striking figure in these UN meetings in New York and Geneva. Small and vivacious, her fair hair now gray, her blue eyes alight and her bright laughter always at the ready, she combined charm with determination, and, with an impressive mastery of scientific and technical detail, she used her powers of analysis and explication with convincing effect. They called her "the conscience of the disarmament movement," and the U.S. representative to the Political Committee later remarked, "I bear many scars testifying to her effectiveness."

On the basis of this experience she produced one of the best studies of the nuclear arms race ever written, *The Game of Disarmament,* published in 1976. Her sharp critique of the superpowers as chiefly responsible for the failure of disarmament efforts was underlined in the subtitle, *How the United States and Russia Run the Arms Race.* While her many articles and books brought home the nuclear danger and made carefully considered recommendations for reasonable policies, she was, at the same time, particularly proud of some "concrete" achievements. She had successfully prevailed upon her government to appropriate funds both for seismological research to improve verification techniques for observing test ban treaties and for the establishment of the Swedish International Peace Research Institute, aimed at buttressing peace and disarmament efforts with scholarly data and documentation.

When the Nobel award ceremony took place, Alva Myrdal was nearing her eighty-first birthday and was in poor health. She had to be helped up to the podium, where, looking frail and somewhat shaky, but always dignified, she received a rising ovation. She gave a very brief statement of thanks, conserving her energy for the lecture expected of her the next day.

She started out that lecture saying that if she were unable to go on to the end, her two daughters were standing by to read it in two sections (one was Dr. Sissela Bok, wife of the president of Harvard University and a scholar in her own right). But Alva Myrdal rose to the occasion. As if "filled with wind," as one observer reported, she grew stronger as she proceeded and delivered unfalteringly the whole text she had prepared.

It was a hard-hitting speech. The little figure at the podium denounced the leaders of the superpowers as guilty of "a clearly irredeemable misconception: that the use of war, violence, can lead to victory." Their nuclear rivalry not only faced the world with the threat of extinction but had helped produce the cult of violence that made our age one of barbarism. Everyday violence, in the streets and in the media, was "to a large extent a result of the spread of arms."

Yet the building up of armaments was so unnecessary, since experts agreed that something like four hundred intercontinental missiles were enough for a deterrent. Her attempts to make that truth understood were becoming a "trifle wearying" to her, but, she declared, "I shall go on repeating, until the politicians get it into their heads, that *when one has sufficient, one does not need more.*"

The technology that had been the driving force of our civilization could be used in the service of good or evil. Nobel's nitroglycerine, which he and she both used for their heart disease, could also be used to blow people up. The forces of good had used technology to overcome human misery and raise millions of people to a comfortable standard of living. But the evil forces were concentrating more and more power in their hands and could employ the technology of war to destroy the world.

Alva Myrdal used her half of the prize, the equivalent of $78,500, for peace causes and to provide herself with a secretary. She continued to work for peace as long as she was able, writing, sending out copies of the 1982 edition of *The Game of Disarmament,* even making appearances at peace demonstrations in Stockholm. During the last two years of her life, however, she was hospitalized, and she died in February 1986, the day after her eighty-fourth birthday.

In a moving eulogy at her memorial service in Stockholm, Olof Palme declared that "Alva Myrdal was unique." He said, in part:

> Alva Myrdal had very clear eyes. They reflected the clarity of her thinking, the orderly and methodical way she handled every project, the happy faith in reason that carried her through life. In her eyes, you also encountered warmth, thoughtfulness, her ability to understand the situation of others. . . . When you talk about Alva Myrdal, people become inspired. To them she signifies happiness about life's potential, a bright faith in the future. A person can hardly hope for a better monument.

In 1980, when Alva Myrdal was the first recipient of the Einstein Peace Prize, she had concluded her acceptance speech with the words: "I have, despite all disillusionment, never, never allowed myself to feel like giving up. That is my message today: it is not worthy of a human being to give up." And she never did.

Alfonso García Robles

In naming García Robles as cowinner of the 1982 prize, the committee declared that he had "played a crucial role in launching and implementing the agreement on a denuclearized zone in Latin America," and also cited his central role in the United Nation's work to promote general disarmament. Chairman Aarvik pointed out in his presentation speech that the work for disarmament proceeds on two levels: informing and influencing world opinion, and developing practical solutions in diplomatic negotiations. García Robles, Aarvik declared, was being honored by the committee for his dedicated and effective efforts on both levels.

García Robles was not well known in Norway, and in selecting him the committee may well have also had in mind the geographical distribution of its laureates. The 1982 winners represented a nice balance between the Old World and the New, the North and the South.

García Robles has spent his active life in the foreign service of his country, except for a period when he was a top UN official. He was born in Zamora, Mexico, the capital of Michoacán State. He first thought of becoming a priest, but then decided on the law. After his studies in Mexico City, he went to the University of Paris, where he received his doctorate in law in 1936, when he was twenty-five years old. He attended the Academy of International Law at The Hague and then joined the staff of the Mexican embassy in Sweden, finally returning in 1941 to Mexico to take a post in the Foreign Ministry.

In 1945 García Robles was a member of the Mexican delegation at the San Francisco conference that founded the United Nations. He then joined the UN Secretariat as it was being formed and remained there for eleven years, serving in the important position of director of the Division of Political Affairs. It was while leading a UN mission to the Middle East in

1949 that he met Juanita Sislo of Peru, who became his wife. They were to have two sons.

In 1957 García Robles returned to the Mexican Foreign Ministry to become director general for Europe. In the following years he was also concerned with shaping his country's policy at the Law of the Sea conferences. In 1962 he became ambassador to Brazil, serving until 1964, when he was appointed under secretary for foreign affairs in the Ministry.

In October 1962, the conflict between the United States and the Soviet Union over Soviet missiles in Cuba alarmed Latin Americans about the danger that nuclear arms might be used in their hemisphere. It was the presidents of Brazil, Ecuador, and Bolivia who first proposed making Latin America a nuclear-free zone, but the idea made no headway until García Robles took it up. He first persuaded the president of Mexico and then other Latin American governments to join in an agreement concerning such a zone. By 1963 he had succeeded in generating widespread support for the idea among these governments and secured approval of the concept from the UN General Assembly.

In 1964, on the initiative of García Robles, a conference was held in Mexico City, which set up the Preparatory Commission for the Denuclearization of Latin America with instructions to prepare a preliminary draft of a multilateral treaty. García Robles chaired this commission with considerable skill and was chiefly responsible for the text of the draft that was ready to be signed in 1967. This was the Treaty of Tlatelolco, taking the Aztec name for the site of the Mexican Foreign Ministry, where it was signed. The treaty was the first of its kind in the world. It declared Latin America "forever free of nuclear weapons" and provided for regular reports by the signatory states and for special inspections to ensure observance of their obligations. In the preamble the Latin American states declared:

> The military denuclearization of Latin America . . . will constitute a measure which will spare their peoples from the squandering of their limited resources on nuclear armaments and will protect them against possible nuclear attacks on their territories, and will also constitute a significant contribution towards preventing the proliferation of nuclear weapons and a powerful factor for general and complete disarmament.

The preamble also stated that the signatory states were convinced that "the incalculable destructive power of nuclear weapons has made it imperative that the legal prohibition of war should be strictly observed in practice if the survival of civilization and of mankind itself is to be assured." Nuclear weapons constituted "an attack on the integrity of the human species and ultimately may even render the whole earth uninhabitable."

García Robles continued to work for disarmament as Mexico's permanent representative to the United Nations from 1971 to 1975. He was foreign minister in 1975–76, and when he left office because of a change in government, he was asked what position he would like to have. His friends, who have regarded him as "obsessed" with disarmament, anticipated his choice, which was to become Mexico's representative to the UN Disarmament Commission in Geneva, which position he still held at the time of his Nobel prize.

In this post he helped prepare for the first UN Special Session on disarmament in 1978, at which meeting he played a leading role. He coordinated the various proposals that were advanced, and he was mainly responsible for the drafting and adoption of the final document. Several of its clauses were strikingly similar to the preamble of the Treaty of Tlatelolco.

At the second Special Session in 1982, García Robles again made an important contribution. Although the results of the session were generally disappointing, García Robles did find much agreement with his proposal for a world disarmament campaign. In the following years at the UN Disarmament Commission in Geneva, where in 1987 he was the respected doyen, García Robles worked hard to promote a comprehensive test ban of nuclear weapons.

At the Oslo ceremonies in 1981 García Robles gave his Nobel lecture on "The Latin American Nuclear-Weapon-Free Zone," presenting a synoptic view of both the genesis and the provisions of the Treaty of Tlatelolco. In his speech of acceptance he stressed the urgency of arms control, citing the declaration of the first special UN disarmament session in 1978: "Mankind is confronted with a choice: we must halt the arms race and proceed to disarmament or face annihilation." In the light of this threat to human survival, García Robles urged that the Norwegian Nobel Committee in the future consider contributions to disarmament as the decisive criterion for awarding the Peace Prize.

He recognized the importance of efforts for human rights—he could not be unaware of the active lobby in Oslo that was clamoring for a prize for Lech Wałesa—and he suggested that perhaps a new Maecenas might provide the funds for a Human Rights Prize, just as the Bank of Sweden had financed the Nobel Memorial Prize in Economics. The Nobel Committee would then have two prizes to award.

This novel proposal received some support in the Oslo press, but no new Maecenas stepped forward, and there was no change. The committee continued to emphasize human rights in its Peace Prizes, giving three of the next four awards to leaders in that field, while the grants to champions of disarmament have remained few and far between.

BIBLIOGRAPHIES

Alva Myrdal

Primary Sources

Myrdal, Alva. *Dynamics of European Nuclear Disarmament.* Nottingham: Spokesman, 1981.

———. *The Game of Disarmament: How the United States and Russia Run the Arms Race.* 1976. Rev. ed. New York: Pantheon, 1982.

———. *Nation and Family.* 2d ed. Cambridge: MIT Press, 1965.

———. *War, Weapons and Everyday Violence.* Manchester: University of New Hampshire Press, 1977.

———. *Women's Two Roles.* With V. Klein. Rev. ed. London: Routledge & Kegan Paul, 1968.

Secondary Sources

Bok, Sissela Myrdal. "Alva Myrdal Remembered." *Boston Sunday Globe,* 10 January 1988. A poignant appreciation by her daughter, telling of her mother's years in Eskilstuna and of her last illness. Sissela Bok has written an intimate biography of Alva Myrdal in Swedish: *Alva: Ett kvinnoliv* (Alva: A Woman's Life), (Stockholm: Bonniers, 1987).

"Myrdal, Alva." In *CB,* 1950.

Alfonso García Robles

Primary Sources

García Robles, Alfonso. *The Denuclearization of Latin America.* New York: Carnegie Endowment for International Peace, 1967.

———. "Mésures de Désarmament dans des Zones Particulières." In Academy of International Law, The Hague, *Recueil des Cours 1971.* Vol. 133. Leyden: Sijthoff, 1972, 2:43–134.

———. *México en las Nacionas Unidas.* 2 vols. Ciudad Universitaria: Universidad Nacional Autónoma de México, 1970. Speeches at the United Nations, with introductions.

———. *El Tratado de Tlatelolco.* Mexico City: El Colegio de México, 1967. Speeches and documents.

Secondary Sources

Epstein, William. *Disarmament: Twenty-Five Years of Effort.* Toronto: Canadian Institute of International Affairs, 1971. A succinct summary by the UN official who nominated García Robles for the prize.

Text of Treaty of Tlatelolco. In *WEP,* 3:83–91.

1983
Lech Wałesa (1943–)

Poland

Leader of Solidarity, Polish trade union movement.

At the end of September 1983, Lech Wałesa talked to a visiting journalist pessimistically about his chances for the Nobel Peace Prize: "If they didn't give it to me last year, when the situation was more fluid, at a time when it could have really helped, I cannot see why they should give it to me now." The previous October, when the committee had met to decide the 1982 award, Wałesa was still being held by the Polish government, which had declared martial law in December 1981. There had been much support for his candidacy in Oslo, where there was widespread sympathy for the suppressed Solidarity trade union movement, but the committee made its disarmament awards to Alva Myrdal and García Robles.

Wałesa was released in November 1982, but

his movements were restricted, and throughout the following months the government tried to discredit him. Shortly after he spoke with the journalist, a fabricated tape was played over the government radio, purporting to be Wałesa's voice discussing his million-dollar bank account abroad. The day after the broadcast the Polish people showed how they felt about Wałesa when the crowd spotted him in the stands at a soccer game in Gdansk and gave him a thunderous ovation.

On the morning of 5 October Wałesa was off with friends picking wild mushrooms in the woods near Gdansk, when television crews from the United States and West Germany suddenly turned up with the news that he had won the Nobel Peace Prize. Wałesa returned to Gdansk to find a celebration. He told journalists that with the prize he would embark upon "more effective" tactics to restore the freedom of Solidarity, but he doubted if he would go to Oslo to receive it in person: "How can I go to get this nice prize and sip champagne when my colleagues are in jail and hungry?"

The Nobel Committee's purpose was not primarily to help Wałesa restore Solidarity but to honor him as a campaigner for human rights, just as previous awards had recognized that campaigns for human rights were campaigns for peace. In his case it was the human right, as defined by the United Nations, of the freedom of workers to organize. Moreover, he had gone about this "through negotiation and cooperation without resorting to violence." The committee considered Wałesa "an exponent of the active longing for peace and freedom which exist, in spite of unequal conditions, unconquered in all the peoples of the world." Wałesa was both "an inspiration and an example."

To the spokesman for the Polish government, the committee had allowed itself "to become a tool in the game of confrontation against Poland and socialism," and its action would heighten international tension, not promote peace. The Polish state radio banned from the air the music of Norway and the United States, and the foreign minister summoned the Norwegian ambassador to protest his prime minister's congratulations to Wałesa. The Polish people, on the other hand, were jubilant, and congratulations came to Wałesa from Pope John Paul II and political and labor leaders from all over the Western world, ranging from anticommunist conservatives to socialists.

Lech Wałesa was born during the German occupation of World War II in a village near Lipno, close to the Vistula River. The Wałesas had long been peasants in the region, once with sizable land holdings, but these had been divided up generation after generation by large families, and Bolek, Lech's father, was left with only a small plot. He became a carpenter, building barns and cowsheds, and although he was a skilled craftsman and worked hard, life was difficult with four children to care for. Toward the end of the war, before Lech was two years old, his father died from mistreatment in a German prison. Lech's mother married Bolek's brother, and after the war conditions improved. There were three more children, and the family moved from its clay cottage to a more substantial brick house. After the children were grown, the parents went to visit relatives in the United States, where Lech's mother died in a traffic accident. The stepfather did not return to Poland.

Lech went to primary school in a neighboring town and then to the secondary trade school in Lipno. His report cards show nothing outstanding about his schoolwork. His lowest marks were in deportment, and it was recorded that he was punished three times for smoking cigarettes in the school dormitory. He was remembered, however, for being a leader among his classmates.

Wałesa finished school at the age of eighteen, worked for a time at the State Machinery Center, did his military service, and then in 1967 went to Gdansk to earn more money in the shipyards. Becoming an electrician, he learned fast and was a good worker. In 1969, now twenty-six, he married the bright and comely Danuta, a florist's assistant. The next year Bogdan was born, and the little family lived in a rented room, with the help of a subsidy from the shipyard.

It was in 1970 that Wałesa first emerged as an activist. In December the shipyard workers went on strike to protest the government's raising food prices. Wałesa, an outspoken member of the strike committee, was chosen as a member of the delegation to meet with the authorities in Warsaw and later was elected an officer of the union. He was leading a march of the workers when they were confronted by government forces and fifty-five of his comrades were killed. Wałesa felt responsible for their deaths, and on every anniversary, unless prevented by the government, he has returned to the scene outside the gate of the shipyard, for an act of remembrance.

A reporter who interviewed Wałesa in 1970 for the union paper wrote that this twenty-seven-year-old electrician was much talked about in the shipyard. He had been at the very center of the strike activity and was now experienced and mature for his years. He had even read books about the psychology of crowds.

In 1972 Wałesa and his family were allotted better living quarters in a small flat, but his union activities and his criticisms of the government brought him into difficulties with the authorities. He was dismissed from three jobs on various pretexts, and the police began to keep watch on him and often took him in for questioning.

Wałesa was unemployed in August 1980, when once again the shipyard workers started a protest against higher food prices. A crowd of workers was assembled to listen to the explanations of the director, when Wałesa climbed over the twelve-foot steel fence of the shipyard, which he was no longer permitted to enter, jumped on a piece of machinery, and asked them, "Do you recognize me? I've been working for ten years in the shipyard and feel that I am still a shipyard man. . . . We're now beginning a sit-in strike!"

Wałesa then became the leader of the workers' movement which spread along the coast. He was head of the interfactory committee and chief negotiator with the government representative who was sent from Warsaw. In August 1980, the government accepted the workers' demands, which went beyond economic improvements to include the right to strike, the right to organize unions free of government control, and freedom of expression, liberties unprecedented in the Soviet Union and its satellites.

Over the loudspeakers at the shipyard, where Wałesa reported the progress of the negotiations, his gravelly voice was heard with respect and affection by the workers, and the short, stocky man with the reddish brown walrus mustache and twinkling eyes, always wearing on his lapel the medallion of the Black Madonna of Czestochowa, became a familiar figure in their midst, as well as on television screens and newsmagazine covers in the West. Wałesa talked the language of the workers—"We eat the same bread," he told them—and knew how to use humor and homely anecdotes in the frank and persuasive speeches he gave at meetings. His down-to-earth shrewdness endeared him to the workers and made him a formidable negotiator with the authorities. His religious devotion and his profound love of his country he shared with the great majority of his fellow citizens.

The movement spread throughout Poland to unions of workers and other associations, which were consolidated under the name of Solidarity, with Wałesa as chairman. The Catholic church gave its support to Solidarity, whose members numbered well over 9 million. The government declared that the August agreement with the shipyard workers applied to the rest of the country, but it was slow to implement all the provisions, for it feared Soviet intervention if it appeared to be losing control. Consequently, strikes and protests continued, and the economy was crippled. To strengthen the government's hand, Gen. Wojciech Jaruzelski became both prime minister and head of the Communist party. The radicals in Solidarity pressed for further political gains. Wałesa, however, was always a force for moderation, adamant that the government remain true to its pledges, but realistic about the threat from the East. He always argued for negotiation and insisted on peaceful means.

In December the extremists in Solidarity's leadership, to Wałesa's dismay, put through a proposal to hold a national referendum, asking whether there should be free elections and calling into question the authority of the Communist party and the military alliance with the Soviet Union. The next day General Jaruzelski proclaimed martial law, banned strikes and public gatherings, imposed a blackout on communications, and arrested Wałesa and the other Solidarity leaders. At the first sign of the government action, Wałesa had angrily rebuked the radicals, "Now you've got the confrontation you've been looking for!" In the face of effective military measures, Solidarity's call for a nationwide strike went unheeded.

After December 1981, Jaruzelski's military dictatorship, established in the name of law and order, jailed all Solidarity leaders it could lay its hands on and suppressed all dissent. There was satisfaction in the Kremlin but outrage in Western countries, and the United States applied economic sanctions. Eventually martial law was lifted, although strict controls remained, and after eleven months of detention Wałesa was released, his seventh child having been born in his absence. In view of his international reputation Wałesa was treated more leniently than the others, but he was largely cut off from the other Solidarity leaders, who were in exile, in jail, or in the underground.

Wałesa himself was careful not to provoke the government. He continued to ask for dialogue with Jaruzelski and he even took a public stand against the United States' sanctions. He decided against going to Oslo to receive the prize, not only thinking of his comrades in jail, but fearing that he might not be allowed to return to Poland. Instead, he sent his wife and thirteen-year-old Bogdan to represent him.

Danuta Wałesa had been out of Poland only once before, when she accompanied her husband on a visit to the pope, but from the moment she stepped off the plane at the Oslo airport and gracefully accepted Chairman Aarvik's bouquet, she impressed everyone with her poise and her intelligence. At her press conference she handled difficult questions adroitly, and at the ceremony she gave such an effective reading of her husband's speech that Wałesa, who heard it in Gdansk in a Radio Free Europe broadcast, told reporters afterward that he had fallen in love with her all over again. He got his champagne after all, a bottle sent from Poznan, and he drank to Solidarity and to Danuta. That evening Wałesa attended mass in

Gdansk and the American chargé d'affaires came from Warsaw to convey congratulations from President Ronald Reagan. In Oslo's frigid air the former florist's assistant stood with her son on the balcony of the Grand Hotel to receive the tribute of the torchlight procession below, banner after banner of the trade unions of Norway passing by.

Chairman Aarvik in his speech of presentation declared that perhaps Lech Wałesa could not "be presented as a victor at the end of a struggle full of sacrifice." But had he really been defeated? "The electrician from Gdansk," Aarvik stated, "the carpenter's son from the Vistula valley has managed to lift the banner of freedom and humanity so high that the world can once again see it." And his weapons were "the word, the spirit and the thought of freedom and human rights."

In Wałesa's acceptance speech he received the prize in the name of Solidarity, expressing his sorrow for those who had lost their lives and their freedom in loyalty to its cause. The next day his Nobel lecture was read by a former Solidarity leader now living in exile. "Addressing you," Wałesa began, "is a Polish worker from the Gdansk shipyard," and he told of his own life and the struggles of the Polish workers.

"When I recall my own path of life," he said, "I cannot but speak of the violence, hatred and lies. A lesson drawn from such experiences, however, was that we can effectively oppose violence only if we ourselves do not resort to it. . . . Solidarity, as a trade union movement, did not reach for power, nor did it turn against the established constitutional order. During the fifteen months of Solidarity's legal existence nobody was killed or wounded as a result of its activities. . . . We have won the right to organize in trade unions independent from the authorities, founded and shaped by the working people themselves. . . . Let the veil of silence fall presently over what happened afterwards. Silence, too, can speak out." It had to be said, however, that "the Polish people have not been subjugated," nor would they yield to violence.

Wałesa told of Poland's troubled history, filled with tragedy, but also with "Polish hope," which the prize enhanced. He called for understanding and dialogue in Poland and in the whole world. He wished that the world were free of the threat of nuclear holocaust and of the arms race. Peace and justice went together, he said: "the two are like bread and salt for mankind."

Danuta and Bogdan Wałesa left the cheering crowds of Oslo to return to a grim reception in Warsaw, with militia standing by. Watched by the police, the Wałesas drove to the shrine of Our Lady of Czestochowa, where Lech deposited the Nobel medal and diploma on the altar where Polish kings had laid their crowns and generals their medals. Wałesa prayed, "Everything I do, I do for you. Guide me so I can accomplish my service and multiply your glory." On the way back to Gdansk they were stopped thirteen times by the police and subjected to a body search.

Wałesa had left the prize money, the equivalent of about $195,000, in Oslo intending to contribute it to a fund the Catholic church planned to establish for grants to private farmers. When the government blocked this plan, the money was used to provide much needed medical supplies to Polish hospitals.

The taste of freedom that Poland enjoyed during the heady days of Solidarity has not been forgotten, and Lech Wałesa remains a symbol of Polish hope. But he stands for more. An obscure untutored worker, he rose to lead millions and, rejecting violence, to negotiate as an equal with government leaders; he withstood isolation and vilification. This was no ordinary achievement; yet the Polish worker from the Gdansk shipyard was an ordinary man, a man of the people. His story gives the promise of humanity's potential, the *human* hope.

BIBLIOGRAPHY

Primary Source

Wałesa, Lech. *A Way of Hope. An Autobiography.* New York: Holt, 1987.

Secondary Sources

The Book of Lech Wałesa. Introduced by Neal Ascherson. New York: Simon & Schuster, 1982. A collective portrait by Solidarity members and friends, first published in Gdansk in September 1981.

Craig, Mary. *Lech Wałesa and His Poland.* New York: Continuum, 1987. First published as *The Crystal Spirit.* London: Hodder & Stoughton, 1986. The best biography in English, based on extensive research and interviews by a popular writer who knows Poland well.

Davies, Norman. *Heart of Europe: A Short History of Poland.* Oxford: Clarendon Press, 1984.

Garton Ash, Tim. *The Polish Revolution: Solidarity 1980–1982.* London: Jonathan Cape, 1983.

"Wałesa, Lech." In *CB,* 1981.

Weschler, Lawrence. *Solidarity: Poland in the Season of Its Passion.* New York: Simon & Schuster, 1982. An expanded version of the vivid account published in the *New Yorker* in November 1981.

1984
Archbishop Desmond Mpilo Tutu (1931–)

South Africa

Anglican churchman; leader in nonviolent struggle for racial equality; bishop of Lesotho (1976–78); general secretary, South African Council of Churches (1978–85); bishop of Johannesburg (1985–86); archbishop of Capetown (1986–).

In 1984, for the second time in two years, the committee made a political statement on human rights with the prize. With its avowed intention "to awaken consciences," the committee gave the award to Bishop Desmond Tutu for his struggle "for racial equality as a human right," recognizing him as "a unifying leader figure in the campaign to resolve the problem of apartheid in South Africa." The committee called attention to the nonviolent character of this campaign, which it declared to be "of vital importance for the whole of the continent of Africa and for the cause of peace in the world." Recalling the award to Albert Lutuli in 1960, the committee said this was "a renewed recognition of the courage and heroism shown by black South Africans in their use of peaceful methods in the struggle against apartheid," and an acknowledgment of the contribution to peace of all those throughout the world who struggled for racial equality by such means.

Tutu's name had been before the committee at least since 1981, when he was nominated by the American Friends Service Committee. This time the rumor factory in Oslo had made Tutu such a heavy favorite that when Chairman Aarvik appeared at the Nobel Institute on 16 October to make the announcement, the press cameramen were ready with large pictures of Tutu to hold up when they photographed Aarvik reading the text.

Tutu himself heard the news in New York City, where he was spending six months as visiting professor at the General Theological Seminary. Even before the official word from the committee reached him, the Norwegian ambassador to the United Nations arrived at Tutu's apartment at the seminary with a bouquet of flowers for the bishop and his wife. "I had a big lump in my throat and I thought my heart had stopped," Tutu said later. His first words were: "Hey, justice is going to win!" Soon the bells of the seminary were tolling the glad tidings. Professors and students stopped on their way to class and rushed to the chapel, where the diminutive churchman arrived to be greeted by their applause. Together they all gave thanks and sang hymns, and Tutu read his favorite psalm, the 139th, which meant for him, "I am nothing but the Lord's servant."

Afterward the bishop met the press in the seminary courtyard, telling them that the award was "a tremendous affirmation that our cause is just and our methods are praiseworthy." He called for world economic pressure against the South African government to force it to end apartheid—it was the last chance to avoid a bloodbath. The prize was not for him alone but for his comrades in the struggle as well, and he would interrupt his teaching to go home to celebrate with them.

Would the South African government prevent him from going to Oslo to receive the prize? His passport had been withdrawn and replaced with a travel document in which his citizenship was listed as "undeterminable at present." Tutu was certain, however, that he would be allowed to go—otherwise the South African government would appear in a light similar to the communist government of Poland when Lech Wałesa was the laureate in 1983.

Although the choice of Tutu met with much approval in world opinion, the South African government and the newspapers that supported it treated the news of Tutu's prize much the same as Wałesa's had been treated in Poland. The Office of the Prime Minister had "no comment," the state television gave the first report six seconds, and editorials called Tutu a troublemaker and expressed outrage that such a man should receive a Peace Prize. One Johannesburg daily commented, "To South Africans who have so often read about his vicious verbal attacks, Bishop Desmond

Tutu . . . must be one of the strangest recipients yet to receive a Peace Prize."

Desmond Mpilo Tutu was born in the gold-mining town of Klerksdorp in the Transvaal, the son of a teacher. When he was twelve, the family moved to Johannesburg, where his mother became a cook in a missionary school for the blind. His first jobs were selling peanuts at railway stations and caddying on a golf course. He wanted to be a doctor, but there was no money for medical training, so he studied to be a teacher, like his father.

In his late teens, Tutu was hospitalized for twenty months with tuberculosis. He kept up his studies, however, with the help of an Anglican priest, Trevor Huddleston, who brought schoolbooks on his frequent visits. Huddleston was one of the most eloquent opponents of apartheid in the land and had a lasting influence upon Tutu, who named his first son after him. Tutu was a small boy when he first met the priest: "I was standing with my mother one day, when this white man in a cassock walked past and doffed his big black hat to her. I couldn't believe it—a white man raising his hat to a simple black labouring woman."

Tutu became a high school teacher in 1954 and married Leah Nomalizo the next year. Three years later the Nationalist government decided to limit blacks to a second-rate "Bantu education," and he resigned in protest. Tutu now decided to become an Anglican priest; he had been baptized a Methodist, but the family had all become Anglicans when Tutu's sister went to an Anglican school. In deciding on this new vocation, Tutu's main motivation was not religious. "I was not moved by very high ideals," he has explained. "It just seemed that if the church would accept me, this might be a likely means of service." What deepened his spiritual life was the training he now received from Father Huddleston's religious order, the Community of Redemption, with its practices of daily communion, frequent prayers, and quiet retreats.

After preparation at a theological college in Johannesburg, Tutu was ordained an Anglican priest in 1961. He then moved with his family to London, where from 1962 to 1966 he combined further theological studies with part-time service as a curate and received the bachelor's degree in divinity and the master's in theology from King's College.

Returning to South Africa, Tutu taught theology at seminaries for four years, and then went back to London to become associate director of the Theological Education Fund of the World Council of Churches. After three years in this position, which involved extensive travel in Africa and elsewhere, Tutu was appointed in 1975 the dean of St. Mary's Cathedral in Johannesburg, the first black to be named. He next served two years as bishop of Lesotho, and in 1978 was appointed general secretary of the South African Council of Churches (SACC), the position he still held when named as winner of the 1984 Peace Prize.

Tutu now was a high-ranking churchman. All the Christian churches of South Africa, except the Dutch Reform, are members of the SACC or work with it, and it is the national body that is represented in the World Council of Churches. About 80 percent of the individual members of SACC churches are black, and they hold the top positions.

As SACC general secretary, Tutu led these churches in opposition to the racial segregationist government policies of apartheid as inconsistent with the principles of Christianity. These policies had been introduced by the Nationalist party after it won control of the government in 1948. The objective was to consolidate the hold on political power of 4.5 million whites over 23 million blacks. Along with provision for limited educational opportunities for blacks, apartheid measures included the evacuation of black populations to so-called homelands, restriction of freedom of movement and of association, detention without trial, and the introduction of the pass, which every black had to carry at all times.

Tutu refused to carry a pass and spoke out courageously against these policies. Since the days when Albert Lutuli had headed the African National Congress, this body had been outlawed and driven underground by the government, and its leaders, now based abroad, had moved to methods of violence. Like Lutuli, Tutu led the SACC in a nonviolent struggle for the same aims—a "non-racial, truly democratic and more just society." Tutu declared that the SACC deplored violence, both the structural and legalized violence of apartheid and the violence of those who would overthrow the state. He warned "that oppressed people will become desperate, and desperate people will use desperate methods."

Tutu said he had never learned to hate, and he told his black audiences, "Be nice to whites; they need you to rediscover their humanity." The black militants attacked him for his moderation and were outraged by his willingness to enter dialogue with government leaders. But he insisted that there was no limit to God's grace and that this could change the heart of the prime minister of South Africa. Tutu's faith is deep-rooted and unwavering. He knows that suffering is at the heart of Christianity but also that his religion can be the source of certain hope and great joy. His sermons have lifted up the spirits of his congregations, and often he has danced up and down the church aisles greeting his parishioners.

Before leaving the United States for Oslo, Tutu's new recognition won him an audience with

President Ronald Reagan, whom he sought to persuade to give up his policy of constructive engagement with the government of South Africa. Reagan had publicly expressed his strong opposition to apartheid but felt that it could be changed by "quiet diplomacy," not by taking sides against the government. Tutu was forthright in calling such a policy "evil, immoral and un-Christian," and urged economic measures against South Africa. He pointed out that when the elephant is stepping on the mouse's tail, the mouse cannot appreciate a policy of impartiality.

At Oslo Chairman Aarvik gave an eloquent speech of presentation, ending with the words of the song of the American civil rights movement, "We Shall Overcome." Before he could give Tutu the scroll and the medal, however, there was a bomb scare, and the audience had to clear the hall. No bomb was found, and the ceremony eventually continued. During the intermission, television watchers saw the worried faces of the dignitaries, but Bishop Tutu was standing in front of the Aula happily talking with people in the crowd who ordinarily only get a passing glimpse of the laureate arriving and departing. Tutu's wife and four children and his friends were with him, and after the audience reassembled, he had a trio sing Gospel songs before he gave his acceptance speech, as is often done elsewhere when he speaks, both at the beginning and at the end, and the joyous mood returned.

The next day he delivered his Nobel lecture, vividly describing the oppression in his country and declaring that where there is no justice, there can be no peace. In this sense, South Africa was a microcosm of the world. "When will we learn," he asked, "that human beings are of infinite value because they have been created in the image of God, and that it is blasphemy to treat them as if they were less than this and to do so ultimately recoils on those who do this?" Tutu concluded, his arms in the air, citing the passage he is so fond of quoting, the vision of world peace in the Revelation of St. John the Divine (7:9ff.)

He went back to South Africa to assume the new position to which he had been elected the month before by the bishops of his church; he became the first black Anglican bishop of Johannesburg. In September 1986, he was made the head of the Anglican church of South Africa, with its 2 million members, and was enthroned as archibishop of Capetown and metropolitan of the Province of South Africa.

Tutu used the Nobel prize money of almost $190,000 to establish a scholarship program to enable blacks from South Africa to study in the United States. He has continued to receive honorary degrees from American and European universities, and he could watch with satisfaction as the movement has grown in the United States and elsewhere to bring economic pressure on the government of South Africa.

That government has remained inflexible, however, and has dealt even more severely with its domestic opponents. Tutu continues to speak out and to take action against the policies he condemns as un-Christian, and presumably because of his world reputation the government has left him alone. Although he relentlessly attacks apartheid, he has never ceased to preach conciliation. In his inaugural sermon as archibishop, Tutu spoke of how his people "were thought to be human, but not quite as human as white people, for we lacked what seemed indispensable to that humanity, a particular skin color. . . . We have a wonderful country with truly magnificent people, if only we could be allowed to be human together."

BIBLIOGRAPHY

Primary Source

Tutu, Desmond. *Hope and Suffering: Sermons and Speeches.* Edited by John Webster. Grand Rapids, Mich.: Eerdmans, 1984. With a foreword by Trevor Huddleston.

Secondary Sources

"Bishop Tutu: 'Person of the Year.' " *Christian Century* 102 (2 January 1985): 3–4. The *Christian Century*'s first "Person of the Year in Religion."

Hope, Marjorie, and James Young. "Desmond Mpilo Tutu." *Christian Century* 97 (31 December 1980): 1290–94.

Lelyveld, Joseph. "South Africa's Bishop Tutu." *New York Times Magazine,* 14 March 1982, pp. 22–24ff.

"The Power of the Pulpit." *Time* 128 (15 September 1986): 1986. Tutu as archbishop of Capetown.

"Tutu, Desmond." In *CB,* 1985.

1985

International Physicians for the Prevention of Nuclear War

International federation, founded in 1980.

When Alfred Nobel designated in his will prizes for both medicine and peace, it is unlikely that he anticipated an organization of doctors one day receiving the Peace Prize. This happened in 1985, when the Norwegian committee named International Physicians for the Prevention of Nuclear War (IPPNW), a choice that proved to be among the most controversial and that occasioned the most dramatic incident in the whole history of the prize.

The committee's announcement in October that IPPNW would receive the award came as a surprise. There had been an all-time high of ninety-nine candidates, sixty individuals and thirty institutions. The Oslo newspapers as usual had made their predictions, but there was no mention of the doctors. What the prize watchers failed to take into account was that the committee would be meeting to make its decision just six weeks before a summit meeting between President Reagan and Secretary Gorbachev in Geneva.

Chairman Egil Aarvik said later the committee intended to send a message to the leaders about the crucial importance of arms control. The October announcement declared that the physicians' organization "has performed a considerable service to mankind by spreading authoritative information and by creating an awareness of the catastrophic consequences of atomic warfare. . . . Such an awakening of public opinion can give the present arms limitation negotiations . . . a new seriousness."

The committee had been impressed by the cooperation between Soviet and American physicians, who had founded a new forum that transcended national borders. In an unprecedented move the committee invited the cofounders, cardiologists Dr. Evgeny Chazov of the Soviet Union and Dr. Bernard Lown of the United States, to receive the award at the ceremony on 10 December.

It was the Soviet connection that brought criticism from conservatives. When it was discovered that Chazov had been among the signers of a letter in 1973 denouncing Andrei Sakharov for anti-Sovietism, the leaders of the European Christian Democratic parties, including Chancellor Helmut Kohl of West Germany, sent a letter asking the Oslo committee to reconsider, and conservatives in Britain and the United States sent similar communications.

On the morning of 9 December, the IPPNW officers held a press conference in Oslo to discuss the nature and purposes of their organization. They wanted to explain that the American and Soviet founders had agreed from the beginning to confine themselves to the single issue on which they had full agreement, based on their medical expertise: there could be no adequate medical response to a nuclear war; the only course of action, therefore, was to try to prevent it. All forty national affiliates, united for this purpose, had agreed to exclude all other questions from their agenda.

The 150 representatives of the world's press packed into the hotel conference room gave the IPPNW little chance to make this explanation. Chazov was the target for one question after another about his part in the Sakharov letter. Suddenly a Soviet cameraman collapsed, victim of a cardiac arrest. Immediately the physicians at the head table rushed to where he lay on the floor, Chazov and Lown first among them, and an international rescue team of eminent doctors administered external cardiac massage to the stricken man and kept him alive until ambulance medics could arrive to take him to the hospital.

Lown then told the reporters that what they had just seen was a "strange parable" of IPPNW itself: "When the crisis comes, Soviet and American cardiologists cooperate. We do not ask what are a patient's or a doctor's politics, nationality, or beliefs." The first priority was to save a human life, just as the physicians of IPPNW put all other considerations aside to work together to save the human race from extinction.

The beginnings of IPPNW go back to a lecture on nuclear arms by the Nobel peace laureate Philip Noel-Baker in Boston in 1961. Dr. Bernard Lown was so stirred by what he heard that he set about organizing the Physicians for Social Responsibility (PSR), which publicized scientific studies vividly demonstrating the devastating effects of nuclear warfare.

After initial successes, the organization lost momentum, but at the end of the 1970s it was revived under the leadership of Dr. Helen Caldicott, an Australian pediatrician at Harvard. Meanwhile, Dr. Lown and a younger cardiologist at Harvard, Dr. James Muller, who had had experience in medical exchanges with the Soviet Union, began to discuss the possibility of cooperation with Soviet physicians in the movement against nuclear war. Lown contacted Chazov, with whom he had a professional association and who had high connections in the Kremlin. In December 1980, a small meeting of Soviet and American physicians took place in Geneva to plan an international congress for March 1981. It was here that the Americans persuaded their Soviet colleagues that the agenda should deal only with the prevention of nuclear war and must exclude all political and other issues.

This congress led to the formation of IPPNW, which by 1985 had a total membership of some 135,000 members of the health professions from forty countries, most of which had national affiliates, like PSR in the United States. Under copresidents Lown and Chazov, an international council drew representatives from West Germany, Argentina, Sweden, Hungary, and Australia, and an executive secretary worked out of the central headquarters in Boston.

Visits between Soviet and American physicians were arranged, and discussions between them on the medical effects of nuclear war were telecast widely and uncensored in the Soviet Union. International congresses were held annually, at which IPPNW called for a verifiable freeze on the development and deployment of nuclear weapons, for a declaration of no-first-use by the nuclear powers, and for a moratorium on testing while a comprehensive test ban treaty was negotiated. When in August 1985 Secretary Gorbachev announced that the Soviet Union would unilaterally refrain from nuclear testing and called upon the United States to follow suit, IPPNW claimed that its stand had helped influence the Soviet move. President Reagan declined Gorbachev's proposal, and American conservatives denounced IPPNW as a front for the Soviet Union, disregarding the facts that the IPPNW congresses had adopted their resolutions before the Gorbachev announcement and that there had been worldwide support among nonaligned governments for the test ban.

Although the Nobel Committee could feel that much of world public opinion favored its choice of IPPNW, the Sakharov matter was an embarrassment. On 10 December in Oslo the guests at the award ceremony had to pass demonstrators with placards reading "Free Sakharov" and "Lown, Find Better Friends." Once again, as in the Ossietzky ceremony in 1936, a German ambassador was conspicuously absent. The ambassadors of both the Federal Republic and the United States were represented by subordinates to indicate the displeasure of their governments.

Chairman Aarvik, in his presentation speech, referred to the previous awards to compaigners for human rights, "whose fate the Committee follows with interest," and he declared that freedom is every human being's birthright. This year's prize, he continued, was more concerned with the problem of disarmament, "but it is also at a deeper level concerned with human rights—perhaps even the most fundamental human right of them all—the right to live."

In their speeches Chazov and Lown reiterated familiar IPPNW themes. Chazov frankly admitted how hard it had been for the Soviet doctors and the Americans to resolve the difficulties in their early meetings: "They were not all roses. We had to cope with mistrust, skepticism, indifference, and sometimes animosity." The theme of his Nobel lecture, which he read in English, was indicated in its title "The Tragedy and Triumph of Reason."

Lown's Nobel address also had a positive title, "A Prescription for Hope." "For the physician, whose role is to affirm life," he declared, "optimism is a medical imperative." He pointed out the fact that the diversion of resources to the production of nuclear arms keeps millions living in poverty, undernourished, and diseased, when science and technology have brought humankind to the boundaries of an age of abundance. But, he concluded, "what humanity creates, humanity can and will control."

But for all their eloquence, Chazov and Lown had given their best interpretation of what IPPNW is all about in their actions at that memorable press conference, when they worked together, Soviet and American, to meet a life-and-death emergency. In the same way all the physicians of IPPNW, organized now in fifty-five national affiliates, faithful to their Hippocratic oath, work together to prevent what they regard as "the final epidemic."

BIBLIOGRAPHY

Secondary Sources

Adams, Ruth, and Susan Cullen, eds. *The Final Epidemic: Physicians and Scientists on Nuclear War.* Chicago: Educational Foundation for Nuclear Science, 1981. An anthology by the editors of the *Bulletin of the Atomic Scientists.* Includes an excerpt from the *Proceedings* of the first IPPNW congress.

Caldicott, Helen. *Missile Envy: The Arms Race and Nuclear War.* Rev. ed. New York: Bantam, 1986. By the Harvard pediatrician who headed Physicians for Social Responsibility. With bibliographical notes.

Chivian, Eric, and others, eds. *Last Aid: The Medical Dimensions of Nuclear War.* San Francisco: W. H. Freeman, 1982. Mainly papers from the first congress of IPPNW.

Graham, Loren R. "Scientists, Human Rights, and the Soviet Union." *Bulletin of the Atomic Scientists* 42, no. 4 (April 1986): 8–9. On IPPNW and the Sakharov affair.

Lown, Bernard. "Physicians and Nuclear War." *Journal of the American Medical Association* 246, no. 20 (20 November 1981): 2331–33.

Lown, Bernard, Eric Chivian, James Muller, and Herbert Abrams. "The Nuclear-Arms Race and the Physician." *New England Journal of Medicine* 304 (19 March 1981): 726–29.

Muller, James. "Cardiopulmonary Resuscitation and the 1985 Nobel Peace Prize." *New England Journal of Medicine* 314 (20 March 1986): 790–93. A medical description of the emergency at the Oslo press conference.

Nusbaumer, Michael R., and Judith A. DiIorio. "The Medicalization of Nuclear Disarmament Claims." *Peace and Change* 11, no. 1 (Spring 1985): 63–73.

Warner, Gale, and Michael H. Shuman. *Citizen Diplomats: From Main Street to Red Square and Back.*

New York: Continuum, 1987. Chap. 1: "Physician to the World: Bernard Lown." An excellent portrait.

1986

Elie Wiesel (1928–)

United States

Survivor of Nazi concentration camps and leading interpreter of the Holocaust; journalist, author, university professor.

In presenting the prize to Elie Wiesel (pronounced vē-zel′), Chairman Aarvik noted that it was exactly fifty years since the award to Carl von Ossietzky, who had opposed the forces of militarism in the German Republic and had also been sent to a concentration camp by the Nazis. Ossietzky did not survive his mistreatment, but now, Aarvik declared, the prize was to be presented to one who had:

> In 1945, in the ashes left behind after the sacrificial flames which annihilated six million Jews sat seventeen-year-old Elie Wiesel. . . . He will receive the Nobel Peace Prize today because he too has become a witness for truth and justice.
>
> From the abyss of the death camps he has come as a messenger to mankind—not with a message of hate and revenge, but with one of brotherhood and atonement.
>
> He has become a powerful spokesman for that human view that knows no boundaries, which is, at all times, the foundation of a lasting peace. Elie Wiesel is not only the man who survived—he is also the spirit which has conquered. In him we see a man who has climbed from utter humiliation to become one of our most important spiritual leaders and guides.

Elie(zer) Wiesel was born in Romania in the Transylvanian town of Sighet in the Carpathian Mountains near the Ukrainian border. His father, Shlomo, was a shopkeeper and a leading member of the large Jewish community in the town. Elie grew up deeply rooted in Jewish traditions. He studied the Hebrew scriptures, the Talmud, and the Hassidic teachings, and he delighted in the Hassidic tales told by his grandfather. From his father he also learned about Western rationalism and humanism. He was always a bookish youth, and when he was only about twelve he wrote a set of commentaries on the Bible.

After the war began in 1939, Transylvania became part of Hungary, and in 1944, in accordance with orders from Germany, the Jews of Hungary were rounded up and sent to the death camps. Elie, then fifteen, with his parents and his three sisters was transported in a cattle car to the concentration camp of Auschwitz in Poland, where his mother and little sister were killed. He and his father managed to survive amid unspeakable conditions until the camp was evacuated in 1945 as the Soviet Army moved westward. They were taken to the concentration camp of Buchenwald in Germany, where Elie watched his father die from dysentery and starvation.

In April 1945 the survivors in the camp were liberated by American soldiers. From a photograph of the inmates lying in their rude bunks, Elie Wiesel's emaciated and worn face peers at the camera. The starving men threw themselves upon the food they were given. Three days after the liberation, Elie was in the hospital from food poisoning and almost died. He has told of looking at himself in a mirror for the first time since the deportation: "From the depths of the mirror, a corpse looked back at me. The look in his eyes, as they stared into mine, has never left me."

Alone now in the world—it was only later that he found the two sisters who survived—he was brought to Normandy in France by a relief organization, which later helped him settle in Paris to study philosophy at the Sorbonne. He lived frugally, supporting himself with jobs as choir director, camp counselor, Bible teacher, and translator. Finally he was hired by the foreign desk of a French newspaper, and he traveled to many countries, including India, where he worked on his English, and Palestine, where he reported on the establishment of the state of Israel in 1948. He then became the foreign correspondent of a Tel Aviv daily, which sent him to New York City to report on the United Nations.

In 1956 Wiesel was hit by a taxi in Times Square and seriously injured. During his long convalescence, he decided to apply for U.S. citizenship, which he received in 1963. In 1957 he became a feature writer for the Yiddish-language *Jewish Daily Forward* in New York, but he had already published his first book about his experiences in the camps and was to become a celebrated author. In 1969 he married Marion Erster Rose, also a concentration camp survivor, and they have one son, Shlomo Elisha.

When Wiesel left Buchenwald, he had vowed not to speak of his experiences for at least ten years: "How does one describe the indescribable? How can one be sure that the words . . . will not betray, distort the message they bear?" Then, in 1954, when Wiesel went to interview the Catholic writer, François Mauriac, for his Tel Aviv newspaper, he found himself interviewed instead, and after Mauriac heard Wiesel's story, he persuaded him that it was wrong not to speak out. One year later Wiesel send Mauriac a manuscript. Published in France as *La Nuit* (Night) in 1958, the book has been translated into many languages and has become the most noted and perhaps the most influential personal account of the Holocaust ever written.

Once released from his self-imposed vow, Wiesel became a prolific writer, no longer fearing that his words might do less than justice to the victims of the Holocaust, but feeling it his duty to witness to their suffering, to keep their memory alive and try to prevent anything like it from ever happening again. A stream of some thirty books has come from his pen—novels, short stories, plays, essays. His prose is poetic and no words are wasted. His fiction has often taken the form of the Hassidic tales of his youth.

No one has more vividly conveyed the horrors of the Holocaust or gone more deeply into its implications. He has condemned the world's indifference—*Night* was first entitled *And the World Remained Silent*—probed the nature of God and of evil, and moved compassionately from concern with Jewish suffering to concern with all human suffering. This has taken him not only to the Soviet Union to give moral support to Soviet Jews and to work for their right of emigration but to African and Latin American countries to intercede for victims of injustice and brutality.

Wiesel's mother tongue was Yiddish, but he writes in French, and his French literary prizes stand at the top of the long list of awards he has received. At the same time, he has attained a mastery of English that has equipped him to become an effective teacher in American universities and a popular lecturer.

In recognition of his work for human rights, his contributions to literature, and his service as chairman of the United States Holocaust Memorial Council, President Ronald Reagan presented him in April 1985 with the Congressional Gold Medal of Achievement in a ceremony at the White House. Before millions of television viewers, Wiesel implored the president not to make a projected visit to the military cemetery at Bitburg in the Federal Republic of Germany. This had been planned as a gesture to strengthen both American-German relationships and the political position of Chancellor Helmut Kohl, but it had been discovered that in the cemetery were also graves of members of the SS, Hitler's elite military corps. Wiesel had watched SS men at their murderous work in the camps.

"That place, Mr. President," he now pleaded, "is not your place. Your place is with the victims of the SS." This was a striking confrontation between a moral leader and a politican. The politician, unheeding, went ahead with his plans. Wiesel, who had always called for reconciliation with the German people and emphasized that the children of killers were not to be held responsible for the killing, went to West Germany for frank and friendly discussions with German youth.

At the Nobel presentation ceremony in the university Aula in Oslo Chairman Aarvik made his formal address in Norwegian and then spoke directly to Wiesel in English. He reminded him of his comment when Shlomo Elisha was born. He had questioned bringing a child into such an evil world but then had realized he had no right to break the chain of generations, that three thousand years must not end with him. So, as Wiesel had said, he had put them on the shoulders of a little child.

"Now," declared Aarvik, "your son, with such a precious burden on his shoulders, should follow you to the podium. As you stood with your father in the darkness, your son, with his grandfather's name, should be at your side in this moment of joy and brightness, as you receive the Peace Prize for 1986."

Father and son stood together as Aarvik handed Wiesel the medal and the diploma, an unprecedented happening, but perfectly fitting the occasion. Before giving his speech of acceptance, Wiesel, having asked permission of King Olav, placed his prayer cap on his head and pronounced a Hebrew blessing: "Thank You, O Lord, for giving us this day."

He accepted the award humbly and prayerfully, eloquently bespeaking his tragic memories and his determination not only to oppose those who would forget but to stand up for victims of inhumanity everywhere. The world had been silent during the Holocaust—"and that is why I swore never to be silent whenever and wherever human beings endure suffering and humiliation." Although it would be unnatural for him not to make Jewish priorities his own, he declared, "As long as one dissident is in prison, our freedom will not be true. As long as one child is hungry, our lives will be filled with anguish and shame."

For the award he expressed his deepest gratitude—"No one is as capable of gratitude as one who has emerged from the kingdom of night." Looking out over the hall filled with other survivors of the death camps who had come to be with him, Wiesel thanked the people of Norway "for declaring on this singular occasion that our survival has meaning for mankind."

That evening the Norwegian people expressed their own feelings, thousands marching with their torches past the Grand Hotel where the Wiesels were staying. Later the hotel was the scene of the customary banquet offered by the Norwegian Nobel Committee, this time for the largest number of guests ever, including the twenty-five special friends Elie Wiesel had invited from the United States, France, Israel, and England, several of them survivors from the town of Sighet.

Wiesel introduced his Nobel lecture the next day with an old Jewish song, the erstwhile choir director conducting the chorus of those who knew it and sang with him. He spoke on "Hope, Despair and Memory": "We must remember the suffering of my people," he said, "as we must remember that of the Ethiopians, the Cambodians, the boat people, the Palestinians, the Mesquite Indians, the Argentinian *disappeared ones*. . . . Because I remember, I despair. Because I remember, I have the duty to reject despair."

Wiesel resolves the perplexing questions his terrible experiences have left with him in just such paradoxes. As he once stated his credo: "I believe in God—in spite of God! I believe in Mankind—in spite of Mankind! I believe in the Future—in spite of the Past!"

With the Nobel prize money of about $270,000, Wiesel said he planned to establish a Foundation for Human Rights, which would organize conferences on such subjects as "Hate" and the implications for humanity of the Hiroshima bomb. He was able to realize another idea in January 1988 with the help of his friend President François Mitterand of France. Together they convened a conference in Paris of seventy-six Nobel laureates from all fields to consider the future of the human race. They decided to create an emergency committee to exercise moral authority in crisis situations around the world, and they agreed to meet again in two years.

BIBLIOGRAPHY

Primary Sources

Wiesel, Elie. *The Fifth Son.* Translated by Marion Wiesel. New York: Warner, 1986. The novel that won Le Grand Prix de la Littérature de la Ville de Paris.

———. *The Jews of Silence: A Personal Report on Soviet Jewry.* Rev. ed. New York: Schocken, 1987.

———. *Legends of Our Time.* New York: Schocken, 1982.

———. *The Night Trilogy: Night, Dawn, The Accident.* New York: Hill & Wang, 1987. The book on the Holocaust with which he broke his silence and two autobiographical novels.

Secondary Sources

Abrahamson, Irving. *Against Silence: The Voice and Vision of Elie Wiesel.* 3 vols. New York: Schocken, 1984.

Brown, Robert McAfee. *Elie Wiesel: Messenger to All Humanity.* South Bend, Ind.: University of Notre Dame Press, 1984.

Cargas, Harry J. *In Conversation with Elie Wiesel.* Mahwah, N.J.: Paulist Press, 1976.

Fine, Ellen S. *Legacy of Night: The Literary Universe of Elie Wiesel.* Albany: State University of New York Press, 1982.

1987

Oscar Arias Sánchez (1941–)

Costa Rica

President of Costa Rica (1986–); architect of the Central America peace plan.

To the surprise of the prize watchers in Oslo, who were speculating that the 1987 award would go to President Corazon Aquino of the Philippines, President Raul Alfonsin of Argentina, or Nelson Mandela, the imprisoned black leader in South Africa, the Norwegian Nobel Committee announced on 13 October that the laureate was to be President Oscar Arias Sánchez of Costa Rica, initiator of a plan to end civil wars and conflicts in Central America.

No one was more surprised than Arias himself, who heard the news on a radio broadcast at a remote beach house on the coast, where he had gone with his wife to celebrate her birthday. He hurried back to the capital city of San José, where he told a crowd of well-wishers at the airport, "This is the happiest day of my life. I interpret the prize as a tribute to my country." He said that the prize would enhance the chances of success of the agreement he had persuaded the other four Central American presidents to sign in Guatemala on 4 August to bring peace to the area.

This was the basis of the decision of the committee, whose chairman, Egil Aarvik, declared in making the announcement that the prize should be used not just to award achievement but to promote peace, and that the committee wanted to back the Arias peace plan with the prestige of the prize.

The announcement met general approval in Norway and in the world press, although there was some criticism that the committee had gone beyond its mandate and had intervened in a political process. There were, however, precedents: in 1971 the award was made to Willy Brandt before his treaties of reconciliation with the Soviet Union and Poland had been ratified; and in 1978 Begin and Sadat were given the prize for agreements reached at Camp David that had still not been embodied in a signed treaty.

The obstacles to peace in Central America seemed almost overwhelming. The region had for many years been torn by strife and civil wars. The governments of El Salvador, Guatemala, and Nicaragua had long been engaged in violent conflicts with guerrilla forces. In Nicaragua the antigovernment rebels, the so-called Contras, had been organized and were being openly and covertly supplied by the United States, while the government was given assistance by Cuba and the Soviet Union. President Reagan feared that the continuance in power of the Marxist Sandinista government would bring a Soviet beachhead to Nicaragua, and his subordinates were apparently willing to go to any lengths to prevent this. In Guatemala and El Salvador the rebels were leftists, and the government of El Salvador claimed that their opponents were being supplied by the Sandinistas.

In these conflicts Honduras, Guatemala, and Costa Rica remained ostensibly neutral, but they were all in various degrees critical of the Nicaragua government's authoritarian measures, uneasy about the threat to their security that its armed forces represented, and dependent upon economic and other aid from the United States, which was encouraging them to give aid to the Contras. Consequently, Honduras permitted the establishment of Contra military bases on its territory, and agents from the United States were even able to build a private airport in Costa Rica, from which supplies could be flown to the Contras.

In 1983 Mexico, Venezuela, Columbia, and Panama cooperated to develop the Contadora peace plan for Central America. The five countries of the region agreed to support the proposal but were unable to carry it through. With the Contadora effort at a standstill, Oscar Arias, on his election to the presidency of Costa Rica, now took the initiative. In his inaugural address on 8 May 1986, he announced, "We will keep Costa Rica out of the armed conflicts of Central America and we will endeavor through diplomatic and political means to keep our Central American brothers from killing each other."

Arias soon moved to close the secret airport, and on 24–25 May he met with the presidents of the other four Central American states to discuss the Contadora plan again. There was some agreement, but fundamental differences remained to be resolved. The following February at another such summit meeting at San José Arias put forward his own plan, based upon Contadora but both broader and more detailed.

The plan met with wide approval in Latin America and Western Europe, and the U.S. Senate passed a resolution endorsing it with only one dissenting vote. President Reagan, however, thought it made concessions to the Nicaraguan government and called the plan "fatally flawed." Meeting with the American president at the White House, the Costa Rican president tried to explain that in his view the Contras were not a solution to the problem; "they *were* the problem."

President Daniel Ortega of Nicaragua had initially been very critical of the peace plan himself, but Arias persuaded Ortega to give up his objections. The document entitled "Procedure for the Establishment of the Firm and Lasting Peace in Central America" that was finally signed ended with these words: "The Presidents of the five Central American States, with the political will to answer to the vehement desire of Peace of our Countries, subscribe it in the City of Guatemala the seventh day of the month of August of Nineteen Eighty-Seven." It was reported that Arias had kept his colleagues in session, refusing to break for a meal, until they were willing to sign.

The Guatemala accord provided for national reconciliation of all the raging conflicts, including dialogue between the governments and unarmed oppositions, and the establishment of national reconciliation commissions to oversee amnesty for rebels, cease-fire agreements, freedom of public expression, and free elections both within individual nations and for a Central American parliament. Aid to the Contras and other insurgent groups from outside governments was to be ended, as well as the use of the territory of any of the signatory states for forces attacking another state. Verification of the agreement was to be conducted by an international verification committee, composed of the secretaries-general of the United Nations and the Association of American States and the foreign ministers of Central America and the Contadora group. Measures were to be taken simultaneously, and a calendar of implementation was set up, with an evaluation meeting of the five presidents set for January 1988.

Oscar Arias Sánchez was born in Heredia near San José, the son of a wealthy coffee-producing family whose members have been prominent in Costa Rican politics. After completing secondary school, where he played on the soccer team, Arias went to the United States to Boston University, with the intention of studying to be a physician. He was already interested in politics, however, and he followed closely the election contest of 1960 between John F. Kennedy and Richard Nixon, Kennedy becoming a role model for him.

Deciding against a medical career, Arias returned home in 1961 to spend the next six years studying law and economics at the University of Costa Rica in San José. During these years his concern with political affairs developed further. He organized students to support the candidates of the Partido Liberación Nacional (PLN; the party of democratic socialism), and he won a newspaper competition with an essay on the confrontation of freedom and totalitarianism during the Soviet blockade of West Berlin in 1948–49.

After obtaining his degree in 1967, Arias went to England with a British government grant to take up advanced study at the London School of Economics and Political Science and the University of Essex. In 1969 he returned to Costa Rica to become professor of political science at the University of Costa Rica. In 1970 he published his first book, a study of pressure groups in Costa Rica, which won him a national prize for essays. He continued his research on his doctoral dissertation, a socioeconomic analysis of Costa Rican political leadership, which earned him the Ph.D. from Essex in 1974 and was published in 1976.

Both these studies have been deemed significant by political scientists abroad, but it was in the field of development economics that Arias was first to make his mark. In 1970, when José "Don Pepe" Figueres, the hero of the Costa Rican revolution and founder of the PLN, returned to the presidency after an absence of twelve years, he appointed the promising young professor to his economic council. Two years later Figueres brought him into the cabinet as minister of national planning and economics policy, a position he held under the next presidency as well.

Arias became a cabinet minister in 1972 when he was only thirty-one years of age and still unmarried. The next year he married Margarita Penón Góngora, a biochemist who had studied in the United States and graduated from Vassar College. They were to have two children.

Although Arias resigned from the university to take the cabinet post, he subsequently served on a number of educational commissions, including the board of directors of Costa Rica's Technological Institute, the national council of rectors, and the board of directors of the International University Exchange Fund, based in Geneva, Switzerland. Because of his own fruitful experience as a student abroad, he became a strong advocate of foreign study and cultural exchanges.

Beginning in 1970 Arias became a well-known figure in international conferences on third world and economic development affairs. From 1975, as international secretary of the PLN, he represented his party at the international congresses of the democratic socialist parties. In 1977 Willy Brandt, then president of the Socialist International, invited Arias to lecture in West Germany on "Socialism and Freedom." Ten years later, at the invitation of Arias, Brandt came to Oslo to attend the Peace Prize ceremony.

In 1978, when the PLN lost the presidency to a conservative, Arias was a leading critic of the administration in the legislature as deputy from Heredia. This led to his election as general secretary of the PLN in 1979 and his reelection in 1983 after having helped his party regain the presidency. In 1986 the PLN elected him to run for the presidency himself. The *New York Times* reported that Arias had "rolled up his usually carefully pressed sleeves and bruised his way through the opposition of the party's aging bosses."

Arias campaigned on a platform of "roofs, jobs, and peace," promising to maintain the country's high standard of living while meeting the crushing national debt of about $4.5 billion dollars that had largely been incurred in the development of Costa Rica's welfare state and had been aggravated by world economic problems. There were few differences between Arias and his conservative opponent in domestic issues and in most matters of foreign policy, but Arias took a far stronger stand in refusing to let Costa Rica be drawn into any war in Central America. In the election of February 1986, in which about 80 percent of the electorate voted, Arias received over 52 percent of the total, becoming at forty-six years of age Costa Rica's youngest president. The PLN also won control of the unicameral legislature.

In his speech presenting the Nobel Peace Prize to Arias, Chairman Aarvik noted that it was no coincidence that it was the president of a country like Costa Rica, a haven of peace in an area of conflict, who had won the prize. It had actually been because of what Costa Rica stood for, not because of his peace plan, that Arias had been nominated. His name had been proposed by a Swedish parliamentary deputy who for several years regularly submitted the name of the chief executive of Costa Rica, whoever he was, in order to give recognition to the country's tradition of peace and democracy. This nomination, the only one for Arias, had been made before the deadline of 1 February, so his name was before the committee when it met after the Guatemala accord of August to consider its decision.

That tradition of peace and democracy had arisen from the country's history. Costa Rica's first settlers had not been looking for gold or for large landholdings to be worked by enslaved Indians; they had been landowning small farmers. The country had thus avoided the pattern so often found in the third world of an aristocratic upper class exploiting a poverty-stricken majority. There was much idealism among the well-to-do members of the middle class who became the political leaders after Costa Rica became independent in 1821. Education has been compulsory and free since 1869, and since the 1890s the country has had a stable democratic system that has been interrupted only once, in 1948, by a brief armed uprising.

This was the revolution that brought to power the liberal leader, José Figueres, responsible for the new constitution that abolished the armed forces. The key to the military barracks in San José was presented to the minister of education to establish a national museum there. Arias had hoped that Figueres could accompany him to Oslo, where he planned to introduce him as the man who "set our history on a new course," but Don Pepe, now in his eighties, was unable to come.

Aarvik in his speech emphasized two points about the Arias peace plan that had impressed the committee: first that it was a product of the Central American presidents themselves, who wanted outside intervention to cease, and second, the plan coupled democracy with peace. Arias always stressed the indivisibility of democracy and peace, explaining that "democracy is never an end in itself. Democracy is a means. The end is always a human being."

When Aarvik had concluded and Arias ascended to the podium to receive the gold medal and the diploma, he was attired in a dark blue suit, in contrast to the tails and white ties of the other Nobel laureates at the Stockholm ceremony later that afternoon. Arias spoke slowly and thoughtfully, simply but most impressively. He gave his speech in English, which his Norwegian audience well understood, and there was a burst of applause when he finished. He declared:

> Peace is a never-ending process. It is an attitude, a way of life, a way of solving problems and resolving conflicts. We seek in Central America not peace alone, no peace to be followed some day by political progress, but peace and democracy, together, indivisible, an end to the shedding of human blood, which is inseparable from an end to the suppression of human rights.

Arias spoke of the "marvelous coincidence" that the day he received the prize was the eighth birthday of his son, Oscar Felipe: "I say to him, and through him to all the children of my country, that we shall never resort to violence, we shall never support military solutions to the problems of Central America."

The day of the awarding of the prize was also the day when President Reagan and General Secretary Gorbachev were meeting at the Washington summit. Without naming names, Arias concluded with a plea to them—the head of a tiny unarmed state, smaller than West Virginia, speaking to the leaders of the greatest military powers on earth, a David addressing Goliaths:

> I say to them with the utmost urgency: let Central Americans decide the future of Central America. . . . Send our people ploughshares instead of swords, pruning hooks instead of spears. If they, for their own purposes, cannot refrain from amassing the weapons of war, then, in the name of God, at least they should leave us in peace.

The next day Arias gave his Nobel lecture, "Only Peace Can Write the New History," this time speaking in Spanish so that his address could be broadcast to Latin America. He declared that he received the prize not as Oscar Arias but as one of 400 million Latin Americans who are seeking to overcome misery and injustice: "I come from a world in a hurry; hunger cannot wait." He accepted the prize as one of 27 million Central Americans, who "want to create a new future with hope for the young and dignity for the old." He accepted the prize as one of 2.7 million Costa Ricans, an unarmed people, a symbol of peace, a country of teachers, its fortress "stronger than a thousand armies": "the power of liberty." He accepted the prize as one of five presidents who have pledged to the world to seek a firm and lasting peace, "a commitment which consists, very largely, in the fact of desiring peace with all one's soul."

Oscar Arias's term as president of Costa Rica will end in 1990, and according to the constitution he cannot be elected again. The odds against his peace plan increased in the weeks after the award, when the cease-fire agreements that Arias considered basic were not concluded, and when President Reagan used his veto power to elicit congressional approval of further aid to the Contras, thus undercutting a key provision of the Guatemala agreement. Later, prospects brightened for peace in Nicaragua when Congress cut off military aid to the Contras, who entered negotiations with the government. But whether or not the Arias plan succeeds, there can be little doubt that he will continue to work "to keep our Central American brothers from killing each other." Whatever the commitment or the priorities of the other four presidents who signed the agreement, Arias impressed those who heard him speak at Oslo as a man of genuine sincerity—indeed, a man desiring peace with all his soul.

BIBLIOGRAPHY

Primary Sources

Arias Sánchez, Oscar. *Dawn of a New Political Era.* Address to the forty-second session of the UN General Assembly, 23 September 1987. San José: Presidencia de la República, 1987.

———. *Grupos de Presión en Costa Rica.* San José: Editorial Costa Rica, 1971. A study of pressure groups.

———. *Let Us Go Together on the Road to Peace.* Address, Harvard University, 24 September 1987. San José: Presidencia de la República, 1987.

———. *¿Quien Gobierna en Costa Rica?* ("Who Governs?") San José: EDUCA, 1976. A study of political leadership in Costa Rica.

Secondary Sources

Abrams, Irwin. "Behind the Scenes: The Nobel Committee and Oscar Arias." *Antioch Review* 46, no. 3 (Summer 1988).

Ameringer, Charles D. *Democracy in Nicaragua.* New York: Praeger, 1982.

———. *Don Pepe: A Political Biography of José Figueres of Costa Rica.* Albuquerque: University of New Mexico Press, 1978. Carefully done, with use of his private papers.

"Arias Sánchez, Oscar." In *CB,* 1987.

Bell, John Patrick. *Crisis in Costa Rica: The 1948 Revolution.* Austin: University of Texas Press, 1971. An authoritative study.

Biesanz, Richard. *The Costa Ricans.* Englewood Cliffs, N.J.: Prentice-Hall, 1982. Good introduction.

Appendixes

Appendix A
Tables

Table 1. Prizewinners by Category

	I. 1901–18	II. 1919–39	III. 1940–59	IV. 1960–87	Total: 1901–87
The Organized Peace Movement	Passy Ducommun Gobat Cremer von Suttner Moneta Arnoldson Bajer d'Estournelles Int'l Peace Bur. Fried La Fontaine	Lange Quidde Buisson Addams Butler Angell Ossietzky Cecil	Balch Noel-Baker	Pauling Williams Corrigan Myrdal IPPNW	27
Humanitarian	Dunant Int'l Red Cross	Nansen Nansen Off. for Ref.	Int'l Red Cross Mott English Quakers Amer. Quakers Boyd-Orr Jouhaux Schweitzer H.C. Ref. Pire	Int'l Red Cross League Red Cr. UNICEF ILO Borlaug M. Teresa H.C. Ref.	20
Int'l Jurists	Inst. Int'l Law Renault Beernaert Asser	None	None	None	4
Statesman	T. Roosevelt Root	Wilson Bourgeois Branting Chamberlain Dawes Briand Stresemann Kellogg Henderson C.S. Lamas	Hull Bunche Marshall Pearson	Hammarskjöld Brandt Sato Kissinger Le Duc Tho* Sadat Begin Robles Arias	25

Reli-gious	None	Söderblom	None	None	1
Human Rights	None	None		Luturi King Cassin MacBride Sakharov Amn. Int'l Pérez Esquivel Wałesa Tutu Wiesel	10
Total	20	21	15	31	87

*declined

Table 2. The Withholding of the Prize in Peacetime

	I. 1901–14	II. 1919–39	III. 1945–59	IV. 1960–87	Total
Award reserved	1912	8 { 1919, 1923, 1924 1928, 1929 1932, 1933 1935	7 { 1948, 1952 1954, 1955 1956, 1960 1962	4 { 1966 1967 1972 1976	20
Award given following year	1912	4 { 1919 1929 1933 1935	4 { 1952 1954 1960 1962	1976	10
No award	0	4 { 1922 1924 1928 1932	3 { 1948 1955 1956	3 { 1966 1967 1972	10

Table 3. Divided Prizes

	I. 1901–18	II. 1919–39	III. 1940–59	IV. 1960–87	Total 1901–87
	1901 1902 1907 1908 1909 1911	1921 1925 *1926 1927 1931	1946 *1947 *1963	*1973 1974 *1976 *1978 1982	
Total Number:	6	5	3	5	19

*For a shared achievement

Table 4. Prizewinners by Country

Nation	I. 1901–18	II. 1919–39	III. 1940–59	IV. 1960–87	Total
Switzerland	4***		1***	1***	6
France	3	2	2		7
Great Britain	1	4	3**	2	10
Austria	2				2
United States	2	5	7**	4	18
Italy	1				1
Denmark	1				1
Belgium	2		1		3
Netherlands	1				1
Sweden	1	2	1	1	5
Norway		2			2
Germany (and West Germany)		3		1	4
Argentina		1		1	2
Canada			1		1
South Africa				2	2
(North Vietnam)*				(1)*	(1)*
Ireland				1	1
Japan				1	1
USSR				1	1
Egypt				1	1
Israel				1	1
India				1	1
Mexico				1	1
Poland				1	1
Costa Rica				1	1
Total Countries (incl. North Vietnam): 26	10	7	7	16	

*Declined the prize
**Includes one institution, the Quakers
***Includes one institution, the International Committee of the Red Cross

Table 5. Awards to Institutions and Associations

I. 1901–18	II. 1919–39	III. 1940–59	IV. 1960–87	Total: 1901–87
Institute of Int'l Law (1904) Permanent Int'l Peace Bur. (1910) Int'l Committee of the Red Cross (1917)	Nansen Int'l Office for Refugees (1938)	Int'l Committee of the Red Cross (1944) English Quakers/ American Quakers (1947) UN High Comm. for Refugees (1954) Int'l Committee of the Red Cross/League of Red Cross Soc. (1963)	UNICEF (1965) Int'l Labor Org. (1969) Amnesty Int'l (1977) UN High Comm. for Refugees (1981) Int'l Physicians for the Prevention of Nuclear War (1985)	
Total 3	1	6	5	15

Table 6. Women Laureates

I. 1901–18	II. 1919–39	III. 1940–59	IV. 1960–87	Total 1901–87
Suttner (1905)	Addams* (1931)	Balch* (1946)	Williams/ Corrigan (1976) Mother Teresa (1979) Myrdal* (1982)	
Total 1	1	1	4	7

*Divided prize

Table 7. Age Distribution of Prizewinners

Age	I. 1901–18	II. 1919–39	III. 1940–59	IV. 1960–87	Total 1901–87
30–39				3	3
40–49	2	2	2	3	9
50–59	3	2		7	12
60–69	6	11	2	6	25
70–79	5	4	6	3	18
80–89	1	1	1	2	5
Total:	17	20	11	24	72

Appendix B
Alfred Nobel's Will

"The whole of my remaining realizable estate shall be dealt with in the following way: the capital, invested in safe securities by my executors, shall constitute a fund, the interest on which shall be annually distributed in the form of prizes to those who, during the preceding year, shall have conferred the greatest benefit on mankind. The said interest shall be divided into five equal parts, which shall be apportioned as follows: one part to the person who shall have made the most important discovery or invention within the field of physics; one part to the person who shall have made the most important chemical discovery or improvement; one part to the person who shall have made the most important discovery within the domain of physiology or medicine; one part to the person who shall have produced in the field of literature the most outstanding work of an idealistic tendency; and one part to the person who shall have done the most or the best work for fraternity between nations, for the abolition or reduction of standing armies and for the holding and promotion of peace congresses. The prizes for physics and chemistry shall be awarded by the Swedish Academy of Sciences; that for physiological or medical works by the Karolinska Institutet in Stockholm; that for literature by the Academy in Stockholm; and that for champions of peace by a committee of five persons to be elected by the Norwegian Storting. It is my express wish that in awarding the prizes no consideration whatever shall be given to the nationality of the candidates, but that the most worthy shall receive the prize, whether he be a Scandinavian or not."

Paris, November 27, 1895.

Appendix C

Invitation to nominate candidates for

THE NOBEL PEACE PRIZE

All proposals for candidates for the Nobel Peace Prize, to be awarded December 10th must, in order to be taken into consideration, be presented to the Norwegian Nobel Committee by a duly qualified person *before the* first of February of the same year.

Any one of the following persons is entitled to submit proposals: (a) Members and former members of the Norwegian Nobel Committee as well as the advisers appointed at the Norwegian Nobel Institute; (b) Members of the National Assembly and Members of the Government in the respective States, as well as Members of the Interparliamentary Union; (c) Members of the International Arbitration Court and of the International Court of Justice at the Hague; (d) Members and Associates of the Institute of International Law; (e) Members of the executive committee of the International Peace Bureau; (f) University professors of Political Science and of Law, of History and of Philosophy; and (g) Persons who have received the Nobel Peace Prize.

The Nobel Peace Prize may also be accorded to institutions or associations.

The nominators are strongly requested not to publish their proposals.

Proposals should be sent to the Norwegian Nobel Committee, Drammensveien 19, Oslo 2, Norway.

Appendix D
Nobel Peace Prize Winners

Year	Laureate
1901	H. Dunant (Swi)
	F. Passy (F)
1902	E. Ducommun (Swi)
	A. Gobat (Swi)
1903	W.R. Cremer (GB)
1904	Institute for Int'l Law, Ghent
1905	Bertha von Suttner (Au)
1906	T. Roosevelt (US)
1907	E. T. Moneta (I)
	L. Renault (F)
1908	K. P. Arnoldson (Swe)
	F. Bajer (D)
1909	A. M. F. Beernaert (B)
	P. H. d'Estournelles-de Constant (F)
1910	Int'l Peace Bureau, Bern
1911	T. M. C. Asser (Nl)
	A. H. Fried (Au)
1912	Elihu Root (US)
1913	H. La Fontaine (B)
1914	None
1915	None
1916	None
1917	Int'l Red Cross, Geneva
1918	None
1919	T. W. Wilson (US)
1920	L. Bourgeois (F)
1921	K. H. Branting (Swe)
	C. L. Lange (N)
1922	F. Nansen (N)
1923	None
1924	None

Year	Laureate
1925	C. G. Dawes (US)
	A. Chamberlain (GB)
1926	A. Briand (F)
	G. Stresemann (G)
1927	F. Buisson (F)
	L. Quidde (G)
1928	None
1929	F. B. Kellogg (US)
1930	N. Söderblom (Swe)
1931	N. M. Butler (US)
	J. Addams (US)
1932	None
1933	N. Angell (GB)
1934	A. Henderson (GB)
1935	C. von Ossietzky (G)
1936	C. Saavedra Lamas (Ar)
1937	E. A. R. G. Cecil (GB)
1938	Nansen Int'l Office for Refugees, Geneva
1939	None
1940	None
1941	None
1942	None
1943	None
1944	Int'l Committee of the Red Cross, Geneva
1945	C. Hull (US)
1946	E. G. Balch (US)
	J. R. Mott (US)
1947	The Friends Service Council (GB)
	The American Friends Service Committee (US)
1948	None

1949 J. Boyd-Orr (GB)
1950 J. Bunche (US)
1951 L. Jouhaux (F)
1952 A. Schweitzer (F)
1953 G. C. Marshall (US)
1954 Office of the UN High Commissioner for Refugees, Geneva
1955 None
1956 None
1957 L. B. Pearson (Ca)
1958 G. Pire (B)
1959 P. J. Noel-Baker (GB)
1960 A. J. Lutuli (SA)
1961 D. Hammarskjöld (Swe)
1962 L. C. Pauling (US)
1963 Int'l Committee of the Red Cross, Geneva
League of Red Cross Societies, Geneva
1964 M. L. King (US)
1965 UN Children's Fund (UNICEF)
1966 None
1967 None
1968 R. Cassin (F)
1969 Int'l Labor Organization, Geneva
1970 N. E. Borlaug (US)
1971 W. Brandt (G)
1972 None
1973 H. A. Kissinger (US)
[Le Duc Tho (N. Vietnam) (declined the prize)]
1974 S. MacBride (Ir)
E. Sato (J)
1975 A. Sakharov (USSR)
1976 M. Corrigan (GB)
B. Williams (GB)
1977 Amnesty Int'l
1978 M. Begin (Is)
A. Sadat (Egypt)
1979 Mother Teresa (In)
1980 A. Pérez Esquivel (Ar)
1981 Office of the High Commissioner for Refugees, Geneva
1982 A. Myrdal (Swe)
A. García Robles (Mexico)
1983 L. Wałesa (Pol)
1984 D. Tutu (SA)
1985 Int'l Physicians for the Prevention of Nuclear War
1986 E. Wiesel (US)
1987 O. Arias Sanchez (CR)

Country abbreviations: (Ar)-Argentina; (B)-Belgium; (Ca)-Canada; (CR)-Costa Rica; (D)-Denmark; (F)-France; (G)-Germany; (GB)-Great Britain; (In)-India; (Ir)-Ireland; (Is)-Israel; (I)-Italy; (J)-Japan; (Nl)-Netherlands; (N)-Norway; (Pol)-Poland; (Swe)-Sweden; (Swi)-Switzerland; (SA)-Union of South Africa; (US)-United States; (USSR)-Soviet Union

Index

Figures in italics indicate page numbers of biographical entries.

The Author

Irwin Abrams is Distinguised University Professor Emeritus at Antioch University in Yellow Springs, Ohio, where he has taught European history and International Relations for more than three decades. He received his B.A. degree from Stanford University, and his M.A. and Ph.D. from Harvard University. One of the early pioneers of peace research, Mr. Abram's dissertation was on the history of European peace societies. During and after the war, he served with the American Friends Service Committee in relief and reconstruction work. A theorist and practitioner of international education, he was coordinator of international programs for the Great Lakes Colleges Association, and served as president of the International Society for Educational, Cultural, and Scientific Interchanges. He has published widely and has lectured on the Nobel Peace Prize at various college and university campuses here and abroad. He has had the opportunity to meet with a number of laureates over the years, including Linus Pauling, Willy Brandt, Martin Luther King, Jr., Adolfo Perez Esquivel, Alva Myrdal, Elie Wiesel, and Oscar Arias.

© PER ANDERS ROSENKVIST/SAMFOTO

A leading authority on the Nobel Peace Prize, Abrams dispels the myths that have surrounded the award over the years—such as the popular misconception that Alfred Nobel, the inventor of dynamite and later a wealthy munitions-maker, established the prize to assuage his guilt. In fact, the money Nobel made from dynamite came mostly from peacetime use in mining and in the building of great canals and tunnels. A sincere interest in the pacifist movement, not guilt, was what motivated the father of the Nobel Peace Prize.

Certainly the Peace Prize has been controversial at times. In 1973, for example, the prize was awarded jointly to Henry Kissinger, then the U.S. secretary of state, and Le Duc Tho, of North Vietnam, for their attempts at negotiating an end to the Vietnam War. When the U.S. ambassador showed up to accept Kissinger's prize, furious Norwegians pelted him with snowballs.

The Nobel Peace Prize and the Laureates will serve as an invaluable resource for anyone who wants to find a concise account of each laureate, the historical context of the prize and its winners, and recommendations for further reading. Abrams's exhaustive work is the culmination of a lifelong fascination with the prize, personal meetings with winners over the last half-century, interviews with members and advisors of the Nobel Committee, and extensive research into their archives.

While the Nobel Peace Prize may have been controversial at times, in its finest moments, Abrams notes, ". . . the peace award has turned the attention of the world to those whose distinguished services to peace and human rights and humanitarian causes may at least temper our cynicism with hope."